Networks
Volume I

Critical Studies in Economic Institutions

Series Editor: Geoffrey M. Hodgson
Research Professor, University of Hertfordshire Business School, UK

1. Competing Capitalisms: Institutions and Economies (Volumes I and II)
   Richard Whitley

2. Foundations of Social Capital
   Elinor Ostrom and T.K. Ahn

3. Trust
   Elias L. Khalil

4. Knowledge, Learning and Routines (Volumes I and II)
   Nathalie Lazaric and Edward Lorenz

5. Recent Developments in Institutional Economics
   Geoffrey M. Hodgson

6. Networks (Volumes I and II)
   Gernot Grabher and Walter W. Powell

Future titles will include:

Markets
Mitchel Y. Abolafia

Concepts of Money: Interdisciplinary Perspectives from Economics, Sociology and Political Science
Geoffrey Ingham

Knowledge and Learning in the Firm
Bart Nooteboom

The State
Klaus Nielsen

Wherever possible, the articles in these volumes have been reproduced as originally published using facsimile reproduction, inclusive of footnotes and pagination to facilitate ease of reference.

For a list of all Edward Elgar published titles visit our site on the World Wide Web at
www.e-elgar.com

Networks
Volume I

Edited by

Gernot Grabher

Professor of Economic Geography
University of Bonn, Germany

and

Walter W. Powell

Professor of Education, Organizational Behavior and Sociology
Stanford University, USA

CRITICAL STUDIES IN ECONOMIC INSTITUTIONS

An Elgar Reference Collection
Cheltenham, UK • Northampton, MA, USA

Published by
Edward Elgar Publishing Limited
Glensanda House
Montpellier Parade
Cheltenham
Glos GL50 1UA
UK

Edward Elgar Publishing, Inc.
136 West Street
Suite 202
Northampton
Massachusetts 01060
USA

A catalogue record for this book is available from the British Library

ISBN   1 84376 035 5 (2 volume set)

Printed and bound in Great Britain by MPG Books Ltd, Bodmin, Cornwall

Contents

Acknowledgements

The editors and publishers wish to thank the authors and the following publishers who have kindly given permission for the use of copyright material.

Administrative Science Quarterly for articles: Oliver E. Williamson (1991), 'Comparative Economic Organization: The Analysis of Discrete Structural Alternatives', *Administrative Science Quarterly*, **36** (2), June, 269–96; Brian Uzzi (1997), 'Social Structure and Competition in Interfirm Networks: The Paradox of Embeddedness', *Administrative Science Quarterly*, **42** (1), March, 35–67.

American Economic Association for article: Bengt Holmström and John Roberts (1998), 'The Boundaries of the Firm Revisited', *Journal of Economic Perspectives*, **12** (4), Fall, 73–94.

Blackwell Publishing Ltd for article: G.B. Richardson (1972), 'The Organisation of Industry', *Economic Journal*, **82** (327), September, 883–96.

Elsevier for articles and excerpt: Walter W. Powell (1990), 'Neither Market Nor Hierarchy: Network Forms of Organization', *Research in Organizational Behavior*, **12**, 295–336, reset; Harrison C. White (1993), 'Markets, Networks and Control', in Siegwart M. Lindenberg and Hein Schreuder (eds), *Interdisciplinary Perspectives on Organization Studies*, 223–39; Mari Sako and Susan Helper (1998), 'Determinants of Trust in Supplier Relations: Evidence from the Automotive Industry in Japan and the United States', *Journal of Economic Behavior and Organization*, **34**, 387–417.

Diego Gambetta for his own article: (1988), 'Mafia: The Price of Distrust', in Diego Gambetta (ed.), *Trust: Making and Breaking Cooperative Relations*, Chapter 10, 158–75.

Macmillan Publishers Ltd for article: Réka Albert, Hawoong Jeong and Albert-László Barabási (2000), 'Error and Attack Tolerance of Complex Networks', *Nature*, **406**, 27 July, 378–82.

Alexandra Milgram and Jeffrey Travers for article: Jeffrey Travers and Stanley Milgram (1969), 'An Experimental Study of the Small World Problem', *Sociometry*, **32** (4), December, 425–43.

Northwestern University School of Law and Ian R. Macneil for article: Ian R. Macneil (1978), 'Contracts: Adjustment of Long-Term Economic Relations Under Classical, Neoclassical, and Relational Contract Law', *Northwestern University Law Review*, **72** (6), 854–905.

Kari Polanyi Levitt for excerpt: K. Polanyi (1968), 'Our Obsolete Market Mentality', in George Dalton (ed.), *Primitive, Archaic, and Modern Economies: Essays of Karl Polanyi*, Chapter 4, 59–77, reset.

Population Council for article: Yoram Ben-Porath (1980), 'The F-Connection: Families, Friends, and Firms and the Organization of Exchange', *Population and Development Review*, **6** (1), March, 1–30.

Taylor and Francis Ltd (http://www.tandf.co.uk/journals) for article: Ronald Dore (1983), 'Goodwill and the Spirit of Market Capitalism', *British Journal of Sociology*, **XXXIV** (4), December, 459–82.

Thomson Learning for excerpt: Gernot Grabher (1993), 'The Weakness of Strong Ties: The Lock-in of Regional Development in the Ruhr Area', in Gernot Grabher (ed.), *The Embedded Firm: On the Socioeconomics of Industrial Networks*, Chapter 12, 255–77.

University of Chicago Press for articles: Mark S. Granovetter (1973), 'The Strength of Weak Ties', *American Journal of Sociology*, **78** (6), May, 1360–80; Peter V. Marsden (1983), 'Restricted Access in Networks and Models of Power', *American Journal of Sociology*, **88** (4), January, 686–717; Mark Granovetter (1985), 'Economic Action and Social Structure: The Problem of Embeddedness', *American Journal of Sociology*, **91** (3), November, 481–510; John F. Padgett and Christopher K. Ansell (1993), 'Robust Action and the Rise of the Medici, 1400–1434', *American Journal of Sociology*, **98** (6), May, 1259–319; Duncan J. Watts (1999), 'Networks, Dynamics, and the Small-World Phenomenon', *American Journal of Sociology*, **105** (2), September, 493–527; Joel M. Podolny (2001), 'Networks as the Pipes and Prisms of the Market', *American Journal of Sociology*, **107** (1), July, 33–60.

Every effort has been made to trace all the copyright holders but if any have been inadvertently overlooked the publishers will be pleased to make the necessary arrangement at the first opportunity.

In addition the publishers wish to thank the Marshall Library of Economics, Cambridge University, the Library of the University of Warwick and the Library of Indiana University at Bloomington, USA for their assistance in obtaining these articles.

Introduction

Gernot Grabher and Walter W. Powell

Networks as Governance Structures and the Governance of Networks

For much of the second half of the twentieth century, research on networks was largely confined to the fields of sociology, communication, and social psychology. These fields produced a considerable corpus of research on reference groups and role sets, on the importance of networks to social support, and the key role of networks in the diffusion of information. During the 1970s, attention began to shift to the workplace and to corporate governance. Mark Granovetter's (1973) important research on the strength of weak ties, which showed how linkages to acquaintances trumped formal channels for obtaining a job, and research on the extensive interlocks among boards of directors of large US firms (Useem, 1984; Mintz and Schwartz, 1985; Mizruchi, 1996), signaled new attention to the varied ways in which networks influenced economic life.[1]

The success of Japanese automakers and their extensive reliance on networks of subcontractors attracted the attention of many management scholars (Clark, 1979; Asanuma, 1985, 1989). Growing recognition that patterns of repeated exchange were an essential component in many craft industries (Eccles, Volume II, Chapter 16; Faulkner, 1983; Powell, 1985; Faulkner and Anderson, Volume II, Chapter 17) and ethnic enterprises (Ben-Porath, Volume I, Chapter 10), as well as critical to the success of regional economies (Brusco, 1982; Saxenian, 1994), meant that scholars from a wide array of social science and professional disciplines became interested in networks.

Today, the literature on networks and economic institutions is quite broad and growing rapidly. Indeed, it is difficult to draw disciplinary boundaries around the field of network research because new developments are abundant, occurring rapidly, and often surprising in their source. In just the past five years, physicists have shown a strong interest in networks, and made key contributions to understanding the ubiquitous nature of small worlds and scale-free networks (Albert and Barabási, 2002; Barabási, 2002; Newman, 2003; Strogatz, 2003; Watts, 1999, 2003). Economists studying topics as diverse as international trade (Feenstra *et al.*, 1999; Rauch, 1999, 2001) and fish markets (Kirman, 2001) have stressed the relational features of exchange. In fact, some argue that the overlapping reproduction of multiple networks is the analytical lever to account for the origins of banking in Renaissance Florence and, in turn, the rise of mercantile capitalism (Padgett and Ansell, Volume I, Chapter 15; Padgett, 2001).

Given such an expansive literature, it is not our task in these two volumes to cover all the various branches of research on networks. We aim, instead, at surveying major empirical research and key theoretical statements concerning how actors (whether individuals, organizations, or large collectivities) forge enduring exchange relations, based on diverse motivations (e.g. incentives, loyalty, trust, etc).[2]

Our collection is, of course, but one possible path through a wide conceptual terrain. Although we aimed at keeping our path accessible and clear, our choices were inevitably molded by our respective academic backgrounds.[3]

Network analysis is not a specific or unitary theory that specifies distinctive laws and propositions, but rather a broad strategy for investigating social structure. Network analysis, in other words, is not (yet) a deductive system in which lower order propositions follow as logical conclusions from more general propositions. Network analysis offers a particular, *relational* view on society and economy (Collins, 1988, p. 413; Emirbayer, 1997).[4] From this basic understanding, network research tends to proceed along two main paths: a social network perspective and a governance perspective (Powell and Smith-Doerr, 1994; Ebers, 1997; Grandori, 1999; Thompson, 2003).

A pivotal starting-point of social network analysis is what Emirbayer and Goodwin (1994, p. 1414) call the 'anticategorical imperative', which rejects explanations of 'social behavior as the result of individuals' common possession of attributes and norms rather than as the result of their involvement in structural social relations' (Wellmann, 1983, p. 165). Social network analysis, then, begins with the assumption that social behavior cannot simply be explicated by the individual attributes of actors. Explanations stem from analyses of patterns of relations. Burt (1986, p. 106) describes network analysis aptly: 'It captures causal factors in the social structural bedrock of society, bypassing the spuriously significant attributes of people temporarily occupying particular positions in social structure.' Behavior and processes, in this perspective, are interpreted by reference to networks of social relations that link actors or 'nodes'. Moreover, position in a network has important behavioral, perceptual and attitudinal consequences for individual actors. The hallmark of social network analysis, in Laumann's (1979, p. 349) words, is to account for 'the behavior of network elements (i.e. the nodes) and of the system as a whole by appeal to specific features of the interconnections among the elements'. This approach thus investigates the constraining and enabling dimensions of patterned relationships among social actors.

The focus of the structural approach is on a set of nodes and the pattern of ties among nodes. Location in a network can provide leverage to those who are in brokerage positions (Burt, 1992), or fast access to timely information and skills to nodes that are linked to well-connected partners (Powell, Koput, and Smith-Doerr, Volume II, Chapter 5; Stuart, 1998). Seen in this view, networks are the 'plumbing' of market relations, channeling and directing flows of information and resources, and shaping the accumulation of stocks of resources and knowledge.

An alternative view of networks stresses governance, focusing on the institutional mechanisms by which networks are initiated, coordinated, monitored, recombined, and terminated. This perspective focuses less on the structural properties of relationships and concentrates more on the particular institutional and social contexts in which actors are embedded. Our selections feature work from both traditions. Thus while Volume I, Part I, and Volume II, Part II, of this collection highlight the governance perspective, Volume I, Part II, and Volume II, Part I, survey the structural approach.

The governance strand of literature is organized around two key foci (Oliver and Ebers, 1998), both of which are featured in this collection. One line of research aims at tracing the formation of networks and their configurations to specific features of the broader institutional environment. For example, with regard to the formation of business networks in Japan and East Asia, scholars have emphasized the interdependencies with particular forms of state intervention, labor market arrangements, and specific cultural norms prevailing in these societies (Dore, 1986; Hamilton and Biggart, 1988; Lincoln, Gerlach, and Ahmadjian, 1996; Westney,

1996). Other studies have focused on variation in the institutional settings between different European countries and the USA, exploring how these differences play out in the particular inter- and intrafirm networks that prevail in these societies (Lane and Bachmann, 1997; Sako, 1998; Sako and Helper, Volume I, Chapter 9). At a regional level, the emergence and decay of networks have been attributed to institutional conditions and particular local conventions in numerous studies of industrial districts and regional clusters (Brusco, 1982; Amin and Thrift, Volume II, Chapter 20; Grabher, Volume I, Chapter 19; Storper, 1993; Saxenian, 1994; Malmberg and Maskell, Volume II, Chapter 21; Powell *et al.*, 2002).

A more managerial approach is evinced in a line of research on governance that seeks to answer how to design, manage, and control networks in order to reduce uncertainties and improve competitive position. This perspective is concerned with the salience of different types of resources and, characteristically, conceptualizes network ties in organizational, contractual, and ownership terms. Scholars have studied, for example, how pre-existing social ties foster and support the development of more formal relationships between organizations (Galaskiewicz and Wasserman, 1989; Gulati, 1995; Gulati and Gargiulo, 1999). Other research has explored how interdependencies and asset complementarities between organizations influence processes of network formation and specific forms of interorganizational networks (Contractor and Lorange, 1988; Kogut, 1988; Teece, 1992; Dyer, 1996; Hagedoorn, 1996; Doz and Hamel, 1998; Nooteboom, 1999).

Networks as Governance Structure

We begin our collection with a focus on networks as a particular type of governance structure. There has been a lively debate in the social science literature concerning the institutional forms that govern economic exchange. Put simply, this line of inquiry asks where the boundaries are drawn between markets and firms, and between social and economic organization. The goal is to account for the heterogeneity of arrangements that are found in contemporary economies, ranging from spot markets to global franchise operations, from informal rotating credit associations to multinational banks, and from joint ventures to complex multi-party consortia.

The study of the boundaries between markets and firms was sparked by Coase (1937), who asked the simple, compelling question of why so much activity takes place inside formal organizations if markets are regarded as the optimal mechanism for resource allocation. With this insight, Coase brought attention to the firm as a governance structure, and not solely a production function. Coase answered his question by attending to the costs of exchange: when the transaction costs of market exchange are high, it may be less costly to coordinate transactions through a formal organization. This important paper, however, lay fallow for almost four decades until it was picked up by Williamson and proponents of transaction cost economics in the 1970s. By theorizing both governance structures and organizational forms, the economics of organization moved much closer to the fields of law, economic sociology, organization theory, and business studies.

Williamson (Volume I, Chapter 4) asked under what circumstances economic functions are performed within the boundaries of hierarchical firms rather than by market exchanges that cross these boundaries. His answer was that transactions involving high uncertainty about their outcome, that recur frequently, and require substantial 'transaction-specific investments' are likely to take place within hierarchically organized firms. Exchanges that are straightforward and non-repetitive, requiring few transaction-specific investments, should take place across a market interface. Two behavioral assumptions (bounded rationality and opportunism) and three transaction variables (frequency, uncertainty, and asset specificity) defined the basic logic of a useful model that offered a dichotomous view of markets and hierarchies as distinct building-blocks for institutional analysis. Competitors are located outside the boundaries of firms, whereas managers exercise authority and curb opportunistic behavior inside those boundaries.

This perspective attracted both followers and critics throughout the social sciences, law, and management. The economist Geoffrey Hodgson (1988, p. 211), reacting to the basic assumptions of the approach, concluded that 'following the tradition of individualistic social scientists, Williamson puts forward a model of individual nature (i.e. 'opportunism') and recklessly assumes that this applies equally to quite different forms of institutional arrangement ... No recognition is made of the effect of the institutional environment in moulding actions and beliefs'. Opportunism and bounded rationality are conceived as generalized 'human conditions', exogenously given rather than as factors that are shaped, intentionally or unintentionally, in the course of recurrent interaction.

In the transaction-cost approach, under- and over-socialized concepts of economic action (Granovetter, Volume I, Chapter 7) complement one another. The market resembles the under-socialized conception of the atomized and anonymous exchange of classical political economy, which neglects the role of social relations and local cultures that can provide order in economic life. Not far from Hobbes's 'state of nature' or Rawls's 'original position', this perception invokes an idealized state of affairs in which behavior and institutions are unaffected by social structure and relations. Interactions among actors are confined to discrete exchanges between independently acting individuals or organizations: 'Sharp in by clear agreement; sharp out by clear performance' (Macneil, 1974, p. 378).

As in Hobbes's *Leviathan*, the problem of disorder is 'solved' with an over-socialized concept of hierarchical power within the firm, which deflects opportunism by making potentially divisive decisions by 'fiat'. The efficacy of hierarchical power within organizations has long been questioned, however. The over-socialized view that orders within a hierarchy elicit easy obedience does not stand scrutiny against a wealth of studies in which the firm appears as an arena of resistance to the encroachment of organizational interests on personal ones. In addition, cross-cutting social ties evolve that frequently transcend vertical lines of hierarchy. As an illustration of these lines of research, we include a classic article by Dalton (Volume II, Chapter 13) on factions inside firms and a paper by White (Volume I, Chapter 14) on cross-cutting linkages within organizations.

A second line of response to Coase and Williamson focused on the dichotomous view of markets and hierarchies. Richardson (Volume I, Chapter 1) drew attention to the increasing involvement of firms in non-market arrangements with other firms and agencies: involvement that refutes the commonplace picture of firms simply as 'islands of planned coordination in a sea of market relations'. In practice, firms build wide and substantial barriers between themselves and such tempestuous seas by entering into all kinds of arrangements or deals with each other. They often, for instance, make use of traditional ties of loyalty and use personal exchanges of goods and resources, rather than turning to the open market and seeking one-off competitive deals (Hodgson, 1988). In referring to these intermediate areas, Richardson (1972) hoped to show that the excluded phenomena are of crucial importance. He argued that viewing industrial activity in terms of a sharp dichotomy between firm and market offers a distorted view of how the economy works. We thus begin our collection with this classic paper by Richardson, which opens inquiry into the varied forms of governance that facilitate economic exchange.

In subsequent work, Williamson became 'persuaded that transactions in the middle range are much more common' than he previously recognized (Williamson, 1985, p. 83). These transactions in the middle range are arrayed by Williamson along a continuum with market exchanges at one end and hierarchies at the other. Moving from the market towards the hierarchy pole, one encounters putting-out systems, regional networks, subcontracting arrangements, strategic partnerships, franchising, joint ventures, and decentralized profit centers. Explaining the existence of these intermediate forms usually involves cataloging the deficiencies of fully integrated hierarchies and competitive markets and then arguing that the new intermediate forms offer a solution to these problems. Williamson (Volume I, Chapter 4) offers a succinct statement about the collection of activities that constitute this 'swollen middle' (Hennart, 1993).

Many social scientists and legal scholars were profoundly dissatisfied with the continuum view, however. Macneil (Volume I, Chapter 2) argues that much exchange is entangled in strings of obligation, duty, and friendship. Bradach and Eccles (1989, p. 116) suggested that while the ideal types of market and hierarchy may serve as a useful starting-point, these polar types also point to the weaknesses of this approach: 'The assumption that these mechanisms are mutually exclusive, however, obscures rather than clarifies our understanding ... [P]rice, authority, and trust are combined with each other in assorted ways in the empirical world.' Much of the complexity of the varied combinations that Bradach and Eccles (1989) characterize as overlapping and nested result because only rarely are control mechanisms created *de novo*. The perspective that economic exchanges can be usefully arranged along a continuum both misses the interweaving of social and economic exchange and undervalues the importance of reciprocity or reputation as alternative governance mechanisms. By conceiving of markets and hierarchies as pure forms, intermediate organizational designs are portrayed as mongrel hybrids (Powell, Volume I, Chapter 3). As this collection seeks to elucidate, the notion of networks can be more fruitfully exploited when viewed as a distinctive form, rather than as idiosyncratic hybrids.

Key Features of Networks

Network analysis is based on the view that how either an individual or an organization performs depends to a considerable extent on how that actor is tied into a larger web of social connections. Considering the stress on genealogy in ancient times, the idea of embeddedness is perhaps as old as mankind itself. Karl Polanyi, writing in the middle of the last century, was especially critical of the economics of his time, and its development of a simple abstract model of the economy that ignored how economies were embedded in communities (Polanyi, Volume I, Chapter 6). The embeddedness argument, most prominently stated in Mark Granovetter's (Volume I, Chapter 7) oft-cited article, stresses that economic relationships cannot be easily separated from social ties (but see also Krippner, 2001). Consider the stylized analysis of a buyer–seller relationship, a dyad viewed outside of a social context, with no connections to other buyers and sellers, and no history of past exchanges. With scant attention paid to issues of trust, reputation, access, or power, the terms of trade are stripped of their relational context.

The embeddedness approach also attempts to avoid 'temporal reductionism', which stems from a discrete view of transactions (Macneil, 1974) that focuses solely on the isolated act of exchange. A relational view of exchange situates actors within ongoing patterns of trust and distrust, in which the identity and reputation of participants loom large. Our selections indicate that trust is not easily accomplished, however. Suspicion and rivalry can pervade both criminal activity (Gambetta, 1993) and trading relations (Sako, 1998; Sako and Helper, Volume I, Chapter 9). Location in social structure commonly determines how parties evaluate one another, and the terms on which they trade, and the advantages they reap. Thus position is strongly shaped by identity and reputation, whether in an ethnic community of diamond traders (Ben-Porath, Volume I, Chapter 10), textile merchants in Japan (Dore, Volume I, Chapter 11), or venture capital syndicates in the USA (Podolny, Volume I, Chapter 12).

Much discussion of networks emphasizes their cohesiveness and reach. Early research on networks of acquaintances revealed a surprising degree of connectivity within groups and the key role of weak ties in transmitting information (Travers and Milgram, Volume I, Chapter 16; Granovetter, Volume I, Chapter 17). Watts (Volume I, Chapter 18) has shown that 'small-world' networks can be created by adding only a handful of remote links to a network where the level of local clustering is high (that is, friends of friends are also friends). Thus, a small proportion of random ties added to several tightly clustered nodes can produce small-world effects. These ideas have been popularized in the theatre (John Guare's play, *Six Degrees of Separation*) and in entertainment (the Kevin Bacon game), as well as applied to the studies of scientific collaborations (Newman, 2003), corporate ownership ties (Kogut and Walker, 2001), and the World Wide Web (Albert, Jeong, and Barabási, 1999).

Connectivity may facilitate the exchange and flow of information and resources, but position can also be used to restrict access to some parties (Marsden, Volume I, Chapter 13) or to mobilize and control multiple, overlapping networks to gain advantage (White, Volume I, Chapter 14; Padgett and Ansell, Volume I, Chapter 15). Ties that bind parties together can also ossify into ties that blind. When repeat trading becomes extensive, it can turn to parochialism. Grabher (Volume I, Chapter 19) illustrates how a tightly linked network calcified into a regional lock-in, culminating in the decline of the Ruhr area. Uzzi's work (Volume I, Chapter 20) stresses that strong bonds have to be blended with weaker ties in order for firms to reap the advantages of network diversity. Moreover, networks that are overly dependent upon highly central 'hubs' are very much prone to collapse if those hubs are eliminated (Albert, Jeong, and Barabási, Volume I, Chapter 21).

Many scholars studying the dynamics of organizational performance have shifted attention from a static focus on minimizing transaction costs to an evolutionary view of the emergence and development of competencies and learning processes (Kogut and Zander, 1992; Teece and Pisano, 1994; Langlois and Robertson, 1995; Nonaka and Takeuchi, 1995). These researchers have noted that the diffusion of knowledge plays an important role in the creation and distribution of wealth. Access to information (Boorman, Volume II, Chapter 1), the ability to utilize and recombine information (Lane and Maxfield, Volume II, Chapter 8; Stark, Volume II, Chapter 9), and the strategic use of information, either by hoarding it for arbitrage or spreading it widely at an opportune moment (Burt, Volume II, Chapter 3), are critical to both individual advancement and organizational performance.

One line of research has emphasized the role of networks in enhancing organizational learning (Lundvall, 1988; Lundvall and Johnson, 1994; Ahuja, 2000; Nooteboom, 2000). Dense social networks facilitate the assimilation and interpretation of information (Brown and Duguid, Volume II, Chapter 4; Wenger, 1998), while centrality in networks affords the opportunity to access multiple views on a problem and marshall diverse resources to tackle the problem. The advantages of centrality in networks are particularly salient in fast-moving industries, where knowledge is developing rapidly and the centers of knowledge production are dispersed (Powell, Koput, and Smith-Doerr, Volume II, Chapter 5).

An older, more developed strand of research has analyzed the diffusion of information, such as the adoption of patterns of agricultural or medical innovations (Ryan and Gross, 1943; Coleman, Katz, and Menzel, Volume II, Chapter 10; Rogers, 1962), or the flow of corporate governance practices through corporate boardrooms (Davis and Greve, Volume II, Chapter 12). Initially, computational limitations precluded the analysis of large-scale networks, but advances in computing power and combinatorial theory (especially graph theory), along with important advances in network methodology (see, for example, Wasserman and Faust, 1994; de Nooy *et al.*, 2004; Scott, 2000), have produced major strides in the scale and scope of network research.

Varieties of Network Forms

In this collection, we differentiate types of networks in terms of their duration and stability, as well as whether they are, in some sense, primordial (that is, steeped in pre-existing relations) or purposive (i.e. created for specific purposes to accomplish a task). Networks vary considerably, from short-term projects to enduring, long-run relationships bolstered by familial or locational connections. Different temporal dimensions have important consequences for the types of governance found in networks. Long-term networks, on the one hand, benefit from well-established channels of exchange and patterns of collaboration. Stable networks economize on past experiences of collaboration and expectations emerging from the 'shadow of the future' (Axelrod, 1984). On the other hand, however, long-term stability seems to increase cohesion and tighten patterns of exchange which, in turn, exposes networks to the risks of obsolescence or lock-in (Powell, 1985, pp. 202–7; Grabher, Volume I, Chapter 19; Uzzi, Volume I, Chapter 20).

The governance of networks can vary from authoritative to distributed. Some networks are more hierarchical, while others are more heterarchical (Sydow, 2001). In hierarchical networks, control is exerted by a more or less clearly identifiable center or coordinator. There is, to describe it more vividly, a spider in the web. The coordinator regulates network practices and rules, such as the selection of network members, the allocation of resources, the evaluation of network practices, and the maintenance of network boundaries. In heterarchical networks, in contrast, the regulation of interaction and relations is distributed and associative (Hedlund, 1986, 1993). Heterarchical networks exhibit patterns of emergent self-organization, strong lateral ties, and a diverse distribution of authority (Stark, 2001).

Both temporal stability and forms of governance provide general coordinates for differentiating four key types: informal networks, project networks, regional networks, and business networks. To be sure, these forms do not represent distinct or essentialist categories, but rather overlap and interpenetrate one another to varying degrees. The particular network forms evolve as complex combinations of overlapping, juxtaposed, and nested government mechanisms. Thus the origins of networks are highly contingent: 'in some cases the formation of networks anticipates the need for this particular form of exchange; in other situations, there is a slow pattern of development which ultimately justifies the form; and, in other cases, networks are a response to the demand for a mode of exchange that resolves exigencies that other forms are ill-equipped to handle' (Powell, Volume I, Chapter 3).

Informal Networks

Membership in an informal network is typically based on shared experience, pre-existing social ties, or some bond of familiarity that draws participants together. Given that such relationships emerge out of repeated exchanges, informal networks often involve long time horizons. But the wide variation in factors that spawn informal networks creates a rich, diverse pool of possible forms. The multiplicity of types of informal networks render this form more diffuse and opaque with respect to critical dimensions such as their internal structure, the regulation of access, and the boundaries between the network and the larger environment.

Informal networks can evolve in contexts that, at first glance, seem to resemble rather clear instances of market-driven exchange relations, or in large organizations governed by hierarchical rule. The Moroccan bazaar, to refer to a classic example, appears to approximate neoclassical market conditions since highly competitive bargaining is price driven (Geertz, Volume II, Chapter 14). Yet, in order to improve the richness and reliability of information, buyers and sellers establish continuing relationships based on reciprocity. Using informal relational contracts to cope with volatility is not confined to ostensibly 'pre-modern' contexts. Similar to the traders in the noisy informational environments of a bazaar, traders on financial markets, Wall Street, or the City of London create trust-based ties with other market participants to collect and evaluate information, rumors and gossip (Abolafia, 1997; Baker, 1984; Amin and Thrift, Volume II, Chapter 20; Thrift, 1994; Beunza and Stark, 2003). Even in these most competitive of arenas, economic exchange is framed by ongoing networks of informal relationships.

Informal networks are not only established to filter and process information in volatile market settings. Due to their informality, these networks are also particularly well suited to collectively distort, suppress or manipulate market information. Consequently, informal networks can provide a context for practices ranging from corruption and conspiracy to organized crime in violent Mafia-type networks (Gambetta, Volume I, Chapter 8; Della Porta and Vanucci, 1999). Secrecy considerations favor close-knit connections. The imperatives of concealment, however, have to be balanced with the need for concerted action and efficient task performance, which demand tighter coupling not unlike in legal business networks (Baker and Faulkner, Volume II, Chapter 15).

Informal networks also evolve in organizational contexts that are governed by formal, hierarchical control. And like in market environments, informal ties in hierarchical organizations fulfill multiple roles. They can compensate for the structural weaknesses of hierarchies when they, for example, constitute 'communities of practice' (Brown and Duguid, Volume II, Chapter 4; Wenger, 1998). Such lateral, self-organized networks, 'informally bound together by shared expertise and passion for a joint enterprise' (Wenger and Snyder, 2000, p. 139), provide decentralized means of learning as well as repositories of experience. Such communities seek to enhance individual competences and thus are usually not in conflict with organizational goals. In fact, they have become acknowledged and valued more and more by organizations despite serious challenges in strategically managing informal emergent networks (Swan, Scarbrough, and Robertson, 2002).

In contrast to this compensatory role, however, informal networks are also forged as lateral coalitions against organizational interests and procedures. Indeed, Dalton (Volume II, Chapter 13) asserted that the success of informal coalitions in evading organizational rules and contradictions involved joined action 'of a kind rarely, if ever, shown in carrying on official activities'. Attempts at implementing hierarchical rule in large bureaucracies, such as in state-socialist economies, have proven, paradoxically, to be fertile grounds for lateral coalitions. These informal networks played a critical role in the post-socialist transformation with regard to both (proto-)entrepreneurial activities and pathways of privatization (Burawoy and Krotov, 1992; Sík, 1992; Stark, Volume II, Chapter 9; Sedaitis, 1997).

Project Networks

Displaying a much higher level of hierarchical coordination than informal networks, project-based networks are highly purposive assemblies of participants with complementary skills. While informal networks are based on interpersonal ties and business networks are configured as interorganizational alliances, project networks interweave interorganizational and inter-personal relationships (Boltanski and Chiapello, 1999). In contrast to other network forms, projects are temporarily limited by definition. Deadlines are the key feature of projects, which are temporary systems with institutionalized termination (Goodman and Goodman, 1976; Lundin and Söderholm, 1995; De Fillippi and Arthur, 1998). While more stable and enduring network forms are primarily devoted to the advancement of particular goals or interests, the aim of project networks is the accomplishment of a specific task.

This temporal limitation and task orientation poses formidable challenges with regard to coordination, control, and learning (Ekstedt *et al.*, 1999). Projects often entail high-risk outcomes; however, they seem to lack normative safeguards that minimize the likelihood of failure. Projects depend on an elaborate body of collective knowledge, yet they often begin without clarifying the responsibilities of project members in advance. Moreover, there is rarely sufficient time to develop personal confidence that could compensate for the absence of shared experience, familiarity, or social coherence. A paradox of project networks is that participation in them presupposes trust, but their temporal limitation seems to hinder its development (Meyerson, Weick, and Kramer, Volume II, Chapter 18).

This abiding tension in project networks finds its solution in the widespread practice of drawing on core members and relationships from (successful) prior projects as a foundation for new tasks. Empirical studies in canonical 'one-off' industries, such as construction (Eccles, 1981) and film (De Fillippi and Arthur, 1998; Jones, 2001), have demonstrated that project networks operate in a context of recurrent collaboration and repeated contracting. Project networks are built on 'latent' ties that facilitate the coordination of experience and expectations (Lundin and Hartmann, 2000; Starkey, Barnatt, and Tempest, 2000; Sydow and Windeler, 1999; Grabher, 2002a). The practice of project organizing is thus shaped by past experience and affected by the shadow of potential future collaboration.

These chains of repeated collaboration are held together (or cut off) by the reputation that members gain (or lose) in previous collaborations. Reputation refers not only to human, but also to social capital: 'whom you know' becomes as important as 'what you know' (Gann and Salter, 2000; Christopherson, 2002; Grabher, 2002b). In addition, project networks rely on various sources of 'swift trust' (Meyerson, Weick, and Kramer, Volume II, Chapter 18). Swift trust, most importantly, is category-driven, based on expectations that participants can deal with one another more as performers of roles than as unique individuals. Expectations, consequently, are more standardized and stable and defined in terms of tasks rather than actor attributes. Frequently, roles in project networks are highly institutionalized – i.e. plumber on a construction site, or sound man on a film set. Increasingly, the use of new information and communication technologies as well as managerial techniques enables novel combinations of globally dispersed virtual teams and highly concentrated local networks (Nonaka and Konno, 1998; Thrift, 2000; Amin and Cohendet, 2004).

Regional Networks

Many accounts of geographically based networks draw, at least implicitly, on the influential writings of Alfred Marshall (1890) and his ideas about industrial districts. In the 1980s and 1990s, numerous success stories proliferated regarding the 'Third Italy', the north-central region of Emilia-Romagna, where decentralized, spatially concentrated production of sophisticated consumer goods thrived (Becattini, 1978; Brusco, 1982; Piore and Sabel, 1984; Pyke, Becattini, and Sengenberger, 1990; Lazerson, 1995). Regional economic networks evolve over longer time periods, but have some of the spontaneous, multiplex features of informal networks. In successful industrial districts, a complex division of labor arises in which diverse small and medium-sized organizations play specialized roles that contribute to a mode of production that is technologically sophisticated and able to sustain competition on a global scale. Smaller organizations thus derive benefits from this division of labor that would not be available were they not located in proximity to other similarly connected organizations (Bresnahan, Gambardella, and Saxenian, 2001). The combination of geographic propinquity and functional specialization generates, as Marshall (1890, 1920) stressed, a distinctive 'industrial atmosphere' that facilitates the exchange of ideas and personnel and the transfer and accumulation of tacit knowledge. In Marshall's (1890, p. 25) felicitous phrase, 'the mysteries of the trade ... are in the air'.

Regional networks are connected through a variety of personal relations – kinship, neighborhoods, political parties, social clubs, technological communities, and industrial specializations. These multiple, overlapping affiliations produce 'region-wide assets', among them skills, trust, and a reputation for reliability (Amin and Thrift, Volume II, Chapter 20). Rather than hierarchical control, regional networks are governed by fluid membership based on technological cycles and local 'conventions' that entail mutually coherent routines and expectations (Storper, 1993). The Italian industrial districts, which were the fountainhead for research on spatial agglomeration, may well have been an unusual case of collective governance because of their dense familial and political bonds. But other successful regions, most notably Baden-Württemberg (Herrigel, 1996) and Silicon Valley (Saxenian, 1994; Kenney, 2000), suggest that robust districts can be based on a variety of mechanisms and network configurations that foster reciprocal forms of exchange. The literature on industrial districts has developed a wide array of relational concepts, including 'clusters' (Porter, 1990) and 'learning regions' (Florida, 1995).

The Marshallian analysis of regional networks focuses on a specialized division of labor, in which firms contribute distinctive skills to a complex production chain. More recent analyses, however, suggest that regional networks also benefit from rivalry, mutual observation, and imitation (Almeida and Kogut, 1999). The sharing of common regional conditions, opportunities, and threats affords comparability and thus elucidates the strengths and weaknesses of particular strategies (Gertler, 1995; Brown and Duguid, 2000; Malmberg and Maskell, Volume II, Chapter 21).

While much of the research on regional networks has focused on the local embeddedness of relationships, more recent studies have stressed how successful industrial districts have extensive extra-local connections as well (Amin and Cohendet, 2004). The extent to which regional networks are integrated into global exchange relations has profound impact on their internal governance, as well as their ability to avoid closure and sclerosis (Markusen, 1996; Bunnell and Coe, 2001; Bresnahan, Gambardella, and Saxenian, 2001; Owen-Smith and Powell, 2003). Trans-regional pipelines can supply crucial resources and information, whereas local ties are more amenable to the interpretation and translation of information (Storper, 1997; Grabher, 2002b).

Business Networks

Formal interorganizational relations are, by their very nature, more strategic and orchestrated than either informal or regional networks. While less tightly controlled than the chain of command in large hierarchical firms, business networks are much more centrally organized than informal or regional networks in terms of the selection of network members, the allocation of resources and distribution of revenues, and definition of network boundaries (Jarillo, 1988; Lorenzoni and Baden-Fuller, 1995). In general, communication channels and information flows are also less open and permeable than in regional and informal networks. Ties in business networks are forged, in a much more distinct and manifest fashion than in other forms, by power (Håkansson and Johanson, Volume II, Chapter 22). Despite these principal features, business networks also cover a broad spectrum of types that stretch from hierarchical configurations in marketing alliances or multinational supply chain networks to more horizontal ties in strategic R&D partnerships (Axelsson and Easton, 1992; Nooteboom, 1999).

Hierarchical relations and the attendant asymmetries of power are key governance mechanisms in large corporations. The efficacy of 'fiat', however, is particularly limited in multinational and global corporations because subsidiaries often control strategic resources and key competences, as well as critical linkages with key actors in their local environments (Ghoshal and Bartlett, Volume II, Chapter 23). Typically, in such large, dispersed, and interdependent organizations, hierarchical authority coexists with significant levels of local autonomy (Hedlund, 1993; Sölvell and Zander, 1995). Thus, intra-organizational ties and external network relations with customers, distributors, and suppliers interpenetrate one another (Johanson and Mattson, 1987). The specific configuration of these networks is more and more driven by attempts to stimulate interactive learning and innovation, then by straightforward transaction-cost considerations (Cantwell and Santangelo, 1999; Amin and Cohendet, 1999, 2004).

The need to concentrate on core competencies has led firms to take vertical disintegration further and shift from internal ties to external supplier relations and global commodity chains. This route of disintegration forks into a variety of paths, ranging from market-driven adversarial transactions to cooperative ties of mutual learning and interactive innovation processes. These two principal variants of adversarial versus cooperative ties have also been conceived in terms of exit- versus voice-based supplier systems (Helper, 1993), in which exit-based relations are driven by opportunistic behavior while voice-based systems benefit from high levels of trust. But cross-country comparisons reveal, however, that opportunism and trust are highly variable and dependent on specific institutional settings (Asanuma, 1985, 1989; Lane and Bachmann, 1997; Sako and Helper, Volume I, Chapter 9; Helper, MacDuffie, and Sabel, 1999).

Trust-based ties form the basic social fabric of Japanese *keiretsu* (Gerlach, 1992; Lincoln, Gerlach, and Takahashi, Volume II, Chapter 24; Westney, 1996, 2001). These corporate networks can be tightly integrated into vertical structures of cascading shareholding or more loosely coupled in multiple horizontal relationships of mutual support and defense between large industrial corporations and financial institutions. Although the lengthy Japanese recession has led to a loosening of ties within the *keiretsu* and an overall weakening of the *keiretsu*'s influence on the domestic economy, long-term, overlapping and multiplex relational patterns persist as a distinctive feature of Japanese capitalism (Westney, 2001). A similarly opaque combination of vertical and horizontal ties also characterizes the 'business groups' that operate in many industrial and developing nations (Granovetter, 1995).

In contrast to overlapping networks of vertical and horizontal ties, strategic alliances and partnerships are typically confined to horizontal inter-firm ties (Contractor and Lorange, 1988; Gomes-Casseres, 1996). Although these networks may be based on trust or mutual forbearance, they typically are, as the adjective 'strategic' suggests, less firmly embedded in social webs of regional and informal networks. As with other network forms, the analysis of alliances more recently has shifted from a concern with governance of transactions to the efficacy of learning processes (Parkhe, 1991; Doz, 1996; Powell, Koput, and Smith-Doerr, 1996; Inkpen, 2000). Joint ventures – i.e. organizational units created by different parent companies – represent an important, more traditional variant of strategic partnerships (Kogut, 1988; Mowery, 1988). Over the last two decades, however, joint ventures have been replaced by non-equity partnerships, such as R&D pacts and joint development agreements (Hagedoorn, Volume II, Chapter 25). These inter-firm arrangements involve a lower degree of organizational dependence and a shorter time horizon than joint ventures. Through the explicit temporal limitation, this flexible fabric of alliance capitalism (Gerlach, 1992) comes rather close to the form of project-based networks.

Future Directions

A key tension in network studies is that the focus on the structure of relationships is not matched by attention to the content of ties. Too much emphasis on the structure of linkages can lead to treating all ties as comparable, without regard to their content or context. Detailed longitudinal studies of networks can mitigate the lack of attention to context, as well as reveal how multiple, overlapping relations shape the dynamics of networks.

A related tension arises between quantitative and qualitative studies of networks, with the latter providing richer analysis of how ties form and evolve. The strength of such studies is the insight they provide into the content of relationships. The limitation is that, in addition to concerns about generalizability, detailed process-based research is often restricted to dyadic relationships or a single focal organization. Quantitative studies are much more likely to involve larger units of analysis that better capture the wider topography of network configurations.

Much current network research focuses on inter-organizational relations. One consequence is that 'lower-level' networks, such as among individuals or groups, are subsumed under 'higher-level' networks among firms. Thus, inter-personal trust may be confounded with inter-organizational trust (Ettlinger, 2003), without consideration for whether the personal or corporate ties came first, or which relationship sustains or thwarts the other. We need to be much more attentive to the multiple levels at which networks coexist.

One alternative approach that aims at embracing the multi-dimensionality of actors and the multiplicity of network logics has been developed by actor-network theory (Callon, Volume II, Chapter 7; Latour, 1987; Callon and Law, 1989; Law and Hassard, 1999). Actor-network theory pursues a relational approach to issues of agency that does not recognize the distinction between society and nature, and between the social and the technical. Actor and network are not perceived as separate, but combined in an actor-network that is a collectivity that includes humans and non-humans. Rather than treat ideas, technical artifacts, tools, and rules as impervious to the context in which they are produced or imported, actor-network theory looks at how problems are translated, support mobilized, and practices transformed through interaction within a network.

One benefit of actor-network theory is that it straddles familiar distinctions between weak and strong ties, and instrumental and primordial relations. As scholars in different disciplines and countries began investigating the importance of networks, there has been a focus, perhaps inevitably, on one type of relation at the expense of others. Thus, Burt's (1992) research on the arbitrage advantages of networks provoked a reaction by some scholars that his analyses were too instrumental, and ignored embedded, trust-based ties. On the other hand, approaches that stress the importance of high-trust, communal strong ties tend to neglect the salient role of weaker ties in accessing novel ideas and opportunities.

The challenge for network analysis is to develop a robust program of research that captures, to paraphrase the early twentieth-century German social theorist Tönnies (1979), both the *Gemeinschaft* and *Gesellschaft* aspects of networks. Neither dimension – the primordial or highly embedded communal elements nor the more calculative, strategic aspects – represents the complete picture. The papers we have included in these two volumes capture the diversity of types of networks. A key goal for future research is to develop the tools and concepts needed to analyze the multiplex features of all types of networks. Much progress is being made in studying strong *and* weak ties, the structure *and* dynamics of networks, as well as the character *and* content of relationships. This attention to both process and structure and the multiplicity of network rationalities and configurations is critical to understanding the anatomy and chemistry of economic exchange. The articles we have collected highlight, we hope, the importance of networks as one of the key constitutive elements that sustain, nurture, and transform economic life.

Notes

1. For general reviews of the field of network research see Burt, 1980, 1992; Powell and Smith-Doerr, 1994; Podolny and Page, 1998; Scott, 2000.
2. There are other volumes in the Edward Elgar series *Critical Studies in Economic Institutions* on

'social capital' and 'trust', hence our selections focus less on these issues, and more on relational and structural aspects.

3. To overcome our disciplinary blind spots, we utilized the strength of weak ties, calling on colleagues for advice and comments on our selections. We are grateful to Ash Amin, Reinhard Bachmann, Fred Block, Jerry Davis, Anna Grandori, Kevin Heatherington, John Law, Mark Lazerson, David Stark, Jörg Sydow, Nigel Thrift, Brian Uzzi and Andreas Wittel for their helpful suggestions.

4. Wellman and Berkowitz (1988, p. 5) locate organizational network research within a fundamental relational turn in science more generally: in quantum physics, the very properties of parts are defined by the interaction between them (Schrödinger, 1951); at the opposite end of the physical scale, this approach has spread to cosmology, in which the universe is now defined relationally (Gregory and Thompson, 1982). In biology, 'constrained relationalism' argues that the properties of organisms are consequences of particular interactions between bits and pieces of matter; and in much the same vein, philosophers of language have maintained that mutual understanding of any utterance is possible 'only by having implicit theory about how to understand a network of possible utterances' (Wellman and Berkowitz, 1988, p. 5).

References

Abolafia, M. (1997), *Making Markets*, Cambridge, MA: Harvard University Press.

Ahuja, G. (2000), 'Collaboration Networks, Structural Holes, and Innovation', *Administrative Science Quarterly*, **45**, 425–55.

Albert, R. and A.-L. Barabási (2002), 'Statistical Mechanics of Complex Networks', *Reviews of Modern Physics*, **T4**, 47–97.

Albert, R., H. Jeong, and A.-L. Barabási (1999), 'Diameter of the World Wide Web', *Nature*, **401**, 130–31.

Albert, R., H. Jeong, and A.-L. Barabási (2000), 'Attack and Error Tolerance in Complex Networks', *Nature*, **406**, 378–82.

Almeida, P. and B. Kogut (1999), 'Localization of Knowledge and the Mobility of Engineers in Regional Networks', *Management Science*, **45**, 905–18.

Amin, A. and P. Cohendet. (1999), 'Learning and Adaptation in Decentralized Business Networks', *Environment and Planning D*, **17**, 87–104.

Amin, A. and P. Cohendet (2004), *Architectures of Knowledge: Firms, Capabilities, and Communities*, Oxford: Oxford University Press.

Amin, A. and N. Thrift (1992), 'Neo-Marshallian Nodes in Global Networks', *International Journal of Urban and Regional Research*, **16**, 571–87.

Asanuma, B. (1985), 'The Organization of Parts Purchases', *Japanese Economic Studies*, Summer, 32–53.

Asanuma, B. (1989), 'Manufacturer–Supplier Relations in Japan and the Concept of Relation-Specific Skill', *Journal of the Japanese and International Economies*, **3**, 1–30.

Axelrod, Robert (1984), *The Evolution of Cooperation*, New York: Basic Books.

Axelson, B. and G. Easton (1992), *Industrial Networks: A New View of Reality*, London: Routledge.

Baker, W.E. (1984), 'The Social Structure of a National Securities Market', *American Journal of Sociology*, **89**, 775–811.

Baker, W.E. and R.R. Faulkner (1993), 'The Social Organization of Conspiracy: Illegal Networks in the Heavy Electrical Equipment Industry', *American Sociological Review*, **58**, 837–60.

Barabási, A. (2002), *Linked: The New Science of Networks*, Cambridge, MA: Perseus.

Becattini, G. (1978), 'The Development of Light Industry in Tuscany: An Interpretation', *Economic Notes*, **2** (3), 107–23.

Ben-Porath, Y. (1980), 'The F-Connection: Families, Friends, and Firms in the Organization of Exchange', *Population and Development Review*, **6**, 1–30.

Beunza, D. and D. Stark (2003), 'Tools of the Trade: The Socio-Technology of Arbitrage in a Wall Street Trading Room', *Socio-Economic Review*, **1**, 135–64.

Boltanski, L. and E. Chiapello (1999), *Le Nouvel Esprit du Capitalisme*, Paris: Gallimard.

Boormann, S.A. (1975), 'A Combinatorial Optimization Model for Transmission of Job Information through Contact Networks', *Bell Journal of Economics*, **6**, 216–49.

Bradach, J.L. and R. Eccles (1989), 'Price, Authority, and Trust', *Annual Review of Sociology*, **15**, 97–118.

Bresnahan, T., A. Gambardella, and A. Saxenian (2001), '"Old Economy Inputs" for "New Economy" Outcomes: Cluster Formation in the New Silicon Valleys', *Industrial and Corporate Change*, **10** (4), 835–60.

Brown, J.S. and P. Duguid (1991), 'Organizational Learning and Communities-of-Practice', *Organization Science*, **2**, 40–57.

Brown, J.S. and P. Duguid (2000), 'Mysteries of the Region: Knowledge Dynamics in Silicon Valley', in C.-M. Lee, W.F. Miller, M.G. Hancock and H.S. Rowen (eds), *The Silicon Valley Edge. A Habitat for Innovation and Entrepreneurship*, Stanford, CA: Stanford University Press, pp. 16–39.

Brusco, S. (1982), 'The Emilian Model: Productive Decentralization and Social Integration', *Cambridge Journal of Economics*, **6**, 167–84.

Bunnell, T.G. and N.M. Coe (2001), 'Spaces and Scales of Innovation', *Progress in Human Geography*, **25** (4), 569–89.

Burawoy, M. and P. Krotov (1992), 'The Soviet Transition from Socialism to Capitalism: Worker Control and Economic Bargaining in the Wood Industry', *American Sociological Review*, **57**, 16–38.

Burt, R.S. (1980), 'Models of Network Structure', *Annual Review of Sociology*, **6**, 79–141.

Burt, R.S. (1986), 'Comment', in S. Lindenberg, J. Coleman and S. Nowak (eds), *Approaches to Social Theory*, New York: Russell Sage Foundation, pp. 105–7.

Burt, R.S. (1992), *Structural Holes*, Cambridge, MA: Harvard University Press.

Burt, R.S. (1993), 'The Social Structure of Competition', in R. Swedberg (ed.), *Exploration in Economic Sociology*, New York: Russell Sage Foundation, pp. 65–103.

Callon, M. (1986), 'The Sociology of an Actor-Network: The Case of the Electric Vehicle', in M. Callon, J. Law and A. Rip (eds), *Mapping the Dynamics of Science and Technology*, London: Macmillan, pp. 19–34.

Callon, M. and J. Law (1989), 'On the Construction of Sociotechnical Networks: Content and Context Revisited', *Knowledge and Society*, **8**, 57–83.

Cantwell, J.A. and G.D. Santangelo (1999), 'The Frontier of International Technology Networks: Sourcing Abroad the Most Highly Tacit Capabilities', *Information Economics and Policy*, **11**, 101–23.

Christopherson, S. (2002), 'Project Work in Context: Regulatory Change and the New Geography of Media', *Environment and Planning A*, **34**, 2003–17.

Clark, R. (1979), *The Japanese Company*, New Haven, CT: Yale University Press.

Coase, R. (1937), 'The Nature of the Firm', *Economica*, **4**, 386–405.

Coleman, J., E. Katz, and H. Menzel (1957), 'The Diffusion of an Innovation among Physicians', *Sociometry*, **20**, 253–70.

Collins, R. (1988), *Theoretical Sociology*, San Diego, CA: Academic Press.

Contractor, F.J. and P. Lorange (1988), *Cooperative Strategies in International Business*, Lexington, MA: Lexington Books.

Dalton, M. (1959), 'Power Struggles in the Line', in *Men Who Manage*, New York: Wiley, ch. 3.

Davis, G.F. and H.R. Greve (1997), 'Corporate Elite Networks and Governance Changes in the 1980s', *American Journal of Sociology*, **103**, 1–37.

De Fillippi, R. and M. Arthur (1998), 'Paradox in Project-Based Enterprise', *California Management Review*, **40** (2), 125–38.

Della Porta, D. and A. Vanucci (1999), *Corrupt Exchanges: Actors, Resources and Mechanisms of Political Corruption*, New York: Aldine de Gruyter.

de Nooy, W., A. Mrvar, and V. Batagelj (2004), *Exploratory Social Network Analysis with Pajek*, New York: Cambridge University Press.

Dore, R. (1983), 'Goodwill and the Spirit of Market Capitalism', *British Journal of Sociology*, **34**, 459–82.

Dore, R. (1986), *Flexible Rigidities: Industrial Policy and Structural Adjustment in the Japanese Economy, 1970–1980*, Stanford, CA: Stanford University Press.

Doz, Y. (1996), 'The Evolution of Cooperation in Strategic Alliances: Initial Conditions or Learning Processes?' *Strategic Management Journal*, **17**, 55–83.

Doz, Y. and G. Hamel (1998), *Alliance Advantage: The Art of Creating Value through Partnering*, Boston, MA: Harvard Business School Press.

Dyer, J.H. (1996), 'Specialized Supplier Networks as a Source of Competitive Advantage: Evidence from the Auto Industry', *Strategic Management Journal*, **17**, 55–83.

Ebers, M. (1997), *The Formation of Inter-Organizational Networks*, Oxford: Oxford University Press.

Eccles, R. (1981), 'The Quasifirm in the Construction Industry', *Journal of Economic Behavior and Organization*, **2**, 335–57.

Ekstedt, E., R.A. Lundin, A. Söderholm, and H. Wirdenius (1999), *Neo-Industrial Organising. Renewal by Action and Knowledge in a Project-Intensive Economy*, London: Routledge.

Emirbayer, M. (1997), 'Manifesto for a Relational Sociology', *American Journal of Sociology*, **103** (2), 281–317.

Emirbayer, M. and J. Goodwin (1994), 'Network Analysis, Culture, and the Problem of Agency', *American Journal of Sociology*, **99** (6), 1411–54.

Ettlinger, N. (2003), 'Cultural Economic Geography and a Relational and Microspace Approach to Trusts, Rationalities, Networks, and Change in Collaborative Workplaces', *Journal of Economic Geography*, **3**, 145–71.

Faulkner, R.R. (1983), *Music on Demand*, Rutgers, NJ: Transaction Books.

Faulkner, R.R. and A. Anderson (1987), 'Short-Term Projects and Emergent Careers: Evidence from Hollywood', *American Journal of Sociology*, **92**, 879–909.

Feenstra, R.C., T.H. Yang, and G.G. Hamilton (1999), 'Business Groups and Product Variety in Trade: Evidence from South Korea, Taiwan, and Japan', *Journal of International Economics*, **48** (1), 71–101.

Florida, R. (1995), 'Toward the Learning Region', *Futures*, **27**, 527–36.

Galaskiewicz, J. and S. Wasserman (1989), 'Mimetic Processes within an Organizational Field: An Empirical Test', *Administrative Science Quarterly*, **34**, 454–79.

Gambetta, D. (1988), 'Mafia: The Price of Distrust', in *Trust*, Oxford: Blackwell, pp. 158–74.

Gambetta, D. (1993), *The Sicilian Mafia: The Business of Private Protection*, Cambridge, MA: Harvard University Press.

Gann, D.M. and A.J. Salter (2000), 'Innovation in Project-Based, Service-Enhanced Firms: The Construction of Complex Products and Systems', *Research Policy*, **29**, 955–72.

Geertz, C. (1978), 'The Bazaar Economy', *American Economic Review*, **68**, 28–32.

Gerlach, M.L. (1992), *Alliance Capitalism: The Social Organization of Japanese Business*, Berkeley, CA: University of California Press.

Gertler, M. (1995), '"Being There": Proximity, Organization, and Culture in the Development and Adoption of Advanced Manufacturing Technologies', *Economic Geography*, **71**, 1–26.

Ghoshal, S. and C. Bartlett (1990), 'The Multinational Corporation as an Interorganizational Network', *Academy of Management Review*, **15**, 561–85.

Gomes-Casseres, B. (1996), *The Alliance Revolution: The New Shape of Business Rivalry*, Cambridge, MA: Harvard University Press.

Goodman, R.A. and L.P. Goodman (1976), 'Some Management Issues in Temporary Systems: A Study of Professional Development of Manpower – the Theatre Case', *Administrative Science Quarterly*, **21**, 494–501.

Grabher, G. (1993), 'The Weakness of Strong Ties: The Lock-in of Regional Development in the Ruhr Area', in G. Grabher (ed.), *The Embedded Firm*, London: Routledge, pp. 255–77.

Grabher, G. (2002a), 'Cool Projects, Boring Institutions: Temporary Collaboration in Social Context', in G. Grabher (ed.), *Production in Projects: Economic Geographies of Temporary Collaboration* (Regional Studies Special Issue), **36**, 3.

Grabher, G. (2002b), 'The Project Ecology of Advertising: Tasks, Talents, and Teams', in G. Grabher (ed.), *Production in Projects: Economic Geographies of Temporary Collaboration* (Regional Studies Special Issue) **36**, 3.

Grandori, A. (1999), *Interfirm Networks: Organizational Mechanisms and Economic Outcomes*, London: Routledge.

Granovetter, M. (1973), 'The Strength of Weak Ties', *American Journal of Sociology*, **78**, 1360–80.

Granovetter, M. (1974), *Getting a Job*, Cambridge, MA: Harvard University Press.

Granovetter, M. (1985), 'Economic Action and Social Structure: The Problem of Embeddedness', *American Journal of Sociology*, **91**, 481–501.

Granovetter, M. (1995), 'Coase Revisited: Business Groups in the Modern Economy', *Industrial and Corporate Change*, **4** (1), 93–130.

Gregory, S. and L. Thompson (1982), 'Superclusters and Voides in the Distribution of Galaxies', *Scientific American*, **246**, 6–14.

Gulati, R. (1995), 'Does Familiarity Breed Trust? – the Implications of Repeated Ties for Contractual Choice in Alliances', *Academy of Management Journal*, **38**, 85–112.

Gulati, R. and M. Gargiulo (1999), 'Where do Interorganizational Networks come from?' *American Journal of Sociology*, **104**, 1439–93.

Hagedoorn, J. (1996), 'Trends and Patterns in Strategic Technology Partnering since the Early Seventies', *Review of Industrial Organization*, **11**, 601–16.

Hagedoorn, J. (2002), 'Inter-Firm R&D Partnerships – An Overview of Major Trends and Patterns since 1960', *Research Policy*, **31**, 477–92.

Håkansson, H. and J. Johanson (1988), 'Formal and Informal Cooperation Strategies in International Industrial Networks', in F.J. Contractor and P. Lorange (eds), *Cooperative Strategies in International Business*, Lexington, MA: Lexington Books, pp. 369–79.

Hamilton, G.G. and N.W. Biggart (1988), 'Market, Culture, and Authority: A Comparative Analysis of Management and Organization in the Far East', *American Journal of Sociology (Supplement)*, **94**, s52–s94.

Hedlund, G. (1986), 'The Hypermodern MNC: A Heterarchy?' *Human Resource Management*, **25** (1), 9–35.

Hedlund, G. (1993), 'Assumptions of Hierarchy and Heterarchy, with Application to the Management of the Multinational Corporation', in S. Ghoshal and O.E. Westney (eds), *Organization Theory and the Multinational Corporation*, New York: Free Press, pp. 211–36.

Helper, S. (1993), 'An Exit-Voice Analysis of Supplier Relations: The Case of the US Automobile Industry', in G. Grabher (ed.), *The Embedded Firm*, London: Routledge, pp. 141–60.

Helper, S., J.P. MacDuffie, and C. Sabel (2000), 'Pragmatic Collaborations: Advancing Knowledge While Controlling Opportunism', *Industrial and Corporate Change*, **9** (3), 443–87.

Hennart, J.F. (1993), 'Explaining the Swollen Middle: Why Most Transactions are a Mix of "Market" and "Hierarchy"', *Organization Science*, **4**, 529–47.

Herrigel, G. (1996), *Industrial Constructions: The Sources of German Industrial Power*, New York: Cambridge University Press.

Hodgson, G. (1988), *Economics and Institutions*, Cambridge: Polity Press.

Inkpen, A.C. (2000), 'Learning through Joint Ventures: A Framework of Knowledge Acquisition', *Journal of Management Studies*, **37**, 1019–43.

Jarillo, J.C. (1988), 'On Strategic Networks', *Strategic Management Journal*, **9** (1), 31–41.

Johanson, J. and L.G. Mattson (1987), 'Interorganizational Relations in Industrial Systems: A Network Approach Compared with the Transaction-Cost Approach', *International Studies of Management and Organization*, **17** (1), 34–48.

Jones, C. (2001), 'Coevolution of Entrepreneurial Careers, Institutional Rules and Competitive Dynamics in American Film, 1895–1920', *Organization Studies*, **6**, 911–44.

Kenney, M. (ed.) (2000), *Understanding Silicon Valley: The Anatomy of an Entrepreneurial Region*, Stanford, CA: Stanford University Press.

Kirman, A. (2001), 'Market Organization and Individual Behavior. Evidence from Fish Markets', in J.E. Rauch and A. Casella (eds), *Networks and Markets*, New York: Russell Sage Foundation, pp. 155–95.

Kogut, B. (1988), 'Joint Ventures: Theoretical and Empirical Perspectives', *Strategic Management Journal*, **9**, 319–32.

Kogut, B. and U. Zander (1992), 'Knowledge of the Firm, Combinative Capabilities, and the Replication of Technology', *Organization Science*, **3**, 383–97.

Kogut, B. and G. Walker (2001), 'The Small World of Germany and the Durability of National Networks', *American Sociological Review*, **66** (3), 317–35.

Krippner, G. (2001), 'The Elusive Market: Embeddedness and the Paradigm of Economic Sociology', *Theory and Society*, **30**, 775–810.

Lane, C. and R. Bachmann (1997), 'Cooperation in Inter-Firm Relations in Britain and Germany: The Role of Social Institutions', *British Journal of Sociology*, **48**, 226–54.

Lane, D. and R. Maxfield (1996), 'Strategy Under Complexity: Fostering Generative Relationships', *Long Range Planning*, **29**, 215–31.

Langlois, R. and P.L. Robertson (1995), *Firms, Markets and Economic Change*, London: Routledge.

Latour, M. (1987), *Science in Action*, Cambridge, MA: Harvard University Press.

Laumann, E.O. (1979), 'Network Analysis in Large Social Systems: Some Theoretical and Methodological Problems', in P.W. Holland and S. Leinhard (eds), *Perspectives in Social Network Research*, New York: Academic Press, pp. 379–402.

Law, J. and J. Hassard (1999), *Actor Network Theory and After*, Oxford: Basil Blackwell.

Lazerson, M.H. (1995), 'A New Phoenix?: Modern Putting-Out in the Modena Knitwear Industry', *Administrative Science Quarterly*, **40**, 34–59.

Lincoln, J., M. Gerlach, and C. Ahmadjian (1996), '*Keiretsu* Networks and Corporate Performance in Japan', *American Sociological Review*, **61**, 67–88.

Lincoln, J., M. Gerlach and P. Takahashi (1992), '*Keiretsu* Networks in the Japanese Economy', *American Sociological Review*, **57**, 561–85.

Lorenzoni, G. and C. Baden-Fuller (1995), 'Creating a Strategic Center to Manage a Web of Partners', *California Management Review*, **37** (3), 146–63.

Lundin, R.A. and A. Söderholm (1995), 'A Theory of Temporary Organization', *Scandinavian Journal of Management*, **11**, 437–55.

Lundin, R.A. and F. Hartmann (2000), *Projects as Business Constituents and Guiding Motives*, Boston, MA: Kluwer.

Lundvall, B.-Å. (1988), 'Innovation as an Interactive Process: From User–Producer Interaction to National Systems of Innovation', in G. Dosi, C. Freeman, R. Nelson, G. Silverberg and L. Soete (eds), *Technical Change and Economic Theory*, London: Pinter, pp. 349–69.

Lundvall, B.-Å. and B. Johnson (1994), 'The Learning Economy', *Journal of Industry Studies*, **1**, 23–42.

Macneil, I.R. (1974), 'The Many Futures of Contract', *Southern California Law Review*, **47**, 691–816.

Macneil, I.R. (1978), 'Contracts: Adjustment of Long-Term Economic Relations under Classical, Neoclassical, and Relational Contract Law', *Northwestern University Law Review*, **72**, 854–905.

Malmberg, A. and P. Maskell (2002), 'The Elusive Concept of Localization Economies: Towards a Knowledge-Based Theory of Spatial Clustering', *Environment & Planning A*, **34**, 429–49.

Marsden, P. (1983), 'Restricted Access in Networks and Models of Power', *American Journal of Sociology*, **88**, 686–715.

Markusen, A. (1996), 'Sticky Places in Slippery Space: A Typology of Industrial Districts', *Economic Geography*, **72**, 293–313.

Marshall, A. (1890), *Principles of Economics*, London: Macmillan.

Marshall, A. (1920), *Industry and Trade*, London: Macmillan.

Meyerson, D., K.E. Weick, and R. Kramer (1996), 'Swift Trust and Temporary Groups', in R. Kramer and T. Tyler (eds), *Trust in Organizations*, London: Sage, pp. 166–95.

Mintz, B. and M. Schwartz (1985), *The Power Structure of American Business*, Chicago: University of Chicago Press.

Mizruchi, M.S. (1996), 'What do Interlocks Do? An Analysis, Critique, and Assessment of Research on Interlocking Directorates', *Annual Review of Sociology*, **22**, 271–98.

Mowery, D.C. (ed.) (1988), *International Collaborative Ventures in US Manufacturing*, Cambridge, MA: Ballinger.

Newman, M. (2003), 'The Structure and Function of Complex Networks', *SIAM Review*, **45**, 167–256.

Nonaka, I. and H. Takeuchi (1995), *The Knowledge-Creating Company: How the Japanese Companies Create the Dynamics of Innovation*, Oxford: Oxford University Press.

Nonaka, I. and N. Konno (1998), 'The Concept of Ba: Building a Foundation for Knowledge Creation', *California Management Review*, **40** (3), 40–54.

Nooteboom, B. (1999), *Inter-Firm Alliances – Analysis and Design*, London: Routledge.

Nooteboom, B. (2000), 'Learning by Interaction, Absorptive Capacity, Cognitive Distance and Governance', *Journal of Management and Governance*, **4**, 69–92.

Oliver, A.L. and M. Ebers (1998), 'Networking Network Studies: An Analysis of Conceptual Configurations in the Study of Interorganizational Relationships', *Organization Studies*, **19** (4), 549–83.

Owen-Smith, J. and W.W. Powell (2004), 'Knowledge Networks as Channels and Conduits: The Effects of Spillovers in the Boston Biotechnology Community', *Organization Science*, **15** (1), 5–21.

Padgett, J.F. (2001), 'Organizational Genesis, Identity, and Control: The Transformation of Banking in Renaissance Florence', in J.E. Rauch and A. Casella (eds), *Markets and Networks*, New York: Russell Sage Foundation, pp. 211–57.

Padgett, J.F. and C. Ansell (1993), 'Robust Action and the Rise of the Medici, 1400–34', *American Journal of Sociology*, **98**, 1259–319.

Parkhe, A. (1991), 'Interfirm Diversity, Organizational Learning, and Longevity in Global Strategic Alliances', *Journal of International Business Studies*, **22**, 579–602.

Piore, M. and C. Sabel (1984), *The Second Industrial Divide*, New York: Basic Books.

Podolny, J.M. (2001), 'Networks as the Pipes and Prisms of the Market', *American Journal of Sociology*, **107**, 33–60.

Podolny, J.M. and K.L. Page (1998), 'Network Forms of Organization', *Annual Review of Sociology*, **24**, 57–76.

Polanyi, K. (1968), 'Our Obsolete Market Mentality', in G. Dalton (ed.), *Primitive, Archaic and Modern Economies: Essays of Karl Polanyi*, Boston, MA: Beacon Press, pp. 59–78.

Porter, M. (1990), *The Competitive Advantage of Nations*, New York: Free Press.

Powell, W.W. (1985), *Getting into Print: The Decision-Making Process in Scholarly Publishing*, Chicago: University of Chicago Press.

Powell, W.W. (1990), 'Neither Market nor Hierarchy: Network Forms of Organization', *Research in Organizational Behaviour*, **12**, 295–336.

Powell, W.W., K.W. Koput, J.I. Bowie, and L. Smith-Doerr (2002), 'The Spatial Clustering of Science and Capital: Accounting for Biotech Firm–Venture Capital Relationships', in G. Grabher (ed.), *Production in Projects: Economic Geographies of Temporary Collaboration* (Regional Studies Special Issue), **36**, 3.

Powell, W.W., K. Koput, and L. Smith-Doerr (1996), 'Interorganizational Collaboration and the Locus of Innovation: Networks of Learning in Biotechnology', *Administrative Science Quarterly*, **41** (1), 116–45.

Powell, W.W. and L. Smith-Doerr (1994), 'Networks and Economic Life', in N.J. Smelser and R. Swedberg (eds), *The Handbook of Economic Sociology*, Princeton, NJ: Princeton University Press/Russell Sage Foundation, pp. 368–402.

Pyke, F., G. Becattini, and W. Sengenberger (1990), *Industrial Districts and Interfirm Cooperation in Italy*, Geneva: International Institute for Labor Studies.

Rauch, J.E. (1999), 'Networks versus Markets in International Trade', *Journal for International Economics*, **48** (1), 7–37.

Rauch, J.E. (2001), 'Business and Social Networks in International Trade', *Journal of Economic Literature*, **39** (4), 1137–76.

Richardson, G.B. (1972), 'The Organization of Industry', *Economic Journal*, **82**, 883–96.

Rogers, E.M. (1962), *Diffusion of Innovations*, New York: Free Press.

Ryan, B. and N.C. Gross (1943), 'The Diffusion of Hybrid Seed Corn in Two Iowa Communities', *Rural Sociology*, **8**, 15–24.

Sako, M. (1998), 'Does Trust Improve Business Performance?', in C. Lane and R. Bachman (eds), *Trust within or between Organizations*, Oxford: Oxford University Press.

Sako, M. and S. Helper (1998), 'Determinants of Trust in Supplier Relations', *Journal of Economic Behavior and Organization*, **34**, 387–417.

Saxenian, A. (1994), *Regional Advantage: Culture and Competition in Silicon Valley and Route 128*, Cambridge, MA: Harvard University Press.

Schrödinger, E. (1951), *Science and Humanism*, Cambridge, Cambridge University Press.

Scott, J. (2000), *Network Analysis: A Handbook* (2nd edn), London: Sage.

Sedaitis, J.B. (1997), 'Network Dynamics of New Firm Formation: Developing Russian Commodity Markets', in G. Grabher and D. Stark (eds), *Restructuring Networks in Post-Socialism: Legacies, Linkages, and Localities*, Oxford: Oxford University Press, pp. 132–58.

Sík, E. (1992), 'From the Second Economy to the Informal Economy', *Journal of Public Policy*, **12**, 153–75.

Sölvell, Ö. and U. Zander (1995), 'Organization of the Dynamic Multinational Enterprise', *International Studies of Management and Organization*, **25**, 17–38.

Stark, D. (1996), 'Recombinant Property in East European Capitalism', *American Journal of Sociology*, **101**, 993–1027.

Stark, D. (2001), 'Ambiguous Assets for Uncertain Environments: Heterarchy in Postsocialist Firms', in P. DiMaggio (ed.), *The Twenty-First Century Firm*, Princeton, NJ: Princeton University Press, pp. 69–104.

Starkey, K., C. Barnatt, and S. Tempest (2000), 'Beyond Networks and Hierarchies: Latent Organizations in the UK Television Industry', *Organization Science*, **11**, 299–305.

Storper, M. (1993), 'Regional "Worlds" of Production: Learning and Innovation in the Technology Districts of France, Italy and the USA', *Regional Studies*, **27**, 433–55.

Storper, M. (1997), *The Regional World. Territorial Development in a Global Economy*, New York: Guilford Press.

Strogatz, S. (2003), *Sync: The Emerging Science of Spontaneous Order*, New York: Hyperion.

Stuart, T.E. (1998), 'Network Positions and Propensities to Collaborate', *Administrative Science Quarterly*, **43**, 668–98.

Sydow, J. (2001), 'Management von Netzwerkorganisationen – Zum Stand der Forschung', in J. Sydow (ed.), *Management von Netzwerkorganisationen*, Wiesbaden: Gabler, pp. 293–354.

Sydow, J. and A. Windeler (1999), 'Projektnetzwerke: Management von (mehr als) temporären Systemen', in J. Engelhardt and E. Sinz (eds), *Kooperation im Wettbewerb*, Wiesbaden: Gabler, pp. 213–35.

Swan, J., H. Scarbrough, and M. Robertson (2002), 'The Construction of "Communities of Practice" in the Management of Innovation', *Management Learning*, **33**, 477–96.

Teece, D.J. (1992), 'Competition, Cooperation, and Innovation: Organizational Arrangements for Regimes of Rapid Technological Progress', *Journal of Economic Behavior and Organization*, **18**, 1–25.

Teece, D.J. and G. Pisano (1994), 'The Dynamic Capabilities of Firms: An Introduction', *Industrial and Corporate Change*, **3**, 537–56.

Thompson, G.F. (2003), *Between Hierarchies and Markets. The Logic and Limits of Network Forms of Organization*, Oxford: Oxford University Press.

Thrift, N. (1994), 'On the Social and Cultural Determinants of International Financial Centers: The Case of the City of London', in S. Corbridge, R. Martin and N. Thrift (eds), *Money, Power and Space*, Oxford: Blackwell, pp. 327–55.

Thrift, N. (2000), 'Animal Spirits: Performing Cultures in the New Economy', *Annals of the Association of American Geographers*, **90**, 674–92.

Tönnies, F. (1979), *Gemeinschaft und Gesellschaft: Grundbegriffe der reinen Soziologie* (8th edn), Darmstadt: Wissenschaftliche Buchgemeinschaft.

Travers, J. and S. Milgram (1969), 'An Experimental Study of the Small World Problem', *Sociometry*, **32**, 425–43.

Useem, M. (1984), *The Inner Circle: Large Corporations and the Rise of Business Political Activity*, New York: Oxford University Press.

Uzzi, B. (1996), 'The Sources and Consequences of Embeddedness for the Economic Performance of Organizations: The Network Effect', *American Sociological Review*, **61**, 674–98.

Uzzi, B. (1997), 'Social Structure and Competition in Interfirm Networks: The Paradox of Embeddedness', *Administrative Science Quarterly*, **42**, 35–67.

Wasserman, S. and K. Faust (1994), *Social Network Analysis: Methods and Applications*, New York: Cambridge University Press.

Watts, D. (1999), *Small Worlds*, Princeton, NJ: Princeton University Press.

Watts, D. (2003), *Six Degrees: The Science of a Connected Age*, New York: Norton.

Wellmann, B. (1983), 'Network Analysis: Some Basic Principles', in R. Collins (ed.), *Sociological Theory*, San Francisco, CA: Jossey-Bass, pp. 155–200.

Wellmann, B. and S.D. Berkowitz (1988), *Social Structures*, New York: Cambridge University Press.

Wenger, E. (1998), *Communities of Practice: Learning, Meaning, and Identity*, Cambridge: Cambridge University Press.

Wenger, E. and W. M. Snyder (2000), 'Communities of Practice: The Organizational Frontier', *Harvard Business Review*, January–February, 139–45.

Westney, E.D. (1996), 'The Japanese Business System: key features and prospects for change', *Journal of Asian Business*, **12**, 21–50.

Westney, E.D. (2001), 'Japan', in A.M. Rugman and T.L. Brewer (eds), *Oxford Handbook of International Business*, Oxford: Oxford University Press, pp. 623–29.

White, H.C. (1993), 'Markets, Networks and Control', in S.M. Lindenberg and H. Schreuder (eds), *Interdisciplinary Perspectives on Organizations*, Oxford: Pergamon, pp. 221–40.

Williamson, O.E. (1975), *Markets and Hierarchies*, New York: The Free Press.

Williamson, O.E. (1985), *The Economic Institutions of Capitalism*, New York: The Free Press.

Williamson, O.E. (1991), 'Comparative Economic Organization', *Administrative Science Quarterly*, **36**, 269–96.

Part I
Networks as Governance Structures

[1]

THE ORGANISATION OF INDUSTRY[1]

I

I was once in the habit of telling pupils that firms might be envisaged as islands of planned co-ordination in a sea of market relations. This now seems to me a highly misleading account of the way in which industry is in fact organised. The underlying idea, of course, was of the existence of two ways in which economic activity could be co-ordinated, the one, conscious planning, holding sway within firms, the other, the price mechanism, operating spontaneously on the relations between firms and between firms and their customers. The theory of the firm, I argued, had as its central core an elaboration of the logic of this conscious planning; the theory of markets analysed the working of the price mechanism under a variety of alternative structural arrangements.

I imagine that this account of things might be acceptable, as a harmless first approximation, to a large number of economists. And yet there are two aspects of it that should trouble us. In the first place it raises a question, properly central to any theory of economic organisation, which it does not answer; and, secondly, it ignores the existence of a whole species of industrial activity which, on the face of it, is relevant to the manner in which co-ordination is achieved. Let us deal with each of these matters in turn.

Our simple picture of the capitalist economy was in terms of a division of labour between the firm and the market, between co-ordination that is planned and co-ordination that is spontaneous. But what then is the principle of this division? What kinds of co-ordination have to be secured through conscious direction within firms and what can be left to the working of the invisible hand? One might reasonably maintain that this was a key question—perhaps the key question—in the theory of industrial organisation, the most important matter that the Divine Maker of market economies on the first day of creation would have to decide. And yet, as I hope soon to show, it is a matter upon which our standard theories, which merely assume but do not explain a division between firm and market, throw little light.

Let me now turn to the species of industrial activity that our simple story, based as it is on a dichotomy between firm and market, leaves out of account. What I have in mind is the dense network of co-operation and affiliation by which firms are inter-related. Our theoretical firms are indeed islands, being characteristically well-defined autonomous units buying and selling at arms' length in markets. Such co-operation as takes place between them is normally studied as a manifestation of the desire to restrict competition and features in chapters about price agreements and market sharing.

[1] I am grateful to Mr. J. F. Wright, Mr. L. Hannah and Mr. J. A. Kay, each of whom gave helpful comments on a draft of this article.

But if the student closes his textbook and takes up a business history, or the financial pages of a newspaper, or a report of the Monopolies Commission, he will be presented with a very different picture.   Firm A, he may find, is a joint subsidiary of firms B and C, has technical agreements with D and E, sub-contracts work to F, is in marketing association with G—and so on. So complex and ramified are these arrangements, indeed, that the skills of a genealogist rather than an economist might often seem appropriate for their disentanglement.[1]   But does all this matter?   Theories necessarily abstract and it is always easy to point to things they leave out of account.   I hope to show that the excluded phenomena in this case are of importance and that by looking at industrial reality in terms of a sharp dichotomy between firm and market we obtain a distorted view of how the system works.   Before doing so, however, I wish to dwell a little longer on the several forms that co-operation and affiliation may take; although the arrangements to be described are no doubt well known to the reader, explicit mention may nevertheless help to draw attention to their variety and extent.

II

Perhaps the simplest form of inter-firm co-operation is that of a trading relationship between two or more parties which is stable enough to make demand expectations more reliable and thereby to facilitate production planning.   The relationship may acquire its stability merely from goodwill or from more formal arrangements such as long-term contracts or share-holding.   Thus, for example, the Metal Box Company used to obtain a discount from its tin plate suppliers in return for undertaking to buy a certain proportion of its requirements from them, and the same company owned 25% of the share capital of the firm supplying it with paints and lacquers.   In the same way Imperial Tobacco owned shares in British Sidac, which made cellophane wrapping, and in Bunzl, which supplied filter tips. Occasionally shareholdings of this kind may be simply investments held for their direct financial yield, but more generally they give stability to relation-ships through which the activities of the parties are co-ordinated both quanti-

---

[1] The sceptical reader might care to look up a few cases in the reports of the Monopolies Com-mission.   The following example is found in the report on cigarette filter tips.   Cigarette Com-ponents Ltd. made filter tips for Imperial Tobacco and Gallaher using machines hired from these companies.   It has foreign subsidiaries, some wholly and some partially owned.   It was both licensee and licensor of various patents one of which was held by the Celfil Trust, registered in Liechtenstein, with regard to the ultimate control of which Cigarette Components told the Mono-polies Commission they could only surmise.   Nevertheless, this patent was of key importance in that the Celfil licensees, of which Cigarette Components was only one, were bound by price and market sharing arrangement.   Cigarette Components was itself owned by Bunzl Ltd., in which Imperial Tobacco had a small shareholding.   The raw material for the tips is cellulose acetate tow which was made by Ectona Fibres Ltd., a company in which Bunzl had a 40% interest and a subsidiary of Eastman Kodak 60%.   Agreements had been made providing that, should Bunzl lose control of Cigarette Components, then Eastman could buy out their shares in Ectona . . . etc., etc.

tatively and qualitatively. Not only is it made easier to adjust the quantity of, say, lacquer to the quantity of cans which it is used to coat but the specification and development of the lacquers can be made appropriate to the use to be made of them. And in the synthetic fibre industry likewise, linkages between firms at the various stages—polymer manufacture, yarn spinning and finishing, textile weaving—help bring about the co-ordinated development of products and processes. The habit of working with models which assume a fixed list of goods may have the unfortunate result of causing us to think of co-ordination merely in terms of the balancing of quantities of inputs and outputs and thus leave the need for qualitative co-ordination out of account.

Co-operation may frequently take place within the framework provided by sub-contracting. An indication of the importance of this arrangement is provided by the fact that about a quarter of the output of the Swedish engineering industry is made up of sub-contracted components, while for Japan the corresponding figure is about a third and in that country's automobile industry almost a half. Sub-contracting on an international basis, moreover, is said to be becoming more widespread and now a dense network of arrangements links the industries of different countries.[1] Now the fact that work has been sub-contracted does not by itself imply the existence of much co-operation between the parties to the arrangement. The plumbing work on a building contract may be sub-contracted on the basis of competitive tenders for the individual job. Frequently, however, the relationship between the parties acquires a degree of stability which is important for two reasons. It is necessary, in the first place, to induce sub-contractors to assume the risks inherent in a rather narrow specialisation in skills and equipment; and, secondly, it permits continuing co-operation between those concerned in the development of specifications, processes and designs.

Co-operation also takes place between firms that rely on each other for manufacture or marketing and its fullest manifestation is perhaps to be found in the operations of companies such as Marks and Spencer and British Home Stores. Nominally, these firms would be classified as retail chains, but in reality they are the engineers or architects of complex and extended patterns of co-ordinated activity. Not only do Marks and Spencer tell their suppliers how much they wish to buy from them, and thus promote a quantitative adjustment of supply to demand, they concern themselves equally with the specification and development of both processes and products. They decide, for example, the design of a garment, specify the cloth to be used and control the processes even to laying down the types of needles to be used in knitting and sewing. In the same way they co-operate with Ranks and Spillers in order to work out the best kind of flour for their cakes and do not neglect to specify the number of cherries and walnuts to go into them.

---

[1] See the *Economic Bulletin for Europe*, Vol. 21, No. 1.

Marks and Spencer have laboratories in which, for example, there is development work on uses of nylon, polyester and acrylic fibres. Yet all this orchestration of development, manufacture and marketing takes place without any shareholding by Marks and Spencer in its suppliers and without even long-term contracts.

Mention should be made, finally, of co-operative arrangements specifically contrived to pool or to transfer technology. Surely the field of technical agreements between enterprises is one of the under-developed areas of economics. These agreements are commonly based on the licensing or pooling of patents but they provide in a quite general manner for the provision or exchange of know-how through the transfer of information, drawings, tools and personnel. At the same time they are often associated with the acceptance by the parties to them of a variety of restrictions on their commercial freedom—that is to say with price agreements, market sharing and the like.

This brief description of the varieties of inter-firm co-operation purports to do no more than exemplify the phenomenon. But how is such co-operation to be defined? And how in particular are we to distinguish between co-operation on the one hand and market transactions on the other? The essence of co-operative arrangements such as those we have reviewed would seem to be the fact that the parties to them accept some degree of obligation—and therefore give some degree of assurance—with respect to their future conduct. But there is certainly room for infinite variation in the scope of such assurances and in the degree of formality with which they are expressed. The blanket manufacturer who takes a large order from Marks and Spencer commits himself by taking the appropriate investment and organisational decisions; and he does so in the expectation that this company will continue to put business in his way. In this instance, the purchasing company gives no formal assurance but its past behaviour provides suppliers with reason to expect that they can normally rely on getting further orders on acceptable terms. The qualification " normally " is, of course, important, and the supplier is aware that the continuation of orders is conditional on a sustained demand for blankets, satisfaction with the quality of his manufacture and so on. In a case such as this any formal specification of the terms and conditions of the assurance given by the supplier would scarcely be practicable and the function of goodwill and reputation is to render it unnecessary.

Where buyer and seller accept no obligation with respect to their future conduct, however loose and implicit the obligation might be, then co-operation does not take place and we can refer to a pure market transaction. Here there is no continuing association, no give and take, but an isolated act of purchase and sale such, for example, as takes place on an organised market for financial securities. The pure market transaction is therefore a limiting case, the ingredient of co-operation being very commonly present, in some degree, in the relationship between buyer and seller. Thus although

I shall have occasion to refer to co-operation and market transactions as distinct and alternative modes of co-ordinating economic activity, we must not imagine that reality exhibits a sharp line of distinction; what confronts us is a continuum passing from transactions, such as those on organised commodity markets, where the co-operative element is minimal, through intermediate areas in which there are linkages of traditional connection and goodwill, and finally to those complex and inter-locking clusters, groups and alliances which represent co-operation fully and formally developed. And just as the presence of co-operation is a matter of degree, so also is the sovereignty that any nominally independent firm is able to exercise on a *de facto* basis, for the substance of autonomy may often have been given up to a customer or a licensor. A good alliance, Bismarck affirmed, should have a horse and a rider, and, whether or not one agrees with him, there is little doubt that in the relations between firms as well as nation states, the condition is often met.

III

It is time to revert to the main line of our argument. I had suggested that theories of the firm and of markets normally provide no explanation of the principle of the division of labour between firms and markets and of the roles within a capitalist economy of planned and spontaneous co-ordination. And I also maintained that these theories did not account for the existence of inter-firm co-operation and affiliation. It is upon the first of these two deficiencies that I now wish to concentrate.

Probably the simplest answer to the question as to the division of labour between firm and market would be to say that firms make products and market forces determine how much of each product is made. But such an answer is quite useless. If " products " are thought of as items of final expenditure such as cars or socks, then it is clear that very many different firms are concerned with the various stages of their production, not only in the sense that firms buy in components and semi-manufactures from other firms but also in that there may be a separation of manufacture and marketing (as in the case of Marks and Spencer and its suppliers) or of development and manufacture (as in the case of licensors and licencees). If, alternatively, we simply define " products " as what firms do, then the statement that firms make products is a tautology which, however convenient, cannot be the basis of any account of the division of labour between firm and market.

It is worth observing that we learn nothing about this division of labour from the formal theory of the firm. And this is perhaps not surprising as the theory, in its bare bones, is little more than an application of the logic of choice to a particular set of problems. It may be that the theory indeed makes it more difficult to answer our question in that, in order the better to exhibit this logic of choice, it is formulated on the assumption of " given production functions " which represent the maximum output obtainable from different input combinations. However useful this representation of productive possibilities, it leaves one important class of ingredients out of account. It abstracts totally from the roles of organisation, knowledge, experience and skills, and thereby makes it the more difficult to bring these back into the theoretical foreground in the way needed to construct a theory of industrial organisation. Of course I realise that production functions presume a certain level of managerial and material technology. The point is not that production is thus dependent on the state of the arts but that it has to be undertaken (as Mrs. Penrose has so very well explained)[1] by human organisations embodying specifically appropriate experience and skill. It is this circumstance that formal production theory tends to put out of focus, and justifiably, no doubt, given the character of the optimisation problems that it is designed to handle; nevertheless, it seems to me that we cannot hope to construct an adequate theory of industrial organisation and in particular to answer our question about the division of labour between firm and market, unless the elements of organisation, knowledge, experience and skills are brought back to the foreground of our vision.

It is convenient to think of industry as carrying out an indefinitely large number of *activities*, activities related to the discovery and estimation of future wants, to research, development and design, to the execution and co-ordination of processes of physical transformation, the marketing of goods and so on. And we have to recognise that these activities have to be carried out by organisations with appropriate *capabilities*, or, in other words, with appropriate knowledge, experience and skills. The capability of an organisation may depend upon command of some particular material technology, such as cellulose chemistry, electronics or civil engineering, or may derive from skills in marketing or knowledge of and reputation in a particular market. Activities which require the same capability for their undertaking I shall call *similar activities*. The notion of capability is no doubt somewhat vague, but no more so perhaps than that of, say, liquidity and, I believe, no less useful. What concerns us here is the fact that organisations will tend to specialise in activities for which their capabilities offer some comparative advantage; these activities will, in other words, generally be similar in the sense in which I have defined the term although they may nevertheless lead the firm into a variety of markets and a variety of product lines. Under capitalism, this degree of specialisation will come about through competition but it seems to me likely to be adopted under any alternative system for reasons of manifest convenience. Mrs. Penrose has provided us with excellent accounts of how companies grow in directions set by their capabilities and how these capabilities themselves slowly expand and alter.[2] Dupont, for example, moved from a basis in nitro-cellulose

[1] E. T. Penrose, *The Theory of the Growth of the Firm* (Oxford University Press, 1959).
[2] E. T. Penrose, *ibid.*

explosives to cellulose lacquers, artificial leather, plastics, rayon and cellophane and from a basis in coal tar dyestuffs into a wide range of synthetic organic chemicals, nylon and synthetic rubber. Similarly, Marks and Spencer, having acquired marketing and organisational techniques in relation to clothing were led to apply them to foodstuffs.

There is therefore a strong tendency for the activities grouped within a firm to be similar, but this need not always be so. In the history of any business random factors will have left an influence, and the incentive to take up a particular activity will sometimes be provided, not by the prior possession of an appropriate capability, but by the opportunity of a cheap acquisition, through a family or business connection or because of management's belief that the profitability of investment in some direction was being generally under-estimated. There is no need to deny, moreover, that a variety of potential gains are provided by grouping activities irrespective of their character; risks can be spread, the general managerial capability of the firm can be kept fully employed and the allocation of finance can be planned from the centre. None of this is in contradiction with the principle that it will pay most firms for most of the time to expand into areas of activity for which their particular capabilities lend them comparative advantage. A firm's activities may also, on occasions, be more similar than they superficially appear. If a firm acquired companies irrespective of the character of their activities we should term it conglomerate; but if the motive for the purchases were the belief that the companies were being badly managed, the hope being to restore them to health before re-selling them at a profit, the management would be exercising a particular capability.

IV

I have argued that organisations tend to specialise in activities which, in our special sense of the term, are similar. But the organisation of industry has also to adapt itself to the fact that activities may be *complementary*. I shall say that activities are complementary when they represent different phases of a process of production and require in some way or another to be co-ordinated. But it is important that this notion of complementarity be understood to describe, for instance, not only the relationship between the manufacture of cars and their components, but also the relationship of each of these to the corresponding activities of research and development and of marketing. Now it is clear that similarity and complementarity, as I have defined them, are quite distinct; clutch linings are complementary to clutches and to cars but, in that they are best made by firms with a capability in asbestos fabrication, they are similar to drain-pipes and heat-proof suits. Similarly, the production of porcelain insulators is complementary to that of electrical switchgear but similar to other ceramic manufacture. And while the activity of retailing toothbrushes is complementary to their manufacture, it is similar to the activity of retailing soap. This notion of complementarity will require closer definition at a later stage, but it will be convenient first to introduce one further (and final) set of conceptual distinctions.

It is clear that complementary activities have to be co-ordinated both quantitatively and qualitatively. Polymer production has to be matched, for example, with spinning capacity, both in terms of output volume and product characteristics, and investment in heavy electrical equipment has likewise to be appropriate, in scale and type, to the planned construction of power stations. Now this co-ordination can be effected in three ways; by *direction*, by *co-operation* or through *market transactions*. Direction is employed when the activities are subject to a single control and fitted into one coherent plan. Thus where activities are to be co-ordinated by direction it is appropriate that they be *consolidated* in the sense of being undertaken jointly by one organisation. Co-ordination is achieved through co-operation when two or more independent organisations agree to match their related plans in advance. The institutional counterparts to this form of co-ordination are the complex patterns of co-operation and affiliation which theoretical formulations too often tend to ignore. And, finally, co-ordination may come about spontaneously through market transactions, without benefit of either direction or co-operation or indeed any purposeful intent, as an indirect consequence of successive interacting decisions taken in response to changing profit opportunities. Let us now make use of this somewhat crude categorisation to re-interpret the questions with which we started.

V

What is the appropriate division of labour, we should now ask, between consolidation, co-operation and market transactions?

If we were able to assume that the scale on which an activity was undertaken did not affect its efficiency, and further that no special capabilities were ever required by the firm undertaking it, then there would be no limit to the extent to which co-ordination could be affected by direction within one organisation. If production could be set up according to " given " production functions with constant returns, no firm need ever buy from, or sell to, or co-operate with any other. Each of them would merely buy inputs, such as land and labour, and sell directly to consumers—which, indeed, is what in our model-building they are very often assumed to do. But, of course, activities do exhibit scale economies and do require specialised organisational capabilities for their undertaking, the result being that self-sufficiency of this kind is unattainable. The scope for co-ordination by direction within firms is narrowly circumscribed, in other words, by the existence of scale economies and the fact that complementary activities need not be similar. The larger the organisation the greater the number of capabilities with which one may conceive it to be endowed and the greater the number of complementary activities that can, in principle, be made subject to co-ordination through direction; but even if a national economy were to be run as a single business, it would prove expedient to trade with the rest of the world. Some co-ordination, that is to say, must be left either to co-operation or to market transactions and it is to the respective roles of each of these that our attention must now turn.

Building and brick-making are dissimilar activities and each is undertaken by large numbers of enterprises. Ideally, the output of bricks ought to be matched to the volume of complementary construction that makes use of them and it is through market transactions that we expect this to come about. Brickmakers, in taking investment and output decisions, estimate future market trends; and errors in these estimates are registered in stock movements and price changes which can lead to corrective actions. As we all know, these adjustments may work imperfectly and I have myself argued elsewhere [1] that the model which we often use to represent this type of market is unsatisfactory. But this is a matter with which we cannot now concern ourselves. What is important, for our present purposes, is to note that impersonal co-ordination through market forces is relied upon where there is reason to expect aggregate demands to be more stable (and hence predictable) than their component elements. If co-ordination were to be sought through co-operation, then individual brick-makers would seek to match their investment and output plans *ex ante* with individual builders. Broadly speaking, this does not happen, although traditional links between buyers and sellers, such as are found in most markets, do introduce an element of this kind. Individual brick manufacturers rely, for the most part, on having enough customers to ensure some cancelling out of random fluctuations in their several demands. And where sales to final consumers are concerned, this reliance on the law of large numbers becomes all but universal. Thus we rely on markets when there is no attempt to match complementary activities *ex ante* by deliberately co-ordinating the corresponding plans; salvation is then sought, not through reciprocal undertakings, but on that stability with which aggregates, by the law of large numbers, are providentially endowed.

Let us now consider the need to co-ordinate the production of cans with tin plate or lacquers, of a particular car with a particular brake and a particular brake lining, of a type of glucose with the particular beer in which it is to be used, or a cigarette with the appropriate filter tip. Here we require to match not the aggregate output of a general-purpose input with the aggregate output for which it is needed, but of particular activities which, for want of a better word, we might call *closely complementary*. The co-ordination, both quantitative and qualitative, needed in these cases requires the co-operation of those concerned; and it is for this reason that

[1] In *Information and Investment* (Oxford University Press, 1961).

the motor car companies are in intimate association with component makers, that Metal Box interests itself in its lacquer suppliers, Imperial Tobacco with Bunzl and so on. Co-ordination in these cases has to be promoted either through the consolidation of the activities within organisations with the necessary spread of capabilities, or through close co-operation, or by means of institutional arrangements which, by virtue of limited shareholdings and other forms of affiliation, come somewhere in between.

Here then we have the prime reason for the existence of the complex networks of co-operation and association the existence of which we noted earlier. They exist because of the need to co-ordinate closely complementary but dissimilar activities. This co-ordination cannot be left entirely to direction within firms because the activities are dissimilar, and cannot be left to market forces in that it requires not the balancing of the aggregate supply of something with the aggregate demand for it but rather the matching, both qualitative and quantitative, of individual enterprise plans.

VI

It is perhaps easiest to envisage co-ordination in terms of the matching, in quantity and specification, of intermediate output with final output, but I have chosen to refer to activities rather than goods in order to show that the scope is wider. The co-operation between Marks and Spencer and its suppliers is based most obviously on a division of labour between production and marketing; but we have seen that it amounts to much more than this in that Marks and Spencer performs a variety of services in the field of product development, product specification and process control that may be beyond the capability of the supplying firms. And one may observe that inter-firm co-operation is concerned very often with the transfer, exchange or pooling of technology. Thus a sub-contractor commonly complements his own capabilities with assistance and advice from the firm he supplies. New products also frequently require the co-operation of firms with different capabilities, and it was for this reason that I.C.I. originally co-operated with Courtaulds in the development of nylon spinning and now co-operates with British Sidac in developing polypropylene film.

It is indeed appropriate to observe that the organisation of industry has to adapt itself to the need for co-ordination of a rather special kind, for co-ordination, that is to say, between the development of technology and its exploitation. A full analysis of this important subject cannot be attempted here but it is relevant to consider those aspects of it that relate to our principal themes. What then are the respective roles, in relation to this kind of co-ordination, of direction, co-operation and market transactions? Obviously there are reasons why it may be convenient to co-ordinate the activities of development and manufacture through their consolidation within a single organisation. Manufacturing activity is technology-producing as

well as technology-dependent; in the process of building aircraft or turbo-
alternators difficulties are encountered and overcome and the stock of
knowledge and experience is thereby increased.   But there are also good
reasons why a firm might not be content to seek the full exploitation of its
development work through its own manufacturing activity.   The company
that develops a new product may itself lack sufficient capacity to manufacture it on the scale needed to meet the demand and may not have time
enough to build up the required additional organisation and material
facilities.   It could, of course, seek to acquire appropriate capacity by buying
firms that already possessed it, but this policy might prove unattractive if it
entailed taking over all the other interests to which these firms were committed.   The innovating firm might judge that its comparative advantage
lay in developing new products and be reluctant therefore to employ its
best managerial talents in increasing the output of old ones.   It would be
aware, moreover, that not only manufacturing but marketing capability
would be needed and might properly consider that it neither possessed nor
could readily acquire this, especially in foreign countries.   All these considerations may lead firms to seek some indirect exploitation of a product
development.   And, in the case of the new process, the incentive might be
even stronger in that there might be a wide variety of fields of production
in which the process could be used.

The indirect exploitation of new technology could be sought, in terms
of our nomenclature, either through market transactions or through cooperation with other firms.   But technology is a very special commodity
and the market for it a very special market.   It is not always easy, in the
first place, to stop knowledge becoming a free good.   The required scarcity
may have to be created artificially through a legal device, the patent system,
which establishes exclusive rights in the use or the disposal of new knowledge.
Markets may then develop in licences of right.   But these are very special
markets in that the commercial freedom of those operating within them is
necessarily restricted.   For suppose that A were to sell to B for a fixed sum
a licence to make a new product, but at the same time retained the unfettered
right to continue to produce and sell the product himself.   In this case the
long- and short-run marginal costs of production of the good would, for both
parties, be below unit costs (because of the fixed cost incurred by A in the
development work and by B as a lump sum paid for the licence) so that un-
restrained competition would drive prices to unremunerative levels.   It
might at first seem that this danger could be avoided if licences were charged
for as a royalty on sales, which, unlike a fixed sum, would enter into variable
costs.   But the licensee might still require assurance that the licensor, un-
burdened by this cost element, would not subsequently set a price disadvantageous to him or even license to others on more favourable terms.   These
dangers could be avoided if the parties were to bind themselves by price or
market-sharing agreements or simply by the prudent adoption of the policy

of live and let live. But, in one way or another, it seems likely that competition would in some degree have been diminished.[1]

It would appear, therefore, on the basis of these considerations, that where the creation and exploitation of technology is co-ordinated through market transactions—transactions in licences—there will already be some measure of co-operation between the parties. The co-operation may, of course, amount to little more than is required not to rock, or at any rate not to sink, the boat. But there are reasons why it will generally go beyond this.

---

[1] Professor Arrow reaches a different conclusion. The matter is considered in his article " Economic Welfare and the Allocation of Resources for Invention " published in *The Rate and Direction of Inventive Activity*, (edited by National Bureau of Economic Research, Princeton University Press, 1962). Professor Arrow maintains that " an incentive to invent can exist even under perfect competition in the product markets though not, of course, in the ' market ' for the information containing the invention " and that " provided only that suitable royalty payments can be demanded, an inventor can profit without disturbing the competitive nature of the industry."

The issue is simplest in the case of a cost-saving invention. Professor Arrow considers a product made under constant costs both before and after the invention and shows how the inventor can charge a royalty that makes it just worth while for firms making the product to acquire a licence. On the face of it one might then conclude that the licensor would have no need to bind himself not to reduce price below the level that provided licensees with a normal profit or to re-license for a lesser royalty, for, if he were to do either of these things, existing licensees would make losses, stop producing and therefore discontinue royalty payments. But this conclusion is valid only under the highly special assumption of there being no fixed costs. For firms will in general continue in production so long as price does not fall below variable costs. Thus the licensor could find it in his interest, having sold as many licences as he could at the higher royalty, to license others at a lower royalty, or to enter the market himself. He would thus extend the market for the product and increase his earnings provided, of course, that price were kept above variable costs and therefore high enough to induce the original (and by then no doubt aggrieved) licensees to stay in business. It is true, of course, that *in the long run* fixed plant would wear out and firms deprived of their quasi-rents would cease producing, but the fact that an opportunity for exploitation is merely temporary does not warrant our assuming that it will not be seized. In general the licensor would stand to gain by " cheating " the licensees in the manner described and the latter would therefore want some measure of assurance (which need not be formal) that he would not do so. There would be a market for licences, that is to say, only if the commercial freedom of the licensor were in this way reduced.

It may be that Professor Arrow would not consider this to represent a significant restriction of competition; and indeed the important practical issue concerns the manner and degree in which the parties accept limitations on their freedom of action. I have suggested that the licensor would be in a position, having licensed other firms, subsequently to deprive them of expected profits. A firm will therefore seek a licence only if it believes that this will not happen, but it may consider that sufficient assurance is provided by the fact that the licensor, in his own long-run interest, will not wish to acquire the reputation for such sharp practice. Much the same situation obtains in the context of the relationship between a large purchaser and a small supplier. Marks and Spencer, having offered attractive enough terms to induce the blanket manufacturer to devote a large proportion of his capacity to meet its needs, might subsequently press for a price reduction that left him with a poor return. The hapless supplier, in the short run at any rate, might have no option but to give way. But although the purchaser could thus act, it could scarcely be in his own long-run interest to acquire the reputation for doing so.

The upshot would therefore seem to be this. A market for licences can function only if the parties to the transactions accept some restraints, but, in certain circumstances, no more restraint might be required than enlightened self-interest could be depended upon by itself to ensure. In practice, of course, licensing arrangements are commonly associated with much more—and often more formal—restraint of trade, the extent of which may or may not be greater than is necessary for the transfer of technology to take place.

Technology cannot always be transferred simply by selling the right to use a process. It is rarely reducible to mere information to be passed on but consists also of experience and skills. In terms of Professor Ryle's celebrated distinction, much of it is " knowledge how " rather than " knowledge that." Thus when one firm agrees to provide technology to another it will, in the general case, supply not only licences but also continuing technical assistance, drawings, designs and tools. At this stage the relation between the firms becomes clearly co-operative and although, at its inception, there may be a giver and a receiver, subsequent development may lead to a more equal exchange of assistance and the pooling of patents. Arrangements of this kind form an important part of the networks of co-operation and affiliation to which I have made such frequent reference.

VII

This article began by referring to a vision of the economy in which firms featured as islands of planned co-ordination in a sea of market relations. The deficiencies of this representation of things will by now be clear. Firms are not islands but are linked together in patterns of co-operation and affiliation. Planned co-ordination does not stop at the frontiers of the individual firm but can be effected through co-operation between firms. The dichotomy between firm and market, between directed and spontaneous co-ordination, is misleading; it ignores the institutional fact of inter-firm co-operation and assumes away the distinct method of co-ordination that this can provide.

The analysis I presented made use of the notion of activities, these being understood to denote not only manufacturing processes but to relate equally to research, development and marketing. We noted that activities had to be undertaken by organisations with appropriate capabilities. Activities that made demands on the same capabilities were said to be similar; those that had to be matched, in level or specification, were said to be complementary. Firms would find it expedient, for the most part, to concentrate on similar activities. Where activities were both similar and complementary they could be co-ordinated by direction within an individual business. Generally, however, this would not be the case and the activities to be co-ordinated, being dissimilar, would be the responsibility of different firms. Co-ordination would then have to be brought about either through co-operation, firms agreeing to match their plans *ex ante*, or through the processes of adjustment set in train by the market mechanism. And the circumstances appropriate to each of these alternatives were briefly discussed.

Let me end with two further observations. I have sought to stress the co-operative element in business relations but by no means take the view that where there is co-operation, competition is no more. Marks and Spencer can drop a supplier; a sub-contractor can seek another principal; technical agreements have a stated term and the conditions on which they may be re-negotiated will depend on how the strengths of the parties change and develop; the licensee of today may become (as the Americans have found in Japan) the competitor of tomorrow. Firms form partners for the dance but, when the music stops, they can change them. In these circumstances competition is still at work even if it has changed its mode of operation.

Theories of industrial organisation, it seems to me, should not try to do too much. Arguments designed to prove the inevitability of this or that particular form of organisation are hard to reconcile, not only with the differences between the capitalist and socialist worlds, but also with the differences that exist within each of these. We do not find the same organisation of industry in Jugoslavia and the Soviet Union, or in the United States and Japan. We ought to think in terms of the substitutability of industrial structures in the same way as Professor Gerschenkron has suggested in relation to the prerequisites for economic development. It will be clear, in some situations, that co-ordination has to be accomplished by direction, by co-operation or through market transactions, but there will be many others in which the choice will be difficult but not very important. In Great Britain, for example, the artificial textile industry is vertically integrated and the manufacturers maintain that this facilitates co-ordination of production and development. In the United States, on the other hand, anti-trust legislation has checked vertical integration, but the same co-ordination is achieved through close co-operation between individual firms at each stage. It is important, moreover, not to draw too sharp lines of distinction between the techniques of co-ordination themselves. Co-operation may come close to direction when one of the parties is clearly predominant; and some degree of *ex ante* matching of plans is to be found in all markets in which firms place orders in advance. This points, however, not to the invalidity of our triple distinction but merely to the need to apply it with discretion.[1]

G. B. RICHARDSON

St. John's College,
    Oxford.

[1] In his article, " The Nature of the Firm," *Economica*, 1937, pp. 386–405, R. H. Coase explains the boundary between firm and market in terms of the relative cost, at the margin, of the kinds of co-ordination they respectively provide. The explanation that I have provided is not inconsistent with his but might be taken as giving content to the notion of this relative cost by specifying the factors that affect it. My own approach differs also in that I distinguish explicitly between inter-firm co-operation and market transactions as modes of co-ordination.

[2]

Copyright 1978 by Ian R. Macneil

Printed in U.S.A.
Vol. 72, No. 6

CONTRACTS: ADJUSTMENT OF LONG-TERM ECONOMIC RELATIONS UNDER CLASSICAL, NEOCLASSICAL, AND RELATIONAL CONTRACT LAW

Ian R. Macneil*

INTRODUCTION

This article concerns the constant clash in modern economic structures between the need for stability and the need to respond to change.[1]

---

* Ingersoll Professor of Law, Cornell Law School; B.A., University of Vermont, 1950; J.D., Harvard University, 1955.

[1] This paper has grown out of prior published work and of working papers prepared for a number of conferences and seminars: Conference of Polish and American Jurists, Lancut,

72:854 (1978)
                                        Adjustment of Relations

The range of the conflict is, of course, immense. This article is aimed at but one segment of the problem: that centered around contractual ways of organizing production and distribution of goods and services. It focuses initially on the relation between classical and neoclassical contract law[2] and the organization of production and distribution in flexible patterns that stress discrete transactional characteristics.[3] It then treats the changes in planning and dispute resolution techniques required where the need for flexibility and change exceeds the dispute-resolving capabilities of a system of neoclassical law.

Variations of the following four questions form the core of the article:

1. How is flexibility planned into economic relations and what is the legal response to such planning?

2. How is conflict between specific planning and needs to adapt to subsequent change in circumstances treated?

3. How are contractual relations preserved when conflicts arise?

4. How are economic activities terminated when they have out-lived their usefulness?

The first section focuses on these issues in a system dominated by discrete transactions, the second on a system with substantial infusions of rela-tional patterns. The third section deals with highly relational patterns, where the first three questions tend to merge, and contains a separate discussion of the fourth question.

Poland, 1974; Hungarian-American Conference on Contract Law and Problems of Large-Scale Enterprise, The Parker School of Foreign and Comparative Law, Columbia Univer-sity, 1975; Legal Theory Workshop, Yale Law School, 1975; Harvard Law School Faculty Seminar, 1977; Organizations Workshop, University of Pennsylvania, 1977. I am indebted to the sponsors of these conferences and seminars for providing opportunities to air these and other ideas and to the many participants for supplying insights, criticism, and encour-agement. In order to make the article complete within itself, it has been necessary at a number of points to repeat parts of articles published earlier—a fact noted where it occurs. This article was written in summer 1977, and references have not been updated across-the-board since then.

2 Classical contract law refers (in American terms) to that developed in the 19th century and brought to its pinnacle by Samuel Williston in THE LAW OF CONTRACTS (1920) and in the RESTATEMENT OF CONTRACTS (1932). Neoclassical contract law refers to a body of contract law founded on that system in overall structure but considerably modified in some, although by no means all, of its detail. The latter is epitomized by the U.C.C. Art. 2, and RESTATE-MENT (SECOND) OF CONTRACTS (Tent. Drafts, 1973-78). *See generally* Macneil, *Restatement (Second) of Contracts and Presentiation*, 60 VA. L. REV. 589 (1974), [hereinafter cited as *Presentiation*], where, however, both classical and neoclassical contract law are de-nominated "traditional contract law."

The Uniform Commercial Code is hereinafter cited as U.C.C. or Code. All citations are to the 1972 official text unless otherwise indicated.

3 *See* note 9 and accompanying text *infra*.

NORTHWESTERN UNIVERSITY LAW REVIEW

DISCRETE TRANSACTIONS: CLASSICAL CONTRACT LAW

The Nature of Discrete Transactions

A *truly* discrete exchange transaction would be entirely separate not only from all other present relations but from all past and future relations as well. In short, it could occur, if at all, only between total strangers, brought together by chance (not by any common social structure, since that link constitutes at least the rudiments of a relation outside the transaction). Moreover, each party would have to be completely sure of never again seeing or having anything else to do with the other. Such an event could involve only a barter of goods, since even money available to one and acceptable to the other postulates some kind of common social structure. Moreover, everything must happen quickly lest the parties should develop some kind of a relation impacting on the transaction so as to deprive it of discreteness. For example, bargaining about quantities or other aspects of the transaction can erode discreteness, as certainly does any effort to project the transaction into the future through promises.

The characteristics of entirely discrete transactions, if they could occur at all,[4] deprive them of any utility as social tools of production and distribution of scarce goods and services. That fact by no means, however, renders the construct useless as a tool of economic or legal analysis, because some discreteness is present in all exchange transactions and relations. One must simply not forget that great modification is required before the model can represent a reasonably accurate picture of actual economic life. (Unfortunately, this kind of forgetfulness is an endemic problem in both economics and law.) When so modified, the construct will no longer represent an entirely discrete transaction, but will retain substantial discreteness while nevertheless remaining relatively realistic.

We do find in real life many quite discrete transactions: little personal involvement of the parties, communications largely or entirely linguistic[5] and limited to the subject matter of transaction, the subjects of exchange consisting of an easily monetized commodity and money,[6] little

---

[4] The transactions of the theoretical perfectly competitive market defined in old-fashioned terms come very close, but only because the relational effects of social structures such as acceptable money are stripped out in the model: *e.g.*, money is treated like coconuts in the sense that it is assumed to have some value to the seller, but has zero impact in creating any extra-transactional relation between the participants in the market. *See* notes 5, 6, 10 *infra*.

[5] The existence of a common language itself erodes discreteness since it postulates a common social structure.

[6] The availability of money presupposes a strong, existing socioeconomic relation between the parties; nevertheless the "cash nexus" relationship is such an impersonal one as to have little effect in reducing many of the characteristics of discreteness in the transaction.

or no social[7] or secondary exchange,[8] and no significant past relations nor likely future relations.[9] For example, a cash purchase of gasoline at a station on the New Jersey Turnpike by someone rarely traveling the road is such a quite discrete transaction.[10] Such quite discrete transactions[11] are no rarity in modern technological societies. They have been and continue to be an extremely productive economic technique both to achieve distribution of goods[12] and to encourage their production.

Thus far we have dealt only with present exchanges of existing goods.[13] Such exchanges can, however, play but a limited role in advanced economies. Advanced economies require greater specialization of effort and more planning than can be efficiently achieved by present exchanges through discrete transactions; they require the projection of exchange into the future through planning of various kinds, that is, planning permitting and fostering the necessary degree of specialization of effort. The introduction of this key factor of futurity gives rise to the question: what happens to discreteness when exchanges are projected into the future?

---

7 *See generally* P. BLAU, EXCHANGE AND POWER IN SOCIAL LIFE (1964).

8 *See* T. PARSONS & N. SMELSER, ECONOMY AND SOCIETY 109 (1956).

9 The column headed "Extreme Transactional Pole" in the chart from Macneil, *The Many Futures of Contracts*, 47 S. CAL. L. REV. 691, 738-40 (1974) [hereinafter cited as *Many Futures*], set out in the Appendix, *infra*, gives the characteristics of discrete transactions in more detail.

10 In real life, even the most apparently discrete transaction is deeply embedded in social relations. Thus, the gasoline purchase is embedded in a great system of property and social relations: money, a social construct, is accepted in payment; the buyer will pay instead of simply taking the gasoline because of his acquiescence in various property rights; the social structure permits the customer to approach the service station attendant, and vice versa, on the assumption that most strangers in such circumstances are not physically dangerous; communication is possible through a common language; the product, simply by being delivered through a certain pump, is not merely gasoline, but gasoline of a certain type, *e.g.*, 89 octane and free of lead, etc. For many practical purposes of analysis, whether of behavior, norms, law, or what have you, these relational aspects can be and are ignored and the transaction sensibly viewed as very discrete. But such analysis invariably must be of limited scope, and when pushed beyond a certain point is defective if the relational elements continue to be excluded from consideration. For example, an analysis of the application of caveat emptor to this "discrete" sale would be highly defective if the brand relationship were omitted from consideration.

11 From here forward, unless the context indicates otherwise, the terms *discrete transaction, discrete*, and *transaction* will be used to describe near-discreteness, not theoretical pure discreteness. I recognize that the words *transaction* and *transactional* are often used to describe circumstances far from discreteness, but here they are always used in that more limited manner.

12 Some services could also be included (*e.g.*, haircuts), but services tend generally to involve less discreteness than transactions in goods, unless the goods have service-like qualities, which is true, for example, of durables.

13 While money itself projects exchanges into the future, inasmuch as it is simply a promise to pay, in a money-saturated economy such as ours we treat it as present wealth, *i.e.*, like an existing good. Our treatment of money is the ultimate in presentiation. *See* note 25 *infra*.

NORTHWESTERN UNIVERSITY LAW REVIEW

The answer is that a massive erosion of discreteness occurs. This is obvious when projection of exchange into the future occurs within structures such as the family, corporations, collective bargaining, and employment, structures obviously relational in nature. Similarly obvious are various relational ways of organizing and controlling markets, for example, the guilds of the feudal era or the planning described by Professor Galbraith in *The New Industrial State*.[14] But this erosion of discreteness occurs even when the projection is by direct and fairly simple promise and where the subject of exchange, if transferred immediately, would permit high levels of discreteness.[15]

Discreteness is lost even in the simple promise situation, because a basis for trust must exist if the promise is to be of any value. Trust in turn presupposes some kind of a relation between the parties. Whether it is that created by a shared morality, by prior experience, by the availability of legal sanction, or whatever, trust depends upon some kind of mutual relation into which the transaction is integrated. And integration into a relation is the antithesis of discreteness.[16]

In spite of the great leap away from pure discreteness occurring when exchange is projected into the future, promises themselves inherently create or maintain at least a certain minimum of discreteness. A promise presupposes that the promisor's individual will can affect the future at least partially free of the communal will, thus separating the individual from the rest of his society. Such separation is an element of discreteness. Promise also stresses the separateness of the promisor and the promisee, another element of discreteness. Moreover, some specificity and measured reciprocity is essential to an exchange of promises— no one in his right mind promises the world. This, again, results in an irreducible level of discreteness.

The foregoing can be seen in the following definition of contract promise: present communication of a commitment to future engagement in a specified reciprocal measured exchange. Thus, the partially discrete nature of promise permits the retention of a great deal of discreteness in

---

[14] J. GALBRAITH, THE NEW INDUSTRIAL STATE 354-62 (1967). *See* A. CHANDLER, THE VISIBLE HAND: THE MANAGERIAL REVOLUTION IN AMERICAN BUSINESS (1977).

[15] Other projectors of exchange are inherently more relational: command, status, social role, kinship, bureaucratic patterns, religious observation, habit, and other internalizations, to mention some. Even a market, however "free" it appears, is inevitably part of a great intertwining of property, personal, social, economic, and legal relations. (Existence of markets is, of course, one of the most important projectors of exchange into the future.)

[16] *See* Lowry, *Bargain and Contract Theory in Law and Economics*, 10 J. ECON. ISSUES 1 (1976). Unfortunately, after making this point Lowry attributes all benefits derived from the transaction to the relation in which it is embedded and concludes erroneously that bargain is therefore a zero-sum game. *See* I. MACNEIL, CASES & MATERIALS ON CONTRACTS: EXCHANGE TRANSACTIONS AND RELATIONS 1-10 (2d ed. 1978) [hereinafter cited as MACNEIL, CASES 2].

transactions where promise projects exchange into the future.[17] Where no massive relational elements counterbalance this discreteness (as they do, for example, in the case of collective bargaining), sense is served by speaking of the contract as discrete, even though the contract is inevitably less discrete than would be an equivalent present exchange.

The combination of exchange with promise has been one of the most powerful social tools ever developed for the production of goods and services. Moreover, discreteness in transactions so projected has its own special virtues. Just as a system of discrete transactions for exchanging present goods may be an effective way to conduct business free of all sorts of extraneous social baggage, so too may discrete transaction contracts serve this function.[18] With this background we can now turn to the questions set out above as they relate to a system of discrete transactions.

Adjustment and Termination of Economic Relations in a System of Discrete Transactions

An economic and legal system dominated by discrete transactions deals with the conflict between various needs for stability and needs for flexibility in ways described below. (The treatment following deals both with present exchanges of existing goods and with forward contracts where exchange is projected into the future. But the latter are assumed to be of a fairly discrete nature, *e.g.*, a contract for 100 tons of iron at a fixed price, delivery in one month.)

Planning Flexibility into Economic Relations.—Within itself, a discrete transaction is rigid, there being no intention to achieve internal flexibility. Planning for flexibility must, therefore, be achieved outside the confines of the transaction. Consider, for example, a nineteenth century manufacturer of stoves who needs iron to be cast into stove parts but does not know how many stoves he can sell. The required flexibility has to be achieved, in a pattern of discrete transactions, by keeping each iron purchase contract small in amount, thereby permitting adjustments of quantity up or down each time a contract is entered. Thus, the needed flexibility comes from the opportunity to enter or to refrain from entering the market for iron. This market is external to the transaction rather than within it. The epitome of this kind of flexibility is the purchasing of needs for immediate delivery, rather than using any kind of a forward contract

---

17 Indeed, it ensures some measure of discreteness even in highly relational exchange patterns whenever promises so defined are utilized, as they often are, *e.g.*, in corporate indentures and collective bargaining agreements.

18 As is plain upon reflection, to give effect to discreteness is to ignore externalities. Such externalities, however, are not necessarily external to the parties; they are simply external to the transaction. For example, the collateral economic loss or emotional pain suffered by a poor person having to repay a bank loan is external to that relatively discrete transaction but is borne by one of the parties. (Such costs may, of course, also have effect as externalities in the usual economic sense, *e.g.*, if the borrower robs a store in desperation.)

NORTHWESTERN UNIVERSITY LAW REVIEW

for future delivery. Such flexibility is reduced by use of forward contracts; the larger and longer they are, the greater is the reduction.

Dealing with Conflict between Specific Planning and Needs to Adapt to Change Arising Thereafter.—Only rarely in a discrete transaction will the items contracted for become useless before the forward contract is performed or become of such lessened value that the buyer either will not want them or will want them in greatly changed form.[19] To put this another way, only rarely will there be *within* the transaction a serious conflict between specific planning and changed needs. To return to the stove manufacturer as an example, seldom will the demand for iron stoves drop so much that the manufacturer comes to regret that he contracted for as much iron as he did.[20]

The discrete transaction technique does not, however, produce a paradise of stability for economic activity; the conflict between specific planning and the need to adapt to change arising thereafter still remains. In those relatively rare cases of difficulties arising while the contract remains unperformed, the conflict exists but is resolved entirely in favor of the specific planning and against the party desiring flexibility. Moreover, outside the discrete transaction, planning must go on; *e.g.*, the seller earlier built an iron smelter in order to sell in the iron market to organizations like the stove manufacturer. Except to the modest extent that the iron producer can shift the risks to the stove manufacturer and other buyers by forward contracts, the risks of change remain with the iron producer. If the demand for iron decreases greatly, the capital invested in building the iron smelter may be largely or entirely lost. Thus, in an economy built on discrete transactions, the risks of change remain but in large measure are not shifted by the transactions. When they are shifted they are shifted totally; *e.g.*, the stove manufacturer bears all those risks to the extent of the quantity for which he contracted.[21] In effect, the contract system does not provide planning for changes; it leaves that to the internal planning of each firm.

Preserving Relations When Conflicts Arise.—Where the mode of

---

19 This *has* to be the case or else the system will not work and will be replaced by techniques that do work.

20 This is a different matter from price fluctuations, which may, of course, cause a buyer regret or euphoria for having entered a contract at a particular price. Only fluctuations seriously and adversely affecting the market in which the manufacturer sells his own finished product will cause him not to want the iron at all.

21 They may, of course, be widely distributed among the stove manufacturer's stockholders and employees, for example, the stake of each of which may be relatively small compared to the whole enterprise (although not necessarily small for the stockholder or employee relative to his own assets). It will be noted, however, that such distribution occurs not by discrete transactions, but by relational contract, i.e., the web of relationship of stockholders-corporation-employees. *See* the last column in the chart in the Appendix, *infra*.

operation is a series of discrete transactions, no significant relations exist to be preserved when conflicts arise. Inside the discrete transaction all that remains is a dispute. Outside the discrete transaction no relation (other than legal rights arising out of the dispute) exists to be preserved. Thus, all that remains is a dispute to be settled or otherwise resolved. The existence of the market that the discrete transactional system presupposes eliminates the necessity for economic relations between the firms to continue in spite of the disputes. That market, rather than continued relations between these particular parties, will supply their future needs.

Terminating Economic Activities Outliving Their Usefulness.— This economic need is simply a particular aspect of the need for planning flexibility into economic relations, the ultimate example of which is to scrap the specific planning altogether. If sheet steel becomes the only technologically sensible substance with which to make stoves, then the stove manufacturer simply makes no more contracts to buy iron. The iron manufacturer continues to produce iron if remaining markets make it worthwhile, or he shifts his production facilities to their next most valuable use. In extreme cases that may mean selling the facilities for scrap or even their abandonment.

                                     *   *   *

The foregoing description of the responses of the discrete transaction system to the conflict between needs for stability and needs for flexibility may be summarized as follows. Except interstitially, such a system does not shift the risks of loss resulting from such conflicts. Such losses are left to fall largely on the suppliers of goods and services. To the extent that shifting does occur it is total shifting, not a sharing of risks. Given this format, minimizing of risk through planning comes in the *internal* planning of firms, not in *mutual* planning between them through contract. Thus, the iron manufacturer plans for its concern about a declining demand for iron by building a smaller smelter, repairing rather than replacing on old one, etc. It will try, of course, to shift as much of that risk as possible through forward contracts with buyers like the stove manufacturer, but prevailing patterns of relatively short discrete transactions preclude much shifting by that method. In any event, there will be no planning or dealing with the conflicts or possible conflicts through cooperative risk sharing between the iron manufacturer and stove manufacturer.[22]

---

22 Professor Oliver E. Williamson pointed out to me that the foregoing description ignores the effect on risk distribution of the possible use of inventory-holding market intermediaries, *e.g.*, warehouses. The use of an inventory-holding market intermediary in a discrete system does not, however, seem to me to affect the analysis in the text. The existence of such risk pooling enterprises will, of course, affect behavior of the markets in which both the iron manufacturer and the stove manufacturer are dealing. But, in the discrete transactional system postulated, risks of loss resulting from conflicts between

NORTHWESTERN UNIVERSITY LAW REVIEW

Classical Contract Law and Discrete Transactions

Any contract law system necessarily must implement certain norms. It must permit and encourage participation in exchange, promote reciprocity, reinforce role patterns appropriate to particular kinds of exchange relations, provide limited freedom for exercise of choice, effectuate planning, and harmonize the internal and external matrixes of particular contracts.[23] A contract law system reinforcing discrete contract transactions, however, must add two further goals: enhancing discreteness and enhancing presentiation.[24]

---

needs for stability and flexibility will continue and not be shifted very much by the contracts. Such risks will continue to fall largely on the suppliers of goods and services; and minimizing of risk through planning will continue to come through the internal planning of firms, not through mutual planning between them with contracts. All that will have happened is the introduction of an additional kind of firm which, because of its expertise and participation in a range of markets, is likely to be particularly efficient at dealing with aspects of the conflict between stability and flexibility. This more efficient handler may make markets work better and also lower costs to both the iron manufacturer and the stove manufacturer, but this will be done, in the system postulated, by intra-firm planning, not by inter-firm contract. It would be stretching the relational contract system too far to be useful to encompass within its scope consequences mediated among firms solely by the competitive market operating through discrete transactions. (As mentioned earlier, organized markets are a different matter and may well come within a useful definition of relational contract.)

[23] These norms are explored in more detail in the postscript to *Many Futures, supra* note 9, at 808-16. I am only slowly beginning their more extensive development.

[24] As already noted in the text, providing limited freedom for exercise of choice is a norm of all contracts, whether discrete or relational. But in a discrete contract the importance of this norm is elevated, perhaps ahead of all other norms. Moreover, the two particularly discrete norms singled out in the text may be viewed in large measure as implementations of this more fundamental norm of freedom of exercise of choice. It might very well have been better to analyze discrete transactions from this standpoint; that is, in terms of enhancing freedom of choice, rather than solely in terms of enhancing discreteness and enhancing presentiation. My reluctance to do so is part of a broader pattern of avoidance of the hard issue of the social impact of the kind of analysis appearing in *Many Futures*, note 9 *supra*, and work following it. Since its writing I have lacked the extended periods for reflection necessary to embark on those fascinating issues. I hope to do so during a sabbatical leave in the near future. Meanwhile, I feel confident in doing no more than hinting at the broad policy issues and largely limiting analysis to a micro level.

Where it is desired to carve out certain parts of relations and treat them as discrete, these will be goals of law pertaining to such carved out "discrete transactions" as well. For example, suppose the legislature or court decides that a claim for pay allegedly due a worker should be decided outside the grievance and arbitration processes of the collective bargaining agreement because back pay is a vested individual right. This in effect treats the claim for pay as a relatively discrete transaction in which the discrete norms will likely play a large role in decision making.

Relational norms also exist: (1) harmonizing conflict within the internal social matrix of the relation, including especially harmonizing the conflict between discrete and presentiated behavior with nondiscrete and nonpresentiated behavior; and (2) preservation of the relation. (These are tentative categorizations.)

72:854 (1978)   *Adjustment of Relations*

Presentiation[25] is a way of looking at things in which a person perceives the effect of the future on the present. It is a recognition that the course of the future is so unalterably bound by present conditions that the future has been brought effectively into the present so that it may be dealt with just as if it were in fact the present. Thus, the presentiation of a transaction involves restricting its expected future effects to those defined in the present, *i.e.*, at the inception of the transaction.[26] No eternal distinctions prevent treating the contract norm of enhancing presentiation as simply an aspect of the norm of enhancing discreteness. It is, however, such an important aspect of the projection of exchange into the future in discrete contracts—to say nothing of microeconomic theory—that separate treatment aids analysis significantly.

A classical contract law system implements these two norms in a number of ways.[27] To implement discreteness, classical law initially treats as irrelevant the identity of the parties to the transaction. Second, it transactionizes or commodifies as much as possible the subject matter of contracts, *e.g.*, it turns employment into a short-term commodity by interpreting employment contracts without express terms of duration as terminable at will.[28] Third, it limits strictly the sources to be considered in establishing the substantive content of the transaction. For example, formal communication (*e.g.*, writings) controls informal communication (*e.g.*, oral statements); linguistic communication controls nonlinguistic communication; and communicated circumstances (to the limited extent that any circumstances outside of "agreements" are taken into account at all) control noncommunicated circumstances (*e.g.*, status). Fourth, only

---

25 *Presentiate* is defined in the Oxford English Dictionary as "[t]o make or render present in place or time; to cause to be perceived or realized as present." 8 OXFORD ENGLISH DICTIONARY 1306 (1933).

26 Rarely do we view future events as completely presentiated, but we often come very close, especially respecting the near term. Discreteness plays an essential role in our doing this. No one even thinks he knows enough to presentiate the future, even for a few seconds, of, say, all of New York City, or even of all of a particular industrial plant. But we might feel considerable confidence in presentiating the soon-to-come purchase of goods in our shopping cart as we wait in line at a supermarket checkout. We can do this because we think of that purchase discretely from all the rest of our own lives, the rest of society (other than the checkout clerk and the rest of the people in the line) and all the physical world more than a few feet away.

27 Details of this implementation are spelled out in I. Macneil, Contracts: The Discrete Transactional Norms (unpublished manuscript). The simplifications appearing in this paragraph inevitably sound a bit like a parody of the classical contract system. Needless to say, the real life system, even as distilled in appellate court opinions, is far richer in complexity and conflicting aims and accomplishment than is suggested here. For example, *see* Childres & Spitz, *Status in the Law of Contract*, 47 N.Y.U.L. REV. 1 (1972). Their treatment of the effect of status on the application of the parol evidence rule is built on modern cases only, and hence pertains only to the neoclassical contract law system. But certainly the real life classical system of 1880-1910, to name one period, was never so pure as to prevent analogous analyses of actual decision-making.

28 *See* Note, *Implied Contract Rights to Job Security*, 26 STAN. L. REV. 335 (1974).

NORTHWESTERN UNIVERSITY LAW REVIEW

limited contract remedies are available, so that should the initial presentiation fail to materialize because of nonperformance, the consequences are relatively predictable from the beginning and are not open-ended, as they would be, for example, if damages for unforeseeable or psychic losses were allowed. Fifth, classical contract law draws clear lines between being in and not being in a transaction; *e.g.*, rigorous and precise rules of offer and acceptance prevail with no half-way houses where only some contract interests are protected or where losses are shared. Finally, the introduction of third parties into the relation is discouraged since multiple poles of interest tend to create discreteness-destroying relations.

Since discreteness enhances the possibility and likelihood of presentiation, all of the foregoing implementations of discreteness by the classical law also tend to enhance presentiation. Other classical law techniques, however, are even more precisely focused on presentiation.[29] The first of these is the equation of the legal effect of a transaction with the promises creating it. This characteristic of classical contract law is commonly explained in terms of freedom of contract, providing maximum scope to the exercise of choice. Nevertheless, a vital consequence of the use of the technique is presentiation of the transaction. Closely related to the first technique is the second: supplying a precise, predictable body of law to deal with all aspects of the transaction not encompassed by the promises.[30] In theory, if not practice, this enables the parties to know exactly what the future holds, no matter what happens to disrupt performance. Finally, stress on expectation remedies, whether specific performance or damages measured by the value of performance, tends to bring the future into the present, since all risks, including market risks, are thereby transferred at the time the "deal is made."[31]

---

[29] These could also be analyzed in terms of enhancing discreteness.

[30] *See Presentiation, supra* note 2, at 592-94.

[31] A considerable amount of quizzical writing exists concerning the function and efficacy of expectation damages, as actually implemented in the law, *e.g.*, Vernon, *Expectancy Damages for Breach of Contract: A Primer and Critique*, 1976 WASH. U.L.Q. 179, 201-03. Such analyses commonly overlook the function of rules of law as models of customary (and by definition "desirable") behavior.

For example, the law of expectation damages says to the lender of money: "You may treat the promises of the borrower to repay the principal and agreed interest as presentiating the future, because the law measures your remedy for nonperformance exactly in terms of those promises." Similarly, it says to buyers and sellers of goods: "As of the time of your contract, you have shifted the market risks of the goods from seller to buyer and you have shifted the market risks of the purchase price from the buyer to the seller." These abstract statements of legal rights may be viewed as simply mirroring the economic effects of what will happen in the vast majority of contracts which will, of course, be performed as agreed. Their function, so viewed, is to tell the world of contractors: "Your customary behavior is in accord with the aims of the law; go to it. To do otherwise is legally wrong." Problems arise with *this* function of the law not so much when particular parties do not "go to it" and the limitations of implementing the principles are revealed, but when the legal mirror is an

In summary, classical contract law very closely parallels the discrete transactional patterns described in the preceding section. Such a legal system, superimposed on economic patterns of such a nature, constitutes the stereotype of interfirm (or firm and consumer or firm and employee) contracting of the laissez faire era.

VARIATIONS FROM THE DISCRETE TRANSACTION: NEOCLASSICAL CONTRACT LAW

The discrete transaction is at one end of a spectrum, at the other end of which are contractual relations.[32] Were we to push far in the direction of contractual relations, we would come to the firm itself, since a firm is, in significant ways, nothing more than a very complex bundle of contractual relations.[33] It is not my intention at this point to push that far, but rather to confine consideration of adjustment and termination of long-term economic relations to those where it is clear that the contractual relations are *between* firms rather than *within* a firm. They are, even in traditional terms, contracts. Again, this section will be organized around variations of the questions appearing in the introduction.

Planning Flexibility into Long-Term Contractual Relations and the Neoclassical Response

Two common characteristics of long-term contracts are the existence of gaps in their planning and the presence of a range of processes and techniques used by contract planners to create flexibility in lieu of either leaving gaps or trying to plan rigidly. Prior to exploring the legal response to such planning, an examination of the major types of planning for flexibility used in modern American contracts is in order.[34]

---

inadequate reflection of customary behavior. Thus, if some level of nonperformance becomes both routine and acceptable, at least to the extent that the injured party does not seek expectation damages, an expectation rule becomes a distorted mirror of actual contractual behavior, and "go to it" falls on deaf ears. Distortion in the mirror of legally assumed custom thwarts one of the goals of contract law: implementing intent.

32 *See* text accompanying note 9 *supra*, and chart in the Appendix, *infra*, under the heading "Extreme Relational Pole."

33 I am indebted to Professor Oliver E. Williamson for alerting me to a potential danger of saying this. The statement *appears* to accept the Alchian and Demsetz view of the firm, since they too refer to "the contractual form, called the firm." Alchian & Demsetz, *Production, Information Costs, and Economic Organization*, 62 AM. ECON. REV. 777, 778 (1972). He is perfectly correct about the danger of misinterpretation. Anyone who persists in thinking of contract solely in the unrealistic and fallacious manner in which it is typically used in the microeconomic model (as Professor Williamson himself certainly does not) will indeed conclude that the statement is an acceptance of the Alchian and Demsetz theory of the firm. Those who are aware of those fallacies should, however, have little difficulty in understanding that it is not. Two articles by economists fall in the latter category: Goldberg, *Toward an Expanded Economic Theory of Contract*, 10 J. ECON. ISSUES 45 (1976); Williamson, Wachter & Harris, *Understanding the Employment Relation: The Analysis of Idiosyncratic Exchange*, 6 BELL J. ECON. 250 (1975).

34 They are based on Macneil, *A Primer of Contract Planning*, 48 S. CAL. L. REV. 627,

NORTHWESTERN UNIVERSITY LAW REVIEW

Standards.—The use of a standard uncontrolled by either of the parties to plan the contractual relation is very common. One important example is the provision in many collective bargaining agreements for adjustments of wages to reflect fluctuations in the Consumer Price Index.[35]

The standard incorporated may sometimes be established by third parties not altogether unrelated to the contractual relation. For example, it is common to find building contracts requiring compliance with regulations, plans, or standards of the Federal Housing Administration or the Veterans' Administration. Both of these agencies insure mortgage loans, and their regulations are promulgated to deal with mortgages they insure. Thus, although the regulations are drafted with no particular contract in mind, they aim at a class of contracts, some of which incorporate them by reference. This kind of planning merges into the technique of using direct third-party determination of performance, the subject of the following section.

Direct Third-Party Determination of Performance.—The role of the architect under form construction contracts of the American Institute of Architects (AIA) provides a good example of direct third-party determination of performance. The architect is responsible for determining many aspects of the performance relation, including everything from "general administration" of the contract and making final decisions "in matters relating to artistic effect" to approving the contractor's selection of a superintendent.[36] The use of an expert relatively independent of the parties to determine contract content is, however, no guarantee of smooth performance; witness the fairly large amount of litigation arising under the AIA contracts with respect to delays, payments, and completion of the work. This occurs in spite of the broad authority given the architect, perhaps because a recurrent problem is the scope of finality to be accorded to his determinations.

A particularly important and increasingly used technique for third-party determination of performance content is arbitration. Arbitration is best known for its utilization in resolving "rights disputes,"[37]—disputes about existing rights, usually growing out of existing contracts[38] and

---

657-63 (1975) [hereinafter cited as *Primer*]. The text is a somewhat barebones treatment of the subject. Readers wishing to examine the subject in richer detail would do well to read Goldberg, *Regulation and Administered Contracts*, 7 BELL J. ECON. 426 (1976), and Williamson, *Franchise Bidding for Natural Monopolies—In General and with Respect to CATV*, 7 BELL J. ECON. 73 (1976).

[35] *See* Hurst, *Drafting Contracts in an Inflationary Era*, 28 U. FLA. L. REV. 879, 889-93 (1976); Rosenn, *Protecting Contracts from Inflation*, 33 BUS. LAW. 729 (1978).

[36] In addition, the architect has important functions respecting trouble and dispute resolution.

[37] This is a term common in industrial relations.

[38] An example of arbitration of a noncontract rights dispute would be the submission to arbitration of claims relating to the collision of two ships.

always substantially defined and narrowed by law at the time the arbitration takes place. Planning for the arbitration of rights disputes is an important aspect of risk planning. But arbitration is also used for filling gaps in performance planning, *e.g.*, in industrial relations where the inability of management and labor to negotiate on their own the performance terms of a collective bargaining agreement is known as an "interest dispute."[39] Collective bargaining agreements are not, however, the only agreements that leave open issues relating to future performance and provide for their arbitration. For example, certain joint ventures among design professionals may leave important aspects open to arbitration to provide necessary flexibility.[40]

Interest disputes and hence their arbitration are inherently more open-ended than rights disputes. In the latter, the very notion of "rights"—whether they are based on contract terms or other legal sources, such as the rules of tort law—circumscribes the scope of poten-

---

[39] *See* NATIONAL ACADEMY OF ARBITRATORS, ARBITRATION OF INTEREST DISPUTES (1974). Although the distinction between a rights dispute and an interest dispute can be easily verbalized, it may be difficult to perceive both in practice and in theory. In an interest dispute the status quo may be as rigid a definer of future rights as would be any express agreement.

> Throughout the history of interest arbitration in the newspaper publishing industry, there has been one principle upon which all of the decisions have been based, regardless of whether the specific issue was wages, hours, or manning. Arbitrators will leave the parties where they found them unless that party which seeks a change in the previous bargain, assuming that it was equitable, demonstrates that sufficient changes have occurred which warrant the alteration of the previous bargain.

Adair, *The Arbitration of Wage and Manning Disputes in the Newspaper Industry*, in *id.*, at 31, 47. The current great growth area of interest arbitration is in public employment collective bargaining. *See* Anderson, MacDonald, & O'Reilly, *Impasse Resolution in Public Sector Collective Bargaining—An Examination of Compulsory Interest Arbitration in New York*, 51 ST. JOHN'S L. REV. 453 (1977).

[40] *See* Aksen, *Legal Considerations in Using Arbitration Clauses to Resolve Future Problems Which May Arise During Long-Term Business Agreements*, 28 BUS. LAW. 595, 599 (1973):

> One or more architects will join with various engineers to provide complete design work and supervision for a large project and generally the intention is to use the strengths of each firm and provide for a maximum of efficiency and profit at the negotiation stage. Before the job has been undertaken, the parties must attempt to ascertain the percentage contribution of each party and division of labor and income. But, in this type of arrangement it is often impossible to predict dependably what each contribution will be in terms of work or time and it may have no relationship to the relative size of the joint ventures. Blueprints and specifications may take considerably longer than anticipated, structural design work may be more intricate than was orginally believed or supervision of the job may turn out to be a much more time consuming element. If the joint venturers have tied themselves to fixed percentages of the contract price, there are gross inequities which can result. A negotiated solution which sets tentative percentages and permits arbitral adjustments in the event of changed circumstances guarantees a means of reallocating income in terms of actual work performed without either endangering the project or creating the possibility of economic oppression for one or more of the parties.

Close corporations constitute another example where such issues may arise, although most such issues are probably more likely to be risk and trouble disputes. *See generally* Note, *Mandatory Arbitration as a Remedy for Intra-Close Corporate Disputes*, 56 VA. L. REV. 271 (1970).

NORTHWESTERN UNIVERSITY LAW REVIEW

tial arbitral resolution. In theory, if not in fact, such limits are far looser or perhaps even nonexistent in interest disputes.[41] This calls for particular care in planning arbitration aimed at filling gaps in performance planning, and consideration must always be given to the need to include substantive limits on arbitrator authority.[42] In any event, the planner should be fully aware that identical general language of broad arbitration clauses applied to interest disputes lacks the situational limits usually present when the same language is applied to rights disputes.[43]

One-Party Control of Terms.—Rather than use external standards or independent third parties, the contract may provide that one of the parties to the contract will define, directly or indirectly, parts of the relation. This may go so far as to allow one party a completely free will to terminate the relation. For example, in an option contract a party may purchase the privilege of either going ahead with a contract or not doing so. One-party control of terms in the form of a "deal no-deal" option is important in certain areas of enterprise such as the financial markets, commercial real estate transactions, some kinds of commercial sales of goods,[44] and certain types of consumer transactions, *e.g.*, insurance.

---

[41] *But see* note 39 *supra*. The lack of "rights" as the basis for resolving interest disputes has in the past led courts to hold such disputes to be nonarbitrable because they raise nonjusticiable questions. *See* M. DOMKE, THE LAW AND PRACTICE OF COMMERCIAL ARBITRATION § 12.02 (1968). This has been a particularly lively area of industrial relations, and one not necessarily settled yet. *See, e.g.*, NLRB v. Sheet Metal Workers, Local 38, [1978] LAB. REL. REP. (BNA) (98 L.R.R.M. 2147) (2d Cir. 1978); NATIONAL ACADEMY OF ARBITRATORS, note 39 *supra*.

[42] For example, in the design contracts described in note 40 *supra*, thought might be given to the inclusion of floors or ceilings on percentages to be allowed the various parties. These may also help in some jurisdictions to make legally arbitrable issues the court might otherwise possibly find nonarbitrable because it finds them nonjusticiable.

[43] While arbitrators are less bound by terms of agreements and legal rules than are courts in the sense that a court may often be unable to overrule arbitrators as readily as it could the decision of a lower court in similar circumstances, arbitrators too are part of a society of contract and law. They too in rights disputes tend to follow both agreement terms and law. Even the more expansive proponents of arbitrator discretion in labor relations are very modest in suggesting departures from those hoary standards. For a good summary of varying views of the arbitrator's role in labor arbitration, see Fuller, *Collective Bargaining and the Arbitrator*, 1963 WIS. L. REV. 3.

[44] One example is blanket orders, used extensively by some manufacturers, particularly automobile manufacturers.

The term "blanket order" is often applied to requirements contracts, particularly those in which the obligation of the buyer to purchase may be quite illusory. This is commonly the case with automobile manufacturers' parts orders reserving broad rights to cancel. Under its terms, such a blanket order becomes a firm obligation of the automobile manufacturer only when it sends the supplier a direction to ship a certain number of parts "contracted for" earlier under the blanket order. Nevertheless, the position of the manufacturer is so strong that even such a one-sided arrangement elicits a great deal of cooperation from the supplier. Professor Stewart Macaulay recorded the following from an interview of a supplier:

When you deal with Ford, you get a release which tells you to ship so many items in January and gives an estimate on February and March. Ford is committed to take or pay for the February estimate even if it cancels. However, it is not bound to take the parts estimated for March if it cancels in February. One fabricates the

72:854 (1978)   *Adjustment of Relations*

Whenever a party is not clearly paying for the privilege of retaining a free will not to perform his own contractual "obligations," the contract drafter wanting to give that party such freedom walks a narrow line between rigid planning and the danger that the consideration doctrine will make that party's "rights" unenforceable.[45] To cope with the difficulties created by its own doctrine of consideration, the transactional legal structure has produced a wide range of concepts, provisions, techniques, and other devices limiting the impact of the doctrine.[46] The drafter desiring to achieve workable flexibility must be aware both of the limitations the law imposes on available techniques and the opportunities the law offers.

Cost.—A very common technique for achieving flexibility is to provide that compensation for goods or services shall be the cost to the provider, with or without an additional fee (specified in amount or a percentage of the cost or otherwise determined) and with or without definition of what constitutes cost. This technique in a sense combines all of the preceding three. First, this technique utilizes a standard, namely, those of the markets in which the goods and services are purchased. Second, this technique utilizes an element of direct third-party determination in that, while the prices in those markets may be determined without regard to this particular contract, in many cases subcontractors and suppliers will be fixing their own prices with complete awareness of the contract. Finally, there is an element of one-party control since the supplier of the goods and services inevitably has some control over his own costs and hence over the price term of the contract. In general this important technique raises no problems for neoclassical contract law. It may, of course, raise many problems in applying that law to particular situations, over such issues as the definition of costs, assignment of overhead, and the like.

March parts at his own risk, but Ford tries to encourage its suppliers to take this risk so there will be an inventory to handle sudden increased orders. In the example just given, it would be in Ford's interest to pay some of the cost of the March parts to encourage companies to go ahead. If you are a good supplier, it might give you some consideration, but it doesn't have to.

I. MACNEIL, CASES & MATERIALS ON CONTRACTS: EXCHANGE TRANSACTIONS AND RELATIONSHIPS 70 (1971). The legal enforceability of blanket orders in the absence of a specific order is, however, far from clear; their enforcement mechanism apparently turns largely, if not entirely, on the desire of the supplier to continue doing business with the manufacturer.

[45] To the extent, if any, that the doctrine of mutuality adds to the scope of nonenforceability beyond the scope imposed by simple consideration doctrine, the line may be narrowed even further. *See* J. MURRAY, MURRAY ON CONTRACTS § 90 (2d rev. ed. 1974).

[46] For example, protection of contract interests such as the restitutionary and perhaps reliance interests, even when "contracts" are not fully enforceable; developing good faith limitations of various kinds on exercise of one-party controls; manipulation of consideration doctrines; implied obligations; and judicial interpretations contrary to complete one-sideness. *See generally* Farnsworth, *Good Faith Performance and Commercial Reasonableness Under the Uniform Commercial Code*, 30 U. CHI. L. REV. 666 (1963); Summers, *"Good Faith" in General Contract Law and the Sales Provisions of the Uniform Commercial Code*, 54 VA. L. REV. 195 (1968).

NORTHWESTERN UNIVERSITY LAW REVIEW

Agreement to Agree.—A flexible technique used more often than one might initially expect is an "agreement to agree." Since parties can almost always agree later to fill gaps in their relation, such an express provision seems pointless, particularly since, if taken literally, it is meaningless. But common human behavior patterns are seldom if ever pointless, and this is no exception. In general, parties probably use the technique because they are not yet prepared to agree on details requiring agreement, but they want to emphasize to each other that resolution will be required and to express a willingness to engage in the processes of agreement at the appropriate time. These processes undoubtedly more often than not lead to future agreement; but when and if difficulty later ensues in trying to reach agreement, a gap in the contract is revealed. The law should treat such gaps quite similarly to other gaps. The cases are legion,[47] however, in which courts have said "an agreement to agree is not a contract" or some similar bit of doggerel. Often these cases involve circumstances where the court would have held a contract to exist if the gap had occurred in any other manner than a breakdown of an explicit "agreement to agree."[48] Thus, the enunciation of an agreement to agree can be fatal to later securing judicial gap-filling. The planner may avoid this difficulty either by avoiding the technique entirely or by adding an alternative gap-filling technique to come into operation if the parties are unable to agree. Which of these routes is chosen depends at least in part upon how important it is to alert the parties to the need for further negotiation at the appropriate time.

As some of the legal references in the foregoing paragraphs suggest, flexible planning techniques and gaps in planning inevitably raise difficulties for any legal system implementing contractual relations. They raise particular difficulties for classical contract law systems. As already noted, one of the key goals of such a system is enhancing presentation, a goal inimical to flexibility in contract planning because the latter precludes complete predictability as of the time of the acceptance of an offer.

The neoclassical contract law system may be seen as an effort to escape partially from such rigorous presentation, but since its overall structure is essentially the same as the classical system it may often be ill-designed to raise and deal with the issues.[49] Nevertheless, the present neoclassical system permits a great deal of flexibility and gap-filling, as is

---

[47] For a discussion of agreements to agree and citations, see 1 P. BONASSIES, G. GORLA, J. LEYSER, W. LORENZ, I. MACNEIL, K. NEUMAYER, I. SAXENA, R. SCHLESINGER, & W. WAGNER, FORMATION OF CONTRACTS 458-64 (R. Schlesinger ed. 1968).

[48] The courts quite often draw the inference that the parties intended the expression "agreement to agree" or similar language to mean more about the consequences of non-agreement than they would have intended if they had said nothing or dealt with the issue by some other flexible technique which also failed. Such an inference is only rarely correct where extensive agreement has occurred relating to other matters, especially where some or all of the remainder of the agreement has been performed.

[49] This proposition is developed at length in *Presentiation*, note 2 *supra*.

72:854 (1978)   *Adjustment of Relations*

demonstrated by the following extract from Professor Murray's recent contract law text, an extract conveying well a sense of the limits beyond which the American neoclassical contract law system will not go in implementing flexibility.

> **Proposals that are too indefinite to constitute offers.**—It seems self-evident that before a proposal can ripen into a contract, upon the exercise of the power of acceptance by the one to whom it is made, it must be definite enough so that when it is coupled with the acceptance it can be determined, with at least a reasonable degree of certainty, what the nature and extent of the obligation is which the proposer has assumed. Otherwise no basis exists for determining liability. However, it is to be emphasized that the requirement of definiteness cannot be pushed to its extreme limits. The fact is that people seldom express their intentions with complete clarity, so that if we were to take the position that any uncertainty in regard to the intentions of the parties invalidates the offer, few offers could be found. The law must of necessity draw a line short of complete definiteness. If we are to have a workable rule, all that can be safely required is that the proposal be reasonably definite. . . .
>
> . . . .
>
> Certain more or less common types of indefiniteness are uniformly held not to invalidate offers. Thus if one undertakes to perform definite services, or to sell ascertainable goods, or to render some other definite performance without, explicitly or by implication, specifying the price to be paid in return for the same, it is generally held that the proposal is a valid offer and that a reasonable price is the measure of the acceptor's undertaking. At least this is true where the performance offered has a market value, or the equivalent, so that some proper standard exists for determining the extent of the acceptor's liability. The theory back of this holding seems to be that a reasonable price is implicit in the offer. It is submitted that the result thus reached is desirable and that in most cases, if not in all, it agrees with the actual intention of the parties. So also, if an undertaking, that is in other respects definite, leaves indefinite the time of performance, it is uniformly held, in the absence of evidence of a contrary intention, that a reasonable time must have been understood, and the agreement will be upheld on that basis. This holding probably also agrees with the parties' actual intention, or at least with what their intention would have been had they given the matter any consideration. It is to be observed, however, that the foregoing principles are applicable only if the parties have omitted any attempt to express any intention in regard to the matters mentioned. *If they have purported to fix a price, or a time of performance, and their expression is so indefinite that its meaning cannot be determined with at least a reasonable degree of certainty, then it will be held that the agreement does not constitute a contract for want of definiteness. This is so because their very attempt to state the matter, or their understanding that it should be left for future determination through mutual agreement, makes it clear that an objectively determined reasonable price or reasonable time, as the case may be, was not contemplated and might be inconsistent with their intention.*

NORTHWESTERN UNIVERSITY LAW REVIEW

. . . .

It is also to be noted that an agreement which is too indefinite in some material aspect for enforcement at the outset, may later become definite as the result of part performance. If performance is rendered by one party in such a way as to make definite what before was indefinite, and this performance is acquiesced in by the other party, there is no apparent reason why the agreement should not be regarded as obligatory from that time forth. The performance may be regarded as the offer which is accepted by the acquiescence of the other party. This is the result usually reached in the decided cases.[50]

While the foregoing extract expresses well the spirit of the neoclassical contract law system, it fails to focus on what I believe to be the fundamental principle underlying the reluctance in such a system to enforce contractual relations in the face of excessive indefiniteness. This principle is founded on the nature of choice-generated exchange and the underlying assumption that the function of a classical or neoclassical contract law system is to enhance the utilities created by choice-generated exchange but not necessarily those created by other kinds of exchange.

When *A* and *B* agree to exchange *A*'s good *X* in return for *B*'s good *Y*, we conclude, in the absence of factors other than desires for *X* and *Y* causing the agreement to occur, that the exchange will enhance the utility levels of each. Where, however, the parties neglect—to take an absurd example—to define in any way what *X* and *Y* are, the operators of a contract law system—judge or jury—can have no assurance whatever that judicial definition of *X* and *Y*, and enforcement of the exchange, will enhance the utility levels of either *A* or *B*, let alone both. The example is absurd, but it demonstrates the limits beyond which enhancement of individual utility levels cannot serve as an adequate reason for enforcing a sufficiently indefinite agreement. Beyond such a point, if enforcement is to be had, other justifications must be found, *e.g.*, avoiding unjust enrichment. Moreover, as Professor Murray suggests, parties can and do fail to define *X* and *Y* sufficiently to provide reasonable assurance to a court that enforcing the "contract" would enhance utilities on both sides as those utilities were originally viewed by the parties.[51] If, as is typical of discrete transactions (especially as treated by a classical or neoclassical contract law system), no other reason exists to enforce the exchange, that is the end of it.[52]

---

50 J. MURRAY, *supra* note 45, § 27 (footnotes omitted) (emphasis supplied) (reprinted with permission of the author and the publisher, the Bobbs-Merrill Co.).

51 Of course, by the time the legal system becomes involved in this kind of dispute it is, in relatively discrete transactions, normally no longer possible to raise utilities of both. That is why stress in the text is on the phrase "as these utilities were originally viewed by the parties."

52 The analysis in the text is consistent with that in R. POSNER, ECONOMIC ANALYSIS OF LAW § 4.2 at 69-70 (2d ed. 1977). Posner, however, does not appear to recognize that the analysis is circumscribed by the assumptions of a discrete transactional system; such a

72:854 (1978)   *Adjustment of Relations*

It will also be noted that one of the goals, mentioned earlier, of a classical contract law system is complete presentiation at the time of agreement. The greater the degree of indefiniteness in an agreement, the more a court must fly in the face of this goal in enforcing the agreement. The increasing laxity of the neoclassical system about definiteness, in contrast to the classical system, reflects relaxation of this goal.

Since the neoclassical contract law system remains structured on the classical model in large measure, it too is limited by the foregoing considerations. On the other hand, the neoclassical system, being significantly more relational in nature,[53] can go much further than the classical system, just so long as it does not break out of the classical structure altogether. What happens when a system pushes beyond the limits even of a neoclassical structure will be discussed later.[54]

Conflict between Specific Planning and Needs for Flexibility: The Neoclassical Response

As a general proposition in American neoclassical contract law, specific planning in contractual relations governs in spite of changes in circumstances making such planning undesirable to one of the parties. The same principle of freedom of contract[55] leading to this result permits the parties, however, to adjust their relations by subsequent agreement. A description of these processes and some of the legal considerations follows.[56]

Adjustments of existing contractual relations occur in numerous ways. Performance itself is a kind of adjustment from original planning. Even meticulous performance of the most explicit planning transforms figments of the imagination, however precise, into a new, and therefore different, reality. A set of blueprints and specifications, however detailed, and a newly built house simply are not the same. Less explicit planning is changed even more by performance. For example, the vaguely articulated duties of a secretary are made concrete by his or her actual performance of a day's work. Perhaps this is merely a way of saying that planning is inherently filled with gaps, and that performance fills the gaps, thereby altering the relations as originally planned.

Events outside the performance of the parties also may effect adjustments in contractual relationships. The five dollars per hour promised an employee for his work in 1977 is not the same when paid in November

---

circumscribed analysis may be and often is singularly inadequate when applied to indefiniteness in ongoing contractual relations.

53 For a discussion of this, see *Presentiation*, note 2 *supra*.

54 *See* text accompanying notes 104-40 *infra*.

55 Freedom of contract here means, of course, power of contract, *e.g.*, the power to bind oneself, by agreement, to further action or consequences to which one otherwise would not have been bound.

56 The following paragraphs are based on *Primer, supra* note 34, at 663-66.

NORTHWESTERN UNIVERSITY LAW REVIEW

1977 as it was when promised at the beginning of the year; inflation and other economic developments have seen to that. More or less drastic changes in outside circumstances constantly effect contractual adjustments, however firmly the parties may appear to be holding to their original course.

Nonperformance by one of the parties without the consent of the other also alters contractual relations, although in a way different from performance. This is true no matter how many powers are available to the other party to redress the situation.

Another kind of adjustment occurring in any contractual relation is that based either on mutual agreement or on unilateral concession by one of the parties of a planned right beneficial to him. These alterations, additions, subtractions, terminations, and other changes from original planning may take place at any time during any contractual relation. This is vividly illustrated by various processes of collective bargaining, including periodic renegotiation of the "whole" contract.

When disputes arise out of contractual relations after adjustment by mutual assent or concession, does the original planning or the adjusted planning govern? Keeping in mind the exchange element basic to contractual relations and the various problems the legal system has in dealing with contractual disputes, the answer might seem to depend in any given situation on answers to the following kinds of questions:

1. How sure is it that the adjustment really was mutually agreed upon or conceded?
2. Did one party take improper advantage of the other in securing the concession or agreement?
3. Was the adjustment mutually beneficial, *e.g.*, was there an exchange element in the adjustment itself, or did only one of the parties benefit?
4. If the adjustment benefited only one party, was its purpose to alleviate some difficulty resulting from lack of prior planning or from unplanned consequences of prior planning?
5. How much had the adjustment become integrated into the relation when disputes concerning it arose, *e.g.*, was there unjust enrichment or reliance, among other things?[57]

No comprehensive doctrinal structure has developed in American neoclassical contract law to answer systematically the foregoing ques-

---

[57] Other possible questions are: To what extent was the adjustment part of an ongoing and still viable relation, and to what extent was it only a settlement of disputes arising from a defunct relation? What is the reason for the attack on the adjustments?

Moreover, other ways of stating the issues are perfectly possible and perhaps more useful to anyone setting out to organize the now disorganized legal thinking in the area. For example, overlapping many of the above questions is the following: Was the adjustment in harmony with the rest of the relation, not just as originally planned, but as it had developed to the time of the adjustment in issue and thereafter?

tions.[58] The closest it comes to providing such a structure is the doctrine of consideration, which pervades much thinking on the subject.[59] Consideration doctrine, however, by no means deals comprehensively with all the questions. For one thing the doctrine normally impedes change if it operates at all, thus implementing discreteness and presentation as of the "original formation."

Where the parties are unable to agree to adjustments to reflect changes in circumstances, neoclassical contract law provides a limited array of doctrines whereby one party may escape some or all the consequences of the change. Doctrines of impossibility of performance, frustration, and mistake are used with varying degress of frequency to relieve parties.[60] More covert techniques such as interpretation or manipulations of technical doctrines such as offer and acceptance and rules governing conditions are also available. But as a general proposition these doctrines aim not at continuing the contractual relations but at picking up the pieces of broken contracts and allocating them between the parties on some basis deemed equitable.

Generally speaking, doctrines of the kind described in the last paragraph achieve such goals as preventing a party from recovering expectation damages when the other party has not performed or preventing unjust enrichment by allowing a party to recover a down payment (restitution) when its purpose in entering the contract has been frustrated. A slowly growing tendency in American law to go farther than this may be discerned. The following sections of the Restatement (Second) of Contracts are illustrative:

Section 292. RELIEF INCLUDING RESTITUTION; SUPPLY-
              ING A TERM

(1) In any case governed by the rules stated in this Chapter [Impracticability of Performance and Frustration of Purpose], either party may have a claim for relief including restitution under the rules stated in Section 265. . . .

(2) In any case governed by the rules stated in this Chapter, if those rules . . . will not avoid injustice, the court may, under the

---

[58] This is not to suggest the absence of such structures respecting particular kinds of contractual relations. Certainly labor law is not only replete with doctrines centering on such adjustments, but also institutions such as the National Labor Relations Board (NLRB) produce and are affected by those doctrines. The law relating to the internal workings of corporations is another example of legal doctrines centered on constant adjustments of exchange relations.

[59] The cases and problems in MACNEIL, CASES 2, *supra* note 16, at 890-927, suggest a range of the kinds of legal issues raised. For more traditional treatment see J. CALAMARI & J. PERILLO, THE LAW OF CONTRACTS, chs. 4 & 5 (2d ed. 1977); J. MURRAY, *supra* note 45, §§ 72-90.

[60] *See generally*, J. MURRAY, *supra* note 45, §§ 30, 124-30, 197-205. These doctrines are generally keyed back by presentation notions into the status quo of the original contract as the base point, *e.g.*, use of the idea of tacit assumptions about the continued existence of property being transferred under the contract.

NORTHWESTERN UNIVERSITY LAW REVIEW

rule stated in Section 230, supply a term which is reasonable in the circumstances.[61]

Section 230. SUPPLYING AN OMITTED ESSENTIAL TERM
When the parties to a bargain sufficiently defined to be a contract have not agreed with respect to a term which is essential to a determination of their rights and duties, a term which is reasonable in the circumstances is supplied by the court.[62]

To the extent that the courts apply these rules in a suit, they will begin to provide a legal framework for continuing contractual relations in spite of major changes in circumstances. More explicit on this score are Uniform Commercial Code sections 2-614, 2-615, and 2-616.

Section 2-614 requires tender and acceptance of commercially reasonable substitute berthing, loading or unloading facilities, type of carrier or manner of delivery where those agreed upon become commercially impracticable without fault of either party. It also permits, in certain circumstances, alternative means of payment from those agreed upon. Section 2-615 requires a seller unable to meet his obligations because of specified changed circumstances to allocate his production among his customers (including, at his option, regular customers not under contract) in any manner fair and reasonable. If he does so and gives proper notice, he has not breached his duty under the contract. Under section 2-616 the buyer may then either terminate the contract (thereby discharging any unexecuted portion) or modify the contract by agreeing to take his available quota in substitution for the originally agreed-upon amount. The process under sections 2-615 and 2-616 is something more than simply a voluntary agreement adjusting the situation, since the seller must make the allocation; and the buyer refuses a proper allocation only at the expense of a discharge of the seller.

In summary, two themes may be seen in the development of neoclassical contract law. One is a gradually increasing willingness to recognize conflict between specific planning and subsequent changes in circumstances and to do something about them. The other is a more truncated recognition of the possibility of doing something when such conflicts occur beyond simply picking up the pieces of a dead contract by awarding monetary judgments to someone or refusing to do so. The latter theme merges into the more general issue of continuing relations in the face of trouble, the subject of the following section.

Planning for Nondisruptive Dispute Settlement: The Neoclassical System and Prevention of Disruption

The common presumption of human institutions is that internal conflict, even quite serious conflict, does not necessarily terminate the

---

61 RESTATEMENT (SECOND) OF CONTRACTS § 292 (Tent. Draft No. 9, 1974).
62 RESTATEMENT (SECOND) OF CONTRACTS § 230 (Tent. Draft Nos. 1-7, 1973).

institution; indeed, only the most basic and grievous of conflict, if that, will do so.[63] In this respect, the classical contract, along with the discrete transaction it parallels, is a sport. Generally speaking, a serious conflict, even quite a minor one such as an objection to a harmlessly late tender of the delivery of goods, terminates the discrete contract as a live one and leaves nothing but a conflict over money damages to be settled by a lawsuit. Such a result fits neatly the norms of enhancing discreteness and intensifying and expanding presentation. These norms never, however, completely dominated classical law and certainly do not completely dominate neoclassical law.[64] Nevertheless, the thrust, even of the neoclassical system, is such that explicit planning is often necessary if the participants in a contractual relation desire to continue in the face of serious conflict or even in the face of some kinds of minor conflict.

In light of the above, it often behooves contract planners to plan for continuing relations in the face of conflict. A major example is the "no strike" clause very common in collective bargaining agreements. Normally a "no lockout" clause binding management parallels the "no strike" clause, and grievance procedures and arbitration for disputes accompany them.[65] Another example is found in United States government procurement contracts. The typical disputes clause in such contracts not only provides a mechanism for dispute resolution,[66] but also provides: "Pending final decision of a dispute hereunder, the Contractor shall proceed diligently with the performance of the contract and in accordance with the Contracting Officer's decision."[67] The widely used construction contract forms of the American Institute of Architects (AIA) contain a similar provision: "Unless otherwise agreed in writing, the Contractor shall carry on the Work and maintain its progress during any arbitration proceedings, and the Owner shall continue to make payments to the Contractor in accordance with the Contract Documents."[68]

---

[63] Witness our surviving our own Civil War or the conflict in the interrelation of church and state in any given area in the Middle Ages.

[64] For example, prevailing rules respecting conditions go a long way to keep the relation going in the face of dispute.

[65] The collective bargaining relation typically would continue even if a strike or lockout occurs; what such clauses preserve is the normal operating relation. For a strong statement of employees' duties to perform as commanded and to grieve later, see Dean Shulman's arbitration decision in Ford Motor Co., 3 LAB. ARB. 779 (1944), *quoted in* A. COX, D. BOK, & R. GORMAN, CASES & MATERIALS ON LABOR LAW 571-72 (8th ed. 1977).

[66] The initial decision is by the Contracting Officer, with a right to appeal to a Board of Contracts Appeals (an administrative court). Further appeal is possible in some circumstances, usually to the Court of Claims. This is an oversimplified statement of an immensely complex procedural structure. *See* S. & E. Contractors, Inc. v. United States, 406 U.S. 1 (1972); 4 Report of the Commission on Government Procurement (1972).

[67] Dispute clause required by Armed Services Procurement Regulations, 32 C.F.R. § 7-103.12 (1976). *See* Vacketta & Wheeler, *A Government Contractor's Right to Abandon Performance*, 65 GEO. L.J. 27 (1976).

[68] AMERICAN INSTITUTE OF ARCHITECTS, GENERAL CONDITIONS OF THE CONTRACT FOR

NORTHWESTERN UNIVERSITY LAW REVIEW

Methods of enforcing provisions such as the foregoing vary. Injunctions are granted against strikes and lockouts carried out in violation of no-strike and no-lockout clauses.[69] Conceivably, the provisions in the federal government contracts and in the AIA forms could be enforced specifically. But the government seldom takes that route. And efforts to enforce the AIA provision specifically would run into the general reluctance of American courts to grant specific performance of complicated construction contracts.[70] While this reluctance seems to be diminishing,[71] it has not disappeared. In principle, provisions of this nature should be enforceable specifically by American courts whenever the other requisites for securing specific performance are met, *e.g.*, inadequacy of damage remedies. Indeed, the reluctance to step into complex situations may be less evident where the court views the relief as merely interim relief granted while the main issue is resolved in another forum, such as arbitration.[72]

Provisions such as those discussed above also can be enforced through damage remedies. Violations of no-strike clauses, for example, give rise to rights to damages.[73] Likewise, failure of a contractor to continue performance in spite of a dispute appears to constitute a default irrespective of the merits of the dispute. Presumably similar remedies would be available for breach of other such clauses. Thus, if a contractor quits over a dispute on a construction contract, the owner should be able to recover damages for losses resulting from the quitting irrespective of the merits of the dispute itself.[74] While damage remedies operate retrospectively and, where actually used, do not keep the relation going, the *threat* of their being used may do so.

Apart from providing explicitly for relations to continue during conflicts, the parties may plan processes or agree to substantive terms tending to have that effect. An example of the latter would be a provision

---

CONSTRUCTION, AIA Document A201, art. 7.9.3 (1976).

69 The provisions of federal and state labor laws prohibiting the issuance of injunctions in labor disputes do not necessarily apply to injunctions enforcing no-strike clauses. *See* Boys Markets, Inc. v. Retail Clerks Union, Local 770, 398 U.S. 235 (1970). How effective such injunctions are is another matter.

70 D. DOBBS, HANDBOOK ON THE LAW OF REMEDIES § 12.22 (1973).

71 *Id*. But some of the cases reflecting this change have involved enforcement of arbitrators' orders to perform specifically, and normally no such order will be available when the owner seeks relief against a contractor under Article 7.9.3 during the pendency of the arbitration proceedings.

72 If the clause provided for continuation of performance while the parties battled their disputes out in court rather than before an arbitrator this reason would not be pertinent. I have never seen such a contract provision, but some are probably lurking out there somewhere.

73 *See, e.g.*, Local 174, Teamsters v. Lucas Flour Co., 369 U.S. 95 (1962) (no-strike clause inferred from presence of compulsory binding arbitration provision).

74 The owner's claim would, under the AIA form contract, be subject to arbitration, just as the original dispute was subject to arbitration.

in a sale and installation of complicated machinery giving the seller ninety days after installation in which to adjust the machinery and cure any problems. Provisions for meeting together to discuss problems, for mediation in event of a dispute, and for arbitration are all examples of planning which tends to keep relations going, even without a statement that the parties will do so.[75] The neoclassical contract system provides its normal enforcement mechanisms for such provisions, including limited availability of specific performance.[76] In the case of arbitration, under modern statutes, the system strongly reinforces the process,[77] although reinforcement of arbitration itself does not necessarily mean that the relation will continue.[78]

Where party planning fails to focus on maintaining the relation in the face of conflict, many factors may nevertheless keep it going while the parties iron out disputes. This is, of course, the common human experience, since self-interest, custom, morality, and many other factors may make it more desirable to do so than to terminate the relation. In addition, the neoclassical contract law system offers a range of assistance. Specific performance is the most obvious means, but in spite of expansion in the availability of specific performance in the past decades, it is hardly the primary neoclassical contract remedy.[79] The existence of any contract law remedy tends to have this effect of maintaining the relation. To whatever extent a party is unsure of the legal correctness of his position in a dispute, he will have some desire to continue performing to avoid liability should he turn out to be wrong.[80] Certainly the importance of this in governing a party's actions will depend upon the effectiveness of the remedy.

Some substantive legal rules focus quite particularly on this subject, for example, the general contract principle that the victim of a contract breach cannot recover damages avoidable "through the exercise of reasonable diligence, and without incurring undue risk, expense, or humiliation."[81] In some circumstances this may prevent recovery of damages

---

[75] *See Primer, supra* note 34, at 681-91.

[76] *See* text accompanying note 79 *infra*.

[77] *See Primer, supra* note 34, at 685-91.

[78] If the arbitrators award specific performance and the court enforces the award effectively, this will, of course continue the relation. *See, e.g., In re* Staklinski and Pyramid Elec. Co., 6 N.Y.2d 159, 160 N.E.2d 78, 188 N.Y.S.2d 541 (1959).

[79] For an expression of hope that it will become so by one of the leading neoclassical contract scholars, see Braucher, *Contracts,* in N.Y.U. SCHOOL OF LAW, AMERICAN LAW: THE THIRD CENTURY—THE LAW BICENTENNIAL VOLUME 121, 127 (B. Schwartz ed. 1976).

[80] This applies to duties from whatever source derived, not just from those agreed upon. For example, an employer who discharges an employee for activity that may be protected by the National Labor Relations Act, 29 U.S.C. §§ 151-169 (1970 & Supp. V 1975), not only must reinstate the employee but also must pay back pay if the discharge is later held to be an unfair labor practice.

[81] J. MURRAY, *supra* note 45, at § 227 (footnote omitted). *See* Hillman, *Keeping the Deal*

NORTHWESTERN UNIVERSITY LAW REVIEW

avoidable by continuing the relation. Another example, in the Uniform Commercial Code, provides that a seller aggrieved by a buyer's breach respecting unfinished goods may

> in the exercise of reasonable commercial judgment for the purposes of avoiding loss and of effective realization either complete the manufacture and wholly identify the goods to the contract or cease manufacture and resell for scrap or salvage value or proceed in any other reasonable manner.[82]

This section permits the seller unilaterally to maintain the relation in spite of the dispute, since identification of the goods to the contract will, within limits, permit the seller to recover the price of the goods[83] rather than merely damages for the breach. (The latter may be far less in amount and more difficult to prove.)

In summary, both planning by parties and the neoclassical system acting in either a supplementary or independent manner, can provide extensively for the continuance of relations even in the face of serious disputes. When, however, self-interest or other motives of the parties are inadequate to accomplish continuation, the reinforcement of the neoclassical contract law system often proves inadequate to the task. We should not, however, sell short that system as a supporter of customs and habits of behavior internalized in such a way that motives to "keep on with it" will prevail.

Terminating Economic Activities and Allocating Losses from Termination

As noted earlier, planning for the termination of economic relations is simply a particular kind of planning for flexibility. For that reason, all the techniques for planning of flexibility discussed before are available for the purpose of planning terminations as well. In addition, the simple technique of putting a time limit on the duration of the contract is not only available, but fits very well with the concept of the discrete transaction, a fixed duration being fundamental to the concept of discreteness. Since discreteness underlies the concepts of the neoclassical contract law structure, some of the kinds of legal difficulties respecting flexibility discussed earlier will not affect provisions respecting termination. For example, a court that might be very reluctant to effectuate a provision giving a seller complete freedom to fix the price would have little doctrinal trouble with a provision allowing the seller complete freedom to terminate the contract.

The generality of the foregoing comments must be limited in certain respects. First, one-sided powers to terminate the relations give rise to

---

Together after Material Breach—Common Law Mitigation Rules, the UCC, and the Restatement (Second) of Contracts, 47 U. COLO. L. REV. 553 (1976).

[82] U.C.C. § 2-704.

[83] U.C.C. § 2-709.

problems of mutuality and to questions of enforceability. For example, suppose that Seller agrees to supply Buyer with all Buyer's requirements for transistors for a five-year period, and Buyer agrees to buy all its requirements for transistors during a five-year period with an option to terminate the relation at any time after the first year upon sixty days notice. The contract establishing this one-sided arrangement could be drafted clearly enough so that a court would enforce it in spite of the absence of substantial mutuality of obligations after the first year. But careless draftsmanship could easily permit a court to hold the contract divisible into two parts: (1) the first year (and perhaps sixty days) during which there was mutuality of obligation and therefore consideration for seller's promise; and (2) the remainder of the time, during which buyer had promised nothing. Under such an analysis, after the first year (and maybe sixty days), consideration for a seller's promise would be lacking and its promise would not be enforceable.[84]

The doctrine of consideration as applied above may be viewed as a regulatory control discouraging parties from providing for unilateral rights of termination of agreements. Occasionally, in contracts where one party is more powerful than the other, American law has gone farther than simply discouraging provisions for such rights. For example, a federal statute[85] confers upon an automobile dealer rights to sue the manufacturer for "failure . . . to act in good faith in . . . terminating, canceling, or not renewing the franchise with said dealer . . . ."[86] This language supersedes any rights, however carefully planned, the manufacturer would otherwise possess to terminate at will. Specific legislation of this kind is relatively rare,[87] although legislation governing employment may have similar effect. For example, civil servants typically have great protection of tenure in their positions, and unemployment insurance schemes imposed on private employers by statute may inhibit discharging employees. Moreover, since collective bargaining almost invariably leads

---

[84] The technique used results in neither being bound, not in both being bound. It is therefore consistent with notions of discreteness, since it shortens the relation.

[85] Automobile Dealers' Day in Court Act, 15 U.S.C. §§ 1221-1225 (1976). While this statute might be viewed as outside the system of neoclassical law, its approach is so consonant with the structure of that system that it may sensibly be viewed as an internal development respecting a particular kind of contract.

[86] 15 U.S.C. § 1222 (1976). The statute also includes the following language: "*Provided*, That in any such suit the manufacturer shall not be barred from asserting in defense of any such action the failure of the dealer to act in good faith." *Id*. (emphasis in original).

This statute and its relative lack of effectiveness are discussed extensively in Macaulay, *The Standardized Contracts of United States Automobile Manufacturers*, in 7 INTERNATIONAL ENCYCLOPEDIA OF COMPARATIVE LAW, ch. 3, 18 (1974). For a recent dealer victory see Shor-Line Rambler, Inc. v. American Motors Sales Corp., 543 F.2d 601 (7th Cir. 1976); for a recent dealer loss, see Autohaus Brugger, Inc. v. Saab Motors, Inc., 567 F.2d 901 (9th Cir. 1978).

[87] A leading state example is Wisconsin's Fair Dealership Law, WIS. STAT. §§ 135.01-.07 (1975). *See* Boatland, Inc. v. Brunswick Corp., 558 F.2d 818 (6th Cir. 1977).

NORTHWESTERN UNIVERSITY LAW REVIEW

to job security for individual employees, the many statutory reinforcements of collective bargaining may reasonably be viewed as legislation of similar nature.

Moving in similar directions are cases such as *Shell Oil Co. v. Marinello*,[88] requiring good cause for the termination of a service station lease-franchise relation. This particular decision was influenced by a New Jersey statute so providing, although, because of its effective date, inapplicable to the dispute in question.[89] No such statute, however, was involved in a recent federal case applying Missouri law.[90] It held that while a franchise agreement silent as to duration is normally terminable at will, the franchisor cannot terminate for a reasonable time from its formation—a reasonable time being long enough to allow franchisee to recover its initial investment and expenses. The court held that in the circumstances of the case eight or nine years was long enough. Also moving in similar direction are common law cases "interpreting" employment contracts without specified duration as being terminable by the employer only for cause[91] and those cases prohibiting terminations or refusals to renew contractual relations for "improper reasons."[92]

Unlike the consideration and mutuality limitations discussed earlier, the foregoing kinds of legal intervention are anti-discrete, since, where effective, they lengthen rather than shorten enforceable contractual relations. Thus, interstitially and gradually, increasingly tight limits are being

---

[88] 63 N.J. 402, 307 A.2d 598 (1973), *cert. denied*, 415 U.S. 920 (1974).

[89] In William C. Cornitius, Inc. v. Wheeler, 276 Or. 747, 556 P.2d 666 (1976), the Oregon Supreme Court refused to follow the decision in Shell Oil Co. v. Marinello, 63 N.J. 402, 307 A.2d 598 (1973), *cert. denied*, 415 U.S. 920 (1974). The court described *Marinello* as the only case holding that service station lease-franchises must be renewable (except for good cause for refusal) and distinguished cases holding unenforceable reserved rights to terminate service station lease-franchises without good cause, *e.g.*, Ashland Oil, Inc. v. Donahue, 223 S.E.2d 433 (W. Va. 1976). *Cornitius* held that the service station owner could omit renewal terms from its leases, the court stating that it was not considering "enforceability of a one-sided cancellation clause in a contract of adhesion." 556 P.2d at 670-71. Careful drafting should enable franchisors in Oregon to avoid ever having such an issue raised against them; they need simply omit renewal provisions, even though renewal will be the normal procedure.

[90] Lockewill, Inc. v. United States Shoe Corp., 547 F.2d 1024 (8th Cir. 1976), *cert. denied*, 431 U.S. 956 (1977).

[91] Monge v. Beebe Rubber Co., 114 N.H. 130, 316 A.2d 549 (1974); Pstragowski v. Metropolitan Life Ins. Co., 553 F.2d 1 (1st Cir. 1977) (applying New Hampshire law).

[92] *E.g.*, L'Orange v. Medical Protective Co., 394 F.2d 57 (6th Cir. 1968) (refusal to renew medical malpractice policy because policyholder testified for plaintiff in a malpractice case); Dickhut v. Norton, 45 Wis. 2d 389, 173 N.W.2d 297 (1970) (eviction of tenant for making a complaint to authorities about housing violations). The Oregon Supreme Court refused to apply the principle in William C. Cornitius, Inc. v. Wheeler, 276 Or. 747, 556 P.2d 666 (1976), without recognizing that this principle is not limited to residential leases and ignoring the court's own recent decision holding tortious the firing of an employee for requesting jury duty after being told not to do so. Nees v. Hocks, 272 Or. 210, 536 P.2d 512 (1975). See note on improper motivations in MACNEIL, CASES 2, *supra* note 16, at 514-15.

imposed on the general principle that parties may plan for unilateral termination of contractual relations and that the courts will effectuate their planning.

Apart from legislatively imposed requirements, unilateral rights to terminate may be exercised leaving losses to fall where they happen to fall. This is analogous to what happens in a system of very discrete transactions, in which most risks of change have to be borne within the firm rather than being shifted to the other party or somehow shared. The difference lies in the option available to the party enjoying the right to terminate unilaterally; with the longer term relational contract that party has the advantages both of the security of the longer term and of short-term discreteness. Parties are, of course, often fully aware of this and may, rather than having the disadvantaged party charge more to cover the added risk, allocate in advance the costs of termination. Perhaps the most complex provisions of this kind are found in the great administrative structure built around the federal government's right to terminate contracts for its convenience.[93] A very general summary of these provisions is that costs incurred in performance of the contract, including overhead and profit on work performed, are allowed, but profit on the parts of the contract not performed because of the termination is not. Franchise agreements giving the franchisor rights to terminate often provide another example of advance allocation of costs so that not all of the costs of termination otherwise falling on the franchisee remain there.[94]

Thus, in summary, the neoclassical system generally poses few doctrinal hurdles to termination, even unilateral termination, if carefully enough planned. But relational limits on unilateral termination are creeping into the neoclassical system.

Overview of the Limits of a Neoclassical Contract Law System

As noted earlier, the two special norms of a classical contract law system are enhancement of discreteness, and expansion and intensification of presentiation. Both of these norms aim toward ideals no social or legal system could ever come close to achieving; pure discreteness is an impossibility, as is pure presentiation. Thus even the purest classical contract law system is itself a compromise; its spirit and its conceptual structures may be those of pure discreteness and presentiation, but its details and its application never can be.

Even apart from these theoretical limitations of a classical contract law system, the limited extent to which it is possible for people to consent

---

[93] Armed Services Procurement Regulations, 32 C.F.R. §§ 8-000 to 8-406, 8-701 to 8-712 (1976). Quite similar rights are reserved by blanket supply contracts automobile manufacturers enter with their suppliers. *See* Macaulay, note 86 *supra*.

[94] *See generally* E. McGuire, Franchised Distribution (The Conference Board, publ., 1971).

NORTHWESTERN UNIVERSITY LAW REVIEW

to all the terms of a transaction, even a relatively simple and very discrete one, soon forces the development of legal fictions expanding the scope of "consent" far beyond anything remotely close to what the parties ever had in mind. The greatest of these in American law is the objective theory of contract. The classical American contract is founded not upon actual consent but upon objective manifestations of intent. Moreover, in classical law manifestations of intent include whole masses of contract content one, or even both, parties did not know in fact. For example, ordinary run-of-the-mill purchasers of insurance are, in classical law, deemed to have consented not only to all the terms in the policy, which they did not read and could not have understood if they had, but also to all the interpretations the law would make of those terms. While in theory this enhances presentation (the law presumably being perfectly clear or at least struggling to be so), and may indeed have done so for the insurer, for the insured it commonly has precisely the opposite effect. Nevertheless, it is necessary to cram such absurdities into "objective consent" in order to avoid recognizing the relational characteristics of the system.

Neoclassical contract law partially, but only partially, frees itself of the foregoing difficulties. The freeing comes in the details, not in the overall structure. As suggested above, for example, the neoclassical system displays a good bit of flexibility in adjusting to change, and by no means always does so in terms of fictions about the original intent of the parties. Perhaps one of the most vivid examples of this is Restatement (Second) of Contracts, sections 266 and 267.[95] These define when a failure to perform is material and when unperformed duties under a contract are discharged by the other party's uncured material failure to perform (or offer to perform).[96] Section 267 lists seven circumstances significant in determining the time when the injured party is discharged:

1. the extent to which the injured party will be deprived of the benefit which he reasonably expected;
2. the extent to which the injured party can be adequately compensated for the part of that benefit of which he will be deprived;
3. the extent to which the party failing to perform or to offer to perform will suffer forfeiture;
4. the likelihood that the party failing to perform or to offer to perform will cure his failure, taking account of all the circumstances including any reasonable assurances;
5. the extent to which the behavior of the party failing to perform or to offer to perform comports with standards of good faith and fair dealing;
6. the extent to which it reasonably appears to the injured party that delay may prevent or hinder him in making reasonable substitute arrangements;
7. the extent to which the agreement provides for performance without delay, but a material failure to perform or to offer to per-

---

[95] RESTATEMENT (SECOND) OF CONTRACTS §§ 266-67 (Tent. Draft No. 8, 1973).

[96] *Id.* For other examples, see *Presentiation, supra* note 2, at 603-06.

form on a stated day does not of itself discharge the other party's remaining duties unless the circumstances, including the language of the agreement, indicate that performance or tender by that day is important.[97]

Of the seven factors, four (3, 4, 5, and 6) clearly focus on circumstances at the time of the difficulties, rather than following the presentiation approach and trying to key back to the original agreement. An element of that is also present in the others. In 1 and 2 "the benefit he reasonably expected" appears to permit more consideration of post-agreement circumstances than would, for example, the phrase "what he was promised." And 7 puts a burden on the injured party to show that timely performance was important beyond simply providing initially in the contract that performance be without delay. (That is only one of the circumstances to be considered.) This too is anti-presentiation.

The burgeoning concept of good faith, in large measure within the neoclassical framework, is another largely anti-presentiating, and very much anti-discrete, concept.[98]

But neoclassical contract law can free itself only partially from the limitations posed by obeisance to the twin classical goals of discreteness and presentiation. This obeisance is imposed by adherence to an overall structure founded on full consent at the time of initial contracting.[99] As long as such adherence continues, *i.e.*, as long as it remains a neoclassical system, there are limits to the ignoring of discreteness and presentiation in favor, for example, of such factors as those listed above respecting Restatement (Second) of Contracts § 267.[100] Nevertheless, the constantly increasing role of ongoing contractual relations in the American economy continues to put immense pressure on the legal system to respond in relational ways.

In the past such pressures have led to the spin-off of many subject areas from the classical, and later the neoclassical, contract law system, *e.g.*, much of corporate law and collective bargaining (to say nothing of marriage, which was never really in). They have thus led to a vast shrinkage of the areas of socioeconomic activity to which the neoclassical system applies.[101] As the earlier discussion in this paper indicates, they

---

[97] RESTATEMENT (SECOND) OF CONTRACTS § 267 (Tent. Draft No. 8, 1973). The first five circumstances are from § 266, where they determine materiality of the failure to perform.

[98] *See generally* Summers, *supra* note 46.

[99] This characteristic of the neoclassical system is explored in *Presentiation*, note 2 *supra*.

[100] RESTATEMENT (SECOND) OF CONTRACTS § 267 (Tent. Draft No. 8, 1973).

[101] *See* L. FRIEDMAN, CONTRACT LAW IN AMERICA (1965); Macneil, *Whither Contracts?*, 21 J. LEGAL EDUC. 403 (1969). The mistake is sometimes made of concluding that because a subject area has spun off and is widely considered to be a special area, that all elements underlying the classical or neoclassical system disappear from the area. There are hints, or more, of this in G. GILMORE, THE DEATH OF CONTRACT (1974), and Friedman & Macaulay, *Contract Law and Contract Teaching: Past, Present, and Future*, 1967 WIS. L. REV. 805.

NORTHWESTERN UNIVERSITY LAW REVIEW

have also led to very significant changes leading to the transformation of the Willistonian classical system to what might be called the Realist neoclassical system. The spin-offs can and will continue.

Equally likely, the neoclassical system will continue to evolve in relational directions, while courts and scholars still strive to keep it within the overall classical structure. (This is especially likely in first-year contracts courses in many American law schools and in the casebooks and texts aimed at first-year contracts students and their teachers.) The spin-offs will, however, render the system, as a total system, of less and less practical interest.[102] At the same time, trying to squeeze increasing relational content into the neoclassical system will encounter the same kinds of strains some of my generation are finding in trying to put on the older parts of their wardrobes. Thus, rewards of expanding the neoclassical system will decrease at the same time that intellectual and perhaps other costs of doing so increase.

Elsewhere, I have suggested the possibility that a more encompassing conceptual structure of contract jurisprudence may emerge from the situation just described.[103] Part of such a structure must focus on the issues raised by this paper, adjustment of long-term contractual relations. The concluding section of this paper will deal with some of the consequences of slipping the bounds of the classical contract system altogether, of reducing discreteness and presentation from dominant roles to roles equal or often subordinate to relational norms such as preserving the relation and harmonization of all aspects of the relation, whether discrete or relational.

CONTRACTUAL RELATIONS: RELATIONAL CONTRACT LAW

The introduction to the preceding section carefully limits that section

(Probably the most extreme view I have found along this line is Lowry, *supra* note 16, at 16-17.) Nothing could be farther from the truth. Discreteness and presentation are ever with us in the modern world and will continue to be so; the fact that we now recognize them as integrated into ongoing relations does not eliminate them. Nor does it eliminate the need to respond to them as particular facets of ongoing relations. And such response very often will be to enhance them and give them full effect. In such instances, not just neoclassical contract law, but sometimes good old-fashioned classical contract law, may supply the best solutions. But those solutions will be "best" because the overall relational circumstances so indicate, not because of the general dominance of jurisprudential systems based on enhancing discreteness and presentation.

102 Relatively little of "the action" in contractual transactions and relations lies in that system now, as the examination of any law school curriculum will demonstrate. Not only is the first-year neoclassical course shrinking in semester hours in many schools, but also the major part of the teaching of contracts in law school is to be found in subject-specific courses such as commercial law, corporations, labor law, securities regulation, and creditors' rights.

103 *Many Futures*, note 9 *supra*; *Presentiation, supra* note 2, at 608-10. Work such as that of Eisenberg, Goldberg, Williamson, and others reinforces my feeling that surely a structure not only is possible, but that some of its outlines are starting to emerge.

to situations where "it is clear that" the long-term economic relations in question are "*between* firms rather than *within* a firm." The situations treated there were, "even in traditional terms, contracts." Such a limitation is unnecessary in introducing the present section. Interfirm contractual relations follow the kinds of patterns discussed here—*e.g.*, in a long-term consortium—but more typical relations of this nature would include such structures as the internal workings of corporations, including relations among management, employees, and stockholders. Corporate relations with long- and short-term creditors, law firms, accounting firms, and managerial and financial consultants may also acquire many of the characteristics discussed and increasingly seem to do so. Collective bargaining, franchising, condominiums, universities, trade unions themselves, large shopping centers, and retirement villages with common facilities of many kinds are other examples now existent. If present trends continue, undoubtedly we shall see new examples, now perhaps entirely unforeseen.

As noted earlier,[104] discreteness and presentation do not disappear from life or law simply because ongoing contractual relations become the organizational mode dominating economic activity. Because they remain with us and because they drastically affect contractual relations, this section will start with an analysis of their role in ongoing relations.

Presentiation and Discreteness in Contractual Relations

However important flexibility for change becomes in economic relations, great need will nevertheless always remain for fixed and reliable planning. Or in the terms emphasized here, presentiation will always occur in economic relations, since it tends to follow planning as a matter of course. Nor does a modern technological economy permit the demise of discreteness. Very specialized products and services, the hallmark of such an economy, produce a high degree of discreteness of behavior, even though their production and use are closely integrated into ongoing relations. When, for example, an automobile manufacturer orders from another manufacturer with which it regularly deals, thousands of piston rings of a specified size, no amount of relational softening of discreteness and presentiation will obscure the disaster occurring if the wrong size shows up on the auto assembly line. Nor would the disaster be any less if the failure had occurred in an even more relational pattern, *e.g.*, if the rings had been ordered from another division of the auto manufacturer. Both discreteness and presentiation must be served in such an economic process, whether it is carried out between firms by discrete separate orders, between firms under long-established blanket contracts, or within the firm.[105]

---

[104] *See* note 100 *supra*.

[105] It would take the imagination of a good science-fiction writer to dream up a technological economy in which this was not true.

NORTHWESTERN UNIVERSITY LAW REVIEW

Even apart from high demands for reliable planning in a technological society, discreteness is a characteristic inherent in human perception. Moreover, as I have suggested elsewhere, any given "present situation," no matter what its origin, tends to be perceived as highly discrete compared to what lies in the past and what is to come in the future.[106] Thus, the status quo, whatever it is, inevitably has about it a fairly high level of discreteness. This fact, coupled with the human propensity to presentiate on the basis of what is currently in the forefront of the mind, creates strong expectations of the future consistent with the status quo. Such expectations tend to be very strong. It is impossible to overstress this phenomenon—it describes not only the conservatism of the nineteenth century Russian peasant but also the intense commitment to change and growth where patterns of change and growth constitute the status quo, *e.g.*, the tenacity in America to patterns of constantly increasing energy consumption.

Expectations created by the above processes can be, and often are, of a magnitude and tenacity as great or greater than those created by good, old-fashioned discrete transactional contracts. Thus, when the phenomenon occurs in contractual relations, any tolerable contract law system must necessarily pay attention to at least some implementation of this kind of discreteness and presentiation.

In view of the foregoing, the need for a contract law system enhancing discreteness and presentiation will never disappear.[107] Moreover, it is possible, even likely, that a neoclassical contract law system will continue in existence to deal with those genuine needs. Such a system will, however, continue to rub in an unnecessarily abrasive manner against the realities of coexistence with relational needs for flexibility and change. Only when the parts of the contract law system implementing discreteness and presentiation are perceived, intellectually and otherwise, not as an independent system, but only as integral parts of much larger systems, will unnecessary abrasion disappear. By no means will all abrasion disappear, of course, because real conflict exists between the need for reliability of planning and the need for flexibility in economic relations.[108] What will disappear is the abrasion resulting from application of contract law founded on the assumption that all of a contractual relation is encompassed in some original assent to it, where that assumption is manifestly false. The elimination of that assumption not only would eliminate the unnecessary abrasion but also would remove the

---

106 *Many Futures, supra* note 9, at 754-56.

107 A formal, sovereign-imposed system conceivably could disappear, if contractual relations develop extensively enough to be able to depend entirely on self-generated internal legal systems. But the internal systems too will need to serve these needs.

108 A point nicely brought out in the context of particular kinds of contracts by Goldberg, *supra* note 34, at 441-42 (university food service contracts) and Williamson, note 34 *supra*.

72:854 (1978)   Adjustment of Relations

penultimate classical characteristic justifying calling a contract law system neoclassical.[109]

What replaces the neoclassical system when, and if, all that remains of classical contract law are discreteness and presentation-enhancing segments of far larger systems, segments perhaps often playing roles subordinate to countless other goals, including those of achieving flexibility and change? The remainder of this paper is an introduction to possible answers to that question.

Processes for Flexibility and Change in Contractual Relations

Change, whether caused by forces beyond social control or actively sought, appears to be a permanent characteristic of modern technological societies. Willy-nilly, flexibility comes along with the phenomenon, since the only alternative is a breakdown of the society. But there are processes of flexibility beyond simply bending with each wind of change on an ad hoc basis. Indeed, we have already seen many such processes respecting contracts and have explored the response to them of a neoclassical legal system. We shall look at them again here to see the response of a legal system which is more frankly relational and which has cast off conceptual obeisance to discreteness and presentation by some all-encompassing original assent. Although no such system as yet exists in American law, I shall speak in the present tense; this is justified, perhaps, by the existence of specific terms of contract law, such as collective bargaining, coming close to the patterns described.

The most important processes used for maintaining flexibility are those of exchange itself, whether the sharply focused bargaining characteristic of labor contract renewals or the subtle interplays of day-to-day activities, or a host of other forms taken by exchange. These patterns of exchange take place against the power and normative positions in which the parties find themselves.[110] This means that exchange patterns occur, *inter alia*, against the background of the discrete and presentated aspects of the relations, whether those aspects were created by explicit prior

---

[109] Penultimate, not ultimate. If we think of the classical contract law system as the antithesis of the status contractual relations of primitive societies—as I believe Maine did in his famous statement about the move from status to contract—one vital characteristic of the classical contract system will remain: the great effect given to planning. Rightly or wrongly we do not think of primitive societies as engaging in a great deal of planning beyond that arising from habit, custom, mores, and customary law of the society. However accurate or inaccurate this view of primitive societies may be, it is a completely inaccurate view of modern technological society with its immense, indeed insatiable, demands for planning and performance of planning. Thus, as already noted, a relational, post-neoclassical contract law system will necessarily retain *in context* a large measure of the respect for presentation and discreteness shown by the classical system.

[110] *See generally* Eisenberg, *Private Ordering through Negotiation: Dispute-Settlement and Rulemaking,* 89 HARV. L. REV. 637 (1976).

NORTHWESTERN UNIVERSITY LAW REVIEW

planning, other existential circumstances, or combinations thereof.[111] This requires harmonization of changes with such a status quo but does not require doctrines such as the doctrine of consideration or the more discrete formulations of concepts like executory accord and accords intended as satisfactions. Instead questions like those raised previously are appropriate.[112] There is, however, a substantial difference. In the neoclassical system, the reference point for those questions about the change tends to be the original agreement. In a truly relational approach the reference point is the entire relation as it had developed to the time of the change in question (and in many instances as it has developed since the change). This may or may not include an "original agreement;" and if it does, may or may not result in great deference being given it.

Since contractual relations, such as the employment relation, commonly involve vertical or command-and-subordinate positions[113] of an ongoing nature, *e.g.*, the vice-president in charge of plant operations and his subordinates, much change is brought about by command. As the commands inevitably relate to exchange, as in an order to an employee to report for overtime work, they are techniques for achieving change through nonhorizontal processes, in contrast to those of agreed-upon, horizontal exchange.[114] Again, a relational contract system implements, modifies, or refuses to implement such commands only in the overall context of the whole relation.

---

111 *Cf. id.* at 672-80 (exchange patterns in a context of dependence).

112 *See* text accompanying note 57 *supra.*

The 1978 American Law Institute meeting approved Restatement (Second) of Contracts (Tent. Draft No. 13, 1978), which, consistent with the overall neoclassical pattern of Restatement (Second) deals with changes in contracts in a chapter entitled "Discharge by Assent or Alteration." Its only black-letter doctrinal tool is consideration, although relational notions such as good faith do creep into the comments occasionally, *e.g.*, § 351, Comment d. At one point the old battle about Foakes v. Beer, 9 App. Cas. 605 (1884), the principle of which is approved in § 348, almost led to a motion not only to revise § 348, but also the more basic section dealing with the pre-existing duty rule, § 76A, approved by the Institute over a decade earlier. I had a strong feeling that passage of such a motion might well have led ultimately to the complete unraveling of Restatement (Second), the most current tapestry of American neoclassical contract law. But so, I suspect, did others who would have greeted that occurrence with less enthusiasm, and the dangerous moment passed without the motion being made.

113 As does, of course, not only the discrete transactional technique of allowing one side to specify terms but also any contract as to the rights conferred thereby. The horizontal nature of the formation of contracts and the fact that both sides have rights, too, often is allowed to obscure their command nature once formed.

114 I do not adhere to the Coasian view recently espoused by Posner, differentiating contract from the firm, *i.e.*, from the command structure. Coase, *The Nature of the Firm*, 4 ECONOMICA 386, 386 n.5, 390-91 (1937); R. POSNER, *supra* note 52, at § 14.1. The corporate firm is no more and no less, in my view, than an immensely complex bundle of ongoing contractual relations. See note 33 *supra* for an expansion of this view. But as is suggested above, those relations are also command relations.

When the conflict levels in exchange processes, wherever they may lie on the command-horizontal spectrum, exceed the resolution capacity of bargaining and other exchange processes, other techniques of dispute resolution must be utilized. Here we find the most dramatic change from the classical or even neoclassical litigation (or rights arbitration[115]) models. Their function is to put an end to the dispute; and, since resolution of the dispute is all that remains of the discrete transaction, the process is a relatively simple and clean one. This process is rather like the discrete transaction itself: sharp in (by commencing suit) and sharp out (by judgment for defendant or collection of a money judgment by plaintiff).[116] Professor Chayes has recently described this model:

(1) The lawsuit is *bipolar*. Litigation is organized as a contest between two individuals or at least two unitary interests, diametrically opposed, to be decided on a winner-takes-all basis.
(2) Litigation is *retrospective*. The controversy is about an identified set of completed events: whether they occurred, and if so, with what consequences for the legal relations of the parties.
(3) *Right and remedy are interdependent.* The scope of the relief is derived more or less logically from the substantive violation under the general theory that the plaintiff will get compensation measured by the harm caused by the defendant's breach of duty—in contract by giving plaintiff the money he would have had absent the breach; in tort by paying the value of the damage caused.
(4) The lawsuit is a *self-contained* episode. The impact of the judgment is confined to the parties. If plaintiff prevails there is a simple compensatory transfer, usually of money, but occasionally the return of a thing or the performance of a definite act. If defendant prevails, a loss lies where it has fallen. In either case, entry of judgment ends the court's involvement.
(5) The process is *party-initiated* and *party-controlled*. The case is organized and the issues defined by exchanges between the parties. Responsibility for fact development is theirs. The trial judge is a neutral arbiter of their interactions who decides questions of law only if they are put in issue by an appropriate move of a party.[117]

Naturally, no such model will do when the relation is supposed to continue in spite of the dispute, and where a main goal must always be its successful carrying on after the dispute is resolved or otherwise eliminated or avoided.

Professor Chayes went on to develop a morphology of what he terms

---

115 *See* note 39 and accompanying text *supra*.

116 This is, of course, a parody, especially the very last point. Contrary to the fantasies of the law school classroom, the real beginning of many contract dispute cases won by plaintiffs comes *after* rendering of a judgment. Then the deficiencies of execution, and with it the legal remedial system itself, become apparent.

117 Chayes, *The Role of the Judge in Public Law Litigation*, 89 HARV. L. REV. 1281, 1282-83 (1976) (footnotes omitted) (emphasis in original). For critical comments concerning the developments Chayes describes, see Kirkham, *Complex Civil Litigation: Have Good Intentions Gone Awry?*, 3 LAW & LIBERTY 1 (Winter 1977).

NORTHWESTERN UNIVERSITY LAW REVIEW

"public law litigation."[118] Although he does not direct this morphology at contract disputes, I have found it helpful in organizing my thoughts about the processes of dispute resolution in contractual relations. (So modified it focuses on the processes of change in such relations when bargaining and other exchange processes fail.) The following is his morphology, modified where appropriate for use in contractual relations.

1. The scope of the dispute is not exogenously given by contract terms but is shaped by both the parties and the resolver of the dispute—*e.g.*, the arbitrator—and by the entire relation as it has developed and is developing.
2. The party structure is not rigidly bilateral but sprawling and amorphous.
3. The fact inquiry is not only historical and adjudicative but also predictive and legislative.[119]
4. Relief is not conceived primarily (or sometimes at all) as compensation for past wrong in a form logically derived from the substantive liability and confined in its impact to the immediate parties; instead, it is in great (or even entire) measure forward-looking, fashioned ad hoc on flexible and broadly remedial lines, often having important consequences for many persons, including absentees.
5. The remedy is not imposed but negotiated and mediated.
6. The award does not terminate the dispute-resolver's role in the relation; instead, the award will require continuing administration by this or other similarly situated dispute-resolvers.
7. The dispute-resolver is not passive, that is, his function is not limited to analysis and statement of governing rules; he is active, with responsibility not only for credible fact evaluation but also for organizing and shaping the dispute processes to ensure a just and viable outcome.
8. The subject matter of the dispute is not between private individuals about private rights but is a grievance about the operation of policies of the overall contractual relation.[120]

In almost every respect the foregoing approaches contrast sharply with a classical contract law system and with the conceptual assumptions of a neoclassical system. For example, two ways by which a classical

---

[118] This is an unfortunately narrow choice of words. His summary appears in Chayes, *supra* note 117, at 1302.

[119] Chayes states this one: "The fact inquiry is not historical and adjudicative but predictive and legislative." *Id.* In his context this seems to me an overstatement; I have no doubt it is if applied to contractual relations.

[120] Readers who examine the chart in the Appendix *infra* will probably have a sense of déjà vu here, as will those familiar with the long-standing debate about the role of the labor arbitrator, and as will readers with a background in legal anthropology. The latter are likely to recognize a kind of neotribalism in the process described, and the labor law experts will see the statement as a generalizing of views expressed by Dean Shulman.

contract law system implements its goals of enhancing discreteness and presentation are by limiting strictly the sources considered in establishing the substantive content of the transaction in resolving disputes and by utilizing strictly defined (and narrow) remedies.[121] Both of these methods sharply conflict with the relational approaches outlined above. Similarly, although the neoclassical system can accomplish some of the flexibility of these relational patterns, and utilizes some of them, in toto the patterns go far beyond it. In the neoclassical system the parol evidence rule is hardly dead; the fact inquiry is nowhere nearly as wide-ranging; development of flexible and broad remedies is modest indeed; at the end of the day, remedies are imposed, rather than simply negotiated and mediated until some kind of uneasy (and probably temporary) consensus is reached; more often than not a dispute-resolver does expect to wipe his hands of the matter after the appropriate remedy has been determined; the dispute-resolver, at least when he is a judge, tends to remain passive; and the subject matter of dispute often tends to remain, at least formally and often more substantially, between clear poles of interest and polar rights, rather than overall policies of the contractual relation.

The sharp contrast between the classical (and even neoclassical) limitation of sources of substantive content mentioned above and the broad ranging inquiries of a relational system brings us to a key question concerning the interplay of presentiated and discrete aspects of relations with their nondiscrete, nonpresentiated aspects. The premise of the classical system is that no interplay could occur, because all aspects of the contract are presentiated and discrete. This premise continues to underlie the structure of the neoclassical system, but in actual operation that system shifts to a presumption in favor of limitation, although one subject to considerable erosion. In implementing their premises both classical and neoclassical contract law establish hierarchies for determining content (as noted earlier). Formal communications such as writings control informal communications; linguistic communications control nonlinguistic communications; communicated circumstances control noncommunicated circumstances; and finally utilization of noncommunicated circumstances is always suspect.

Do such hierarchies continue in a relational system? The answer is both yes and no. To the extent that presentiated and discrete aspects of contractual relations are created by written documents, they may reflect very sharp focus of party attention and strong intentions to be governed by them in the future. Certainly the wage and seniority structures in most collective bargaining agreements exemplify this. Thus, such documents may occupy very dominant positions in the priorities of values of the relation. When this is the case, something analogous to the classical notions previously set out may very properly be applied by the dispute-

---

121 *See* text accompanying note 27 *supra*.

NORTHWESTERN UNIVERSITY LAW REVIEW

resolver. There is, however, one big difference. In a system of relational contract law the simple existence of formal communications does not automatically trigger application of the neoclassical hierarchy of presumptions. Rather, a preliminary question must always be asked: do the formal communications indeed reflect the sharp past focus and strong intentions necessary to put these communications high in the priorities of values created by the contractual relation? This question can be answered only by looking at the whole relation, not in the grudging manner of the neoclassical system, but as the very foundation for proceeding further with the hierarchical assumptions, or without them, or with other hierarchies. (An example of the latter occurs in marital disputes: nonlinguistic conduct and informal communications typically far outweigh in importance for resolving such disputes any formal agreements—except sometimes as to property—the parties may have made.)

I feel some temptation to think of the written parts of contractual relations, especially very formal parts, such as collective bargaining agreements and corporate charters and bylaws, as constitutions establishing legislative and administrative processes for the relation.[122] Indeed, that is what many of them are. Nevertheless, danger lurks in this formulation. The danger lies in reintroducing into the law of contractual relations[123] such things as the hierarchies discussed above—not on an ad hoc basis but as a matter of general principle emanating from the concept of "constitution." If that concept or terminology is used to resurrect "constitutions" long decayed and made obsolete by less formally established patterns of communications and behavior, we are, as a matter of principle, back to a relationally dysfunctional neoclassicism.[124] Moreover, only one party or class of parties may know the content of these "constitutions," and they may suffer from other adhesion characteristics. In such circumstances giving them constitutional weight may be very dubious indeed.

---

122 This is hardly an original thought. *See, e.g.*, Fuller, *supra* note 43, at 5. *See also* Cox, *Reflections upon Labor Arbitration*, 72 HARV. L. REV. 1482, 1490-93, 1498-1501 (1959); Shulman, *Reason, Contract, and Law in Labor Relations*, 68 HARV. L. REV. 999, 1004-05 (1955).

123 I mean by this term law not only of the sovereign, but also both internal law of the relation—*e.g.*, that established by agreement or internal bodies such as boards of directors—and external law other than that of the sovereign, such as trade association rules.

124 The following language from IBM v. Catamore Enterprises, Inc., 548 F.2d 1065, 1073 (1st Cir. 1976), *cert. denied*, 431 U.S. 960 (1977), while appropriate enough to the facts of the case, is the kind that can be sadly misused in the face of long time erosion of "constitutions" of contractual relations:

> The first is the substantive principle that when, in the course of business transactions between people or corporations, free and uncoerced understandings purporting to be comprehensive are solemnized by documents which both parties sign and concede to be their agreement, such documents are not easily bypassed or given restrictive interpretations.

In fact, over time, parties to complex relations do "easily bypass" such agreements and give them "restrictive" (or expansive) interpretations. Courts not recognizing this are likely to reach unsatisfactory results.

72:854 (1978)   *Adjustment of Relations*

This brief treatment of processes of flexibility and change in contractual relations can now serve as a background for consideration of characteristics of substantive change in contractual relations.

The Substance of Change in Contractual Relations

All aspects of contractual relations are subject to the norms characterizing contracts generally, whether they are discrete or relational. As noted earlier[125] these are: (1) permitting and encouraging participation in exchange, (2) promoting reciprocity, (3) reinforcing role patterns appropriate to the various particular kinds of contracts, (4) providing limited freedom for exercise of choice, (5) effectuating planning, and (6) harmonizing the internal and external matrixes of particular contracts. These norms affect change in contractual relations just as they affect all their other aspects.

In addition, I have identified two norms particularly applicable to contractual relations:[126] (1) harmonizing conflict within the internal matrix of the relation, including especially, discrete and presentiated behavior with nondiscrete and nonpresentiated behavior; and (2) preservation of the relation.[127] These norms affect change in contractual relations, just as they affect all their aspects.

A great deal of change in ongoing contractual relations comes about glacially, through small-scale, day-to-day adjustments resulting from an interplay of horizontally arranged exchange—*e.g.*, workers creating new ways of cooperatively defining their work or minor changes in the way in which deliveries are made—and from the flow of day-to-day commands through the vertical patterns of the relation. In addition, within a broad range, change will come about through commands of a more sweeping nature, *e.g.*, to sell the appliance division of the firm or develop a major new line of products. This is, of course, focused change and raises all kinds of problems, not the least of which involve the two relational norms. Moreover, command changes of this magnitude in a modern society almost invariably overlap areas that must be dealt with by horizontal arrangements, *e.g.*, the terms of the collective bargaining agreement governing severance or transfer of old employees and the hiring of new employees. Finally, there are horizontal changes in contractual

---

125 *See* text accompanying note 23 *supra*; *Many Futures, supra* note 9, at 808-16. The word norm is used here generally to include the way people actually behave, the "oughts" that their behavior generates vis-à-vis each other, and the "oughts" their behavior generates externally to their relation, *e.g.*, in sovereign contract law. There may, of course, be occasion to differentiate, but commonly this usage is fine enough.

126 *See* note 24 *supra*.

127 The discrete norms—enhancing discreteness and presentation—were not truly separate from the general norms of effectuating planning and exercising choice but were an intensification of these general norms that was so great and opened up so many facets as to justify new labels. This is also true of the relational norms. Both grow out of the last of the general norms and could be treated as part of it.

NORTHWESTERN UNIVERSITY LAW REVIEW

relations themselves partially or wholly horizontal in origin. If, for example, we consider a collective bargaining agreement as an arrangement separate from the firm itself (by my lights, a somewhat artificial thing to do), the shifting of a major part of a wage increase from cash into layoff compensation would constitute a focused horizontal change.[128] Similarly, a consortium of businesses determining whether to go into a new line of activity would be engaged in horizontally focused change.

We have thus far considered change coming about either through gradual accretion, through command operating within acceptable limits of the relation, or through successful negotiation and agreement. While these offer many problems for a relational contract system and its related legal structure, the big *legal* difficulties come when change is pushed that has failed to come about in those ways. What happens when this occurs?

In answering that question it is well to remember that we are dealing with situations where the desire is to continue the relation, not to terminate it. Moreover, my sense is that normally the most important factor is the status quo; that is to say, that the dispute-resolver will be conservative and will not move far from the status quo. This is borne out by the sense of arbitrators experienced in "interest arbitration" that the base point of such arbitration is the presentiated status quo.[129] Anyone interested in change through the dispute-resolution process has a heavy burden of persuasion. Dispute-resolution processes governed by the norm of continuing the relation are, if this view is correct, essentially conservative.

The foregoing conclusion does not lead to the conclusion that change will not result from this kind of interest-dispute-resolution process. Anyone the least familiar with arbitration of public employee interest disputes knows this.[130] The very fact that a party is willing to press this far suggests in most cases a basis for some change, although bargaining being what it is, probably not as much as the aggressive party tries to get. Moreover, status quo in a dynamic society does not mean a static status quo; as noted earlier in another connection, the status quo itself may very well be one in which changes in a certain direction are expected. If they do not come or come less than expected, then the interest-dispute-resolver is faced with a situation where the status quo calls for change, not for simply sticking to patterns now viewed as obsolete.[131]

---

[128] In the growth society of the past 40 years, such patterns have largely dealt with increments to the wage package, and hence their nature as a fundamental change has been somewhat disguised. In a no-growth or slow-growth society, trade-offs may have to be made between existing cash wages and fringe benefits. Such trade-offs will indeed be perceived as changes.

[129] *See* note 39 *supra*.

[130] I confess to overlooking this obvious point until someone at the Harvard Seminar, *see* note 1 *supra*, I think it was Professor Chayes, mentioned it.

[131] "In some cases, such as wages, change over time actually becomes the norm, so that a

72:854 (1978)   *Adjustment of Relations*

Exploration of the other relational norm—harmonizing conflicts within the internal social matrix of the relation—reinforces the foregoing conclusions. Such harmonization is unlikely to come through revolutionary changes[132] that conflicting interests have been unable to accede to through negotiation or mediation. Changes typically can be harmonized with the remainder of the relation only by making them consistent with the status quo, again a conservative notion. But it must be noted that if the status quo is a dynamic one moving over time in certain directions—*e.g.*, increasing levels of real wages—change in accord with those patterns is essential to preserve the status quo itself. This is the kind of harmonization we should expect from a dispute-resolver implementing this norm.

My work on developing general contractual norms and relational norms has progressed slowly since *The Many Futures of Contracts.*[133] Certainly other norms besides the two mentioned will have a bearing on change in a system of relational contract law. Two categories should be mentioned, the first of which will have a ring of familiarity to all students of contracts: the restitution, reliance and expectation interests. In a system of discrete transactions, it is now generally accepted that protection of these three interests constitutes a basic norm of contract law. This does not change as we move from classical to neoclassical contract law and on to relational contract law; such interests remain fundamental.

One important change, however, does occur. In classical contract law it is expectations created solely by defined promises and reliance on defined promises that are protected. Only the restitution interest had a broader foundation, and restitution fitted uneasily in the structure of classical contract law, often being conceptualized as not part of that law at all. In neoclassical contract law the expectation and reliance interests remain based primarily on promise, although exceptions do exist. For example, *Drennan v. Star Paving Co.*[134] can be read as holding that reliance on something (industry patterns or common decency?) created the promise rather than the other way around.[135] Restitution, increasingly recognized in neoclassical contract law as an integral part of the system (again perhaps slightly uneasily), stands out as perhaps the least promise-

---

party who resists an accustomed change may be perceived as himself the proponent of change." Eisenberg, *supra* note 110, at 676 n.122.

132 This is to say nothing about the efficacy of revolution for other purposes; soothing conflict within a structure is simply not one of its goals.

133 Note 9 *supra*.

134 51 Cal. 2d 409, 333 P.2d 757 (1958).

135 More recent examples are: Lockewill, Inc. v. United States Shoe Corp., 547 F.2d 1024 (8th Cir. 1976), *cert. denied*, 431 U.S. 956 (1977) (*see* text accompanying note 90 *supra*); Carlson v. Olson, 256 N.W.2d 249 (1977); Reisman & Sons v. Snyder's Potato Chips, 32 Somerset Leg. J. 3 (Pa. C.P. Somerset County 1976) (in spite of a holding that a franchisor had no promissory obligation to continue the franchise, the court held that the franchisee's reliance on the relation precluded termination). *Cf.* Sheridan, *The Floating Trust: Mutual Wills*, 15 ALBERTA L. REV. 211 (1977) (agreements to make mutual wills may impose restrictions on revoking or altering the arrangement).

NORTHWESTERN UNIVERSITY LAW REVIEW

oriented part of the system. In this sense restitution paves the way for treatment of the three contract interests in relational contract law. No longer are those interests bottomed primarily on defined promises, nor are efforts necessary to squeeze them within promissory contexts. In such a system recognition is easily accorded to the creation of such interests arising naturally from *any* behavior patterns within the relation. Substantive changes in relations must therefore take into account the three basic contract interests of restitution, reliance, and expectations, irrespective of their sources.

As illustrative of the foregoing, consider an employee of a small business who has been treated very decently by his employer for thirty years. He quite naturally comes to expect decent treatment throughout the relation including through retirement. Moreover, he relies on that expectation; and if the expectation is not realized, the employer may very well have derived benefits from the reliance by the employee that, in terms of the relation as it existed, are unjustified. We can, and do, infer promises in such situations, but they are far from the defined promises of discrete transactions. Moreover, something besides promise lies behind the social desiderata of seeing that these interests of the employee do not go unprotected. Expectations, as noted earlier, are a form of presentiation however they may be created. When they are reasonable under the circumstances, irrespective of how the circumstances were created, societies tend to be very loath to see them thwarted. An already mentioned example is the reluctance of virtually all of American society to accept even the temporary thwarting of post-World War II expectations of continued economic growth.

The final category of relational norm to be considered here is very open-ended. As contractual relations expand, those relations take on more and more the characteristics of minisocieties and ministates. Indeed, even that is an understatement. In the case of huge bundles of contractual relations, such as a major national or multinational corporation, they take on the characteristics of large societies and large states. But whether small or large, the whole range of social and political norms become pertinent *within* the contractual relations. In ongoing contractual relations we find such broad norms as distributive justice, liberty,[136] human dignity, social equality and inequality, and procedural justice, to mention some of the more vital. Changes in such contractual relations must accord with norms established respecting these matters, just as much as they do the more traditional contract norms. Changes made ignoring this fact may be very disruptive indeed.[137]

---

[136] *See* D. EWING, FREEDOM INSIDE THE ORGANIZATION (1977); Keeffe Bros. v. Teamsters Local Union No. 592, 562 F.2d 298 (4th Cir. 1977).

[137] At this point, just as contractual relations exceed the capacities of the neoclassical contract law system, so too the issues exceed the capacities of neoclassical contract law scholars. They must become something else—anthropologists, sociologists, economists,

72:854 (1978)   *Adjustment of Relations*

Termination of Contractual Relations

Termination of contractual relations is an extremely complex sub-ject, far too complex to do more than touch here.[138] Nevertheless a number of points should be made. One is that, unlike discrete transac-tions, many contractual relations are, for all practical purposes, expected never to end. IBM, the relation between the United Auto Workers and General Motors, and Harvard University are expected to go on forever. Even in the face of great trouble, relations of this kind often do not end, but continue on in new forms; *e.g.*, Northeast Airlines is merged into Delta, or rail passenger service is transferred to Amtrak, along with physical facilities, the labor force, and much of the management. The realities of such transformations often evoke processes very similar to relational patterns of change already discussed, rather than clean-cut application of clear rights and obligations in the discrete transactional tradition.

Of course, many long-term contractual relations are recognized (by outsiders, if not always by the participants) as vulnerable to traumatic termination. Small businesses, branch plant operations of large busi-nesses, and in part, marriages, clubs, and many franchises, serve as illustrations. Depending in part on the relations themselves and in part on such external factors as their importance to the community and the political heft of various of their participants, their termination may or may not be treated by the legal system in relational ways, procedurally or substantively.[139] To the extent that they are treated relationally, their terminations will be similar to those massive contractual relations that had not been expected to end at all.

On the other hand, many long-term contractual relations are, from the start, expected to terminate. A small partnership expecting not to take in new members, or marriage without progeny are examples. Many business consortiums are of this nature. When such relations terminate

---

political theorists, and philosophers—to do reasonable justice to the issues raised by contractual relations. Exchange and planning, the basic areas of expertise of the contracts scholar, have now become just two of the many factors in a complete social organism.

138 For an earlier discussion of this subject, see *Many Futures, supra* note 9, at 750-53.

139 *E.g.*, McGrath v. Hilding, 41 N.Y.2d 625, 363 N.E.2d 328, 394 N.Y.S.2d 603 (1977). Plaintiff divorced defendant after three months of marriage and remarried her former husband. During the brief marriage plaintiff contributed money to building an addition to defendant's house relying on an oral premarital promise to give her a tenancy by the entirety. The promise was not performed, and plaintiff sought equitable relief based on a constructive trust. The lower courts rejected as collateral defendant's offer to prove marital misconduct by plaintiff. The New York Court of Appeals remanded for a new trial, stating that whether defendant's enrichment was unjust could not be determined by inquiring only about an "isolated transaction." Rather it must be a "realistic determination based on a broad view of the human setting involved." *Id.* at 629, 363 N.E.2d at 331, 394 N.Y.S.2d at 606.

NORTHWESTERN UNIVERSITY LAW REVIEW

traumatically early, their treatment will follow patterns already discussed. When they follow the expected course, the legal system will treat their termination as it does other aspects of the relation. Some discrete aspects may be given effect; *e.g.*, legacies to the widow will be enforced explicitly. Some aspects may instead invoke relational norms; *e.g.*, the widow, even by will or maybe even by mutual agreement, cannot be cut out of the estate entirely or lose her rights in community property.

A final point to be made is the distinction between termination of a contractual relation and termination of an individual's participation in a contractual relation. Sometimes the two coincide, *e.g.*, the death of a spouse in a childless marriage. But contractual relations outside the nuclear family tend in modern society to be multiperson and to survive the departure or death of individual participants. Further, typically it is the ongoing relation rather than the individual that is the more powerful of the two.[140] Where, as in employment, this fact is coupled with a high degree of dependency of the individual on the particular relation, we are likely to find considerable protection of that dependency. Such protection may grow up internally (*e.g.*, through collective bargaining), may perhaps be coerced in considerable measure from outside (*e.g.*, labor laws and tax provisions favoring pensions), or may simply be imposed (*e.g.*, mandatory contributions by both employer and employee to Social Security).

In sum, terminations of long-term contractual relations tend to be like other aspects of relations, messily relational rather than cleanly transactional.

SUMMARY

A system of discrete transactions and its corresponding classical contract law provides for flexibility and change through the market outside the transactions, rather than within them. This enables the system to work while the transactions themselves remain highly discrete and presentiated, characteristics preserved and enhanced by classical contract law.

A system of more relational contract and its corresponding neoclassical contract law remains theoretically structured on the discrete and classical models, but involves significant changes. Such contracts, being more complex and of greater duration than discrete transactions, become dysfunctional if too rigid, thereby preventing the high level of presentiation of the discrete transaction. Thus, flexibility, often a great deal of it, needs to be planned into such contracts, or gaps need to be left in the planning to be added as needed. The neoclassical system responds to this by a range of techniques. These run from some open evasion of its

---

140 In his later years this appears to have been true even of someone as extraordinarily powerful as Howard Hughes.

primary theoretical commitment to complete presentation through initial consent on to the more common techniques of stretching consent far beyond its actual bounds and by fictions to squeeze later changes within an initial consent framework.

Somewhere along the line of increasing duration and complexity, trying to force changes into a pattern of original consent becomes both too difficult and too unrewarding to justify the effort, and the contractual relation escapes the bounds of the neoclassical system. That system is replaced by very different adjustment processes of an ongoing-administrative kind in which discreteness and presentiation become merely two of the factors of decision, not the theoretical touchstones. Moreover, the substantive relation of change to the status quo has now altered from what happens in some kind of a market external to the contract to what can be achieved through the political and social processes of the relation, internal and external. This includes internal and external dispute-resolution structures. At this point, the relation has become a minisociety with a vast array of norms beyond the norms centered on exchange and its immediate processes.

NORTHWESTERN UNIVERSITY LAW REVIEW

APPENDIX[141]

Transactional and Relational Axes

CONCEPT	EXTREME TRANSAC-TIONAL POLE	EXTREME RELATION-AL POLE
1. Overall relation type	Nonprimary	Primary
A. Personal involvement	Segmental, limited, non-unique, transferable	Whole person, unlimit-ed, unique, non-transfer-able
B. Types of communication	Limited, linguistic, formal	Extensive, deep, not limited to linguistic, in-formal in addition to or in lieu of formal
C. Subject matter of satisfactions	Simple, monetizable economic exchange only	In addition to economic, complex personal non-economic satisfactions very important; social exchange; non-exchange
2. Measurability and ac-tual measurement of exchange and other factors	One side of exchange is money; other side is easily monetized; both are actual-ly measured; no other aspects	Both exchanges and other factors are relatively dif-ficult to monetize or other-wise measure, and the par-ties do not monetize or measure them
3. Basic sources of socio-economic support	Apart from exchange moti-vations themselves, exter-nal to the transaction	Internal to the relation, as well as external
4. Duration	Short agreement process; short time between agree-ment and performance; short time of performance	Long term; no finite begin-ning; no end to either rela-tion or performance, ex-cept perhaps upon death of parties
5. Commencement and termination	Sharp in by clear agree-ment; sharp out by clear performance	Commencement and termi-nation, if any, of relation likely to be gradual; indi-vidual entry into existing relation often gradual, as may be withdrawal; indi-vidual entry may be by birth, and withdrawal by death

---

[141] From *Many Futures, supra* note 9, at 738–40, slightly modified.

6. Planning

A. Primary focus of planning	Substance of exchanges	Structures and processes of relation; planning of substance of exchanges primarily for initial period
B. Completeness and specificity		
(1) Possible when planning occurs	Can be very complete and specific; only remote contingencies (if those) are beyond reasonable planning capacity	Limited specific planning of substance possible; extensive specific planning of structures and processes may be possible
(2) Actual planning accomplished	Very complete and specific; only the practically unplanable (of which there is little) left unplanned	Limited specific planning of substance carried out; extensive planning of structures may or may not occur
C. Sources and forms of mutual planning		
(1) Bargaining and adhesion	Specific consent to price of a good produced unilaterally by seller; short bid-ask bargaining, if any	Adhesion without bargaining unlikely except in case of entry of new members into existing relation; otherwise extended mutual planning merging imperceptibly into ongoing relation being established; a "joint creative effort"
(2) Tacit assumptions	Inevitably present, but inherently relational and anti-transactional	Recognized aspect of relational planning, without which relations cannot survive
(3) Sources and forms of post-commencement planning	No post-commencement planning	Operation of relation itself is prime source of further planning, which is likely to be extensive; may or may not be extensive explicit post-commencement planning
D. Bindingness of planning	Planning is entirely binding	Planning may be binding, but often some or all of it is characterized by some degree of tentativeness
E. Conflicts of interest in planning	Enterprise planning can be expressed only through partially zero-sum allocative planning, hence all mutual planning is conflict laden.	Enterprise planning may be separable at least in part from allocative planning, and hence relatively low in conflict; merger of non-allocative enterprise plan-

903

NORTHWESTERN UNIVERSITY LAW REVIEW

			ning with allocative planning may occur in ways muting conflict and providing nonnegotiational ways for dealing with it.
7.	Future cooperation required in post-commencement planning and actual performance	Almost none required	Success of relation entirely dependent on further cooperation in both performance and further planning
8.	Incidence of benefits and burdens	Shifting or other specific assignment of each particular benefit and burden to one party or the other	Undivided sharing of both benefits and burdens
9.	Obligations undertaken		
	A. Sources of content	Genuinely expressed, communicated and exchanged promises of parties	Relation itself develops obligations which may or may not include genuinely expressed, communicated and exchanged promises of the parties
	B. Sources of obligation	External to parties and transaction except for their triggering it by manifestation of consent	Both external and internal to the relation; same as the sources of content of the obligation as to internal element
	C. Specificity of obligation and sanction	Specific rules and rights specifically applicable and founded on the promises; monetizable or monetized (whether by mutual party planning i.e. promissory or otherwise i.e. by rule)	Nonspecific; nonmeasurable, whether based on customs, general principles or internalizations all arising from relation or partly from external sources; restorative unless breach results in termination, then may become transactional in nature
10.	Transferability	Entirely transferable with the sole exception of an obligor's ultimate liability for nonperformance	Transfer likely to be uneconomic and difficult to achieve even when it is not impossible[142]
11.	Number of participants	Two	May be as few as two, but likely to be more than two and often large masses
12.	Participant views of transaction or relation		
	A. Recognition of exchange	High	Low or perhaps even none

---

142 I no longer believe this to be accurate; corporations can, for example, be sold and the work force may go right along. *See* MACNEIL, CASES 2, *supra* note 16, at 778.

B. Altruistic behavior	None expected or occurring	Significant expectations of occurrence
C. Time-sense	Presentiation of the future	Futurizing of the present, i.e. to the extent past, present and future are viewed as separate, the present is viewed in terms of planning and preparing for a future not yet arrived
D. Expectations about trouble in performance or among the participants	None expected, except perhaps that planned for; if it occurs expected to be governed by specific rights	Possibility of trouble anticipated as normal part of relation, to be dealt with by cooperation and other restorational techniques

[3]

Neither Market Nor Hierarchy: Network Forms of Organization

Walter W. Powell

Network forms of organization – typified by reciprocal patterns of communication and exchange – represent a viable pattern of economic organization. Networks are contrasted with market and hierarchical governance structures, and the distinctive features of networks are highlighted. Illustrative examples of network arrangements – in craft and high-technology industries, in regional economies, and in formerly vertically integrated fields – are presented. The paper concludes with a discussion of the conditions that give rise to network forms.

In recent years, there has been a considerable amount of research on organizational practices and arrangements that are network-like in form. This diverse literature shares a common focus on lateral or horizontal patterns of exchange, interdependent flows of resources, and reciprocal lines of communication. Yet this rich vein of work has had much impact on students of organizational behavior. This is not particularly surprising, given the many divergent strands of this work. One would need to have followed the fields of international business, technology strategy, industrial relations, organizational sociology, and the new institutional economics, as well as interdisciplinary work on such themes as cooperation, the embeddedness of economic life in social structure, and the proliferation of small business units to have kept abreast. The purpose of this chapter is to render this literature more accessible to scholars in the organizational behavior field. I do so by arguing that relational or network forms of organization are a clearly identifiable and viable form of economic exchange under certain specifiable circumstances.

I begin by discussing why the familiar market-hierarchy continuum does not do justice to the notion of network forms of organization. I then contrast three modes of organization – market, hierarchy, and network – and stress the salient features of each. The logic of network forms is explored systematically in order to demonstrate how networks differ from other forms. I cull the literature in a number of social science and management fields and provide examples of a wide range of organizational arrangements that can be characterized as networks. This review affords considerable insight into the etiology of network forms, and allows me to develop a number of empirically disconfirmable arguments about the circumstances that give rise to networks and allow them to proliferate. I close with some thoughts on the research agenda that follows from these arguments.

Markets and Firms

In his classic article on the nature of the firm, the economist Ronald Coase (1937) conceived of the firm as a governance structure, breaking with orthodox accounts of the firm as a 'black box' production function. Coase's key insight was that firms and markets were alternative means for organizing similar kinds of transactions. This provocative paper, however, lay fallow, so to speak, for nearly four decades, until it was picked up by Williamson and other proponents of transaction costs economics in the 1970s. This work took seriously the notion that organizational form matters a great deal, and in so doing moved the economics of organization much closer to the fields of law, organization theory, and business history.

The core of Williamson's (1975; 1985) argument is that transactions that involve uncertainty about their outcome, that recur frequently and require substantial 'transaction-specific investments' – of money, time or energy that cannot be easily transferred – are more likely to take place within hierarchically organized firms. Exchanges that are straightforward, non-repetitive and require no transaction-specific investments will take place across a market interface. Hence, transactions are moved out of markets into hierarchies as knowledge specific to the transaction (asset specificity) builds up. When this occurs, the inefficiencies of bureaucratic organization will be preferred to the relatively greater costs of market transactions. There are two reasons for this: (1) bounded rationality – the inability of economic actors to write contracts that cover all possible contingencies; when transactions are internalized, there is little need to anticipate such contingencies since they can be handled within the firm's 'governance structure'; and (2) 'opportunism' – the rational pursuit by economic actors of their own advantage, with every means at their disposal, including guile and deceit; opportunism is mitigated by authority relations and by the stronger identification that parties presumably have when they are joined under a common roof.

This dichotomous view of markets and hierarchies (Williamson, 1975) sees firms as separate from markets or more broadly, the larger societal context. Outside the boundaries of firms are competitors, while inside managers exercise authority and curb opportunistic behavior. This notion of sharp firm boundaries was not just an academic view. A good deal of management practice as well as antitrust law shared the belief that, in Richardson's (1972) colorful language, firms are 'islands of planned co-ordination in a sea of market relations.'

But just as many economists have come to view firms as governance structures, and are providing new insights into the organization of the employment relationship and the multidivisional firm (to cite only two examples), firms appear to be changing in significant ways and forms of relational contracting have assumed much greater importance. Firms are blurring their established boundaries and engaging in forms of collaboration that resemble neither the familiar alternative of arm's length market contracting nor the former ideal of vertical integration.

Some scholars respond to these changes by arguing that economic changes can be arrayed in a continuum-like fashion, with discrete market transactions located at one end and the highly centralized firm at the other. In between these poles, we find various intermediate or hybrid forms of organization.[1] Moving from the market pole, where prices capture all the relevant information necessary for exchange, we find putting-out systems, various kinds of repeated trading, quasi-firms, and subcontracting arrangements; toward the hierarchy pole, franchising, joint ventures, decentralized profit centers, and matrix management are located.

Is this continuum view satisfactory? Can transaction costs logic meet the task of explaining this rich array of alternative forms? Williamson clearly thinks that it can. Shifting gears somewhat, he remarks that he is 'now persuaded that transactions in the middle range are much more common' than he previously recognized (Williamson, 1985, p. 83).[2] But, he avers, the distribution of transactions are such that the tails of this continuum from market to hierarchy are 'thick.'

I do not share the belief that the bulk of economic exchange fits comfortably at either of the poles of the market–hierarchy continuum. The legal theorist Ian Macneil (1985, p. 485) also disputes this view, arguing that, 'discrete exchange can play only a very limited and specialized function in any economy.'[3] Moreover, although I was earlier of the view that nonmarket, nonhierarchical forms represented hybrid modes (Powell, 1987), I now find that this mixed mode or intermediate notion is not particularly helpful. It is historically inaccurate, overly static, and it detracts from our ability to explain many forms of collaboration that are viable means of exchange.[4]

The view that transactions are distributed at points along a continuum implies that markets are the starting point, the elemental form of exchange out of which other methods evolve. Such a view is, obviously, a distortion of historical and anthropological evidence. As Moses Finley (1973) tells us so well, there was no market in the modern sense of the term in the classical world, only money in the nature of free booty and treasure trove. Nor did markets spring full blown with the Industrial Revolution. Economic units emerged from the dense webs of political, religious and social affiliations that had enveloped economic activity for centuries. Agnew (1986) documents that the word market first enters the English language during the twelfth century to refer to specific locations where provisions and livestock were sold. The markets of medieval England had a highly personal, symbolic, and hierarchical flavor. E.P. Thompson (1971) used the term 'the moral economy' to characterize the intricate pattern of symbolic and statutory expectations that surrounded the eighteenth century marketplace. It was not until the latter part of the eighteenth century that among the British educated classes the term market became separated from a physical and social space and came to imply a boundless and timeless phenomenon of buying and selling (Agnew, 1986).[5]

By the same token, hierarchies do not represent an evolutionary end-point of economic development. A long view of business history would suggest that firms with strictly defined boundaries and highly centralized operations are quite atypical.[6] The history of modern commerce, whether told by Braudel, Polanyi, Pollard, or Wallerstein, is a story of family businesses, guilds, cartels, and extended trading companies – all enterprises with loose and highly permeable boundaries.

Recent work on the growth of small firms also casts doubt on the utility of a continuum view of economic exchange. Larson (1988) and Lorenzoni and Ornati (1988) draw similar portraits from very different settings – high tech start-ups in the United States and craft-based firms in Northern Italy – which do not follow the standard model of small firms developing internally through an incremental and linear process. Instead, they suggest an entirely different model of externally-driven growth in which pre-existing networks of relationships enable small firms to gain an established foothold almost overnight. These networks serve as conduits to provide small firms with the capacity to meet resource and functional needs.[7]

The idea that economic exchanges can be usefully arrayed along a continuum is thus too quiescent and mechanical. It fails to capture the complex realities of exchange.[8] The continuum view also misconstrues patterns of economic development and blinds us to the role played by reciprocity and collaboration as alternative governance mechanisms. By sticking to the twin pillars of markets and hierarchies, our attention is deflected from a diversity of organizational designs that are neither fish nor fowl, nor some mongrel hybrid, but a distinctly different form.

To be sure, there are a number of social scientists who question whether the distinction between market and hierarchy is particularly useful in the first place.[9] They contend that no sharp demarcation exists and that the argument is more a matter of academic pigeon-holing than of substantive operational differences. These analysts are united, however, more by their dislike of stylized models of economic exchange than by any shared alternative perspective.

One group of critics emphasizes the embeddedness of economics in social and cultural forces. Markets, in this view, are structured by a complex of local, ethnic, and trading cultures, and by varying regimes of state regulation (Gordon, 1985). Historians and sociologists contend that the market is not an amoral self-subsistent institution, but a cultural and social construction (Agnew, 1986; Reddy, 1984; Zelizer, 1988).[10] Others maintain that markets cannot be insulated from social structure because differential social access results in information asymmetries, as well as bottlenecks, thus providing some parties with considerable benefits and leaving others disadvantaged (Granovetter, 1985; White, 1981).

Another chorus of skeptics point to the intermingling of various forms of exchange. (See Bradach and Eccles, 1989, for a good review of this literature.) Stinchcombe (1985) shows that there are strong elements of hierarchy and domination in written contracts. Goldberg (1980, p. 338) notes that many market exchanges have been replaced by interorganizational collaborations. He contends that much economic activity 'takes place within long-term, complex, multiparty contractual (or contract-like) relationships; behavior is in various degrees sheltered from market forces.' Similarly, much of the observed behavior in hierarchical firms seems unrelated to either top management directives or the logic of vertical integration. For example, a firm's relationships with its law, consulting, accounting, and banking firms may be much more enduring and personal than its employment relationship with even its most senior employees.[11] The introduction of market processes into the firm also appears to be widespread. Eccles (1985) observes that large firms commonly rely on such market-like methods as transfer pricing and performance-based compensation schemes, while Eccles and Crane (1987) report that dual reporting relationships, internal competition, and compensation based on services provided to clients are the current norm in investment banking.

Markets, Hierarchies, and Networks

I have a good deal of sympathy regarding the view that all economic exchange is embedded in a particular social structural context. Yet it is also the case that certain forms of exchange are more social – that is, more dependent on relationships, mutual interests, and reputation – as well as less guided by a formal structure of authority. My aim is to identify a coherent set of factors that make it meaningful to talk about networks as a distinctive form of coordinating economic activity. We can then employ these ideas to generate arguments about the frequency, durability, and limitations of networks.

When the items exchanged between buyers and sellers possess qualities that are not easily measured, and the relations are so long-term and recurrent that it is difficult to speak of the parties as separate entities, can we still regard this as a market exchange? When the entangling strings of obligation and reputation reach a point that the actions of the parties are interdependent, but there is no common ownership or legal framework, do we not need a new conceptual tool kit to describe and analyze this relationship? Surely this patterned exchange looks more like a marriage than a one-night stand, but there is no marriage license, no common household, no pooling of assets. In the language I employ below, such an arrangement is neither a market transaction nor a hierarchical governance structure, but a separate, different mode of exchange, one with its own logic, a network.

Many firms are no longer structured like medieval kingdoms, walled off and protected from hostile outside forces. Instead, we find companies involved in an intricate latticework of collaborative ventures with other firms, most of whom are ostensibly competitors. The dense ties that bind the auto and biotechnology industries, discussed below, cannot be easily explained by saying that these firms are engaged in market transactions for some factors of production, or by suggesting that the biotechnology business is embedded in the international community of science. At what point is it more accurate to characterize these alliances as networks rather than as joint ventures among hierarchical firms?

We need fresh insights into these kinds of arrangements. Whether they are new forms of exchange that have recently emerged or age-old practices that have gained new prominence (more on the etiology of networks below), they are not satisfactorily explained by existing approaches. Markets, hierarchies, and networks are pieces of a larger puzzle that is the economy. The properties of the parts of this system are defined by the kinds of interaction that take place among them. The behaviors and interests of individual actors are shaped by these patterns of interaction. Stylized models of markets, hierarchies, and networks are not perfectly descriptive of economic reality, but they enable us to make progress in understanding the extraordinary diversity of economic arrangements found in the industrial world today.

Table 1 represents a first cut at summarizing some of the key differences among markets, hierarchies, and networks. In market transactions the benefits to be exchanged are clearly specified, no trust is required, and agreements are bolstered by the power of legal sanction. Network forms of exchange, however, entail indefinite, sequential transactions within the context of a general pattern of interaction. Sanctions are typically normative rather than legal. The value of the goods to be exchanged in markets is much more important than the relationship itself; when relations do matter, they are frequently defined as if they were commodities. In hierarchies, communication occurs in the context of the employment contract. Relationships matter and previous interactions shape current ones, but the patterns and context of intraorganizational exchange are most strongly shaped by one's position within the formal hierarchical structure of authority.

The philosophy that undergirds exchange also contrasts sharply across forms. In markets the standard strategy is to drive the hardest possible bargain in the immediate exchange. In networks, the preferred option is often one of creating indebtedness and reliance over the long haul. Each approach thus devalues the other: prosperous market traders would be viewed as petty and untrustworthy shysters in networks, while successful participants in networks who carried those practices into competitive markets would be viewed as naïve and foolish. Within hierarchies, communication and exchange are shaped by concerns with career mobility – in this sense, exchange is bound up with considerations of personal advancement. At the same time, intraorganizational communication takes place among parties who generally know one another,

Table 1   Stylized Comparison of Forms of Economic Organization

Key Features	Forms		
	Market	Hierarchy	Network
Normative Basis	Contract–Property Rights	Employment Relationship	Complementary Strengths
Means of Communication	Prices	Routines	Relational
Methods of Conflict Resolution	Haggling–resort to courts for enforcement	Administrative fiat–Supervision	Norm of reciprocity–Reputational concerns
Degree of Flexibility	High	Low	Medium
Amount of Commitment Among the Parties	Low	Medium to High	Medium to High
Tone or Climate	Precision and/or Suspicion	Formal, bureaucratic	Open-ended, mutual benefits
Actor Preferences or Choices	Independent	Dependent	Interdependent
Mixing of Forms	Repeat transactions (Geertz, 1978)	Informal organization (Dalton, 1957)	Status Hierarchies
	Contracts as hierarchical documents (Stinchcombe, 1985)	Market-like features: profit centers, transfer pricing (Eccles, 1985)	Multiple Partners Formal rules

have a history of previous interactions, and possess a good deal of firm-specific knowledge, thus there is considerable interdependence among the parties. In a market context, it is clear to everyone concerned when a debt has been discharged, but such matters are not nearly as obvious in networks or hierarchies.

Markets, as described by economic theory, are a spontaneous coordination mechanism that imparts rationality and consistency to the self-interested actions of individuals and firms. One need not go as far as Polanyi (1957) did, when he argued that market transactions are characterized by an 'attitude involving a distinctive antagonistic relationship between the partners,' but it is clear that market exchanges typically entail limited personal involvement. 'A contract connects two people only at the edges of their personalities' (Walzer, 1983, p. 83). The market is open to all comers, but while it brings people together, it does not establish strong bonds of altruistic attachments. The participants in a market transaction are free of any future commitments. The stereotypical competitive market is the paradigm of individually self-interested, noncooperative, unconstrained social interaction. As such, markets have powerful incentive effects for they are the arena which each party can fulfill its own internally defined needs and goals.

Markets offer choice, flexibility, and opportunity. They are a remarkable device for fast, simple communication. No one need rely on someone else for direction, prices alone determine production and exchange. Because individual behavior is not dictated by a supervising agent, no organ of systemwide governance or control is necessary. Markets are a form of noncoercive organization, they have coordinating but not integrative effects. As Hayek (1945) suggested, market coordination is the result of human actions but not of human design.

Prices are a simplifying mechanism; consequently they are unsuccessful at capturing the intricacies of idiosyncratic, complex, and dynamic exchange. As a result, markets are a poor device for learning and the transfer of technological know-how. In a stylized perfect market, information is freely available, alternative buyers or sellers are easy to come by, and there are no carry-over effects from one transaction to another. But as exchanges become more frequent and complex, the costs of conducting and monitoring them increase, giving rise to the need for other methods of structuring exchange.

Organization, or hierarchy, arises when the boundaries of a firm expand to internalize transactions and resource flows that were previously conducted in the marketplace. The visible hand of management supplants the invisible hand of the market in coordinating supply and demand. Within a hierarchy, individual employees operate under a regime of administrative procedures and work roles defined by higher level supervisors. Management divides up tasks and positions and establishes an authoritative system of order. Because tasks are often quite specialized, work activities are highly interdependent. The large vertically-integrated firm is thus an eminently social institution, with its own routines, expectations, and detailed knowledge.

A hierarchical structure – clear departmental boundaries, clean lines of authority, detailed reporting mechanisms, and formal decision making procedures – is particularly well-suited for mass production and distribution. The requirements of high volume, high speed operations demand the constant attention of a managerial team. The strength of hierarchical organization, then, is its reliability – its capacity for producing large numbers of goods or services of a given quality repeatedly – and its accountability – its ability to document how resources have been used (DiMaggio and Powell, 1983; Hannan and Freeman, 1984). But when hierarchical forms are confronted by sharp fluctuations in demand and unanticipated changes, their liabilities are exposed.

Networks are 'lighter on their feet' than hierarchies. In network modes of resource allocation, transactions occur neither through discrete exchanges nor by administrative fiat, but through networks of individuals engaged in reciprocal, preferential, mutually supportive actions. Networks can be complex: they involve neither the explicit criteria of the market, nor the familiar paternalism of the hierarchy. The basic assumption of network relationships is that one party is dependent on resources controlled by another, and that there are gains to be had by the pooling of resources.[12] In essence, the parties to a network agree to forego the right to pursue their own interests at the expense of others.

In network forms of resource allocation, individual units exist not by themselves, but in relation to other units. These relationships take considerable effort to establish and sustain, thus they constrain both partners' ability to adapt to changing circumstances. As networks evolve, it becomes more economically sensible to exercise voice rather than exit. Benefits and burdens come to be shared. Expectations are not frozen, but change as circumstances dictate. A mutual orientation – knowledge which the parties assume each has about the other and upon which they draw in communication and problem solving – is established. In short, complementarity and accommodation are the cornerstones of successful production networks. As Macneil (1985) has suggested, the 'entangling strings' of reputation, friendship, interdependence, and altruism become integral parts of the relationship.

Networks are particularly apt for circumstances in which there is a need for efficient, reliable information. The most useful information is rarely that which flows down the formal chain of command in an organization, or that which can be inferred from shifting price signals. Rather, it is that which is obtained from someone whom you have dealt with in the past and found to be reliable. You trust best information that comes from someone you know well. Kaneko and Imai (1987) suggest that information passed through networks is 'thicker' than information obtained in the market, and 'freer' than that communicated in a hierarchy. Networks, then, are especially useful for the exchange of commodities whose value is not easily measured. Such qualitative matters as know-how, technological capability, a particular approach or style of production, a spirit of innovation or experimentation, or a philosophy of zero defects are very hard to place a price tag on. They are not easily traded in markets nor communicated through a corporate hierarchy. The open-ended, relational features of networks, with their relative absence of explicit quid pro quo behavior, greatly enhance the ability to transmit and learn new knowledge and skills.

Reciprocity is central to discussions of network forms of organization. Unfortunately, it is a rather ambiguous concept, used in different ways by various social science disciplines. One key point of contention concerns whether reciprocity entails exchanges of roughly equivalent value in a strictly delimited sequence or whether it involves a much less precise definition of equivalence, one that emphasizes indebtedness and obligation. Game theoretic treatments of reciprocity by scholars in political science and economics tend to emphasize equivalence. Axelrod (1984) stresses that reciprocal action implies returning ill for ill as well as good for good. As Keohane (1986) notes, the literature in international relations 'emphatically' associates reciprocity with equivalence of benefits.[13] As a result, these scholars take a view of reciprocity that is entirely consistent with the pursuit of self-interest.

Sociological and anthropological analyses of reciprocity are commonly couched in the language of indebtedness. In this view, a measure of imbalance sustains the partnership, compelling another meeting (Sahlins, 1972). Obligation is a means through which parties remain connected to one another. Calling attention to the need for equivalence might well undermine and devalue the relationship.[14] To be sure, sociologists have long emphasized that reciprocity implies conditional action (Gouldner, 1960). The question is whether there is a relatively immediate assessment or whether 'the books are kept open,' in the interests of continuing satisfactory results. This perspective also takes a different tack on the issue of self-interest. In his classic work *The Gift*, Marcel Mauss (1967 [1925]), attempted to show that the obligations to give, to receive, and to return were not to be understood simply with respect to rational calculations, but fundamentally in terms of underlying cultural tenets that provide objects with their meaning and significance, and provide a basis for understanding the implications of their passage from one person to another. Anthropological and sociological approaches, then, tend to focus more on the normative standards that sustain exchange; game theoretic treatments emphasize how individual interests are enhanced through cooperation.

Social scientists do agree, however, that reciprocity is enhanced by taking a long-term perspective. Security and stability encourage the search for new ways of accomplishing tasks, promote learning and the exchange of information, and engender trust. Axelrod's (1984) notion of 'the shadow of the future' – the more the immediate payoff facing players is shaped by future expectations – points to a broadened conception of self-interest. Cooperation thus emerges out of mutual interests and behavior is based on standards that no one individual can determine alone. Trust is thereby generated. Trust is, as Arrow (1974) has noted, a remarkably efficient lubricant to economic exchange. In trusting another party, one treats as certain those aspects of life which modernity rendered uncertain (Luhmann, 1979). Trust reduces complex realities far more quickly and economically than prediction, authority, or bargaining.

It is inaccurate, however, to characterize networks solely in terms of collaboration and concord. Each point of contact in a network can be a source of conflict as well as harmony. Recall that the term alliance comes from the literature of international relations where it describes relations among nation states in an anarchic world. Keohane (1986) has stressed that processes of reciprocity or cooperation in no way 'insulate practitioners from considerations of power.' Networks also commonly involve aspects of dependency and particularism.[15] By establishing enduring patterns of repeat trading, networks restrict access (Powell, 1985). Opportunities are thus foreclosed to newcomers, either intentionally or more subtly through such barriers as unwritten rules or informal codes of conduct. In practice, subcontracting networks and research partnerships influence who competes with whom, thereby dictating the adoption of a particular technology and making it much harder for unaffiliated parties to join the fray. As a result of these inherent complications, most potential partners approach the idea of participating in a network with trepidation. In the various examples presented below, all of the parties to network forms of exchange have lost some of their ability to dictate their own future and are increasingly dependent on the activities of others.

Illustrative Cases of Network Forms

It is time to add some flesh to these stylized models. Substantive details enable us to see how these abstractions operate in economic life. I provide examples of networks from a diversity of industries, ranging from highly traditional sectors to the most technologically advanced ones. These disparate examples share some important commonalities. They all involve intricate, multifaceted, durable relationships in which horizontal forms of exchange are paramount. My argument is based on the Simmelian notion that similar patterns of exchange are likely to entail similar behavioral consequences, no matter what the substantive context.

I begin this section with craft industries, a setting where network forms have long been dominant. I turn next to a discussion of industrial districts, where network forms have made a resurgence. I then move to high technology fields; here, networks are a much more novel phenomenon.

They are being established for strategic purposes because neither market nor hierarchical forms have delivered the goods. Networks, in this case, are very much associated with the early stages of product life cycles. I conclude with the case of vertical disaggregation, where networks represent an effort to introduce collaboration into well-established contexts in which trust and cooperation have long been absent. The logic is to move from arenas in which networks are common and easy to form to settings where they are developed almost as a last resort.

Networks in Craft Industries

The distinction between craft-based work and formal organization revolves around not only the dissimilar way in which work is organized in the two settings, but also on a different set of expectations about where authority is located. Craft work tends to be project-based, while in bureaucratic organizations a product moves through a series of functional departments where different activities are performed. In craft work each product is relatively unique, search procedures are non-routine, and the work process depends to a considerable degree on intuition and experimentation (Perrow, 1967). The examples presented below represent well-researched cases that highlight the many network features associated with craft production.

Construction. Robert Eccles (1981), in his research on the construction industry, found that in many countries the relations between a general contractor and his subcontractors are stable and continuous over long time periods, and only rarely established through competitive bidding. This type of quasi-integration results in what Eccles calls the 'quasi-firm.' Although most contracts are set under fixed price terms, no hierarchical organization arises, even though there are clear 'incentive for shirking performance requirements.' Instead, long-term and fairly exclusive association obviates the need for costly organizational monitoring. In an empirical study of residential construction in Massachusetts, Eccles found that it was unusual for a general contractor to employ more than two or three subcontractors in a given trade. This relationship obtained even when a large number of projects were done in the same year, and despite the fact that a number of alternative subcontractors were available.

Publishing. The book industry is, to a considerable extent, based on network relationships (Coser, Kadushin and Powell, 1982). One effort to recognize and profit from these linkages is the establishment of personal imprint lines within large trade publishing houses. Under these arrangements, successful editors enjoy freedom from corporate constraints, and authors enjoy the intimacy and closeness associated with a small company. These extended networks allow an editor to rely on his or her own judgment and not have to appeal for higher level approval. The large firm is able to keep top-flight editors content and, at the same time, give them a greater financial stake in the books they bring in. Personal imprint editors are on their own as far as acquiring and nurturing authors, yet retain corporate clout for financing, sales, and distribution. Other publishers, in a related effort to hold on to key personnel, have 'spun off' subsidiaries that operate in an autonomous fashion within the loose boundaries of the larger company. These 'boutique' operations permit, in the words of the head of one such company, 'the intimacy of a small operation with no committee meetings and no bureaucracy' (Coser et al., 1982, p. 53).

But these developments are merely reflections of a general phenomenon that is characteristic of certain sectors of the book trade. In trade and scholarly publishing, much of the time editors behave as if they are optimizing not their organization's welfare, but the welfare of the social networks to which they belong. In scholarly publishing, editorial research and evaluation relies extensively on personal networks, which are based on loyalty and friendship, cemented over time. Bonds of allegiance shape the processes of access and discovery. These personal relationships are also vital to economic success. While competition among firms does, to some extent, influence the success or failure of particular publishing houses, these selection pressures are dampened by the dense associational ties and personal relations that support all publishing transactions. The fortunes of a scholarly publishing house often depend more on the rise and fall of various academic paradigms than on the efficiency of a firm's internal operations. In a sense, companies do not so much compete with one another as hitch their fate to the success or failure of different academic networks and intellectual fashions.

Both the spinoff arrangements and the quasi-organizations based on personal networks reflect the fact that editors are located in structurally ambivalent positions: loyalty to their authors and their craft often outweighs allegiance to the firm that employs them. From the employer's perspective, the only means of responding to circumstances in which the most valued assets of the organization – the editor and his or her contacts – are highly mobile is to either allow the editor to set up shop on their own within the corporate boundaries or to try to influence editorial behavior in an unobtrusive manner (Powell, 1985, pp. 144–57).

Film and Recording Industries. Sociologists who study popular culture have long known that the music and movie businesses were external economy industries in which there was heavy reliance on subcontracting and freelance talent. But recent research has shed new light on this particular method of matching investment capital and human capital. These industries thrive on short-term contracts, minimization of fixed overhead, mutual monitoring of buyers and sellers, and a constant weaving and interweaving of credits, relationships, and successes or failures. But the ostensibly open competition that one might expect to pervade these markets is minimal (Peterson and White, 1981). Instead, recurrent small-numbers contracting appears to be the norm.

Cultural industries are characterized by high variance and great unpredictability; conditions which breed high rates of social reconstruction or reproduction (Faulkner and Anderson, 1987). These 'project markets' are complex, dynamic, and uncertain. The participants in the film industry – producers, directors, cinematographers, actors, and musicians – appear at first glance to be highly mobile. They move from studio to studio, from one project to another, with few stable ties to any formal organization. But as Faulkner and Anderson (1987) show, in their analysis of participation in 2430 films over a fifteen-year period (1965–1980), considerable stability and recurrent contracting among the participants is the norm. It is the networks of participants, however, that are stable and enduring, not the film studios, where employees come and go and ownership changes frequently.

Not surprisingly, the key players in the film industry trust others with whom they have worked in the past and found to be reliable. What is striking about Faulkner and Anderson's analysis is how dramatic the patterns of inclusion and exclusion are. Reproduction persists within film genres and between big money and small money films. They observe (p. 907) that 'distinct networks crystallize out of a persistent pattern of contracting when particular buyers of expertise and talent (film producers), with given schedules of resources and alternatives, settle into self-reproducing business transactions with distinct (and small) sets of sellers (directors, cinematographers, and fashionable actors and actresses).' Commercial results feedback and then historically shape the next round of contracting.

These network patterns are interesting in their own right; but Peterson and White (1981) point out that even though they are powerful and long-lasting, they tend to be invisible to most observers. Instead of long-term rates of reproduction, most participants observe individual acts of ranking, favors, and contacts.

These craft-based examples are not particularly unique. Network forms of social organization are found in many cultural industries, in research and knowledge production, and in various industrial districts – such as the diamond trade (Ben-Porath, 1980), the garment and fashion business in Milan and New York, the Lyonese silk industry (Piore and Sabel, 1984), or the 'Third Italy,' discussed below. And many of the professions exhibit some network-like features. Architecture is a prime example; but so apparently is engineering where, to judge from one recent study (Von Hippel, 1987), the informal trading of proprietary know-how among technical professionals in competing firms is extensive.[16] What these different activities share in common is a particular kind of skilled labor force, one with hands-on experience with production and the strategic ability to generate new products to keep pace with changing market demands. The people who perform the work have a kind of knowledge that is fungible, i.e., not limited to an individual task but applicable to a wide range of activities. The organizations that complement these human capital inputs are highly porous – with boundaries that are ill-defined, where work roles are vague and responsibilities overlapping, and where work ties both across teams and to members of other organizations are strong.

Regional Economies and Industrial Districts

Recent economic changes have created, or perhaps recreated is a more apt description, new forms of collaboration among for-profit firms. In the previous century, a number of regions and industries were closely identified because both the social life and the economic health of such areas as Lyon and Sheffield were closely linked to the fate of the silk and cutlery trades, respectively (see Piore and Sabel, 1984; Sabel, 1989). This rediscovery or reinvigoration of the 19th century industrial districts points to the advantages of agglomeration, in which firms choose to locate in an area not because of the presence of an untapped market, but because of the existence of a dense, overlapping cluster of firms, skilled laborers, and an institutional infrastructure (for a good discussion of the economics of agglomeration, see Arthur, 1987).

German textiles.   Charles Sabel et al. (1987) describe the German textile industry, centered in the prosperous state of Baden-Wurttemberg in southwestern Germany, as an 'association of specialists, each with unmatched expertise and flexibility in a particular phase or type of production.' This flourishing traditional craft industry employs a highly refined system of production that links small and medium-size firms with a wide range of institutional arrangements that further the well-being of the industry as a whole. These support services include industry research institutes, vocational training centers, consulting firms, and marketing agencies. Most textile producers are highly specialized; and, as Sabel et al. (1987) argue, the more distinctive each firm is, the more it depends on the success of the other firms' products that complement its own. This production system depends on an extensive subcontracting system in which key technologies are developed in a collaborative manner. The subcontractors are also connected to overlapping inter-industry supplier networks. These linkages allow textile makers to benefit from the subcontractors' experiences with customers in other industries, and the suppliers are, in turn, buffered from downturns in any one industry. All of these arrangements serve to strengthen the social structure in which textile firms are embedded and to encourage cooperative relations that attenuate the destructive aspects of competition.

The Emilian Model. Perhaps nowhere have socially integrated, decentralized production units had more of an impact than in Italy, where the economy has outgrown Britain's and is catching up to France's.[17] Modena, the microcosm of Latin Europe's renaissance, is the center of Emilia-Romagna, in north central Italy, and it is here that Italy's economic performance has been most exceptional. Behind this success is both a set of unusual, to an American eye, political and social institutions, and a size distribution of firms that seem more suited to the nineteenth century than the late twentieth.[18]

Firms employing fewer than 50 employees engaged 49 per cent of the Italian labor force, and the average manufacturing firm has only 9.19 employees (Lazerson, 1988, p. 330). The proportion of the labor force grouped in smaller units of employment is greater in Emilia than in Italy as a whole (Brusco, 1982). The success of these small enterprises rests on a different logic of production than found in a typical vertically-integrated firm.

These small firms are frequently grouped in specific zones according to their product, and give rise to industrial districts in which all firms have a very low degree of vertical integration (Brusco, 1982). Production is conducted through extensive, collaborative subcontracting agreements. Only a portion of the firms market final products, the others execute operations commissioned by the group of firms that initiate production. The owners of small firms typically prefer subcontracting to expansion or integration (Lazerson, 1988). The use of satellite firms allows them to remain small and preserve their legal and organizational structure as a small company. Often satellite firms outgrow the spawning firms. Though closely related and highly cooperative, the firms remain strictly independent entities.

These industrial districts embrace a wide range of consumer goods and engineering components and machines: knitwear in Modena, clothes and ceramic tiles in Modena and Reggio, cycles, motorcycles, and shoes in Bologna, food processing machinery in Parma, and woodworking machine tools in Capri, to name but a few (see Brusco, 1982, pp. 169–70).

Why is production so widely decentralized and so spatially concentrated? The answer appears to be rather idiosyncratic to the Italian case. It is partly a response to labor union power in large firms, where union influence has proved to be a disincentive to job expansion. The small firms exhibit high wage dispersion, with highly skilled workers who have registered as artisans in order to make more than is standard in large-firm industrial relations agreements, and unskilled, temporary employees – students, the elderly, immigrants, who work off the books for much less than they would receive in a large factory, if they could find employment. The districts are also a response to changing tastes and technology, in particular the emerging popularity of custom rather than the standardized goods and the availability of high quality, flexible technologies that are compatible with the needs and budgets of small firms.

These decentralized organizational arrangements depend on a unique set of political and social institutions, most notably the fact that almost all local political authorities are controlled by the Communist party (Brusco, 1982; Lazerson, 1988). A combination of familial, legislative, ideological, and historical factors buttress Emilia-Romagna's economic progress. The continued existence of the extended family provides for economic relations based on cooperation and trust, and facilitates the search for new employees through family and friendship networks (Lazerson, 1988). The CNA, a national organization with close ties to the Italian Communist party, represents some 300,000 artisanal firms and provides them with a rich array of administrative services. These artisanal associations prepare pay slips, keep the books, and pay the taxes, as well as establish consulting, marketing, and financial services (Brusco, 1982). By coordinating these various administrative activities, the associations establish on a cooperative basis the conditions for achieving economies of scale.

Brusco (1982) and Sabel (1989) make a persuasive case that the Emilian model fosters the skills and initiative of artisanal entrepreneurs. The number of entrepreneurs previously employed by large firms, particularly as foremen, is very high. By tapping both initiative and detailed production knowledge, the small firms are able to offer a vast array of new products. And these small firms, through their multitude of collaborative networks, are able to give shape to new ideas with a speed unimaginable in larger enterprises.

Extended Trading Groups.   The kind of collaboration that obtains in the industrial districts of southwestern Germany or north central Italy is based in part on a set of local circumstances, but the principles of mutual organization on which the districts are based are more widely applicable. Interfirm cooperation is often found in economic activities based in a particular region, such as in Japan or Scandinavia, or in locales where firms from similar industries are spatially concentrated, such as Silicon Valley or Route 128 in the United States. The extended trading relationships that develop under these circumstances of physical proximity may vary considerably in their details, but their underlying logic is constant.

Ronald Dore (1983) argues that networks of preferential, stable trading relationships are a viable alternative to vertical integration. His work on the regionally concentrated Japanese textile industry, particularly its weaving segment, aptly illustrates this point. The industry was dominated in the 1950s by large mills, most of which were vertically integrated enterprises with cotton-importing, spinning, and finishing operations. By 1980 the larger mills had closed and the integrated firms had divested and returned to their original base in spinning. This 'devolution' has led to a series of stable relationships among firms of different sizes. The key to this system is mutual assistance. Dore (1983) gives the example of a finisher who re-equips with a more efficient process, which gives him a cost advantage. This finisher, however, does not win much new business by offering a lower price. The more common consequence is that merchants go to their own finishers and say: 'Look how X has got his price down. We hope you can do the same because we really would have to reconsider our position if the price difference goes on for months. If you need bank financing to get the new type of vat we can probably help by guaranteeing the loan.' This type of relationship is, of course, not limited to the Japanese textile industry; similar patterns of reciprocal ties are found in many other sectors of the Japanese economy.[19]

What are the performance consequences of these kinds of trading relationships? Dore suggests that the security of the relationship encourages investment by suppliers, as the spread of robotics among Japan's engineering subcontractors amply attests. Trust and mutual dependency result in a more rapid flow of information. In textiles, changes in consumer markets are passed quickly upstream to weavers, and technical changes in production also flow downstream rapidly. There is, Dore asserts, a general emphasis on quality. One would not terminate a relationship when a party cannot deliver the lowest price, but it is perfectly proper to terminate a relationship when someone is not maintaining quality standards.

More recently, Dore (1987) has maintained that Japanese economic relations in general do not have the properties (i.e., opportunism, short-term profit-maximization, and distrust) that we commonly associate with capitalist enterprise and on which we build our theories of economic organization (in particular, transaction cost economics). He contends that the costs of doing business in Japan are lower than in Britain or the United States because of concerns for reputation and goodwill and considerations of trust and obligation. Moreover, he argues, this embedding of business relations in moral and social concerns does not reduce economic vitality, it sustains it and provides Japan with a considerable edge (for further discussion on this point, see the chapter by Lincoln).

But is Japan all that unique? Perhaps it is true, as Dore (1987) suggests, that as a nation, Japanese industry is organized more along the principles of an extended network (see also, Imai and Itami, 1984), but it does not appear to have a monopoly on these practices. Hagg and Johanson (1983), in an analysis of the industrial markets which comprise the core of the Swedish economy, describe a series of long-term, stable relationships among industrial producers who share R&D resources and personnel. They suggest that the companies are actually investing in their connections with other companies, and in the process, losing their own identity to some extent. Instead of a competitive environment, there is a sharing of risks and resources and a pooling of information. Hagg and Johanson argue that these arrangements eliminate costly safeguards and defensive measures and are better adapted to uncertainty. Competition in intermediate producer markets is not eliminated, rather coalitions of firms compete with other coalitions, not on the basis of price, but in terms of product development and knowledge accumulation.

Swedish researchers have chronicled numerous such collaborative projects, principally among large manufacturing companies (Hakansson, 1987; Johanson and Mattson, 1987). Most of the ventures involve at least one firm with a home base in Sweden, but the researchers do not speculate whether Swedish industry has a particular proclivity for coordinating product development activities with suppliers, consumers, and producers of complementary products. These 'network forms of interorganizational relations' tend to be long-term, costly, project-based efforts at product development or technological innovation (Hakansson, 1987). They differ, however, in a number of respects from some of the examples discussed above. They usually involve very large firms, such as Volvo, Saab-Scandia, Ericsson, and Fairchild, and are typically heavy manufacturing projects in fields such as aerospace, metallurgy, mining, and marine engines. Unlike many of the subcontracting relationships, in which one firm serves as a principal and various satellite firms as agents, these production ventures bring companies together as co-contractors. In the language of agency theory, they are both principals and agents: risk-takers who allocate tasks and share in the gains or losses and contributors to the final product.

It was not all that long ago that notions of industrial districts and spatially concentrated production were largely ignored – both intellectually and geographically.[20] Now, every municipality seems busy at work trying to create their own Route 128 or Modena.[21] The success of these forms of extended trading networks has several key ramifications:

1. One of the main consequences has been to blur the boundaries of the firm – boundaries are being expanded to encompass a larger community of actors and interests that would previously have either been fully separate entities or absorbed through merger;
2. A new constellation of forces is being recognized as crucial to economic success: whether in the Third Italy or Silicon Valley, spatially concentrated production involves the cooperation of local government, proximity to centers of higher education, a highly skilled

labor pool, extensive ties to research institutes and trade associations, and cooperation among firms with specialized skills and overlapping interests;

3. The spread of technologically advanced, smaller units of enterprise – a growth that comes at the expense of larger companies and is not explained solely by the shift from manufacturing to services (Loveman, Piore and Sengenberger, 1987), and occurs without notable direct investment or significant employment increase, but rather as a result of expansion through various cooperative interorganizational relationships (Lorenzoni and Ornati, 1988).

Strategic Alliances and Partnerships

In many respects, partnerships and joint ventures are not new developments. They have been common among firms involved in oil extraction and petroleum refining as a means of spreading risks. Chemical and pharmaceutical firms have long conducted basic research jointly with university scientists. And some of the most complex partnerships have taken place in the commercial aircraft industry. Three major global players – Boeing, McDonnell Douglas, and Airbus Industrie – construct their planes via complex joint ventures among firms from many nations (Mowery, 1987). Boeing and Rolls-Royce teamed up to produce the Boeing 757, and much of the construction of the Boeing 767 is done, through joint ventures, in Japan and Italy. Airbus Industrie is a four nation European aircraft consortium, supported in part through loans (or subsidies, if you take the competition's view) from European governments.[22]

There is widespread evidence, however, that experimentation within various new kinds of interfirm agreements, collaborations, and partnerships have mushroomed in an unprecedented fashion (Friar and Horwitch, 1985; Teece, 1986; Zagnoli, 1987; Hergert and Morris, 1988; Mowery, 1988). Firms are seeking to combine their strengths and overcome weaknesses in a collaboration that is much broader and deeper than the typical marketing joint ventures and techhnology licensing that were used previously. These new ventures may take the form of novel cooperative relationships within suppliers, or collaboration among several small firms to facilitate research and new product development. More generally, internally generated and financed research is giving way to new forms of external R&D collaboration among previously unaffiliated enterprises. Indeed, in some industries, there appears to be a wholesale stampede into various alliance-type combinations that link large generalist firms and specialized entrepreneurial start-ups. Nor are these simply new means to pursue research and development; the new arrangements also extend to production, marketing, and distribution. And, in some circumstances, large firms are joining together to create 'global strategic partnerships' (Perlmutter and Heenan, 1986) that shift the very basis of competition to a new level – from firm vs. firm to rival transnational groupings of collaborators.[23]

In the past, the most common way in which large companies gained expertise or products that they were unable to develop on their own was to acquire another company with the needed capability. Mergers and acquisitions in high technology fields have not disappeared, but their track record is generally poor (Doz, 1988). Partnerships are more frequent now because of growing awareness that other options have serious drawbacks. Recent efforts at various kinds of more limited involvement represent an important alternative to outright takeover. Equity arrangements – deals that combine direct project financing and varying degrees of ownership – are an example. A larger firm invests, rather than purchases, primarily for reasons of speed and creativity. The movement in large companies away from in-house development to partial ownership reflects an awareness that small firms are much faster at, and more capable of, innovation and product development. General Motors explained its 11 per cent investment in Teknowledge, a maker of diagnostic systems that use a type of artificial intelligence, by noting that 'if we purchased the company outright, we would kill the goose that laid the golden egg.' Equity arrangements can be quite complex. Some small companies have several equity partners, and large companies find themselves in the novel position of negotiating product development contracts and licensing arrangements with companies that they partly own. Equity investments are typically 'complemented by various agreements, such as research contracts from the larger firm to the smaller one, exclusive licensing agreements to the larger firm, and often loan and other financial agreements provided by the larger firm to the smaller one' (Doz, 1988, p. 32).

These developments, not surprisingly, are particularly common in technology-intensive industries (Mariti and Smiley, 1983; Zagnoli, 1987; Contractor and Lorange, 1988). Both the motivations for collaboration and the organizational forms that result are quite varied. Firms pursue cooperative agreements in order to gain fast access to new technologies or new markets, to benefit from economies of scale in joint research and/or production, to tap into sources of know-how located outside the boundaries of the firm, and to share the risks for activities that are beyond the scope or capability of a single organization. The ensuing organizational arrangements include joint ventures, strategic alliances, equity partnerships, collaborative research pacts of large scale research consortia, reciprocity deals, and satellite organizations. There is no clear cut relationship between the legal form of cooperative relationships and the purposes they are intended to achieve. The form of the agreement appears to be individually tailored to the needs of the respective parties, and to tax and regulatory considerations. The basic thrust, however, is quite obvious: to pursue new strategies of innovation through collaboration without abrogating the separate identity and personality of the cooperating partners.

In these process-oriented fields, knowing how to make a product and how to make it work is absolutely critical to success. In recent years, as product life cycles shorten and competition intensifies, timing considerations and access to know-how have become paramount concerns. Teece and Pisano (1987) suggest that, increasingly, the most qualified centers of excellence in the relevant know-how are located outside the boundaries of the large corporation. Fusfeld and Haklisch (1985) argue that corporations are becoming less self-sufficient in their ability to generate the science and technology necessary to fuel growth. The larger and more technology-intensive the firm, the greater the amount of technical expertise it requires to maintain its position. Whether it is the case that one firm's technological competence has outdistanced the others, or that innovations would be hard to replicate internally, as suggested by the growing reliance on external sources of research and development (see Friar and Horwitch, 1985; Graham, 1985; and Hamilton, 1985), network forms of organization represent a fast means of gaining access to know-how that cannot be produced internally. The network-like configurations that have evolved in high technology can process information in multiple directions. They create complex webs of communication and mutual obligation. By enhancing the spread of information, they sustain the conditions for further innovation by bringing together different logics and novel combinations of information.

Collaborative agreements involve a wide variety of organizations. While the joining together of small firms that possess entrepreneurial commitment and expertise in technology innovation with large scale corporate organizations that have marketing and distribution power represents the prototypical example, these arrangements are certainly not the only option. Many large firms are linking up with other large companies, particularly in international joint ventures.[24] These partnerships are unusual in that they involve the creation of dependencies and linkages among very large firms, such as Toyota and General Motors.

Porter and Fuller (1986) suggest that such coalitions seem well suited to the process of industry and firm globalization, as evidenced by AT&T's alliances with Olivetti, Phillips, NTT, Toshiba and Ricoh. Large telecommunications companies have been very active participants in collaborative international research efforts. Siemens and ICL both have links with Fujitsu, while ICL, Siemens, and Machines Bull have formed a joint research institute in Munich to pool their basic research. Machines Bull is also a partner in a joint venture with Honeywell and N.E.C. Indeed, firms often have stakes in several projects with different partners (and potential competitors) and are engaged in ventures involving several technologies of different stages of development, creating a 'loose network of sometimes interlocking companies' (Contractor and Lorange, 1988, p. 24).

Traditionally, international joint ventures were not regarded favorably by multinational firms, especially those based in the United States. International manufacture and marketing occurred through either direct foreign investment or export, and occasionally international licensing was utilized when a firm wished to exploit a process technology. Joint ventures were sometimes resorted to when political exigencies or protectionist policies prevented operating fully owned subsidiaries. This was the standard reason for joint ventures in Japan, certain third world nations, and socialist countries.

Recent collaborations differ substantially from previous strategies. In these new global partnerships, all of the participants contribute technological and managerial expertise, as well as capital. The relationships are multidimensional and long-term, rather than one-shot transfers of technologies. What has happened to cause firms to prefer cooperation to full ownership, or a 'go-it-alone' approach?

There are numerous factors both pushing and pulling US multinationals into global alliances. On the push side are technological constraints. Much sophisticated technological knowledge is tacit in character (Nelson and Winter, 1982) and cannot easily be transferred by licensing. Indeed, it is the unwritten, intangible character of much firm-specific knowledge that has led US firms, particularly the automakers, to form joint ventures with Japanese manufacturers in an effort to better understand their production processes. Similarly, Japanese companies have been attracted to joint projects with US high tech firms because technological innovation cannot be simply purchased, it requires cumulative knowledge of the linkages among design, production, and sales.

On the pull side are financial concerns and the advantages of risk reduction. In joining a coalition with another firm, both partners may enjoy options that otherwise would not be available to them, ranging from better access to markets, pooling or exchanging technologies, and enjoying economies of scale and scope. Risk-sharing is very attractive in industries where each successive generation of products is expensive to develop, and product life cycles are short.

In some instances, international joint ventures do appear to represent an intermediate position between contracting among independent firms and vertical integration of the entire production chain. This is most common when the venture involves securing complementary inputs representing successive stages of production, or contracting for specific services or distribution arrangements. But this intermediate stage does not appear to be a temporary or unstable arrangement. Indeed, firms in such situations are ceding a good deal of their autonomy and facing considerable interorganizational dependence. Moreover, alliances that involve the pooling of know-how, the ceding of proprietary information, and the sharing of common assets are not intermediate in either an analytical or a developmental sense. They represent a very different form of interorganizational exchange, one in which ongoing vitality rests on continuing mutual dependence.

While US firms have been recently active in international business alliances, collective industrial research is considerably less advanced here than in Japan or Western Europe,[25] where research consortia have proven to be valuable in eliminating costly, duplicative R&D, in achieving economies of scale in research, and in diversifying the search for solutions to technical problems. But it was not until 1984 that Congress passed the National Cooperative Research Act, easing antitrust laws and permitting collaborative research among competing firms. Since then, more than 100 R&D consortiums have been founded, involving more than 500 companies in such fields as biotechnology, telecommunications, automobiles, energy, and steel. Collective industrial research is, nevertheless, still viewed by many in the US industry and government as a form of collusion and as a seedbed for anticompetitive practices.[26]

Despite a growing consensus that the changing nature of technology development encourages collective R&D, firms have been reluctant to share their best scientists and most attractive projects.[27] It may well be the perceived threat of Japan, with its extensive government-sponsored networks of collective research, that is the greatest spur to collaboration among large US firms. Cries of economic nationalism were motivating forces in the establishment of research consortia such as Sematech. This consortium of semiconductor firms may signal a new awareness of the need for collective research. Both IBM and AT&T are, for the first time, surrendering proprietary designs and processes to competitors in hopes of aiding the consortium's efforts at trying to revive the domestic semiconductor industry.

Cooperative arrangements are not necessarily easy to sustain, nor do they always entail success.[28] They can create a host of management problems and they also raise serious questions about effective industrial policy. On the organizational front, Doz (1988) has cautioned that convergence of purpose is often difficult to achieve, consistency of effort can be undermined by parochial subunit goals, and middle managers and technical specialities may not share top management's enthusiasm for cooperation. Similarly, Borys and Jemison (1989) suggest that because partners have not previously worked together, they may misperceive one another's actions. They observe that collaborations often begin with considerable resources, heavy obligations, and lofty expectations. Thus, the pressures to perform successfully may be considerable.

Collaboration can be fraught with other risks. Parties may bring hidden agendas to the venture. There is an ever-present threat that one party will capture the lion's share of the benefits, or defect with the other party's knowledge and expertise.[29] Some analysts worry that US partners to global alliances may provide 'mundane' services such as assembly, distribution, and marketing, which add little value to the product.[30] The key development work and the higher-paying, value-added jobs are taken overseas, and the US firm merely completes the final stages. These issues are far from being resolved, but they point out the complex ways in which collaborative networks may or may not contribute to a country's stock of organizational talents.

Vertical Disaggregation

Evidence is accumulating that many firms are choosing to shrink their operations in response to the liabilities of large-scale organization. For example, Mariotti and Cainarca (1986) describe a 'downsizing' pattern in the Italian textile industry, where there has been a decline in the number of vertically-integrated firms and growth in 'intermediate governance structures.' They attribute this development to three failures that plague vertically-integrated firms: an inability to respond quickly to competitive changes in international markets; resistance to process innovations that alter the relationship between different stages of the production process; and systematic resistance to the introduction of new products.[31] Interestingly, in an earlier era, firms actively pursued a strategy of vertical integration in an effort to reap the benefits of administrative coordination, economies of scale, and risk reduction (Chandler, 1977). Today, these 'strengths' have resulted in various weaknesses: structural inertia, slow response times, and decreased employee satisfaction.

Large organizations are designed to do certain things well over and over again. The more that behaviors are repeated, the more predictable they become; thus, the greater likelihood that these actions will become formalized. Child (1972) found that large organizations tend to be more rule-bound and to require greater documentation of their efforts. For certain kinds of activities, such practices are useful, but for others it can result in informational logjams and a serious mismatch between organizational outcomes and the demands of clients and customers in a changing environment. Thus, the very factors that make a large organization efficient and reliable at some tasks render it cumbersome and resistant to change when it comes to other actions (Nelson and Winter, 1982; Hannan and Freeman, 1984).

The information costs in large organizations are further compounded by motivational difficulties as well. One point that Alchian and Demsetz (1972) and Williamson (1975) implicitly demonstrate is that much of the internal structure of large organizations is designed to prevent collective action by employees. This basic attitude of suspicion may explain the finding by social psychologists that job satisfaction (as measured by turnover, absenteeism, and morale) declines with increases in organizational size and/or centralization (Porter and Lawler, 1965; Berger and Cummings, 1979). The design of organizations can affect the behavior of their members in a number of powerful ways.[32] In large hierarchical organizations, promotions up the career ladder are a key part of the reward structure. You have, then, little incentive to disagree with the operating decisions made by people above you in rank because they are the people who must decide on your promotion. Research suggests that hierarchical design dampens employee motivation because individuals are likely to be more committed when they have participated in a decision, and much less enthusiastic when they have been ordered by superiors to undertake a particular task (Hackman and Oldham, 1980).

When the pace of technological change was relatively slow, production processes were well understood and standardized, and production runs turned out large numbers of similar products, vertical integration was a highly successful strategy. But the disadvantages of large-scale vertical integration can become acute when the pace of technological change quickens, product life cycles shorten, and markets become more specialized. Firms are trying to cope with these new pressures in a variety of ways: by explicitly limiting the size of work units, by contracting work out, or through more collaborative ventures with suppliers and distributors. One route leads firms to a rediscovery of the market, to the hostile world of arm's length relationships. Associated with a greater reliance on external contracts are strong efforts at cost-cutting, and greater managerial freedom in the deployment of resources and personnel. Another route leads firms to try to reorganize production, not so much through eliminating jobs, but by searching for new methods of collaboration among formerly antagonistic and/or competitive parties (Walton, 1985; Weitzman, 1984). Both responses entail some form of vertical disaggregation, or the shrinking of large corporate hierarchies.

The US auto industry provides a good example of the crossroads many firms are at as they encounter the limits of vertical integration. The auto industry has undergone a profound shake-up, but the ultimate consequences of these changes have yet to be determined (see Dyer et al., 1987; Quinn, 1987). Prior to the mid-1970s, the big three automakers operated in a comfortable environment with little competitive pressure and scant customer demands for gas-efficient, high quality cars. The auto companies pursued a strategy of tight integration of production, which provided a means to guarantee supplies during periods of peak demand, as well as to protect the secrecy of annual styling changes. Vertical integration also kept down the prices of the independent parts suppliers with whom the companies traded. There was neither any give and take nor trust between the automakers and the subcontractors. Contracts were lost because a supplier bid .01 cent per item higher than a competitor (Porter, 1983). Automakers rigorously inspected supplier facilities, quality control procedures, stability of raw material sources, cost data, and management quality and depth (Porter, 1983, p. 278). They were reluctant to permit a supplier to manufacture a complete system. Instead, automakers preferred a competitive situation in which several firms supplied various components and the final assembly was done in-house.

Today this old system has crumbled in the face of international competition and fallen prey to the contradictions and short-term logic of the regime of competitive supplier relations. Heightened competition exposed a number of serious defects in this system. Abernathy (1978) has argued that vertical integration in the auto industry led to inflexibility. One consequence of tight technological interdependence is that change in any one part means the entire process must be altered. Pursuit of a cost-minimization strategy also reduced the automakers' ability to innovate. Susan Helper (1987), in an excellent analysis of supplier relations in the auto industry, observes that the old methods prevented suppliers from developing expertise, thereby reducing the skill requirements of their employees. This made it hard for them to develop any nonautomotive contracts and kept them dependent on the auto companies. It also had a chilling effect on innovation. There was neither any incentive nor capability for the suppliers to update equipment, suggest technological changes, or make long-range plans.

Because of their declining market share and lower profits, automakers are experimenting with an enormous variety of new approaches. A complex web of ties has developed among US automakers, their Japanese rivals, American labor, and auto parts suppliers. These changes are transforming the way the US auto industry operates, changing the nature of competition worldwide, and sharply blurring the distinction between domestic and imported cars. Joint venture activity is extensive: between Ford and Mazda, General Motors and Toyota, GM and Volvo, and Chrysler and Mitsubishi. Ownership is also held in tandem: Ford owns 25 per cent of Mazda, GM 42 per cent of Isuzu and 5 per cent of Suzuki, Chrysler 12 per cent of Mitsubishi Motors. These relationships involve close collaboration and joint production on some projects, and secrecy and exclusiveness on other models.

Equally extensive tinkering is underway with respect to subcontracting arrangements (Helper, 1987). The length of contracts has been expanded, from one year to three to five. More joint design work is being undertaken and sole-sourcing agreements are becoming more common. These new, more collaborative arrangements involve less monitoring and costly inspections, yet defect rates are much reduced. The automakers are becoming more dependent on the technological expertise of the suppliers, whose long-run health is now a factor in the automakers' profits.

At the same time, however, the automakers are pursuing a second strategy: outsourcing to low wage areas. They are simultaneously deciding which suppliers are worth investing in a long-term relationship with and determining which components can be obtained on the basis of price rather than quality. In these cases, there is little concern for collaboration or supplier design work; instead, the effort is aimed at finding third-world suppliers that can provide parts at the lowest possible price.

These disparate options graphically illustrate how practices such as subcontracting have a double edge to them: they may represent a move toward relational contracting (Macneil, 1978), with greater emphasis on security and quality; or they could be a return to earlier times, a part of a campaign to slash labor costs, reduce employment levels, and limit the power of unions even further. Hence, many of the current downsizing efforts seem, at the first glance, to be illogical. Some firms are seeking new collaborative alliances with parts suppliers while at the same time they are trying to stimulate competition among various corporate divisions and between corporate units and outside suppliers. Firms are proposing new cooperative relationships with labor unions and in the same motion reducing jobs and outsourcing them to foreign producers.

Are companies really as confused as it seems? Are these various actions merely the faulty experimentation of poor and indecisive managements? Not necessarily. Though many of the efforts at vertical disaggregation appear to work at cross purposes, there does appear to be an underlying theme. Strong competitive pressures within an industry reduce the number of levels of hierarchy within firms and push companies to redefine the boundaries of their organizations. Firms are externalizing the production of highly standardized components, and searching for new collaborative methods to produce components that require highly skilled, innovative efforts. These collaborations may entail new relationships with labor, close relationships with 'outsiders' who are no longer viewed merely as providers of a component but rather as sources of technological creativity that large firms cannot duplicate internally, and new cooperative ventures with competitors to pool risks and to provide access to markets.

The Etiology of Network Forms

Examples, as the old adage goes, are never proof. Qualitative data are often vulnerable to charges of being selectively presented. But qualitative materials are very useful for theory generation. The cases presented above are, in my view, much more than anecdotes, because taken together they represent a number of highly competitive and/or resurgent industries, and more importantly, they tell a consistent story that enables us to understand the circumstances under which network forms arise. These examples suggest that non-market, non-hierarchical modes of exchange represent a particular form of collective action, one in which:

- cooperation can be sustained over the long run as an effective arrangement;
- networks create incentives for learning and the dissemination of information, thus allowing ideas to be translated into action quickly;
- the open-ended quality of networks is most useful when resources are variable and the environment uncertain;
- networks offer a highly feasible means of utilizing and enhancing such intangible assets as tacit knowledge and technological innovation.

The examples presented above suggest that the conditions that give rise to network forms are quite diverse. The immediate causes, to the extent that they can be discerned, reveal a wide variety of reasons for the proliferation of network-like arrangements. In only a minority of instances is it sensible to maintain that the genesis of network forms is driven by a concern for minimizing transaction costs. Strategic considerations – such as efforts to guarantee access to critical resources, to obtain crucial skills that cannot be produced internally, to pacify the concerns of professional communities or national governments, or even, as in the case of global partnerships, to remake the very nature of international competition – certainly seem to outweigh a simple concern with cost minimization.

The origins and development of network forms seldom reveal a simple chain of events. The loose informal ties that sustain the Japanese keiretsu – the powerful trading companies such as Mitsui, Mitsubishi, and Sumitomo – developed because in the years immediately following the Second World War the US Occupation Authority dissolved the tightly centralized prewar zaibatsu (Gerlach, 1990). In Italy, the extended trading groups of small firms in the north central region emerged as a consequence of restricted job opportunities available to educated young people, due in part to labor union power and large firm rigidities (Sabel, 1989). Thus in some cases, the formation of networks anticipates the need for this particular form of exchange; in other situations, there is a slow pattern of development which ultimately justifies the form; and in still other circumstances, networks are a response to the demand for a mode of exchange that resolves exigencies that other forms are ill-equipped to handle. The network story, then, is a complex one of contingent development, tempered by an adjustment to the social and economic conditions of the time.

The absence of a clear developmental pattern and the recognition that network forms have multiple causes and varied historical trajectories suggest that no simple explanation ties all the cases together. Economizing is obviously a relevant concern in many instances, especially in infant industries where competitive preserves are strong. But it alone is not a particularly robust story, it is but one among a number of theoretically possible motives for action – all of which are consonant with a broad view of self-interest. Clearly many of the arrangements discussed above actually increase transaction costs, but in return they provide concrete benefits or intangible assets that are far more valuable. The reduction of uncertainty, fast access to information, reliability, and responsiveness are among the paramount concerns that motivate the participants in exchange networks.

My claims about network forms of organization obviously have broader ramifications. To the extent that these arguments are persuasive, they suggest that some of the basic tenets of other approaches to economic organization are problematic. For example, an exclusive focus on the transaction – rather than the relationship – as the primary unit of analysis is misplaced. Similarly, approaches that neglect the role of the state in shaping the context in which exchange is conducted are too narrow. The degree to which economic actors rely on the marketplace, private enterprise, or network forms of relational contracting is determined, to a considerable extent, by state policies. From a sociologist's perspective, it makes little sense to separate organizational behavior from its social, political, and historical context. To make serious progress in understanding the diversity of organizational forms, we need arguments that are much more historically contingent and context dependent.

Rationale for Network Forms

Does the diversity of network arrangements imply that their pattern of development is largely idiosyncratic? Or do the cases have sufficient generality that we can point to specific enabling conditions that foster the formation and proliferation of networks? If we are able to identify these conditions, then it would be possible to make refutable arguments about the circumstances that promote and sustain network forms. My own modest contribution to the theory of network forms highlights three factors – know-how, the demand for speed, and trust – which are critical components of networks.

Know-how.   There are a number of jobs that are based, in large measure, on either intellectual capital or craft-based skills, both of which have been honed through years of education, training, and experience. Many of these kinds of knowledge-intensive activities, such as cultural production, scientific research, design work, mathematical analysis, computer programming or software development, and some professional services, require little in the way of costly physical resources. They are based on know-how and detailed knowledge of the abilities of others who possess similar or complementary skills. Know-how typically involves a kind of tacit knowledge that is difficult to codify (Nelson and Winter, 1982; Teece and Pisano, 1987). These assets are both largely intangible and highly mobile. They exist in the minds of talented people whose expertise cannot be easily purchased or appropriated and who commonly prefer to ply their trade in a work setting that is not imposed on them 'from above' or dictated to them by an outside authority. Indeed, markets or hierarchical governance structures may hinder the development of these capabilities because the most critical assets – the individuals themselves – may choose to walk away.

Network forms of organization, with their emphasis on lateral forms of communication and mutual obligation, are particularly well-suited for such a highly skilled labor force, where participants possess fungible knowledge that is not limited to a specific task but applicable to a wide range of activities. Thus, networks are most likely to arise and proliferate in fields in which knowledge and/or skills do not lend themselves to either monopoly control or expropriation by the wealthiest bidder.

Exchange relations vary both in terms of how they are organized, as well with respect to the object of exchange. Transactions can take place in a variety of contexts; but, as Williamson and others have alerted us, certain kinds of goods and services lend themselves more readily to particular forms of exchange. The more general, and more substitutable are resources, the more likely they will be secured through short-term market transactions. Similarly, some kinds of exchanges fit more comfortably under the rubric of networks. Take the case of joint ventures, either domestic or international, which are organized for the purposes of exchanging skills or services between two or more firms. What kind of ventures are more likely to promote long-term collaboration and shared responsibility? Agreements that are based on contracting for the performance of particular services, such as sales or distribution, are not likely to promote cooperation. Indeed, joint ventures of this kind are often discontinued when one party's capabilities 'catch up' with those of the other. In contrast, when partners are involved in ongoing, complementary activities – such as pooling of research staffs or joint production arrangements – the relationship is more likely to lead to the sharing of critical information and the development of some measure of trust in one another. The sharing of information, as Buckley and Casson (1988) suggest, often leads to the emergence of common values. This cooperation is particularly likely to develop either in circumstances that require operational integration or under conditions of uncertainty about how to obtain desired outcomes. In both cases, there is a strong motive for parties to share information with one another (Buckley and Casson, 1988).

Thus, the exchange of distinctive competencies – be they knowledge or skills – is more likely to occur in networks. The transfer of resources – tangible items, such as equipment, services, patents, and the like – more commonly occurs through a market transaction or among organizational units, depending on the frequency and the distinctiveness of the items that are exchanged.

The *demand for speed* is based on a compelling economic logic. A regime of intense technological competition robs incumbents of their clout and brings upstarts to the fore. Firms join forces with other companies and/or with university scientists to reduce the risks and to share the expense of developing costly products that have very short life spans. Porter and Fuller (1986) argue that partnerships and coalitions are a more rapid means of repositioning than internal development and are less costly, less irreversible, and more successful than mergers. This view suggests that the business environment has changed in such a manner that it now rewards many of the key strengths of network forms of organization: fast access to information, flexibility, and responsiveness to changing tastes. Networks, then, possess some degree of comparative advantage in coping with an environment that places a premium on innovation and customized products.

What is it about networks that makes them more adaptive and well-suited to coping with change? One of the key advantages of network arrangements is their ability to disseminate and interpret new information. Networks are based on complex communication channels. Kaneko and Imai (1987) emphasize this dynamic property of networks, noting that they are particularly adept at generating new interpretations; as a result of these new accounts, novel linkages are often formed. This advantage is seen most clearly when networks are contrasted with markets and hierarchies. Passing information up or down a corporate hierarchy or purchasing information in the marketplace is merely a way of processing information or acquiring a commodity. In either case the flow of information is controlled. No new meanings or interpretations are generated. In contrast, networks provide a context for learning by doing. As information passes through a network, it is both freer and richer; new connections and new meanings are generated, debated, and evaluated.

Thus, to the extent that competition is based on such factors as the ability to innovate and translate ideas into products quickly, network forms of organization are more likely to proliferate. When competition occurs on the basis of price or manufacturing intensity, networks are likely to be less in evidence.

Trust. Several of the examples, particularly the cases of craft-based networks and industrial districts, suggest that certain social contexts encourage cooperation and solidarity, or a sense of generalized reciprocity. In these situations, exchange relations have been long-term and continuous, hence there is scant need to formalize them. What are the specific attributes that create circumstances in which collaboration is so easily accomplished? Axelrod (1984) has demonstrated the powerful consequences of repeated interaction among individuals. When there is a high probability of future association, persons are not only more likely to cooperate with others, they are also increasingly willing to punish those who do not cooperate. When repeat trading occurs, quality becomes more important than quantity. The reputation of a participant is the most visible signal of their reliability. Reputation bulks large in importance in many network-like work settings because there is little separation of formal business statuses and personal social roles. One's standing in one arena often determines one's place in the other. As a result, there is limited need for hierarchical oversight because the desire for continued participation successfully discourages opportunism. Monitoring is generally easier and more effective when done by peers than when done by superiors. Consensual ideologies substitute for formal rules and compliance procedures.

Networks should be most common in work settings in which participants have some kind of common background – be it ethnic, geographic, ideological, or professional. The more homogeneous the group, the greater the trust, hence the easier it is to sustain network-like arrangements. When the diversity of participants increases, trust recedes, and so does the willingness to enter into long-term collaborations. Calculative attitudes replace cooperative ones, and formal agreements – either contractual or bureaucratic – supplant informal understandings.

It also stands to reason that certain kinds of institutional contexts, that is, particular combinations of legal, political, and economic factors, are especially conducive to network arrangements as well as interorganizational collaborations. Yet we know very little about what kinds of political and economic conditions support network forms. As a result, I hold this discussion for the next section on unresolved issues. It is, however, worth noting that networks appear to involve a distinctive combination of factors – skilled labor, some degree of employment security, salaries rather than piece rates, some externally-provided mechanisms for job training, relative equity among the participants, a legal system with relaxed antitrust standards, and national policies that promote research and development and encourage linkages between centers of higher learning and industry – which seldom exist in sufficient measure without a political and legal infrastructure to sustain them.

A Research Agenda

The discussion thus far points to a number of key issues that require more sustained attention, as well as suggests several new topics for the research agenda. We need to know a good deal more about the factors that explain the ecology of network forms. Why is there such considerable cross-national variation in the frequency of network forms? Why are network arrangements so common in some nations and some sectors and not others? The evidence that I have presented suggests that state policies make a difference in the ease with which collaborative arrangements are formed and are sustained, but we have only begun to investigate the relationship between governance structures and state policies. Similarly, network forms are found in a diverse set of industries – craft-based occupations and professions, high technology sectors, and even mature ones such as auto. Can we make sense of this diversity? Do rates of formation vary across industries? Some early research (Friar and Horwitch, 1985; Hamilton, 1985; Hergert and Morris, 1988; Mariti and Smiley, 1983; Zagnoli, 1987) suggests that alliances are much more common in high technology fields, but we do not yet know whether this is a function of a youthful stage in an industry's life cycle or of basic structural features of activities that are highly dependent on the creation of new forms of knowledge.

A good deal more research is needed on the durability of networks. I have suggested above that the distinction between very specific resources and intangible assets might account for divergent patterns. The need to acquire resources may lead to network arrangements that are an interim step, either a half way point between market procurement and outright merger or a transitional move until internal capability is built up. Tacit knowledge, however, is inherently difficult to exchange; it may well lead to repeated, reciprocal interactions, transforming what was initially a relationship approached with some caution and fear into one that is institutionalized and enduring. In these circumstances, collaboration would be expected to shift from a means to an end in itself. Careful comparative research along these lines would be highly useful.

We know very little about the phenomenology of work under different governance structures. Do participants 'experience' networks as qualitatively different from market transactions or careers in hierarchical firms? If the argument that markets, hierarchies, and networks are distinctive forms, with their own logic and procedures, is correct, then we should find important behavioral differences among them. Do members of networks exhibit greater loyalty or commitment? Do participants in network arrangements face novel problems of control? How do people cope with relationships that are both collaborative and competitive, with circumstances in which control is not direct and immediate, and conformity to well-established administrative routines not guaranteed?

What are the performance liabilities of networks? There are, in all likelihood, certain tasks for which networks are poorly suited. When do networks create new levels of complexity that are incommensurate with their intended benefits? Are the gains from network relationships appropriated asymmetrically due to differences in the learning capacity of the participants? Some researchers (Cole, 1985; Pucik, 1988) suggest that much of the imbalance between Western and Japanese partners to joint ventures can be attributed to disparities in learning. Many Japanese firms have in place systematic methods that encourage the transfer of information and know-how from a joint venture throughout their organization (Imai, Nonaka and Takeuchi, 1985). More work is needed to understand how information is processed through networks and how learning is sustained.

Does participation in a network arrangement alter one's orientation toward future collaboration? Do the partners to a successful network relationship change their calculus and decide to act in different ways because of this experience? Does a reputation for being a fair-minded and successful exchange partner translate into clear economic benefits? These are fundamental questions and they suggest that much work remains to be done. This is not a daunting prospect, however. Indeed, one of my goals in this paper has been to suggest that students of organizational behavior are particularly well-equipped to study and explain the circumstances under which cooperation and collaboration proceed with only limited reliance on contracts and the legal system on the one hand, and on administrative fiat and bureaucratic routines on the other.

Acknowledgments

This paper has had a long gestation period. It began as a talk to the Industrial Relations Workshop at MIT's Sloan School of Management. The comments and encouragement of Mel Howitch and Mike Piore are greatly appreciated. A second iteration was presented at the Law, Economics, and Organization Workshop at Yale Law School and at the 1986 meetings of The American Sociological Association. The suggestions of Mitch Abolafia, Wayne Baker, Dick Nelson, Oliver Williamson, and Sid Winter were most helpful. An earlier draft of the paper was prepared while I was a fellow at the Center for Advanced Study in the Behavioral Sciences. The writing of the final draft was supported by funds from the Karl Eller Center for the Study of the Private Market Economy at the University of Arizona. I have benefited from comments by a great many people. Space limitations preclude me from thanking everyone properly, but several people who provided yeoman's help should be singled out: Michael Gerlach, Dave Jemison, Bob Keohane, Andrea Larson, Claus Offe and Charles Perrow. I also profited from comments by members of the audience at seminars at the Berkeley, Stanford, and UCLA business schools and the sociology departments at Arizona, Chicago, and Santa Barbara. Of course, I remain responsible for any errors or omissions.

Notes

1. See Koenig and Thietart (1988) on intermediate forms in the aerospace industry, Thorelli (1986) on industrial marketing networks, Eccles and White (1986) on transfer pricing, and Powell (1987) on hybrid forms in craft and high technology industries.
2. This recognition of intermediate forms has not, however, been accompanied by much in the way of concerted analysis. *The Economic Institutions of Capitalism* may include relational contracting in its subtitle, but the index lists a scant four pages of references to the topic. Similarly, Riordan and Williamson (1985) emphasize polar firm and market choices throughout their analysis, and then acknowledge in their last paragraph that 'hybrid modes of organization are much more important than had hitherto been realized.'
3. Transaction costs reasoning borrows freely from legal scholars, such as Macaulay and Macneil, who are noted for the development of ideas regarding relational contracting. Gordon (1985), however, questions whether this assimilation is satisfactory, noting that the price of success by economists is the 'exclusion of the very elements of contract relations to which Macneil and Macaulay have given most prominence: culture, politics, and power' (p. 575).
4. Transaction cost logic involves the comparison of discrete structural alternatives, typically the comparison that is made is that between market and hierarchy. The problem I have with this analysis is that in many cases where transaction cost reasoning predicts internalization, we find other kinds of governance structures, particularly networks. But one can read Williamson (1985) in a different manner, ignoring the argument about the predominance of markets and hierarchies, and focus instead on the highly important role of credible commitments. The book discusses a marvelous array of mechanisms for creating mutually reliant and self-enforcing agreements. If one conceives of production as a chain of activities in which value is added (Porter, 1985), the question is thus posed: which activities does a firm choose to perform internally and which activities are either downplayed or 'farmed out' so members of a network who presumably can carry theirs out more effectively, due to benefits of specialization, focus, or size (see Jarillo, 1988 for an extended discussion of this network value chain). When production is viewed in this manner, Williamson's arguments about credible commitments are quite useful in assessing what kinds of network agreements are likely to prove durable.

5. This does not mean that market forces were of little consequence before the eighteenth century. Braudel (1982) argues that economic history is the story of slowly-evolving mixtures of institutional forms. He suggests that we can speak of a market economy when the prices in a given area appear to fluctuate in unison, a phenomenon that has occurred since ancient times. But this does not imply that transactions between individuals were of a discrete, impersonal nature.

6. I owe this observation to comments made by Jim Robins.

7. What is remarkable about the firms in these two studies is how explicitly the entrepreneurs follow a 'network' strategy, intentionally eschewing internalization for such crucial and recurrent activities as manufacturing, sales, and research and development.

8. On this point, Macneil (1985, p. 496) suggests that 'the transaction costs approach is far too unrelational a starting point in analyzing' relational forms of exchange. Richardson (1972, p. 884) provides an apt example of these densely connected forms of exchange: 'Firm A, . . . is a joint subsidiary of firms B and C, has technical agreements with D and E, subcontracts work to F, is in marketing association with G – and so on. So complex and ramified are these arrangements, indeed, that the skills of a genealogist rather than an economist might often seem appropriate for their disentanglement.'

9. Bob Eccles and Mark Granovetter have repeatedly made this point to me in personal communications, insisting that all forms of exchange contain elements of networks, markets, and hierarchies. Since they are smarter than me, I should listen to them. Nevertheless, I hope to show that there is merit in thinking of networks as an empirically identifiable governance structure.

10. This line of work is both novel and promising, but it has yet to demonstrate how social ties and cultural patterns transform economic exchange in a systematic fashion; nor do we as yet have any clear cut notions about how cultural or historical factors create or introduce comparative variations in economic life. The focus, thus far, has been more on the intriguing question of how are economic motives culturally constructed.

11. Some economists (Alchian and Demsetz, 1972; Klein, 1983) go so far as to regard the firm as merely a set of explicit and implicit contracts among owners of different factors of production.

12. Many other scholars have their own definitions. Jarillo (1985, p. 32) defines strategic networks as 'long-term, purposeful arrangements among distinct but related for-profit organizations that allow those firms in them to gain or sustain competitive advantage vis-à-vis their competitors outside the network.' Kaneko and Imai (1987) conceive of networks as a particular form of multifaceted, inter-organizational relationships through which new information is generated. Johanson and Mattson (1987) regard networks as a method of dividing labor such that firms are highly dependent upon one another. Coordination is not achieved through hierarchy or markets, but through the interaction and mutual obligation of the firms in the network. Gerlach (1990) suggests that alliances among Japanese firms are an important institutional alternative that links Japanese firms to one another in ways that are fundamentally different from US business practices. Alliances, in his view, are coherent networks of rule-ordered exchange, based on the mutual return of obligations among parties bound in durable relationships.

   I find these various definitions very helpful, but also limited. They all describe networks as a form of dense interorganizational relationships. But networks can also evolve out of personal ties, or market relationships among various parties. Many of the arrangements discussed below, commonly found in the publishing, fashion, computer software, construction, and entertainment businesses are among individuals, independent production teams, or very small business units. Thus, my conceptions of networks is closer to Macneil's (1978; 1985) ideas about relational contracts than to the above views.

13. In an illuminating essay, Keohane (1986, p. 8) defines reciprocity as exchanges of roughly equivalent values in which the actions of each party are contingent on the prior actions of the others in such a way that good is returned for good, and bad for bad.

14. For example, successful reciprocal ties in scholarly book publishing – between authors and editors or between editors in competing houses – were highly implicit, of long-standing duration, and not strictly balanced (Powell, 1985). It was widely believed that the open-ended quality of the relationship meant that the goods being exchanged – advice, recommendations, or manuscripts – were more valuable and reliable.

15. Parties are, of course, free to exit from a network. But the difficulty of abandoning a relationship around which a unit or a company has structured its operations and expectations can keep a party locked into a relationship that it experiences as unsatisfactory. This problem of domination in networks obviously lends itself to transaction costs discussions of credible commitments.

16. In his study of the US steel minimill industry, Von Hippel (1987) found the sharing of know-how to be based on professional networks, which develop among engineers with common research interests. When a request for technical assistance is made, the person being asked typically makes two calculations: (1) is the information being requested vital to the health of the firm or just useful, but not crucial? and (2) how likely is the requester to reciprocate at a later date? Even though no explicit accounting is made, assistance is commonly offered. Von Hippel argues that this 'economically feasible and novel form of cooperative R&D' is probably found in many other industries as well.

17. For useful reports on Italy's economy, see 'Europe's sun belt also rises,' *U.S. News and World Report*, 7/18/88, pp. 27–29; and 'The Italian Economy: A Special Survey,' *The Economist*, 2/27/88, pp. 3–34. Both surveys point to the remarkable transformation of Italian industry, led by vast battalions of small firms, but caution that huge government budget deficits, inefficient public services, and an antiquated financial system could hold back further progress.

18. While the organizational structure of Italian firms may not seem modern, they are decidedly successful and high-tech in their operations. Benetton, the fashionable clothing company, is an oft-cited example. With some 2000 employees, the company orchestrates relations backward with more than 350 subcontractors throughout western Europe and forward with some 100 selling agents and over 4000 retail stores worldwide. The company's spectacular growth from small family business to far-flung empire has not been built on internalization or economies of scale, but on external relations for manufacturing, design, distribution and sales. These extended networks have both advantages in terms of speed and flexibility and liabilities with regard to maintaining quality standards. See Jarillo and Martinez (1987) and Belussi (1986) for detailed case studies of the company.

19. For more discussion of the interfirm networks that pervade the Japanese economy, see Okumura (1982), Shimokawa (1985), and Gerlach (1990).

20. For a thoughtful analysis of regional economies and changes in the scale of production, see Sabel (1989).

21. Such efforts, alas, will be hard pressed to succeed. See Dorfman (1983) on the largely idiosyncratic, hard-to-duplicate origins of the Route 128 technology corridor.

22. The commercial aircraft industry is unusual with respect to the very active role played by governments in insuring that their countries maintain a major presence in the industry. In this case, coalitions and joint ventures are driven as much by political factors and pressures for economic nationalism as by organizational and economic logic. See several of the chapters in Porter (1986) for a discussion of the political aspects of international alliances.

23. Competition over the marketing of tissue plasminogen activator (TPA), an enzyme many expect to be a major drug in treating heart attacks, is the most severe and complicated in biotechnology today. This competitive struggle illustrates how rival transnational alliances race for global market share. The US firm Genentech is allied with Mitsubishi Chemical and Kyowa Hakko in Japan, while another American firm, Biogen, is collaborating with Fujisawa. Numerous other Japanese and European pharmaceutical alliances, ignoring Genentech's claims for patent priority for TPA, are busy with their own TPA research. This contest shows the intensity of transnational alliance competition, but at the same time that Genentech and Fujisawa are at odds over TPA, they are collaborating in the marketing of another biotech drug, tumor necrosis factor (TNF). Yoshikawa (1988) offers a good road map to the complex, crosscutting terrain of biotechnology strategic alliances.

24. The label 'joint venture' implies the creation of a separate organization, but this need not be the case. Rather than form a new entity, partners can agree to a co-production arrangement. This is common in manufacturing, particularly aerospace, where each partner produces a section of the final product. Or firms may agree to a research partnership in which scientists and laboratories are shared. Similarly, exploration consortia in extractive industries need not create a new firm, but rather pool the costs and risks of existing activities.

25. The founding chairman of Sematech (a research consortium of 14 semiconductor firms), Charles Sporck, bemoaned that, 'We are trailing a pack of nations that are far ahead of us in forming

consortiums. We're especially trailing the Japanese.' Quoted in Peter Lewis, 'Are US Companies Learning to Share?' *New York Times*, 2/1/88, Week in Review, p. 5.

26. Ouchi and Bolton (1988) provide a good summary of the factors that account for the present stage of mixed support in the US for collective industrial research.

27. For a detailed discussion of the origins, development, and initial problems of one large cooperative R&D venture, the Microelectronics and Computer Technology Corporation (MCC) in Austin, Texas, see Peck (1986).

28. Ed Zajac has emphasized to me that the termination of a relationship does not necessarily imply failure. Collaboration is often intended as a means for the transfer of knowledge. Once this process is realized, termination may well be a sign of success.

29. Analysts have cautioned against alliances that involve a relative power imbalance, in which either one partner receives undue benefits or where one partner becomes so dependent on another that they may have no option other than to continue a relationship in which their share is increasingly inferior (see Teece, 1986). This fear, along with the worry that the partner will not perform according to expectations, explains why most potential partners approach an agreement with trepidation. These are typical and well-founded misgivings about any asymmetric exchange relationship.

30. Many commentators have voiced particular concerns about global partnerships, issues that are contested in the current 'manufacturing matters' debate (see Cohen and Zysman, 1987). Reich and Mankin (1986) warn that friendly colleagues often revert to hostile competitors. In the Pentax-Honeywell and Canon-Bell & Howell alliances, Japanese partners took advantage of valuable US technology and know-how only to later discard their American partners. *Business Week*, in its well-known March 3, 1986 issue, cautioned against the growth of 'hollow corporations,' that is, firms that have disaggregated so radically that they are left without any core expertise.

31. Wilkinson (1983) details related developments in Britain, where retailing, clothing, shoemaking, printing, and foodstuffs have undergone vertical disintegration, with the subsequent rise of small firms and numerous subcontracting relationships.

32. Top-down controls create distance between supervisors and subordinates, between powerful executives and less powerful employees. A vertical chain of command, and its accompanying layers of administration, undercuts management's ability to see its directives implemented and creates an environment in which employees see their work as but a tiny cog in a large impersonal machine. The diffuse control structure in large firms both dampens management's ability to move quickly and labor's sense of commitment to the enterprise.

References

Abernathy, W. (1978), *The Productivity Dilemma*, Baltimore: Johns Hopkins University Press.

Agnew, J. (1986), *Worlds Apart: The Market and the Theater in Anglo-American Thought, 1550–1750*, New York: Cambridge University Press.

Alchian, A. and H. Demsetz (1972), 'Production, information costs, and economic organization', *American Economic Review*, **62** (5), 777–95.

Arrow, K. (1974), *The Limits of Organization*, New York: Norton.

Arthur, B. (1987), 'Urban systems and historical path-dependence', to appear in R. Herman and J. Ansubel (eds), *Urban Systems and Infrastructure*, NAS/NAE, forthcoming.

Axelrod, R. (1984), *The Evolution of Cooperation*, New York: Basic Books.

Belussi, F. (1986), 'New technologies in a traditional sector: The Benetton case', Berkeley Roundtable on the International Economy working paper no. 19.

Ben-Porath, Y. (1980), 'The F-connection: Families, friends, and firms in the organization of exchange', *Population and Development Review*, **6**, 1–30.

Berger, C. and L.L. Cummings (1979), 'Organizational structure, attitudes and behavior', in Barry Staw (ed.), *Research in Organizational Behavior*, **1**, 169–208.

Borys, B. and D.B. Jemison (1989), 'Hybrid organizations as strategic alliances: Theoretical issues in organizational combinations', *Academy of Management Review*, **14** (2), 234–49.

Bradach, J.L. and R.G. Eccles (1989), 'Markets versus hierarchies: From ideal types to plural forms', *Annual Review of Sociology*, **15**, 97–118.

Braudel, F. (1982), *The Wheels of Commerce*, New York: Harper and Row.

Brusco, S. (1982), 'The Emilian model: Productive decentralization and social integration', *Cambridge Journal of Economics*, **6**, 167–84.

Buckley, P.J. and M. Casson (1988), 'A theory of cooperation in international business', in P. Contractor and P. Lorange (eds), *Cooperative Strategies in International Business*, Lexington, MA: Lexington Books, pp. 31–53.

Chandler, A.D. (1977), *The Visible Hand*, Cambridge, MA: Harvard University Press.

Child, J. (1972), 'Organizational structure and strategies of control: A replication of the Aston Study', *Administrative Science Quarterly*, **18**, 168–85.

Coase, R. (1937), 'The nature of the firm', *Economica*, **4**, 386–405.

Cohen, S. and J. Zysman (1987), *Manufacturing Matters*, New York: Basic Books.

Cole, R. (1985), 'The macropolitics of organizational change: A comparative analysis of the spread of small-group activities', *Administrative Science Quarterly*, **30**, 560–85.

Contractor, F.J. and P. Lorange (1988), *Cooperative Strategies in International Business*, Lexington, MA: Lexington Books.

Coser, L., C. Kadushin and W.W. Powell (1982), *Books: The Culture and Commerce of Publishing*, New York: Basic Books.

Dalton, M. (1957), *Men Who Manage*, New York: Wiley.

DiMaggio, P. and W.W. Powell (1983), 'The iron cage revisited: Institutional isomorphism and collective rationality in organizational fields', *American Sociological Review*, **48**, 147–60.

Dore, R. (1983), 'Goodwill and the spirit of market capitalism', *British Journal of Sociology*, **34** (4), 459–82.

Dore, R. (1987), *Taking Japan Seriously*, Stanford, CA: Stanford University Press.

Dorfman, N. (1983), 'Route 128: The development of a regional high-tech economy', *Research Policy*, **12**, 299–316.

Doz, Y. (1988), 'Technology partnerships between larger and smaller firms: some critical issues', *International Studies of Management and Organization*, **17** (4), 31–57.

Dyer, Davis, M.S. and A. Webber (1987), *Changing Alliances*, Boston, MA: Harvard Business School Press.

Eccles, R. (1981), 'The quasifirm in the construction industry', *Journal of Economic Behavior and Organization*, **2**, 335–7.

Eccles, R. (1985), *The Transfer Pricing Problem: A Theory for Practice*, Lexington, MA: Lexington Books.

Eccles, R.G. and D. Crane (1987), 'Managing through networks in investment banking', *California Management Review*, **30** (1), 176–95.

Eccles, R.G. and H.C. White (1986), 'Firm and market interfaces of profit center control', in S. Lindenberg, J.S. Coleman and S. Novak (eds), *Approaches to Social Theory*, New York: Russell Sage, pp. 203–20.

Faulkner, R.R. and A. Anderson, (1987), 'Short-term projects and emergent careers: Evidence from Hollywood', *American Journal of Sociology*, **92** (4), 879–909.

Finley, M. (1973), *The Ancient Economy*, Berkeley: University of California Press.

Friar, J. and M. Horwitch (1985), 'The emergence of technology strategy: A new dimension of strategic management', *Technology in Society*, **7** (2/3), 143–78.

Fusfeld, H. and C. Haklisch (1985), 'Cooperative R&D for competitors', *Harvard Business Review*, **85** (6), 60–76.

Geertz, C. (1978), 'The bazaar economy: Information and search in peasant marketing', *American Economic Review*, **68** (2), 28–32.

Gerlach, M.L. (1990), *Alliances and the Social Organization of Japanese Business*, Berkeley: University of California Press.

Goldberg, V.P. (1980), 'Relational exchange: Economics and complex contracts', *American Behavioral Scientist*, **23** (3), 337–52.

Gordon, R.W. (1985), 'Macaulay, Macneil, and the discovery of solidarity and power in contract law', *Wisconsin Law Review*, **3**, 565–80.

Gouldner, A. (1960), 'The norm of reciprocity: A preliminary statement', *American Sociological Review*, **25**, 161–78.

Graham, M. (1985), 'Corporate research and development: The latest information', *Technology in Society*, **7** (2/3), 179–96.

Granovetter, M. (1985), 'Economic action and social structure: A theory of embeddedness', *American Journal of Sociology*, **91** (3), 481–510.

Hackman, R. and G. Oldham (1980), *Work Redesign*, Reading, MA: Addison-Wesley.

Hagg, I. and J. Johanson (1983), *Firms in Networks: A New View of Competitive Power*, Stockholm: Business and Social Research Institute.

Hakansson, H. (ed.) (1987), *Industrial Technological Development: A Network Approach*, London: Croom Helm.

Hamilton, W.F. (1985), 'Corporate strategies for managing emerging technologies', *Technology in Society*, **7** (2/3), 197–212.

Hannan, M. and J.H. Freeman (1984), 'Structural inertia and organizational change', *American Sociological Review*, **49**, 149–64.

Hayek, F. (1945), 'The use of knowledge in society', *American Economic Review*, **35**, 519–30.

Helper, S. (1987), *Supplier Relations and Technical Change*, Ph.D. dissertation, Dept. of Economics, Harvard University.

Hergert, M. and D. Morris (1988), 'Trends in international collaborative agreements', in F. Contractor and P. Lorange (eds), *Cooperative Strategies in International Business*, Lexington, MA: Lexington Books, pp. 99–109.

Imai, K. and H. Itami (1984), 'Interpenetration of organization and market', *International Journal of Industrial Organization*, **2**, 285–310.

Imai, K., I. Nonaka and H. Takeuchi (1985), 'Managing the new product development process: How Japanese companies learn and unlearn', in Kim B. Clark et al. (eds), *The Uneasy Alliance*, Boston, MA: Harvard Business School Press, pp. 337–75.

Jarillo, J.-C. (1988), 'On strategic networks', *Strategic Management Journal*, **9**, 31–41.

Jarillo, J.-C. and J.I. Martinez (1987), 'Benetton S.p.A.: A case study', working paper, Barcelona, Spain: IESE.

Johanson, J. and L.-G. Mattson (1987), 'Interorganizational relations in industrial systems: A network approach compared with the transaction-cost approach', *International Studies of Management and Organization*, **18** (1), 34–48.

Kaneko, I. and K. Imai (1987), 'A network view of the firm', paper presented at first Hitotsubashi–Stanford conference.

Keohane, R. (1986), 'Reciprocity in international relations', *International Organization*, **40** (1), 1–27.

Klein, B. (1983), 'Contracting costs and residual claims: The separation of ownership and control', *Journal of Law and Economics*, **26**, 367–74.

Koenig, C. and R.A. Thietart (1988), 'Managers, engineers and government', *Technology in Society*, **10**, 45–69.

Larson, A. (1988), 'Cooperative alliances: A study of entrepreneurship', Ph.D. dissertation, Harvard Business School.

Lazerson, M. (1988), 'Organizational growth of small firms: An outcome of markets and hierarchies?', *American Sociological Review*, **53** (3), 330–42.

Lorenzoni, G. and O. Ornati (1988), 'Constellations of firms and new ventures', *Journal of Business Venturing*, **3**, 41–57.

Loveman, G., M. Piore and W. Sengenberger (1987), 'The evolving role of small business in industrial economies', paper presented at conference on New Developments in Labor Market and Human Resource Policies, Sloan School, M.I.T.

Luhmann, N. (1979), *Trust and Power*, New York: Wiley.

Macneil, I. (1978), 'Contracts: Adjustment of long-term economic relations under classical, neoclassical, and relational contract law', *Northwestern University Law Review*, **72** (6), 854–905.

Macneil, I. (1985), 'Relational contract: What we do and do not know', *Wisconsin Law Review*, **3**, 483–526.

Mariotti, S. and G.C. Cainarca (1986), 'The evolution of transaction governance in the textile-clothing industry', *Journal of Economic Behavior and Organization*, **7**, 351–74.

Mariti, P. and R.H. Smiley (1983), 'Co-operative agreements and the organization of industry', *Journal of Industrial Economics*, **31** (4), 437–51.

Mauss, M. (1967, 1925), *The Gift*, New York: Norton.

Mowery, D.C. (1987), *Alliance Politics and Economics*, Cambridge, MA: Ballinger.

Mowery, D.C. (ed.) (1988), *International Collaborative Ventures in U.S. Manufacturing*, Cambridge, MA: Ballinger.

Nelson, R. and S. Winter (1982), *An Evolutionary Theory of Economic Change*, Cambridge: Harvard University Press.

Okumura, H. (1982), 'Interfirm relations in an enterprise group: The case of Mitsubishi', *Japanese Economic Studies*, **10** (4), 53–82.

Ouchi, W.G. and M.K. Bolton (1988), 'The logic of joint research and development', *California Management Review*, **30** (3), 9–33.

Peck, M.J. (1986), 'Joint R&D: The case of microelectronics and computer technology corporation', *Research Policy*, **15**, 219–31.

Perlmutter, H. and D. Heenan (1986), 'Cooperate to compete globally', *Harvard Business Review*, **86** (2), 136–52.

Perrow, C. (1967), 'A framework for the comparative analysis of organizations', *American Sociological Review*, **32**, 194–208.

Peterson, R.A. and H. White (1981), 'Elements of simplex structure', *Urban Life*, **10** (1), 3–24.

Piore, M.J. and C.F. Sabel (1984), *The Second Industrial Divide*, New York: Basic Books.

Polanyi, K. (1957), *The Great Transformation*, Boston: Beacon.

Porter, L. and E. Lawler (1965), 'Properties of organization structure in relation to job attitudes and job behavior', *Psychological Bulletin*, **64** (1), 23–51.

Porter, M. (1983), *Cases in Competitive Strategy*, New York: Free Press.

Porter, M. (1985), *Competitive Advantage*, New York: Free Press.

Porter, M. (1986), *Competition in Global Industries*, Boston, MA: Harvard Business School Press.

Porter, M. and M.B. Fuller (1986), 'Coalitions and global strategy', in M. Porter (ed.), *Competition in Global Industries*, Boston, MA: HBS Press, pp. 315–44.

Powell, W.W. (1985), *Getting into Print: The Decision Making Process in Scholarly Publishing*, Chicago: University of Chicago Press.

Powell, W.W. (1987), 'Hybrid organizational arrangements: New form or transitional development?', *California Management Review*, **30** (1), 67–87.

Pucik, V. (1988), 'Strategic alliances with the Japanese: Implications for human resource management', in P. Contractor and P. Lorange (eds), *Cooperative Strategies in International Business*, Lexington, MA: Lexington Books, pp. 487–98.

Quinn, D.P. (1987), 'Dynamic markets and mutating firms: The changing organization of production in automotive firms', working paper presented at APSA meetings, Chicago.

Reddy, W.M. (1984), *The Rise of Market Culture*, New York: Cambridge University Press.

Reich, R.B. and E. Mankin (1986), 'Joint ventures with Japan give away our future', *Harvard Business Review*, **86** (2), 78–86.

Richardson, G.B. (1972), 'The organization of industry', *Economic Journal*, **82**, 883–96.

Riordan, M.H. and O.E. Williamson (1985), 'Asset specificity and economic organization', *International Journal of Industrial Organization*, **3**, 365–78.

Sabel, C.F. (1989), 'Flexible specialization and the re-emergence of regional economies', in P. Hirst and J. Zeitlin (eds), *Reversing Industrial Decline?* Oxford, UK: Berg, pp. 17–70.

Sabel, C., G. Herrigel, R. Kazis and R. Deeg (1987), 'How to keep mature industries innovative', *Technology Review*, **90** (3), 26–35.

Sahlins, M. (1972), *Stone Age Economics*, Chicago: Aldine.

Shimokawa, K. (1985), 'Japan's keiretsu system: The case of the automobile industry', *Japanese Economic Studies*, **13** (4), 3–31.

Stinchcombe, A. (1985), 'Contracts as hierarchical documents', in A. Stinchcombe and C. Heimer (eds), *Organization Theory and Project Management*, Oslo: Norwegian University Press, pp. 121–71.

Teece, D. (1986), 'Profiting from technological innovation: Implications for integration, collaboration, licensing and public policy', *Research Policy*, **15** (6), 785–805.

Teece, D. and G. Pisano (1987), 'Collaborative arrangements and technology strategy', paper presented at conference on New Technology and New Intermediaries, Stanford: Center for European Studies.

Thompson, E.P. (1971), 'The moral economy of the English crowd in the eighteenth century', *Past and Present*, **50**, 78–98.

Thorelli, H.B. (1986), 'Networks: Between markets and hierarchies', *Strategic Management Journal*, **7**, 37–51.

Von Hippel, E. (1987), 'Cooperation between rivals: Informal know-how trading', *Research Policy*, **16**, 291–302.

Walton, R. (1985), 'From control to commitment in the workplace', *Harvard Business Review*, **85** (2), 76–84.

Walzer, M. (1983), *Spheres of Justice*, New York: Basic Books.

Weitzman, M. (1984), *The Share Economy*, Cambridge, MA: Harvard University Press.

White, H.C. (1981), 'Where do markets come from?', *American Journal of Sociology*, **87**, 517–47.

Wilkinson, F. (1983), 'Productive systems', *Cambridge Journal of Economics*, **7**, 413–29.

Williamson, O.E. (1975), *Markets and Hierarchies: Analysis and Antitrust Implications*, New York: Free Press.

Williamson, O.E. (1985), *The Economic Institutions of Capitalism*, New York: Free Press.

Yoshikawa, A. (1988), 'Japanese biotechnology: New drugs, industrial organization, innovation, and strategic alliances', BRIE working paper no. 33.

Zagnoli, P. (1987), 'Interfirm agreements as bilateral transactions?', paper presented at conference on New Technology and New Intermediaries, Stanford: Center for European Studies.

Zelizer, V. (1988), 'Beyond the polemics of the market: Establishing a theoretical and empirical agenda', paper presented at conference on Economy and Society, Santa Barbara: University of California.

[4]

Comparative Economic Organization: The Analysis of Discrete Structural Alternatives

Oliver E. Williamson
University of California, Berkeley

This paper combines institutional economics with aspects of contract law and organization theory to identify and explicate the key differences that distinguish three generic forms of economic organization—market, hybrid, and hierarchy. The analysis shows that the three generic forms are distinguished by different coordinating and control mechanisms and by different abilities to adapt to disturbances. Also, each generic form is supported and defined by a distinctive type of contract law. The cost-effective choice of organization form is shown to vary systematically with the attributes of transactions. The paper unifies two hitherto disjunct areas of institutional economics—the institutional environment and the institutions of governance—by treating the institutional environment as a locus of parameters, changes in which parameters bring about shifts in the comparative costs of governance. Changes in property rights, contract law, reputation effects, and uncertainty are investigated.•

Although microeconomic organization is formidably complex and has long resisted systematic analysis, that has been changing as new modes of analysis have become available, as recognition of the importance of institutions to economic performance has grown, and as the limits of earlier modes of analysis have become evident. Information economics, game theory, agency theory, and population ecology have all made significant advances.

This paper approaches the study of economic organization from a comparative institutional point of view in which transaction-cost economizing is featured. Comparative economic organization never examines organization forms separately but always in relation to alternatives. Transaction-cost economics places the principal burden of analysis on comparisons of transaction costs—which, broadly, are the "costs of running the economic system" (Arrow, 1969: 48).

My purpose in this paper is to extend and refine the apparatus out of which transaction-cost economics works, thereby to respond to some of the leading criticisms. Four objections to prior work in this area are especially pertinent. One objection is that the two stages of the new institutional economics research agenda—the institutional environment and the institutions of governance—have developed in disjunct ways. The first of these paints on a very large historical canvas and emphasizes the institutional rules of the game: customs, laws, politics (North, 1986). The latter is much more microanalytic and focuses on the comparative efficacy with which alternative generic forms of governance—markets, hybrids, hierarchies—economize on transaction costs. Can this disjunction problem be overcome? Second, transaction-cost economics has been criticized because it deals with polar forms—markets and hierarchies—to the neglect of intermediate or hybrid forms. Although that objection has begun to be addressed by recent treatments of long-term contracting in which bilateral dependency conditions are supported by a variety of specialized governance features (hostages, arbitration, take-or-pay procurement clauses, tied sales, reciprocity, regulation, etc.), the abstract attributes

© 1991 by Cornell University.
0001-8392/91/3602-0269/$1.00.

•

The author is Transamerica Professor of Business, Economics, and Law at the University of California, Berkeley and Senior Research Scientist of the Institute for Policy Reform. The paper benefitted from presentations at workshops at the University of California, Berkeley, the University of California, Los Angeles/University of Southern California, the University of California, Irvine, the University of Michigan, and the Netherlands Institute for Advanced Studies. Helpful comments from workshop participants and from Glenn Carroll, Melvin Eisenberg, Bengt Holmstrom, David Kreps, Gillian Hadfield, Scott Masten, Vai-Lam Mui, Richard Nelson, Dan Ostas, Michael Riordan, Roberta Romano, Richard Stewart, Jean Tirole, and Birger Wernerfelt as well as the referees, editor, and managing editor of this journal are gratefully acknowledged. A much shorter version was prepared for and presented as the opening address to the annual meeting of German Academic Business Economists at Frankfurt, Germany in June 1990. A German translation of that address has since been published in the papers and proceedings. The final version of this paper was produced while I was at Saarbrücken University as Distinguished U.S. Senior Scientist, Alexander von Humboldt-Stiftung, for which support I express appreciation.

that characterize alternative modes of governance have remained obscure. What are the key attributes and how do they vary among forms? This is responsive to the third objection, namely, that efforts to operationalize transaction-cost economics have given disproportionate attention to the abstract description of transactions as compared with the abstract description of governance. The dimensionalization of both is needed. Finally, there is the embeddedness problem: Transaction-cost economics purports to have general application but has been developed almost entirely with reference to Western capitalist economies (Hamilton and Biggart, 1988). Is a unified treatment of Western and non-Western, capitalist and noncapitalist economies really feasible? This paper attempts to address these objections by posing the problem of organization as one of discrete structural analysis.

DISCRETE STRUCTURAL ANALYSIS

The term discrete structural analysis was introduced into the study of comparative economic organization by Simon (1978: 6–7), who observed that

As economics expands beyond its central core of price theory, and its central concern with quantities of commodities and money, we observe in it . . . [a] shift from a highly quantitative analysis, in which equilibration at the margin plays a central role, to a much more qualitative institutional analysis, in which discrete structural alternatives are compared. . . .

[S]uch analyses can often be carried out without elaborate mathematical apparatus or marginal calculation. In general, much cruder and simpler arguments will suffice to demonstrate an inequality between two quantities than are required to show the conditions under which these quantities are equated at the margin.

But what exactly is discrete structural analysis? Is it employed only because "there is at present no [satisfactory] way of characterizing organizations in terms of continuous variation over a spectrum" (Ward, 1967: 38)? Or is there a deeper rationale?

Of the variety of factors that support discrete structural analysis, I focus here on the following: (1) firms are not merely extensions of markets but employ different means, (2) discrete contract law differences provide crucial support for and serve to define each generic form of governance, and (3) marginal analysis is typically concerned with second-order refinements to the neglect of first-order economizing.

Different Means

Although the study of economic organization deals principally with markets and market mechanisms, it is haunted by a troublesome fact: a great deal of economic activity takes place within firms (Barnard, 1938; Chandler, 1962, 1977). Conceivably, however, no novel economizing issues are posed within firms, because technology is largely determinative—the firm is mainly defined by economies of scale and scope and is merely an instrument for transforming inputs into outputs according to the laws of technology—and because market mechanisms carry over into firms. I have taken exception with the technology view elsewhere (Williamson, 1975). Consider, therefore, the latter.

In parallel with von Clausewitz's (1980) views on war, I
maintain that hierarchy is not merely a contractual act but is
also a contractual instrument, a continuation of market relations by other means. The challenge to comparative contractual analysis is to discern and explicate the different means.
As developed below, each viable form of governance—market, hybrid, and hierarchy—is defined by a syndrome of attributes that bear a supporting relation to one another. Many
hypothetical forms of organization never arise, or quickly die
out, because they combine inconsistent features.

Contract Law

The mapping of contract law onto economic organization has
been examined elsewhere (Williamson, 1979, 1985). Although some of that is repeated here, there are two significant differences. First, I advance the hypothesis that each
generic form of governance—market, hybrid, and hierarchy—
needs to be supported by a different form of contract law.
Second, the form of contract law that supports hierarchy is
that of forbearance.

Classical contract law. Classical contract law applies to the
ideal transaction in law and economics—"sharp in by clear
agreement; sharp out by clear performance" (Macneil, 1974:
738)—in which the identity of the parties is irrelevant.
"Thick" markets are ones in which individual buyers and sellers bear no dependency relation to each other. Instead, each
party can go its own way at negligible cost to another. If
contracts are renewed period by period, that is only because
current suppliers are continuously meeting bids in the spot
market. Such transactions are monetized in extreme degree;
contract law is interpreted in a very legalistic way: more formal terms supercede less formal should disputes arise between formal and less formal features (e.g., written
agreements versus oral amendments), and hard bargaining,
to which the rules of contract law are strictly applied, characterizes these transactions. Classical contract law is congruent with and supports the autonomous market form of
organization (Macneil, 1974, 1978).

Neoclassical contract law and excuse doctrine. Neoclassical contract law and excuse doctrine, which relieves parties
from strict enforcement, apply to contracts in which the parties to the transaction maintain autonomy but are bilaterally
dependent to a nontrivial degree. Identity plainly matters if
premature termination or persistent maladaptation would
place burdens on one or both parties. Perceptive parties reject classical contract law and move into a neoclassical contracting regime because this better facilitates continuity and
promotes efficient adaptation.

As developed below, hybrid modes of contracting are supported by neoclassical contract law. The parties to such contracts maintain autonomy, but the contract is mediated by an
elastic contracting mechanism. Public utility regulation, in
which the relations between public utility firms and their customers are mediated by a regulatory agency, is one example
(Goldberg, 1976; Williamson, 1976). Exchange agreements
or reciprocal trading in which the parties experience (and respond similarly to) similar disturbances is another illustration

(Williamson, 1983). Franchising is another way of preserving semi-autonomy, but added supports are needed (Klein, 1980; Hadfield, 1990). More generally, long-term, incomplete contracts require special adaptive mechanisms to effect realignment and restore efficiency when beset by unanticipated disturbances.

Disturbances are of three kinds: inconsequential, consequential, and highly consequential. Inconsequential disturbances are ones for which the deviation from efficiency is too small to recover the costs of adjustment. The net gains from realignment are negative for minor disturbances because (as discussed below) requests for adjustments need to be justified and are subject to review, the costs of which exceed the prospective gains.

Middle-range or consequential disturbances are ones to which neoclassical contract law applies. These are transactions for which Karl Llewellyn's concept of "contract as framework" is pertinent. Thus Llewellyn (1931: 737) refers to contract as "a framework highly adjustable, a framework which almost never accurately indicates real working relations, but which affords a rough indication around which such relations vary, an occasional guide in cases of doubt, and a norm of ultimate appeal when the relations cease in fact to work." The thirty-two-year coal supply agreement between the Nevada Power Company and the Northwest Trading Company illustrates the elastic mechanisms employed by a neoclassical contract. That contract reads in part as follows:

. . . In the event an inequitable condition occurs which adversely affects one Party, it shall then be the joint and equal responsibility of both Parties to act promptly and in good faith to determine the action required to cure or adjust for the inequity and effectively to implement such action. Upon written claim of inequity served by one Party upon the other, the Parties shall act jointly to reach an agreement concerning the claimed inequity within sixty (60) days of the date of such written claim. An adjusted base coal price that differs from market price by more than ten percent (10%) shall constitute a hardship. The Party claiming inequity shall include in its claim such information and data as may be reasonably necessary to substantiate the claim and shall freely and without delay furnish such other information and data as the other Party reasonably may deem relevant and necessary. If the Parties cannot reach agreement within sixty (60) days the matter shall be submitted to arbitration.

By contrast with a classical contract, this contract (1) contemplates unanticipated disturbances for which adaptation is needed, (2) provides a tolerance zone (of ±10%) within which misalignments will be absorbed, (3) requires information disclosure and substantiation if adaptation is proposed, and (4) provides for arbitration in the event voluntary agreement fails.

The forum to which this neoclassical contract refers disputes is (initially, at least) that of arbitration rather than the courts. Fuller (1963: 11–12) described the procedural differences between arbitration and litigation:

[T]here are open to the arbitrator . . . quick methods of education not open to the courts. An arbitrator will frequently interrupt the examination of witnesses with a request that the parties educate

Comparative Economic Organization

him to the point where he can understand the testimony being received. This education can proceed informally, with frequent interruptions by the arbitrator, and by informed persons on either side, when a point needs clarification. Sometimes there will be arguments across the table, occasionally even within each of the separate camps. The end result will usually be a clarification that will enable everyone to proceed more intelligently with the case.

Such adaptability notwithstanding, neoclassical contracts are not indefinitely elastic. As disturbances become highly consequential, neoclassical contracts experience real strain, because the autonomous ownership status of the parties continuously poses an incentive to defect. The general proposition here is that when the "lawful" gains to be had by insistence upon literal enforcement exceed the discounted value of continuing the exchange relationship, defection from the spirit of the contract can be anticipated.

When, in effect, arbitration gives way to litigation, accommodation can no longer be presumed. Instead, the contract reverts to a much more legalistic regime—although, even here, neoclassical punitive contract law averts truly punitive consequences by permitting appeal to exceptions that qualify under some form of excuse doctrine. The legal system's commitment to the keeping of promises under neoclassical contract law is modest, as Macneil (1974: 731) explained:

. . . contract remedies are generally among the weakest of those the legal system can deliver. But a host of doctrines and techniques lies in the way even of those remedies: impossibility, frustration, mistake, manipulative interpretation, jury discretion, consideration, illegality, duress, undue influence, unconscionability, capacity, forfeiture and penalty rules, doctrines of substantial performance, severability, bankruptcy laws, statutes of frauds, to name some; almost any contract doctrine can and does serve to make the commitment of the legal system to promise keeping less than complete.

From an economic point of view, the tradeoff that needs to be faced in excusing contract performance is between stronger incentives and reduced opportunism. If the state realization in question was unforeseen and unforeseeable (different in degree and/or especially in kind from the range of normal business experience), if strict enforcement would have truly punitive consequences, and especially if the resulting "injustice" is supported by (lawful) opportunism, then excuse can be seen mainly as a way of mitigating opportunism, ideally without adverse impact on incentives. If, however, excuse is granted routinely whenever adversity occurs, then incentives to think through contracts, choose technologies judiciously, share risks efficiently, and avert adversity will be impaired. Excuse doctrine should therefore be used sparingly—which it evidently is (Farnsworth, 1968: 885; Buxbaum, 1985).

The relief afforded by excuse doctrine notwithstanding, neoclassical contracts deal with consequential disturbances only at great cost: arbitration is costly to administer and its adaptive range is limited. As consequential disturbances and, especially, as highly consequential disturbances become more frequent, the hybrid mode supported by arbitration and excuse doctrine incurs added costs and comes under added strain. Even more elastic and adaptive arrangements warrant consideration.

Forbearance. Internal organization, hierarchy, qualifies as a still more elastic and adaptive mode of organization. What type of contract law applies to internal organization? How does this have a bearing on contract performance?

Describing the firm as a "nexus of contracts" (Alchian and Demsetz, 1972; Jensen and Meckling, 1976; Fama, 1980) suggests that the firm is no different from the market in contractual respects. Alchian and Demsetz (1972: 777) originally took the position that the relation between a shopper and his grocer and that between an employer and employee was identical in contractual respects:

The single consumer can assign his grocer to the task of obtaining whatever the customer can induce the grocer to provide at a price acceptable to both parties. That is precisely all that an employer can do to an employee. To speak of managing, directing, or assigning workers to various tasks is a deceptive way of noting that the employer continually is involved in renegotiation of contracts on terms that must be acceptable to both parties. . . . Long-term contracts between employer and employee are not the essence of the organization we call a firm.

That it has been instructive to view the firm as a nexus of contracts is evident from the numerous insights that this literature has generated. But to regard the corporation only as a nexus of contracts misses much of what is truly distinctive about this mode of governance. As developed below, bilateral adaptation effected through fiat is a distinguishing feature of internal organization. But wherein do the fiat differences between market and hierarchy arise? If, moreover, hierarchy enjoys an "advantage" with respect to fiat, why can't the market replicate this?

One explanation is that fiat has its origins in the employment contract (Barnard, 1938; Simon, 1951; Coase, 1952; Masten, 1988). Although there is a good deal to be said for that explanation, I propose a separate and complementary explanation: The implicit contract law of internal organization is that of forbearance. Thus, whereas courts routinely grant standing to firms should there be disputes over prices, the damages to be ascribed to delays, failures of quality, and the like, courts will refuse to hear disputes between one internal division and another over identical technical issues. Access to the courts being denied, the parties must resolve their differences internally. Accordingly, hierarchy is its own court of ultimate appeal.

What is known as the "business judgment rule" holds that "Absent bad faith or some other corrupt motive, directors are normally not liable to the corporation for mistakes of judgment, whether those mistakes are classified as mistakes of fact or mistakes of law" (Gilson, 1986: 741). Not only does that rule serve as "a quasi-jurisdictional barrier to prevent courts from exercising regulatory powers over the activities of corporate managers" (Manne, 1967: 271), but "The courts' abdication of regulatory authority through the business judgment rule may well be the most significant common law contribution to corporate governance" (Gilson, 1986: 741). The business judgment rule, which applies to the relation between shareholders and directors, can be interpreted as a particular manifestation of forbearance doctrine, which applies to the management of the firm more

Comparative Economic Organization

generally. To review alleged mistakes of judgment or to adjudicate internal disputes would sorely test the competence of
courts and would undermine the efficacy of hierarchy.

Accordingly, the reason why the market is unable to replicate the firm with respect to fiat is that market transactions
are defined by contract law of an altogether different kind.
There is a logic to classical market contracting and there is a
logic for forbearance law, and the choice of one regime precludes the other. Whether a transaction is organized as
make or buy—internal procurement or market procurement,
respectively—thus matters greatly in dispute-resolution respects: the courts will hear disputes of the one kind and will
refuse to be drawn into the resolution of disputes of the
other. Internal disputes between one division and another
regarding the appropriate transfer prices, the damages to be
ascribed to delays, failures of quality, and the like, are thus
denied a court hearing.

To be sure, not all disputes within firms are technical. Personnel disputes are more complicated. Issues of worker
safety, dignity, the limits of the "zone of acceptance," and
the like sometimes pose societal spillover costs that are un-
dervalued in the firm's private net benefit calculus. Under-
provision of human and worker rights could ensue if the
courts refused to consider issues of these kinds. Also, executive compensation agreements can sometimes be written
in ways that make it difficult to draw a sharp line between
personnel and technical issues. Even with personnel disputes, however, there is a presumption that such differences will be resolved internally. For example, unions may
refuse to bring individual grievances to arbitration (Cox,
1958: 24):

[G]iving the union control over all claims arising under the collective
agreement comports so much better with the functional nature of a
collective bargaining agreement. . . . Allowing an individual to carry
a claim to arbitration whenever he is dissatisfied with the adjustment worked out by the company and the union . . . discourages
the kind of day-to-day cooperation between company and union
which is normally the mark of sound industrial relations—a relationship in which grievances are treated as problems to be solved and
contracts are only guideposts in a dynamic human relationship.
When . . . the individual's claim endangers group interests, the
union's function is to resolve the competition by reaching an accommodation or striking a balance.

As compared with markets, internal incentives in hierarchies
are flat or low-powered, which is to say that changes in effort expended have little or no immediate effect on compensation. That is mainly because the high-powered incentives
of markets are unavoidably compromised by internal organization (Williamson, 1985, chap. 6; 1988). Also, however, hierarchy uses flat incentives because these elicit greater
cooperation and because unwanted side effects are checked
by added internal controls (see Williamson, 1988; Holmstrom, 1989). Not only, therefore, will workers and managers
be more willing to accommodate, because their compensation is the same whether they "do this" or "do that," but an
unwillingness to accommodate is interpreted not as an excess of zeal but as a predilection to behave in a noncooperative way. Long-term promotion prospects are damaged as a

consequence. Defection from the spirit of the agreement in favor of litigiousness is quite perverse if neither immediate nor long-term gains are thereby realized. The combination of fiat with low-powered incentives is a manifestation of the syndrome condition of economic organization to which I referred earlier (and develop more fully below).

The underlying rationale for forbearance law is twofold: (1) parties to an internal dispute have deep knowledge—both about the circumstances surrounding a dispute as well as the efficiency properties of alternative solutions—that can be communicated to the court only at great cost, and (2) permitting internal disputes to be appealed to the court would undermine the efficacy and integrity of hierarchy. If fiat were merely advisory, in that internal disputes over net receipts could be pursued in the courts, the firm would be little more than an "inside contracting" system (Williamson, 1985: 218–222). The application of forbearance doctrine to internal organization means that parties to an internal exchange can work out their differences themselves or appeal unresolved disputes to the hierarchy for a decision. But this exhausts their alternatives. When push comes to shove, "legalistic" arguments fail. Greater reliance on instrumental reasoning and mutual accommodation result. This argument contradicts Alchian and Demsetz's (1972: 777) claim that the firm "has no power of fiat, no authority, no disciplinary action any different in the slightest degree from ordinary market contracting." That is exactly wrong: firms can and do exercise fiat that markets cannot. Prior neglect of contract law differences and their ramifications explain the error.

First-Order Economizing

Although the need to get priorities straight is unarguable, first-order economizing—effective adaptation and the elimination of waste—has been neglected. Adaptation is especially crucial. As developed below, it is the central economic problem. But as Frank Knight (1941: 252) insisted, the elimination of waste is also important:

. . . men in general, and within limits, wish to behave economically, to make their activities and their organization "efficient" rather than wasteful. This fact does deserve the utmost emphasis; and an adequate definition of the science of economics . . . might well make it explicit that the main relevance of the discussion is found in its relation to social policy, assumed to be directed toward the end indicated, of increasing economic efficiency, of reducing waste.

Relatedly, but independently, Oskar Lange (1938: 109) held that "the real danger of socialism is that of the bureaucratization of economic life, and not the impossibility of coping with the problem of allocation of resources." Inasmuch, however, as Lange (1938: 109) believed that this argument belonged "in the field of sociology" he concluded that it "must be dispensed with here." Subsequent informed observers of socialism followed this lead, whereupon the problems of bureaucracy were, until recently, given scant attention. Instead, the study of socialism was preoccupied with technical features—marginal cost pricing, activity analysis, and the like—with respect to which a broadly sanguine consensus took shape (Bergson, 1948; Montias, 1976; Koopmans, 1977).

Comparative Economic Organization

The natural interpretation of the organizational concerns expressed by Knight and Lange—or, at least, the interpretation that I propose here—is that economics was too preoccupied with issues of allocative efficiency, in which marginal analysis was featured, to the neglect of organizational efficiency, in which discrete structural alternatives were brought under scrutiny. Partly that is because the mathematics for dealing with clusters of attributes is only now beginning to be developed (Topkis, 1978; Milgrom and Roberts, 1990; Holmstrom and Milgrom, 1991). Even more basic, however, is the propensity to focus exclusively on market mechanisms to the neglect of discrete structural alternatives. The argument, for example, that all systems of honest trade are variants on the reputation-effect mechanisms of markets (Milgrom, North, and Weingast, 1990: 16) ignores the possibility that some ways of infusing contractual integrity (e.g., hierarchy) employ altogether different means. Market-favoring predispositions need to be disputed, lest the study of economic organization in all of its forms be needlessly and harmfully truncated.

DIMENSIONALIZING GOVERNANCE

What are the key attributes with respect to which governance structures differ? The discriminating alignment hypothesis to which transaction-cost economics owes much of its predictive content holds that transactions, which differ in their attributes, are aligned with governance structures, which differ in their costs and competencies, in a discriminating (mainly, transaction-cost-economizing) way. But whereas the dimensionalization of transactions received early and explicit attention, the dimensionalization of governance structures has been relatively slighted. What are the factors that are responsible for the aforementioned differential costs and competencies?

One of those key differences has been already indicated: market, hybrid, and hierarchy differ in contract law respects. Indeed, were it the case that the very same type of contract law were to be uniformly applied to all forms of governance, important distinctions between these three generic forms would be vitiated. But there is more to governance than contract law. Crucial differences in adaptability and in the use of incentive and control instruments are also germane.

Adaptation As the Central Economic Problem

Hayek (1945: 523) insistently argued that "economic problems arise always and only in consequence of change" and that this truth was obscured by those who held that "technological knowledge" is of foremost importance. He disputed the latter and urged that "the economic problem of society is mainly one of rapid adaptation in the particular circumstances of time and place" (Hayek, 1945: 524). Of special importance to Hayek was the proposition that the price system, as compared with central planning, is an extraordinarily efficient mechanism for communicating information and inducing change (Hayek, 1945: 524–527).

Interestingly, Barnard (1938) also held that the main concern of organization was that of adaptation to changing circumstances, but his concern was with adaptation within internal organization. Confronted with a continuously fluctuating

environment, the "survival of an organization depends upon
the maintenance of an equilibrium of complex character. . . .
[This] calls for readjustment of processes internal to the organization. . . , [whence] the center of our interest is the processes by which [adaptation] is accomplished" (Barnard,
1938: 6).

That is very curious. Both Hayek and Barnard hold that the
central problem of economic organization is adaptation. But
whereas Hayek locates this adaptive capacity in the market,
it was the adaptive capacity of internal organization on which
Barnard focused attention. If the "marvel of the market"
(Hayek) is matched by the "marvel of internal organization"
(Barnard), then wherein does one outperform the other?

The marvel to which Hayek (1945: 528) referred had spontaneous origins: "The price system is . . . one of those formations which man has learned to use . . . after he stumbled
on it without understanding it." The importance of such
spontaneous cooperation notwithstanding, it was Barnard's
experience that intended cooperation was important and un-
dervalued. The latter was defined as "that kind of cooperation among men that is conscious, deliberate, purposeful"
(Barnard, 1938: 4) and was realized through formal organization, especially hierarchy.

I submit that adaptability is the central problem of economic
organization and that both Hayek and Barnard are correct,
because they are referring to adaptations of different kinds,
both of which are needed in a high-performance system.
The adaptations to which Hayek refers are those for which
prices serve as sufficient statistics. Changes in the demand
or supply of a commodity are reflected in price changes, in
response to which "individual participants . . . [are] able to
take the right action" (Hayek, 1945: 527). I will refer to adaptations of this kind as adaptation (A), where (A) denotes autonomy. This is the neoclassical ideal in which consumers
and producers respond independently to parametric price
changes so as to maximize their utility and profits, respectively.

That would entirely suffice if all disturbances were of this
kind. Some disturbances, however, require coordinated responses, lest the individual parts operate at cross-purposes
or otherwise suboptimize. Failures of coordination may arise
because autonomous parties read and react to signals differently, even though their purpose is to achieve a timely and
compatible combined response, The "nonconvergent
expectations" to which Malmgren (1961) referred is an illustration. Although, in principle, convergent expectations could
be realized by asking one party to read and interpret the signals for all, the lead party may behave strategically—by dis-
torting information or disclosing it in an incomplete and
selective fashion.

More generally, parties that bear a long-term bilateral dependency relation to one another must recognize that incomplete contracts require gapfilling and sometimes get out of
alignment. Although it is always in the collective interest of
autonomous parties to fill gaps, correct errors, and effect
efficient realignments, it is also the case that the distribution
of the resulting gains is indeterminate. Self-interested bargaining predictably obtains. Such bargaining is itself costly.

Comparative Economic Organization

The main costs, however, are that transactions are mal-
adapted to the environment during the bargaining interval.
Also, the prospect of ex post bargaining invites ex ante pre-
positioning of an inefficient kind (Grossman and Hart, 1986).

Recourse to a different mechanism is suggested as the
needs for coordinated investments and for uncontested (or
less contested) coordinated realignments increase in frequency and consequentiality. Adaptations of these coordinated kinds will be referred to as adaptation (C), where (C)
denotes cooperation. The conscious, deliberate, and purposeful efforts to craft adaptive internal coordinating mechanisms were those on which Barnard focused. Independent
adaptations here would at best realize imperfect realignments and could operate at cross-purposes. Lest the aforementioned costs and delays associated with strategic
bargaining be incurred, the relation is reconfigured by sup-
planting autonomy by hierarchy. The authority relation (fiat)
has adaptive advantages over autonomy for transactions of a
bilaterally (or multilaterally) dependent kind.

Instruments

Vertical and lateral integration are usefully thought of as organization forms of last resort, to be employed when all else
fails. That is because markets are a "marvel" in adaptation
(A) respects. Given a disturbance for which prices serve as
sufficient statistics, individual buyers and suppliers can repo-
sition autonomously. Appropriating, as they do, individual
streams of net receipts, each party has a strong incentive to
reduce costs and adapt efficiently. What I have referred to
as high-powered incentives result when consequences are
tightly linked to actions in this way (Williamson, 1988). Other
autonomous traders have neither legitimate claims against
the gains nor can they be held accountable for the losses.
Accounting systems cannot be manipulated to share gains or
subsidize losses.

Matters get more complicated when bilateral dependency
intrudes. As discussed above, bilateral dependency introduces an opportunity to realize gains through hierarchy. As
compared with the market, the use of formal organization to
orchestrate coordinated adaptation to unanticipated disturbances enjoys adaptive advantages as the condition of bilateral dependency progressively builds up. But these
adaptation (C) gains come at a cost. Not only can related divisions within the firm make plausible claims that they are
causally responsible for the gains (in indeterminate degree),
but divisions that report losses can make plausible claims
that others are culpable. There are many ways, moreover, in
which the headquarters can use the accounting system to
effect strategic redistributions (through transfer pricing
changes, overhead assignments, inventory conventions,
etc.), whatever the preferences of the parties. The upshot is
that internal organization degrades incentive intensity, and
added bureaucratic costs result (Williamson, 1985: chap. 6;
1988).

These three features—adaptability of type A, adaptability of
type C, and differential incentive intensity—do not exhaust
the important differences between market and hierarchy.
Also important are the differential reliance on administrative

controls and, as developed above, the different contract law regimes to which each is subject. Suffice it to observe here that (1) hierarchy is buttressed by the differential efficacy of administrative controls within firms, as compared with between firms, and (2) incentive intensity within firms is sometimes deliberately suppressed. Incentive intensity is not an objective but is merely an instrument. If added incentive intensity gets in the way of bilateral adaptability, then weaker incentive intensity supported by added administrative controls (monitoring and career rewards and penalties) can be optimal.

Markets and hierarchies are polar modes. As indicated at the outset, however, a major purpose of this paper is to locate hybrid modes—various forms of long-term contracting, reciprocal trading, regulation, franchising, and the like—in relation to these polar modes. Plainly, the neoclassical contract law of hybrid governance differs from both the classical contract law of markets and the forbearance contract law of hierarchies, being more elastic than the former but more legalistic than the latter. The added question is How do hybrids compare with respect to adaptability (types A and C), incentive intensity, and administrative control?

The hybrid mode displays intermediate values in all four features. It preserves ownership autonomy, which elicits strong incentives and encourages adaptation to type A disturbances (those to which one party can respond efficiently without consulting the other). Because there is bilateral dependency, however, long-term contracts are supported by added contractual safeguards and administrative apparatus (information disclosure, dispute-settlement machinery). These facilitate adaptations of type C but come at the cost of incentive attenuation. Concerns for "equity" intrude. Thus the Nevada Power Company–Northwest Trading Company coal contract, whose adaptation mechanics were set out above, begins with the following: "It is the intent of the Parties hereto that this agreement, as a whole and in all of its parts, shall be equitable to both Parties throughout its term." Such efforts unavoidably dampen incentive-intensity features.

One advantage of hierarchy over the hybrid with respect to bilateral adaptation is that internal contracts can be more incomplete. More importantly, adaptations to consequential disturbances are less costly within firms because (1) proposals to adapt require less documentation, (2) resolving internal disputes by fiat rather than arbitration saves resources and facilitates timely adaptation, (3) information that is deeply impacted can more easily be accessed and more accurately assessed, (4) internal dispute resolution enjoys the support of informal organization (Barnard, 1938; Scott, 1987), and (5) internal organization has access to additional incentive instruments—including especially career reward and joint profit sharing—that promote a team orientation. Furthermore, highly consequential disturbances that would occasion breakdown or costly litigation under the hybrid mode can be accommodated more easily. The advantages of hierarchy over hybrid in adaptation C respects are not, however, realized without cost. Weaker incentive intensity (greater bureaucratic costs) attend the move from hybrid to hierarchy, ceteris paribus.

Comparative Economic Organization

Summarizing, the hybrid mode is characterized by semi-strong incentives, an intermediate degree of administrative apparatus, displays semi-strong adaptations of both kinds, and works out of a semi-legalistic contract law regime. As compared with market and hierarchy, which are polar opposites, the hybrid mode is located between the two of these in all five attribute respects. Based on the foregoing, and denoting strong, semi-strong, and weak by + +, +, and 0, respectively, the instruments, adaptive attributes, and contract law features that distinguish markets, hybrids, and hierarchies are shown in Table 1.

Table 1

Distinguishing Attributes of Market, Hybrid, and Hierarchy Governance Structures*

Attributes		Governance structure	
	Market	Hybrid	Hierarchy
Instruments			
Incentive intensity	+ +	+	0
Administrative controls	0	+	+ +
Performance attributes			
Adaptation (A)	+ +	+	0
Adaptation (C)	0	+	+ +
Contract law	+ +	+	0

* + + = strong; + = semi-strong; 0 = weak.

DISCRIMINATING ALIGNMENT

Transaction-cost economics subscribes to Commons' view (1924, 1934) that the transaction is the basic unit of analysis. That important insight takes on operational significance upon identifying the critical dimensions with respect to which transactions differ. Without purporting to be exhaustive, these include the frequency with which transactions recur, the uncertainty to which transactions are subject, and the type and degree of asset specificity involved in supplying the good or service in question (Williamson, 1979). Although all are important, transaction-cost economics attaches special significance to this last (Williamson, 1975, 1979; Klein, Crawford, and Alchian, 1978; Grossman and Hart, 1986).

Asset specificity has reference to the degree to which an asset can be redeployed to alternative uses and by alternative users without sacrifice of productive value. Asset-specificity distinctions of six kinds have been made: (1) site specificity, as where successive stations are located in a cheek-by-jowl relation to each other so as to economize on inventory and transportation expenses; (2) physical asset specificity, such as specialized dies that are required to produce a component; (3) human-asset specificity that arises in learning by doing; (4) brand name capital; (5) dedicated assets, which are discrete investments in general purpose plant that are made at the behest of a particular customer; and (6) temporal specificity, which is akin to technological nonseparability and can be thought of as a type of site specificity in which timely responsiveness by on-site human assets is vital (Masten, Meehan, and Snyder, 1991). Asset specificity, especially in its first five forms, creates bilateral dependency and poses added contracting hazards. It has played a central role in the conceptual and empirical work in transaction-cost economics.

The analysis here focuses entirely on transaction costs: neither the revenue consequences nor the production-cost savings that result from asset specialization are included. Although that simplifies the analysis, note that asset specificity increases the transaction costs of all forms of governance. Such added specificity is warranted only if these added governance costs are more than offset by production-cost savings and/or increased revenues. A full analysis will necessarily make allowance for effects of all three kinds (Riordan and Williamson, 1985). Only a truncated analysis appears here.

Reduced-Form Analysis

The governance-cost expressions set out herein are akin to reduced forms, in that governance costs are expressed as a function of asset specificity and a set of exogenous variables. The structural equations from which these reduced forms are derived are not set out. The key features that are responsible for cost differences among governance structures are nonetheless evident in the matrix version of the model set out below.[1]

Although asset specificity can take a variety of forms, the common consequence is this: a condition of bilateral dependency builds up as asset specificity deepens. The ideal transaction in law and economics—whereby the identities of buyers and sellers is irrelevant—obtains when asset specificity is zero. Identity matters as investments in transaction-specific assets increase, since such specialized assets lose productive value when redeployed to best alternative uses and by best alternative users.

Assume, for simplicity, that asset specificity differences are entirely due to physical or site specificity features. I begin with the situation in which classical market contracting works well: autonomous actors adapt effectively to exogenous disturbances. Internal organization is at a disadvantage for transactions of this kind, since hierarchy incurs added bureaucratic costs to which no added benefits can be ascribed. That, however, changes as bilateral dependency sets in. Disturbances for which coordinated responses are required become more numerous and consequential as investments in asset specificity deepen. The high-powered incentives of markets here impede adaptability, since each party to an autonomous exchange that has gotten out of alignment and for which mutual consent is needed to effect an adjustment will want to appropriate as much as possible (ideally, all but epsilon) of the adaptive gains to be realized. When bilaterally dependent parties are unable to respond quickly and easily, because of disagreements and self-interested bargaining, maladaptation costs are incurred. Although the transfer of such transactions from market to hierarchy creates added bureaucratic costs, those costs may be more than offset by the bilateral adaptive gains that result.

1
Developing the deeper structure that supports the reduced forms—by explicating contractual incompleteness and its consequences in a more microanalytic way and by developing the bureaucratic cost consequences of internal organization more explicitly—is an ambitious but important undertaking.

Let M = M($k;\theta$) and H = H($k;\theta$) be reduced-form expressions that denote market and hierarchy governance costs as a function of asset specificity (k) and a vector of shift parameters (θ). Assuming that each mode is constrained to choose the same level of asset specificity, the following comparative-cost relations obtain: M(0) < H(0) and M' > H' > 0.[2] The first of these two inequalities reflects the fact that the bureaucratic costs of internal organization exceed those of the market because the latter is superior in adaptation (A) respects—which is the only kind that matters if asset specificity is negligible. The intercept for market governance is thus lower than is the intercept for hierarchy. The second inequality reflects the marginal disability of markets as compared with hierarchies in adaptation (C) respects as asset specificity, hence bilateral dependency, becomes more consequential.

As described above, the hybrid mode is located between market and hierarchy with respect to incentives, adaptability, and bureaucratic costs. As compared with the market, the hybrid sacrifices incentives in favor of superior coordination among the parts. As compared with the hierarchy, the hybrid sacrifices cooperativeness in favor of greater incentive intensity. The distribution of branded product from retail outlets by market, hierarchy, and hybrid, where franchising is an example of this last, illustrates the argument.

Forward integration out of manufacturing into distribution would be implied by hierarchy. That would sacrifice incentive intensity but would (better) assure that the parts do not operate at cross-purposes with one another. The market solution would be to sell the good or service outright. Incentive intensity is thereby harnessed, but suboptimization (free riding on promotional efforts, dissipation of the brand name, etc.) may also result. Franchising awards greater autonomy than hierarchy but places franchisees under added rules and surveillance as compared with markets. Cost control and local adaptations are stronger under franchising than hierarchy, and suboptimization is reduced under franchising as compared with the market. The added autonomy (as compared with hierarchy) and the added restraints (as compared with the market) under which franchisees operate nevertheless come at a cost. If, for example, quality assurance is realized by constraining the franchisee to use materials supplied by the franchisor, and if exceptions to that practice are not permitted because of the potential for abuse that would result, then local opportunities to make "apparently" cost-effective procurements will be prohibited. Similarly, the added local autonomy enjoyed by franchisees may get in the way of some global adjustments.

Transactions for which the requisite adaptations to disturbances are neither predominantly autonomous nor bilateral, but require a mixture of each, are candidates to be organized under the hybrid mode. Over some intermediate range of k, the mixed adaptation (A/C) that hybrids afford could well be superior to the A-favoring or C-favoring adaptations supported by markets and hierarchies, respectively.

Letting X = X($k;\theta$) denote the governance costs of the hybrid mode as a function of asset specificity, the argument is

2
A more general optimizing treatment in which the level of asset specificity varies with organization form is set out in Riordan and Williamson (1985). Also see Masten (1982).

that $M(0) < X(0) < H(0)$ and that $M' > X' > H' > 0.$[3] The relations shown in Figure 1 then obtain. Efficient supply implies operating on the envelope, whence, if k^* is the optimal value of k, the rule for efficient supply is as follows: I, use markets for $k^* < \overline{k}_1$; II, use hybrids for $\overline{k}_1 < k^* < \overline{k}_2$; and III, use hierarchy for $k^* > \overline{k}_2$.

Figure 1. Governance costs as a function of asset specificity.

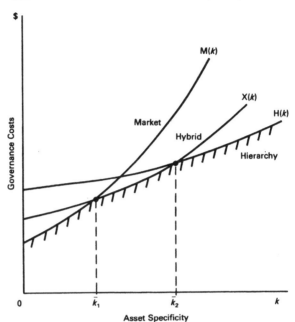

In a very heuristic way, moreover, one can think of moving along one of these generic curves as moving toward more intrusive controls. Thus, consider two forms of franchising, one of which involves less control than the other. If $X^1(k)$ and $X^2(k)$ refer to franchising with little and much control, respectively, then $X^2(k)$ will be located to the right of $X^1(k)$ in Figure 2. Or consider the M-form (multidivisional) and U-form (unitary or functionally organized) corporation. Because the former provides more market-like divisionalization than does the latter, the M-form is given by $H^1(k)$ and is located closer to $\overline{k}_2$ in Figure 2.

A Matrix Representation

Suppose that disturbances are distinguished in terms of the type of response—autonomous or bilateral—that is needed to effect an adaptation. Suppose further that the type of adaptation depends on the degree of asset specificity. Let asset specificity be denoted by k_j and suppose that it can take on any of three values: $k_1 = 0$ (generic investment), $k_2 > 0$ (semi-specific investment), or $k_3 \gg 0$ (highly specific investment). Assume that adjustments to disturbances can be any

3
This assumes that X(0) is less than H(0) to a nontrivial degree, since otherwise the hybrid mode could be dominated throughout by the least-cost choice of either market or hierarchy, which may occur for certain classes of transactions, as discussed below.

Comparative Economic Organization

Figure 2. Governance differences within discrete structural forms.

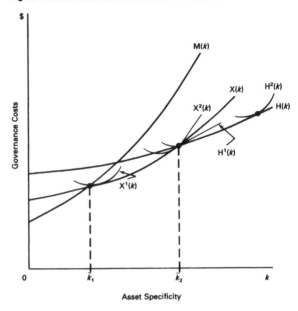

Asset Specificity

of four kinds: I, strictly autonomous; II, mainly autonomous; III, mainly coordinated; or IV, strictly coordinated. Let p_{ij} be the probability that an adaptation of type $i = $ I, II, . . . , IV will be required if asset-specificity condition k_j ($j = 1, 2, 3$) obtains and let the matrix $[p_{ij}]$ be given by

		k_1	k_2	k_3
	I	1.00	.25	.10
$[p_{ij}]$:	II	.00	.25	.10
	III	.00	.25	.40
	IV	.00	.25	.40

Note that, the k_1 column excepted, positive probability is associated with every element in the matrix. What added asset specificity does is shift the distribution of required responses in favor of greater cooperativeness.

Assume that each adaptation, if costlessly and successfully implemented, would yield identical expected cost savings. For the reasons given above, however, the efficacy with which different modes adapt to disturbances of different kinds varies. Let e_{im} be the efficacy with which mode m (m = M, X, H) is able to implement adaptations of type i ($i = $ I, II, . . . , IV) and assume that the matrix e_{im} is given by

		M	X	H
	I	1.0	0.9	0.7
$[e_{im}]$:	II	0.7	0.9	0.4
	III	0.2	0.5	0.5
	IV	-0.2	0.0	0.5

where 1.0 is the ideal degree of adaptiveness and 0.0 is equivalent (in terms of efficacy) to no adaptation.

The efficacy assumptions embedded in this last matrix warrant remark: (1) Only the entry e_{IM} has a value of 1.0. This condition—market adaptations to a disturbance for which strictly autonomous adaptation is appropriate—corresponds to the ideal transaction in law and economics (classical market contracting); (2) The efficacy of the market falls off as bilateral dependency builds up, becoming negative (worse than no adaptation at all) for the strictly cooperative case (IV). This last reflects the conflictual nature of market exchange for transactions of the bilaterally dependent kind; (3) The hybrid mode is almost as good as the market for strictly autonomous adaptations, is better than the market in all other adaptation categories, and is as good or better than hierarchy in all categories save that for which strict coordination is indicated; (4) Hierarchy is burdened by bureaucracy and never scores high in efficacy for any category of adaptation.[4] What matters, however, is comparative efficacy. The hierarchy comes into its own (comparatively) where adaptations of a strictly cooperative kind are needed; and (5) The efficacy of hierarchy is lowest for disturbances requiring a mainly autonomous adaptation. As compared with strictly autonomous disturbances, where bureaucratic costs are held in check by an objective market standard, ready recourse to the market is compromised by the need for some coordination. Because, however, the gains from coordination are not great, efforts to coordinate are problematic. If efforts to adapt autonomously are protested (my costs are greater because you moved without consulting me) while failures to adapt quickly are costly, the hierarchy is caught between the proverbial rock and a hard place.

Let C_{jm} be the expected maladaptation costs of using mode m to effect adaptations if asset specificity is of type k_j. Since inefficacy is given by $1 - e_{jm}$, the expected maladaptation costs are $C_{jm} = \Sigma_i\, p_{ij} (1 - e_{im})$. That matrix is given by

		M	X	H
$[C_{jm}]$:	k_1	.000	.100	.300
	k_2	.575	.425	.475
	k_3	.830	.620	.490

The lowest values in each row are realized by matching market, hybrid, and hierarchy with asset specificity conditions k_1, k_2, and k_3, respectively. These costs are consonant with the reduced-form relations shown in Figure 1. Thus if $\beta \geq 0$ is the irreducible setup costs of economic participation, then the bureaucratic cost intercepts associated with zero asset specificity (k_1) for market, hybrid, and hierarchy will be given by β plus .000, .100, and .300, respectively. Also, the relation between the implied slopes associated with each mode in the matrix (expressed as a function of asset specificity) is that $M' > X' > H'$, which corresponds exactly to the relations shown in Figure 1.

COMPARATIVE STATICS

Transaction-cost economics maintains that (1) transaction-cost economizing is the "main case," which is not to be confused with the only case (Williamson, 1985: 22–23; 1989: 137–138), and (2) transaction costs vary with governance structures in the manner described above. Assuming

---

4
Hierarchy is able to deal with type I (strictly autonomous) disturbances reasonably well by instructing the operating parts to respond to local disturbances on their own motion and by using the market as an alternate source of supply and/or standard.

that the institutional environment is unchanging, transactions should be clustered under governance structures as indicated. Variance will be observed, but the main case should be as described.

The purpose of this section is to consider how equilibrium distributions of transactions will change in response to disturbances in the institutional environment. That is a comparative static exercise. Both parts of the new institutional economics—the institutional environment and the institutions of governance—are implicated. The crucial distinctions are these (Davis and North, 1971: 6–7):

The *institutional environment* is the set of fundamental political, social and legal ground rules that establishes the basis for production, exchange and distribution. Rules governing elections, property rights, and the right of contract are examples. . . .

An *institutional arrangement* is an arrangement between economic units that governs the ways in which these units can cooperate and/or compete. It . . . [can] provide a structure within which its members can cooperate . . . or [it can] provide a mechanism that can effect a change in laws or property rights.

The way that I propose to join these two is to treat the institutional environment as a set of parameters, changes in which elicit shifts in the comparative costs of governance. An advantage of a three-way setup—market, hybrid, and hierarchy (as compared with just market and hierarchy)—is that much larger parameter changes are required to induce a shift from market to hierarchy (or the reverse) than are required to induce a shift from market to hybrid or from hybrid to hierarchy. Indeed, as developed below, much of the comparative static action turns on differential shifts in the intercept and/or slope of the hybrid mode. The critical predictive action is that which is located in the neighborhood of $\bar{k}_1$ (M to X) and $\bar{k}_2$ (X to H) in Figure 1. Parameter changes of four kinds are examined: property rights, contract law, reputation effects, and uncertainty.

Among the limitations of the discrete structural approach is that parameter changes need to be introduced in a special way. Rather than investigate the effects of increases (or decreases) in a parameter (a wage rate, a tax, a shift in demand), as is customary with the usual maximizing setup, the comparative governance cost setup needs to characterize parameter changes as improvements (or not). It is furthermore limited by the need for these improvements to be concentrated disproportionately on one generic mode of governance. Those limitations notwithstanding, it is informative to examine comparative static effects.

Property Rights

What has come to be known as the economics of property rights holds that economic performance is largely determined by the way in which property rights are defined. Ownership of assets is especially pertinent to the definition of property rights, where this "consists of three elements: (a) the right to use the asset [and delimitations that apply thereto] . . . , (b) the right to appropriate returns from the asset . . . , and (c) the right to change the asset's form and/or substance" (Furubotn and Pejovich, 1974: 4).

Most discussions of property rights focus on definitional issues. As is generally conceded, property rights can be costly
to define and enforce and hence arise only when the expected benefits exceed the expected costs (Demsetz, 1967).
That is not my concern here. Rather, I focus on the degree
to which property rights, once assigned, have good security
features. Security hazards of two types are pertinent: expropriation by the government and expropriation by commerce
(rivals, suppliers, customers).

Governmental expropriation. Issues of "credible
commitments" (Williamson, 1983) and "security of
expectations" (Michelman, 1967) are pertinent to expropriation by the government. If property rights could be efficiently
assigned once and for all, so that assignments, once made,
would not subsequently be undone—especially strategically
undone—governmental expropriation concerns would not
arise. Firms and individuals would confidently invest in productive assets without concern that they would thereafter
be deprived of their just desserts.

If, however, property rights are subject to occasional reas-
signment, and if compensation is not paid on each occasion
(possibly because it is prohibitively costly), then strategic
considerations enter the investment calculus. Wealth will be
reallocated (disguised, deflected, consumed) rather than invested in potentially expropriable assets if expropriation is
perceived to be a serious hazard. More generally, individuals
or groups who either experience or observe expropriation
and can reasonably anticipate that they will be similarly disadvantaged in the future have incentives to adapt.

Michelman (1967) focused on cost-effective compensation.
He argued that if compensation is costly and if the "demoralization costs" experienced by disadvantaged individuals
and interested observers are slight, then compensation is
not needed. If, however, demoralization costs can be expected to be great and losses can be easily ascertained,
compensation is warranted. Michelman proposed a series of
criteria by which to judge how this calculus works out. Suppose that the government is advised of these concerns and
"promises" to respect the proposed criteria. Will such promises be believed? This brings us to the problem of credible
commitments.

Promises are easy to make, but credible promises are another thing. Kornai's (1986: 1705–1706) observation that
craftsmen and small shopkeepers fear expropriation in Hun-
gary despite "repeated official declarations that their activity
is regarded as a permanent feature of Hungarian socialism"
is pertinent. That "many of them are myopic profit maximizers, not much interested in building up lasting goodwill . . .
or by investing in long-lived fixed assets" (1986: 1706) is
partly explained by the fact that "These individuals or their
parents lived through the era of confiscations in the forties"
(Kornai, 1986: 1705).

But there is more to it than that. Not only is there a history
of expropriation, but, as of 1986, the structure of the government had not changed in such a way as to assuredly forestall subsequent expropriations. Official declarations will be
more credible only with long experience or if accompanied

Comparative Economic Organization

by a credible (not easily reversible) reorganization of politics. As one Polish entrepreneur recently remarked, "I don't want expensive machines. If the situation changes, I'll get stuck with them" (Newman, 1989: A10). Note, in this connection, that the objectivity of law is placed in jeopardy if the law and its enforcement are under the control of a one-party state (Berman, 1983: 37). Credibility will be enhanced if a monarch who has made the law "may not make it arbitrarily, and until he has remade it—lawfully—he is bound by it" (Berman, 1983: 9). Self-denying ordinances and, even more, inertia that has been crafted into the political process have commitment benefits (North and Weingast, 1989).

That this has not fully registered on Eastern Europe and the Soviet Union is suggested by the following remarks of Mikhail Gorbachev (advising U.S. firms to invest quickly in the Soviet Union rather than wait): "Those [companies] who are with us now have good prospects of participating in our great country . . . [whereas those who wait] will remain observers for years to come—*we will see to it*" (*International Herald Tribune*, 1990: 5). That the leadership of the Soviet Union "will see to it" that early and late movers will be rewarded and punished, respectively, reflects conventional carrot-and-stick incentive reasoning. What it misses is that ready access to administrative discretion is the source of contractual hazard. The paradox is that fewer degrees of freedom (rules) can have advantages over more (discretion) because added credible commitments can obtain in this way. Effective economic reform thus requires that reneging options be foreclosed if investor confidence is to be realized.

Lack of credible commitment on the part of the government poses hazards for durable, immobile investments of all kinds—specialized and unspecialized alike—in the private sector. If durability and immobility are uncorrelated with asset specificity, then the transaction costs of all forms of private-sector governance increase together as expropriation hazards increase. In that event, the values of $\bar{k}_1$ and $\bar{k}_2$ might then change little or not at all. What can be said with assurance is that the government sector will have to bear a larger durable investment burden in a regime in which expropriation risks are perceived to be great. Also, private-sector durable investments will favor assets that can be smuggled or are otherwise mobile—such as general-purpose human assets (skilled machinists, physicians) that can be used productively if emigration is permitted to other countries.

Leakage. Not only may property rights be devalued by governments, but the value of specialized knowledge and information may be appropriated and/or dissipated by suppliers, buyers, and rivals. The issues here have recently been addressed by Teece (1986) in conjunction with "weak regimes of appropriability" and are related to earlier discussions by Arrow (1962) regarding property rights in information. If investments in knowledge cannot lawfully be protected or if nominal protection (e.g., a patent) is ineffective, then (1) the ex ante incentives to make such investments are impaired and (2) the ex post incentives to embed such investments in protective governance structures are increased. As Teece (1986) discussed, vertical or lateral integration into related stages of production where the hazards of leakage are greatest is sometimes undertaken for precisely these protective purposes. Trade secret protection is an example.

Interpreted in terms of the comparative governance cost apparatus employed here, weaker appropriability (increased risk of leakage) increases the cost of hybrid contracting as compared with hierarchy. The market and hybrid curves in Figure 1 are both shifted up by increased leakage, so that $\bar{k}_1$ remains approximately unchanged and the main effects are concentrated at $\bar{k}_2$. The value of $\bar{k}_2$ thus shifts to the left as leakage hazards increase, so that the distribution of transactions favors greater reliance on hierarchy.

Contract Law

Improvements or not in a contract law regime can be judged by how the relevant governance-cost curve shifts. An improvement in excuse doctrine, for example, would shift the cost of hybrid governance down. The idea here is that excuse doctrine can be either too lax or too strict. If too strict, then parties will be reluctant to make specialized investments in support of one another because of the added risk of truly punitive outcomes should unanticipated events materialize and the opposite party insist that the letter of the contract be observed. If too lax, then incentives to think through contracts, choose technologies judiciously, share risks efficiently, and avert adversity will be impaired.

Whether a change in excuse doctrine is an improvement or not depends on the initial conditions and on how these trade-offs play out. Assuming that an improvement is introduced, the effect will be to lower the cost of hybrid contracting—especially at higher values of asset specificity, where a defection from the spirit of the contract is more consequential. The effect of such improvements would be to increase the use of hybrid contracting, especially as compared with hierarchy.

Hadfield (1990: 981–982) has recently examined franchise law and has interpreted the prevailing tendency by the courts to fill in the gaps of an incomplete contract "by according the franchisor unfettered discretion, much as it would enjoy if it [the franchisor] were a vertically integrated corporation" as a mistaken application of forbearance reasoning from hierarchy (where the logic holds) to neoclassical contracting (where the logic fails). Such a failure of franchise law would increase the cost of franchising in relation to forward integration into distribution (Hadfield, 1990: 954). This would imply a shift in the value of $\bar{k}_2$ in Figure 1 to the left.

A change in forbearance doctrine would be reflected in the governance cost of hierarchy. Thus, mistaken forbearance doctrine—for example, a willingness by the courts to litigate intrafirm technical disputes—would have the effect of shifting the costs of hierarchical governance up. This would disadvantage hierarchy in relation to hybrid modes of contracting ($\bar{k}_2$ would shift to the right).

Reputation Effects

One way of interpreting a network is as a nonhierarchical contracting relation in which reputation effects are quickly

Comparative Economic Organization

and accurately communicated. Parties to a transaction to which reputation effects apply can consult not only their own experience but can benefit from the experience of others. To be sure, the efficacy of reputation effects is easily overstated (Williamson, 1991b), but comparative efficacy is all that concerns us here and changes in comparative efficacy can often be established.

Thus, assume that it is possible to identify a community of traders in which reputation effects work better (or worse). Improved reputation effects attenuate incentives to behave opportunistically in interfirm trade—since the immediate gains from opportunism in a regime where reputation counts must be traded off against future costs. The hazards of opportunism in interfirm trading are greatest for hybrid transactions—especially those in the neighborhood of $\bar{k}_2$. Since an improvement in interfirm reputation effects will reduce the cost of hybrid contracting, the value of $\bar{k}_2$ will shift to the right. Hybrid contracting will therefore increase, in relation to hierarchy, in regimes where interfirm reputation effects are more highly perfected, ceteris paribus. Reputation effects are pertinent within firms as well. If internal reputation effects improve, then managerial opportunism will be reduced and the costs of hierarchical governance will fall.

Ethnic communities that display solidarity often enjoy advantages of a hybrid contracting kind. Reputations spread quickly within such communities and added sanctions are available to the membership (Light, 1972). Such ethnic communities will predictably displace nonethnic communities for activities for which interfirm reputation effects are important. Nonethnic communities, to be viable, will resort to market or hierarchy (in a lower or higher k niche, respectively).

Uncertainty

Greater uncertainty could take either of two forms. One is that the probability distribution of disturbances remains unchanged but that more numerous disturbances occur. A second is that disturbances become more consequential (due, for example, to an increase in the variance).

One way of interpreting changes of either kind is through the efficacy matrix, above. I conjecture that the effects of more frequent disturbances are especially pertinent for those disturbances for which mainly coordinated or strictly coordinated responses are required. Although the efficacy of all forms of governance may deteriorate in the face of more frequent disturbances, the hybrid mode is arguably the most susceptible. That is because hybrid adaptations cannot be made unilaterally (as with market governance) or by fiat (as with hierarchy) but require mutual consent. Consent, however, takes time. If a hybrid mode is negotiating an adjustment to one disturbance only to be hit by another, failures of adaptation predictably obtain (Ashby, 1960). An increase in market and hierarchy and a decrease in hybrid will thus be associated with an (above threshold) increase in the frequency of disturbances. As shown in Figure 3, the hybrid mode could well become nonviable when the frequency of disturbances reaches high levels.[5]

5
The range of asset specificity is from zero (purely generic) to complete (purely firm-specific). The range of frequency is from "low" (a positive lower bound in a nearly unchanging environment) to "very high."

Figure 3. Organization form responses to changes in frequency.

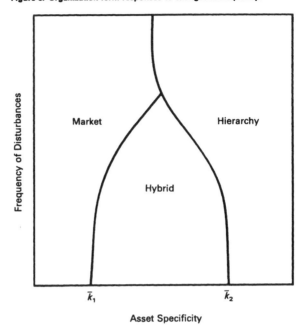

Asset Specificity

If an increase in the variance of the disturbances uniformly increases the benefits to be associated with each successful adaptation, then the effect of increasing the consequentiality of disturbances can again be assessed through the effects on efficacy. Since outliers induce greater defection on the spirit of the agreement for hybrid modes, the efficacy of the hybrid is adversely affected by added variance. Unless similar disabilities can be ascribed to market or hierarchy, the hybrid is disfavored by greater variance, ceteris paribus.

DISCUSSION

The foregoing is concerned with the organization of transactions for mature goods and services and introduces parameter shifts one at a time. Added complications arise when innovation is introduced and when a series of parameter shifts occur together.

Innovation

Some of the added problems posed by innovation take the form of weak property rights. These are discussed above in conjunction with leakage. A second class of problems that confront innovation is that of timeliness. Nonstandard forms of organization, such as parallel R&D (Nelson, 1961) and joint ventures, are sometimes employed because these facilitate timely entry.

Timing can be crucial if a party expects to be a "player" when events are fast-moving or if learning-by-doing is essential. Although transaction-cost economics can relate to some

of the pertinent issues, such as those posed by tacit knowledge (Polanyi, 1962) and the limits of imitation (Williamson,
1975: 31–32, 203–207), added apparatus is needed to deal
with the full set of issues that arise when responsiveness in
real time, rather than equilibrium contracting, is the central
concern. Awaiting such developments, the apparatus developed here should not be applied uncritically. For example,
joint ventures are sometimes described as hybrids. If, however, joint ventures are temporary forms of organization that
support quick responsiveness, and if that is their primary purpose, then both successful and unsuccessful joint ventures
will commonly be terminated when contracts expire. Successful joint ventures will be terminated because success
will often mean that each of the parties, who chose not to
merge but, instead, decided to combine their respective
strengths in a selective and timely way, will have learned
enough to go it alone. Unsuccessful joint ventures will be
terminated because the opportunity to participate will have
passed them by. Joint ventures that are designed to give a
respite should be distinguished from the types of hybrid
modes analyzed here, which are of an equilibrium kind.

The need to distinguish continuing from temporary supply
does not, however, mean that transaction-cost economizing
principles do not apply to each. To the contrary, although the
particulars differ, I would urge that the same general transaction-cost economizing framework has application (Williamson, 1985). The quasi-firms described by Eccles (1981), for
example, can be interpreted as the efficient solution to a particular type of recurrent contracting problem. But the details
do matter.

Simultaneous Parameter Shifts

The comparative static analysis set out above treats each
generic form of organization as a syndrome of attributes and
introduces parameter shifts one at a time. Suppose, instead,
that a series of shifts were to occur together. Could these
be processed as a sequence of independent changes? If
such changes were in fact independent, that is precisely
what I would propose. If, however, a related set of changes
is made simultaneously, it will not do to treat these independently. If strong interaction effects exist, these must be
treated as a cluster.

Relying extensively on the recent work of Aoki (1988, 1990),
I have elsewhere interpreted the Japanese corporation as
follows: (1) three key factors—employment, subcontracting,
and banking—are fundamentally responsible for the success
of the Japanese firm; (2) the efficacy of each of these rests
on distinctive institutional supports; and (3) the three factors
bear a complementary relation to each other (Williamson,
1991a).

The search for key factors and their institutional supports is
wholly consistent with the spirit of this paper. Because employment, subcontracting, and banking changes are linked,
however, the American corporation cannot expect to replicate the Japanese corporation by making changes in only
one of these practices and not in the others. That is not to

say that American firms cannot learn by observing subcontracting practices in Japanese firms. Exact replication of individual practices will be suboptimal, however, if linkages are important.

Similar considerations apply to economic reforms in China and Eastern Europe. If, for example, the efficacy of privatization turns crucially on the manner in which banking is organized and on the security of property rights, then piecemeal proposals that ignore the support institutions are fraught with hazard. The study of viable clusters of organization is a combined law, economics, and organizations undertaking. Although the apparatus in this paper is pertinent, applications to economic reform need to make express provision for contextual differences between alternative forms of capitalism (Hamilton and Biggart, 1988).

CONCLUSION

This paper advances the transaction-cost economics research agenda in the following five respects: (1) the economic problem of society is described as that of adaptation, of which autonomous and coordinated kinds are distinguished; (2) each generic form of governance is shown to rest on a distinctive form of contract law, of which the contract law of forbearance, which applies to internal organization and supports fiat, is especially noteworthy; (3) the hybrid form of organization is not a loose amalgam of market and hierarchy but possesses its own disciplined rationale; (4) more generally, the logic of each generic form of governance—market, hybrid, and hierarchy—is revealed by the dimensionalization and explication of governance herein developed; and (5) the obviously related but hitherto disjunct stages of institutional economics—the institutional environment and the institutions of governance—are joined by interpreting the institutional environment as a locus of shift parameters, changes in which parameters induce shifts in the comparative costs of governance. A large number of refutable implications are derived from the equilibrium and comparative static analyses of governance that result. The growing empirical literature, moreover, is broadly corroborative (for summaries, see Williamson, 1985: chap. 5; Joskow, 1988; Shelanski, 1990).

Further developments of conceptual, theoretical, and empirical kinds are needed. Taken together with related developments in information economics, agency theory, and population ecology, there is reason to be optimistic that a "new science of organization" will take shape during the decade of the 1990s (Williamson, 1990). Whether that materializes or not, organization theory is being renewed in law, economics, and organizational respects. These are exciting times for interdisciplinary social theory.

REFERENCES

Alchian, Armen, and Harold Demsetz
1972 "Production, information costs, and economic organization." American Economic Review, 62: 777–795.

Aoki, Masahiko
1988 Information, Incentives, and Bargaining in the Japanese Economy. New York: Cambridge University Press.

1990 "Toward an economic model of the Japanese firm." Journal of Economic Literature, 28: 1–27.

Comparative Economic Organization

Arrow, Kenneth J.
1962 "Economic welfare and the allocation of resources of invention." In National Bureau of Economic Research (ed.), The Rate and Direction of Inventive Activity: Economic and Social Factors: 609–625. Princeton, NJ: Princeton University Press.
1969 "The organization of economic activity: Issues pertinent to the choice of market versus nonmarket allocation." In The Analysis and Evaluation of Public Expenditure, Vol. 1: The PPB System: 59–73. U.S. Joint Economic Committee, 91st Congress, 1st Session. Washington, DC: U.S. Government Printing Office.

Ashby, W. Ross
1960 Design for a Brain. New York: Wiley.

Barnard, Chester
1938 The Functions of the Executive. Cambridge, MA: Harvard University Press.

Bergson, Abram
1948 "Socialist economics." In Howard Ellis (ed.), Survey of Contemporary Economics: 430–458. Philadelphia: Blakiston.

Berman, Harold
1983 Law and Revolution. Cambridge, MA: Harvard University Press.

Buxbaum, Richard M.
1985 "Modification and adaptation of contracts: American legal developments." Studies in Transnational Economic Law, 3: 31–54.

Chandler, Alfred D., Jr.
1962 Strategy and Structure. Cambridge, MA: MIT Press.
1977 The Visible Hand: The Managerial Revolution in American Business. Cambridge, MA: Harvard University Press.

Clausewitz, Karl von
1980 Vom Kriege, 19th ed. (Originally published in 1832.) Bonn: Dremmler.

Coase, R. H.
1952 "The nature of the firm." In George J. Stigler and Kenneth E. Boulding (eds.), Readings in Price Theory: 331–351. Homewood, IL: Irwin.

Commons, John R.
1924 "Law and economics." Yale Law Journal, 34: 371–382.
1934 Institutional Economics. Madison, WI: University of Wisconsin Press.

Cox, Archibald
1958 "The legal nature of collective bargaining agreements." Michigan Law Review, 57: 1–36.

Davis, Lance E., and Douglass C. North
1971 Institutional Change and American Economic Growth. Cambridge: Cambridge University Press.

Demsetz, Harold
1967 "Toward a theory of property rights." American Economic Review, 57: 347–359.

Eccles, Robert
1981 "The quasifirm in the construction industry." Journal of Economic Behavior and Organization, 2: 335–357.

Fama, Eugene F.
1980 "Agency problems and the theory of the firm." Journal of Political Economy, 88: 288–307.

Farnsworth, Edward Allan
1968 "Disputes over omissions in contracts." Columbia Law Review, 68: 860–891.

Fuller, Lon L.
1963 "Collective bargaining and the arbitrator." Wisconsin Law Review, January: 3–46.

Furubotn, Eirik, and Svetozar Pejovich
1974 The Economics of Property Rights. Cambridge, MA: Ballinger.

Gilson, Ronald
1986 The Law and Finance of Corporate Acquisitions. Mineola, NY: Foundation Press.

Goldberg, Victor
1976 "Regulation and administered contracts." Bell Journal of Economics, 7: 426–452.

Grossman, Sanford J., and Oliver D. Hart
1986 "The costs and benefits of ownership: A theory of vertical and lateral integration." Journal of Political Economy, 94: 691–719.

Hadfield, Gillian
1990 "Problematic relations: Franchising and the law of incomplete contracts." Stanford Law Review, 42: 927–992.

Hamilton, Gary, and Nicole Biggart
1988 "Market, culture, and authority." American Journal of Sociology (Supplement), 94: S52–S94.

Hayek, Friedrich
1945 "The use of knowledge in society." American Economic Review, 35: 519–530.

Holmstrom, Bengt
1989 "Agency costs and innovation." Journal of Economic Behavior and Organization, 12: 305–327.

Holmstrom, Bengt, and Paul Milgrom
1991 "Multi-task principal-agent analysis." Journal of Law, Economics, and Organization (in press).

International Herald Tribune
1990 "Soviet economic development." June 5: 5.

Jensen, Michael, and William Meckling
1976 "Theory of the firm: Managerial behavior, agency costs, and capital structure." Journal of Financial Economics, 3: 305–360.

Joskow, Paul
1988 "Asset specificity and the structure of vertical relationships." Journal of Law, Economics, and Organization, 4: 95–117.

Klein, Benjamin
1980 "Transaction cost determinants of 'unfair' contractual arrangements." American Economic Review, 70: 356–362.

Klein, Benjamin, R. A. Crawford, and A. A. Alchian
1978 "Vertical integration, appropriable rents, and the competitive contracting process." Journal of Law and Economics, 21: 297–326.

Knight, Frank H.
1941 Review of Melville J. Herskovits, Economic Anthropology. Journal of Political Economy, 49: 247–258.

Koopmans, Tjalling
1977 "Concepts of optimality and their uses." American Economic Review, 67: 261–274.

Kornai, Janos
1986 "The Hungarian reform process." Journal of Economic Literature, 24: 1687–1737.

Lange, Oskar
1938 "On the theory of economic socialism." In Benjamin Lippincott (ed.), On the Economic Theory of Socialism: 55–143. Minneapolis: University of Minnesota Press.

Light, Ivan
1972 Ethnic Enterprise in America: Business and Welfare among Chinese, Japanese, and Blacks. Berkeley, CA: University of Calfornia Press.

Llewellyn, Karl N.
1931 "What price contract? An essay in perspective." Yale Law Journal, 40: 704–751.

Macneil, Ian R.
1974 "The many futures of contracts." Southern California Law Review, 47: 691–816.
1978 "Contracts: Adjustments of long-term economic relations under classical, neoclassical, and relational contract law." Northwestern University Law Review, 72: 854–906.

Malmgren, Harold
1961 "Information, expectations and the theory of the firm." Quarterly Journal of Economics, 75: 399–421.

Manne, Henry
1967 "Our two corporation systems: Law and economics." University of Virginia Law Review, 53: 259–285.

Masten, Scott
1982 "Transaction costs, institutional choice, and the theory of the firm." Unpublished Ph.D. dissertation, University of Pennsylvania.
1988 "A legal basis for the firm." Journal of Law, Economics, and Organization, 4: 181–198.

Masten, Scott, James Meehan, and Edward Snyder
1991 "The costs of organization." Journal of Law, Economics, and Organization, Vol. 7 (in press).

Michelman, Frank
1967 "Property, utility and fairness: The ethical foundations of 'just compensation' law." Harvard Law Review, 80: 1165–1257.

Milgrom, Paul, Douglass North, and Barry Weingast
1990 "The role of institutions in the revival of trade." Economics and Politics, 2: 1–23.

Milgrom, Paul, and John Roberts
1990 "The economics of modern manufacturing: Technology, strategy, and organization." American Economic Review, 80: 511–528.

Montias, Michael
1976 The Structure of Economic Systems. New Haven, CT: Yale University Press.

Nelson, Richard R.
1961 "Uncertainty, learning, and the economics of parallel R&D." Review of Economics and Statistics, 43: 351–364.

Newman, Barry
1989 "Poland's farmers put the screws to leaders by holding back crops." Wall Street Journal, October 25: A1 and A10.

North, Douglass
1986 "The new institutional economics." Journal of Theoretical and Institutional Economics, 142: 230–237.

North, Douglass, and Barry Weingast
1989 "Constitutions and commitment: The evolution of institutions governing public choice in 17th century England." Journal of Economic History, 49: 803–832.

Polanyi, Michael
1962 Personal Knowledge: Towards a Post-Critical Philosophy. New York: Harper & Row.

Riordan, Michael, and Oliver Williamson
1985 "Asset specificity and economic organization." International Journal of Industrial Organization, 3: 365–378.

Scott, W. Richard
1987 Organizations, 2d ed. Englewood Cliffs, NJ: Prentice-Hall.

Shelanski, Howard
1990 "A survey of empirical research in transaction cost economics." Unpublished manuscript, University of California, Berkeley:

Simon, Herbert
1951 "A formal theory of the employment relation." Econometrica, 19: 293–305.
1978 "Rationality as process and as product of thought." American Economic Review, 68: 1–16.

Teece, David J.
1986 "Profiting from technological innovation." Research Policy, 15 (December): 285–305.

Topkis, Donald
1978 "Maximizing a submodular function on a lattice." Operations Research, 26: 305–321.

Ward, B. N.
1967 The Socialist Economy: A Study of Organizational Alternatives. New York: Random House.

Williamson, Oliver E.
1975 Markets and Hierarchies. New York: Free Press.
1976 "Franchise bidding for natural monopoly—In general and with respect to CATV." Bell Journal of Economics, 7: 73–104.
1979 "Transaction-cost economics: The governance of contractual relations." Journal of Law and Economics, 22: 233–261.
1983 "Credible commitments: Using hostages to support exchange." American Economic Review, 73: 519–540.
1985 The Economic Institutions of Capitalism. New York: Free Press.
1988 "The logic of economic organization." Journal of Law, Economics, and Organization, 4: 65–93.
1989 "Transaction cost economics." In Richard Schmalensee and Robert Willig (eds.), Handbook of Industrial Organization, 1: 136–182. New York: North-Holland.
1990 "Chester Barnard and the incipient science of organization." In Oliver E. Williamson (ed.), Organization Theory: 172–207. New York: Oxford University Press.
1991a "Strategizing, economizing, and economic organization." Strategic Management Journal (in press).
1991b "Economic institutions: Spontaneous and intentional governance." Journal of Law, Economics, and Organization (in press).

Journal of Economic Perspectives—Volume 12, Number 4—Fall 1998—Pages 73–94

The Boundaries of the Firm Revisited

Bengt Holmström and John Roberts

Why do firms exist? What is their function, and what determines their scope? These remain the central questions in the economics of organization. They are also central questions for business executives and corporate strategists. The worldwide volume of corporate mergers and acquisitions exceeded $1.6 trillion in 1997. It is hard to imagine that so much time, effort and investment bankers' fees would be spent on adjusting firm boundaries unless there was some underlying economic gain. Indeed, the exceptional levels of merger and acquisition activity over the past two decades are a strong indication that economically significant forces do determine organizational boundaries.

The study of firm boundaries originated with the famous essay by Coase (1937), who raised the question of why we observe so much economic activity inside formal organizations if, as economists commonly argue, markets are such powerful and effective mechanisms for allocating scarce resources. Coase's answer was in terms of the costs of transacting in a world of imperfect information. When the transaction costs of market exchange are high, it may be less costly to coordinate production through a formal organization than through a market.

In large part thanks to the work of Williamson (1975, 1985), recent decades have seen a resurgence of interest in Coase's fundamental insight that firm boundaries can be explained by efficiency considerations. Our understanding of firm boundaries has been sharpened by identifying more precisely the nature and sources of transaction costs in different circumstances. In the process, the focus of

■ *Bengt Holmström is Paul A. Samuelson Professor of Economics, Massachusetts Institute of Technology, Cambridge, Massachusetts. John Roberts is Jonathan B. Lovelace Professor of Economics and Strategic Management, Graduate School of Business, Stanford University, Stanford, California.*

attention has shifted away from the coordination problems originally emphasized by Coase and towards the role of firm boundaries in providing incentives. In particular, the most influential work during the last two decades on why firms exist, and what determines their boundaries, has been centered on what has come to be known as the "hold-up problem."

The classic version of the hold-up story is told by Klein, Crawford and Alchian (1978); its essence is modeled in Grout (1984). One party must make an investment to transact with another. This investment is relation-specific; that is, its value is appreciably lower (perhaps zero) in any use other than supporting the transaction between the two parties.[1] Moreover, it is impossible to draw up a complete contract that covers all the possible issues that might arise in carrying out the transaction and could affect the sharing of the returns from the investment. The classic example, cited by Klein, Crawford and Alchian (1978), involves the dies used to shape steel into the specific forms needed for sections of the body of a particular car model (say, the hood or a quarter panel). These dies are expensive—they can cost tens of millions of dollars. Further, they are next-to-worthless if not used to make the part in question. Suppose the dies are paid for and owned by an outside part supplier. Then the supplier will be vulnerable to hold-up. Because any original contract is incomplete, situations are very likely to arise after the investment has been made that require the two parties to negotiate over the nature and terms of their future interactions. Such ex post bargaining[2] may allow the automobile manufacturer to take advantage of the fact that the dies cannot be used elsewhere to force a price reduction that grabs some of the returns to the investment that the supplier had hoped to enjoy. The supplier may then be unwilling to invest in the specific assets, or it may expend resources to protect itself against the threat of hold-up. In either case, inefficiency results: either the market does not bring about optimal investment, or resources are expended on socially wasteful defensive measures. Having the auto company own the dies solves the problem.

If the supply relationship faces more extensive hold-up problems, the best solution may be vertical integration, with all the parts of the body being procured internally rather than outside. The organization and governance structure of a firm are thus viewed as a mechanism for dealing with hold-up problems.

The next section of the paper will review the two strains of work that have dominated the research on the boundaries of the firm: transaction cost economics and property rights theory. Both theories, while quite different in their empirical implications, focus on the role of ownership in supporting relationship-specific

---

[1] Thus, once the investment has been sunk, it generates quasi-rents—amounts in excess of the return necessary to keep the invested assets in their current use. There could, but need not, be pure rents—returns in excess of those needed to cause the investment to be made in the first place.

[2] The terms ex ante and ex post—"before the fact" and "after the fact"—are widely used in this literature. In the hold-up story, the investment must be made ex ante, before a binding agreement is reached, while the renegotiation is ex post, after the investment. More generally, the literature refers to negotiations that occur after some irreversible act, including the establishing of the relationship, as ex post bargaining.

investments in a world of incomplete contracting and potential hold-ups. There is much to be learned from this work.

In this essay, however, we argue for taking a much broader view of the firm and the determination of its boundaries. Firms are complex mechanisms for co-ordinating and motivating individuals' activities. They have to deal with a much richer variety of problems than simply the provision of investment incentives and the resolution of hold-ups. Ownership patterns are not determined solely by the need to provide investment incentives, and incentives for investment are provided by a variety of means, of which ownership is but one. Thus, approaches that focus on one incentive problem that is solved by the use of a single instrument give much too limited a view of the nature of the firm, and one that is potentially misleading.

We support our position first by pointing to situations where relationship-specific investments appear quite high and contracting is incomplete, yet the patterns of ownership are hard to explain either with transaction cost theory or property rights models. The comparison of traditional procurement and subcontracting practices across the U.S. and Japanese automobile industries is the best and most detailed example of this sort that we discuss. Another set of examples illustrates settings in which hold-up problems seem to be small, and therefore boundary choices must be driven by other considerations. Our examples suggest that ownership patterns are responsive to, among other things, agency problems, concerns for common assets, difficulties in transferring knowledge, and the benefits of market monitoring. These suggestions are tentative, and we confess that they are mostly without a good theoretical foundation. They are offered in the hope of inspiring new theoretical research.

We emphasize that this paper is not a survey. We make no claim to having been complete in either our exposition or our citations. Indeed, we are aware of many excellent papers that bear on our arguments or that relate to our examples but that we could not cite because of space considerations. We hope those whose work we have slighted will understand and forgive.

Theoretical Background

Discussions of the hold-up problem and its implications for firm boundaries typically list a standard string of references—including Williamson (1975, 1985), Klein et al. (1978), Grossman and Hart (1986), and Hart and Moore (1990)—as if they were the building blocks in a single coherent theory of ownership. This is not the case. There are certainly points of similarity, particularly that contractual incompleteness necessitates ex post bargaining, causing potential problems for efficiency. But the detailed logic of the stories differs, resulting in quite different empirical predictions.[3] Our brief review of the transaction cost and property rights theories aims at highlighting these distinctions.

---

[3] Whinston (1997) takes a close look at the empirical distinctions of transaction cost theory and property rights theory.

Modern transaction cost economics originated with Williamson. His views have evolved somewhat over the years. His early work (Williamson, 1975) tended to emphasize ex post inefficiencies that arise in bilateral relationships—for example, when bargaining occurs under asymmetric information—rather than relationship-specific investments and hold-ups, while his later work has paid more attention to initial, specific investments (Williamson, 1979, 1985). But this shift in emphasis has not significantly affected the operational content of his theory, which remains premised on the idea that one can identify key dimensions of individual transactions such that, when described in terms of these dimensions, every transaction can be mapped into a most efficient institutional arrangement.

Williamson (1985) suggests that three transaction characteristics are critical: frequency, uncertainty, and most especially, asset specificity (as measured by the foregone economic benefits of discontinuing a relationship). Each characteristic is claimed to be positively related to the adoption of internal governance. The basic logic is that higher levels of uncertainty and higher degrees of asset specificity, particularly when they occur in combination, result in a more complex contracting environment and a greater need for adjustments to be made after the relationship has begun and commitments have been made. A hierarchical relationship, in which one party has formal control over both sides of the transaction, is presumed to have an easier time resolving potential disputes than does a market relationship. The frequency of a transaction matters because the more often it takes place, the more widely spread are the fixed costs of establishing a non-market governance system.

For the purpose of later comparison, we want to single out a few distinguishing features of Williamson's three-factor paradigm. First, it makes no reference to the direct costs of up-front, ex ante investments. For example, there is no differentiation between a case where a specialized asset costs $10 million and one in which the asset costs $100 million, provided that the assets in both cases are worth the same amount more inside the relationship than outside it. There need not even be any up-front expenditures at all: the original, ex ante "investment" could just be an initially costless choice of partner or standard or something similar that limits a party's later options. Williamson (1985) places particular weight on this last case, referring to "The Fundamental Transformation" that occurs when an exchange relationship moves from an ex ante competitive situation, with large numbers of potential trading partners, to an ex post, small-numbers one, once commitments have been made. The theory's indifference to the level of initial investments is consistent with the assumption that the carrying out of such investments is fully contractible (as might well be the case with the investment in automobile dies) and hence poses no incentive problems.

Second, in Williamson's approach the implicit measure of asset specificity is the *aggregate level* of quasi-rents created by the investment. With two parties, say a buyer B and a seller S, asset specificity and aggregate quasi-rents are measured as $V - V_B - V_S$, where V is the capitalized value of the jointly controlled assets in a continued relationship and V_B and V_S are the go-alone values of the individually controlled assets in case B and S separate. In this expression, only the sum $V_B + V_S$

rather than the individual values V_B and V_S matters. On this account, an asymmetric relationship with one party in a dominant position is no different from a symmetric one with the same level of aggregate asset specificity.

Third, taking the transaction as the unit of analysis runs into problems when one starts to consider the costs of bureaucracy and hierarchy more generally, because these costs quite clearly relate not to one single transaction, but to the whole collection of transactions that the hierarchy covers (Milgrom and Roberts, 1992, pp. 32–33).

Finally, Williamson treats market trade as a default that is assumed superior to within-organization trade unless levels of uncertainty, frequency and asset specificity are high enough to pull the transaction out of the market. Because the market is the default, its benefits are not spelled out as clearly as its costs. In transaction cost economics, the functioning market is as much a black box as is the firm in neoclassical microeconomic theory. An assortment of conditions have been adduced by Williamson and others to limit firm size—costs of bureaucracy, the weakening of individual incentives, the hazards of internal politicking, and so on—but none of these costs are easy to measure, and (perhaps for this reason) they have not played much of an empirical role.[4]

A major strength of the modern property rights approach, pioneered by Grossman and Hart (1986),[5] is that it spells out the costs and benefits of integration in a manner that does not rely on the presence of an impersonal market. The theory takes ownership of non-human assets as the defining characteristic of firms: a firm is exactly a set of assets under common ownership. If two different assets have the same owner, then we have a single, integrated firm; if they have different owners, then there are two firms and dealings between them are market transactions. Decisions about asset ownership—and hence firm boundaries—are important because control over assets gives the owner bargaining power when unforeseen or uncovered contingencies force parties to negotiate how their relationship should be continued. The owner of an asset can decide how it should be used and by whom, subject only to the constraints of the law and the obligations implied by specific contracts. Assets become bargaining levers that influence the terms of new agreements and hence the future payoffs from investing in the relationship. In contrast to transaction cost economics, the standard property rights models assume that *all* bargaining, including any that occurs after investments are made, is efficient. Thus, everything turns on how ownership affects initial investments, but unlike Klein et al. (1978), it is essential that these investments are non-contractible.[6]

---

[4] This is changing. Recently, for example, influence cost ideas (Milgrom and Roberts, 1988, 1990; Meyer, Milgrom and Roberts, 1992) have been used to explain observed inefficiencies in internal capital markets (Scharfstein, 1998; Shin and Stulz, 1998).

[5] Hart and Moore (1990) and many others have developed the property rights approach further. See Hart (1995). Recent additions include DeMeza and Lockwood (1998) and Rajan and Zingales (1998). Holmström (1996) offers a critical commentary.

[6] If the parties can contract on the investments, the assumption of efficient bargaining means that they will be made at the efficient levels, irrespective of ownership patterns.

To illustrate, in Hart and Moore (1990) each agent makes (non-contractible) investments in human capital that are complementary with a set of non-human assets. Each agent necessarily owns his or her own human capital. The ownership of the non-human assets, however, affects the incentives to invest in human capital. Once the investment is made, ex post bargaining determines the allocation of the returns from the investments. This bargaining is assumed to give each party—that is, the buyer B or the seller S—what it could have obtained on its own, V_B or V_S, plus a share of the surplus created by cooperation.

Specifically, payoffs to the parties take the form $P_i = V_i + \frac{1}{2}(V - V_i - V_j)$, $i,j = B,S$, where as before V is the capitalized value of cooperation. Ownership influences the separation payoffs V_B and V_S since the owner of a particular asset gets to deny the other party the use of it if cooperation is not achieved. Ownership does not influence V, since all assets are in use when the parties cooperate. Neither party's investment affects the other's separation payoff, because if they do not cooperate then neither has access to the other's human capital and the investment in it. Individual incentives to invest are driven by the derivatives of the payoff functions P_B and P_S. If $V \equiv V_B + V_S$ for all levels of investment, then individual returns to investments coincide exactly with the social returns, as measured by the derivatives of V. This case corresponds to a competitive market, because no extra value is created by the particular relationship between B and S; both parties would be equally well off if they traded with outsiders. In general, however, the social returns and the individual returns differ, resulting in inefficient investments. In particular, if the payoff functions are supermodular,[7] so that the payoff to incremental investment by one party is increasing in both the volume of non-human assets available to that party and the amount of the other party's investment, then there is underinvestment. One can strengthen the incentives of one party by giving that party control over more assets, but only at the expense of weakening the incentives of the other party. There is a trade-off, because ownership shares cannot add up to more than 100 percent. This trade-off determines the efficient allocation of ownership.

Several conclusions follow from this model. For instance, as investment by the buyer B becomes more important (for generating surplus V) relative to investments by the seller S, B should be given more assets. B should be given those assets that make V_B most sensitive to B's investment. If an asset has no influence on B's investment it should be owned by S. For this reason, no outsider should ever own an asset—that would waste bargaining chips that are precious for incentive provision. For the same reason, joint ownership—meaning that both parties have the right to veto the use of the asset—is never optimal. As a consequence, assets that are worthless unless used together should never be separately owned.

---

[7] Supermodularity of a function means that an increase in one argument increases the incremental return from all the other arguments. With differentiable functions, the cross-partials are all non-negative. In the Hart-Moore model, supermodularity refers both to human capital and to assets, so that having more assets implies a higher marginal return to all investments. See Milgrom and Roberts (1994).

While these implications regarding joint ownership, outside ownership and co-ownership of perfectly complementary assets are often stressed, it is important to keep in mind that they are easy to overturn by slight changes in assumptions. For instance, joint ownership may be desirable when investments improve non-human assets. Third-party control can be desirable if parties would otherwise invest too much in improving their outside opportunities to strengthen their bargaining positions (Holmström and Tirole, 1991; Holmström and Milgrom, 1991, 1994; Rajan and Zingales, 1998). And most conclusions are sensitive to the particular bargaining solution being used (de Meza and Lockwood, 1998). What does survive all variations of the model is the central idea that asset ownership provides levers that influence bargaining outcomes and hence incentives.

In contrast to Williamson's three-factor framework, there is no uncertainty in this model. Frequency plays no role either (although it can be introduced with interesting results, as in Baker, Gibbons and Murphy, 1997, or Halonen, 1994). Most strikingly, the *level* of asset specificity has no influence on the allocation of ownership: the predictions of the model remain unchanged if one increases the total surplus V by adding an arbitrarily large constant to it, because investments are driven by marginal, not total, returns. This is problematic for empirical work, partly because margins are hard to observe when there are no prices and partly because some of the key margins relate to returns from hypothetical investments that in equilibrium are never made. Indeed, as Whinston (1997) has noted, the extensive empirical research geared to testing Williamson's three-factor framework casts no light on the modern property rights models.

As noted earlier, a virtue of the property rights approach is that it simultaneously addresses the benefits *and* the costs of ownership. Markets are identified with the right to bargain and, when necessary, to exit with the assets owned. This greatly clarifies the market's institutional role as well as its value in providing entrepreneurial incentives. On the other hand, firms are poorly defined in property rights models and it is not clear how one actually should interpret the identities of B and S. In an entrepreneurial interpretation, B and S are just single individuals, but this seems of little empirical relevance. If, on the other hand, firms consist of more than one individual, then one has to ask how one should interpret the unobserved investments (in human capital) that cannot be transferred. An even more fundamental question is why firms, as opposed to individuals, should own any assets. At present, the property rights models are so stylized that they cannot answer these questions.[8]

---

[8] Holmström and Milgrom (1994) and Holmström (1996) argue that the function of firms cannot be properly understood without considering additional incentive instruments that can serve as substitutes for outright ownership. Employees, for instance, typically own no assets, yet they often do work quite effectively. In these theories asset ownership gives access to many incentive instruments and the role of the firm is to coordinate the use of all of them. That may also explain why non-investing parties, including the firm itself, own assets.

Investment Incentives Are Not Provided by Ownership Alone

There is no doubt that hold-up problems are of central concern to business people. In negotiating joint venture agreements, venture capital contracts, or any of a number of other business deals, much time is spent on building in protections against hold-ups. At the same time, such contracts are *prima facie* evidence that hold-up problems do not get resolved solely by integration of buyer and seller into a single party—the firm. Indeed, there seems to be something of a trend today toward disintegration, outsourcing, contracting out, and dealing through the market rather than bringing everything under the umbrella of the organization. This trend has seen the emergence of alternative, often ingenious solutions to hold-up problems.

Japanese Subcontracting

The pattern of relations between Japanese manufacturing firms and their suppliers offers a prominent instance where the make-buy dichotomy and related theorizing have been less than satisfactory. Although the basic patterns apply in a number of industries (including, for example, electronics), the practices in the automobile industry are best documented (Asanuma, 1989, 1992). These patterns have spread from Japan to the auto industry in the United States and elsewhere, and from autos to many other areas of manufacturing. These practices feature long-term, close relations with a limited number of independent suppliers that seem to mix elements of market and hierarchy. Apparently, these long-term relations substitute for ownership in protecting specific assets.

Two points of contrast in the treatment of specific investments between traditional U.S. practice and the Japanese model present particular problems for the received theory. The first concerns investments in designing specialized parts and components. Traditional U.S. practice featured either internal procurement or arm's length, short-term contracting. Design-intensive products were very often procured internally (Monteverde and Teece, 1982).[9] When products were outsourced, the design was typically done by the automaker, with the drawings being provided to the suppliers. This pattern is what hold-up stories would predict, for the investment in design is highly specific and probably cannot be protected fully by contracts; thus, external suppliers will not make such relationship-specific investments, for fear that they will be held up by buyers after their investments are in place. In stark contrast, it is normal practice for Japanese auto firms to rely on their suppliers to do the actual design of the products supplied. The design costs are then to be recovered through the sale price of the part, with the understanding that this price will be adjusted in light of realized volumes.

A second contrast: traditional U.S. practice has been that physical assets specific

---

[9] However, this pattern did not become standard until decades after the founding of the industry. Earlier, something akin to the practices associated now with the Japanese was the norm. See Helper (1991).

to an automaker's needs are owned by the automaker. This clearly applies in the case of internally procured items, but it also holds in cases where the assets are used by the external supplier in its own factory. For example, the dies used in making a particular car part will belong to the automaker, even though they are used in the supplier's plant on the supplier's presses. Again, this accords well with the transaction cost story of potential hold-up by the automaker.[10] In Japan, in contrast, these specific investments are made by the supplier, who retains ownership of the dies. This would seem to present the automaker with temptations to appropriate the returns on these assets, once the supplier has made the relationship-specific investment. Moreover, because the Japanese auto manufacturers typically have a very small number of suppliers of any part, component or system, the supplier would also seem to be in a position to attempt opportunistic renegotiation by threatening to withhold supply for which there are few good, timely substitutes.

The Japanese pattern is directly at odds with transaction cost theory. Meanwhile, the divergence in ownership of the dies between the two countries presents problems for attempts to explain ownership allocation solely in terms of providing incentives for investment.[11]

In Japanese practice, explicit contracting is not used to overcome the incentive problems involved in outsourced design and ownership of specific assets. In fact, the contracts between the Japanese automakers and their suppliers are short and remarkably imprecise, essentially committing the parties only to work together to resolve difficulties as they emerge. Indeed, they do not even specify prices, which instead are renegotiated on a regular basis. From the hold-up perspective, the prospect of frequent renegotiations over the prices of parts that are not yet even designed would certainly seem problematic.

The key to making this system work is obviously the long-term, repeated nature of the interaction.[12] Although supply contracts are nominally year-by-year, the shared understanding is that the chosen supplier will have the business until the model is redesigned, which lasts typically four or five years. Moreover, the expectation is that the firms will continue to do business together indefinitely. There has been very little turnover of Japanese auto parts suppliers: over a recent eleven-year period, only three firms out of roughly 150 ceased to be members of *kyohokai*, the association of first-level Toyota suppliers (Asanuma, 1989).

The familiar logic of repeated games, that future rewards and punishments motivate current behavior, supports the on-going dealings.[13] An attempted hold-up

---

[10] An alternative story is more in the line of Williamson's earlier discussions emphasizing inefficiencies in ex post bargaining. The useful life of a die far exceeds the one-year contracting period. If the supplier owned the die, changing suppliers would require negotiating the sale of the die to the new supplier, and this could be costly and inefficient.

[11] Interestingly, Toyota followed U.S. practice in supplying the dies used by at least some of the suppliers to its Kentucky assembly plant (Milgrom and Roberts, 1993).

[12] Taylor and Wiggins (1997) argue that these long-term relations are also the means used in the Japanese system to solve moral hazard problems with respect to quality.

[13] Baker et al. (1997) present a formal analysis of the choice between external and internal procurement,

would presumably bring severe future penalties. As importantly, the amount of future business awarded to a supplier is linked to ratings of supplier performance. The auto companies carefully monitor supplier behavior—including cost reductions, quality levels and improvements, general cooperativeness, and so on—and frequent redesigns allow them to punish and reward performance on an on-going basis. In this sense, supplier relationships in Japan are potentially *less*, not more, locked in than in the traditional U.S. model, where at the corresponding point in the value chain, the supplier is typically an in-house division or department.

Having a small number of suppliers is crucial to the Japanese system. It reduces the costs of monitoring and increases the frequency of transacting, both of which strengthen the force of reputation. Also, the rents that are generated in the production process do not have to be shared too widely, providing the source for significant future rewards. This logic underlies the normal "two-supplier system" used at Toyota. There is more than one supplier to permit comparative performance evaluation, to allow shifting of business as a reward or punishment, to provide insurance against mishaps, and perhaps to limit the hold-up power of each supplier, but the number is not chosen to minimize hold-ups.

The relationship is marked by rich information sharing, including both schedules of production plans necessary for just-in-time inventory management and also details of technology, operations and costs. The automakers also assist the suppliers in improving productivity and lowering costs: technical support engineers are a major part of the automakers' purchasing staff, and they spend significant amounts of time at the suppliers' facilities. All this in turn means that potential information asymmetries are reduced, which presumably facilitates both performance evaluation and the pricing negotiations.[14]

Perhaps the major problem in the system may be that the automakers are inherently too powerful and thus face too great a temptation to misbehave opportunistically. Indeed, many Japanese observers of the system have interpreted it in terms of the automakers' exploitation of their power. One counterbalance to this power asymmetry is the supplier association, which facilitates communication among the suppliers and ensures that if the auto company exploits its power over one, all will know and its reputation will be damaged generally. This raises the cost of misbehavior. In this regard, the fact that Toyota itself organized an association of the leading suppliers for its Kentucky assembly plant is noteworthy (Milgrom and Roberts, 1993).

An alternative solution to this imbalance would be for the automaker to own

---

taking into account the important fact that long-term relational contracts can be maintained both within a firm as well as across firms.

[14] Strikingly, as automobile electronics have become more sophisticated and a greater part of the cost of a car, Toyota has ceased to rely exclusively on its former sole supplier, Denso, and has developed its own in-house capabilities in this area. Arguably, this was to overcome information asymmetries and their associated costs (Ahmadjian and Lincoln, 1997). In contrast, see the discussion of the effects of Ford's complete reliance on Lear for developing seats for the redesigned 1997 Taurus (Walton, 1997).

the dies, as in the United States. Here a property rights explanation may be useful: under this arrangement, the supplier would not have the same incentives to maintain the dies, since it must be very hard to contract over the amount of wear and tear and its prevention.[15]

Mini-mills, Exclusive Sourcing and Inside Contracting

Another significant shift in the organization of production is illustrated by Nucor, the most successful steel maker in the United States over the past 20 years. Nucor operates mini-mills, which use scrap (mainly car bodies) as raw material for steel production. After an initial technological breakthrough, Nucor started to expand aggressively (Ghemawat, 1995). The strategy required much capital, and to save on capital outlays, Nucor decided to outsource its entire procurement of steel scrap. Traditionally, mini-mills had integrated backwards, partly to secure an adequate supply of raw material and partly because sourcing entails substantial know-how and so was considered "strategically critical." Chaparral Steel, another big mini-mill operator, continues to be integrated backwards, for instance.

In a break with the tradition, Nucor decided to make a single firm, the David J. Joseph Company (DJJ), its sole supplier of scrap. Total dependence on a single supplier would seem to carry significant hold-up risks, but for more than a decade, this relationship has been working smoothly and successfully. Unlike in the Japanese subcontracting system, there are certain contractual supports. Prices are determined by a cost-plus formula to reflect market conditions, and an "evergreen" contract specifies that the parties have to give advance warning (about half a year in advance) if they intend to terminate the relationship. Even so, there is plenty of room for opportunism. Despite transparent cost accounting (essentially, open books), DJJ can misbehave, since realized costs need not be the same as potential costs. Asset specificity remains significant even with the six-month warning period, since a return to traditional sourcing and selling methods would be quite disruptive and expensive for both sides. Indeed, one reason why the partnership has been working so well may be the high degree of mutual dependence: Nucor's share of DJJ's scrap business is estimated to be over 50 percent.

The success of Nucor's organizational model has led other mini-mills to emulate and refine it. In England, Co Steel has gone as far as relying on its sole supplier to make ready-to-use "charges," the final assemblage of materials to go into the steel-making ovens. The production technology for charges is quite complicated: about 20–30 potential ingredients go into each mixture, with the mix depending on the desired properties of the final product, and big cost savings can be had by optimizing the use of the different inputs. This activity entails much know-how and requires extensive information exchange with the steel plant to match inputs with final product demand. The charges must be prepared by the supplier on Co Steel's premises, both for logistical reasons and to facilitate information sharing. In trans-

---

[15] See Segal and Whinston (1997) for a model in the property rights spirit that is relevant to these issues.

action cost economics, such a cheek-by-jowl situation would be an obvious candidate for integration. Yet, the industry is moving in the direction of disintegration in the belief that specialization will save on costs by eliminating duplicate assets, streamlining the supply chain, and providing better incentives for the supplier through improved accountability.

Related experiments of "inside contracting" include Volkswagen's new car manufacturing plant in Brazil, where the majority of the production workers in the factory are employees, not of Volkswagen, but of subcontractors that provide and install components and systems on the cars as they move along the line. It is too early to tell whether other firms will return to inside contracting, which used to be quite common in the United States up to World War I (Buttrick, 1952), and whether such a move will be successful. But evidently, even potentially large hold-up problems have not deterred recent experimentation.

Airline Alliances

Another illustration of close coordination without ownership is provided by airline alliances, which have proliferated in recent years. Coordinating flight schedules to take advantage of economies of scope requires the parties to resolve an intricate set of issues, particularly ones related to complex "yield management" decisions on how to allocate seats across different price categories and how to shift prices as the flight date approaches. Information and contracting problems abound, and it is hardly surprising that tensions occasionally surface. For instance, KLM and Northwest Airlines recently ran into a dispute that had to be resolved by dismantling their cross-ownership structure. But interestingly, this did not prevent KLM and Northwest from deepening their commitment to their North Atlantic alliance by agreeing to eliminate, over a period of years, all duplicate support operations in the United States and Europe. With the completion of this deal, KLM and Northwest have made themselves extraordinarily interdependent in one of the most profitable segments of their business. A 13-year exclusive contract, with an "evergreen" provision requiring a three-year warning before pull-out, is the main formal protection against various forms of opportunism, but undoubtedly the real safeguard comes from the sizable future rents that can be reaped by continued good behavior.

Why don't the two airlines instead integrate? Regulations limiting foreign ownership and potential government antitrust objections are a factor, as may be tax considerations. However, an explanation we have been given is that airline cultures (and labor unions) are very strong and merging them is extremely difficult. Pilot seniority is a particularly touchy issue.

Contractual Assets and Network Influence

In property rights theory, the boundaries of the firm are identified with the ownership of assets, but in the real world, control over assets is a more subtle matter. "Contractual assets" can often be created rather inexpensively to serve some of the same purposes that the theory normally assigns to ownership: to provide levers that give bargaining power and thereby enhance investment incentives. What we have in mind here are contracts that allocate decision rights much like ownership; for instance, exclusive dealing contracts such as Nucor's, or licensing agreements of various kinds. Such "governance contracts" are powerful vehicles for regulating market relationships. With increased disintegration, governance contracts seem to have become more nuanced and sophisticated. They place firms at the center of a network of relationships, rather than as owners of a clearly defined set of capital assets.

BSkyB, a satellite broadcasting system in Rupert Murdoch's media empire, is an example of a highly successful organization that has created its wealth, not by owning physical assets, but by crafting ingenious contracts that have given it influence over an effective network of media players. Satellite broadcasting requires a variety of highly complementary activities, including acquisition and development of programming, provision of the distribution system (satellites, transmitters and home receivers) and development of encryption devices (to limit reception to those who pay), all of which must be carried out before the service can be offered. Other similarly complex and innovative systems of complements, like electric lighting systems or early computer systems, were largely developed within a single firm. BSkyB instead relies on alliances with other firms. Topsy Tail is even more of a "virtual company." It employs three people, but has sales of personal appearance accessories (combs, hair clips and such) approaching $100 million. Topsy Tail conceives of new products, but essentially everything involved in developing, manufacturing and distributing them is handled through an extensive contractual network. Benetton and Nike, to take some bigger and more conventional firms, also extensively rely on outsourcing and a small asset base. The critical asset in these cases is of course control of the brand name, which gives enormous power to dictate how relationships among the various players are to be organized.

Microsoft and the web of inter-firm relations centered around it provide another illustration. The stock market values Microsoft at around $250 billion, which is more than $10 million per employee. Surely very little of this is attributable to its ownership of physical assets. Instead, by leveraging its control over software standards, using an extensive network of contracts and agreements that are informal as well as formal and that include firms from small start-ups to Intel, Sony and General Electric, Microsoft has gained enormous influence in the computer industry and beyond. We are not experts on Microsoft's huge network of relationships, but it seems clear that the traditional hold-up logic does poorly in explaining how the network has developed and what role it serves. If one were to measure asset specificity simply in terms of separation costs, the estimates for breaking up some of the relationships—say, separating Intel from Microsoft—would likely be large. Yet these potential losses do not seem to cause any moves in the direction of ownership integration.

A similar pattern can be observed in the biotechnology industry (Powell, 1996). As in the computer industry, the activities of the different parties are highly interrelated, with different firms playing specialized roles in the development and marketing of different products. Most firms are engaged in a large number of partnerships; for instance, in 1996 Genentech was reported to have 10 marketing partnerships, 20 licensing arrangements, and more than 15 formal research collaborations (Powell, p. 205). Significant relationship-specific investments are made by many parties, and potential conflicts must surely arise after these investments are in place. Yet the system works, thanks to creative contractual assets—patents and licensing arrangements being the oldest and most ingenious—but also to the force of reputation in a market that is rather transparent, because of the close professional relationships among the researchers.

Firm Boundaries are Responsive to More than Investment Incentives

The examples above make clear that there are many alternatives to integration when one tries to solve hold-up problems. The examples also suggest that ownership may be responsive to problems other than underinvestment in specific assets. Speaking broadly, the problems relate to contractual externalities of various kinds, of which hold-ups are just one.

Resolving Agency Problems

An example of how agency issues can affect the boundaries of an organization is whether a firm employs its sales force directly, or whether it uses outside sales agents. The best-known example here involves electronic parts companies, some of which hire their own sales agents while others sell through separate supply companies (Andersen, 1985; Andersen and Schmittlein, 1984). Originally, Andersen (1985) appears to have expected that the observed variation in this choice would relate to the degree of asset specificity; for example, the extent to which investment by sales people with knowledge about products was specific to a particular company. Instead, measurement costs and agency concerns turned out to be central. An employee sales force is used when individual performance is difficult to measure and when non-selling activities (like giving customer support or gathering information about customers' needs) are important to the firm; otherwise, outside companies are used.

Holmström and Milgrom (1991, 1994) rationalize this pattern with a model of multi-task agency, in which sales people carry out three tasks: making current sales, cultivating long-term customer satisfaction, and gathering and relaying information on customer needs. If the latter two activities are important and if the three activities compete for the agent's time, then the marginal rewards to improved performance on each must be comparable in strength; otherwise, the ill-paid activities will be slighted. Because performance in non-selling activities is arguably hard to measure, it may be best to provide balanced, necessarily lower-powered incentives for all three activities.

Offering weak incentives to an outside sales agent can be problematic, however, because the agent may then divert all effort to selling other firms' products that come with stronger rewards for sales. With an employee, this problem can be handled with a salary and a low commission rate, because the employee's outside activities are more easily constrained and promotion and other broader incentives can be used within the firm to influence the agent's behavior.[16] This logic also explains why outside agents commonly receive higher commission rates than does an inside sales force.

A less familiar illustration of how ownership responds to agency concerns comes from multi-unit retail businesses. Some of these businesses are predominantly organized though traditional franchise arrangements, in which a manufacturer contracts with another party to sell its products in a dedicated facility, as in gasoline retailing. Others, including fast-food restaurants, hotels and pest-control services, are organized in what is called "business concept" franchising. The franchiser provides a brand name and usually other services like advertising, formulae and recipes, managerial training and quality control inspections, collecting a fee from the franchisee in return, but the physical assets and production are owned and managed by the franchisee. Sometimes franchisers (like McDonald's) own and operate a number of outlets themselves. Finally, other businesses are commonly organized with a single company owning all the multiple outlets and hiring the outlet managers as employees. Examples are grocery supermarkets and department stores. What accounts for such differences?

It is hard to see how the specificity of the assets—real estate, cash registers, kitchens and inventories—differs between supermarkets and restaurants in such a way that transactions cost arguments would lead to the observed pattern. Indeed, the assets involved are often not very specific at all. Alternatively, applying the Hart-Moore property rights model here would involve identifying non-contractible investments that are unavailable to the other party if the franchise agreement is terminated or the store manager's employment should end. Noncontractible investments by the center in building the brand might qualify on the one hand, but in many cases it is hard to see what the investments of the operator might be. For example, a fast-food restaurant manager might invest in training the workers and building a clientele, but these investments would presumably still be effective even if the manager were replaced by another. Further, these should also be investments that vary across cases in such a way that it is more important to provide the strong incentives of ownership to the manager of the outlet in one case and to the central party in the other.[17]

An alternative approach based on the need to offer incentives for effort has been proposed by Maness (1996). This approach begins by noting that any elements of the retail outlet's financial costs that are sufficiently difficult to measure must

---

[16] For a further discussion of the idea that low-powered incentives are a major virtue of firm organization and can help explain firm boundaries, see Holmström (1996).

[17] See Lutz (1995) for a formal model of franchising along these lines.

accrue to the owner of the outlet as residual claimant, because they cannot be passed by contract to another party. Suppose then that all costs are non-contractible in this sense; that is, since the level or appropriateness of various costs cannot be well-monitored from outside, such costs cannot be part of an agreed-upon contract. Then, the only possibility for payments from the owner to the other party is on the basis of revenues. Indeed, actual franchise fees are almost always based on revenues and not on costs (Maness, p. 102) and incentive pay for employee managers is also often based on sales. In such a structure, the employee-manager has no direct incentive to control costs under central ownership, while the franchiser has no incentives for cost-reduction under local ownership. Because the efforts of either party might affect costs, this creates a potential inefficiency. The solution is to lodge ownership with the party to whom it is most important to give incentives for cost control. Maness then argues that cost control in a fast-food operation is more influenced by the local manager's efforts at staffing, training, controlling waste and the like, while costs in supermarkets are most influenced by the inventory and warehousing system, which can be centrally managed. Thus, an explanation emerges for the observed patterns: ownership is assigned to give appropriate incentives for cost control.

A more complex example involves gasoline retailing in the United States and Canada, which has been studied by Shepard (1993) and Slade (1996), respectively. They document a variety of contractual arrangements that are used in each country between the gasoline refining company and the station operator and, in the United States, significant variation in ownership of the station. While the physical assets used in gasoline retailing are quite specific to that use, a station can be switched from one brand to another with a little paint and new signs. Consequently, neither study attempted to explain the variation in contractual and ownership arrangements in terms of specific assets and hold-up.

Both studies find that the observed patterns are consistent with the arrangements being chosen to deal with problems of inducing effort and its allocation among tasks. These arrangements differ over the strengths of the incentives given to sell gasoline and other, ancillary services like repairs, car washes, or convenience store items. In turn, these ancillary services differ in the ease and accuracy of performance measurement. The observed patterns were generally consistent with their being selected to provide appropriately balanced incentives. For example, Shepard's (1993) work notes that in repair services, effort is hard to measure and, more importantly, monitoring the realized costs and revenues by the refiner may be tricky. This should make it less likely that the refinery will own the station and employ the operator and more likely that an arrangement will be adopted where the operator is residual claimant on sales of all sorts, either owning the station outright or leasing it from the refiner on a long-term basis. This is what the data show. In Slade's (1996) data, the presence of repair did not affect the ownership of the station (essentially all the stations were refiner-owned). It did, however, favor leasing arrangements, where the operator is residual claimant on all sales, and diminished the likelihood of commission arrangements, which would offer unbalanced incentives because the operator is residual claimant on non-gasoline business but is paid only a small commission on gasoline sales. The presence of full service rather than just self-serve gasoline sales also favors moving away from the company-owned model, since it matches the returns to relationship-building with the costs, which are borne by the local operator.[18] However, adding a convenience store actually increases the likelihood of using company-owned and -operated stations in the U.S. data, which goes against this logic unless one assumes that monitoring of such sales is relatively easy.

Considering a broad variety of retailing businesses more generally, LaFontaine and Slade (1997) document that the contractual and ownership arrangements that are used are responsive to agency considerations.

Market Monitoring

Ownership also influences agency costs through changes in the incentives for monitoring and the possibilities for performance contracting. A firm that is publicly traded can take advantage of the information contained in the continuous bidding for firm shares. Stock prices may be noisy, but they have a great deal more integrity than accounting-based measures of long-term value. For this reason, stock-related payment schemes tend to be superior incentive instruments. This factor can come to play a decisive role in organizational design as local information becomes more important and firms are forced to delegate more decision authority to sub-units and lower-level employees. Such moves require stronger performance incentives and in many cases the incentives can be offered most effectively by spinning off units and exposing them to market evaluation.

This, at least, is the underlying philosophy of Thermo Electron Corporation and its related companies. Thermo is an "incubator." It finances and supports start-up companies and entrepreneurs within a modern-day variant of the conglomerate. As soon as a unit is thought to be able to stand on its own feet, it is spun off. A minority stake is offered to outside investors, with Thermo and its family of entrepreneurs (particularly the head of the new operation) retaining a substantial ownership share. The principal owners of Thermo, the Hatsapolous brothers, make it very clear that getting to the spin-off stage is the final objective and a key element in their strategy to foster a true entrepreneurial spirit within the company. Besides making managerial incentives dependent on market information, spin-offs limit the

---

[18] A hold-up story is consistent with the fact that the presence of repair services favors dealer ownership over leasing arrangements in the U.S. data: a lessee who invests in building a clientele for repair work might worry that the refining company will raise the lease payments to appropriate the returns from this investment. This argument, however, does not do much to explain the pattern in the Canadian data, where the refiners own all the stations. One might also attempt to apply this logic to the choice between company-owned and leased stations by arguing that if the company owns the station it cannot motivate the employee-manager to invest in building a clientele because it will appropriate all the returns. However, this argument is not compelling without explaining how firms in other industries succeed in motivating their employees to undertake similar investments.

amount of intervention that Thermo can undertake in the independent units. This, too, will enhance entrepreneurial incentives.[19]

While Thermo has been remarkably successful (at least until recently), few companies have emulated its strategy. One likely reason is that Thermo's approach requires real commitment not to interfere inappropriately in the management of the spun-off units as this would undercut entrepreneurial incentives and would also destroy the integrity of the independent businesses in the eyes of outside investors. While laws protecting minority shareholders help to achieve this commitment to some extent, Thermo's founders have worked for over a decade to establish a reputation for neither intervening excessively nor cross-subsidizing their units. Another reason may be that Thermo has enjoyed all the benefits of a booming stock market since the early 1980s; it is not clear how well Thermo's strategy would work in a flat stock market like the 1970s.

Knowledge Transfers and Common Assets

Information and knowledge are at the heart of organizational design, because they result in contractual and incentive problems that challenge both markets and firms. Indeed, information and knowledge have long been understood to be different from goods and assets commonly traded in markets. In light of this, it is surprising that the leading economic theories of firm boundaries have paid almost no attention to the role of organizational knowledge.[20] The subject certainly deserves more scrutiny.

One of the few economic theory papers to discuss knowledge and firm boundaries is Arrow (1975), who argued that information transmission between upstream and downstream firms may be facilitated by vertical integration. As we saw in the examples of Nucor and the case of Japanese subcontracting, however, this type of information transfer may actually work fairly well even without vertical integration. More significant problems are likely to emerge when a firm comes up with a better product or production technology. Sharing this knowledge with actual or potential competitors would be socially efficient and could in principle enrich both parties, but the dilemma is how to pay for the trade. Until the new ideas have been shown to work, the potential buyer is unlikely to want to pay a lot. Establishing the ideas' value, however, may require giving away most of the relevant information for free. Again, repeated interactions can help here; in fact, even competing firms engage in continuous information exchange on a much larger scale than commonly realized. A common example is the extensive use of benchmarking, in which the costs of particular processes and operations are compared between firms. But when big

---

[19] See Aghion and Tirole (1997) for a model along these lines. In general, the role of firm boundaries in limiting interventions by more senior managers, thereby improving subordinates' incentives in various ways, has been a basic theme in the influence cost literature (Milgrom and Roberts 1990; Meyer et al., 1992).

[20] In contrast, researchers outside economic theory have made much of the role of knowledge. See, for instance, Teece et al. (1994).

leaps in knowledge occur, or when the nature of the knowledge transfer will involve ongoing investments or engagements, the issues become more complex. A natural option in that case is to integrate. Any claims about the value of knowledge are then backed up by the financial responsibility that comes with pairing cash flow and control rights.[21]

We think that knowledge transfers are a very common driver of mergers and acquisitions and of horizontal expansion of firms generally, particularly at times when new technologies are developing or when learning about new markets, technologies or management systems is taking place. Given the current level of merger and acquisition activity, and the amount of horizontal rather than vertical integration, it seems likely that many industries are experiencing such a period of change. The trend towards globalization of businesses has put a special premium on the acquisition and sharing of knowledge in geographically dispersed firms.

Two organizations that we have studied in which the development and transfer of knowledge are particularly central are ABB, Asea Brown Boveri, the largest electrical equipment manufacturer, and British Petroleum, the fourth-largest integrated oil company. Both firms see the opportunity to learn and share information effectively as key to their competitive advantage, and both operate with extremely lean headquarters that are too small to play a central, direct role in transferring knowledge across units. ABB spends a huge amount of time and effort sharing technical and business information across its more than 1,300 business units around the world through a variety of mechanisms. This would hardly be possible if these businesses were not under the single ABB umbrella. Similarly, BP's 100 business units have been encouraged to share information extensively through "peer assists," which involve business units calling on people from other units to help solve operating problems. BP also has a network of different "federal groups," each of which encourages technologists and managers from units around the world to share knowledge about similar challenges that they face.

The problem with knowledge transfers can be viewed as part of the more general problem of free-riding when independent parties share a common asset. If bargaining is costly, the situation is most easily solved by making a single party responsible for the benefits as well as the costs of using the asset. Brand-names are another example of common assets that typically need to be controlled by a single entity.

Concluding Remarks

It seems to us that the theory of the firm, and especially work on what determines the boundaries of the firm, has become too narrowly focused on the hold-up problem and the role of asset specificity. Think of arraying the set of coordi-

---

[21] Stuckey (1983), in his extraordinary study of the aluminum industry, reports that knowledge transfer was an important driver of joint ventures.

nation and motivation problems that the firm solves along one dimension of a matrix, and the set of instruments it has available along the other. Put the provision of investment incentives in column one and ownership-defined boundaries in row one. Let an element of the matrix be positive if the corresponding instrument is used to solve the corresponding problem, and zero otherwise. So there is certainly a positive entry in row one, column one: ownership does affect incentives for investment. We have argued, however, that both the first column and the first row have many other positive elements; ownership boundaries serve many purposes and investment incentives are provided in many ways.

Admittedly, most of the evidence we have offered in support of this claim is anecdotal and impressionistic. Our stories are largely based on newspaper reports, case studies, and our own consulting work and they are not the sort of systematic evidence one would ideally want. Nevertheless, we think that of the significant organizational change that seems to be taking place, only a small part can be easily understood in terms of traditional transaction cost theory in which hold-up problems are resolved by integration. Many of the hybrid organizations that are emerging are characterized by high degrees of uncertainty, frequency and asset specificity, yet they do not lead to integration. In fact, high degrees of frequency and mutual dependency seem to support, rather than hinder, ongoing cooperation across firm boundaries. This issue deserves to be explored in future work.[22]

It is also questionable whether it makes sense to consider one transaction at a time when one tries to understand how the new boundaries are drawn. In market networks, interdependencies are more than bilateral, and how one organizes one set of transactions depends on how the other transactions are set up. The game of influence is a complicated one and leads to strategic considerations that transcend simple two-party relationships.

The property rights approach, with its emphasis on incentives driven by ownership, may be a good starting point for investigating these new hybrid structures. These appear to be emerging in response to, among other things, an increase in the value of entrepreneurship and the value of human capital, both of which are features that the property rights approach can in principle model. But this approach also needs to expand its horizon and recognize that power derives from other sources than asset ownership and that other incentive instruments than ownership are available to deal with the joint problems of motivation and coordination. We do not believe that a theory of the firm that ignores contracts and other substitutes for ownership will prove useful for empirical studies. The world is replete with alternative instruments and, as always, the economically interesting action is at the margin of these substitutions.

---

[22] See Halonen (1994) for a first modeling effort along these lines.

■ *We thank Bradford De Long, Robert Gibbons, Oliver Hart, David Kreps, Timothy Taylor and Michael Whinston for their helpful comments. We are also indebted to the members of the Corporation of the Future initiative at McKinsey & Co., especially Jonathan Day, with whom we have collaborated on the issues discussed here.*

References

Aghion, Philippe, and Jean Tirole, "Formal and Real Authority in Organizations," *Journal of Political Economy*, 1997, *105*, 1–27.

Ahmadjian, Christina, and James Lincoln, "Changing Firm Boundaries in Japanese Auto Parts Supply Networks," draft, Columbia Business School, 1997.

Andersen, Erin, "The Salesperson as Outside Agent or Employee: A Transaction Cost Analysis," *Marketing Science*, 1985, *4*, 234–54.

Andersen, Erin, and David Schmittlein, "Integration of the Sales Force: An Empirical Examination," *Rand Journal of Economics*, 1984, *15*, 385–95.

Arrow, Kenneth, "Vertical Integration and Communication," *Bell Journal of Economics*, 1975, *6*, 173–82.

Asanuma, Banri, "Manufacturer-Supplier Relationships in Japan and the Concept of Relation-Specific Skill," *The Journal of the Japanese and International Economies*, 1989, *3*, 1–30.

Asanuma, Banri, "Japanese Manufacturer-Supplier Relationships in International Perspective." In Paul Sheard, ed., *International Adjustment and the Japanese Economy*. St. Leonards, Australia: Allen & Unwin, 1992.

Baker, George, Robert Gibbons, and Kevin J. Murphy, "Relational Contracts and the Theory of the Firm," draft, Massachusetts Institute of Technology, 1997.

Buttrick, John, "The Inside Contracting System," *Journal of Economic History*, 1952, *12*, 205–21.

Coase, Ronald, "The Nature of the Firm," *Economica*, November 1937, *4*, 386–405.

De Meza, David, and Ben Lockwood, "Does Asset Ownership Always Motivate Managers? Outside Options and the Property Rights Theory of the Firm," *Quarterly Journal of Economics*, 1998, *113*:2, 361–86.

Ghemawat, Pankaj, "Competitive Advantage and Internal Organization: Nucor Revisited," *Journal of Economics and Management Strategy*, 1995, *3*, 685–717.

Grossman, Sanford, and Oliver Hart, "The Costs and Benefits of Ownership: A Theory of Lateral and Vertical Integration," *Journal of Political Economy*, 1986, *94*, 691–719.

Grout, Paul, "Investment and Wages in the Absence of Binding Contracts: A Nash Bargaining Approach," *Econometrica*, 1984, *52*, 449–60.

Halonen, Maija, "Reputation and Allocation of Ownership," STICERD Theoretical Economics Discussion Paper, London School of Economics, 1994.

Hart, Oliver, *Firms, Contracts, and Financial Structure*. Oxford: Clarendon Press, 1995.

Hart, Oliver, and John Moore, "Property Rights and the Nature of the Firm," *Journal of Political Economy*, 1990, *98*, 1119–1158.

Helper, Susan, "Strategy and Irreversibility in Supplier Relations: The Case of the U.S. Automobile Industry," *Business History Review*, 1991, *65*, 781–824.

Holmström, Bengt, "The Firm as a Subeconomy," draft, Department of Economics, Massachusetts Institute of Technology, 1996.

Holmström, Bengt, and Paul Milgrom, "Multitask Principal-Agent Analyses: Incentive Contracts, Asset Ownership, and Job Design," *Journal of Law, Economics, and Organization*, 1991, *7*, 24–51.

Holmström, Bengt, and Paul Milgrom, "The Firm as an Incentive System," *American Economic Review*, 1994, *84*, 972–91.

Holmström, Bengt, and Jean Tirole, "Transfer Pricing and Organizational Form," *Journal of Law, Economics, and Organization*, 1991, *7*:2, 201–28.

Klein, Benjamin, Robert Crawford, and Armen Alchian, "Vertical Integration, Appropriable Rents, and the Competitive Contracting Process," *Journal of Law and Economics*, 1978, *21*, 297–326.

LaFontaine, Francine, and Margaret Slade, "Retail Contracting: Theory and Practice," *Journal of Industrial Economics*, 1997, *45*, 1–25.

Lutz, Nancy, "Ownership Rights and Incentives in Franchising," *Journal of Corporate Finance*, 1995, *2*, 103–31.

Maness, Robert, "Incomplete Contracts and the Choice between Vertical Integration and Franchising," *Journal of Economic Behavior and Organization*, 1996, *32*, 101–15.

Meyer, Margaret, Paul Milgrom, and John Roberts, "Organizational Prospects, Influence Costs and Ownership Changes," *Journal of Economics and Management Strategy*, 1992, *1*:1, 9–35.

Milgrom, Paul, and John Roberts, "An Economic Approach to Influence Activities and Organizational Responses," *American Journal of Sociology*, 1988, *94* (supplement), S154–S179.

Milgrom, Paul, and John Roberts, "Bargaining Costs, Influence Costs and the Organization of Economic Activity." In J. Alt and K. Shepsle, eds., *Perspectives on Positive Political Economy*. Cambridge: Cambridge University Press, 1990, 57–89.

Milgrom, Paul, and John Roberts, *Economics, Organization and Management*. Englewood Cliffs, NJ: Prentice-Hall, 1992.

Milgrom, Paul, and John Roberts, "Johnson Controls, Inc. — Automotive Systems Group:

The Georgetown Kentucky Plant," Stanford Graduate School of Business, Case S-BE-9, 1993.

Milgrom, Paul, and John Roberts, "Comparing Equilibria," *American Economic Review,* 1994, *84,* 441–59.

Monteverde, Kirk, and David Teece, "Supplier Switching Costs and Vertical Integration in the Automobile Industry," *Bell Journal of Economics,* 1982, *13,* 206–13.

Powell, Walter, "Inter-Organizational Collaboration in the Biotechnology Industry," *Journal of Institutional and Theoretical Economics,* 1996, *152:*1, 197–215.

Rajan, Raghuram, and Luigi Zingales, "Power in a Theory of the Firm," *Quarterly Journal of Economics,* 1998, *113:*2, 387–432.

Scharfstein, David, "The Dark Side of Internal Capital Markets II: Evidence from Diversified Conglomerates," NBER Working Paper No. 6352, 1998.

Segal, Ilya, and Michael Whinston, "Exclusive Dealing and Protection of Investments," draft, Department of Economics, University of California, Berkeley, 1997.

Shepard, Andrea, "Contractual Form, Retail Price, and Asset Characteristics," *Rand Journal of Economics,* 1993, *24,* 58–77.

Shin, Hyun-Han, and Rene M. Stulz, "Are Internal Capital Markets Efficient?" *Quarterly Journal of Economics,* 1998, *113:*2, 531–52.

Slade, Margaret, "Multitask Agency and Contract Choice: An Empirical Assessment," *International Economic Review,* 1996, *37,* 465–86.

Stuckey, John, *Vertical Integration and Joint Ventures in the Aluminum Industry.* Cambridge: Harvard University Press, 1983.

Taylor, Curtis, and Steven Wiggins, "Competition or Compensation: Supplier Incentives Under the American and Japanese Subcontracting Systems," *American Economic Review,* 1997, *87:*4, 598–618.

Teece, David, Richard Rumelt, Giovanni Dosi, and Sidney Winter, "Understanding Corporate Coherence, Theory and Evidence," *Journal of Economic Behavior and Organization,* 1994, *23,* 1–30.

Walton, Mary, *Car: A Drama of the American Workplace.* New York: W.W. Norton, 1997.

Whinston, Michael, "On the Transaction Cost Determinants of Vertical Integration," draft, Department of Economics, Northwestern University, 1997.

Williamson, Oliver, *Markets and Hierarchies: Analysis and Antitrust Implications.* New York: The Free Press, 1975.

Williamson, Oliver, "Transaction-Cost Economics: The Governance of Contractual Relations," *Journal of Law and Economics,* 1979, *22,* 233–71.

Williamson, Oliver, *The Economic Institutions of Capitalism.* New York: The Free Press, 1985.

Part II
Governance of Networks

A
Embeddedness

[6]

Our Obsolete Market Mentality*

Karl Polanyi

The first century of the Machine Age is drawing to a close amid fear and trepidation. Its fabulous material success was due to the willing, indeed the enthusiastic, subordination of man to the needs of the machine. Liberal capitalism was in effect man's initial response to the challenge of the Industrial Revolution. In order to allow scope to the use of elaborate, powerful machinery, we transformed human economy into a self-adjusting system of markets, and cast our thoughts and values in the mold of this unique innovation.

Today, we begin to doubt the truth of some of these thoughts and the validity of some of these values. Outside the United States, liberal capitalism can hardly be said to exist any more. How to organize human life in a machine society is a question that confronts us anew. Behind the fading fabric of competitive capitalism there looms the portent of an industrial civilization, with its paralyzing division of labor, standardization of life, supremacy of mechanism over organism, and organization over spontaneity. Science itself is haunted by insanity. This is the abiding concern.

No mere reversion to the ideals of a past century can show us the way. We must brave the future, though this may involve us in an attempt to shift the place of industry in society so that the extraneous fact of the machine can be absorbed. The search for industrial democracy is not merely the search for a solution to the problems of capitalism, as most people imagine. It is a search for an answer to industry itself. Here lies the concrete problem of our civilization. Such a new dispensation requires an inner freedom for which we are but ill equipped. We find ourselves stultified by the legacy of a market economy which bequeathed us oversimplified views of the function and role of the economic system in society. If the crisis is to be overcome, we must recapture a more realistic vision of the human world and shape our common purpose in the light of that recognition.

Industrialism is a precariously grafted scion upon man's age-long existence. The outcome of the experiment is still hanging in the balance. But man is not a simple being and can die in more than one way. The question of individual freedom, so passionately raised in our generation, is only one aspect of this anxious problem. In truth, it forms part of a much wider and deeper need – the need for a new response to the total challenge of the machine.

Our condition can be described in these terms: Industrial civilization may yet undo man. But since the venture of a progressively artificial environment cannot, will not, and indeed, should not, be voluntarily discarded, the task of adapting life *in such a surrounding* to the requirements of human existence must be resolved if man is to continue on earth. No one can foretell whether such an adjustment is possible, or whether man must perish in the attempt. Hence the dark undertone of concern.

Meanwhile, the first phase of the Machine Age has run its course. It involved an organization of society that derived its name from its central institution, the market. This system is on the downgrade. Yet our practical philosophy was overwhelmingly shaped by this spectacular episode. Novel notions about man and society became current and gained the status of axioms. Here they are: As regards *man*, we were made to accept the heresy that his motives can be described as 'material' and 'ideal,' and that the incentives on which everyday life is organized spring from the 'material' motives. Both utilitarian liberalism and popular Marxism favored such views. As regards *society*, the kindred doctrine was propounded that its institutions were 'determined' by the economic system. This opinion was even more popular with Marxists than with liberals.

Under a market economy both assertions were, of course, true. *But only under such an economy.* In regard to the past, such a view was no more than an anachronism. In regard to the future, it was a mere prejudice. Yet under the influence of current schools of thought, reinforced by the authority of science and religion, politics and business, these strictly time-bound phenomena came to be regarded as timeless, as transcending the age of the market. To overcome such doctrines, which constrict our minds and souls and greatly enhance the difficulty of the life-saving adjustment, may require no less than a reform of our consciousness.

Market Society

The birth of laissez faire administered a shock to civilized man's views of himself, from the effects of which he never quite recovered. Only very gradually are we realizing what happened to us as recently as a century ago.

Liberal economy, this primary reaction of man to the machine, was a violent break with the conditions that preceded it. A chain-reaction was started – what before was merely isolated markets was transmuted into a self-regulating *system* of markets. And with the new economy, a new society sprang into being. The crucial step was this: labor and land were made into commodities, that is, they were treated *as if* produced for sale. Of course, they were not actually commodities, since they were either not produced at all (as land) or, if so, not for sale (as labor). Yet no more thoroughly effective fiction was ever devised. By buying and selling labor and land freely, the mechanism of the market was made to apply to them. There was now supply of labor, and demand for it; there was supply of land, and demand for it. Accordingly, there was a market price for the use of labor power, called wages, and a market price for the use of land, called rent. Labor and land were provided with markets of their own, similar to the commodities proper that were produced with their help. The true scope of such a step can be gauged if we remember that labor is only another name for man, and land for nature. The commodity fiction handed over the fate of man and nature to the play of an automaton running in its own grooves and governed by its own laws.

Nothing similar had ever been witnessed before. Under the mercantile regime, though it deliberately pressed for the creation of markets, the converse principle still operated. Labor and land were not entrusted to the market; they formed part of the organic structure of society. Where land was marketable, only the determination of price was, as a rule, left to the parties; where labor was subject to contract, wages themselves were usually assessed by public authority. Land stood under the custom of manor, monastery, and township, under common-law limitations concerning rights of real property; labor was regulated by laws against beggary and vagrancy, statutes of laborers and artificers, poor laws, guild and municipal ordinances. In effect, all societies known to anthropologists and historians restricted markets to commodities in the proper sense of the term.

Market-economy thus created a new type of society. The economic or productive system was here entrusted to a self-acting device. An institutional mechanism controlled human beings in their everyday activities as well as the resources of nature. This instrument of material welfare was under the sole control of the incentives of hunger and gain – or, more precisely, fear of going without the necessities of life, and expectation of profit. So long as no propertyless person could satisfy his craving for food without first selling his labor in the market, and so long as no propertied person was prevented from buying in the cheapest market and selling in the dearest, the blind mill would turn out ever-increasing amounts of commodities for the benefit of the human race. Fear of starvation with the worker, lure of profit with the employer, would keep the vast establishment running.

In this way an 'economic sphere' came into existence that was sharply delimited from other institutions in society. Since no human aggregation can survive without a functioning productive apparatus, its embodiment in a distinct and separate sphere had the effect of making the 'rest' of society dependent upon that sphere. This autonomous zone, again, was regulated by a mechanism that controlled its functioning. As a result, the market mechanism became determinative for the life of the body social. No wonder that the emergent human aggregation was an 'economic' society to a degree previously never even approximated. 'Economic motives' reigned supreme in a world of their own, and the individual was made to act on them under pain of being trodden under foot by the juggernaut market. Such a forced conversion to a utilitarian outlook fatefully warped Western man's understanding of himself.

This new world of 'economic motives' was based on a fallacy. Intrinsically, hunger and gain are no more 'economic' than love or hate, pride or prejudice. No human motive is per se economic. There is no such thing as a *sui generis* economic experience in the sense in which man may have a religious, aesthetic, or sexual experience. These latter give rise to motives that broadly aim at evoking similar experiences. In regard to material production these terms lack self-evident meaning.

The economic factor, which underlies all social life, no more gives rise to definite incentives than the equally universal law of gravitation. Assuredly, if we do not eat, we must perish, as much as if we were crushed under the weight of a falling rock. But the pangs of hunger are not automatically translated into an incentive to produce. Production is not an individual, but a collective affair. If an individual is hungry, there is nothing definite for him to do. Made desperate, he might rob or steal, but such an action can hardly be called productive. With man, the political animal, everything is given not by natural, but by social circumstance. What made the nineteenth century think of hunger and gain as 'economic' was simply the organization of production under a market economy.

Hunger and gain are here linked with production through the need of 'earning an income.' For under such a system, man, if he is to keep alive, is compelled to buy goods on the market with the help of an income derived from selling other goods on the market. The name of these incomes – wages, rent, interest – varies accordingly to what is offered for sale: use of labor power, of land, or of money; the income called profit – the remuneration of the entrepreneur – derives from the sale of goods that fetch a higher price than the goods that go into the producing of them. Thus all incomes derive from sales, and all sales – directly or indirectly – contribute to production. The latter is, in effect, *incidental to the earning of an income*. So long as an individual is 'earning an income,' he is, automatically, contributing to production. Obviously, the system works only so long as individuals have a reason to indulge in the activity of 'earning an income.' The motives of hunger and gain – separately and conjointly – provide them with such a reason. These two motives are thus geared to production and, accordingly, are termed 'economic.' The semblance is compelling that hunger and gain are *the* incentives on which any economic system must rest. This assumption is baseless. Ranging over human societies, we find hunger and gain not appealed to as incentives to production, and where so appealed to, they are fused with other powerful motives.

Aristotle was right: man is not an economic, but a social being. He does not aim at safeguarding his individual interest in the acquisition of material possessions, but rather at ensuring social good will, social status, social assets. He values possessions primarily as a means to that end. His incentives are of that 'mixed' character which we associate with the endeavor to gain social approval – productive efforts are no more than incidental to this. *Man's economy is, as a rule, submerged in his social relations.* The change from this to a society which was, on the contrary, submerged in the economic system was an entirely novel development.

The evidence of facts, I feel, should at this point be adduced. *First*, there are the discoveries of primitive economics. Two names are outstanding: Bronislaw Malinowski and Richard Thurnwald. They and some other research workers revolutionized our conceptions in this field and, by so doing, founded a new discipline. The myth of the individualistic savage had been exploded long ago. Neither the crude egotism, nor the apocryphal propensity to barter, truck, and exchange, nor even the tendency to cater to one's self was in evidence. But equally discredited was the legend of the communistic psychology of the savage, his supposed lack of appreciation for his own personal interests. (Roughly, it appeared that man was very much the same all through the ages. Taking his institutions not in isolation, but in their interrelation, he was mostly found to be behaving in a manner broadly comprehensible to us.) What appeared as 'communism' was the fact that the productive or economic system was usually arranged in such a fashion as not to threaten any individual with starvation. His place at the campfire, his share in the common resources, was secure to him, whatever part he happened to have played in hunt, pasture, tillage, or gardening. Here are a few instances: Under the *kraalland* system of the Kaffirs, 'destitution is impossible; whosoever needs assistance receives it unquestioningly' (L.P. Mair, *An African People in the Twentieth Century*, 1934). No Kwakiutl 'ever ran the least risk of going hungry' (E.M. Loeb, *The Distribution and Function of Money in Early Society*, 1936). 'There is no starvation in societies living on the subsistence margin' (M.I. Herskovits, *The Economic Life of Primitive Peoples*, 1940). In effect, the individual is not in danger of starving unless the community as a whole is in a like predicament. It is this absence of the menace of individual destitution that makes primitive society, in a sense, more humane than nineteenth-century society, and at the same time less 'economic.'

The same applies to the stimulus of individual gain. Again, a few quotations: 'The characteristic feature of primitive economics is the absence of any desire to make profits from production and exchange' (R. Thurnwald, *Economics in Primitive Communities*, 1932). 'Gain, which is often the stimulus for work in more civilized communities, never acts as an impulse to work under the original native conditions' (B. Malinowski, *Argonauts of the Western Pacific*, 1922). If so-called economic motives were natural to man, we would have to judge all early and primitive societies as thoroughly unnatural.

Secondly, there is no difference between primitive and civilized society in this regard. Whether we turn to ancient city-state, despotic empire, feudalism, thirteenth-century urban life, sixteenth-century mercantile regime, or eighteenth-century regulationism – invariably the economic system is found to be merged in the social. Incentives spring from a large variety of sources, such as custom and tradition, public duty and private commitment, religious observance and political allegiance, judicial obligation and administrative regulation as established by prince, municipality, or guild. Rank and status, compulsion of law and threat of punishment, public praise and private reputation, insure that the individual contributes his share to production. Fear of privation or love of profit need not be altogether absent. Markets occur in all kinds of societies, and the figure of the merchant is familiar to many types of civilization. But isolated markets do not link up into an economy. The motive of gain was specific to merchants, as was valor to the knight, piety to the priest, and pride to the craftsman. The notion of making the motive of gain universal never entered the heads of our ancestors. At no time prior to the second quarter of the nineteenth century were markets more than a subordinate feature in society.

Thirdly, there was the startling abruptness of the change. Predominance of markets emerged not as a matter of degree, but of kind. Markets through which otherwise self-sufficient householders get rid of their surplus neither direct production nor provide the producer with his income.[1] This is only the case in a market-economy where *all* incomes derive from sales, and commodities are obtainable exclusively by purchase. A free market for labor was born in England only about a century ago. The ill-famed Poor Law Reform (1834) abolished the rough-and-ready provisions made for the paupers by patriarchal governments. The poorhouse was transformed from a refuge of the destitute into an abode of shame and mental torture to which even hunger and misery were preferable. Starvation or work was the alternative left to the poor. Thus was a competitive national market for labor created. Within a decade, the Bank Act (1844) established the principle of the gold standard; the making of money was removed from the hands of the government regardless of the effect upon the level of employment. Simultaneously, reform of land laws mobilized the land, and repeal of the Corn Laws (1846) created a world pool of grain, thereby making the unprotected Continental peasant-farmer subject to the whims of the market. Thus were established the three tenets of economic liberalism, the principle on which market economy was organized: that labor should find its price on the market; that money should be supplied by a self-adjusting mechanism; that commodities should be free to flow from country to country irrespective of the consequences – in brief, a labor market, the gold standard, and free trade. A self-inflammatory process was induced, as a result of which the formerly harmless market pattern expanded into a sociological enormity.

These facts roughly outline the genealogy of an 'economic' society. Under such conditions the human world must appear as determined by 'economic' motives. It is easy to see why. Single out whatever motive you please, and organize production in such a manner as to make that motive the individual's incentive to produce, and you will have induced a picture of man as altogether absorbed by that particular motive. Let that motive be religious, political, or aesthetic; let it be pride, prejudice, love, or envy; and man will appear as essentially religious, political, aesthetic, proud, prejudiced, engrossed in love or envy. Other motives, in contrast, will appear distant and shadowy since they cannot be relied upon to operate in the vital business of production. The particular motive selected will represent 'real' man.

As a matter of fact, human beings will labor for a large variety of reasons as long as things are arranged accordingly. Monks traded for religious reasons, and monasteries became the largest trading establishments in Europe. The Kula trade of the Trobriand Islanders, one of the most intricate barter arrangements known to man, is mainly an aesthetic pursuit. Feudal economy was run on customary lines. With the Kwakiutl, the chief aim of industry seems to be to satisfy a point of honor. Under mercantile despotism, industry was often planned so as to serve power and glory. Accordingly, we tend to think of monks or villeins, Western Melanesians, the Kwakiutl, or seventeenth-century statesmen, as ruled by religion, aesthetics, custom, honor, or politics, respectively.

Under capitalism, every individual has to earn an income. If he is a worker, he has to sell his labor at current prices; if he is an owner, he has to make as high a profit as he can, for his standing with his fellows will depend upon the level of his income. Hunger and gain – even if vicariously – make them plow and sow, spin and weave, mine coal, and pilot planes. Consequently, members of such a society will think of themselves as governed by these twin motives. In actual fact, man was never as selfish as the theory demanded. Though the market mechanism brought his dependence upon material goods to the fore, 'economic' motives never formed with him the sole incentive to work. In vain was he exhorted by economists and utilitarian moralists alike to discount in business all other motives than 'material' ones. On closer investigation, he was still found to be acting on remarkably 'mixed' motives, not excluding those of duty toward himself and others – and maybe, secretly, even enjoying work for its own sake.

However, we are not here concerned with actual, but with assumed motives, not with the psychology, but with the ideology of business. *Not on the former, but on the latter, are views of man's nature based.* For once society expects a definite behavior on the part of its members, and prevailing institutions become roughly capable of enforcing that behavior, opinions on human nature will tend to mirror the ideal whether it resembles actuality or not. Accordingly, hunger and gain were defined as economic motives, and man was supposed to be acting on them in everyday life, while his other motives appeared more ethereal and removed from humdrum existence. Honor and pride, civic obligation and moral duty, even self-respect and common decency, were now deemed irrelevant to production, and were significantly summed up in the word 'ideal.' Hence man was believed to consist of two components, one more akin to hunger and gain, the other to honor and power. The one was 'material,' the other 'ideal'; the one 'economic,' the other 'non-economic'; the one 'rational,' the other 'non-rational.' The Utilitarians went so far as to identify the two sets of terms, thus endowing the economic side of man's character with the aura of rationality. He who would have refused to imagine that he was acting for gain alone was thus considered not only immoral, but also mad.

Economic Determinism

The market mechanism, moreover, created the delusion of economic determinism as a general law for all human society. Under a market economy, of course, this law holds good. Indeed, the working of the economic system here not only 'influences' the rest of society, but determines it – as in a triangle the sides not merely influence, but determine, the angles. Take the stratification of classes. Supply and demand in the labor market were *identical* with the classes of workers and employers, respectively. The social classes of capitalists, landowners, tenants, brokers, merchants, professionals, and so on, were delimited by the respective markets for land, money, and capital and their uses, or for various services. The income of these social classes was fixed by the market, their rank and position by their income. This was a complete reversal of the secular practice. In Maine's famous phrase, 'contractus' replaced 'status'; or, as Tönnies preferred to put it, 'society' superseded 'community'; or, in terms of the present article, *instead of the economic system being embedded in social relationships, these relationships were now embedded in the economic system.*

While social classes were directly, other institutions were indirectly determined by the market mechanism. State and government, marriage and the rearing of children, the organization of science and education, of religion and the arts, the choice of profession, the forms of habitation, the shape of settlements, the very aesthetics of private life – everything had to comply with the utilitarian pattern, or at least not interfere with the working of the market mechanism. But since very few human activities can be carried on in the void; even a saint needing his pillar, the indirect effect of the market system came very near to determining the whole of society. It was almost impossible to avoid the erroneous conclusion that as 'economic' man was 'real' man, so the economic system was 'really' society.

Yet it would be truer to say that the basic human institutions abhor unmixed motives. Just as the provisioning of the individual and his family does not commonly rely on the motive of hunger, so the institution of the family is not based on the sexual motive. Sex, like hunger, is one of the most powerful of incentives when released from the control of other incentives. That is probably why the family in all its variety of forms is never allowed to center on the sexual instinct, with its intermittences and vagaries, but on the combination of a number of effective motives that prevent sex from destroying an institution on which so much of man's happiness depends. Sex in itself will never produce anything better than a brothel, and even then it might have to draw on some incentives of the market mechanism. An economic system actually relying for its mainspring on hunger would be almost as perverse as a family system based on the bare urge of sex.

To attempt to apply economic determinism to all human societies is little short of fantastic. Nothing is more obvious to the student of social anthropology than the variety of institutions found to be compatible with practically identical instruments of production. Only since the market was permitted to grind the human fabric into the featureless uniformity of selenic erosion has man's institutional creativeness been in abeyance. No wonder that his social imagination shows signs of fatigue. It may come to a point where he will no longer be able to recover the elasticity, the imaginative wealth and power, of his savage endowment.

No protest of mine, I realize, will save me from being taken for an 'idealist.' For he who decries the importance of 'material' motives must, it seems, be relying on the strength of 'ideal' ones. Yet no worse misunderstanding is possible. Hunger and gain have nothing specifically 'material' about them. Pride, honor, and power, on the other hand, are not necessarily 'higher' motives than hunger and gain.

The dichotomy itself, we assert, is arbitrary. Let us once more adduce the analogy of sex. Assuredly, a significant distinction between 'higher' and 'lower' motives can here be drawn.

Yet, whether hunger or sex, it is pernicious to *institutionalize* the separation of the 'material' and 'ideal' components of man's being. As regards sex, this truth, so vital to man's essential wholeness, has been recognized all along; it is at the basis of the institution of marriage. But in the equally strategic field of economy, it has been neglected. This latter field has been 'separated out' of society as the realm of hunger and gain. Our animal dependence upon food has been bared and the naked fear of starvation permitted to run loose. Our humiliating enslavement to the 'material,' which all human culture is designed to mitigate, was deliberately made more rigorous. This is at the root of the 'sickness of an acquisitive society' that Tawney warned of. And Robert Owen's genius was at its best when, a century before, he described the profit motive as 'a principle entirely unfavorable to individual and public happiness.'

The Reality of Society

I plead for the restoration of that unity of motives which should inform man in his everyday activity as a producer, for the reabsorption of the economic system in society, for the creative adaptation of our ways of life to an industrial environment.

On all these counts, laissez-faire philosophy, with its corollary of a marketing society, falls to the ground. It is responsible for the splitting up of man's vital unity into 'real' man, bent on material values, and his 'ideal' better self. It is paralyzing our social imagination by more or less unconsciously fostering the prejudice of economic determinism. It has done its service in that phase of industrial civilization which is behind us. At the price of impoverishing the individual, it enriched society. Today, we are faced with the vital task of restoring the fullness of life to the person, even though this may mean a technologically less efficient society. In different countries in different ways, classical liberalism is being discarded. On Right and Left and Middle, new avenues are being explored. British Social-Democrats, American New Dealers, and also European fascists and American anti-New Dealers of the various 'managerialist' brands, reject the liberal utopia. Nor should the present political mood of rejection of everything Russian blind us to the achievement of the Russians in creative adjustment to some of the fundamental aspects of an industrial environment.

On general grounds, the Communist's expectation of the 'withering away of the state' seems to me to combine elements of liberal utopianism with practical indifference to institutional freedoms. As regards the withering state, it is impossible to deny that industrial society is complex society, and no complex society can exist without organized power at the center. Yet, again, this fact is no excuse for the Communist's slurring over the question of concrete institutional freedoms. It is on this level of realism that the problem of individual freedom should be met. No human society is possible in which power and compulsion are absent, nor is a world in which force has no function. Liberal philosophy gave a false direction to our ideals in seeming to promise the fulfillment of such intrinsically utopian expectations.

But under the market system, society as a whole remained invisible. Anybody could imagine himself free from responsibility for those acts of compulsion on the part of the state which he, personally, repudiated, or for unemployment and destitution from which he, personally, did not benefit. Personally, he remained unentangled in the evils of power and economic value. In good conscience, he could deny their reality in the name of his imaginary freedom. Power and economic value are, indeed, a paradigm of social reality. Neither power nor economic value spring from human volition; non-cooperation is impossible in regard to them. The function of power is to insure that measure of conformity which is needed for the survival of the group: as David Hume showed, its ultimate source is opinion – and who could help holding opinions of some sort or other? Economic value, in any society, insures the usefulness of the goods produced; it is a seal set on the division of labor. Its source is human wants – and how could we be expected not to prefer one thing to another? Any opinion or desire, no matter what society we live in, will make us participants in the creation of power and the constituting of value. No freedom to do otherwise is conceivable. An ideal that would ban power and compulsion from society is intrinsically invalid. By ignoring this limitation on man's meaningful wishes, the marketing view of society reveals its essential immaturity.

Freedom in Industrial Society

The breakdown of market-economy imperils two kinds of freedoms: some good, some bad.

That the freedom to exploit one's fellows, or the freedom to make inordinate gains without commensurable service to the community, the freedom to keep technological inventions from being used for the public benefit, or the freedom to profit from public calamities secretly engineered for private advantage, may disappear, together with the free market, is all to the good. But the market economy under which these freedoms throve also produced freedoms that we prize highly. Freedom of conscience, freedom of speech, freedom of meeting, freedom of association, freedom to choose one's job – we cherish them for their own sake. Yet to a large extent they were by-products of the same economy that was also responsible for the evil freedoms.

The existence of a separate economic sphere in society created, as it were, a gap between politics and economics, between government and industry, that was in the nature of a no man's land. As division of sovereignty between pope and emperor left medieval princes in a condition of freedom sometimes bordering on anarchy, so division of sovereignty between government and industry in the nineteenth century allowed even the poor man to enjoy freedoms that partly compensated for his wretched status. Current skepticism in regard to the future of freedom largely rests on this. There are those who argue, like Hayek, that since free institutions were a product of market-economy, they must give place to serfdom once that economy disappears. There are others, like Burnham, who assert the inevitability of some new form of serfdom called 'managerialism.'

Arguments like these merely prove to what extent economistic prejudice is still rampant. For such determinism, as we have seen, is only another name for the market mechanism. It is hardly logical to argue the effects of its absence on the strength of an economic necessity that derives from its presence. And it is certainly contrary to Anglo-Saxon experience. Neither the freezing of labor nor selective service abrogated the essential freedoms of the American people, as anybody can witness who spent the crucial years 1940–43 in these States. Great Britain during the war introduced an all-round planned economy and did away with that separation of government and industry from which nineteenth-century freedom sprang, yet never were public liberties more securely entrenched than at the height of the emergency. In truth, we will have just as much freedom as we will desire to create and to safeguard. There is no *one* determinant in human society. Institutional guarantees of personal freedom are compatible with any economic system. In market society alone did the economic mechanism lay down the law.

What appears to our generation as the problem of capitalism is, in reality, the far greater problem of an industrial civilization. The economic liberal is blind to this fact. In defending capitalism as an economic system, he ignores the challenge of the Machine Age. Yet the dangers that make the bravest quake today transcend economy. The idyllic concerns of trust-busting and Taylorization have been superseded by Hiroshima. Scientific barbarism is dogging our footsteps. The Germans were planning a contrivance to make the sun emanate death rays. We, in fact, produced a burst of death rays that blotted out the sun. Yet the Germans had an evil philosophy, and we had a humane philosophy. In this we should learn to see the symbol of our peril.

Among those in America who are aware of the dimensions of the problem, two tendencies are discernible: some believe in elites and aristocracies, in managerialism and the corporation. They feel that the whole of society should be more intimately adjusted to the economic system, which they would wish to maintain unchanged. This is the ideal of the Brave New World, where the individual is conditioned to support an order that has been designed for him by such as are wiser than he. Others, on the contrary, believe that in a truly democratic society, the problem of industry would resolve itself through the planned intervention of the producers and consumers themselves. Such conscious and responsible action is, indeed, one of the embodiments of freedom in a complex society. But, as the contents of this article suggest, such an endeavor cannot be successful unless it is disciplined by a total view of man and society very different from that which we inherited from market-economy.

Notes

*   From 'Our Obsolete Market Mentality', *Commentary*, **3**, February 1947, 109–17. Reprinted by permission of *Commentary*, copyright 1947 by the American Jewish Committee.
1.   On such peripheral or petty markets as they function in Africa, see Paul Bohannan and George Dalton, 'Introduction' to *Markets in Africa*, New York: Natural History Press, 1965.

[7]

Economic Action and Social Structure: The Problem of Embeddedness[1]

Mark Granovetter
State University of New York at Stony Brook

How behavior and institutions are affected by social relations is one of the classic questions of social theory. This paper concerns the extent to which economic action is embedded in structures of social relations, in modern industrial society. Although the usual neoclassical accounts provide an "undersocialized" or atomized-actor explanation of such action, reformist economists who attempt to bring social structure back in do so in the "oversocialized" way criticized by Dennis Wrong. Under- and oversocialized accounts are paradoxically similar in their neglect of ongoing structures of social relations, and a sophisticated account of economic action must consider its embeddedness in such structures. The argument is illustrated by a critique of Oliver Williamson's "markets and hierarchies" research program.

INTRODUCTION: THE PROBLEM OF EMBEDDEDNESS

How behavior and institutions are affected by social relations is one of the classic questions of social theory. Since such relations are always present, the situation that would arise in their absence can be imagined only through a thought experiment like Thomas Hobbes's "state of nature" or John Rawls's "original position." Much of the utilitarian tradition, including classical and neoclassical economics, assumes rational, self-interested behavior affected minimally by social relations, thus invoking an idealized state not far from that of these thought experiments. At the other extreme lies what I call the argument of "embeddedness": the argu-

[1] Earlier drafts of this paper were written in sabbatical facilities kindly provided by the Institute for Advanced Study and Harvard University. Financial support was provided in part by the institute, by a John Simon Guggenheim Memorial Foundation fellowship, and by NSF Science Faculty Professional Development grant SPI 81-65055. Among those who have helped clarify the arguments are Wayne Baker, Michael Bernstein, Albert Hirschman, Ron Jepperson, Eric Leifer, Don McCloskey, Charles Perrow, James Rule, Michael Schwartz, Theda Skocpol, and Harrison White. Requests for reprints should be sent to Mark Granovetter, Department of Sociology, State University of New York at Stony Brook, Stony Brook, New York 11794-4356.

American Journal of Sociology

ment that the behavior and institutions to be analyzed are so constrained by ongoing social relations that to construe them as independent is a grievous misunderstanding.

This article concerns the embeddedness of economic behavior. It has long been the majority view among sociologists, anthropologists, political scientists, and historians that such behavior was heavily embedded in social relations in premarket societies but became much more autonomous with modernization. This view sees the economy as an increasingly separate, differentiated sphere in modern society, with economic transactions defined no longer by the social or kinship obligations of those transacting but by rational calculations of individual gain. It is sometimes further argued that the traditional situation is reversed: instead of economic life being submerged in social relations, these relations become an epiphenomenon of the market. The embeddedness position is associated with the "substantivist" school in anthropology, identified especially with Karl Polanyi (1944; Polanyi, Arensberg, and Pearson 1957) and with the idea of "moral economy" in history and political science (Thompson 1971; Scott 1976). It has also some obvious relation to Marxist thought.

Few economists, however, have accepted this conception of a break in embeddedness with modernization; most of them assert instead that embeddedness in earlier societies was not substantially greater than the low level found in modern markets. The tone was set by Adam Smith, who postulated a "certain propensity in human nature . . . to truck, barter and exchange one thing for another" ([1776] 1979, book 1, chap. 2) and assumed that since labor was the only factor of production in primitive society, goods must have exchanged in proportion to their labor costs—as in the general classical theory of exchange ([1776] 1979, book 1, chap. 6). From the 1920s on, certain anthropologists took a similar position, which came to be called the "formalist" one: even in tribal societies, economic behavior was sufficiently independent of social relations for standard neoclassical analysis to be useful (Schneider 1974). This position has recently received a new infusion as economists and fellow travelers in history and political science have developed a new interest in the economic analysis of social institutions—much of which falls into what is called the "new institutional economics"—and have argued that behavior and institutions previously interpreted as embedded in earlier societies, as well as in our own, can be better understood as resulting from the pursuit of self-interest by rational, more or less atomized individuals (e.g., North and Thomas 1973; Williamson 1975; Popkin 1979).

My own view diverges from both schools of thought. I assert that the level of embeddedness of economic behavior is lower in nonmarket societies than is claimed by substantivists and development theorists, and it has changed less with "modernization" than they believe; but I argue

Embeddedness

also that this level has always been and continues to be more substantial than is allowed for by formalists and economists. I do not attempt here to treat the issues posed by nonmarket societies. I proceed instead by a theoretical elaboration of the concept of embeddedness, whose value is then illustrated with a problem from modern society, currently important in the new institutional economics: which transactions in modern capitalist society are carried out in the market, and which subsumed within hierarchically organized. firms? This question has been raised to prominence by the "markets and hierarchies" program of research initiated by Oliver Williamson (1975).

OVER- AND UNDERSOCIALIZED CONCEPTIONS OF HUMAN ACTION IN SOCIOLOGY AND ECONOMICS

I begin by recalling Dennis Wrong's 1961 complaint about an "oversocialized conception of man in modern sociology"—a conception of people as overwhelmingly sensitive to the opinions of others and hence obedient to the dictates of consensually developed systems of norms and values, internalized through socialization, so that obedience is not perceived as a burden. To the extent that such a conception was prominent in 1961, it resulted in large part from Talcott Parsons's recognition of the problem of order as posed by Hobbes and his own attempt to resolve it by transcending the atomized, *undersocialized* conception of man in the utilitarian tradition of which Hobbes was part (Parsons 1937, pp. 89–94). Wrong approved the break with atomized utilitarianism and the emphasis on actors' embeddedness in social context—the crucial factor absent from Hobbes's thinking—but warned of exaggerating the degree of this embeddedness and the extent to which it might eliminate conflict:

> It is frequently the task of the sociologist to call attention to the intensity with which men desire and strive for the good opinion of their immediate associates in a variety of situations, particularly those where received theories or ideologies have unduly emphasized other motives. . . . Thus sociologists have shown that factory workers are more sensitive to the attitudes of their fellow workers than to purely economic incentives. . . . It is certainly not my intention to criticize the findings of such studies. My objection is that . . . [a]lthough sociologists have criticized past efforts to single out one fundamental motive in human conduct, the desire to achieve a favorable self-image by winning approval from others frequently occupies such a position in their own thinking. [1961, pp. 188–89]

Classical and neoclassical economics operates, in contrast, with an atomized, *under*socialized conception of human action, continuing in the utilitarian tradition. The theoretical arguments disallow by hypothesis any impact of social structure and social relations on production, distribution, or consumption. In competitive markets, no producer or consumer

American Journal of Sociology

noticeably influences aggregate supply or demand or, therefore, prices or other terms of trade. As Albert Hirschman has noted, such idealized markets, involving as they do "large numbers of price-taking anonymous buyers and sellers supplied with perfect information . . . function without any prolonged human or social contact between the parties. Under perfect competition there is no room for bargaining, negotiation, remonstration or mutual adjustment and the various operators that contract together need not enter into recurrent or continuing relationships as a result of which they would get to know each other well" (1982, p. 1473).

It has long been recognized that the idealized markets of perfect competition have survived intellectual attack in part because self-regulating economic structures are politically attractive to many. Another reason for this survival, less clearly understood, is that the elimination of social relations from economic analysis removes the problem of order from the intellectual agenda, at least in the economic sphere. In Hobbes's argument, disorder arises because conflict-free social and economic transactions depend on trust and the absence of malfeasance. But these are unlikely when individuals are conceived to have neither social relationships nor institutional context—as in the "state of nature." Hobbes contains the difficulty by superimposing a structure of autocratic authority. The solution of classical liberalism, and correspondingly of classical economics, is antithetical: repressive political structures are rendered unnecessary by competitive markets that make force or fraud unavailing. Competition determines the terms of trade in a way that individual traders cannot manipulate. If traders encounter complex or difficult relationships, characterized by mistrust or malfeasance, they can simply move on to the legion of other traders willing to do business on market terms; social relations and their details thus become frictional matters.

In classical and neoclassical economics, therefore, the fact that actors may have social relations with one another has been treated, if at all, as a frictional drag that impedes competitive markets. In a much-quoted line, Adam Smith complained that "people of the same trade seldom meet together, even for merriment and diversion, but the conversation ends in a conspiracy against the public, or in some contrivance to raise prices." His laissez-faire politics allowed few solutions to this problem, but he did suggest repeal of regulations requiring all those in the same trade to sign a public register; the public existence of such information "connects individuals who might never otherwise be known to one another and gives every man of the trade a direction where to find every other man of it." Noteworthy here is not the rather lame policy prescription but the recognition that *social atomization is prerequisite to perfect competition* (Smith [1776] 1979, pp. 232–33).

Embeddedness

More recent comments by economists on "social influences" construe these as processes in which actors acquire customs, habits, or norms that are followed mechanically and automatically, irrespective of their bearing on rational choice. This view, close to Wrong's "oversocialized conception," is reflected in James Duesenberry's quip that "economics is all about how people make choices; sociology is all about how they don't have any choices to make" (1960, p. 233) and in E. H. Phelps Brown's description of the "sociologists' approach to pay determination" as deriving from the assumption that people act in "certain ways because to do so is customary, or an obligation, or the 'natural thing to do,' or right and proper, or just and fair" (1977, p. 17).

But despite the apparent contrast between under- and oversocialized views, we should note an irony of great theoretical importance: both have in common a conception of action and decision carried out by atomized actors. In the undersocialized account, atomization results from narrow utilitarian pursuit of self-interest; in the oversocialized one, from the fact that behavioral patterns have been internalized and ongoing social relations thus have only peripheral effects on behavior. That the internalized rules of behavior are social in origin does not differentiate this argument decisively from a utilitarian one, in which the source of utility functions is left open, leaving room for behavior guided entirely by consensually determined norms and values—as in the oversocialized view. Under- and oversocialized resolutions of the problem of order thus merge in their atomization of actors from immediate social context. This ironic merger is already visible in Hobbes's *Leviathan,* in which the unfortunate denizens of the state of nature, overwhelmed by the disorder consequent to their atomization, cheerfully surrender all their rights to an authoritarian power and subsequently behave in a docile and honorable manner; by the artifice of a social contract, they lurch directly from an undersocialized to an oversocialized state.

When modern economists do attempt to take account of social influences, they typically represent them in the oversocialized manner represented in the quotations above. In so doing, they reverse the judgment that social influences are frictional but sustain the conception of how such influences operate. In the theory of segmented labor markets, for example, Michael Piore has argued that members of each labor market segment are characterized by different styles of decision making and that the making of decisions by rational choice, custom, or command in upper-primary, lower-primary, and secondary labor markets respectively corresponds to the origins of workers in middle-, working-, and lower-class subcultures (Piore 1975). Similarly, Samuel Bowles and Herbert Gintis, in their account of the consequences of American education, argue that different social classes display different cognitive processes because

485

American Journal of Sociology

of differences in the education provided to each. Those destined for lower-level jobs are trained to be dependable followers of rules, while those who will be channeled into elite positions attend "elite four-year colleges" that "emphasize social relationships conformable with the higher levels in the production hierarchy. . . . As they 'master' one type of behavioral regulation they are either allowed to progress to the next or are channeled into the corresponding level in the hierarchy of production" (Bowles and Gintis 1975, p. 132).

But these oversocialized conceptions of how society influences individual behavior are rather mechanical: once we know the individual's social class or labor market sector, everything else in behavior is automatic, since they are so well socialized. Social influence here is an external force that, like the deists' God, sets things in motion and has no further effects—a force that insinuates itself into the minds and bodies of individuals (as in the movie *Invasion of the Body Snatchers*), altering their way of making decisions. Once we know in just what way an individual has been affected, ongoing social relations and structures are irrelevant. Social influences are all contained inside an individual's head, so, in actual decision situations, he or she can be atomized as any *Homo economicus*, though perhaps with different rules for decisions. More sophisticated (and thus less oversocialized) analyses of cultural influences (e.g., Fine and Kleinman 1979; Cole 1979, chap. 1) make it clear that culture is not a once-for-all influence but an ongoing process, continuously constructed and reconstructed during interaction. It not only shapes its members but also is shaped by them, in part for their own strategic reasons.

Even when economists do take social relationships seriously, as do such diverse figures as Harvey Leibenstein (1976) and Gary Becker (1976), they invariably abstract away from the history of relations and their position with respect to other relations—what might be called the historical and structural embeddedness of relations. The interpersonal ties described in their arguments are extremely stylized, average, "typical"— devoid of specific content, history, or structural location. Actors' behavior results from their named role positions and role sets; thus we have arguments on how workers and supervisors, husbands and wives, or criminals and law enforcers will interact with one another, but these relations are not assumed to have individualized content beyond that given by the named roles. This procedure is exactly what structural sociologists have criticized in Parsonian sociology—the relegation of the specifics of individual relations to a minor role in the overall conceptual scheme, epiphenomenal in comparison with enduring structures of normative role prescriptions deriving from ultimate value orientations. In economic models, this treatment of social relations has the paradoxical effect of preserving atomized decision making even when decisions are

Embeddedness

seen to involve more than one individual. Because the analyzed set of individuals—usually dyads, occasionally larger groups—is abstracted out of social context, it is atomized in its behavior from that of other groups and from the history of its own relations. Atomization has not been eliminated, merely transferred to the dyadic or higher level of analysis. Note the use of an oversocialized conception—that of actors behaving exclusively in accord with their prescribed roles—to implement an atomized, undersocialized view.

A fruitful analysis of human action requires us to avoid the atomization implicit in the theoretical extremes of under- and oversocialized conceptions. Actors do not behave or decide as atoms outside a social context, nor do they adhere slavishly to a script written for them by the particular intersection of social categories that they happen to occupy. Their attempts at purposive action are instead embedded in concrete, ongoing systems of social relations. In the remainder of this article I illustrate how this view of embeddedness alters our theoretical and empirical approach to the study of economic behavior. I first narrow the focus to the question of trust and malfeasance in economic life and then use the "markets and hierarchies" problem to illustrate the use of embeddedness ideas in analyzing this question.[2]

EMBEDDEDNESS, TRUST, AND MALFEASANCE IN ECONOMIC LIFE

Since about 1970, there has been a flurry of interest among economists in the previously neglected issues of trust and malfeasance. Oliver Williamson has noted that real economic actors engage not merely in the pursuit of self-interest but also in "opportunism"—"self-interest seeking with guile; agents who are skilled at dissembling realize transactional advantages.[3] Economic man . . . is thus a more subtle and devious creature than the usual self-interest seeking assumption reveals" (1975, p. 255).

---

[2] There are many parallels between what are referred to here as the "undersocialized" and "oversocialized" views of action and what Burt (1982, chap. 9) calls the "atomistic" and "normative" approaches. Similarly, the embeddedness approach proposed here as a middle ground between under- and oversocialized views has an obvious family resemblance to Burt's "structural" approach to action. My distinctions and approach also differ from Burt's in many ways that cannot be quickly summarized; these can be best appreciated by comparison of this article with his useful summary (1982, chap. 9) and with the formal models that implement his conception (1982, 1983). Another approach that resembles mine in its emphasis on how social connections affect purposive action is Marsden's extension of James Coleman's theories of collective action and decision to situations where such connections modify results that would occur in a purely atomistic situation (Marsden 1981, 1983).

[3] Students of the sociology of sport will note that this proposition had been put forward previously, in slightly different form, by Leo Durocher.

American Journal of Sociology

But this points out a peculiar assumption of modern economic theory, that one's economic interest is pursued only by comparatively gentlemanly means. The Hobbesian question—how it can be that those who pursue their own interest do not do so mainly by force and fraud—is finessed by this conception. Yet, as Hobbes saw so clearly, there is nothing in the intrinsic meaning of "self-interest" that excludes force or fraud.

In part, this assumption persisted because competitive forces, in a self-regulating market, could be imagined to suppress force and fraud. But the idea is also embedded in the intellectual history of the discipline. In *The Passions and the Interests,* Albert Hirschman (1977) shows that an important strand of intellectual history from the time of *Leviathan* to that of *The Wealth of Nations* consisted of the watering down of Hobbes's problem of order by arguing that certain human motivations kept others under control and that, in particular, the pursuit of economic self-interest was typically not an uncontrollable "passion" but a civilized, gentle activity. The wide though implicit acceptance of such an idea is a powerful example of how under- and oversocialized conceptions complement one another: atomized actors in competitive markets so thoroughly internalize these normative standards of behavior as to guarantee orderly transactions.[4]

What has eroded this confidence in recent years has been increased attention to the micro-level details of imperfectly competitive markets, characterized by small numbers of participants with sunk costs and "specific human capital" investments. In such situations, the alleged discipline of competitive markets cannot be called on to mitigate deceit, so the classical problem of how it can be that daily economic life is not riddled with mistrust and malfeasance has resurfaced.

In the economic literature, I see two fundamental answers to this problem and argue that one is linked to an undersocialized, and the other to an oversocialized, conception of human action. The undersocialized account is found mainly in the new institutional economics—a loosely defined confederation of economists with an interest in explaining social institutions from a neoclassical viewpoint. (See, e.g., Furubotn and Pejovich 1972; Alchian and Demsetz 1973; Lazear 1979; Rosen 1982; Williamson 1975, 1979, 1981; Williamson and Ouchi 1981.) The general story told by members of this school is that social institutions and arrangements previously thought to be the adventitious result of legal, historical, social, or political forces are better viewed as the efficient solution to certain economic problems. The tone is similar to that of structural-functional sociology of the 1940s to the 1960s, and much of the argumentation fails the elementary tests of a sound functional explanation laid down by

---

[4] I am indebted to an anonymous referee for pointing this out.

Embeddedness

Robert Merton in 1947. Consider, for example, Schotter's view that to understand any observed economic institution requires only that we "infer the evolutionary problem that must have existed for the institution as we see it to have developed. Every evolutionary economic problem requires a social institution to solve it" (1981, p. 2).

Malfeasance is here seen to be averted because clever institutional arrangements make it too costly to engage in, and these arrangements— many previously interpreted as serving no economic function—are now seen as having evolved to discourage malfeasance. Note, however, that they do not produce trust but instead are a functional substitute for it. The main such arrangements are elaborate explicit and implicit contracts (Okun 1981), including deferred compensation plans and mandatory retirement—seen to reduce the incentives for "shirking" on the job or absconding with proprietary secrets (Lazear 1979; Pakes and Nitzan 1982)—and authority structures that deflect opportunism by making potentially divisive decisions by fiat (Williamson 1975). These conceptions are undersocialized in that they do not allow for the extent to which concrete personal relations and the obligations inherent in them discourage malfeasance, quite apart from institutional arrangements. *Substituting* these arrangements for trust results actually in a Hobbesian situation, in which any rational individual would be motivated to develop clever ways to evade them; it is then hard to imagine that everyday economic life would not be poisoned by ever more ingenious attempts at deceit.

Other economists have recognized that some degree of trust *must* be assumed to operate, since institutional arrangements alone could not entirely stem force or fraud. But it remains to explain the source of this trust, and appeal is sometimes made to the existence of a "generalized morality." Kenneth Arrow, for example, suggests that societies, "in their evolution have developed implicit agreements to certain kinds of regard for others, agreements which are essential to the survival of the society or at least contribute greatly to the efficiency of its working" (1974, p. 26; see also Akerlof [1983] on the origins of "honesty").

Now one can hardly doubt the existence of some such generalized morality; without it, you would be afraid to give the gas station attendant a 20-dollar bill when you had bought only five dollars' worth of gas. But this conception has the oversocialized characteristic of calling on a generalized and automatic response, even though moral action in economic life is hardly automatic or universal (as is well known at gas stations that demand exact change after dark).

Consider a case where generalized morality does indeed seem to be at work: the legendary (I hesitate to say apocryphal) economist who, against all economic rationality, leaves a tip in a roadside restaurant far from home. Note that this transaction has three characteristics that make it

American Journal of Sociology

somewhat unusual: (1) the transactors are previously unacquainted, (2) they are unlikely to transact again, and (3) information about the activities of either is unlikely to reach others with whom they might transact in the future. I argue that it is only in situations of this kind that the absence of force and fraud can mainly be explained by generalized morality. Even there, one might wonder how effective this morality would be if large costs were incurred.

The embeddedness argument stresses instead the role of concrete personal relations and structures (or "networks") of such relations in generating trust and discouraging malfeasance. The widespread preference for transacting with individuals of known reputation implies that few are actually content to rely on either generalized morality *or* institutional arrangements to guard against trouble. Economists *have* pointed out that one incentive not to cheat is the cost of damage to one's reputation; but this is an undersocialized conception of reputation as a generalized commodity, a ratio of cheating to opportunities for doing so. In practice, we settle for such generalized information when nothing better is available, but ordinarily we seek better information. Better than the statement that someone is known to be reliable is information from a trusted informant that he has dealt with that individual and found him so. Even better is information from one's own past dealings with that person. This is better information for four reasons: (1) it is cheap; (2) one trusts one's own information best—it is richer, more detailed, and known to be accurate; (3) individuals with whom one has a continuing relation have an economic motivation to be trustworthy, so as not to discourage future transactions; and (4) departing from pure economic motives, continuing economic relations often become overlaid with social content that carries strong expectations of trust and abstention from opportunism.

It would never occur to us to doubt this last point in more intimate relations, which make behavior more predictable and thus close off some of the fears that create difficulties among strangers. Consider, for example, why individuals in a burning theater panic and stampede to the door, leading to desperate results. Analysts of collective behavior long considered this to be prototypically irrational behavior, but Roger Brown (1965, chap. 14) points out that the situation is essentially an *n*-person Prisoner's Dilemma: each stampeder is actually being quite rational given the absence of a guarantee that anyone else will walk out calmly, even though all would be better off if everyone did so. Note, however, that in the case of the burning houses featured on the 11:00 P.M. news, we never hear that everyone stampeded out and that family members trampled one another. In the family, there is no Prisoner's Dilemma because each is confident that the others can be counted on.

490

Embeddedness

In business relations the degree of confidence must be more variable, but Prisoner's Dilemmas are nevertheless often obviated by the strength of personal relations, and this strength is a property not of the transactors but of their concrete relations. Standard economic analysis neglects the identity and past relations of individual transactors, but rational individuals know better, relying on their knowledge of these relations. They are less interested in *general* reputations than in whether a particular other may be expected to deal honestly with *them*—mainly a function of whether they or their own contacts have had satisfactory past dealings with the other. One sees this pattern even in situations that appear, at first glance, to approximate the classic higgling of a competitive market, as in the Moroccan bazaar analyzed by Geertz (1979).

Up to this point, I have argued that social relations, rather than institutional arrangements or generalized morality, are mainly responsible for the production of trust in economic life. But I then risk rejecting one kind of optimistic functionalism for another, in which networks of relations, rather than morality or arrangements, are the structure that fulfills the function of sustaining order. There are two ways to reduce this risk. One is to recognize that as a solution to the problem of order, the embeddedness position is less sweeping than either alternative argument, since networks of social relations penetrate irregularly and in differing degrees in different sectors of economic life, thus allowing for what we already know: distrust, opportunism, and disorder are by no means absent.

The second is to insist that while social relations may indeed often be a necessary condition for trust and trustworthy behavior, they are not sufficient to guarantee these and may even provide occasion and means for malfeasance and conflict on a scale larger than in their absence. There are three reasons for this.

1. The trust engendered by personal relations presents, by its very existence, enhanced opportunity for malfeasance. In personal relations it is common knowledge that "you always hurt the one you love"; that person's trust in you results in a position far more vulnerable than that of a stranger. (In the Prisoner's Dilemma, knowledge that one's coconspirator is certain to deny the crime is all the more rational motive to confess, and personal relations that abrogate this dilemma may be less symmetrical than is believed by the party to be deceived.) This elementary fact of social life is the bread and butter of "confidence" rackets that simulate certain relationships, sometimes for long periods, for concealed purposes. In the business world, certain crimes, such as embezzling, are simply impossible for those who have not built up relationships of trust that permit the opportunity to manipulate accounts. The more complete the trust, the greater the potential gain from malfeasance. That such

American Journal of Sociology

instances are statistically infrequent is a tribute to the force of personal relations and reputation; that they do occur with regularity, however infrequently, shows the limits of this force.

2. Force and fraud are most efficiently pursued by teams, and the structure of these teams requires a level of internal trust—"honor among thieves"—that usually follows preexisting lines of relationship. Elaborate schemes for kickbacks and bid rigging, for example, can hardly be executed by individuals working alone, and when such activity is exposed it is often remarkable that it could have been kept secret given the large numbers involved. Law-enforcement efforts consist of finding an entry point to the network of malfeasance—an individual whose confession implicates others who will, in snowball-sample fashion, "finger" still others until the entire picture is fitted together.

Both enormous trust and enormous malfeasance, then, may follow from personal relations. Yoram Ben-Porath, in the functionalist style of the new institutional economics, emphasizes the positive side, noting that "continuity of relationships can generate behavior on the part of shrewd, self-seeking, or even unscrupulous individuals that could otherwise be interpreted as foolish or purely altruistic. Valuable diamonds change hands on the diamond exchange, and the deals are sealed by a handshake" (1980, p. 6). I might add, continuing in this positive vein, that this transaction is possible in part because it is not atomized from other transactions but embedded in a close-knit community of diamond merchants who monitor one another's behavior closely. Like other densely knit networks of actors, they generate clearly defined standards of behavior easily policed by the quick spread of information about instances of malfeasance. But the temptations posed by this level of trust are considerable, and the diamond trade has also been the scene of numerous well-publicized "insider job" thefts and of the notorious "CBS murders" of April 1982. In this case, the owner of a diamond company was defrauding a factoring concern by submitting invoices from fictitious sales. The scheme required cooperation from his accounting personnel, one of whom was approached by investigators and turned state's evidence. The owner then contracted for the murder of the disloyal employee and her assistant; three CBS technicians who came to their aid were also gunned down (Shenon 1984).

3. The extent of disorder resulting from force and fraud depends very much on how the network of social relations is structured. Hobbes exaggerated the extent of disorder likely in his atomized state of nature where, in the absence of sustained social relations, one could expect only desultory dyadic conflicts. More extended and large-scale disorder results from coalitions of combatants, impossible without prior relations. We do not generally speak of "war" unless actors have arranged themselves into two

Embeddedness

sides, as the end result of various coalitions. This occurs only if there are insufficient crosscutting ties, held by actors with enough links to both main potential combatants to have a strong interest in forestalling conflict. The same is true in the business world, where conflicts are relatively tame unless each side can escalate by calling on substantial numbers of allies in other firms, as sometimes happens in attempts to implement or forestall takeovers.

Disorder and malfeasance do of course occur also when social relations are absent. This possibility is already entailed in my earlier claim that the presence of such relations inhibits malfeasance. But the *level* of malfeasance available in a truly atomized social situation is fairly low; instances can only be episodic, unconnected, small scale. The Hobbesian problem is truly a problem, but in transcending it by the smoothing effect of social structure, we also introduce the possibility of disruptions on a larger scale than those available in the "state of nature."

The embeddedness approach to the problem of trust and order in economic life, then, threads its way between the oversocialized approach of generalized morality and the undersocialized one of impersonal, institutional arrangements by following and analyzing concrete patterns of social relations. Unlike either alternative, or the Hobbesian position, it makes no sweeping (and thus unlikely) predictions of universal order or disorder but rather assumes that the details of social structure will determine which is found.

THE PROBLEM OF MARKETS AND HIERARCHIES

As a concrete application of the embeddedness approach to economic life, I offer a critique of the influential argument of Oliver Williamson in *Markets and Hierarchies* (1975) and later articles (1979, 1981; Williamson and Ouchi 1981). Williamson asked under what circumstances economic functions are performed within the boundaries of hierarchical firms rather than by market processes that cross these boundaries. His answer, consistent with the general emphasis of the new institutional economics, is that the organizational form observed in any situation is that which deals most efficiently with the cost of economic transactions. Those that are uncertain in outcome, recur frequently, and require substantial "transaction-specific investments"—for example, money, time, or energy that cannot be easily transferred to interaction with others on different matters—are more likely to take place within hierarchically organized firms. Those that are straightforward, nonrepetitive, and require no transaction-specific investment—such as the one-time purchase of standard equipment—will more likely take place between firms, that is, across a market interface.

American Journal of Sociology

In this account, the former set of transactions is internalized within hierarchies for two reasons. The first is "bounded rationality," the inability of economic actors to anticipate properly the complex chain of contingencies that might be relevant to long-term contracts. When transactions are internalized, it is unnecessary to anticipate all such contingencies; they can be handled within the firm's "governance structure" instead of leading to complex negotiations. The second reason is "opportunism," the rational pursuit by economic actors of their own advantage, with all means at their command, including guile and deceit. Opportunism is mitigated and constrained by authority relations and by the greater identification with transaction partners that one allegedly has when both are contained within one corporate entity than when they face one another across the chasm of a market boundary.

The appeal to authority relations in order to tame opportunism constitutes a rediscovery of Hobbesian analysis, though confined here to the economic sphere. The Hobbesian flavor of Williamson's argument is suggested by such statements as the following: "Internal organization is not beset with the same kinds of difficulties that autonomous contracting [among independent firms] experiences when disputes arise between the parties. Although interfirm disputes are often settled out of court . . . this resolution is sometimes difficult and interfirm relations are often strained. Costly litigation is sometimes unavoidable. Internal organization, by contrast . . . is able to settle many such disputes by appeal to fiat—an enormously efficient way to settle instrumental differences" (1975, p. 30). He notes that complex, recurring transactions require long-term relations between identified individuals but that opportunism jeopardizes these relations. The adaptations to changing market circumstances required over the course of a relationship are too complex and unpredictable to be encompassed in some initial contact, and promises of good faith are unenforceable in the absence of an overarching authority:

> A general clause . . . that "I will behave responsibly rather than seek individual advantage when an occasion to adapt arises," would, in the absence of opportunism, suffice. Given, however, the unenforceability of general clauses and the proclivity of human agents to make false and misleading (self-disbelieved) statements, . . . both buyer and seller are strategically situated to bargain over the disposition of any incremental gain whenever a proposal to adapt is made by the other party. . . . Efficient adaptations which would otherwise be made thus result in costly haggling or even go unmentioned, lest the gains be dissipated by costly subgoal pursuit. *Governance structures* which attenuate opportunism and otherwise infuse confidence are evidently needed. [1979, pp. 241–42, emphasis mine]

This analysis entails the same mixture of under- and oversocialized assumptions found in *Leviathan*. The efficacy of hierarchical power within the firm is overplayed, as with Hobbes's oversocialized sovereign

Embeddedness

state.[5] The "market" resembles Hobbes's state of nature. It is the atomized and anonymous market of classical political economy, minus the discipline brought by fully competitive conditions—an undersocialized conception that neglects the role of social relations among individuals in different firms in bringing order to economic life. Williamson does acknowledge that this picture of the market is not always appropriate: "Norms of trustworthy behavior sometimes extend to markets and are enforced, in some degree, by group pressures. . . . Repeated personal contacts across organizational boundaries support some minimum level of courtesy and consideration between the parties. . . . In addition, expectations of repeat business discourage efforts to seek a narrow advantage in any particular transaction. . . . Individual aggressiveness is curbed by the prospect of ostracism among peers, in both trade and social circumstances. The reputation of a firm for fairness is also a business asset not to be dissipated" (1975, pp. 106–8).

A wedge is opened here for analysis of social structural influences on market behavior. But Williamson treats these examples as exceptions and also fails to appreciate the extent to which the dyadic relations he describes are themselves embedded in broader systems of social relations. I argue that the anonymous market of neoclassical models is virtually nonexistent in economic life and that transactions of all kinds are rife with the social connections described. This is not necessarily more the case in transactions between firms than within—it seems plausible, on the contrary, that the network of social relations within the firm might be more dense and long-lasting on the average than that existing between—but all I need show here is that there is sufficient social overlay in economic transactions across firms (in the "market," to use the term as in Williamson's dichotomy) to render dubious the assertion that complex market transactions approximate a Hobbesian state of nature that can only be resolved by internalization within a hierarchical structure.

In a general way, there is evidence all around us of the extent to which business relations are mixed up with social ones. The trade associations deplored by Adam Smith remain of great importance. It is well known that many firms, small and large, are linked by interlocking directorates so that relationships among directors of firms are many and densely knit. That business relations spill over into sociability and vice versa, espe-

---

[5] Williamson's confidence in the efficacy of hierarchy leads him, in discussing Chester Barnard's "zone of indifference"—that realm within which employees obey orders simply because they are indifferent about whether or not they do what is ordered—to speak instead of a "zone of acceptance" (1975, p. 77), thus undercutting Barnard's emphasis on the problematic nature of obedience. This transformation of Barnard's usage appears to have originated with Herbert Simon, who does not justify it, noting only that he "prefer[s] the term 'acceptance' " (Simon 1957, p. 12).

American Journal of Sociology

cially among business elites, is one of the best-documented facts in the sociological study of business (e.g., Domhoff 1971; Useem 1979). In his study of the extent to which litigation was used to settle disputes between firms, Macaulay notes that disputes are "frequently settled without reference to the contract or potential or actual legal sanctions. There is a hesitancy to speak of legal rights or to threaten to sue in these negotiations. . . . Or as one businessman put it, 'You can settle any dispute if you keep the lawyers and accountants out of it. They just do not understand the give-and-take needed in business.' . . . Law suits for breach of contract appear to be rare" (1963, p. 61). He goes on to explain that the

> top executives of the two firms may know each other. They may sit together on government or trade committees. They may know each other socially and even belong to the same country club. . . . Even where agreement can be reached at the negotiation stage, carefully planned arrangements may create undesirable exchange relationships between business units. Some businessmen object that in such a carefully worked out relationship one gets performance only to the letter of the contract. Such planning indicates a lack of trust and blunts the demands of friendship, turning a cooperative venture into an antagonistic horse trade. . . . Threatening to turn matters over to an attorney may cost no more money than postage or a telephone call; yet few are so skilled in making such a threat that it will not cost some deterioration of the relationship between the firms. [Pp. 63–64]

It is not only at top levels that firms are connected by networks of personal relations, but at all levels where transactions must take place. It is, for example, a commonplace in the literature on industrial purchasing that buying and selling relationships rarely approximate the spot-market model of classical theory. One source indicates that the "evidence consistently suggests that it takes some kind of 'shock' to jolt the organizational buying out of a pattern of placing repeat orders with a favored supplier or to extend the constrained set of feasible suppliers. A moment's reflection will suggest several reasons for this behavior, including the costs associated with searching for new suppliers and establishing new relationships, the fact that users are likely to prefer sources, the relatively low risk involved in dealing with known vendors, and the likelihood that the buyer has established personal relationships that he values with representatives of the supplying firm" (Webster and Wind 1972, p. 15).

In a similar vein, Macaulay notes that salesmen "often know purchasing agents well. The same two individuals may have dealt with each other from five to 25 years. Each has something to give the other. Salesmen have gossip about competitors, shortages and price increases to give purchasing agents who treat them well" (1963, p. 63). Sellers who do not satisfy their customers "become the subject of discussion in the gossip exchanged by purchasing agents and salesmen, at meetings of purchasing agents' associations and trade associations or even at country clubs or

Embeddedness

social gatherings . . ." (p. 64). Settlement of disputes is eased by this embeddedness of business in social relations: "Even where the parties have a detailed and carefully planned agreement which indicates what is to happen if, say, the seller fails to deliver on time, often they will never refer to the agreement but will negotiate a solution when the problem arises as if there never had been any original contract. One purchasing agent expressed a common business attitude when he said, 'If something comes up, you get the other man on the telephone and deal with the problem. You don't read legalistic contract clauses at each other if you ever want to do business again. One doesn't run to lawyers if he wants to stay in business because one must behave decently' " (Macaulay 1963, p. 61).

Such patterns may be more easily noted in other countries, where they are supposedly explained by "cultural" peculiarities. Thus, one journalist recently asserted,

> Friendships and longstanding personal connections affect business connec-
> tions everywhere. But that seems to be especially true in Japan. . . . The
> after-hours sessions in the bars and nightclubs are where the vital personal
> contacts are established and nurtured slowly. Once these ties are set, they
> are not easily undone. . . . The resulting tight-knit nature of Japanese
> business society has long been a source of frustration to foreign companies
> trying to sell products in Japan. . . . Chalmers Johnson, a professor at . . .
> Berkeley, believes that . . . the exclusive dealing within the Japanese indus-
> trial groups, buying and selling to and from each other based on decades-
> old relationships rather than economic competitiveness . . . is . . . a real
> nontariff barrier [to trade between the United States and Japan]. [Lohr
> 1982]

The extensive use of subcontracting in many industries also presents opportunities for sustained relationships among firms that are not orga-nized hierarchically within one corporate unit. For example, Eccles cites evidence from many countries that in construction, when projects "are not subject to institutional regulations which require competitive bidding . . . relations between the general contractor and his subcontractors are stable and continuous over fairly long periods of time and only infre-quently established through competitive bidding. This type of 'quasi-integration' results in what I call the 'quasifirm.' It is a preferred mode to either pure market transactions or formal vertical integration" (1981, pp. 339–40). Eccles describes this "quasifirm" arrangement of extensive and long-term relationships among contractors and subcontractors as an or-ganizational form logically intermediate between the pure market and the vertically integrated firm. I would argue, however, that it is not *empiri-cally* intermediate, since the former situation is so rare. The case of construction is closer to vertical integration than some other situations where firms interact, such as buying and selling relations, since subcon-

American Journal of Sociology

tractors are physically located on the same site as the contractor and are under his general supervision. Furthermore, under the usual fixed-price contracts, there are "obvious incentives for shirking performance requirements" (Eccles 1981, p. 340).

Yet a hierarchical structure associated with the vertically integrated firm does not arise to meet this "problem." I argue this is because the long-term relations of contractors and subcontractors, as well as the embeddedness of those relations in a community of construction personnel, generate standards of expected behavior that not only obviate the need for but are superior to pure authority relations in discouraging malfeasance. Eccles's own empirical study of residential construction in Massachusetts shows not only that subcontracting relationships are long term in nature but also that it is very rare for a general contractor to employ more than two or three subcontractors in a given trade, whatever number of projects is handled in the course of a year (1981, pp. 349–51). This is true despite the availability of large numbers of alternative subcontractors. This phenomenon can be explained in part in investment terms—through a "continuing association both parties can benefit from the somewhat idiosyncratic investment of learning to work together" (Eccles 1981, p. 340)—but also must be related to the desire of individuals to derive pleasure from the social interaction that accompanies their daily work, a pleasure that would be considerably blunted by spot-market procedures requiring entirely new and strange work partners each day. As in other parts of economic life, the overlay of social relations on what may begin in purely economic transactions plays a crucial role.

Some comments on labor markets are also relevant here. One advantage that Williamson asserts for hierarchically structured firms over market transactions is the ability to transmit accurate information about employees. "The principal impediment to effective interfirm experience-rating," he argues, "is one of communication. By comparison with the firm, markets lack a rich and common rating language. The language problem is particularly severe where the judgments to be made are highly subjective. The advantages of hierarchy in these circumstances are especially great if those persons who are most familiar with a worker's characteristics, usually his immediate supervisor, also do the experience-rating" (1975, p. 78). But the notion that good information about the characteristics of an employee can be transmitted only within firms and not between can be sustained only by neglecting the widely variegated social network of interaction that spans firms. Information about employees travels among firms not only because personal relations exist between those in each firm who do business with each other but also, as I have shown in detail (Granovetter 1974), because the relatively high levels of interfirm mobility in the United States guarantee that many workers will be reason-

Embeddedness

ably well known to employees of numerous other firms that might require and solicit their services. Furthermore, the idea that internal information is necessarily accurate and acted on dispassionately by promotion procedures keyed to it seems naive. To say, as Williamson does, that reliance "on internal promotion has affirmative incentive properties because workers can anticipate that differential talent and degrees of cooperativeness will be rewarded" (1975, p. 78) invokes an ideal type of promotion as reward-for-achievement that can readily be shown to have only limited correspondence to existing internal labor markets (see Granovetter 1983, pp. 40–51, for an extended analysis).

The other side of my critique is to argue that Williamson vastly overestimates the efficacy of hierarchical power ("fiat," in his terminology) within organizations. He asserts, for example, that internal organizations have a great auditing advantage: "An external auditor is typically constrained to review written records. . . . An internal auditor, by contrast, has greater freedom of action. . . . Whereas an internal auditor is not a partisan but regards himself and is regarded by others in mainly instrumental terms, the external auditor is associated with the 'other side' and his motives are regarded suspiciously. The degree of cooperation received by the auditor from the audited party varies accordingly. The external auditor can expect to receive only perfunctory cooperation" (1975, pp. 29–30). The literature on intrafirm audits is sparse, but one thorough account is that of Dalton, in *Men Who Manage,* for a large chemical plant. Audits of parts by the central office were supposed to be conducted on a surprise basis, but warning was typically surreptitiously given. The high level of cooperation shown in these internal audits is suggested by the following account: "Notice that a count of parts was to begin provoked a flurry among the executives to hide certain parts and equipment . . . materials *not* to be counted were moved to: 1) little-known and inaccessible spots; 2) basements and pits that were dirty and therefore unlikely to be examined; 3) departments that had already been inspected and that could be approached circuitously while the counters were en route between official storage areas and 4) places where materials and supplies might be used as a camouflage for parts. . . . As the practice developed, cooperation among the [department] chiefs to use each other's storage areas and available pits became well organized and smoothly functioning" (Dalton 1959, pp. 48–49).

Dalton's work shows brilliantly that cost accounting of all kinds is a highly arbitrary and therefore easily politicized process rather than a technical procedure decided on grounds of efficiency. He details this especially for the relationship between the maintenance department and various production departments in the chemical plant; the department to which maintenance work was charged had less to do with any strict time

499

American Journal of Sociology

accounting than with the relative political and social standing of department executives in their relation to maintenance personnel. Furthermore,
the more aggressive department heads expedited their maintenance work
"by the use of friendships, by bullying and implied threats. As all the
heads had the same formal rank, one could say that an inverse relation
existed between a given officer's personal influence and his volume of
uncompleted repairs" (1959, p. 34). Questioned about how such practices
could escape the attention of auditors, one informant told Dalton, "If
Auditing got to snooping around, what the hell could they find out? And
if they did find anything, they'd know a damn sight better than to say
anything about it. . . . All those guys [department heads] have got lines
through Cost Accounting. That's a lot of bunk about Auditing being
independent" (p. 32).

Accounts as detailed and perceptive as Dalton's are sadly lacking for a
representative sample of firms and so are open to the argument that they
are exceptional. But similar points can be made for the problem of transfer pricing—the determination of prices for products traded between
divisions of a single firm. Here Williamson argues that though the trading
divisions "may have profit-center standing, this is apt to be exercised in a
restrained way. . . . Cost-plus pricing rules, and variants thereof, preclude supplier divisions from seeking the monopolistic prices [to] which
their sole source supply position might otherwise entitle them. In addition, the managements of the trading divisions are more susceptible to
appeals for cooperation" (1975, p. 29). But in an intensive empirical study
of transfer-pricing practices, Eccles, having interviewed nearly 150 managers in 13 companies, concluded that no cost-based methods could be
carried out in a technically neutral way, since there is "no universal
criterion for what is cost. . . . Problems often exist with cost-based
methods when the buying division does not have access to the information by which the costs are generated. . . . Market prices are especially
difficult to determine when internal purchasing is mandated and no external purchases are made of the intermediate good. . . . There is no obvious
answer to what is a markup for profit . . ." (1982, p. 21). The political
element in transfer-pricing conflicts strongly affects whose definition of
"cost" is accepted: "In general, when transfer pricing practices are seen to
enhance one's power and status they will be viewed favorably. When they
do not, a countless number of strategic and other sound business reasons
will be found to argue for their inadequacy" (1982, p. 21; see also Eccles
1983, esp. pp. 26–32). Eccles notes the "somewhat ironic fact that many
managers consider internal transactions to be more difficult than external
ones, even though vertical integration is pursued for presumed advantages" (1983, p. 28).

Thus, the oversocialized view that orders within a hierarchy elicit easy

Embeddedness

obedience and that employees internalize the interests of the firm, suppressing any conflict with their own, cannot stand scrutiny against these empirical studies (or, for that matter, against the experience of many of us in actual organizations). Note further that, as shown especially well in Dalton's detailed ethnographic study, resistance to the encroachment of organizational interests on personal or divisional ones requires an extensive network of coalitions. From the viewpoint of management, these coalitions represent malfeasance generated by teams; it could not be managed at all by atomized individuals. Indeed, Dalton asserted that the level of cooperation achieved by divisional chiefs in evading central audits involved joint action "of a kind rarely, if ever, shown in carrying on official activities . . ." (1959, p. 49).

In addition, the generally lower turnover of personnel characteristic of large hierarchical firms, with their well-defined internal labor markets and elaborate promotion ladders, may make such cooperative evasion more likely. When many employees have long tenures, the conditions are met for a dense and stable network of relations, shared understandings, and political coalitions to be constructed. (See Homans 1950, 1974, for the relevant social psychological discussions; and Pfeffer 1983, for a treatment of the "demography of organizations.") James Lincoln notes, in this connection, that in the ideal-typical Weberian bureaucracy, organizations are "designed to function independently of the collective actions which can be mobilized through [internal] interpersonal networks. Bureaucracy prescribes fixed relationships among positions through which incumbents flow, without, in theory, affecting organizational operations" (1982, p. 26). He goes on to summarize studies showing, however, that "when turnover is low, relations take on additional contents of an expressive and personal sort which may ultimately transform the network and change the directions of the organization" (p. 26).

To this point I have argued that social relations between firms are more important, and authority within firms less so, in bringing order to economic life than is supposed in the markets and hierarchies line of thought. A balanced and symmetrical argument requires attention to power in "market" relations and social connections within firms. Attention to power relations is needed lest my emphasis on the smoothing role of social relations in the market lead me to neglect the role of these relations in the conduct of conflict. Conflict is an obvious reality, ranging from well-publicized litigation between firms to the occasional cases of "cutthroat competition" gleefully reported by the business press. Since the effective exercise of power between firms will prevent bloody public battles, we can assume that such battles represent only a small proportion of actual conflicts of interest. Conflicts probably become public only when the two sides are fairly equally matched; recall that this rough equality was pre-

American Journal of Sociology

cisely one of Hobbes's arguments for a probable "war of all against all" in the "state of nature." But when the power position of one firm is obviously dominant, the other is apt to capitulate early so as to cut its losses. Such capitulation may require not even explicit confrontation but only a clear understanding of what the other side requires (as in the recent Marxist literature on "hegemony" in business life; see, e.g., Mintz and Schwartz 1985).

Though the exact extent to which firms dominate other firms can be debated, the voluminous literature on interlocking directorates, on the role of financial institutions vis-à-vis industrial corporations, and on dual economy surely provides enough evidence to conclude that power relations cannot be neglected. This provides still another reason to doubt that the complexities that arise when formally equal agents negotiate with one another can be resolved only by the subsumption of all parties under a single hierarchy; in fact, many of these complexities are resolved by implicit or explicit power relations *among* firms.

Finally, a brief comment is in order on the webs of social relations that are well known from industrial and organizational sociology to be important within firms. The distinction between the "formal" and the "informal" organization of the firm is one of the oldest in the literature, and it hardly needs repeating that observers who assume firms to be structured in fact by the official organization chart are sociological babes in the woods. The connection of this to the present discussion is that insofar as internalization within firms does result in a better handling of complex and idiosyncratic transactions, it is by no means apparent that hierarchical organization is the best explanation. It may be, instead, that the effect of internalization is to provide a focus (see Feld 1981) for an even denser web of social relations than had occurred between previously independent market entities. Perhaps this web of interaction is mainly what explains the level of efficiency, be it high or low, of the new organizational form.

It is now useful to summarize the differences in explanation and prediction between Williamson's markets and hierarchies approach and the embeddedness view offered here. Williamson explains the inhibition of "opportunism" or malfeasance in economic life and the general existence of cooperation and order by the subsumption of complex economic activity in hierarchically integrated firms. The empirical evidence that I cite shows, rather, that even with complex transactions, a high level of order can often be found in the "market"—that is, across firm boundaries—and a correspondingly high level of disorder within the firm. Whether these occur, instead of what Williamson expects, depends on the nature of personal relations and networks of relations between and within firms. I claim that both order *and* disorder, honesty *and* malfeasance have more

Embeddedness

to do with structures of such relations than they do with organizational form.

Certain implications follow for the conditions under which one may expect to see vertical integration rather than transactions between firms in a market. Other things being equal, for example, we should expect pressures toward vertical integration in a market where transacting firms lack a network of personal relations that connects them or where such a network eventuates in conflict, disorder, opportunism, or malfeasance. On the other hand, where a stable network of relations mediates complex transactions and generates standards of behavior between firms, such pressures should be absent.

I use the word "pressures" rather than predict that vertical integration will always follow the pattern described in order to avoid the functionalism implicit in Williamson's assumption that whatever organizational form is most efficient will be the one observed. Before we can make this assumption, two further conditions must be satisfied: (i) well-defined and powerful selection pressures toward efficiency must be operating, and (ii) some actors must have the ability and resources to "solve" the efficiency problem by constructing a vertically integrated firm.

The selection pressures that guarantee efficient organization of transactions are nowhere clearly described by Williamson. As in much of the new institutional economics, the need to make such matters explicit is obviated by an implicit Darwinian argument that efficient solutions, however they may originate, have a staying power akin to that enforced by natural selection in the biological world. Thus it is granted that not all business executives "accurately perceive their business opportunities and faultlessly respond. Over time, however, those [vertical] integration moves that have better rationality properties (in transaction cost and scale-economy terms) tend to have better survival properties" (Williamson and Ouchi 1981, p. 389; see also Williamson 1981, pp. 573–74). But Darwinian arguments, invoked in this cavalier fashion, careen toward a Panglossian view of whatever institution is analyzed. The operation of alleged selection pressures is here neither an object of study nor even a falsifiable proposition but rather an article of faith.

Even if one could document selection pressures that made survival of certain organizational forms more likely, it would remain to show how such forms could be implemented. To treat them implicitly as mutations, by analogy to biological evolution, merely evades the issue. As in other functionalist explanations, it cannot be automatically assumed that the solution to some problem is feasible. Among the resources required to implement vertical integration might be some measure of market power, access to capital through retained earnings or capital markets, and appropriate connections to legal or regulatory authorities.

American Journal of Sociology

Where selection pressures are weak (especially likely in the imperfect markets claimed by Williamson to produce vertical integration) and resources problematic, the social-structural configurations that I have outlined are still related to the efficiency of transaction costs, but no guarantee can be given that an efficient solution will occur. Motives for integration unrelated to efficiency, such as personal aggrandizement of CEOs in acquiring firms, may in such settings become important.

What the viewpoint proposed here requires is that future research on the markets-hierarchies question pay careful and systematic attention to the actual patterns of personal relations by which economic transactions are carried out. Such attention will not only better sort out the motives for vertical integration but also make it easier to comprehend the various complex intermediate forms between idealized atomized markets and completely integrated firms, such as the quasi firm discussed above for the construction industry. Intermediate forms of this kind are so intimately bound up with networks of personal relations that any perspective that considers these relations peripheral will fail to see clearly what "organizational form" has been effected. Existing empirical studies of industrial organization pay little attention to patterns of relations, in part because relevant data are harder to find than those on technology and market structure but also because the dominant economic framework remains one of atomized actors, so personal relations are perceived as frictional in effect.

DISCUSSION

In this article, I have argued that most behavior is closely embedded in networks of interpersonal relations and that such an argument avoids the extremes of under- and oversocialized views of human action. Though I believe this to be so for all behavior, I concentrate here on economic behavior for two reasons: (i) it is the type-case of behavior inadequately interpreted because those who study it professionally are so strongly committed to atomized theories of action; and (ii) with few exceptions, sociologists have refrained from serious study of any subject already claimed by neoclassical economics. They have implicitly accepted the presumption of economists that "market processes" are not suitable objects of sociological study because social relations play only a frictional and disruptive role, not a central one, in modern societies. (Recent exceptions are Baker 1983; Burt 1983; and White 1981.) In those instances in which sociologists study processes where markets are central, they usually still manage to avoid their analysis. Until recently, for example, the large sociological literature on wages was cast in terms of "income attainment," obscuring the labor

Embeddedness

market context in which wages are set and focusing instead on the background and attainment of individuals (see Granovetter 1981 for an extended critique). Or, as Stearns has pointed out, the literature on who controls corporations has implicitly assumed that analysis must be at the level of political relations and broad assumptions about the nature of capitalism. Even though it is widely admitted that how corporations acquire capital is a major determinant of control, most relevant research "since the turn of the century has eliminated that [capital] market as an objective of investigation" (1982, pp. 5–6). Even in organization theory, where considerable literature implements the limits placed on economic decisions by social structural complexity, little attempt has been made to demonstrate the implications of this for the neoclassical theory of the firm or for a general understanding of production or such macroeconomic outcomes as growth, inflation, and unemployment.

In trying to demonstrate that all market processes are amenable to sociological analysis and that such analysis reveals central, not peripheral, features of these processes, I have narrowed my focus to problems of trust and malfeasance. I have also used the "market and hierarchies" argument of Oliver Williamson as an illustration of how the embeddedness perspective generates different understandings and predictions from that implemented by economists. Williamson's perspective is itself "revisionist" within economics, diverging from the neglect of institutional and transactional considerations typical of neoclassical work. In this sense, it may appear to have more kinship to a sociological perspective than the usual economic arguments. But the main thrust of the "new institutional economists" is to deflect the analysis of institutions from sociological, historical, and legal argumentation and show instead that they arise as the efficient solution to economic problems. This mission and the pervasive functionalism it implies discourage the detailed analysis of social structure that I argue here is the key to understanding how existing institutions arrived at their present state.

Insofar as rational choice arguments are narrowly construed as referring to atomized individuals and economic goals, they are inconsistent with the embeddedness position presented here. In a broader formulation of rational choice, however, the two views have much in common. Much of the revisionist work by economists that I criticize above in my discussion of over- and undersocialized conceptions of action relies on a strategy that might be called "psychological revisionism"—an attempt to reform economic theory by abandoning an absolute assumption of rational decision making. This strategy has led to Leibenstein's "selective rationality" in his arguments on "X-inefficiency" (1976), for example, and to the claims of segmented labor-market theorists that workers in different mar-

American Journal of Sociology

ket segments have different kinds of decision-making rules, rational choice being only for upper-primary (i.e., professional, managerial, technical) workers (Piore 1979).

I suggest, in contrast, that while the assumption of rational action must always be problematic, it is a good working hypothesis that should not easily be abandoned. What looks to the analyst like nonrational behavior may be quite sensible when situational constraints, especially those of embeddedness, are fully appreciated. When the social situation of those in nonprofessional labor markets is fully analyzed, their behavior looks less like the automatic application of "cultural" rules and more like a reasonable response to their present situation (as, e.g., in the discussion of Liebow 1966). Managers who evade audits and fight over transfer pricing are acting nonrationally in some strict economic sense, in terms of a firm's profit maximization; but when their position and ambitions in intrafirm networks and political coalitions are analyzed, the behavior is easily interpreted.

That such behavior is rational or instrumental is more readily seen, moreover, if we note that it aims not only at economic goals but also at sociability, approval, status, and power. Economists rarely see such goals as rational, in part on account of the arbitrary separation that arose historically, as Albert Hirschman (1977) points out, in the 17th and 18th centuries, between the "passions" and the "interests," the latter connoting economic motives only. This way of putting the matter has led economists to specialize in analysis of behavior motivated only by "interest" and to assume that other motives occur in separate and nonrationally organized spheres; hence Samuelson's much-quoted comment that "many economists would separate economics from sociology upon the basis of rational or irrational behavior" (1947, p. 90). The notion that rational choice is derailed by social influences has long discouraged detailed sociological analysis of economic life and led revisionist economists to reform economic theory by focusing on its naive psychology. My claim here is that however naive that psychology may be, this is not where the main difficulty lies—it is rather in the neglect of social structure.

Finally, I should add that the level of causal analysis adopted in the embeddedness argument is a rather proximate one. I have had little to say about what broad historical or macrostructural circumstances have led systems to display the social-structural characteristics they have, so I make no claims for this analysis to answer large-scale questions about the nature of modern society or the sources of economic and political change. But the focus on proximate causes is intentional, for these broader questions cannot be satisfactorily addressed without more detailed understanding of the mechanisms by which sweeping change has its effects. My claim is that one of the most important and least analyzed of such mecha-

Embeddedness

nisms is the impact of such change on the social relations in which economic life is embedded. If this is so, no adequate link between macro- and micro-level theories can be established without a much fuller understanding of these relations.

The use of embeddedness analysis in explicating proximate causes of patterns of macro-level interest is well illustrated by the markets and hierarchies question. The extent of vertical integration and the reasons for the persistence of small firms operating through the market are not only narrow concerns of industrial organization; they are of interest to all students of the institutions of advanced capitalism. Similar issues arise in the analysis of "dual economy," dependent development, and the nature of modern corporate elites. But whether small firms are indeed eclipsed by giant corporations is usually analyzed in broad and sweeping macropolitical or macroeconomic terms, with little appreciation of proximate social structural causes.

Analysts of dual economy have often suggested, for example, that the persistence of large numbers of small firms in the "periphery" is explained by large corporations' need to shift the risks of cyclical fluctuations in demand or of uncertain R & D activities; failures of these small units will not adversely affect the larger firms' earnings. I suggest here that small firms in a market setting may persist instead because a dense network of social relations is overlaid on the business relations connecting such firms and reduces pressures for integration. This does not rule out risk shifting as an explanation with a certain face validity. But the embeddedness account may be more useful in explaining the large number of small establishments not characterized by satellite or peripheral status. (For a discussion of the surprising extent of employment in small establishments, see Granovetter 1984.) This account is restricted to proximate causes: it logically leads to but does not answer the questions why, when, and in what sectors does the market display various types of social structure. But those questions, which link to a more macro level of analysis, would themselves not arise without a prior appreciation of the importance of social structure in the market.

The markets and hierarchies analysis, important as it may be, is presented here mainly as an illustration. I believe the embeddedness argument to have very general applicability and to demonstrate not only that there is a place for sociologists in the study of economic life but that their perspective is urgently required there. In avoiding the analysis of phenomena at the center of standard economic theory, sociologists have unnecessarily cut themselves off from a large and important aspect of social life and from the European tradition—stemming especially from Max Weber—in which economic action is seen only as a special, if important, category of social action. I hope to have shown here that this Weberian

American Journal of Sociology

program is consistent with and furthered by some of the insights of modern structural sociology.

REFERENCES

Akerlof, George. 1983. "Loyalty Filters." *American Economic Review* 73 (1): 54–63.
Alchian, Armen, and Harold Demsetz. 1973. "The Property Rights Paradigm." *Journal of Economic History* 33 (March): 16–27.
Arrow, Kenneth. 1974. *The Limits of Organization*. New York: Norton.
Baker, Wayne. 1983. "Floor Trading and Crowd Dynamics." In *Social Dynamics of Financial Markets*, edited by Patricia Adler and Peter Adler. Greenwich, Conn.: JAI.
Becker, Gary. 1976. *The Economic Approach to Human Behavior*. Chicago: University of Chicago Press.
Ben-Porath, Yoram. 1980. "The F-Connection: Families, Friends and Firms in the Organization of Exchange." *Population and Development Review* 6 (1): 1–30.
Bowles, Samuel, and Herbert Gintis. 1975. *Schooling in Capitalist America*. New York: Basic.
Brown, Roger. 1965. *Social Psychology*. New York: Free Press.
Burt, Ronald. 1982. *Toward a Structural Theory of Action*. New York: Academic Press.
———. 1983. *Corporate Profits and Cooptation*. New York: Academic Press.
Cole, Robert. 1979. *Work, Mobility and Participation: A Comparative Study of American and Japanese Industry*. Berkeley and Los Angeles: University of California Press.
Dalton, Melville. 1959. *Men Who Manage*. New York: Wiley.
Doeringer, Peter, and Michael Piore. 1971. *Internal Labor Markets and Manpower Analysis*. Lexington, Mass.: Heath.
Domhoff, G. William. 1971. *The Higher Circles*. New York: Random House.
Duesenberry, James. 1960. Comment on "An Economic Analysis of Fertility." In *Demographic and Economic Change in Developed Countries*, edited by the Universities–National Bureau Committee for Economic Research. Princeton, N.J.: Princeton University Press.
Eccles, Robert. 1981. "The Quasifirm in the Construction Industry." *Journal of Economic Behavior and Organization* 2 (December): 335–57.
———. 1982. "A Synopsis of *Transfer Pricing: An Analysis and Action Plan*." Mimeographed. Cambridge, Mass.: Harvard Business School.
———. 1983. "Transfer Pricing, Fairness and Control." Working Paper no. HBS 83-167. Cambridge, Mass.: Harvard Business School. Reprinted in *Harvard Business Review* (in press).
Feld, Scott. 1981. "The Focused Organization of Social Ties." *American Journal of Sociology* 86 (5): 1015–35.
Fine, Gary, and Sherryl Kleinman. 1979. "Rethinking Subculture: An Interactionist Analysis." *American Journal of Sociology* 85 (July): 1–20.
Furubotn, E., and S. Pejovich. 1972. "Property Rights and Economic Theory: A Survey of Recent Literature." *Journal of Economic Literature* 10 (3): 1137–62.
Geertz, Clifford. 1979. "Suq: The Bazaar Economy in Sefrou." Pp. 123–225 in *Meaning and Order in Moroccan Society*, edited by C. Geertz, H. Geertz, and L. Rosen. New York: Cambridge University Press.
Granovetter, Mark. 1974. *Getting a Job: A Study of Contacts and Careers*. Cambridge, Mass.: Harvard University Press.
———. 1981. "Toward a Sociological Theory of Income Differences." Pp. 11–47 in *Sociological Perspectives on Labor Markets*, edited by Ivar Berg. New York: Academic Press.

Embeddedness

————. 1983. "Labor Mobility, Internal Markets and Job-Matching: A Comparison of the Sociological and Economic Approaches." Mimeographed.

————. 1984. "Small Is Bountiful: Labor Markets and Establishment Size." *American Sociological Review* 49 (3): 323–34.

Hirschman, Albert. 1977. *The Passions and the Interests*. Princeton, N.J.: Princeton University Press.

————. 1982. "Rival Interpretations of Market Society: Civilizing, Destructive or Feeble?" *Journal of Economic Literature* 20 (4): 1463–84.

Homans, George. 1950. *The Human Group*. New York: Harcourt Brace & Co.

————. 1974. *Social Behavior*. New York: Harcourt Brace Jovanovich.

Lazear, Edward. 1979. "Why Is There Mandatory Retirement?" *Journal of Political Economy* 87 (6): 1261–84.

Leibenstein, Harvey. 1976. *Beyond Economic Man*. Cambridge, Mass.: Harvard University Press.

Liebow, Elliot. 1966. *Tally's Corner*. Boston: Little, Brown.

Lincoln, James. 1982. "Intra- (and Inter-) Organizational Networks." Pp. 1–38 in *Research in the Sociology of Organizations*, vol. 1. Edited by S. Bacharach. Greenwich, Conn.: JAI.

Lohr, Steve. 1982. "When Money Doesn't Matter in Japan." *New York Times* (December 30).

Macaulay, Stewart. 1963. "Non-Contractual Relations in Business: A Preliminary Study." *American Sociological Review* 28 (1): 55–67.

Marsden, Peter. 1981. "Introducing Influence Processes into a System of Collective Decisions." *American Journal of Sociology* 86 (May): 1203–35.

————. 1983. "Restricted Access in Networks and Models of Power." *American Journal of Sociology* 88 (January): 686–17.

Merton, Robert. 1947. "Manifest and Latent Functions." Pp. 19–84 in *Social Theory and Social Structure*. New York: Free Press.

Mintz, Beth, and Michael Schwartz. 1985. *The Power Structure of American Business*. Chicago: University of Chicago Press.

North, D., and R. Thomas. 1973. *The Rise of the Western World*. Cambridge: Cambridge University Press.

Okun, Arthur. 1981. *Prices and Quantities*. Washington, D.C.: Brookings.

Pakes, Ariel, and S. Nitzan. 1982. "Optimum Contracts for Research Personnel, Research Employment and the Establishment of 'Rival' Enterprises." NBER Working Paper no. 871. Cambridge, Mass.: National Bureau of Economic Research.

Parsons, Talcott. 1937. *The Structure of Social Action*. New York: Macmillan.

Pfeffer, Jeffrey. 1983. "Organizational Demography." In *Research in Organizational Behavior*, vol. 5. Edited by L. L. Cummings and B. Staw. Greenwich, Conn.: JAI.

Phelps Brown, Ernest Henry. 1977. *The Inequality of Pay*. Berkeley: University of California Press.

Piore, Michael. 1975. "Notes for a Theory of Labor Market Stratification." Pp. 125–50 in *Labor Market Segmentation*, edited by R. Edwards, M. Reich, and D. Gordon. Lexington, Mass.: Heath.

————, ed. 1979. *Unemployment and Inflation*. White Plains, N.Y.: Sharpe.

Polanyi, Karl. 1944. *The Great Transformation*. New York: Holt, Rinehart.

Polanyi, Karl, C. Arensberg, and H. Pearson. 1957. *Trade and Market in the Early Empires*. New York: Free Press.

Popkin, Samuel. 1979. *The Rational Peasant*. Berkeley and Los Angeles: University of California Press.

Rosen, Sherwin. 1982. "Authority, Control and the Distribution of Earnings." *Bell Journal of Economics* 13 (2): 311–23.

Samuelson, Paul. 1947. *Foundations of Economic Analysis*. Cambridge, Mass.: Harvard University Press.

American Journal of Sociology

Schneider, Harold. 1974. *Economic Man: The Anthropology of Economics*. New York: Free Press.

Schotter, Andrew. 1981. *The Economic Theory of Social Institutions*. New York: Cambridge University Press.

Scott, James. 1976. *The Moral Economy of the Peasant*. New Haven, Conn.: Yale University Press.

Shenon, Philip. 1984. "Margolies Is Found Guilty of Murdering Two Women." *New York Times* (June 1).

Simon, Herbert. 1957. *Administrative Behavior*. Glencoe, Ill.: Free Press.

Smith, Adam. (1776) 1979. *The Wealth of Nations*. Edited by Andrew Skinner. Baltimore: Penguin.

Stearns, Linda. 1982. "Corporate Dependency and the Structure of the Capital Market: 1880–1980." Ph.D. dissertation, State University of New York at Stony Brook.

Thompson, E. P. 1971. "The Moral Economy of the English Crowd in the Eighteenth Century." *Past and Present* 50 (February): 76–136.

Useem, Michael. 1979. "The Social Organization of the American Business Elite and Participation of Corporation Directors in the Governance of American Institutions." *American Sociological Review* 44:553–72.

Webster, Frederick, and Yoram Wind. 1972. *Organizational Buying Behavior*. Englewood Cliffs, N.J.: Prentice-Hall.

White, Harrison C. 1981. "Where Do Markets Come From?" *American Journal of Sociology* 87 (November): 517–47.

Williamson, Oliver. 1975. *Markets and Hierarchies*. New York: Free Press.

———. 1979. "Transaction-Cost Economics: The Governance of Contractual Relations." *Journal of Law and Economics* 22 (2): 233–61.

———. 1981. "The Economics of Organization: The Transaction Cost Approach." *American Journal of Sociology* 87 (November): 548–77.

Williamson, Oliver, and William Ouchi. 1981. "The Markets and Hierarchies and Visible Hand Perspectives." Pp. 347–70 in *Perspectives on Organizational Design and Behavior*, edited by Andrew Van de Ven and William Joyce. New York: Wiley.

Wrong, Dennis. 1961. "The Oversocialized Conception of Man in Modern Sociology." *American Sociological Review* 26 (2): 183–93.

B
Trust

[8]

Mafia: the Price of Distrust

Diego Gambetta

There is a number of places around the world where three unfortunate sets of circumstances coexist: where people do not cooperate when it would be mutually beneficial to do so; where they compete in harmful ways; and, finally, where they refrain from competing in those instances when they could all gain considerably from competition. There are probably not many, though, where such a powerful combination has lasted for centuries. Southern Italy – especially the Tyrrhenian regions of Campania, Calabria, and Sicily – is conspicuous among them, in spite of the fact that Italy as a whole is now one of the most successful of industrial countries.[1]

It is tempting to conclude, therefore, that people in the south are either stubbornly irrational or entertain masochistic preferences. While the possibility cannot be excluded that they may have evolved such preferences as a means of reducing the cognitive dissonance caused by prolonged exposure to such an environment, the overall aim of this paper is to reconcile individual rationality with protracted collective disaster. If anything, in this case, the latter results from an excess of individual rationality. This paper is an account of the remarkable responses to a generalized absence of trust and of the mechanisms by which such responses, while reinforcing distrust, have none the less brought about a relatively stable social structure. Its major underlying assumption is that the *mafia* – although by no means its only element – represents the quintessence of this structure, in which all the crucial behavioural patterns converge to form an indissoluble but explosive mixture. In addition, the mafia is exemplary of those cases where the public interest

[1] I wish to thank Keith Hart, Geoffrey Hawthorn, and Anthony Pagden for their helpful and penetrating comments on an earlier version of this paper.

lies in collapsing rather than building *internal* trust and cooperation (Schelling 1984).

In the first section I shall consider the historical background by looking at the effects of Spanish domination in southern Italy and by following Alexis de Tocqueville in his journey to Sicily. In the second, drawing on the classic study by Leopoldo Franchetti ([1876] 1974), I shall outline the causes and long-lasting features of the Sicilian mafia. In the final section I shall consider some of the intended and unintended mechanisms whereby the mafia, while exploiting and reinforcing distrust, has been able to maintain itself for over a century.

I

Anthony Pagden (this volume), standing on the shoulders of two Neapolitan thinkers, Paolo Mattia Doria and Antonio Genovesi, articulates a plausible and enticing account of how a generalized sense of distrust might first have spread under the Habsburg Spanish domination. Most of the component strategies of *divide et impera* were adopted by the Spaniards: a bewildering and sophisticated array ranging from discouraging commerce and the production of wealth to the manipulation of information; from fostering religious superstition to establishing vertical bonds of submission and exploitation at the expense of solidarity between equals; from destroying equality before the law to overturning the relationship between the sexes. As Pagden argues, much of what they did can be seen as the promotion and selective exploitation of distrust.

We do not know whether the accounts of Doria and Genovesi were set against a trust-based society which existed under an allegedly less disagreeable rule – that of the Aragonese – or against the virtues of an ideal society with which southern Italy had never been blessed.[2] We do know, however, that there is something very striking in Pagden's account, something analogous to discovering the first steps in the childhood of an adult we know and whose behaviour has remained something of a mystery to us. We discover that that behaviour has a *genesis*, that the seemingly intractable backwardness of southern Italy emerges from a plausible history. But knowing something of the causes which generate a state of affairs is quite different from understanding how such a state can outlast those causes. The mechanisms of reproduction or – to switch to the language of game theory – the enduring convergence of expectations, constraints, and individual interest on a particular *equilibrium*, must

_____

[2] If Thucydides is right, we should certainly consider going back quite some time. He said of Sicilians that they were 'sui commodi quam publici amantiores' (quoted by Fazello 1558: 28).

Diego Gambetta

have a force of their own, and must lie more in the *adaptive responses* selected by the subjects of the Spanish domination and by their successors than in the strategies of domination themselves. The type of behaviour of which the mafia represents the most radical, aggressive, and perfected expression has been subject to a wide range of mutations and instability, but at a certain level of abstraction it has never been transformed into something radically different; if anything, its essential peculiarities have been strengthened. The use of the term *equilibrium*, therefore, is not just an analogy but is adopted here in the sense of a state of affairs in which all or most agents, in spite of what they may think of the collective outcome, have not found adequate incentives to behave differently and to change that outcome in any significant way. How was it, then, that a social system centred around such notions as *fede privata* and public distrust maintained its equilibrium?

In 1827, approximately 100 years after Doria and 50 after Genovesi, Alexis de Tocqueville, then a young man, undertook the first of his renowned travels and went to Naples and Sicily. Let us leave Naples then, and follow him further south. Most of *Voyage en Sicile*, the first long essay he ever wrote, is lost, and only 30 pages survive.[3] There is an imaginary dialogue, in these few pages, between two fictional characters: one a Sicilian, Don Ambrosio, and the other a Neapolitan, Don Carlo. In spite of their differences, Tocqueville writes, 'tout deux semblaient avoir fait de *la duplicité* une longue habitude; mais chez le premier, c'était plutôt encore un fruit amer de la nécessité et de la servitude; on pouvait croire que le second ne trompait que parce que *la fourberie* était le moyen le plus court d'arriver au but' (1864–67: 154; my italics).

Don Ambrosio blames Don Carlo and his fellow citizens for doing to the Sicilians pretty much the same things that Doria and Genovesi blamed the Spaniards for having done to the Neapolitans: 'Notre noblesse . . . elle n'est plus sicilienne. Vous lui avez ôté *tout intérêt dans les affaires publiques*. . . . Vous l'avez attirée tout entière à Naples . . . vous avez abâtardi son coeur en substituant *l'ambition de cour* au désir de l'illustration, et le pouvoir de *la faveur* à celui du mérite et du courage' (pp. 157–8; my italics). Don Carlo, embittered by the violence of the attack, returns the challenge by asking the Sicilian why it is then that the Sicilians have adapted to rather than rebelled against such an unbearable yoke. To this Don Ambrosio replies that 'dénaturée par l'oppression, [l'énergie] cachée [de notre caractère national] ne se révèle plus que par des *crimes*; pour vous, vous n'avez que des vices. En nous refusant la

---

[3] Its loss is reported by J. P. Mayer, the editor of the 1957 edition of Tocqueville's complete works. A search I conducted at the Bibliothèque Nationale in Paris was equally unfruitful.

justice, en faisant mieux, en nous la vendant, vous nous avez appris à
considérer *l'assassinat comme un droit*' (p. 59, my italics).

Through this fictional account, by which Tocqueville manages to
convey his reflections on the journey, we begin to grasp some of the
elements of the peculiar process of adjustment to – rather than rebellion
against – domination which to different degrees involves both Naples
and Sicily: the absenteeism of an aristocracy lured by the pleasures and
servility of the court; the predominance of private over public concerns,
of duplicity, cunning, and favour over merit; and the fashion for crime
and murder, which have become habitual and are even felt to be legitimate
rights.

Moreover, not only did the Spaniards exploit distrust for the purpose
of domination, but they taught some of their subjects to do so too and to
pass it on to others. The Bourbon Spanish domination, which replaced
the Habsburgs in 1724 and, except for a brief interval, lasted until the
Italian unification in 1861, continued to pursue the policy of *divide et
impera* and took particular care to foster the hatred between Neapolitans
and Sicilians: so much so that, as the Tocqueville dialogue shows, 'in the
minds of Sicilians the Bourbon and the Neapolitan domination became
the same thing' (Franchetti [1876] 1974: 79).

Yet the diffusion throughout southern Italy of the characteristics of
the Spanish rule and of the peculiar responses it received do not tell us
how and why some features of this system, *mutatis mutandis*, have
endured until the present day. It is probably not a coincidence, though,
that only 11 years (1838) after Tocqueville wrote his account, we read for
the first time in an official report of the existence of a thing called *the
mafia* (Hess 1986: 114); and, what is more, we read of it as an already
established social force. The sketchy historical account given thus far
does not amount to an analytical exposition of the causes that generated
the mafia or its less renowned but equally fierce twin entities, the
camorra (Naples) and the *'ndrangheta* (Calabria).[4] But on intuitive
grounds, it makes a criminal response plausible. Most of the ingredients
were there. How they merged into a coherent structure is something we
shall consider below.

II

In 1876 Leopoldo Franchetti – a Tuscan landowner who travelled in
Sicily and was animated by a strong degree of civil passion – wrote what,
still today, remains one of the most coherent and comprehensive accounts
of the Sicilian mafia and its surroundings. His study – *Condizioni*

---

4 On the *camorra* see Walston (1986); on the *'ndrangheta* see Gambino (1975).

politiche ed amministrative della Sicilia – has much the same quality as some of the best nineteenth-century classics in the social sciences.[5] What is striking is not only the freshness of style and the bold disregard of disciplinary boundaries – typical of those (in this respect) happy days – but the fact that he was in a position to come up *then* with remarks which make considerable sense *now*. In other words, Franchetti's book constitutes indirect evidence that the mafia in the nineteenth century has characteristics which are still present today, and makes it possible to think of this phenomenon as something arching over no less than 100 years.[6] Virtually everything Franchetti wrote is supported by the evidence which has since emerged, and what we know about the way the mafia has evolved is largely consistent with his analysis.

Franchetti essentially identifies two related sets of causes for the emergence of the mafia. The first is eminently political and has to do with the absence of credible or effective systems of justice and law enforcement. From at least the time of the sixteenth century (Cancila 1984), Sicilians were able to trust neither the fairness nor the protection of the law.[7] This pre-existing state of affairs caused considerable difficulties to the newly formed Italian state, which, in spite of its weakness and its mistakes, might otherwise have claimed the right to a far higher degree of legitimation than any of the previous regimes (I shall return to the role of the democratic state below).

The second set of causes concerns economic rather than political trust. As Gellner shows (this volume), the lack of a central agency is not in itself an explanation of social disorder: on the contrary, social cohesion and acceptable rules of collective conduct may emerge across a multiplicity of local clusters. Even the presence of an *untrustworthy* central agency – although of course different from the complete lack of one – is not quite sufficient to explain the emergence of the mafia. The untrustworthiness of the state, by interacting with economic relations, sets another process in motion: as Dasgupta and Pagden both argue (this volume), distrust percolates through the social ladder, and the unpredictability of sanctions generates uncertainty in agreements, stagnation in commerce and industry, and a general reluctance towards impersonal and extensive forms of cooperation. Sicilians – as everyone knows – do

[5] Unfortunately it has only been translated into German, and is semi-forgotten or superficially understood in Italy. An exception is providded by Pezzino (1985), who takes Franchetti's arguments seriously, especially those about the role of the then newly formed Italian state.

[6] See Cancila (1984) for interesting evidence suggesting that some elements of mafioso behaviour were already present in the sixteenth century.

[7] There were not just deliberate intentions on the part of the rulers behind the unpredictability and unfairness of the law, but also objective conditions, such as the isolation of Sicily and the scarcity of internal roads, which made other than local law enforcement far from easy (see Pezzino 1985).

not trust the state: beyond the boundaries of limited clusters, they often end up distrusting each other as well.

In turn, economic backwardness 'closes off a multiplicity of channels which could give vent to the activity of private citizens. . . . In such a state of affairs, the only goal one can set for one's activity or ambition [is] to prevail over one's peers' (Franchetti 1974: 71): 'your enemy is the man in your own trade', claims a Sicilian proverb (Gower Chapman 1971: 65). The desire to prevail over one's peers, combined with the lack of a credible central agency, does not lead to ordinary 'market competition: instead of outdoing rivals the most common practice becomes that of doing them in. Individual improvements are seen as desirable and possible, but social mobility is and is believed to be a zero-sum game.

The opportunities for social mobility should be considered as a third concomitant cause. Franchetti does not do so explicitly, yet evidence suggests that the areas in southern Italy where organized crime has traditionally evolved are those where for different reasons social mobility was feasible. As well as in the large urban concentrations such as Naples and Palermo, it emerged in the *latifondo* of western Sicily where landowners were absenteeists (Blok 1974), but not in other parts of Sicily (Franchetti 1974: 53–6), or in Calabria (Crotonese) and Puglia, areas where the presence of landowners left no opportunity open to the rural middle class (Arlacchi 1980; Cosentino 1983). It also developed in those small farming areas which manifested a thriving agriculture, but not in those based on a subsistence economy (Arrighi and Piselli 1986). Lack of trust, matched by heavy constraints on social mobility – such as in the case of the depressing village studied by Banfield (1958) – does not offer sufficient incentive to 'specialize' in prevailing over one's peers, but simply leads to a deeply fragmented social world and to the reproduction of wretchedly poor economic conditions.

By contrast, in a politically and economically untrustworthy world which is not lacking in scope for social mobility, and where *le pouvoir de la faveur* prevails over justice and merit, the sole remaining merit is in fact that of seeking *la faveur* from those above, extorting it out of one's equals, and distributing part of its fruits – the smallest possible part (Franchetti 1974: 27) – to a select group of those below. Here, people cluster in groups, take shelter behind the men who make themselves respected (p. 38). Associations and clusters involve persons of all classes and occupations (p. 38), and only personal relations – where distrust is less threatening – count and are believed to count as means of social mobility (p. 36; see also Pezzino 1985: 49–50).

In this context, we may begin to understand why mafiosi do not emerge as ordinary criminals, acting in isolation as individuals (Franchetti 1974: 101). Or, at least, why they are not perceived as such: the *pubblica*

164 *Diego Gambetta*

opinione in Sicily sees them more as men capable of enforcing privately that public justice the Spaniards had eroded (p. 93) and that nobody could trust. And this is still the way they see themselves today (Arlacchi 1983: 151). To Don Ambrosio, 50 years earlier, recourse to *l'assassinat* still seemed appalling. At the time when Franchetti is writing, it is taken as sign of the capacity to protect (p. 108), as the foremost sign of reputation (pp. 9, 33).[8]

The mafia at any one time can thus be seen as a successful cluster or coalition of clusters. It is successful not just at coping defensively with lack of trust – as in the case of weaker and non-violent forms of association such as clienteles and patron–client relations – but at turning distrust into a profitable business by a relentless, and if necessary violent, search for *exclusivity*. Its single most important activity is the enforcement of monopolies over the largest possible number of resources in any given territory.[9] Each mafioso is either a monopolist or the acolyte of a monopolist. 'Cosa nostra' – as members apparently call it (Staiano 1986) – means that the thing is ours, *not* yours; it stresses inclusion, and inclusion can only subsist by simultaneously postulating exclusion. The long-lasting specificity of the mafia is that it tolerates no competition, and it probably tends to engage precisely in those types of activity and transaction which most lend themselves to monopolization (Schelling 1984: 184): land, cattle, sources of water in a dry land, markets, auctions, ports, building, transport, and public works are all areas which, for different reasons, can be easily controlled, where exclusivity is relatively easy to enforce.

Historically, the *crime* most characteristic of the mafia is the use of violence to enforce the monopoly of otherwise legal goods. As we shall see in the next section, even the profitable practice of extortion in exchange for protection does not always take on the features of an entirely criminal exercise: it is not just applied to recalcitrant victims, and a clear demarcation line between protection against true and protection against deliberately generated threats is often very hard to draw.

The mafia, moreover, is not – as has recently been claimed (see Blok 1974) – something which originates only in the countryside. Since its inception (Franchetti informs us) it has been an urban as well as a rural phenomenon. Prominent mafiosi often belong to *la classe media*, to what elsewhere has managed to become the bourgeoisie (p. 97). The difference is this: that whereas in other places this class has succeeded in guaranteeing a 'legislazione uguale per tutti', in this area, where private

---

[8] For a bitter satire of the 'right' to murder in Sicily see Anonimo del XX secolo (1985).

[9] Some of the literature on the subject has confused a change in the field of undertaking with a change in the specific ubiquitous component of mafioso behaviour (see Gambetta 1986).

power dominates and even 'the mind cannot tell the difference between the public interest and immediate personal interest' (p. 35), it is inevitable, wrote Franchetti, that villains and *classe media* should find themselves in close connection and that they should exchange services (p. 108). But the middle class can sustain the search for exclusivity with the same personal gifts which in other circumstances it invests in peaceful business: order, foresight, caution, and cunning (p. 97). They go so far as to practise understatement about their real power, a style they ostensibly share more with the British than the Italian mentality. This style, moreover, has won them reputation and trust. ('It is strange', wrote Alongi in 1887, 'that in that hot and colourful country where ordinary speech is so honey-sweet, hyperbolic and picturesque, that of the mafiosi is curt, restrained and decisive'; quoted by Hess 1973: 52).

In more recent periods the mafia may have approximated the status of a formal organization,[10] but initially it was probably an uncertain and erratic coalition of local monopolies which cooperated at some times and ignored each other or fought bloody wars at others. The only limit to the expansion of monopoly, wrote Franchetti, is the challenge of 'another coalition, not less strong, bold and fierce' (p. 10). Indeed, one of the theoretical reasons which most strongly suggests that the mafia of any one period is likely to be more or better organized than previously is that competition for monopoly is likely to weed out the less organized clusters. But even if the mafia has evolved into a more organized entity, it has not managed to reach a stage at which stable cooperation can be sustained for any length of time. The reasons, both theoretical and historical, have yet to be properly understood, but the evidence suggests that neither has the mafia evolved towards a single monopoly successful in submitting all others, nor has it dissolved. The characteristics of its persistence suggest those of a turbulent equilibrium.[11]

To the extent to which one cluster does not triumph over all others, and all clusters do not melt peacefully into the fabric of the democratic state, the solution to the problem of trust that mafioso behaviour offers will remain at once individually rational and collectively disastrous. Trust – as we shall see in the next section – here displays the features of a positional good (see Pagano 1986), for one can trust others and be

10 Here I shall not address the question – which I have addressed elsewhere (Gambetta 1986) – of whether the mafia has been able to develop as a proper organization. However, I believe that there is enough evidence (Staiano 1986: 55–61), as well as sufficient theoretical grounds, to think that such an organization – somewhat like a confederation of local governments not always at peace with each other – has indeed existed. What is more difficult is to say whether such a confederation is still capable of operating now, after several years of internal conflict and state repression.
11 The notion of equilibrium does not, that is, apply to any one cluster or coalition of clusters in particular, but to the fact that, in spite of its internal wars and those intermittently waged against it by the state, *a* mafia has so far always managed to re-emerge.

trusted by them only to the extent that trust is subtracted from somewhere else: more trust on one side means less on another. This is a kind of trust that is in endemically short supply and that, unlike the trust which Hirschman (1984), Dasgupta and I myself explore (elsewhere in this volume), does not increase with use. After all, it is perhaps no trust at all, but rather the segmentary and patchily organized exploitation of distrust. The corollaries of distrust – and indeed its self-reinforcing behavioural expressions of secrecy, duplicity, information intelligence (Franchetti 1974: 30), and betrayal – all feature prominently in the lives and careers of mafiosi. Today, as much as 100 years ago, the minds of mafiosi are constantly occupied by thoughts of risks and traps, populated by a threatening array of 'traitors, spies and torturers' (Arlacchi 1983: 151). As an old *capo-mafia* wrote to a young member: 'I beg you to be careful, for the world is all infamous.' Indeed, there is no one we can trust in this world.

III

We have described the causes that may explain the emergence of the mafia. We still have to consider the mechanisms by which it has managed to maintain itself over such a long period.[12] These mechanisms are a combination of intended and unintended consequences. Let us begin with the latter.

Franchetti says that in Sicily those who are clever, energetic, and ambitious can only find a way to improve their social position by dedicating themselves to the 'industria della violenza' (p. 97). If one does not want to have anything to do with the mafia, then, in the absence of a legitimate authority in which to take refuge, the only alternatives are those of migrating and lying low ('se ne stanno neghittosi', p. 109). Both have been widely pursued, thereby – indirectly and unintentionally – enhancing the sense of distrust on which the force of the mafia thrives: as a result of migration and withdrawal into private life, the proportion of 'well-adjusted' or complacent people increases and the system is reinforced. A wide range of evidence (Arlacchi 1983) suggests that, on the margin, people who migrate do so also because of the mafia. Given that 'mafia-averse' people tend to migrate more frequently, the degree of opposition is likely to decrease and the power of the mafia to increase. The effects of migration are clearly unintended, because those who migrate do not do so *in order to* enhance the force of the mafia (although they may of course recognize those effects).

12 For an account of the continuity of the mafia see also Catanzaro (1985).

The second, partially unintentional, mechanism which explains the successful survival of the mafia has to do with the democratic state, which while hostile to such an alternative power as the mafia has also to depend on its capacity to mobilize votes. Geoffrey Hawthorn, elsewhere in this volume, argues that there might be two ways to undermine or override 'vicious circles' such as the mafia: one consists in the emergence of a predictable environment, the other in 'a power which is *independent* of the interests that maintain them'. The former, through the example Hawthorn gives of changing relationships on the land in the western Gangetic plain, consists essentially in the emergence of a reliable market for credit and produce, and is largely unintentional. As I shall argue below, in the world of the mafia monopoly a reliable market is a contradiction in terms and is not likely to come about, or at least to spread, 'naturally'. The latter, through the example Hawthorn gives of South Korea, consists of an authoritarian and military rule which, in itself monopolistic, would not tolerate local monopolies. In a sense, this implies that in order to get rid of the mafia, what we need is simply another – bigger and better – mafia.

Italy did once have a power which was largely independent of the mafia, or at least of the social strata supporting it, and which did contribute to a partial undoing of the mafia (Duggan 1985): this was of course the Fascist regime. In contrast, democracy, by its very nature, has to rely for consensus on larger parts of the population. Thus the temptation to come to terms with those who hold a monopoly of people's votes, regulate the dispensation of political trust, and somehow guarantee local 'law and order', has been strong, and in several instances has proved irresistible. This, of course, has not enhanced the already fragile trust in central authority in Sicily or the country as a whole. Here, it is not possible to go into details. Suffice it to say that it is unlikely that democracy's complicity with the mafia, at least at the national level, has been consistently intentional and conspiratorial, even though there are clearly cases in which this has been so. And as the majority of Italians would certainly agree: 'better the mafia than fascism!' Still today, any attempt to eradicate the mafia is caught between two extremes: that of using too little force and thereby remaining ineffective, and that of using too much, putting civil liberties at risk.

The aggregate and unintended effects of migration go some way towards explaining the lack of opposition to the mafia and its consequent capacity to survive. So does the intrinsic, and otherwise beneficial, weakness of democracy. But the weakness of the state – which has never fully succeeded in acquiring legitimation in the south – can only be measured in comparison with the strength of the local social structure (Franchetti 1974: 101) and its capacity to foster cooperation through intentional action.

Diego Gambetta

The mechanisms which motivate cooperation in any form of human endeavour, as Bernard Williams explains elsewhere in this volume, comprise four basic elements: coercion, interests, values, and personal bonds. People, that is, may decide to cooperate (1) for fear of sanctions; (2) because cooperation enhances their mutual economic interests; (3) because they have general reasons, whether cultural, moral or religious, to believe that cooperation is good irrespective of sanctions and rewards; and finally (4) because they are related to one another by bonds of kin or friendship.[13]

Even without having read Williams's essay, the mafia learnt this lesson well, and relies on *all four* mechanisms simultaneously.[14] Owing to constraints of space, I shall limit myself to detailed consideration of only the first two: coercion, and especially economic interests.[15] Their combination, within a world of deep distrust, is itself a robust pillar of mafia business for, irrespective of values and cultural codes, the force of constraints and opportunities can bring about rational adaptation on the part of people living in proximity with mafioso networks, even if they are not related by kin or do not entertain strong beliefs about the social importance of adhering to the code of honour or that of silence.

> It so happens that a person who would be prepared to make very great sacrifices in order to stop the domination of violence, is compelled to support it, strengthen it and associate with it . . . . He cannot think to resort to the law, because the probability of being shot for those who do so is far too high for him to expose himself lightly . . . . External circumstances impose themselves on everyone, irrespective of the inclinations of his mind (Franchetti 1974: 106–7).

The ability to use violence, whether direct or in the form of a credible threat, is a generalized ingredient of mafioso behaviour. It is the feature which most radically distinguishes the mafia from other forms of southern Italian cluster (see Gribaudi 1980: 69–75). Having recourse to

[13] Although the four basic mechanisms can be usefully distinguished for analytical purposes they are unlikely to represent four distinct motivational sets in people's minds all the time: we cannot always be sure whether our cooperation is motivated by fear of retaliation, economic advantage, or faith in the code of silence, or, finally, because it is our 'friend' who is asking us to cooperate. Within each cluster all possible reasons operate simultaneously to discourage the temptation to defect.

[14] To draw a map of the extent to which organizations of whatever sort rely on the four motivational sets would be well beyond the scope of this paper. Intuitively, however, there do not seem to be many which rely on all four at the same time. This may go some way towards explaining the relative success of organized crime of Italian origin in the United States with respect to other ethnic groups. While all rely on coercion and interest, the Italians probably have a more perfected tradition of suitable values and well-oiled codes of friendship and kinship.

[15] Several other authors have devoted a great deal of attention to the other mechanisms: for the code of honour and instrumental friendship see, for instance, Catanzaro (1985); for the importance of kinship and its manipulation see Arlacchi (1983: 154–64).

Mafia: the Price of Distrust   169

private violence is valuable outside as well as inside the cluster: outside, against unyielding victims, rival mafiosi groups, recalcitrant cooperators, and officials loyal to the state; inside, to punish defectors, discourage internal competitors for the leading positions, or, conversely, to challenge the leaders. Many mafiosi have begun their careers with violent acts (Hess 1973; Arlacchi 1983), but have subsequently relied on the reputation with which such acts provided them: 'basta la fama' wrote Franchetti (p. 104), in line with some of the most advanced game theory (see Milgrom and Roberts 1982, who show that, contrary to the standard economic claim, 'predatory practices' to maintain a monopoly are not irrational if reputation and future challengers are taken into account). They become persons with a reputation and are trusted, and, if interests diverge, they are trusted, in a limited but effective sense, to resort to violence without a second thought.

The relationship between violence and the other mechanisms suitable for inducing cooperation is threefold. First of all there is the relationship of *substitution*: violence substitutes for and can be substituted by (1) values – larger doses of *omertà* ensure lesser ones of violence; (2) interests, which can encourage cooperation and dispense with the need for violence; (3) personal bonds – relatives and friends are by definition more likely to cooperate, and hence there is a lower demand on violence to keep them under control. Next, there is the relationship of mutual *reinforcement*: greater quantities of *omertà* diminish the risks attached to the use of violence; at the same time, the higher the expectation that violence will be used, the higher the likelihood that silence will be scrupulously observed, to the point that it becomes impossible to say whether *omertà* is maintained out of faith or fear (Franchetti 1974: 31). Similarly, a greater capacity to satisfy mutual economic interests within the network, while offering a greater incentive to aggression from rival groups, may call for a more widespread use of violence in protection and at the same time act as an insurance against the undesirable consequences of its use. Conversely, a greater capacity for violence increases the capacity to satisfy mutual economic interests, thereby reinforcing the bonds of economic cooperation.

As I explain in the conclusion to this volume, there are also instances of a third, *contradictory* relationship between coercion and cooperation. An exaggerated use of violence – besides engendering paranoia in the users – can lead to revenge and the breach of *omertà*, as in the case of Tommaso Buscetta who, in 1983, decided to confess all he knew after half of his family was murdered. His confession brought to trial in Palermo nearly 500 persons suspected of a large number and variety of crimes (Staiano 1986).[16]

---

[16] Most cases of defection to the police involve the widows of mafiosi killed by other mafiosi.

170   *Diego Gambetta*

Violence by itself, however, will not do. It is risky, costly, and generates instability and conflict: explaining the persistence of the mafia simply by its capacity for coercion would be nearly as limited as explaining the persistence of capitalism on the same basis (see Przeworski 1985). The promotion of cooperation must also rely on a more powerful weapon: the satisfaction of economic interests. Mutual interests are served in a variety of ways, both within and without the immediate mafioso networks. Within the network, solidarity in case of arrest or death 'in the field' acts as insurance against the risks attached to illegal activities (Schneider and Schneider 1976: 189). Outside it, a wide range of economic bonds are formed: they can involve the corruption of civil servants, the exchange of favours for electoral support, or the handling of labour disputes for the benefit of landowners and entrepreneurs. But they may also be remote and aseptically insulated from the violent core of mafia activity: when private citizens, for instances, are offered extremely high interest rates to invest their money in informal banking systems without needing to know, like most investors, whether that money will be spent in financing philanthropic enterprises or drug trafficking. Thus the network of interests that mafiosi form around themselves can be widely ramified, ranging from active criminality, through corruption, to rational adaptation on the part of ordinary citizens (Franchetti 1974: 101).

Even the fundamental and time-honoured practice of extortion can be so deeply entrenched that it becomes difficult to distinguish between victims and accomplices, for the extortion bonds may take on rather ambiguous connotations. Franchetti's account is striking:[17]

> The distinction between a damage avoided and a benefit gained is up to a point artificial. [In most cases] the line that separates them is impossible to determine, or rather it does not exist in human feeling. When evildoers intrude on and dominate most social relationships, . . . the very act that saves one from their hostility can also bring their friendship with all its associated advantages (p. 129).

The violence of extortion and the self-interest of the 'victim' tend to merge and to provide an inextricable set of reasons for cooperation: the advantage of being a 'friend' of those who extort one's money or goods is not therefore simply that of avoiding the likely damages that would otherwise ensue, but can extend to assistance in disposing of competitors, or protection against the threats of isolated bandits, and against the risk of being cheated in the course of business transactions.

---

[17] Over a century after Franchetti wrote his account exactly the same notions are being expressed by the prosecutors in the current trial in Palermo (see Staiano 1986: 82–3).

The latter risk is particularly interesting with respect to the problem of trust, and worth pursuing in more detail, for it allows us to explore more analytically, if as yet tentatively, the economic heart of mafioso behaviour. We know that the absence of trust in business has a devastating effect: a high expected probability of being cheated (of being saddled with a 'lemon') may lead to the non-emergence or even to the collapse of market exchange, especially in those cases where asymmetric information – concerning the quality of the goods exchanged – is relevant (Akerlof 1970; Dasgupta, this volume). Within the cluster of people they protect, mafiosi offer a peculiar solution to the problem raised by the market of 'lemons'. On this issue, a Neapolitan coachman in 1863 had the following to say (consider that bad used horses were then the counterpart of the bad used cars of today):

> I am a murdered man. I bought a *dead* horse who does not know his way around, wants to follow only the roads he likes, slips and falls on slopes, fears squibs and bells, and yesterday he fledged and crashed into a flock of sheep that was barring the way. A *camorrista* [the Neapolitan version of a mafioso] who protects me and used to control the horse market, would have spared me from this theft. He used to check on the sales and get his tip from both buyers and sellers. Last year I wanted to get rid of a blind horse and he helped me to sell it as a good one, for he protected me. Now he is in jail and I was forced to buy this bad horse without him. He was a great gentleman! (quoted by Monnier [1863] 1965: 73–4)

There are several illuminating points in this amusing yet perfectly realistic account, the substance of which is confirmed by evidence from several other sources referring to more recent times (Arrighi and Piselli 1986: 399–404; Galante 1986: 97). The coachman willingly pays the protection money in compensation for an actual defensive task performed by the mafioso, and he bitterly regrets the latter's forced absence. The mafioso, by means which are left unclear but which presumably involve his reputation for toughness, seems capable of deterring the seller from handing over a 'lemon'. Without that protection the coachman is truly at risk, for he is indeed, as it were, saddled with a bad horse.

More difficult to interpret is the fact that the seller too gives the mafioso a tip. This could suggest, in line with Dasgupta's argument (this volume), that with respect to that particular transaction the protection the mafioso offers is really a *public* good which benefits both sides. If he did not act as guarantor the exchange would not take place at all, for the potential buyer would be deterred from entering the transaction for fear of getting a bad deal. The seller's tip, in other words, might reflect the price he is prepared to pay to be trusted. If the world were made up of only three agents – seller, coachman, and mafioso – the transaction would leave everyone better off: transaction costs would be higher than in a trustworthy world, but returns too would be higher than those yielded by no transaction at all.

If there is not just one seller on the market, however, the seller may also pay the mafioso for a service that has nothing to do with trust: for directing the customer to *him* rather than to another seller, for helping him to fend off the competition.[18] If all sellers look equally untrustworthy, and the mafioso can enforce honest behaviour from and signal *any one* of them to the buyer, then he must find some additional incentive to choose *one* in particular for whom to act as guarantor. Thus the seller's tip to the mafioso might reflect both the price of being considered trustworthy *and* the extra price of being *chosen* from among other potential sellers.

One might ask why the mafioso should not offer his 'mark of guarantee' to all sellers on the market and then let customers choose on the basis of taste, price, and the detectable quality of the goods. He would thus effectively offer trust as a public good: all sellers could chip in to pay him his due for making them appear trustworthy, and transactions would then take place in an 'ordinary' market. The available evidence suggests that this is not the case and that the mafioso tends to guarantee, *and* therefore to select, only a limited number of sellers *at the expense* of others.

One reason the mafioso might prefer to offer trust *in conjunction with* discouraging competition is that if that trust were *too* public he would then be unable to enforce the collection of his fee from all sellers, who would find free-riding particularly easy. He might also find it difficult to check on all transactions carried out by those sellers he guarantees, with the risk of losing his reputation if a 'lemon' were to be sold behind his back. A further reason why his intervention as guarantor must always be identifiable – linked, that is, to specific transactions – is to make sure that the buyer knows that if he gets a good deal this is due to the mafioso's protection and not to the independent honesty of the seller, which could foster the growth of trust directly between buyer and seller and put the mafioso out of business.

This is a crucial point, for it is by acting in such a way that the mafioso ends up selling trust as a positional good – a good, that is, that one seller can 'consume' only if other potential sellers do not (Pagano 1986). And this is presumably why competition develops in harmful ways, for in

---

[18] Here I do not discuss the problem of whether the mafioso is paid in actual cash or, as often happens, in other forms: presents in kind, credit for future transactions, or the exchange of favours. Although scholars have repeatedly stressed its importance, this problem is analytically irrelevant to my purpose.

order to stay in – or enter into – business, other potential sellers are
forced to rely less on improving the quality of their goods and the
competitiveness of their prices, than on developing those (ultimately
'military') skills which might subtract monopolistic power from the
mafioso and his cluster. In other words, they have either to become
mafiosi themselves or to ask for the protection of other mafiosi.

From what the coachman says we also learn that, on another occasion,
the mafioso succeeded in helping him to sell a blind horse as a good one.
This indicates that the mafioso is not offering his protection to *all* buyers
on the horse market: he is not really, in other words, dispensing a public
good to the buyers either. We are not told, however, why the mafioso on
one occasion satisfies the interests of both buyer and seller, while on this
occasion he takes care only of those of the latter, at the expense of those
of the former. It could be that the victim is an occasional buyer to whom
it is not worth offering protection for just a single transaction, whereas
on the other hand it would be advantageous to promote the (in this case
dishonest) interests of his coachman friend.

A more subtle interpretation might be that the mafioso, by 'guaranteeing' the sale of a blind horse to a victim who for whatever reason is
not under his protection (or indeed under that of any more powerful
mafioso),[19] is performing a demonstrative action: reminding everyone that
without his protection it is not just likely but 'guaranteed' that cheating
will occur. The mafioso himself has an interest in *regulated injections of
distrust* into the market to increase the demand for the product he sells –
that is, protection. If agents could trust each other independently of his
intervention he would, on this score at least, be idle. The income he
receives and the power he enjoys are the benefits to him of distrust.

Thus coping with, and at the same time re-creating, distrust would
seem to be the means by which the power of the mafiosi has endured so
long. No matter how distrust is generated, once it has been generated the
important thing from the point of view of the individual buyer is to find
a way of riding away from the market with a good horse rather than a
bad one. From the point of view of the seller, the first priority is to be
able to sell a horse; better still, a bad one. To choose to obtain the
mafioso's protection can hardly be considered irrational. The collective
disaster that is likely to follow from these individually rational premises
– sky-high murder rates, higher transaction costs, lower incentives for
technological innovation other than 'military' innovation, migration of
the best human capital, higher cheating rates, poorer quality of goods
and services – is the sad and largely unwanted result which has kept
southern Italy the way it is.

[19] If the victim has been under more powerful protection this would be another typical
case for the emergence of violent retaliation. It is clear that, in order to prevent tragic
mistakes, it is essential to know who is who.

174 *Diego Gambetta*

REFERENCES

Akerlof, G. 1970: The market for 'lemons': qualitative uncertainty and the market mechanisms. *Quarterly Journal of Economics* 84, 488–500.

Anonimo del XX secolo 1985: *Una modesta proposta per pacificare la citta' di Palermo.* Naples: Qualecultura.

Arlacchi, P. 1980: *Mafia, contadini e latifondo nella Calabria tradizionale.* Bologna: Il Mulino.

Arlacchi, P. 1983: *La mafia imprenditrice.* Bologna: Il Mulino.

Arrighi, G. and Piselli, F. 1986: Parentela, clientela e comunità. In *Storia della Calabria.* Turin: Einaudi, 367–492.

Banfield, E. 1958: *The Moral Basis of a Backward Society.* Glencoe: Free Press.

Blok, A. 1974: *The Mafia of a Sicilian Village, 1860–1960.* Oxford: Basil Blackwell.

Cancila, O. 1984: *Come andavano le cose nel sedicesimo secolo.* Palermo: Sellerio.

Catanzaro, R. 1985: Enforcers, entrepreneurs and survivors: how the mafia has adapted to change. *British Journal of Sociology*, 35, 1, 34–55.

Cosentino, F. 1983: Imprenditori sociali e processi di cambiamento nella Sicilia occidentale. Università degli studi di Modena: Tesi di Laurea.

Duggan, C. 1985: Fascism's campaign against the mafia. Oxford: doctoral thesis.

Fazello, T. 1558: *De rebus siculis decades.* Palermo.

Franchetti, L. [1876] 1974: Condizioni politiche ed amministrative della Sicilia. In L. Franchetti and S. Sonnino: *Inchiesta in Sicilia*, vol. I. Florence: Vallecchi.

Galante, G. 1986: Cent'anni di mafia. In D. Breschi et al., *L'immaginario mafioso*, Bari: Dedalo.

Gambetta, D. 1986: La mafia non esiste! Cambridge: unpublished paper.

Gambino, S. 1975: *La mafia in Calabria.* Reggio Calabria: Edizioni Parallelo.

Gower Chapman, C. 1971: *Milocca: a Sicilian village.* Cambridge, Mass.: Schenkman.

Gribaudi, G. 1980: *Mediatori.* Turin: Rosenberg and Sellier.

Hess, H. 1973: *Mafia and Mafiosi: the structure of power.* Lexington, Mass.: Lexington Books.

Hess, H. 1986: The traditional Sicilian mafia: organized crime and repressive crime. In R. J. Kelly (ed.), *Organized Crime: a global perspective*, Totowa, New Jersey: Rowman and Littlefield.

Hirschman, A. O. 1984: Against parsimony: three easy ways of complicating some categories of economic discourse. *American Economic Review Proceedings*, 74, 88–96.

Milgrom, P. and Roberts, J. 1982: Predation, reputation and entry deterrence. *Journal of Economic Theory* 27, 280–312.

Monnier, M. [1863] 1965: *La camorra.* Naples: Arturo Berisio Editore.

Pagano, U. 1986: The economics of positional goods. Cambridge: unpublished paper.

Pezzino, P. 1985: Alle origini del potere mafioso: stato e società in Sicilia nella seconda metà dell'ottocento. *Passato e Presente* 8, 33–69.

Przeworski, A. 1985: *Capitalism and Social Democracy.* Cambridge: Cambridge University Press.

Mafia: the Price of Distrust   175

Schelling, T. 1984: *Choice and Consequence.* Cambridge, Mass. Harvard University Press.

Schneider, J. and Schneider, P. 1976: *Culture and Political Economy in Western Sicily.* New York: Academic Press.

Staiano, C. (ed.) 1986: *L'atto d'accusa dei giudici di Palermo.* Rome: Editori Riuniti.

Tocqueville, A. de 1864–67: *Voyage en Sicile.* In *Œuvres complètes,* vol. VI, Paris.

Walston, J. 1986: See Naples and die: organized crime in Campania. In R. J. Kelly (ed.), *Organized Crime: a global perspective,* Totowa, New Jersey: Rowman and Littlefield.

ELSEVIER

Journal of Economic Behavior & Organization
Vol. 34 (1998) 387–417

JOURNAL OF
Economic Behavior
& Organization

Determinants of trust in supplier relations: Evidence from the automotive industry in Japan and the United States

Mari Sako[a,*], Susan Helper[b]

[a] Said Business School, University of Oxford, 59 George Street, Oxford OXI 2BE, UK
[b] Department of Economics, Case Western Reserve University, Cleveland OH, USA

Received 30 October 1995; received in revised form 3 October 1996

Abstract

This study examines the determinants of inter-organizational trust by using survey data from over 1000 suppliers in the automotive industry. Drawing on transaction cost economics, game theory and sociological exchange theory, we define trust and derive a model of its determinants. Regression analysis results indicate that determinants of trust are different from determinants of opportunism. US–Japanese differences are found in three respects: (i) the way trust is conceptualised by suppliers is more complex in Japan than in the US; (ii) the level of trust is higher in Japan than in the US; and (iii) the factors facilitating trust and those attenuating opportunism differ in the US and Japan. © 1998 Elsevier Science B.V.

JEL classification: L14; L22; L23; L62

Keywords: Trust; Opportunism; Supplier relations; Auto industry

The advantage to mankind of being able to trust one another penetrates into every crevice and cranny of human life. (Mill, 1891, p. 68)

Virtually every commercial transaction has within itself an element of trust, certainly any transaction conducted over a period of time. It can be plausibly argued that much of the economic backwardness in the world can be explained by the lack of mutual confidence. (Arrow, 1975, p. 24)

---

* Corresponding author.

388   *M. Sako, S. Helper/J. of Economic Behavior & Org. 34 (1998) 387–417*

1. Introduction and review of literature

Recent work on trust between business organizations focuses on the possibility of using it to enhance competitive advantage (Barney and Hansen, 1994, Jarillo, 1988, Mohr and Spekman, 1994). In fact, an increasing number of studies exhort companies to build trust with their business partners (e.g. Dodgson, 1993, SMMT and DTI, 1994). However, trust is sometimes understood to be a by-product of norms embedded in social networks and rarely brought about through rational–instrumental means (Granovetter, 1985). Even if trust could be cultivated intentionally, it is regarded as a scarce commodity which only a few can afford (Gambetta, 1988, pp. 224). Before an explicit strategy of developing and maintaining trust can be considered feasible, the determinants of trust must be identified. This paper is a stepping stone towards developing a strategic framework for trust. It combines the strength of the discipline of economics which has focused on how trust may be created deliberately, and that of psychology which has endeavoured to develop a reliable survey technique for measuring trust. The empirical part of the paper is based on a large-scale survey of automotive parts suppliers in the United States and Japan.

Inter-organisational trust may enhance organizational performance in a number of ways. For instance, trust enables a network of firms to adapt to unforeseen circumstances which are common in a world of risk and uncertainty, thus reducing transaction costs (Jarillo, 1988). Also, trust is said to promote suppliers' willingness to invest in customer-specific and general assets (Dyer, forthcoming). But while theoretical work abounds, empirical work on the link between trust and performance has been rare. In empirical work, as in theory, it is opportunism rather than trust which has attracted more attention (e.g. Anderson, 1988). Moreover, opportunism or trust tend not to be measured directly; instead, these features are assumed to be present in transactions with certain characteristics such as specific assets (Klein et al., 1978) or long-term trading (Gulati, 1995). Therefore, we believe that the operationalisation of trust is an important task.

The central concept explored in this paper is mutual trust between a customer and a supplier organization. Trust is an expectation held by an agent that its trading partner will behave in a mutually acceptable manner (including an expectation that neither party will exploit the other's vulnerabilities). This expectation narrows the set of possible actions, thus reducing the uncertainty surrounding the partner's actions. Sako (1991), Sako (1992) used these different reasons to distinguish between three types of trust: contractual trust (will the other party carry out its contractual agreements?), competence trust (is the other party capable of doing what it says it will do?), and goodwill trust (will the other party make an open-ended commitment to take initiatives for mutual benefit while refraining from unfair advantage taking?).[1]

The study of inter-personal trust has a long history within the discipline of psychology (e.g. Deutsch, 1958, Rotter, 1967; see Clark, 1993 for a good literature survey). Much progress has been made in developing reliable attitudinal measures of trust (Cook and Wall, 1980, Cook et al., 1981). But in the context of business organizations, this focus of

---

[1] Predictable behaviour can also arise because an agent is tightly constrained in its behaviour, not due to a desire to act in a trustworthy manner. In our analysis below, we distinguish between these two sources of predictability.

psychology is deficient. In particular, while psychologists tend to study inter-personal trust, business firms are concerned just as much with inter-organizational trust. It is the latter which might survive a breakdown of inter-personal relationships due to labour turnover or personality clash, and which provides the stability necessary for firms to pursue innovative and competitive activities. For this reason the determinants of inter-personal and inter-organizational trust may well be different (Barney and Hansen, 1994), although similar methods may be applied to analyse them (Smith et al., 1995).[2]

In organizational studies, it has been common to focus on determinants of 'governance structures' or 'governance mechanisms' (such as markets vs hierarchies and intermediate modes including long-term contracts, joint ventures and other forms of alliances, Heide and John, 1990, Joskow, 1988, Walker and Weber, 1984). Trust or opportunism enter into some of these analyses as either one of the determinants of governance structures or a governance structure in itself. As an example of the former, trust is a social norm which lessens the need to use hierarchy to attenuate opportunism. Thus, the higher the general level of trust, the less need there is for vertical integration (Williamson, 1985) or equity-holding (Gulati, 1995). Here, trust tends to be conceptualised as a substitute for various governance mechanisms. Also, trust may be a society-wide norm or a norm which develops in dyadic relationships. As an example of the latter, governance by trust is an informal control mechanism which enhances the effectiveness of transactions *whether* they take place in markets or within a hierarchy (Smitka, 1991). This conceptualisation introduces the possibility that trust may complement, rather than substitute for, hierarchy or market (Bradach and Eccles, 1989, Smitka, 1992). However, unlike equity holding or long-term written contracts, inter-organizational trust as a form of governance remains ill-defined because it is intangible and informal. It has been noted that difficulties in defining the presence or absence of trust in a consistent manner have caused much misunderstanding both within and between disciplinary fields (Hosmer, 1995).

In economics, the interest in trust has come from a rather oblique angle, mainly from two theoretical perspectives, transaction cost economics and game theory. In transaction cost economics, opportunism (self-interest-seeking with guile), rather than trust, has been

---

[2] Recently, Williamson (1993) has objected to the increasingly popular notion of 'calculative trust' which is an assessment of the expected benefits and costs of cooperation. He called for the restriction of the usage of the term trust to personal trust only, a situation in which Williamson assumes that no monitoring occurs. Here, he appears to conflate the absence of continuous calculation with the absence of monitoring. In inter-organizational trust, as in some marriages and friendships, trust tends to be associated with periodic intense mutual observation (Sabel, 1992, 1994, Lorenz, 1993). But this does not necessarily imply that all firms are always calculating benefits and costs of each action they take with respect to another firm.

Despite Williamson's concerns, the concept of inter-organizational trust is widely used in both the marketing and the strategy literature. For examples of empirical work, see Zaheer and Venkatraman (1995), Parkhe (1993), Anderson and Weitz (1989), Morgan and Hunt (1994), Kumar et al. (1995), Ganesan (1994) and Cummings and Bromiley (1996). The scales used by these authors to measure trust meet conventional criteria of validity, such as internal consistency and face validity. In addition, Gulati (1995) finds that firms act as if they gain trust in each other over time; firms which have engaged in alliances with each other before are less likely to use equity, "since interfirm trust based on prior alliances reduces the imperative to use equity." There is also a good deal of case study evidence that inter-organizational trust can survive the departure of the individuals who initially established the relationship. Odaka et al. (1988) describe the close ties that bind Toyota and its long-term suppliers. Eccles (1981) shows that participants in the U.S. construction industry have repeated dealings with each other, dealings which are governed by trust rather than by legally-enforceable guarantees. Similar arrangements are also found in other areas, such as the "Third Italy" (Brusco, 1986), the Japanese textile industry (Dore, 1983) and the Japanese electronics industry (Sako, 1992).

390   *M. Sako, S. Helper / J. of Economic Behavior & Org. 34 (1998) 387–417*

a central concept. In designing organizations, the reliance on trust is seen to be too fragile as compared to devising safeguards against opportunism (Williamson, 1985, p. 64). Opportunistic behaviour is said to be irresistible for parties encountering a cocktail of specific assets and uncertainty. Vertical integration or obligational contracting is put forward as an optimal governance structure for attenuating such behaviour (Williamson, 1979). Attenuating opportunism, however, is not the same as attaining mutual trust, as will be shown in this paper.

In game theory, economists are interested in the evolution of cooperation. Even self-interested agents will cooperate if they expect a positive pay-off from cooperation, a situation more likely with repeated encounters over an infinite or uncertain time horizon than in one-time transactions (Kreps, 1990). However, cooperation cannot be equated with trust. This is because cooperation may emerge where no trust exists (Axelrod, 1984). Also, trust as a subjective state of mind may not have a straightforward linear relationship to cooperation or trust as manifested in behaviour (Kee and Knox, 1970).

This paper is structured as follows. Section 2 develops a conceptual framework for defining trust and analysing its determinants, by borrowing approaches from economic, sociological and psychological theories. This framework is used to develop a number of hypotheses. Section 3 reports the results of factor analysis used to create composite measures of trust, and regression analysis to test the hypotheses. Section 4 concludes by drawing theoretical and empirical implications of this study.

2. Conceptual framework and hypotheses

2.1. Differentiating trust and opportunism

In this paper, we conceptualize trust to be not a mere opposite of opportunism. This is due to a distinction we make among different types of trust, following Sako (1992). A precondition for trust of the contractual and goodwill types is the absence of opportunistic behaviour. However, lack of opportunism is not a sufficient condition for goodwill trust. For example, a supplier that withholds a vital piece of technical information is acting opportunistically according to the goodwill trust definition but not in the strict contractual sense. This amounts to fulfilling the letter, but not the spirit, of the contract. Thus, there seems to be a hierarchy of trust, with fulfilling a minimal set of obligations constituting 'contractual trust,' and honouring a broader set constituting 'goodwill trust.' A move from contractual trust to goodwill trust involves a gradual expansion in the congruence in beliefs about what is acceptable behaviour. Also, as one goes higher up the hierarchy, a looser form of reciprocity applies between the trading partners. Reciprocation may take a broader range of forms, and more time may elapse between the receipt of a favour and its return (Goulder, 1960).

The existence of reciprocity could be tested using a research design which asks both parties in a relationship whether each trusted the other (Currall and Judge, forthcoming). However, such reciprocity also gives grounds for arguing that trust is a self-reinforcing set of expectations (Fox, 1974, Zand, 1972), so that it is not possible for a customer to

M. Sako, S. Helper / J. of Economic Behavior & Org. 34 (1998) 387–417 391

continue to trust a supplier for ever if the supplier starts to distrust the customer. Therefore, it is useful to investigate trust from the supplier's point of view only.

2.2. Conditions for facilitating trust and attenuating opportunism

The main tasks of this paper are to operationalise the concept of trust, and to determine conditions which facilitate the creation and maintenance of trust. The following hypotheses concern eight sets of factors which are thought to facilitate the creation and maintenance of trust between a customer and a supplier. Since the survey data analysis in this paper focuses on suppliers' trust of customers, the hypotheses will be in terms of this. Suppliers' perception of customer opportunism is hypothesized to be distinct from suppliers' trust of customers. Some conditions may prevent opportunism but do not necessarily foster trust, while other factors which enhance trust do not necessarily constitute a safeguard against opportunism. Moreover, we expect all the following hypotheses to be more significant in cases where customers are free to choose from alternative courses of action than when they are constrained, for example, by the lack of alternative suppliers in the marketplace.

Characteristics of the bilateral relationship are dealt with first before moving on to wider environmental and institutional conditions.

2.2.1. Vertical integration and written contracts

Financial vertical integration is one solution given by transaction cost economists to attenuate the effects of supplier opportunism. In theory, integration gives the principal (the customer) better control and ability to monitor the agent's (the supplier's) behaviour. In this sense, vertical integration is considered a substitute for 'governance by trust' (Smitka, 1991). Where there is control via integration, there is no need to rely on trust to coordinate activities. But in reality, vertical integration in itself has not assured better internal administrative coordination. For example, General Motors has had great difficulty in persuading its internal divisions (and in particular its most formidable Fisher Body Division) to share cost information within the corporation (Helper, 1991, pp. 803–804). Transaction cost economics has focused on vertical integration attenuating the *agent's* (supplier's) opportunism. Therefore, it is not at all clear that the *principal's* own opportunism is attenuated by the principal's integration with the supplier.

The customer's ownership of suppliers may be interpreted by the latter as a form of credible commitment for long-term relationship, which in turn may lead to the absence of opportunistic behaviour by the customer (Williamson, 1983). But vertical integration has not stopped the closure or selling off of component divisions by the Big Three in the US. Such recent U.S. experience militates against the case for vertical integration attenuating customer opportunism. Thus, we may hypothesize that:

H1A: Suppliers' trust of customers is not significantly affected by the degree to which they are vertically integrated by their customer, other things being equal.

H1B: Suppliers' perception of customer opportunism is not significantly affected by the degree to which they are vertically integrated by their customer, other things being equal.

392   *M. Sako, S. Helper/J. of Economic Behavior & Org. 34 (1998) 387–417*

Another governance structure is the long-term written contract. Long-term contracts may reduce the expectations of opportunistic behaviour, but may not necessarily enhance trust. In fact where there is trust in a relationship, long-term written contracts are superfluous to the viability of the relationship. According to one strand of thinking (e.g. Kawashima, 1967), appeal to legal authorities in itself introduces, not only rigidity, but suspicion into a relationship. However, some researchers (e.g. Lane and Backman, 1996, Sitkin and Roth, 1993) argue on the contrary that law may help strengthen the foundation upon which trust can grow under certain circumstances. In contrast, our view is that contracts are a partial safeguard against opportunism only. Contracts are almost always incomplete due to uncertainty and complexity; so they provide no guarantee of what the customer might do in unforeseen circumstances. Contracts, therefore, provide no assurance that the customer will act in a mutually beneficial way when not required to do so by the contract. We can therefore hypothesize about opportunism but not about trust because contracts tend to be regarded as safeguards. Thus,

H1C: The longer the duration of written contracts, the lower the supplier's expectation of customer opportunism, other things being equal.

2.2.2. Long-term trading and future expectations of customer commitment

According to Axelrod (1984), it is the expectation of long-term commitment into the future – what he calls "enlarging the shadow of the future" – rather than the record of long-term trading, which matters in making trading partners cooperate with each other (see also Heide and John, 1990). Expectations of repeated transactions have led even litigious American business firms to rely on 'relational contracting' (Macaulay, 1963, Macneil, 1974). To the extent that trust is built by demonstrating trustworthiness over time, the historical duration of a relationship may also matter. That is, expectations of continuity may be induced by past association.

H2A: The longer the informal commitment made by the customer to continue trading with the supplier, the higher is the supplier's trust for its customer.
H2B: The longer the duration of past trading, the higher is the supplier's trust of its customer.

2.2.3. Reciprocity in information exchange

Sharing of information facilitates coordination between organizations. But disclosing proprietary or confidential information to the other party, that is, acting as if one trusted the other, exposes one's vulnerability. In this situation, a two-way flow of information is essential for creating and sustaining trust, which feeds on a loose form of reciprocity over time. One-way flow of information – for example, a supplier being asked to provide information about its detailed process steps without the customer being more open about its future business plan – is likely to be regarded with suspicion by the supplier as a sign of increased control. Information asymmetry resulting from one-way flow of information also gives much scope for opportunistic behaviour (Williamson, 1975).

H3A: The more a supplier's disclosure of information to its customer is matched by the customer's provision of information to the supplier, the higher the supplier's trust for its customer.

M. Sako, S. Helper/J. of Economic Behavior & Org. 34 (1998) 387–417 393

H3B: The more a supplier is asked to provide information to its customer without the customer reciprocating by giving information to the supplier, the greater the supplier's perception of customer opportunism.

2.2.4. Interdependence and asset specificity

Axelrod (1984) wrote about the importance of perceived interdependence for cooperation to evolve. A deliberate strategy of locking oneself into a relationship, thus raising switching costs, may facilitate the creation and maintenance of trust. Investment in assets dedicated to the other party makes mutual commitment to the relationship credible, thus enhancing trust, particularly if both parties have equally good alternatives to turn to.

This proposition is in stark contrast to Williamson's earlier argument that in a situation of bilateral monopoly, "it is in the interest of each party to seek terms most favorable to him, which encourages opportunistic representations and haggling" (Williamson, 1975, p. 27). In contrast, in a situation with large numbers of bidders, "parties who attempt to secure gains by strategic posturing will find, at the contract renewal interval, that such behavior is nonviable."

More recently, however, transactions cost theorists, including Williamson (1983) himself, have argued that the establishment of 'credible commitments' or 'hostages' can bind the parties to trustworthy behaviour even while it creates bilateral monopoly. Empirical support for this idea is provided by Anderson and Weitz (1989) and Heide and John (1990).

H4A: The greater the level of customer-specific assets possessed by the supplier and the more difficult it is for the customer to switch away from the supplier, the higher the supplier's trust in its customer.

H4B: The greater the level of customer-specific assets possessed by the supplier, the higher the supplier's perception of customer opportunism.

2.2.5. Technical assistance

One type of credible commitment that a customer can provide to a supplier is technical assistance, since the customer receives no return on its investment in training if it fires the supplier. In addition, the customer would have more trust in its supplier's competence as a result. To the extent that the customer demonstrates knowledge and skills by providing technical assistance, it enhances supplier's 'competence trust' of the customer. Over time, particularly if technical assistance is not fully paid for, the supplier would interpret it as a manifestation of commitment by the customer, and may become a basis for 'goodwill trust' (Sako, 1992).

In the automobile industry, it is typically the customer which has greater market power in relation to its suppliers. Where there is such differential power between the customer and the supplier, the initiative taken by the more powerful partner – the customer – to commit to a relationship before receiving guarantees of trust from the weaker partner is conducive to the creation of trust. A weaker partner is therefore more grateful for a show of commitment through technical assistance. At the same time, technical assistance provides no protection against opportunism, and therefore we cannot hypothesize about opportunism in this respect.

394   *M. Sako, S. Helper / J. of Economic Behavior & Org. 34 (1998) 387–417*

H5A: The more technical assistance is provided by the customer, the higher the supplier's trust in the customer.

H5B: The smaller the supplier is relative to the customer, the more trusting the supplier is for a given level of technical assistance.

2.2.6. Uncertainty

Unpredictability in business environments makes opportunism difficult to control because a firm, either customer or supplier, would find it difficult to write fully contingent contracts (Williamson, 1975). However, at the same time, the greater the degree of environmental uncertainty, the greater the benefit from being able to trust a trading partner, because trust facilitates decision making in unanticipated circumstances. Here, it may be useful to make a distinction between behavioural uncertainty (the source of which is the customer who may increase the degree of uncertainty by behaving in an unpredictable and/or opportunistic manner) and environmental uncertainty (the source of which is other than the customer, such as the cost of raw materials or the future trajectory of new technology). Environmental uncertainty predisposes agents to behave opportunistically when there are relation-specific investments (Walker and Weber, 1984). However, behavioural uncertainty is reduced when opportunism is contained.

H6: The more uncertain the market and technology environments, and the higher the degree of asset specificity, the greater the level of customer opportunism.

2.2.7. National cultural values, business norms and past investment into trust

Trust between trading partners may vary, not only with the attributes of transaction, but also with the trading environment of which they are a part. Here, societal culture, politics, regulation, professionalisation, networks and corporate culture are said to be a relevant set of attributes in which a bilateral relationship may be embedded (Granovetter, 1985). For example, Smitka (1991) argues that 'governance by trust' is more prevalent in the Japanese than in the U.S. automobile industry due to, among other things, the existence of suppliers' associations (kyoryokukai) in Japan and their absence in the US. These associations enhance communication among suppliers, and therefore act as an extra bulwark against customer opportunism (Sako, 1996). Dore (1983) and Sako (1992) provide evidence that Japanese companies are more predisposed to trusting their trading partners than are British companies. This is in part due to prevailing business norms which are determined by societal-level cultural values.

Societal norms may be self-reinforcing. Over time, a history of good experience with trusting behaviour in Japan may have promoted the diffusion of trust. In fact, cultural norms such as trust can be "the precipitate of history" (Dore, 1987, p. 91). For instance, Japanese suppliers in the automotive industry may trust their customers more today because they have had more customer commitment, more technical assistance, etc. over a much longer period of time than most U.S. suppliers, and their trusting behaviour has been honoured by being given growing orders. In contrast, a typical (though more eloquent) U.S. supplier executive asserted that their customer "would steal a dime from a starving grandmother" (Helper, 1991). Attempts by U.S. companies to imitate the Japanese business norm are costly and difficult because the way in which a network of customer–supplier relations developed in Japan is path-dependent.

M. Sako, S. Helper / J. of Economic Behavior & Org. 34 (1998) 387–417 395

Due to the extent to which norms of trustworthy behaviour are embedded in a society, there is no reason to expect the same model of the determinants of trust to hold in each country (Dore, 1983, Sako, 1992).[3] For this reason, we control for national differences, not only by using a dummy variable in the combined data set, but also by examining the determinants of trust in each country separately.

By extension, we may also hypothesize that because of this accumulated expectation of trust among Japanese companies, Japanese-owned suppliers in the US are likely to trust their customers more than do other suppliers in the US. Due to a reputation effect, even U.S.-owned suppliers may trust Japanese-owned customers more than the Big Three customers.

H7A: Suppliers in Japan tend to have a higher level of trust towards their customer than do suppliers in the US.

H7B: In the US, Japanese-owned suppliers tend to entertain a higher level of trust towards their customer than do other suppliers.

H7C: In the US, suppliers to Japanese-owned automakers tend to entertain a higher level of trust towards their customer than do other suppliers.

2.2.8. Customers' supplier management practices

One caveat to the above generalisation about national culture and business norms is that suppliers' trust of customers may be customer-specific, and that within each country some customers may be perceived to be more trustworthy than others. For example, within Japan, the largest producer, Toyota, has a reputation for having been more consistent than other Japanese automakers in offering help (e.g. technical assistance on Total Quality, Just-in-Time, Value Analysis, etc.) which suppliers have found useful (Sako, 1996). In the US, despite a general trend towards longer-term relationships, General Motors has recently adopted a purchasing strategy which emphasises the benefit of hard-nosed bargaining with little commitment to renew contracts (Helper, 1994).

Over time, each customer may develop a reputation for particular procurement practices among the supplier community. The reputation may be for being receptive to suppliers' suggestions (rather than unwillingness to consider them), or for providing help to reduce costs (rather than switching immediately to an alternative supplier) whenever a competitor offered a lower price or when material prices rose. These beliefs on the part of suppliers, whether they are based on actual past experience with their customer or hearsay, are hypothesized to be associated with high trust.

This hypothesis can also be seen as a test of whether the concept of inter-organizational trust makes sense. If it is true that trust can exist only between individuals, and that trustworthy individuals are randomly allocated across companies, then our data should reject the following hypothesis:

H8: The supplier's trust of customers within a country depends on the customer's supplier management practices.

---

[3] For example, in our field research, we found that U.S. firms considered it untrustworthy for a customer to ask for a price reduction on an existing product, and considered it quite acceptable to win a contract through a low bid and then ask for a price increase later. In contrast, Japanese suppliers were used to reducing prices on their products; their customers considered it untrustworthy to ask for a price increase.

3. Data analysis and discussion

The data used to test the above hypotheses were collected by the authors during 1993. For details on questionnaire design, the sampling framework and response rates, see Appendix A. The data are derived from responses from first-tier component suppliers in the automotive industry. Although single-industry studies may often lack generalisability, they have the advantage of controlling for sources of extraneous variation due to industry characteristics, environmental noise and the like. We solicited answers from one respondent per organization to make a large-scale international survey feasible (a total of more than 3000 questionnaires were sent out).

Trust and opportunism concern subjective judgments and expectations. We relied on composite rather than single measures in order to reduce measurement errors. The measures of trust and opportunism were developed by surveying the academic literature in economics and psychology (e.g. Anderson, 1988, Cook et al., 1981). By contrast, most of the independent variables used for regression analysis, such as contract lengths and company size, are objective data and are therefore based on single-item measures.

3.1. Different types of trust

Eight items used to measure trust and opportunism in the questionnaire are shown in Table 1. Each item is a 5-point scale, ranging from strongly disagree (1) to strongly agree (5). The items were chosen to capture the notion of three types of trust and opportunism. For example, the concept of 'contractual trust' is operationalised by the statement 'We prefer to have everything spelt out in detail in our contract.' The concept of 'competence trust' is captured by a reverse-coded statement 'The advice our customer gives us is not always helpful.' 'Goodwill trust' is operationalised by the statements 'We can rely on our customer to help us in ways not required by our agreement with them' and 'We can depend on our customer always to treat us fairly.' Other items were included to capture the notion of opportunism ('Given the chance, our customer might try to take unfair advantage of our business unit'), the notion of suspicion ('We feel that our customer often uses the information we give to check up on us rather than to solve problems'), and distrust arising from lack of shared goals ('In dealing with this customer, we spend a lot of time haggling unproductively over such issues as prices and responsibility for problems'). Lastly, we attempted to gauge the extent of mutual trust by asking suppliers to assess their own trustworthiness ('Our business unit has a reputation for being more straightforward and open with our customer than are other suppliers').

When each item is examined separately, it is evident that Japanese suppliers tend to entertain a higher level of trust and a lower level of opportunism than U.S. suppliers, except in their assessment of their own honesty and openness. Within the US, Japanese-owned suppliers and those which supply to Japanese customers tend to be more trusting and expect less opportunism from their customers. By contrast, suppliers to General Motors are significantly more suspicious of their customer. Within Japan, suppliers to Toyota are somewhat more trusting of their customer.

In order to examine if survey respondents differentiated between different types of trust, factor analysis was performed on the above items. Principal components analysis

M. Sako, S. Helper/J. of Economic Behavior & Org. 34 (1998) 387–417

Table 1
Differences in trust and opportunism in Japan and the US (Percent agreeing)

	Japan vs. US N=472; N=675		In Japan Toyota (N=103)		In US Japcust (N=92)		In US Japown (N=75)		In US GM (N=242)	
	Japan	USA	No	Yes	No	Yes	No	Yes	No	Yes
We feel that our customer often uses the information we give to check up on us, rather than to solve problems.	1.72 [a]	2.67	1.75	1.62	2.74	2.23 [a]	2.70	2.48 [d]	2.55	2.89 [a]
The advice our customer gives us is not always helpful.	2.51 [a]	3.37	2.61	2.17 [a]	3.42	3.06 [c]	3.40	3.16	3.25	3.59 [b]
We prefer to have everything spelt out in detail in our contract.	3.08 [b]	3.74	3.15	2.84 [b]	3.81	3.24 [a]	3.79	3.37 [a]	3.68	3.85 [c]
Given the chance, our customer might try to take unfair advantage of our business unit.	1.90 [a]	2.87	1.97	1.69 [d]	2.97	2.19 [a,c]	2.92	2.52 [b]	2.63	3.30 [a]
In dealing with this customer, we spend a lot of time haggling unproductively over such issues as prices and responsibility for problems.	2.05 [a]	2.74	2.13	1.79 [a]	2.80	2.28 [a]	2.78	2.44 [b]	2.58	3.02 [a]
We can rely on our customer to help us in ways not required by our agreement with them.	3.17 [c]	3.02	3.13	3.33 [d]	2.92	3.73 [a]	2.96	3.46 [a]	3.26	2.60 [a]
Our business unit has a reputation for being more straightforward and open with our customer than are other suppliers.	3.49 [a]	3.73	3.47	3.56	3.73	3.75	3.72	3.87	3.74	3.73
We can depend on our customer always to treat us fairly.	3.91 [a]	2.97	3.85	4.11 [b]	2.84	3.85 [a]	2.88	3.54 [a]	3.33	2.31 [a]

Note: The figures show the average scores for responses on a 1–5 scale (5=strongly agree; 4=agree; 3=neither agree nor disagree; 2=disagree; 1=strongly disagree). T-test is significant at:
[a] $p<0.001$.
[b] $p<0.01$.
[c] $p<0.05$.
[d] $p<0.10$.

398   M. Sako, S. Helper / J. of Economic Behavior & Org. 34 (1998) 387–417

with varimax (orthogonal) rotation was used throughout. Of the eight items listed in Table 1, one concerning 'contractual trust' ('We prefer to have everything spelt out in detail in our contract') was dropped from the factor analysis because including it produced a factor loading of this item of below 0.2 in all cases. Table 2 shows that the results are substantially different in the U.S. and Japanese surveys. In the US, only one main factor emerged, which combines 6 items with a Cronbach's alpha of 0.811. This factor may be labelled Distrust. The suppliers' self-assessment of their trustworthiness emerged as a separate factor. In Japan, however, the application of the same technique led to the emergence of three separate factors: Factor 1 (combining 4 items with a Cronbach's alpha of 0.726) called Customer Opportunism, Factor 2 (combining 2 items with a Cronbach's alpha of 0.599) called Goodwill Trust, and one item as a separate indicator of Competence Trust.[4] Next, the U.S. and Japanese surveys were combined to perform factor analysis on the overall data. As shown in Table 2, one main factor, Distrust, which is the same as the U.S.-only factor of Distrust, was identified, with a Cronbach's alpha of 0.816.

Thus, it seems from these results that in contrast to U.S. suppliers, Japanese suppliers distinguish among different types of trust. Moreover, as the Goodwill Trust Factor in Japanese data indicates, reciprocity appears to be more embedded in the Japanese conceptualisation of trust than the U.S. counterpart. In the Japanese data, opportunism and trust are not mere opposites; if they were, only one factor should have emerged from the above analysis. (See Deutsch, 1958 who argues that trust and suspicion are not mere opposites.) By contrast, in the US, generalised distrust appears to prevail, possibly because distrust is self-perpetuating; distrust in one area (e.g. contractual) may induce distrust in another area (e.g. competence) due to the lack of information necessary in order to assess the source of misconduct.

3.2. Conditions for facilitating trust and attenuating opportunism

How different are the factors which attenuate opportunism from those factors which enhance trust? Moreover, are there any differences in the facilitating conditions for trust in Japan and the US?

The eight sets of hypotheses in the previous section were tested using ordinary least squares regression, with Distrust, Customer Opportunism and Goodwill Trust as alternative dependent variables.[5] The independent variables are explained in detail in

---

[4] Factor analysis was also conducted by excluding the item on suppliers' self-assessment of their trustworthiness ('Our business unit has a reputation for being more straightforward and open with our customer than are other suppliers'). A single factor emerged for the U.S. sample, but two distinct factors were identified in the Japanese sample. This reinforces the evidence that U.S. and Japanese suppliers conceptualise trust differently.

[5] OLS and ordered probit regressions were run using single item measures as well as composite measures derived from factor analysis. Similar results (with respect to signs and significance of independent variables) were obtained as between Customer Opportunism and the measure 'Given the chance, our customer might take unfair advantage of our business unit,' and between Goodwill Trust and the measure 'We can rely on our customer to help us in ways not required by our agreement with them.'

M. Sako, S. Helper / J. of Economic Behavior & Org. 34 (1998) 387–417   399

Table 2
Factor analysis of trust scales in Japan and the US

	US (N=630)		Japan (N=445)			US and Japan (N=1073)	
	FACTOR 1 Distrust	FCTR 2	FCTR 1 Customer opportunism	FCTR 2 Goodwill trust	FCTR 3 Competence trust	FCTR 1 Distrust	FCTR 2
We feel that our customer often uses the information we give to check up on us rather than to solve problems.	0.60503	0.12658	0.37895	-0.04483	0.31211	0.64480	0.02903
The advice our customer gives us is not always helpful.	0.39588	-0.02763	0.23556	-0.20108	0.28699	0.45445	-0.08273
Given the chance, our customer might try to take unfair advantage of our business unit.	0.81950	0.00883	0.71744	-0.10321	0.07664	0.82441	-0.08989
In dealing with this customer, we spend a lot of time haggling unproductively over such issues as prices and responsibility for problems.	0.68365	0.07649	0.71289	-0.07189	0.06598	0.71701	-0.06391
We can rely on our customer to help us in ways not required by our agreement with them.	-0.61820	0.16127	-0.13264	0.56331	0.04835	-0.41088	0.40548
Our business unit has a reputation for being more straightforward and open with our customer than are other suppliers.	-0.14842	0.17452	-0.12673	0.59547	-0.11507	-0.05079	0.36242
We can depend on our customer always to treat us fairly.	-0.74042	0.15150	-0.56046	0.35477	-0.03758	-0.71806	0.25394
Cronbach's alpha coefficient	0.811		0.726	0.599		0.816	

Appendix B. As the correlation matrices in Appendix B show, there is no problem with multicollinearity. Note that coefficients of the regression equations shown in the subsequent Tables are standardised (i.e. all variables were standardised with mean 0 and standard deviation 1 before regressions were run).

First, the U.S. and Japanese datasets are combined to test the eight sets of hypotheses. Next, we focus our analysis on the question of whether determinants of trust are different from those of opportunism. We also test a meta-hypothesis that more independent variables are significant in determining trust and opportunism in a 'free will' than in a 'constrained' situation. Lastly, we deal with the Japanese and U.S. datasets separately to test the hypothesis that the structural models of trust and opportunism are different in the two countries.

3.2.1. Overall results

A multivariate regression analysis was conducted in order to test the relative importance of the eight sets of hypotheses. The first column of Table 3 shows the results for the dependent variable DISTRUST. Note that DISTRUST is a generalised form which conflates some notion of customer opportunism and the absence of trust. The model fits the data reasonably well, with an adjusted R^2 of 41 percent which is excellent by the standards of cross-sectional research. All the hypotheses were sustained except for H1 (contract length) and H4 (asset specificity and interdependence). A brief summary of the regression results for each hypothesis follows:

H1: As predicted, vertical integration (OWNER) does not have a significant effect on the level of distrust. There was also a weak, yet significant, finding that the longer the contract length (CONTRACT) the higher the level of distrust, contrary to the prediction (see below for an explanation).

H2: As predicted, the longer suppliers expect their customers' commitment (COMMIT) to last, the lower the degree of distrust. But the duration of trading to date (TRADING) does not have a separate effect on distrust.

H3: The act of customers providing information to suppliers (CUSTINFO) in itself reduces distrust. In addition, the gap between suppliers' information to their customers and customers' information to suppliers (INFODIF) has an independent impact. As predicted, the more suppliers are asked to provide information to customers without reciprocation, the higher the level of suppliers' distrust in customers.

H4: A high switching cost on the part of customers (CUSWICH) does not affect distrust significantly. The degree of asset specificity on the part of the supplier (ATSPEC) does not have a significant impact, nor does the extent of interdependence (INTDEP) between the customer and the supplier.

H5: As predicted, the more technical assistance (TECHA) is provided by the customer, the lower the suppliers' distrust. However, the size of the supplier relative to the customer (COMPSIZE) has no significant effect on the level of distrust.

H6: Uncertainty (UNCERT) has a highly significant effect on increasing suppliers' distrust of customers. But uncertainty combined with asset specificity (TCE) does not have a significant impact on distrust.

M. Sako, S. Helper/J. of Economic Behavior & Org. 34 (1998) 387–417 401

Table 3
Regression coefficients on distrust, customer opportunism and goodwill trust

	Distrust	Customer Opportunism	Goodwill Trust
OWNER	−0.017	−0.015	0.034
CONTRACT	0.047 [d]	0.052†	−0.026
TRADING	0.016	0.017	0.001
COMMIT	−0.057 [c]	−0.067 [c]	0.044
CUSTINFO	−0.057 [c]	−0.032	0.051
INFODIF	0.092 [a]	0.087 [b]	0.003
CUSWICH	−0.016	−0.047	−0.006
ATSPEC	−0.057	−0.144	−0.008
INTDEP	−0.030	−0.008	0.076
TECHA	−0.097 [a]	−0.038	0.109 [b]
COMPSIZE	0.036	0.059 [c]	−0.021
UNCERT	0.235 [a]	0.196 [a]	−0.123 [b]
TCE	0.092	0.214 [c]	−0.001
USJAP	−0.044	−0.041	0.041
JAPUS	0.021	0.001	0.020
JAPJAPU	−0.053 [c]	−0.034	0.074 [c]
JAPJAPJ	−0.230 [a]	−0.203 [a]	−0.061
SUGGEST	−0.175 [a]	−0.137 [a]	0.103 [b]
HELP	−0.101 [a]	−0.087 [b]	0.071 [c]
PASS	−0.030	0.006	0.139 [a]
GM	0.163 [a]	0.139 [a]	−0.153 [a]
TOYOTAJ	0.046	−0.027	0.037
Adjusted R^2	0.41	0.31	0.14
N	853	847	848

[a] $p<0.001$.
[b] $p<0.01$.
[c] $p<0.05$.
[d] $p<0.10$.
N.B.: The dependent variable for Customer Opportunism is: 'Given the chance, our customer might try to take unfair advantage of our business unit.'
The dependent variable for Goodwill Trust is: 'We can rely on our customer to help us in ways not required by our agreement with them.'
The table reports OLS regression results. Ordered probit analysis for Customer Opportunism and Goodwill Trust shows that the identical set of independent variables as for OLS is significant.
INTDEP=CUSWICH*ATSPEC.
TCE=UNCERT*ATSPEC.

H7: In order to examine the differential impact of ownership and location, a set of dummy variables were constructed with the U.S.-owned suppliers with U.S. customers located in the US as the reference group. First, as the coefficient on the dummy variable, JAPJAPJ, indicates, the location of suppliers is highly significant: suppliers located in Japan exhibit a much lower level of distrust than those in the US. Next, within the US, Japanese-owned suppliers which traded with Japanese automakers (JAPJAPU) distrust them less. At the same time, Japanese-owned suppliers with U.S. customers (JAPUS) entertained a level of distrust which was not significantly different from U.S.-owned suppliers with U.S. customers. Evidently, the nationality of ownership of customers matters more than the nationality of ownership of suppliers. Even after taking account of ownership and location, we found that U.S. suppliers considered General Motors to be particularly distrustful.[6]

H8: As predicted, suppliers' expectations about customers' supplier management practices had an impact on distrust. The survey asked suppliers about possible customer reactions in different hypothetical situations. In particular, suppliers' expectations that their suggestions would be welcomed without reservation and that benefits arising from the suggestions would be shared (SUGGEST) were associated with low distrust. Also, if a competitor offered a lower price for a product of equal quality, the customer practice of helping suppliers to match competitor's efforts (rather than switching to the competitor) (HELP) was associated with less distrust. Lastly, in the event that a materials supplier raised its prices, the customer practice of providing significant help to reduce costs and of allowing full or partial pass-through of the supplier's cost increases (rather than holding the supplier to its original price) (PASS) was not found to affect distrust significantly in the multiple regression analysis.

3.2.2. Differences in the determinants of trust and opportunism

Table 3 also shows separate regressions for Customer Opportunism and Goodwill Trust. As predicted, the determinants of trust and opportunism are not the same. In particular, the customers' provision of technical assistance to suppliers, interpreted as 'credible commitment' and a 'gift,' enhances trust but does not function as a safeguard against opportunism. A type of information asymmetry – suppliers providing much more information to customers than customers provide suppliers – increases perceptions of customer opportunism but does not affect goodwill trust adversely.

One way of exploring this issue of different determinants for trust and opportunism further is to distinguish between trustworthy customer behaviour when a 'free will' choice exists and the same trustworthy customer behaviour which, however, is predictable due to constraints put upon the customer. We hypothesize that when customers are free rather than constrained or 'enslaved,' more of the variations in suppliers' trust in customers can be explained by the independent variables.[7]

Our sample can be divided into subsamples, one with 'constrained' customers and the other with 'free will' customers using the CUSWICH variable, measuring the number of months it would take the customer to replace the supplier with another supplier. Since the median time was 8 months, those with more than 8 months were classified as 'constrained' (41% of the total sample), and those with 8 months or less as 'free' (59% of the total sample)[8]. Table 4 shows the results of regressions of GOODWILL TRUST and CUSTOMER OPPORTUNISM using these subsamples.

Technical assistance (TECHA) stands out as a significant variable in determining trust when customers are 'free' but not when they are 'constrained.' This implies that when customers have different alternatives (including behaving distrustfully), the provision of

---

[6] The U.S. survey was conducted in April 1993, when Jose Ignacio Lopez, GM's purchasing director, dramatically increased GM's emphasis on price competition. This included at least a few instances in which suppliers proprietary designs were given to their rivals.

[7] Thanks to an anonymous referee for suggesting this distinction.

[8] Just to make sure that neither of the subsamples consisted predominantly of U.S. or Japanese suppliers, it was checked that 40.4% of the U.S. sample and 42.5% of the Japanese sample are in the 'constrained' subsample.

M. Sako, S. Helper/J. of Economic Behavior & Org. 34 (1998) 387–417   403

Table 4
Regression coefficients on goodwill trust and customer opportunism in constrained and free conditions

	Goodwill Trust		Customer Opportunism	
	Constrained	Free	Constrained	Free
OWNER	0.033	0.008	−0.075	0.042
CONTRACT	−0.073	0.026	0.085 [d]	0.027
TRADING	0.029	−0.028	−0.097 [d]	0.087 [c]
COMMIT	0.057	0.011	−0.078	−0.048
CUSTINFO	0.015	0.063	−0.021	−0.039
INFODIF	0.038	−0.037	0.041	0.127 [b]
CUSWICH	−0.087	0.052	0.015	−0.022
ATSPEC	−0.335	0.213	0.209	−0.333 [d]
INTDEP	0.179	−0.053	−0.096	−0.013
TECHA	0.062	0.144 [b]	0.022	−0.080 [d]
COMPSIZE	0.017	−0.047	0.056	0.065 [d]
UNCERT	−0.241 [b]	−0.059	0.281 [a]	0.153 [b]
TCE	0.318	−0.172	−0.113	0.409 [b]
USJAP	0.029	0.040	−0.098 [c]	−0.001
JAPUS	0.040	0.010	−0.058	0.052
JAPJAPU	0.142 [c]	−0.016	−0.087†	0.036
JAPJAPJ	−0.035	−0.075	−0.132†	−0.235 [a]
SUGGEST	0.049	0.125 [b]	−0.206 [a]	−0.073 [d]
HELP	−0.020	0.138 [b]	−0.080†	−0.110 [b]
PASS	0.182 [a]	0.116 [b]	0.044	−0.029
GM	−0.212 [a]	−0.131 [c]	0.158 [b]	0.133 [b]
TOYOTAJ	0.018	0.071	−0.028	−0.032
Adjusted R^2	0.14	0.13	0.33	0.31
N	345	503	345	502

[a] $p<0.001$.
[b] $p<0.01$.
[c] $p<0.05$.
[d] $p<0.10$.
N.B.: 'Constrained' if CUSWICH>8; 'Free' otherwise.
Goodwill Trust: 'We can rely on our customer to help us in ways not required by our agreement with them.'
Customer Opportunism: 'Given the chance, our customer might try to take unfair advantage of our business unit.'
The table reports OLS results only. Ordered probit analysis led to the same set of independent variables being significant in each regression.

technical assistance signals their commitment to behave in a trustworthy manner. When customers are constrained, technical assistance does not matter in creating suppliers' trust.

With respect to customer opportunism, the distinction between 'constrained' and 'free' situations illustrates the following two points which are noteworthy. First, as expected, many more safeguards against opportunism matter in the 'free' than in the 'constrained' situation. In particular, the minimisation of information asymmetry (INFODIF) and technical assistance(TECHA) are significant in reducing customer opportunism in the 'free' subsample but not in the 'constrained' subsample. Second, consistent with transaction cost theory, the combination of uncertainty and asset specificity leads suppliers to expect customers to behave opportunistically in the 'free' situation but not in the 'constrained' situation.

404   M. Sako, S. Helper / J. of Economic Behavior & Org. 34 (1998) 387–417

3.2.3. Differences between Japan and the US

Thus far, we have assumed that there are no U.S.–Japanese differences in the determinants of trust and opportunism, other than those which can be captured by country-specific dummy variables. However, as mentioned in the discussion of hypothesis H7 on national differences, we will now examine the possibility that determinants of trust and opportunism may be different between the US and Japan.

One standard approach to exploring whether the structural model of trust and opportunism is different between the US and Japan is to apply Chow tests (Johnston, 1972, pp. 202–207; Kennedy, 1992, pp. 108–109 and 224). First, we tested whether the U.S. and Japanese data came from a single population, with one probability distribution. The test was significant in all three cases, with $F(17,819)=5.82$ significant at 0.1% in the case of Distrust as the dependent variable, $F(17, 815)=1.80$ significant at 5 percent in the case of Goodwill Trust, and $F(17, 819)=6.03$ significant at 0.1% in the case of Customer Opportunism. These results suggest that the two national samples have distinctly different structural models.

In order to further explore this issue, we examine separate regressions for the two countries. The results are shown in Table 5. Columns 1 and 2 are the regression results for the Japanese data only, and the dependent variables are Goodwill Trust and Customer Opportunism, the two factors identified through factor analysis for the Japanese data. Columns 3 and 4 show the regression results for the U.S. data, using the same Goodwill Trust and Customer Opportunism factors as dependent variables. What Column 3 shows is the conditions for enhancing trust in the US, had the Japanese concept of goodwill trust had existed in the US. Similarly, Column 4 shows the conditions for attenuating customer opportunism if the same concept of customer opportunism as in Japan existed in the US. Only significant differences are reported below.

3.2.3.1. US–Japanese differences in the determinants of opportunism.
The three aspects of long-termism have different impacts in Japan and the US. Column 2 of Table 5 shows that in Japan, the results are as expected. The duration of written contracts has no significant impact on Customer Opportunism because in the Japanese automotive industry, there tend not to be product-specific contracts, and the framework contract is typically renewed annually. Japanese customers therefore do not use long contracts to make credible commitments for long-term trading. Instead, suppliers appear to base their expectations of future customer commitment on the history of long-term trading to date (TRADING).

By contrast, in the US, all the three variables of long-termism are significant, and the results for two out of the three variables are counter-intuitive. A longer duration of written contract is associated with a *higher* degree of Customer Opportunism. Moreover, the longer the history of trading to date (TRADING), the higher the level of opportunism. At the same time informal commitment (COMMIT) reduces opportunism. What appears to be happening in the US is that suppliers with only a recent record of trading to date are given longer duration contracts than suppliers with a long history of trading with the same customer; the median contract length was 3 years for those with a record of supplying the customer for 4 years or less, as compared to one year for those with a record of supplying

Table 5
Regression coefficients on customer opportunism and goodwill trust in the US and Japan separately

	Japan Goodwill Trust	Japan Customer Opportunism	US Goodwill Trust	US Customer Opportunism
OWNER	0.067	0.007	0.003	−0.045
CONTRACT	−0.089 [d]	−0.009	−0.023	0.096 [c]
TRADING	−0.019	−0.094 [d]	0.038	0.100 [c]
COMMIT	0.056	−0.052	0.007	−0.096 [c]
CUSTINFO	0.069	−0.066	0.068	−0.003
INFODIF	0.094 [d]	0.163 [a]	0.049	0.134 [a]
CUSWICH	0.076	−0.019	0.020	0.003
ATSPEC	−0.232	−0.188	−0.010	−0.071
INTDEP	0.046	−0.004	0.020	−0.031
TECHA	0.115 [c]	−0.054	0.025	−0.045
COMPSIZE	−0.048	0.062	−0.041	0.022
UNCERT	−0.221 [b]	0.261 [a]	−0.135 [c]	0.275 [a]
TCE	0.312	0.267	−0.090	0.114
SUGGEST	0.057	−0.187 [a]	0.090 [c]	−0.161 [a]
HELP	0.121 [c]	−0.220 [a]	−0.067	−0.021
PASS	0.140 [b]	0.062	0.072	−0.035
USJAP	—	—	0.022	−0.060
JAPUS	—	—	0.040	−0.012
JAPJAPU	—	—	0.088 [d]	−0.057
JAPJAPJ	—	—	—	—
GM	—	—	−0.111 [c]	0.183 [a]
TOYOTAJ	0.067	−0.058	—	—
Adjusted R^2	0.14	0.26	0.08	0.26
N	349	349	500	504

[a] $p < 0.001$.
[b] $p < 0.01$.
[c] $p < 0.05$.
[d] $p < 0.10$.

the customer for over 40 years. This contract duration is used by suppliers as a basis for projecting future customer commitment. Either written contracts do not attenuate opportunistic behaviour in the US, perhaps because they are not sufficiently contingent, or longer duration contracts are implemented in response to rampant opportunism. The cross-sectional nature of the dataset cannot distinguish between the two possibilities. But it appears that given the past adversarial nature of relations in the US, long-term suppliers have had more experience of opportunism than have newer suppliers. Thus, in contrast to the argument of Axelrod (1984), long-term trading or repeated games are not sufficient to bring about trust in relationships.

3.2.3.2. U.S.–Japanese differences in the determinants of trust. Comparing Columns 1 and 3 in Table 5, it is evident that technical assistance (TECHA) is significant in enhancing trust in Japan but not in the US. Similar notions of customer help and expectations of cost sharing (HELP, PASS) create trust but again in Japan only.

406   *M. Sako, S. Helper/J. of Economic Behavior & Org. 34 (1998) 387–417*

In Japan, but not in the US, longer written contracts (CONTRACT) are associated with lower goodwill trust. This lends support to the notion that contracts breed and institutionalise suspicion. In other words, in Japan, while written contracts are not used to contain customer opportunism, they undermine goodwill trust.[9]

4. Conclusions

The following main conclusions can be drawn from this study.

First, the conceptualisation of trust and opportunism was found to be different for the U.S. and the Japanese suppliers, with the latter group demonstrating a greater capacity to distinguish among different types of trust. Due to this distinction, Japanese suppliers also conceptualised trust and opportunism not to be mere opposites.

Second, the surveys provided empirical support for the eight sets of hypotheses advanced in the paper. The conditions which facilitated the creation and sustenance of trust – and the containing of opportunism – were found to include long-term commitment, information exchange, technical assistance, and customer reputation. Vertical integration was found not to have a significant effect on attenuating customer opportunism in the multivariate analysis. Thus, equity holding of suppliers by customers gives rise to varying levels of opportunism or trust depending on other supplier management techniques (such as information sharing, supplier suggestions and technical assistance) which are practised in specific relationships.

Third, Japanese suppliers were more trusting than U.S. suppliers, even after taking account of these universal facilitating conditions. Within the US, having Japanese customers, but not the Japanese ownership of the suppliers themselves, had an impact on reducing distrust. Also General Motors continues to be perceived as a distrustful customer in all regressions. This indicates that even when it employs all the safeguards against opportunism, GM has not been successful in convincing its suppliers that its commitments are credible.

Fourth, the US–Japanese differences lie, not only in the conceptualisation of trust and in having different levels of trust, but also in the determinants of trust and opportunism. In particular, the length of past trading to date and the length of written contracts were associated with *greater* opportunism in the US. U.S. automotive suppliers have frequently experienced untrustworthy behaviour from their customers in the past, and this bias in expectations is carried forward to current practices. This is a worrying phenomenon because future expectations are often extrapolated from the past. This may be a reason why customers' informal commitment into the future has to backed up by long-term written contracts for the commitment to be credible in the US. By contrast, written contracts were found to be an irrelevant governance mechanism in Japan in so far as its impact on opportunism was concerned. Contracts, however, were associated with lower goodwill trust in Japan, lending support to the view that they institutionalise suspicion.

---

[9] The dummy variable variant of the Chow test (Kennedy, 1992, p. 224) shows that the differences between the U.S. and Japanese datasets lie in the dummy intercept and the slope coefficients for CONTRACT, TECHA, and HELP.

M. Sako, S. Helper/J. of Economic Behavior & Org. 34 (1998) 387–417 407

Fifth, this study found that the determinants of trust and those of opportunism are different. The survey data provide some evidence for this, especially in Japan where trust and opportunism were found to be distinct concepts. In particular, as expected, technical assistance by customers is important for enhancing goodwill trust but not as a safeguard against customer opportunism.

Lastly, trust and opportunism are valid concepts only in situations where actors can choose from alternative courses of action. This study gives support to this notion. We find in particular that customers' provision of technical assistance to suppliers is significant in enhancing trust and attenuating customer opportunism only in cases where customers are free, but not when they are constrained by market structure or technology. In other words, customers can be made to behave in a predictably trustworthy or non-opportunistic manner if they cannot replace their existing suppliers easily, regardless of other factors. It is when easily accessible alternative suppliers exist that suppliers give careful consideration to safeguards in deciding how much opportunistic or trustworthy behaviour to expect from their customers.

Acknowledgements

The authors acknowledge the funding support of the International Motor Vehicle Program (IMVP) at MIT which made this study possible. We also wish to express our gratitude to Pat Coburn for his computing expertise. We benefitted from helpful comments from Patricia Clifford, Ronald Dore, Jeff Dyer, Marvin Lieberman, Edward Lorenz, Riccardo Peccei and Michael Smitka.

Appendix A

Questionnaire development and data collection

Data were collected by the authors during 1993 from 675 first-tier automotive component suppliers in the US and 472 first-tier suppliers in Japan, according to the following procedure.

A.1. Questionnaire design

A questionnaire was developed in English and Japanese in order to enquire into a broad range of questions concerning the nature of suppliers' relationship with their customers, the vehicle manufacturers. As many companies supply their customers with several different types of products, and their relationships with their customers differ by product, we made a decision to ask respondents to answer the questionnaire for their most important customer regarding one product which was typical of their company's output and with which they were familiar.

Many of the questions were taken from an earlier survey undertaken by Helper in North America in 1989 (Helper, 1991) and a short questionnaire on trust and opportunism administered by Sako in the electronics industry in Japan and Britain in 1988–89 (Sako, 1992). In particular, the measures of trust and opportunism were developed by surveying the academic literature in economics and psychology (e.g. Anderson, 1988,Cook et al., 1981). We took the view more common in psychology than in economics that creating composite measures of trust and opportunism would reduce measurement error, as compared to using a single measure. Thus, the questionnaire adopted a number of scales, each reflecting different types of trust and opportunism.

A.2. Piloting the questionnaire

Next, the draft questionnaire was sequentially piloted at a handful of supplier companies in both the US and Japan during 1992. As a result, improvements were made to the clarity of questions and the ease of answering them. Much attention was paid to the phrasing of questions in a vocabulary familiar to managers, and to the consistency of meaning in the English and Japanese languages. For instance, we asked several people to translate some questions from English to Japanese and others to translate them back from Japanese into English. The process of piloting and revision took around nine months.

A.3. Sampling framework

The sample chosen for the North American questionnaire was every automotive supplier and automaker component division named in the *Elm Guide to Automotive Sourcing* (available from Elm, Inc. in East Lansing, Michigan). This guide lists the major first-tier suppliers (both domestic and foreign-owned) to manufacturers of cars and light trucks in the United States and Canada.

In Japan, the sample consisted of all members of the Japan Auto Parts Industries Association (JAPIA), all automotive suppliers named in *Nihon no Jidosha Buhin Kogyo 1992/1993* (Japanese Automotive Parts Industry) (published by Auto Trade Journal Co. Inc. and JAPIA, Tokyo, 1992), and the component divisions of vehicle manufacturers. This publication lists all the first-tier suppliers (both domestic and foreign-owned) to the eleven manufacturers of cars and trucks in Japan.

The target respondent in the US was the divisional director of sales and marketing, and the divisional business manager or director of strategic planning in the case of components divisions of vehicle manufacturers. Since they commonly take a lead in interfacing with customers, they were deemed the most knowledgeable informants about customers' procurement practices. Similarly in Japan, the questionnaire was sent to the Director of Sales and Marketing at independent firms. For member companies of JAPIA, the survey was sent to the main contacts named by JAPIA, many of whom were either chief executives or marketing directors. JAMA (Japan Auto Manufacturers Association) took responsibility to identify the respondents for automaker components divisions.

A.4. Response rates

The questionnaires were sent out in spring 1993 in the US and summer 1993 in Japan. The responses were far above the norm for business surveys. It was 55 percent in North

M. Sako, S. Helper/J. of Economic Behavior & Org. 34 (1998) 387–417 409

America and 30 percent in Japan (45% among JAPIA members), after taking into account those firms which were unreachable (mail sent to them was returned undelivered), and those which were not eligible to answer the survey (they were not first-tier automotive suppliers, or they specialised in supplying for heavy trucks and buses). The respondents had a wealth of experience, and were thus the single individual able to answer all of our questions for the customer/product pair they chose. U.S. respondents averaged more than 18 years in the automobile industry and more than 11 years with their company. Japanese respondents had worked for 22 years on average at their company.

We tested for non-response bias in several ways. First, we compared the characteristics of those who returned the survey to those of the entire population. On the characteristics for which data were available (size and location) no significant differences were found. The survey respondents were also divided into 2 groups based on response data. The hypothesis was that those who responded only after the second follow-up mailing might have more in common with those who did not respond at all than those who responded early. This test showed no significant differences for early and late respondents on any of the measures used in this paper. (We judged statistical significance in both cases using a 10 per cent cutoff.)

Appendix B

Explanations of independent variables

This appendix provides the survey question and explains any manipulation made subsequently to create each independent variable.

VARIABLE NAMES

OWNER 'Please describe the ownership of your business unit.
Independent of automaker
100% subsidiary of an automaker
Partially owned by an automaker
(percentage of automaker ownership)'
Ranges from 0 (for 'independent of automaker')
to 100.

CONTRACT 'What is the length of your written contract or purchase order with this customer for this product' (in years)

TRADING 'Approximately how long has your firm sold products in this product line to this customer?
1 year, 2 years, 3 years, 4 years, 5–10 years, 11–19 years, 20–40 years, 41–60 years, over 60 years.'
The mid-point of each interval was used; thus the variable takes the values of 1, 2, 3, 4, 7.5, 15, 30, 50.5 and 75.

COMMIT   'For how long do you think there is a high probability that your
                       business unit will be supplying this or similar item to your
                       customer?' (in years)

SUPINFO   'What types of information does your business unit provide to
                       your customer about the process you use to the maker the
                       product you listed above? (Please check all that apply).
                       – Detailed breakdown of process steps
                       – Cost of each process step
                       – Financial information not publicly available
                       – Production scheduling information
                       – Type of equipment used
                       – Your sources of supply
                       – Detailed information regarding materials you use'
                       The seven information items were given one point each if
                       checked, and were added.

CUSTINFO   'Does your customer provide you with any of the following
                       types of information? (Please check all that apply.)
                       – Warranty or other data from final consumers
                       – Financial information not publicly available
                       – Information on how your product is used in their process'
                       The information items were given one point each if checked, and
                       added.

INFODIF   SUFINFO – CUSTINFO

TECHA   'Over the last four years, what sorts of technical assistance have
                       you received from your customer? (Please check all that apply,
                       and indicate whether 'provided for zero or nominal charge' or
                       'provided for a fee')
                       – Provided personnel who visited supplier site to aid in
                       implementing improved procedures
                       – Arranged for training of your personnel at their site
                       – Provided personnel who worked two weeks or more on your
                       shop floor to improve your process
                       Given a weight of 2 if 'provided for zero or nominal charge' and a
                       weight of 1 if 'provided for a fee,' and summed over the three items.'

COMPSIZE   'What is the approximate total number of employees at your
                       business unit in 1992?'

CUSWICH   'Please estimate the number of months it would take your
                       customer to replace your business unit with another supplier.
                       Consider the time required to locate, qualify, train, make

M. Sako, S. Helper/J. of Economic Behavior & Org. 34 (1998) 387–417 411

investments, test, and develop a working relationship with another firm. Please exclude legal considerations such as the existence of long-term contracts. 0, 1–3, 4–12, 13–24, 25–48, 48+' The mid-point of each interval was used. The variable therefore takes a value of 0, 2, 8, 18.5, 36.5 and 72.

ATSPEC   'If you were to stop getting these orders from this customer, approximately how much of your investment for this product in plant, equipment, and training would you be unlikely to find alternative uses for and have to write off?
10% or less, 11–33%, 34–66%, 67–89%, 90–100%
Again, the mid-point of each interval was used (5, 22, 50, 78 and 95).
Each supplier is, however, diversified in sectors outside the car industry to a varying degree. In order to derive the extent of asset specificity which is company-wide, the above proportions were multiplied by the percent of the supplier as sales which end up as original equipment for cars or light trucks.

INTDEP   CUSWICH*ATSPEC

UNCERT   'In the production of this product, how much certainty is there regarding the following factors?' (A 1–5 Likert scale (1=fairly certain; 5=completely unpredictable))
– Customer's production schedule 2 weeks ahead
– Customer's production schedule 1 year ahead
– Customer's final product specifications before Job 1
– Customer's final product specifications after Job 1' (Job 1 is the first mass production batch, after pre-production test runs)
– The supplier's production costs over 4 years
– Production technology for this product over 4 years The scores for the six items were summed.

TCE   UNCERT*ATSPEC

COMPLEX   'Please estimate the technical complexity involved in manufacturing this product' Used a 1–5 scale (1=fairly simple; 5=highly complex).

SUGGEST   'Suppose your business unit has an idea that would allow you to reduce your costs, but would require your customer to make a slight modification in its procedures. How would your customer react (Please check all that apply.)

412   M. Sako, S. Helper/J. of Economic Behavior & Org. 34 (1998) 387–417

| | A dummy with 1 if 'Customer eagerly solicits such suggestions' and 'Customer would adopt the suggestion and would *not* seek to capture most of the savings,' 0 otherwise. |

HELP   'How would your customer react if one of your competitors offered a lower price for a product of equal quality?'
A dummy with 1 if 'Help you match competitors' efforts', but not 'Switch at end of contract', nor 'switch as soon as technically feasible'

PASS   'How would your customer react if your material suppliers raised their prices?'
A dummy with 1 if 'Provide significant help for your business unit to reduce costs,' but not 'Hold you to your original price,' 0 otherwise. This is meant to capture the notion of customer help and sharing of costs.

USJAP   A dummy with 1 for US-owned suppliers with a Japanese customer in the US, 0 otherwise.

JAPUS   A dummy with 1 for Japanese-owned suppliers with a US customer in the US, 0 otherwise.

JAPJAPU   A dummy with 1 for Japanese-owned suppliers with a Japanese Customer in the US, 0 otherwise.

JAPJAPJ   A dummy with 1 for Japanese suppliers in Japan, 0 otherwise.

GM   A dummy with 1 for U.S. suppliers supplying to General Motors.

TOYOTAJ   A dummy with 1 for Japanese suppliers supplying to Toyota in Japan.

B.1. Descriptive statistics and correlation matrix

Variable	Obs	Mean	Std. dev.	Min.	Max
owner	1128	6.315532	19.3516	0	100
contract	1060	1.398503	2.526527	0	60
trading	1130	16.82832	14.43125	1	75
commit	961	15.01561	22.88683	0	100

M. Sako, S. Helper/J. of Economic Behavior & Org. 34 (1998) 387–417 413

custinfo	1147	1.37925	0.7461514	0	3
infodif	1147	2.941587	1.758323	−2	7
cuswich	1106	14.45389	13.52287	0	72
atspec	1087	24.5954	24.0723	0.9	85.975
intdep	1076	419.644	698.6211	0	6190.2
techa	1147	1.932868	1.726964	0	9
compsize	1107	779.9621	2597.432	5	45000
uncert	1123	2.288825	0.6500431	1	5
tce	1075	56.87315	60.96052	1.05	358.2292
suggest	1147	0.4603313	0.4986413	0	1
help	1147	0.1517001	0.3588864	0	1
pass	1147	0.1011334	0.3016368	0	1
usjap	1147	0.0383609	0.1921499	0	1
japus	1147	0.0366173	0.1879022	0	1
japjapu	1147	0.374891	0.1900399	0	1
japjapj	1147	0.4115083	0.4923216	0	1
gm	1147	0.2109852	0.4081859	0	1
toyotaj	1147	0.9015432	0.2885058	0	1

(obs=853)

	owner	contract	trading	commit	custinfo	infodif	cuswich
owner	1.0000						
contract	−0.0472	1.0000					
trading	0.0660	−0.1001	1.0000				
commit	0.1768	−0.0044	0.2581	1.0000			
custinfo	0.0999	0.0680	0.0143	0.0876	1.0000		
infodif	−0.0270	0.1342	−0.0485	−0.0919	−0.0522	1.0000	
cuswich	0.1044	0.0930	0.0288	0.0996	0.1626	−0.0274	1.0000
atspec	0.1337	0.0490	0.0698	0.1116	0.0637	0.0157	0.2109
intdep	0.1260	0.0734	0.0507	0.1022	0.1205	−0.0519	0.7447
techa	−0.0293	0.1213	−0.0755	−0.0530	0.1461	0.2552	0.0116
compsize	0.0952	0.0063	0.1533	0.2012	0.0776	−0.0870	0.0858
uncert	−0.1020	−0.0107	−0.0115	−0.1462	−0.1453	0.0532	−0.0797
tce	0.0981	0.0376	0.0466	0.0590	0.0129	0.0447	0.1666
suggest	0.0541	−0.0240	0.0340	0.1080	0.1487	−0.0057	0.0782
help	0.0303	−0.0332	0.1058	0.1322	0.0084	−0.0751	0.0463
pass	0.0835	−0.0711	0.0916	0.0901	0.1295	−0.0209	0.0656
usjap	0.0056	0.0167	−0.1451	−0.0390	−0.0091	0.1241	0.0238
japus	−0.0630	0.0263	−0.0807	−0.0519	0.0344	−0.0006	0.0643
japjapu	0.0252	0.1936	−0.1264	−0.0120	0.0515	0.0607	0.0993
japjapj	0.2838	−0.2602	0.3430	0.3563	0.0899	−0.2714	0.0550
gm	−0.1678	−0.0482	−0.1206	−0.2085	−0.1401	0.1067	−0.1558
toyotaj	0.1066	−0.1002	0.2195	0.2551	0.0625	−0.1684	0.0562

414   M. Sako, S. Helper / J. of Economic Behavior & Org. 34 (1998) 387–417

	atspec	intdep	techa	compsize	uncert	tce	suggest
atspec	1.0000						
intdep	0.6292	1.0000					
techa	0.0505	0.0118	1.0000				
compsize	0.0888	0.0974	-0.0260	1.0000			
uncert	0.0139	-0.0386	0.0479	-0.0623	1.0000		
tce	0.9275	0.5571	0.0942	0.0434	0.2770	1.0000	
suggest	0.0162	0.0185	0.0664	0.0655	-0.1612		1.0000
help	0.0405	0.0548	-0.0830	0.0162	-0.1037	0.0160	0.0347
pass	0.0218	0.0311	0.0326	0.0135	-0.1235	-0.0136	0.1597
usjap	0.0220	0.0013	0.1308	-0.0216	-0.0757	0.0031	-0.0276
japus	-0.0331	0.0276	0.0596	-0.0115	0.0138	-0.0254	-0.0666
japjapu	0.0225	0.0621	0.0656	-0.0309	-0.0827	0.0018	-0.0029
japjapj	0.1584	0.1146	-0.2421	0.0879	-0.1706	0.0987	0.2207
gm	-0.1050	-0.1146	0.0781	-0.0515	0.1902	-0.0408	-0.2537
toyotaj	0.1010	0.1270	-0.1555	0.2458	-0.1452	0.0421	0.1012

	help	pass	usjap	apus	japjapu	japjapj	gm	toyotaj
help	1.0000							
pass	0.1267	1.0000						
usjap	-0.0277	-0.0005	1.0000					
japus	0.0079	-0.0429	-0.0352	1.0000				
japjapu	0.0140	-0.0179	-0.0339	-0.0339	1.0000			
japjapj	0.2108	0.2152	-0.1561	-0.1561	-0.1504	1.0000		
gm	-0.0969	-0.1584	-0.1021	0.0673	-0.0984	-0.4530	1.0000	
toyotaj	0.1148	0.1193	-0.0565	-0.0565	-0.0545	0.3621	-0.1640	1.0000

References

Anderson, E., 1988. Transaction costs as determinants of opportunism in integrated and independent sales force, Journal of Economic Behavior and Organization 9, 247–264.

Anderson, E., and Weitz, B., 1989. Determinants of continuity in conventional industrial channel dyads, Marketing Science 8, 310–323.

Arrow, K.J., 1975. Gifts and exchanges. In: Phelps, E.S. (Ed.), Altruism, Morality and Economic Theory. Russell Sage Foundation, New York.

Axelrod, R., 1984. Evolution of Cooperation. Basic Books, New York.

Barney, Jay B., and Hansen, Mark H., 1994. Trustworthiness as a source of competitive advantage, Strategic Management Journal 7, 175–190.

Bradach, J.L., and Eccles, R.G., 1989. Price, authority and trust: From ideal types to plural forms, Annual Review of Sociology 15, 96–118.

Brusco, S., 1986. Small firms and industrial districts: The experience of Italy. In: Keeble, D., Weever, F. (Eds.), New Firms and Regional Development. Croom Helm, London.

Clark, Murray C., 1993. Interpersonal trust in the coal mining industry: A facet analysis, Unpublished Ph.D. thesis. Manchester Business School, Manchester.

M. Sako, S. Helper/J. of Economic Behavior & Org. 34 (1998) 387–417 415

Cook, J., and Wall, T., 1980. New work attitude measures of trust, organizational commitment and personal need non-fulfilment, Journal of Occupational Psychology 53, 39–52.

Cook, J.D. et al., 1981. The Experience of Work: A Compendium and Review of 249 Measures and Their Use. Academic Press, Orlando, FL.

Cummings, L.L., Bromiley, P., 1996. The organizational trust inventory (OTI): Development and validation. In: Kramer, R.M., Tyler, T.R. (Eds.), Trust in Organizations Frontiers of Theory and Research. Sage, London.

Currall, S.C., Judge T.A., Measuring trust between organizational boundary role persons, Forthcoming, Organizational Behavior and Human Decision Processes.

Deutsch, M., 1958. Trust and suspicion, Journal of Conflict Resolution 2(4), 265–279.

Dodgson, M., 1993. Learning, trust and technological collaboration, Human Relations 46(1).

Dore, R., 1983. Goodwill and the spirit of market capitalism, British Journal of Sociology 34, 459–482.

Dore, R., 1987. Taking Japan Seriously. Stanford University Press, Stanford, CA.

Dyer, J. Does governance matter? Keiretsu alliances and asset specificity as source of Japanese competitive advantage, Forthcoming, Organization Science.

Eccles, R., 1981. The quasi-firm in the construction industry, Journal of Economic Behavior and Organization 2, 335–357.

Fox, A., 1974. Beyond Contract: Work, Power and Trust Relations. Faber and Faber, London.

Gambetta, D. (Ed.), 1988. Trust: Making and Breaking Cooperative Relations. Basil Blackwell, Oxford.

Ganesan, S., 1994. Determinants of long-term orientation in buyer–seller relationships, Journal of Marketing 58, 1–19.

Goulder, A., 1960. The norm of reciprocity: A preliminary statement, American Sociological Review 25(2), 161–177.

Granovetter, M., 1985. Economic action and social structure: The problem of embeddedness, American Journal of Sociology 91, 481–510.

Gulati, R., 1995. Does familiarity breed trust? The implications of repeated ties for contractual choice in alliances, Academy of Management Journal 38, 85–112.

Heide, J.B., and John, G., 1990. Alliances in industrial purchasing: The determinants of joint action in buyer-supplier relationship, Journal of Marketing Research 27, 24–36.

Helper, S., 1991. Strategy and irreversibility in supplier relations: The case of the U.S. automobile industry, Business History Review, 65.

Helper, S., 1994. Three steps forward, two steps back in automotive supplier relations, Technovation 14(10), 1–8.

Hosmer, L.T., 1995. Trust: The connecting link between organizational theory and philosophical ethics, Academy of Management Review 20(2), 379–403.

Joskow, P.L., 1988. Asset specificity and the structure of vertical relationships: Empirical evidence, Journal of Law, Economics and Organization 4(1), 95–118.

Jarillo, J.C., 1988. On strategic networks, Strategic Management Journal 9, 31–41.

Johnston, J., 1972. Econometric Methods. McGraw-Hill, New York.

Kawashima, T., 1967. Nihonhin No Hoishiki, Legal Consciousness of the Japanese. Iwanami shoten, Tokyo.

Kee, H.W., and Knox, R.E., 1970. Conceptual and methodological considerations in the study of trust and suspicion, Journal of Conflict Resolution 14(3), 357–366.

Kennedy, Peter, 1992. A Guide to Econometrics. Blackwell, Oxford.

Klein, B., Crawford, R.A., and Alchian, A.A., 1978. Vertical integration, appropriable rents, and the competitive contracting process, Journal of Law and Economics 21(2), 297–326.

Kreps, D.M., 1990. Corporate Culture and Economic Theory, in Alt, J.E., Schepsle. K.A. (Eds.), Perspectives in Positive Political Economy, Cambridge University Press, Cambridge.

Kumar, N., Scheer, L., and Steenkamp, J., 1995. The effects of perceived interdependence on dealer attitudes, Journal of Marketing Research 32, 348–356.

416   *M. Sako, S. Helper/J. of Economic Behavior & Org. 34 (1998) 387–417*

Lane, C., and Backman, R., 1996. The social construction of trust: Supplier relations in Britain and Germany, Organization Studies 17(3), 365–395.

Lorenz, E.H., 1993. Flexible production systems and the social construction of trust, Politics and Society 21(3), 307–324.

Macaulay, S., 1963. Non-contractual relations in business: Preliminary study, American Sociological Review 28(2), 55–67.

Macneil, I.R., 1974. Contracts: Adjustment of long-term economic relationship under classical, neo-classical, and relational contract law, Northwestern University Law Review 72, 584–906.

Mill, J.S., 1891. Principles of political economy. Longmans, London.

Mohr, J., and Spekman, R., 1994. Characteristics of partnership success: Partnership attributes, communication behavior, and conflict resolution techniques, Strategic Management Journal 15, 135–152.

Morgan, R., and Hunt, S., 1994. The commitment–trust theory of relationship marketing, Journal of Marketing 58, 20–38.

Odaka, K., Ono, K., Adachi, F., 1988. The Automobile Industry in Japan: A Study of Ancillary Firm Development. Oxford University Press, Oxford.

Parkhe, A., 1993. Strategic alliance structuring: A game theoretic and transaction cost examination of inter-firm cooperation, Academy of Management Journal 36, 794–829.

Rotter, J.B., 1967. A new scale for the measurement of interpersonal trust, Journal of Personality 35, 651–665.

SMMT and DTI, 1994. A Review of The Relationships Between Vehicle Manufacturers and Suppliers, Society of Motor Manufacturers and Traders and the U.K. Department of Trade and Industry, London.

Sabel, C.F. 1992. Studied trust: building new forms of co-operation in a volatile economy. In: Pyke, F., Sengenberger W., (Eds.), Industrial Districts and Local Economic Regeneration, International Institute for Labour Studies, Geneva.

Sabel, C.F., 1994. Learning by monitoring: the institutions of economic development. In: Smelser, N.J., Swedberg R. (Eds.), The Handbook of Economic Sociology. Princeton University Press, Princeton, NJ.

Sako, M., 1991. The role of trust in Japanese buyer-supplier relationships, Ricerche Economiche XLV, 449–474.

Sako, M., 1992. Prices, Quality and Trust: Inter-firm Relations in Britain and Japan. Cambridge University Press, Cambridge.

Sako, M., 1996. Suppliers' associations in the Japanese automobile industry: Collective action for technology diffusion, Cambridge Journal of Economics 20(6), 651–71.

Sitkin, S.B., and Roth, N.L., 1993. Explaining the limited effectiveness of legalistic remedies for trust/distrust, Organization Science 4(3), 356–392.

Smith, K.G., Carroll, S.J., and Ashford, S.J., 1995. Intra- and inter-organizational cooperation: Toward a research agenda, Academy of Management Journal 39, 7–23.

Smitka, M., 1991. Competitive Ties: Subcontracting in the Japanese Automotive Industry. Columbia University Press, New York.

Smitka, M., 1992. Contracting without contracts. In: Sitkin, S.B., Bies, R.J. (Eds.), The Legalistic Organisation. London, Sage.

Walker, G., and Weber, D., 1984. A transaction cost approach to make-or-buy decisions, Administrative Science Quarterly 29, 373–391.

Williamson, O.E., 1975. Markets and Hierarchies. The Free Press, New York.

Williamson, O.E., 1979. Transaction-cost economics: The governance of contractual relations, Journal of Law and Economics 22, 3–61.

Williamson, O.E., 1983. Credible commitments: Using hostages to support exchange, American Economic Review 73, 519.

Williamson, O.E., 1985. The Economic Institutions of Capitalism. The Free Press, New York.

Williamson, O.E., 1993. Calculativeness, trust, and economic organization, Journal of Law and Economics 36, 453–486.

Zaheer, A., and Venkatraman, N., 1995. Relational governance as an inter-organizational strategy: An empirical test of the role of trust in economic exchange, Strategic Management Journal 16, 373–392.

Zand, D.E., 1972. Trust and managerial problem solving, Administrative Science Quarterly 17, 229–239.

C
Identity and Reputation

[10]

The F-Connection: Families, Friends, and Firms and the Organization of Exchange

YORAM BEN-PORATH

The family plays a major role in the allocation and distribution of resources. The way in which members of families have dealings with each other, the implicit contract by which they conduct their activities, stands in sharp contrast to the textbook market transaction. Between these two extremes are many other transaction modes and institutions involving elements of both: transactions between friends, business partners, and employers and employees.

The main theme of this essay is that the identity of the people engaged in a transaction is a major determinant of the institutional mode of transaction. Some transactions can take place only between mutually or unilaterally identified parties. Investment in resources specific to a relationship between identified parties can save transaction costs and stimulate trade. Such investment gives rise to what I call specialization by identity—concentration of exchange between the same parties—analogous to specialization by impersonal dimensions of transactions. The organization of activity is determined by the (implicit) attempt to benefit from the returns to scale on the personal and the impersonal dimensions of transactions and the interaction between these returns to scale. The degree to which identity dominates or is subsumed under the impersonal dimensions of specialization shapes the type of transaction or contract. The family is the locale of transactions in which identity dominates; however, identity is also important in much of what we consider the "market," and, in fact, recent developments in economics can be interpreted as a departure from impersonal economics.

1

In recent years economists have devoted extensive efforts to analyzing aspects of family or household behavior using the ordinary tools of price theory and have emphasized the applicability and transferability of this mode of analysis to the nonmarket sector. I do not wish to abandon this approach but to add to it the transactional characteristics. Within this broader framework, one can analyze the transactions in which families have an advantage over other institutions, the conditions that make families of various types more or less efficient than the alternatives in any given transaction, the sorting of individuals into families, and the implications of family membership for transactions with others.

The main advantages of this approach are:

1. It provides a means of explicitly analyzing the implications on the micro level of various economic and institutional changes that on the macro level are considered as part of processes described as economic development, modernization, or Westernization.

2. Such issues and their bearing on the family tend to be tackled by economists and other social scientists in a nonintegrated fashion—sometimes in terms of "economic" as against "social" or "cultural" variables. The present framework seeks to integrate lines of thought generated in different branches of the social sciences and to link the family more closely with other phenomena studied in economics.

3. Demographers have recently been concerned with family demography. Economists have recently begun to question the decision model in which the household (or the firm) is treated as if it were an individual. I hope to shed some light on the link between individual and group analysis.

**The Role of Identity
in Transactions:
The General Framework**

Family and Market Transactions   In the broadest sense, a transaction consists of activities or transfers of property rights by or between at least two individuals or groups, the activities or transfers of the participants being interdependent (at least in a probabilistic sense).

Market transactions are a subset of all transactions no matter how one defines the whole set or what language is used to describe nonmarket transactions. Polanyi distinguished between exchange, reciprocity, and redistribution; he and other economic anthropologists oppose the application of economic analysis to social transactions that bear only a superficial resemblance to market transactions (Polanyi et al., 1957; Dalton, 1976; Sahlins, 1965). Others have stressed the similarity to market transactions of affective relationships (Blau, 1964; Homans, 1974) and used the concepts and analytical modes of economics to describe such relationships. Mauss (1954) has stressed the exchange nature of gifts. While I can sympathize with the aversion to superficial analogies and semantic exercises, I believe that economics can be used to provide a framework for analyzing the delimitation of the subsets of transactions and for identifying the determinants of the distribution of transactions by type.

Among nonmarket transactions, those occurring within kinship groups or families predominate. The family is a group of individuals related by blood, marriage, or adoption, but its significance as a social institution comes from the activities it accommodates. The institution takes the form of rights and obligations associated with and defining the roles of the family members, thus forming a comprehensive transaction, or contract, or a set of interrelated contracts (husband-wife, parent-children, wife-mother-in-law, etc.). Terms such as contract or transaction usually connote voluntary association. This seems natural in the case of marriage, where entry into the roles is voluntary on the part of either the spouses or their families of origin. Where the parent-child relationship is concerned, the usage might be objected to because entry of at least one of the parties into the relationship is involuntary. The transformation of the biological event into a social relationship that may extend over several decades, however, involves voluntary behavior of both parties and options on both sides to break away. Parental decisions to have children and how to behave toward them in infancy and early childhood are unilateral but are probably affected by expectations concerning future mutual relationships.

Let us, thus, accept the treatment of the family connection as a transaction or an exchange and consider some of its characteristics:[1] (a) It extends over long periods of time, but the duration is not specified in advance. (b) While the scope and importance of various activities change, the connection generally encompasses a large variety of activities. (c) Not all terms of the contract are specified explicitly—most activities are contingent on events and are decided sequentially; the response to contingencies remains unspecified, guided by general principles or rules of behavior that tend to apply to sets of similar family contracts in the society. (d) The highly interdependent elements of the contract exist as a package; and prices cannot be used as multipliers or weights for adding up all the various elements of the contract. (e) There is generally no explicit balancing of the exchange in terms of a unit of account, although certain money payments (e.g., dowry or bride price) can be interpreted as approximations to the ex-ante differences in the expected value of the packages being exchanged. What is generally true, here too, is that there is no balancing of individual components, there is no running quid pro quo. Instead, large outstanding balances are tolerated; because of the unspecified nature of the contract, when and how these balances are liquidated remains open. (f) Enforcement is mostly internal, although the contract is supported to some extent by the family of origin and by other social forces. (g) To varying degrees, the family contract creates a collective identity that affects the transactions of each member with people outside the family. (h) The most important characteristic of the family contract is that it is embedded in the identity of the partners, without which it loses its meaning. It is thus specific and nonnegotiable or nontransferable. Most of these characteristics are connected with the issue of identity.

Markets involve many (actual or potential) buyers and sellers. Ideally market transactions are assumed to be perfectly replicable. A market transaction involves a unit price and a value in terms of a common unit of account, which indicate the opportunities gained and forgone by the transacting parties. In terms of such opportunities, the transaction entails a full quid pro quo, and there is no left-over business or outstanding balance. The value in exchange is independent of the identity of the parties; sufficient information is contained in the price-quantity offers, and nothing else about the transacting parties matters. This is an essential part of the perfect replicability of market transactions and the essence of perfect transferability. Thus, as it is pictured through intermediate theory textbooks, economics deals with agents who are stripped of identity. Faceless buyers and sellers, households and firms that grind out decision rules from their objective functions (utility, profits), meet in the market place for an instant to exchange standardized goods at equilibrium prices.

Obviously, an extreme case in which identity matters is that of affective relationships: love and care or hate directed at a particular individual, the desire to be in the company of or avoid certain people, and so on. Such a relationship has by and large been outside the domain of economics. Some attempts by economists to explore some of the consequences of such relationships have taken the form of introducing the utility of others in the individual's utility function in the form of "altruism" (Becker 1974a, 1976). The insertion of the number of children into the utility function in the analysis of fertility is another expression of affective relationships. But such treatment cannot provide a satisfactory solution to the general issue that I raise here in which people are interested in the identity of those with whom they deal for practical reasons that may be only sometimes intermingled with affective relationships.

Unlike the textbook view, recent work in economics deals with many issues in which the identity of the agents and the mechanics of their interaction matter. In order to bring home the general importance of identity, consider the following worlds or models:

A. Every market day people (agents, traders, etc.) change, while the joint distribution of their endowments and tastes is stationary.

B. People stay the same: they have been present on past market days and they expect to be present on future market days. They neither recognize anyone nor expect to be recognized by anyone.

C. People can identify at least some others and be identified by others.

World A is the world of instantaneous transactions, to which much of general equilibrium theory applies. Moving to world B; in which there are permanent actors with a past and a future, broadens the range of issues that can be tackled. Present behavior is affected by accumulated experience and by the expectation that it will have future consequences, so there is room for investment behavior and capital theory. In the absence of identification, however, many activities take a restricted form or do not exist. Obviously there can be no intertemporal transactions; there is room only for the Robinson Crusoe type of capital theory—unidentified individuals cannot take upon themselves obligations for future delivery of goods or money, so there are no financial assets or commodity markets. There is investment in human capital, but only to the extent that the skills acquired can be used or manifest themselves costlessly without resort to identity. People learn the distribution of prices or trading partners confronting them, and they can search for the lowest price, the highest wage offer, or the best quality store, but they will not do so if they cannot identify them for the next transaction. Similarly, there is no incentive to sell more cheaply or to offer higher quality service if one knows one is not going to be identified. It needs but little reflection to realize that giving people an identity (in analysis), in addition to a past and a future, permits the discussion of much that is of interest even in narrowly defined economic activity.

There is a ploy that can solve some of the problem: a Grand Enforcer (sitting next to the Auctioneer and maybe the Invisible Hand) who identifies and is identified by all. He serves as a clearing house—debtors know that because he identifies them they have to pay; by the same token, creditors know they can lend. He declares true quality, he knows all. With free enforcement and free information, identity does not matter. But this is not the world we live in.

Identity and Fixed Transaction Costs   The conduct of transactions itself involves a certain class of costs that are part of what the transactors forgo and that differ from other costs only in that they are associated with the exchange. They include the costs of information collection, advertisement, and negotiations, the creation of provisions and guarantees for enforcement, and so on. They arise because the parties to transactions are different individuals with asymmetric information, divergent motives, and mutual suspicions, and because expenditure of resources can reduce the gap in information and protect the parties against each other.

It is important to examine how transaction costs vary.[2] At one extreme are transaction costs that vary proportionately with the volume of goods being traded (e.g., a turnover tax); at the other extreme are the pure set-up costs associated with engaging in any exchange and not dependent on the volume of trade (e.g., a license to trade). Between the two extremes of pure set-up costs and costs that vary proportionately with the volume of transactions lie many possibilities: some costs may be fixed for any volume of trade between given pairs of people only at a point in time or for only one good or type of service. Some costs may serve one party in its dealings with any other party, and some may be fixed only for trade with a given party.

6   THE ORGANIZATION OF EXCHANGE

Insofar as they can serve specific parties for many periods they create capital. This capital is specific inasmuch as the returns materialize only in the exchange between specific parties, the capital stock losing its value when they separate.

The argument that some costs are fixed for fixed trading parties is based on the following factors:

1. Each person has some stable traits—honesty, reliability, skill, etc.—that interest the other and affect his perception of what he is getting or the terms on which he is getting it. The cost of establishing this mutual view is an investment that facilitates future trading between the parties.

2. Parties to a transaction can establish rules or norms for their exchange relationship, a common view concerning contingencies, and procedures for settling disputes that can serve them beyond a single transaction. The cost of negotiating and establishing these rules will have to be incurred again if the parties change.

3. The expectation of continuing exchange has a favorable effect on the behavior of the parties. Abstention from cheating in the present is an investment that will reap the gains of future trade.

We can see clearly how continuity of relationships can generate behavior on the part of shrewd, self-seeking, or even unscrupulous individuals that could otherwise be interpreted as foolish or purely altruistic. Valuable diamonds change hands on the diamond exchange, and the deals are sealed by a handshake. Major transactions are often concluded over the telephone between long-time business associates. Businessmen shun conflict and litigation when they expect continuing relationships (Macaulay, 1963). Members of a robber band must maintain honor among thieves, and needless to say the word "family" has not reached the mafia by accident. On the other hand, tourists are cheated by traders who deal honestly with their local customers; and anthropologists speak about "contextual morality" in primitive societies—ethical codes that forbid internal cheating within a tribe and allow cheating of others (Sahlins, 1965). The following observation by Arrow seems to correspond to many arrangements: "It is useful for individuals to have some trust in each other's word. In the absence of trust it would become very costly to arrange for alternative sanctions and guarantees and many opportunities for mutually beneficial cooperation would have to be forgone" (1969, p. 62).

The confidence of each party in the degree to which he and his trading partners will go on being tied together influences the amount of their investment commitment and the gains. The expected duration is influenced by exogenous factors (e.g., mortality) and by expectations of future changes in conditions (migration, mobility). Contractual arrangements may include provisions that increase the mutual confidence in continued affiliation, even if they are inefficient in a short-run view. Within institutions involving partners with unequal exit opportunities, part of the bargaining may involve the degree to which the parties are tied to the institution. Even the large expenditure associated with weddings has to do with penalties and signals associated with mutual guarantees of continued relationship.

The strategic advantage of expectation of continued contact is analyzed in game theory under the heading of repeated games, or super games (e.g., Luce and Raiffa, 1957). In a single, noncooperative game, parties may fail to achieve a mutually beneficial solution because each party recognizes the opportunities to cheat or to reap a short-term advantage. Adverse selection in the exchange in goods of uncertain quality is an example (e.g., Akerlof, 1970). However, infinite repetition of the transaction (a super game) can induce the parties to give up short-term benefits in order to realize future gains (Heal, 1976). (If the duration of the game is finite and certain and if there is no enforcement by a third party, then in the final game there is no incentive for good behavior; but then this will apply also to the game before the last and so on back to the first game.)

The investment framework ties together in an overall contract transaction that may be unbalanced or unintelligible when observed separately. Even the most extreme instances of seemingly unilateral giving—gifts and favors—are recognized as forms of exchange (see Mauss, 1954). Often they are given in order to create an obligation. They are accepted by those who cannot afford to refuse, or who believe that they will be able to control the repayment, or who believe that they will not be the losers in the implicit contract.[3] The acceptance of a gift constitutes an obligation to repay out of a set of alternatives, which may be defined narrowly or broadly, explicitly or implicitly. The choice within the set will be made by the original "giver" (whether he is Don Corleone or a tribal chief demanding loyalty) or will be left undecided among friends. The tolerance of large outstanding balances signals the presence of trust or implicit threats. The refusal to accept a gift often signals mistrust. A return gift cancels an obligation. Horizontal friendship and vertical loyalty are often associated with a series of gifts and favors.[4]

In addition to affective relationships, the types of transaction in which identity is important include:

1. Transactions in which, because of imperfect information, there is uncertainty about the quality of the object of exchange or the terms of the transaction. The identity of the seller can reduce this uncertainty: a producer's identity can be a signal of the quality of what is produced, and a worker's identity a signal of the quality of his services.

2. Transactions that are not consummated instantaneously and that involve obligations or consequences that extend over time. In one sense this is an important subset of the first category. The quality of promises to pay or deliver depends on the identity of the promise giver. In contracting for an intertemporal transaction between strangers, it is necessary to specify the contract in a manner that would allow a third party to adjudicate in case of disagreement.

Another special class of transactions, insurance transactions, in which a guarantee against future uncertainty is the commodity exchanged, presents

8   THE ORGANIZATION OF EXCHANGE

problems for buyers and sellers for the solution of which identity is almost a necessary, but not a sufficient, condition. Indeed, transactions in insurance are the classical explanation for the failure of markets and the possible advantage of family contracts. What is known as "moral hazard" comes from the costs associated with making the distinction between the external risk and the incentive effect of insurance; adverse selection is the consequence of the inability of the insurer to assess individual risks. Buyers of insurance also face risks of a transactional nature—the risk of breach of contract in the form of failure to deliver or act and in the form of extortion attempts when the insured is in trouble. When the crop is about to be ruined if it is not harvested immediately, the only workers available can extort most of it; a drowning man or one wounded in battle can be stripped of all his wealth as the price of immediate help. Some risks are thus associated with the insurer's absolute monopoly power, which may allow him to collect not the (ex-ante) expected value of the damage but the ex-post value of the damage to the insured (Landes and Posner, 1978). The deal between Jacob and Esau is a reminder that even within families there is no complete guarantee against such blackmail.

The risks on the two sides do not cancel but add up in generating transaction costs that cause some insurance markets to shrink or vanish. Embedding the insurance contract in a connection between identified parties can provide a partial solution. Of the many examples that one could cite here let me mention the peculiar treatment of food in primitive societies, which put various restrictions on trade and disposal of food even where other items are traded. In one case (an Indian community in Colombia) the researcher notes that trade in food is restricted to trade with special clients: "the individuals must be bound by reciprocal obligation for [an Indian] to consider the transaction worth while, . . . because limiting the exchange in this way has served to minimize the risk of famine" (Ortiz, 1967, pp. 209–210). Special taboos governing food distribution have the same source (Sahlins, 1965, pp. 171–173).

Insurance elements in employer-employee relationships have only recently been mentioned with respect to modern economies but have for long been discussed in connection with the Japanese labor market (see Taira, 1970) and come up in various forms in developing societies. Epstein (1962) describes relationships between peasants and untouchables in Indian villages where the connection is hereditary and remuneration of untouchables by peasants is fixed. In years of famine the peasant receives no more than his worker and by sharing provides subsistence to all. In return, the worker is obligated to be on call: subsistence insurance is exchanged for insurance of labor services. The exchange of mutual obligations to ensure labor supply among farmers is very common.

Specialization by Identity   The approach taken here is that the different modes of transacting—market and nonmarket institutions—can be understood if viewed as the (not necessarily perfect) result of an attempt to minimize all costs, including the costs of transacting. Think of a transaction as the unit of analysis. It can be described in several dimensions—the goods and services being exchanged, the terms, the location, and, what is important here, the identity of those involved in it. The division of labor, or specialization, implies that each individual appears (as a seller) only in those transactions that are similar in most or all of the other dimensions—what is being traded, location, and so on.

In the same way one speaks of specialization by impersonal dimensions of transactions, one can speak of specialization by identity, meaning that individuals deal only with the same person or with small groups.

The Adam Smith tradition links specialization and the division of labor to the presence of returns to scale in production, that is, to the presence of set-up costs that make it cheaper, up to a point, to produce on a large scale. In the preceding section I argued that identity is a form of set-up cost; thus, the rationale for specialization by identity derives from returns to scale. The balance between specialization by identity and other dimensions derives from the minimization of production and transaction costs and reflects the scale economies connected with the different dimensions.

The structure of distribution is sometimes one of a strict hierarchy in specialization with increasingly finer division of labor—each differentiated product being channeled through exclusive wholesalers down to the local store dealing with just one product. But more often, distributors draw from several producers, and the local store draws many products from many producers. This reflects the fact that the economies of scale, or set-up costs, associated with each dimension can often be utilized over more than one dimension, so that at each stage there is a built-in bias toward homogeneity in terms of one dimension and heterogeneity in terms of the other dimension.[5] In buying a used car or taking a personal loan, people often prefer to deal with someone they know well, rather than go to a used car dealer or money lender. When purchasing sophisticated equipment, however, trust in one's friends or relatives cannot compete with the technical know-how of the specialized dealer. A buyer who intends to buy in the future will invest in (search for) a reliable salesman, but the long-term contract will be subsumed under the impersonal dimensions of the transactions. With differences in the importance of identity in various goods and in the specificity of investment of identity to goods or activities, people will be organized in small clusters for some purposes and large ones for others, and these groupings may intersect for different purposes.

Many of the issues that family research is concerned with are associated with specilization by identity. Thus, the class of related individuals engaged in a given set of transactions determines whether we talk about an extended or a nuclear family, and the process of nuclearization is one in which the class narrows until it includes only the spouses and their children.

The range of transactions involving family members has narrowed with modernization. This narrowing has taken the form of a reduction in the range of goods and services supplied within the family; a reduction in the proportion of families acting as producer cooperatives of marketable goods; greater specialization in joint consumption and affective relationships; and changes in the nature of the internal insurance and in capital allocation.

The relevance of household research and the usefulness of the various concepts of the household (Bender, 1967; Laslett, 1972; Goode, 1963) depend on the degree to which coresidence is consistently associated with other family transactions. Caldwell (1976) and others argue against the dominance of the household. Oppong (1976) provides many illustrations from Africa in which individuals are involved with different partners for different transactions and contracts between a pair of individuals defined by kinship differ in content in different settings.

Specialization and Enforcement of Contracts by Competition The point at which specialization by identity occurs in the flow of transactions matters for the nature of the relationship between the transacting parties. When the permanent trading relationship is subsumed under impersonal specialization, trade is organized around specialized traders or firms each typically facing many buyers and sellers. Firms establish their separate identity via a brand name. This can be done through direct spending on advertising and promotion or by selling high-quality goods for low prices until people learn to recognize the quality.[6] Brand names represent *general* signals directed at potential trading partners of unspecified identity. The trading partners of the specialized trader make some investments that are general—becoming "educated" buyers (or sellers), in effect acquiring information that is of service whomever they deal with. They also make *specific* investments that depend for their value on the specific policies of the specialized trader. Workers who sell their labor services to large employers are in the same position.

On the face of it, the specific investment made by individual buyers in their relationship with each specialized trader gives the latter some monopoly power, a range in which prices change and buyers do not switch. A seller who faces many buyers (or a buyer facing many sellers) in ongoing relationships involving new buyers (or sellers) is, however, restrained from reneging on the contracts with each of his trading partners. What restrains him and provides protection for his trading partners' specific investments in him is the effect that failure to keep his promises would have on the terms at which he could get new buyers (sellers). The cheaper the flow of information among buyers and prospective buyers, the more effective is the self-enforcement mechanism of the implicit contract. An employer who wants to shift the cost of acquiring specific skills on to his workers by paying new employees less than the alternative wage and promising them seniority-linked future benefits above it could subsequently take advantage of them to such an extent that they would go elsewhere. What restrains him is that failure to keep the promises would eventually force him to pay higher starting wages.[7]

This form of social enforcement is the more effective, the finer the specialization by impersonal dimensions, the more standardized the transactions with various buyers (sellers), and the easier the flow of information among buyers (sellers). The more standardized the transactions, the closer we are of course to the ideal market transaction.

In relationships that tend to be exclusive, as in the family, the enforcing power of competition is weaker, and the range for informal bargaining is wide. Parties who have already invested specifically in each other are in a short-run position of bilateral monopoly. If the self-enforcement mechanism is imperfect, trust, or fear, or violence, becomes more important. The thrust of the argument of this section is that specific investment in identity is present also in what is regarded as the market. But where it is subsumed under impersonal specialization, enforcement of an explicit or implicit contract is provided by "the market," and is not internal to the contract.

Collective and Individual Identity One can view firms (and families) as contracts between identified parties that form units replacing personal identity in transactions between them and the rest of the world. The set of contracts and rules between partners or shareholders, and between them and the hired management and labor that constitute the firm, establishes the extent and limits of individual liability and mutual responsibility vis-à-vis a third party. (Likewise, a family or a tribe may be regarded as a set of contracts that establishes rules of exchange and cooperation internally and allows the appearance of the collective identity vis-à-vis others to replace individual identity.)[8] An organization is a set of contracts and rules defining roles and establishing their relationships, in which individuals assume or leave roles that have been defined for general purposes and permanent use. Investment in identity takes place in the selection for roles and as individuals select the organizations they join.

In standard economic analysis, households and firms exist as collective identities that completely replace the identity of the individuals affiliated with them. For purposes of transactions between households and firms the collective identities exist as atoms rather than molecules.[9] Standard economic theory is concerned only with the transactions between the collective units, while what goes on within them is the subject-matter of other disciplines.

The sharp dichotomy between the external and the internal serves an analytically useful purpose. A more general view of collective and personal identity, however, would be that the involvement of individuals in a set of contracts can affect the cost of their other transactions, either because of the substance of these transactions or because of their value as signals. Sometimes a connection is preferred mostly for its effects on transactions with those outside it: this may be true of some social clubs, law firms, economics departments, and even marriage contracts. In all these cases, there is reliance on what bears a loose resemblance to the transitivity of the brand name—institutions based on personal investment and sorting provide signals

12   THE ORGANIZATION OF EXCHANGE

that benefit individual members in their dealings with others. The collective name is, in turn, a public good whose value can be diminished by the behavior of each individual and whose survival depends on the internal controls. Internal contracts of the firm that do not provide incentives for (e.g.) quality will damage the brand name. A social club or a university department that does not sort new members carefully will damage its collective name.

The role of family affiliation in the transactions of individuals with those outside the family is particularly evident during the early stages of economic development. Families have played an important part in employment placement (see e.g., Anderson, 1971, on nineteenth-century England and Vogel, 1967, on Japan at the onset of the migration to towns). And family affiliation has also played an important part in the capital market in reducing the transaction costs of individuals (on family capitalism in both Europe and part of the developing world, see e.g., Benedict, 1968). Family relationships also play an important part in the struggle over the establishment of property rights and their physical protection, as is evident in any frontier movie.

The role of family affiliation vis-à-vis others relies partly on its value as a signal of personal traits—honesty, fidelity, skill, and so on—and on the degree to which the family takes responsibility for the obligations and actions of its members. Ascribed status has greater operational significance than achieved status when the family is an important educator and when the set of internal family contracts affects the security of those who deal with family members. Authority, discipline, altruism, and family solidarity affect the value of the signal, "family affiliation," for the rest of the world. The presence of a head of family, serving as director for communication, trust, and redistribution, reduces transaction costs within the family by reducing the need for bilateral relationships.[10] We can speak loosely of transitivity here—the pairwise investment of each member with the center links him to all the others. In his theory of social interaction, Becker (1974a) has shown why a central figure who cares (i.e., has the utility of members at heart, or in his own utility function) can generate socially optimal behavior from all the others, even if they are all egoists.

This concludes the presentation of the general framework. The next two sections of the exposition present, first, a general application of these ideas and, then, an examination of the way the relationship between wealth and family size is related to the functions of the family.

**Families
and the Development
of Markets**

General Trends   Economic and social development affects the importance of identity in given transactions relative to other elements of the cost structure; the relative weight in all transactions of those in which identity is important; the degree to which specialization by identity is subsumed under impersonal specialization, or investment in identity is specific to some activities; and the ability of the family, compared with other institutions, to provide an efficient milieu for transactions and to affect favorably the transactions of its members with others.

Social enforcement of private contracts, ready access to adjudication, morality, and religious pressure for generalized honesty (in contrast to "contextual morality") all tend to reduce the importance of identity, to facilitate transactions between strangers, and to reduce the need for specific mutual investment by trading parties, allowing people to trade with a wider circle of others and narrowing the range of goods and services in which any pair or small group deals.

Impersonal social institutions provide substitutes for family transactions—sometimes at the price of reducing efficiency (by relieving the individual of the cost of collecting information or by raising the threat of inspection, where from a social point of view it would be desirable for him to internalize these costs). Note, however, that certain types of social action change the types of connections created, but do not necessarily reduce their number or importance. The threat of punitive social action on certain transactions (such as trade in drugs, liquor, or sex) induces connections of mutual dependence between buyers and sellers and distributors at different stages. High penalties on crimes in general increase the mutual dependence of the criminals.

Likewise, money as a social institution reduces the role of identity. Its transactional facility, its liquidity and negotiability, rest on the fact that its value is independent of the identity of the seller. Commodities that served as money have tended to be of a fairly uniform and readily observable quality. Money in the form of coins depends on the identity of whoever mints it or vouches for its content. Paper money depends for its value on the identity of those who issue it. Money in the form of personal checks depends for its value on the identity of the banking concern. People acquire information (at some or no cost) about the identity of the third party who issues money. This serves them in many transactions, saves transaction costs, and makes the identity of the "seller" of money immaterial.

As mechanized production and quality control increase standardization of many commodities, there is a decline in the importance of identity in the trade in tangible commodities.

Transactions in Labor   In the exchange of personal services and in capital and insurance transactions, it is more difficult to reduce the relative importance of personal identity than it is in transactions involving produced commodities; but it is, nonetheless, possible. Modern economic growth is associated with the increase in the stock of knowledge and the accumulation of human capital. Information is a consistent source of economies of scale leading to specialization; and behind specialization by identity there is investment in information pertaining to those involved. However, economic development is associated with a greater return to investment in information pertaining to the *impersonal* dimensions, which in turn induces specialized investment in human capital. The transactional advantages of the family cannot compensate for the fact that within its confines the returns from impersonal specialization and division of labor are not fully realizable.

A change in the organization of economic activity that involves a shift from family farm and cottage industry through putting-out system to factory system could be the consequence of purely technological change that increased the advantage of large-scale production, because of economies associated with (e.g.) the harnessing of energy sources. But the emphasis placed on institutional change, at least by traditional economic historians, suggests that institutional innovations may be an important contributing factor, at times even the moving force; the greater efficiency of one organizational structure compared with another is a matter of both technological change in the narrow sense and transactional efficiency, and the two cannot be easily distinguished. Cottage industry, putting out, and the family represent involvement in product markets and division of labor but use mostly the family's own labor and capital or land. The shift to specialized firms, which rests on the concentration of a large volume of labor and capital, means separate sale of labor and capital services in markets that have experienced significant institutional innovations. In labor service transactions (more than elsewhere) buyer and seller differ in the information at their disposal or in the cost of acquiring it; such differences may lead workers to shirk, cheat, or misrepresent their ability. As a result, the use of hired labor has considerable disadvantages over own labor and labor spot markets over the family-type transaction. One (popular) view of the effect of the factory system on the exchange in labor services is that mechanization and automation eliminate the importance of identity in labor transactions. This is the *Modern Times* image of masses of anonymous workers performing mechanical routine tasks requiring little know-how. If this were a realistic image we would find labor spot markets in developed countries. The fact is that such markets exist mostly in less developed countries or sectors. Taira's (1970) interpretation of the emergence of the implicit patriarchal employer-employee contract in Japan is that it provided a solution to the inefficiency of a labor spot market with excessive turnover, rather than being some kind of inert conformity with old customs. Recent studies of the US labor market report on the prevalence of long-term association between employers and employees (Lilien, 1977; Feldstein, 1975).[11] Thus, technological advance and sustained growth have not done away with identity as an element in labor services but, rather, have found ways of dealing with it by permitting increasing interaction between specialization by identity and by impersonal dimensions of transactions.

Another aspect of specialization by impersonal dimensions is the development of standardized (albeit imperfect) signals and certificates produced by organizations specializing in education, sorting, and the production of general signals. Their function is to reduce transaction costs, and one of their effects is to reduce the importance of identity. But increasing complexity of production and fine product differentiation require the services of reliable specialists. The cost of error and the damage that individuals can do both in production and in the financial affairs of large firms, together with the imperfections of the generalized signals, mean that personal identity is still important. Yet clearly, once identity is important mainly when subsumed under impersonal specialization, the family becomes a relatively inefficient institution.

Capital and Insurance Transactions Institutional developments in capital markets have occupied a prominent role in economic historians' account of growth: the emergence of negotiable financial assets and specialized institutions for capital transactions, the rise of the firm as a collective legal identity, and the concept of limited liability. These developments have enabled individuals to separate the sale of their labor and capital services, to separate ownership from operation, and to enjoy the benefits of diversification of ownership; they have enabled firms to mobilize capital from many individuals and to operate on an optimum scale.

The family, particularly in developing countries, often serves as an alternative and very different mode for transacting on the capital account. Thus, a common argument concerning high fertility in developing countries is that children are desirable as partners in capital and insurance transactions and not only as suppliers of labor. The child who receives support is implicitly bound by an obligation to reward his parents by supplying labor and old-age support. These transactions are based on complementarity in the life cycle—children come when they can be provided for and later they assist their parents.

In his pure-loan model, Samuelson (1958) pointed out the inability of a market in pure loans to solve such problems of intertemporal transfers efficiently, in the absence of a general asset. The solution is a "social compact" whereby successive generations implicitly agree not to break the chain of giving and receiving. The absence of general assets is at one end of a spectrum in which assets are partly specific, because of transaction costs, which raise their internal value relative to their market value.

In effecting intertemporal transfers and transacting in contingent claims, the child-parent relationship has the potential advantage that it is reinforced by other transactions and activities. Much of the socialization carried out in the family is concerned with education for roles toward the parents within the family ("Honor thy father and mother" comes before "Thou shalt not kill"). It may be argued that when the family is the major institution for socialization the parents and others have opportunities to invest in family-specific human capital, that is, to create traits that are more valuable within the family than elsewhere, reducing the chances that children will want to leave. Child betrothal serves this function. The cool or even hostile

16   THE ORGANIZATION OF EXCHANGE

reaction to (even free) schools in some traditional contexts may reflect the
objection of the parent generation to the substitution of general human capital for the family-specific human capital and the implied reduction in family
attachment (see, e.g., Oppong, 1973).

Investment in family-specific human capital may not be sufficient to
insure the bond of obligation. Enforcement of the parent-child contract can
be further secured through bequests, giving the parents the last word.[12]
Children, for their part, bear the risk that their parents will need more sup-
port.than the bequest is worth if the parents live "too long." The bequest
may not cover the extended support, but once part of the support has been
paid, it may be worthwhile to carry on rather than lose the whole bequest.
The bargaining position of the parties depends on the size of the estate and
on the ability of parents to choose alternative heirs or to secure services from
other sources. Bargaining and sometimes written contracts deal with the
distribution of the estate, timing of transfer of title and control, the rights
and obligations of each side.[13]

Inheritance laws affect and may reflect various trade-offs and assessment of risks. Inheritance practices that keep property intact enhance the
ability and willingness of *one* of the children to provide old-age insurance.
The timing of transfer of title and the terms of the contract depend on the
parties' bargaining positions, which in turn depend on the alternatives available to each, including the presence of other children. Splitting an inheritance between children can secure support from more people but may
reduce the probability of support from each. The availability of enforcement
of contracts between parents and children makes earlier transfer of title feasible (see Berkner, 1973). Ortiz (1967) mentions children's bargaining over
shares in bequests tied to their readiness to provide labor services; Anderson
(1971) compares rural Ireland with rural Lancashire in the middle of the
nineteenth century and relates the duration of adult children's residence in
the parental home to the amount they expect to inherit. Nor is this just a
rural phenomenon. Describing family business in East Africa, Benedict
(1968) cites examples of parents who finance the education of their children
and then make a transfer of part of the family business conditional on the
son's readiness to work in it. The supply of labor services by children is thus
linked to the transfer-insurance-bequests nexus. The particular form in
which parents hold wealth (and in which children accumulate their own) has
implications for the demand of parents and children for each other, and the
particular choice of assets is affected by returns that reflect both transactional
and nontransactional considerations.

It is probably correct to view the changes in the capital market as a
reduction in the importance of identity and a corresponding rise in ano-
nymity, so clearly expressed in the French term *société anonyme*. But the
importance of identity does not vanish. Investment in identity becomes
more specialized for capital or insurance transactions: the village lender represents specialization in intensive investment in identity, and so does his

heir, the loan officer in a bank. Note also that there is no uniform monotonic decline in the importance of identity and family-type transactions. The private financing of investment in human capital, which constitutes a significant share of total investment, rests on identity much more than does the financing of investment in tangible capital. Some may describe this as an imperfection in the capital market and others as an imperfection in the labor market, where indentures cannot be enforced (Stigler, 1967). The fact remains that the financing of human capital requires nonmarket substitutes, either a family-type contract or alternatively some kind of governmental intervention.

There is also a scale effect: the development of markets implies that each unit of capital can be traded at a lower cost, and there may be a smaller return to investment in identity from a unit transacted; however, greater wealth and more transactions per unit of wealth may actually raise the total return on investment in identity. Moreover there is some complementarity between market and nonmarket transactions. There are returns to scale in the use of information; the identity of whoever transmits or shares information is important in evaluating it; information is important in doing business in the market—all these elements may increase the returns to cooperation based on family-type contracts. Joint ownership of property has often been part of the definition of the family (e.g., Goode, 1963). Its advantages have ranged from the joint protection and acquisition of property rights to more subtle economic benefits. Business cooperation between the members of rich families continues in highly developed economies. Long-term partnerships with nonrelatives simulate some of the properties of the family-type contract, again mutually investing in identity in order to save transaction costs and reap the benefits of joint action vis-à-vis the rest of the world. The need to invest in identity to operate efficiently even in relatively developed markets is an element in the high salaries of top executives and in the dependence of lonely millionaires on trusty henchmen. (Henchmen become famous by betraying their employer or selling his secrets to magazines, and they do it more often than sons or brothers.)

Transition from Family- to Market-Dominated Transactions   Examples of complementarity between market and family-type transactions abound, particularly in the early stages of development. Parental involvement in the labor market may be combined with an attempt to maintain a family farm as well—certainly prevalent in many developing countries. This is a form of market involvement that increases the domestic tasks of wives and children. This practice is particularly prevalent in early stages of development during which market employment is subject to considerable instability and is essentially a spot transaction. Involvement of mothers in the labor market raises the cost of child rearing. The impact of this change again depends on the context: in a large household there is greater flexibility in allocating members between the labor market and the home—older children take care of younger children and older relatives are sought after for the

18   THE ORGANIZATION OF EXCHANGE

purpose, temporarily raising household size. The conflict between child rearing and the labor market is more severe once women get into permanent jobs in which on-the-job training and continuity matter.

The employment of children in the labor market can, in the short run, increase family income in periods of slack internal supply of jobs.[14] If employment is uncertain, children will want to remain part of the parental household. Children entering the labor market more permanently may leave the household but may still want the backing of the parental farm and may maintain the implicit contract with parents. If stable employment at a high enough wage is offered, the inducement to break away is greater. We mentioned earlier the traditional objections to education. If, however, both parents work in the market, public education is a social provision of child care and can reduce the cost of children. To the extent that education is offered in conjunction with or as a consequence of the development of a labor market in which education is rewarded, parents may still maintain direct or indirect control of children and may welcome education as an improved investment for their own support and as support for smaller children.[15] This may temporarily increase parental demand for transactions with children; it can at the same time reduce the number of the first vintage to be exposed to education.

The initial entry into a turbulent labor market is associated with increased risks: parents may gamble and reduce risks by pooling the fortunes of several children. The simultaneous entry into the market of several relatives may have the advantage of information and connections that strengthen rather than weaken family ties. No less important, perhaps more so, are the complementarities between the family and the emerging capital market. The role of the family in the history of European capitalism is well-known. There is also some documentation of the role of families in the business world in developing countries, where expansion and credit position depend on the availability of several sons in the various branches of the family business and sometimes in government or banking or elsewhere where connections matter.

Let me conclude this section with a skeleton of a model: The benefits from a family-type connection can be viewed as the savings in transaction cost per dollar transacted times the volume of transaction. The latter rises with wealth. Thus, within one society, for a given institutional setup, the benefit from a connection tends to rise with wealth; the (upward) slope of such a curve rises with the saving per dollar transacted. The development of markets tends to push this curve downward, that is, for any given level of wealth, the benefits from a connection decline as identity becomes less important. The slope tends to decline too. But: economic growth means accumulation of wealth, that is, a move to the right and toward higher benefits to a connection along any given curve for a given institutional setup. Thus, the ambiguity, and even lack of monotonicity, in the relationship between economic development and the benefit from investment in identity can be viewed as the result of two processes—the reduction in the benefit at any given level of wealth and the increase in the benefit coming from the accumulation of wealth.

The Effect of Wealth on Family Size and Composition

The relationship between family size and composition, on the one hand, and the level of income or wealth, on the other, has been widely researched. The relatively easy-to-measure variables such as household size and fertility have attracted greater attention, however, than more elusive aspects of family relationships. To some extent there is substitution between intensive relationship in a small family and less intensive involvement with a large family. The balance between intensive and extensive family involvement depends on the functions of the family, on the rate at which internal transaction costs rise with family size, on the distribution of individual traits, and on demographic constraints on the supply of partners of a particular status.[16]

We shall distinguish here between three types of family transactions, namely those involving production, consumption, and insurance. In the standard household production model (Becker, 1965), all categories of household activity are treated uniformly—all involve the transformation of own time and purchased goods into activities useful to the members of the family. This is appropriate if indeed all activities are separable and have constant-returns-to-scale technologies. If some of the commodities produced for own use are semi-public goods, in that there is some indivisibility in their provision, or if there is complementarity in consumption between individuals—in other words, if it is either cheaper or more enjoyable to consume the same things and pursue the same activities—there is some merit in distinguishing between the various activities and between the family as a consumer cooperative (including affective relationships) and as a producer cooperative.

Production In a production model of the family in which the head of the family possesses tangible capital and in which the operation of factor markets gives an advantage to the family-type contract, we can expect family size to increase with wealth and with the inequality in its distribution between men, women, and children. In the language of production theory, the complementarity between tangible capital and human time means that more tangible capital should work with more labor; that richer men want to "employ" more wives and children within the family. The same will be true if there is gross complementarity between men's human capital and that of children and women. Men with more human capital will demand more complementary services. The same can be said in terms of a trade analogy: diversity in the composition of endowments creates comparative advantage and promotes intrafamily trade (see Gronau, 1973; and Becker, 1974b). So does diversity in tastes. But the gains from trade depend also on the volume of trade—men with a large endowment may need more trading partners to exploit the potential gains from trade.

The greater the advantages of intrafamily over interfamily trade in terms of transaction costs, the more pronounced will be the positive correlation between family size and wealth. The crude association between family size and income in societies with low or declining fertility tends to be inverse, while cross-section studies in peasant societies show a positive association between family size and land holdings. Positive associations between wealth and family size seem also to have prevailed in Europe before the demographic transition. From the demand side, rather than rely on a vague income effect, one could explain these as a reflection of gross complementarity (using a production model) or of the positive association between endowment and gains from trade. The same argument would apply to the positive association between wealth and the number of wives in polygynous societies (see Grossbard, 1978).

Sorting into families is governed by the same rules that determine the sorting of inputs into firms and the selection of partners in trade.[17] Either analogy suggests a positive association between the endowments of men and women who are paired in marriage, that is, complementarity in production, or greater gains in trade. Given that there are fixed costs associated with identity, obtaining complementary services from one person with a large endowment is preferable to obtaining them from several with small endowments. This modifies what was said before about the relationship between property and size. If women and children have a fairly low and uniform endowment, the better-endowed men can satisfy their demand for a larger volume of trade only by increasing family size. But if women's labor endowment is not uniform, the better-endowed will be sought by the better-endowed men, and will substitute for the men's need for a larger family.

Consumption   Let us move next to the family as a consumer cooperative and assume that it is based on the joint use of indivisible facilities, cheaper provision of commodities on a larger scale, and the enjoyment of joint activities. One could think here of a family whose members derive their income from the market and spend it together on purchased goods or on recreation activities. Again, we need fixed identity costs to account for the preference for (semi) permanent partners.[18] Several statements can be made on size and composition.

The size of a group cooperating in the consumption of a normal semipublic good will diminish with the income of the members. This is a well-known implication of the theory of social clubs (Buchanan, 1965; and Pauly, 1967), which rests on the statment that, as each individual's consumption rises with income, the range of publicness or declining costs is exhausted with fewer participants. As income rises, an increasing variety of commodities is consumed, which may reduce the sensitivity to income of the size of the sharing group. Still, it is quite plausible that the rich are less in need of partners. Another question that comes up here repeats one raised earlier in general terms: to what extent does specialization by identity dominate other forms of specialization—do people team up as one pair or group for many purposes or do they form specialized groups (clubs), each dedicated to a particular activity? As noted, this depends on the relative personal and impersonal economies of scale. For consumption activities requiring high set-up costs and fewer of the identity-related characteristics, people will join a specialized club. Similarly, when the family is a large kinship group, individual members may team up for special purposes.

While specialized clubs are sorted by the similarity in one activity, multipurpose social clubs, neighborhoods with several public amenities, and, of course, families have to be more uniform in terms of tastes and income.[19] Here the theory of localized public goods is applicable also to families. Affiliation to a firm is dictated mostly by a specialized activity that does not directly satisfy the utility of its members, and this limits the range of utility-satisfying public commodities over which a consensus can be established, such as group health insurance and other fringe benefits in kind (see, e.g., Goldstein and Pauly, 1974). Joint consumption tends to equalize real income in the family and is an incentive for intraclass marriage. Laws or social customs that impose restrictions on the internal distribution of real income and the separate ownership of wealth encourage intraclass marriage. On the other hand the fact that Muslim women keep individual property rights facilitates marriage across classes, as do flexible consumption habits, when husbands and wives do not necessarily share the same consumption level, as is common in Africa (see Oppong, 1974).

Insurance   Let us discuss now a third category of family transactions, namely insurance. Here lie all the pitfalls for the operation of markets— moral hazard, adverse selection, the costs or difficulties of explicitly specifying states of the world, and so on. These are some of the reasons why insurance transactions with specialized traders involve specific investment in the identity of the buyer and restrictions on behavior.[20] It is clear why investment in identity is rewarding in these circumstances, why trust is mutually beneficial, why proximity and general involvement create at little expense the information that is lacking among strangers and generate incentives for proper behavior. Typically insurance between family members is mutual, an exchange of promises for aid contingent on the situation of both (or all) parties. Several remarks can be made concerning the sorting of people into groups for mutual insurance.

In discussing the relationship between the size of the coinsurance group and the income of its members, we can begin with some of the club arguments. The security gained by sharing independent risks is analogous to security produced at declining costs. If the size of the group that shares risks

is limited, this can be interpreted to mean that fixed identity costs of investing in an additional member just balance the benefits of adding a member.
Much of the advantage of risk-sharing can be achieved with fairly small numbers, and the marginal contribution to risk reduction of an additional member declines rapidly. The rich are better able to self-insure against losses of a
given size, and a smaller number of coinsurers comes close to exhausting the
benefits of the added security. Likewise, if one thinks of a given profitability
of default in the face of a given loss, the size of the group and the wealth of its
members are substitutes. But "great wealth implies great loss," said Lao-tse
(*The Simple Way*, p. 44).[21] The rich can lose more. Note also that the risks
that threaten all the units of wealth held by an individual are likely to be
correlated—wealth is held in discrete assets, at given locations, subject to
risks associated with the identity of the owner. This is by definition true of
human wealth and also, but to a lesser degree, of nonhuman wealth. What is
clear is that it is worthwhile for the rich to invest significantly in their coinsurers. Beyond this point, statements concerning the connection between
size of group and income will have to bring in the connection between income and risk aversion.

The benefits of sharing risks with others are greater the less is the
direct dependence of the risks across individuals. Ideally, groups of mutual
insurance will consist of people with equal ability to insure each other and
with independent or negatively correlated risks.

These observations have several implications for the ability of families
to cope with the insurance problem. In insuring, for example, for support in
time of sickness or in averaging the randomness of individual incomes, the
family can be an effective insurer, and larger families may serve this function
either through many children or through ties extending beyond the nuclear
family. But it should be noted that if family relationships are intensive, there
is also a greater chance that risks are positively correlated across members,
that fluctuations in the economy or in other external conditions would hit the
coinsurers simultaneously. Of course, pooling the wealth of family members
allows greater diversification than in individual portfolios (because of the
fixed costs of holding single assets), but the gains from pooling with a close
relative on the basis of trust and personal investment in identity have to be
weighed against the benefits of doing it with strangers facing independent or
negatively correlated risks. This may account for the fact that within kinship
networks, groups of coinsurers extend beyond the nuclear and coresident
family. The ability of the market to enter into insurance transactions and
reap the benefits of sharing between even much larger groups may reflect
some success in reducing the fixed costs of investment in additional coinsurers.

The specific investment in relationships with others is subject to risks
that affect the choice between concentrating a large investment in a few
people and spreading it among many. This is relevant for analyzing the
effects of mortality: high mortality means that the expected duration of a

relationship between parties is short, and, up to a point, its variance is high. Low mortality increases the returns to specific investment in one or a few individuals, as against the incentive to diversify investment over a broad group of kin. The high risk of investing in a single partner may be behind the observation of anthropologists that in Africa transactions between husband and wife are fewer or less important than those with the families of origin, particularly in regard to property ownership. Even the fact that child-father contracts are much less intensive than the relationships between the children and the family of origin (particularly maternal kin or uncles, as in parts of Africa) may reflect the greater likelihood that a child in a high-mortality and high-fertility environment will have a surviving uncle than a father. This extends the familiar argument that, in a high infant-mortality regime, there may be a tendency to gamble on many children, while investing little in each. The general argument is that reduced mortality intensifies the relationships within the nuclear family and attenuates those with the wider kinship group (see e.g., Shorter, 1975).

We have seen that in different types of transactions the relationship between wealth and family size may differ. It is more likely to be direct in production and more likely to be inverse in joint consumption, while the picture is more complex concerning insurance. Developments in the labor and capital market discussed here and in the preceding section reduce the role of family in production. When families are confined more to joint consumption and affective relationships, there is less reason to observe the positive relationship between wealth and size. On the other hand, joint consumption induces sorting of people with similar tastes and incomes.

Conclusion

Taking a broad view of transactions, I have discussed the role of identity. I sketched a framework in which the opportunity to reduce transaction costs by making specific investment in the exchanges between identified parties affects the organization of social activity, the division of labor, and, in particular, the interaction between specialization by identity and by other dimensions of transactions. This framework provides channels for linking various aspects of economic and social development to changes in the mode of transacting and to the shifts in the borderlines between the various types of market and nonmarket modes.

The motivation for this essay is the study of the family, the most important institution for nonmarket transactions and probably still the least specialized. The general framework is a result of a search for some elements missing from economists' and others' analyses of families and households and the desire to create a bridge between previous analyses. The framework aspires to generality—I do want to point to common elements in transactions

24   THE ORGANIZATION OF EXCHANGE

that take many institutional forms and to draw examples from many diverse corners of human activity, and the family serves as the chief example.

A Note on Theory

This paper is part of a general attempt to create a new institutional economics. It bears some similarity in approach to Williamson's *Markets and Hierarchies* (1975) and to some extent to Hirschman's *Exit Voice and Loyalty* (1970). This new attempt in contrast to the old institutional school (e.g., Commons, 1924) tries to explain institutions using many developments within economics proper. This was the approach of Coase's (1937) classic work on the nature of the firm, which was maintained partly in the oral tradition at the Universities of Chicago and California at Los Angeles. Some of the theoretical strains underlying this paper are: information economics as positive theory, led by Stigler, and as normative theory (market failure) à la Arrow; the "new" monetarism, which emphasizes the role of transaction costs and institutional constraints (Clower, Leijenhufvud); the implicit contract theory and the theory of agency, starting with Cheung (1969) and elaborated by Stiglitz, Azariadis, Baily, and others; the work on internal labor markets (Doeringer and Piore; Williamson et al.); the theory of repeated games; and the theory of the club. My emphasis on specific investment draws on Oi (1962) and Becker (1964). In the context of the family this approach comes to complement rather than replace the new household economics, as exemplified in the volume sponsored by T.W. Schultz (1974), where again the influence of Becker's work is dominant. Outside the field of economics this paper relates to issues raised by economic anthropologists both in general treatises and in the concerns of many empirical studies (Dalton, Polanyi et al., Sahlins, Firth, Barth). Such issues have also been raised in the demographic work in developing countries (e.g., Caldwell).

Notes

Most of the work toward this paper was done while the author was in residence at the Labor and Population Program of the Rand Corporation and at the Economics Department, University of California at Los Angeles, and completed when he was a fellow of the Institute of Advanced Studies of the Hebrew University of Jerusalem. The work at Rand was financed by a grant from the National Institute of Health.

The author benefited from communications by Peter Diamond, Jack Hirshleifer, Simon Kuznets, Axel Leijonhufvud, T. W. Schultz; comments by William Butz, Robert Clower, Harold Demsetz, Susan Freund, Zvi Griliches, Reuben Gronau, David Harrison, Michael Keren, Ruth Klinov-Malul, Ed Lazear, John McCall, Dale Mortensen, Sam Peltzman, Norman Ryder, Finis Welch, and Menahem Yaari; and seminars at Columbia, Harvard, Jerusalem, the University of California at San Diego, Los Angeles, and Berkeley, and NBER-West.

An earlier, condensed version of this

paper was presented at the 1978 IUSSP conference in Helsinki on Economic and Demographic Change: Issues for the 1980s, and was published in volume 1 of the Proceedings (Liège: IUSSP, 1979).

1. I benefited here from Macneil (1974). Macneil distinguishes between transactional and relational contracts as two extremes of a continuum and suggests their characteristics.

2. For a detailed exposition of this, see Hirshleifer (1973).

3. There is some similarity here to Herbert Simon's description of the implicit employment contract (1951).

4. See, however, Titmuss (1970) for a treatment of anonymous gifts.

5. Contemporary interest in the nature of the division of labor is quite rare. See, however, Stigler (1951) and Leibenstein (1960).

6. These are investments and correspondingly a brand name is an asset that can in part be realized either through deliberate depreciation and debasement (selling bad goods under a good name) or through sale. A brand name is a *specific* asset if its capitalized value exceeds its value in sale. The nature of the information conveyed by a brand name determines whether it can be sold by its original owner at a price equal to the present value of the capitalized services. Franchised names rest on the assumption that there is some monitoring of quality or transmission of patented knowledge. A doctor or a lawyer can sell some of his goodwill, but the trust in his personal knowledge is a *specific* asset (here, it is simply human capital).

7. Thus, the supply function of labor faced by individual employers should include quit rates, layoffs, and discharges in addition to wages. See, e.g., Parsons (1972) and Pencavel (1972).

8. Jones (1976) presents a view of trade within "socially defined enclaves" that is in many respects similar to that presented here.

9. Leibenstein's (1976) first chapter is titled "Atomistic versus molecular economics" and deals with this issue.

10. If the fixed cost of establishing a relationship in a system with m members with a center is F and the cost is F^1 in a system without a center, the former will be superior to the latter in terms of their fixed costs if $(m - 1)F < 1/2m(m - 1)F^1$.

11. The theories of specific human capital, internal labor market, and implicit labor contracts provide various interpretations of this phenomenon. See Oi (1962); Becker (1964); Doeringer and Piore (1971); Baily (1974); Azariadis (1975); Stiglitz (1975); Williamson et al. (1975); and Mortensen (1978).

12. See Hirshleifer's (1977) response to Becker's (1976) handling of altruism. Parsons (1974) interprets old-age support as a contract for income insurance secured by the promise of a bequest.

13. A somewhat extreme example, cited by Anderson (1971), is that of parents losing support once they had "used up" what their children expected to give to them.

14. See the analyses of the relation between child wage and US fertility in Lindert (1974). See also Rosenzweig and Evenson (1977).

15. See, e.g., Caldwell (1965) and Salaff (1975).

16. Thus, for example, the number of brothers who can combine to cooperate in an extended family framework is restricted by the availability of brothers, in turn determined by the mortality-fertility regime. The size of the group participating in such an implicit contract will then depend on the degree to which more distant relatives are good substitutes. [This is the point of the exchange between Levy (1965) and Coale and Faller in Coale et al. (1965).]

17. Becker's (1974b) theory of marriage applies these rules to the sorting of spouses by their traits.

18. In the absence of fixed costs, a semi-public good could be provided by competitive firms (see Berglas, 1976).

19. "It is the wretchedness of being rich that you have to live with rich people" (Logan Pearsall-Smith, *Afterthoughts*), indicating that it is not the pleasure but the cost effectiveness of associating with other rich that causes social stratification.

26   THE ORGANIZATION OF EXCHANGE

20. For example, the cost of check-ups for medical insurance, or safety requirements in home insurance; contrast the anonymous sale of in-flight life insurance, where these problems do not exist.

21. Support for this important empirical observation is found in the old Hebrew saying, "He who multiplies assets, multiplies worries," and the presumably independent observations by Benjamin Franklin, "He who multiplies riches multiplies care" (*Poor Richard*) and Periander "The greater your fortune the greater your cares" (Plus est sollicitius magis beatus).

Bibliography

Akerlof, George A. 1970. "The market for 'lemons': Quality uncertainty and the market mechanism." *Quarterly Journal of Economics* 84 (August):488–500.

Alchian, Armen A., and Harold Demsetz. 1972. "Production, information costs, and economic organization." *American Economic Review* 62 (December):777–795.

Anderson, Michael. 1971. *Family Structure in Nineteenth Century Lancashire*. London: Cambridge University Press.

Arrow, Kenneth J. 1969. "The organization of economic activity: Issues pertinent to the choice of market versus nonmarket allocation." In *The Analysis and Evaluation of Public Expenditures: The PPB System*, Vol. 1. Joint Economic Committee, 91st Cong., 1st Sess., pp. 47–63.

Azariadis, Costas. 1975. "Implicit contracts and underemployment equilibria." *Journal of Political Economy* 83 (December):1183–1202.

Baily, Martin Neil. 1974. "Wages and employment under uncertain demand." *Review of Economic Studies* 41 (January):37–50.

Barth, F. 1966. *Models of Social Organization*. Occasional Paper 23. London: Royal Anthropological Institute.

Becker, Gary S. 1964. *Human Capital: A Theoretical and Empirical Analysis with Special Reference to Education*. National Bureau of Economic Research, General Series No. 80. New York and London: Columbia University Press.

———. 1965. "A theory of the allocation of time." *Economic Journal* 75 (September):493–517.

———. 1974a. "A theory of social interactions." *Journal of Political Economy* 82 (November/December):1063–1093.

———. 1974b. "A theory of marriage." In *Economics of the Family: Marriage, Children, and Human Capital*, ed. T.W. Schultz. A Conference Report of the National Bureau of Economic Research. Chicago and London: University of Chicago Press.

———. 1976. "Altruism, egoism, and genetic fitness: Economics and sociobiology." *Journal of Economic Literature* 14 (September):817–826.

———, Elisabeth M. Landes, and Robert T. Michael. 1977. "An economic analysis of marital instability." *Journal of Political Economy* 85 (December):1141–1187.

Bender, D. R. 1967. "A refinement of the concept of household, families, co-residence, and domestic functions." *American Anthropologist* 69:493–504.

Benedict, Burton. 1968. "Family, firms and economic development." *Southwestern Journal of Anthropology* 24 (Spring):1–19.

Berglas, Eitan. 1976. "On the theory of clubs." *American Economic Review* 66 (May):116–121.

Berkner, Lutz. 1973. "Recent research on the history of the family in Western Europe." *Journal of Marriage and the Family* 35 (August):395–405.

Blau, Peter M. 1964. *Exchange and Power in Social Life.* New York: Wiley.

Buchanan, James M. 1965. "An economic theory of clubs." *Economica* 32 (February):1–13.

Burch, Thomas K., and Murray Gendell. 1970. "Extended family structure and fertility: Some conceptual and methodological issues." *Journal of Marriage and the Family* 32, no. 2: 227–236.

Caldwell, John C. 1965. "Extended family obligations and education: A study of an aspect of demographic transition amongst Ghanaian university students." *Population Studies* 19 (November):183–199.

———. 1976. "Toward a restatement of demographic transition theory." *Population and Development Review* 2, nos. 3/4 (September/December):321–366.

Cheung, Steven. 1969. *The Theory of Share Tenancy.* Chicago: University of Chicago Press.

Clower, Robert W. 1971. "Theoretical foundations of monetary policy." In *Monetary Theory and Monetary Policy in the 1970s,* ed. E. Clayton, J.C. Gilbert, and R. Sedgwick. New York and London: Oxford University Press, pp. 13–28.

Coale, Ansley J., et al. (eds.) 1965. *Aspects of the Analysis of Family Structure.* Princeton, N.J.:Princeton University Press.

Coase, R. H. 1937. "The nature of the firm." *Economica* 4 (N. S.; November):386–405.

Commons, John Rogers. 1974. *Legal Foundations of Capitalism.* Clifton, N.J.: A. M. Kelley. Photocopy of New York edition, 1924.

Dahlman, Carl J. 1977. "Transaction costs, externalities and our two paradigms." Workshop in Law and Economics, University of Los Angeles at California.

Dalton, G. 1976. *Economics, Anthropology and Development.* New York: Basic Books.

Doeringer, Peter B., and Michael J. Piore. 1971. *Internal Labor Markets and Manpower Analysis.* Lexington, Mass.: D. C. Heath.

Epstein, T. S. 1962. *Economic Development and Social Change in South India.* Manchester, Eng.: Manchester University Press.

Feldstein, Martin. 1975. "The importance of temporary layoffs: An empirical analysis." *Brookings Papers on Economic Activity,* no. 3, pp. 725–745.

Firth, Raymond. 1967. "Themes in economic anthropology: A general comment." In *Themes in Economic Anthropology,* ed. Raymond Firth. London: Tavistock Publications.

Goldstein, G. S., and M. V. Pauly. 1974. "Group health insurance as a local public good." In *Conference on the Role of Health Insurance in the Health Services Sector.* National Bureau of Economic Research.

Goode, William J. 1963. *World Revolution and Family Patterns.* London: Collier Macmillan.

Gronau, Reuben. 1973. "The intrafamily allocation of time: The value of the housewives' time." *American Economic Review* 63 (September):634–651.

Grossbard, Amyra. 1978. "The economics of polygamy." Ph.D. dissertation, University of Chicago.

28   THE ORGANIZATION OF EXCHANGE

Heal, Geoffrey. 1976. "The market for lemons, comment." *Quarterly Journal of Economics* 90 (August):499–502.

Hirschman, Albert O. 1970. *Exit Voice and Loyalty*. Cambridge, Mass.: Harvard University Press.

Hirshleifer, Jack. 1973. "Exchange theory: The missing chapter." *Western Economic Journal* 11 (June):129–146.

———. 1977. "Shakespeare vs. Becker on altruism: The importance of hearing the last word." *Journal of Economic Literature* 15 (June):500–502.

Homans, George Caspar. 1974. *Social Behavior: Its Elementary Forms*, rev. ed. New York: Harcourt Brace Jovanovich.

Jones, J. R. 1976. "Market imperfections in peasant societies." In *Paths to Symbolic Self*, ed. J. P. Loucky and J. R. Jones. Department of Anthropology, University of California at Los Angeles.

Landes, William M., and Richard A. Posner. 1978. *Salvors, Finders, Good Samaritans, and Other Rescuers: An Economic Study of Law and Altruism.* Working Paper No. 227. New York: National Bureau of Economic Research.

Laslett, Peter. 1972. "Introduction: The history of the family." In *Household and Family in Past Times*, ed. P. Laslett. Cambridge, Eng.: Cambridge University Press.

Lazear E. 1978. "The economics of retirement." Unpublished paper.

Leibenstein, Harvey. 1960. *Economic Theory and Organizational Analysis*. New York: Harper & Row.

———. 1976. *Beyond Economic Man*. Cambridge, Mass. and London: Harvard University Press.

Levy, Marion J. 1965. "Aspects of the analysis of family structure." In *Aspects of the Analysis of Family Structure*, ed. Ansley J. Coale et al. Princeton, N. J.: Princeton University Press, pp. 40–63.

Lilien, D. 1977. "The cyclical pattern of temporary layoffs: An empirical study." Paper based on M.I.T. dissertation. Labor Workshop, University of California at Los Angeles.

Lindert, Peter H. 1974. "American fertility patterns since the Civil War." Center for Demography and Ecology Working Paper No. 74-27. Madison: University of Wisconsin.

Luce, R. D., and H. Raiffa. 1957. *Games and Decisions*. New York: Wiley.

Macaulay, Stewart. 1963. "Non-contractual relations in business: A preliminary study." *American Sociological Review* 28 (February):55–67.

Macneil, Ian. 1974. "The many futures of contracts." *Southern California Law Review* 47 (May):691–816.

Makowsky, Louis. n.d. [1977]. "Value theory with personalized trading." Unpublished paper.

Mauss, Marcel. 1954. *The Gift: Forms and Functions of Exchange in Archaic Societies*. Glencoe, Ill.: The Free Press.

Mincer, J. 1977. *Family Migration Decisions*. Working Paper No. 199. New York: National Bureau of Economic Research.

Mortensen, D. 1978. "Specific capital bargaining and labor turnover." Unpublished paper.

Nelson, Phillip. 1970. "Information and consumer behavior." *Journal of Political Economy* 78 (March/April):311–329.

Yoram Ben-Porath   29

Oi, Walter Y. 1962. "Labor as a quasi-fixed factor." *Journal of Political Economy* 70 (December):538–555.

Oppong, Christine. 1973. *Growing Up in Dagbon*. Ghana: Ghana Publishing.

———. 1974. *Marriage Among a Matrilineal Elite: A Family Study of Ghanaian Senior Civil Servants*. London: Cambridge University Press.

———. 1976. "Ghanaian household models: Data for processing by the New Home Economists of the developing world." Paper presented at a Seminar on Household Models of Economic Demographic Decision-Making, Mexico City.

Ortiz, Sutti. 1967. "The structure of decision-making among Indians of Colombia." In *Themes in Economic Anthropology*, ed. Raymond Firth. London: Tavistock Publishing.

Parsons, Donald O. 1972. "Specific human capital: An application to quit rates and layoff rates." *Journal of Political Economy* 80 (November/December):1120–1143.

———. 1974. "On the economics of intergenerational relations." Unpublished paper (revised 1976).

Pauly, Mark V. 1967. "Clubs, commonality, and the core: An integration of game theory and the theory of public goods." *Economica* 34 (August):314–324.

Pencavel, John H. 1972. "Wages, specific training, and labor turnover in U.S. manufacturing industries." *International Economic Review* 13, no. 1:53–64.

Polanyi, Karl, Conrad A. Arensberg, and Harry Pearson. 1957. *Trade and Markets in the Early Empires*. New York: The Free Press; London: Collier Macmillan.

Rosen, Sherwin. 1968. "Short-run employment variation on class-I railroads in the U.S., 1947–1963." *Econometrica* 36 (July–October):511–529.

Rosenzweig, Mark R., and Robert Evenson. 1977. "Fertility, schooling and the economic constitution of children in rural India: An econometric analysis." *Econometrica* 45 (July):1065–1079.

Sahlins, Marshall D. 1965. "On the sociology of primitive exchange." In *The Relevance of Models for Social Anthropology*, ed. Michael Banton. New York: Praeger.

Salaff, Janet W. 1975. "The status of unmarried Hong Kong women and the social factors contributing to their delayed marriage." Paper presented at the Population Research Program Conference at Bellagio, Italy, 2–5 May.

Samuelson, Paul A. 1958. "An exact consumption-loan model of interest with or without the social continuance of money." *Journal of Political Economy* 66 (December):467–482.

Schultz, T. W. (ed.) 1974. *Economics of the Family: Marriage, Children, and Human Capital*. A Conference Report of the National Bureau of Economic Research. Chicago and London: University of Chicago Press.

Shorter, Edward. 1975. *The Making of the Modern Family*. New York: Basic Books.

Simon, Herbert A. 1951. "A formal theory of the employment relationship." *Econometrica* 19 (July):293–305.

Stigler, George J. 1951. "The division of labor is limited by the extent of the market." *Journal of Political Economy* 59 (June):185–193.

———. 1961. "The economics of information." *Journal of Political Economy* 69 (June):213–225.

———. 1967. "Imperfections in the capital market." *Journal of Political Economy* 75 (June):287–292.

Stiglitz, Joseph E. 1975. "Incentive risk and information: Notes towards a theory of hierarchy." *Bell Journal of Economics* 6 (Autumn):552–575.

Taira, K. 1970. *Economic Development and the Labor Market in Japan.* New York: Columbia University Press.

Titmuss, Richard M. 1970. *The Gift Relationship: From Human Blood to Social Policy.* London: George Allen & Unwin.

Vogel, E. F. 1967. "Kinship structure, migration to the city and modernization." In *Aspects of Social Change in Modern Japan,* ed. R. P. Dore. Princeton, N. J.: Princeton University Press.

Williamson, Oliver E. 1975. *Markets and Hierarchies: Analysis and Anti Trust Implications.* New York: The Free Press.

———, Michael L. Wachter, and Jeffrey E. Harris. 1975. "Understanding the employment relation: The analysis of idiosyncratic exchange." *Bell Journal of Economics* 6 (Spring):250–278.

[11]

Ronald Dore

Goodwill and the spirit of market capitalism

HOBHOUSE MEMORIAL LECTURE

Why have large factories given way to the co-ordinated production of specialized family units in segments of the Japanese textile industry? One reason is the predominance of 'obligated relational contracting' in Japanese business. Consumer goods markets are highly competitive in Japan, but trade in intermediates, by contrast, is for the most part conducted within long-term trading relations in which goodwill 'give-and-take' is expected to temper the pursuit of self-interest.

Cultural preferences explain the *unusual* predominance of these relations in Japan, but they are in fact more common in Western economies than textbooks usually recognize. The recent growth of relational contracting (in labour markets especially) is, indeed, at the root of the 'rigidities' supposedly responsible for contemporary stagflation. Japan shows that to sweep away these rigidities and give markets back their pristine vigour is not the only prescription for a cure of stagflation. The Japanese economy more than adequately compensates for the loss of allocative efficiency by achieving high levels of other kinds of efficiency — in many respects thanks to, rather than in spite of, relational contracting. We would do well to be more concerned about those kinds of efficiency too.

One of economists' favourite Adam Smith quotations is the passage in the *Wealth of Nations* in which he sets out one of his basic premises.

It is not from the benevolence of the butcher, the brewer and the baker, that we expect our dinner, but from their regard to their own interest. We address ourselves, not to their humanity, but to their self-love, and never talk to them of our necessities but of their advantages.[1]

The British Journal of Sociology Volume XXXIV Number 4
© R.K.P. 1983 0007-1315/83/3404-459 $1.50

I wish to question that sharp opposition between benevolence and self-interest. Perhaps, so that he should be alert for signs of possible bias, the reader should be warned that a prolonged soaking in the writings of Japanese eighteenth- and nineteenth-century Confucianists at an early age has left me with a soft spot for the virtue of benevolence, even a tendency to bristle when anyone too much disparages it. At any rate I wish to argue, apropos of benevolence, or goodwill, that there is rather more of it about than we sometimes allow, further that to recognize the fact might help in the impossible task of trying to run an efficient economy and a decent society – an endeavour which animated Hobhouse's life, and about which, as Ginsburg makes clear in his 1950s preface to *Morals in Evolution*, even the pains of old age and the rise of fascism in the 1920s did not destroy his eventual optimism.

My title refers to goodwill rather than benevolence because benevolence, in my Confucian book, though not I think in Adam Smith's, is something shown in relations between unequals, by superior to inferior, the reciprocal of which is usually called loyalty. Goodwill is more status-neutral, more an expression of Hobhouse's 'principle of mutuality'. And it is that broader meaning which I intend. A formal definition of my subject might be: the sentiments of friendship and the sense of diffuse personal obligation which accrue between individuals engaged in recurring contractual economic exchange. (By 'economic', I mean only that the goods and services exchanged should be commonly subject to market valuation.)

Goodwill, of course, is a term of art in the commercial world. In the world of petty proprietorships, familiar to most of us, if you are selling a corner store you set a price on the premises, a price on the stock and a price on the goodwill. Back in the old Marshallian days when economists took their concepts from everyday life rather than trying to take everyday life from their concepts, goodwill meant the same thing to economists too. Palgrave's 1923 dictionary of economics defines goodwill as:

> The expectancy of a continuance, to the advantage of a successor in an established business, of the personal confidence, or of the habit of recurring to the place or premises or to the known business house or firm, on the part of a circle or connection of clients or customers.[2]

The next economics dictionary I find, McGraw-Hill's exactly half a century later, has a very different definition of goodwill:

> An accounting term used to explain the difference between what a company pays when it buys another company and what it gets in the form of tangible assets.[3]

Samuelson, to his credit one of the very few textbook writers in whose index one will find the word goodwill, illustrates the concept with J. P. Morgan taking over Carnegie's steel interests, making it clear that Morgan paid a premium well over the market value of the fixed assets primarily because he thereby advanced significantly towards a monopoly position.[4] In other words the goodwill concept is extended to cover not just the benefits accruing to the purchaser of a business from the affectionate or inertial habits of its customers, but also those accruing out of his consequent shift from the position of price-taker to that of price-maker — his enhanced ability to hold those customers up to ransom. To be fair to the economists who have adopted this use of the term, and partially to retract my earlier gibe, one could say that the standard definition of the term has changed because everyday life has changed. A world in which the terms appropriate to the small owner-managed business formed the dominant norm, has given way to a world dominated by the large corporations and their accountants' terms. Certainly, if anyone wanted to write an Old Testament Prophet-style denunciation of modern capitalism *à la* Marx, he could hardly ask for a better illustration than the corruption of the concept of 'goodwill', that primordial embodiment of basic social bonds, into a term for some of the more ugly anti-social forms of profit-seeking.

THE DISAGGREGATION OF FACTORY PRODUCTION

I have been caused to ponder the role of goodwill in economic life by the recent experience of studying the organization of the textile industry, or to be more precise, the weaving segment of it, in Britain and Japan. One place I visited in the course of that research was the small town of Nishiwaki in western Japan whose industry is almost wholly devoted to the weaving of ginghams chiefly for export to Hong Kong to be made up into garments for Americans to wear when square-dancing in the Middle West. This is an area where hand-loom weaving goes back some centuries. Power-looms came in in the late nineteenth century and they brought with them the factory system as they did everywhere else. And 25 years ago, although many small weaving establishments had survived, the bulk of the output was accounted for by larger mills, many of which were part of vertically integrated enterprises with their own cotton-importing, spinning and finishing establishments.

By 1980, however, the picture had changed. The larger mills had closed. The integrated firms had retreated, as far as direct production was concerned, to their original base in spinning. Most of them were still, either alone or in collaboration with a trading company, producing their own brand cloth, dyed and finished. But they were doing so through the co-ordination of the activities of a large number of family enterprises. The key family business was that of the merchant-converter who contracted with the spinning company to turn its yarn into a certain type of cloth at a given contract price. The converter would send the yarn to another small family concern specializing in yarn dyeing, then it would go on to a specialist beamer who would wind it on to the warp beams in the desired pattern and also put the warp through the sizing process. Then it would be delivered to the weaver who might do his own weft preparation and the drawing-in (putting the harness on the beams ready for the looms) or might use other family businesses — contract winders or drawers in — for the process. And so on to the finishers who did the bleaching or texturizing or over-printing.

What is the reason for this fragmentation? What changes in Japanese society and the Japanese economy account for what most orthodox notions of the direction of the evolution of modern economies would count as a regression — the replacement of a system of production co-ordination within a vertically integrated firm by a system of production co-ordination between a large number of fragmented small firms; the replacement, to use Williamson's terms, of co-ordination through hierarchy by co-ordination through the market?[5]

I can think of four possible long-term secular trends which might help to explain the change.

1. The first is the rise in wages and the shorter working week of employees in union-organized firms. Wages are commonly lower in small firms — especially in Japan where the privileged position of the large enterprise elite has become firmly conventionalized, and inter-scale wage differentials are very great. But that is not all. Family enterprisers themselves are often willing to work much longer than 40 hours a week for what may or may not be a larger *total* income than wage workers get, but for an *average* return per hour of labour — hence wage cost per metre of cloth — which is below the employee's wage. If you like, family enterprisers are now willing to exploit themselves more than the unions or the law permit employees to be exploited — a condition which did not hold when *employees* were already working close to the human maximum — a 70 hour week for a subsistence level wage. The clear superiority of the factory system at that time may have been lost since.

2. Second, the secular trend to high taxation and higher levels of taxation-allergy make the family enterpriser's advantage in both tax avoidance and tax evasion more attractive — *vide* the growth of the secondary 'black' and quasi-black economy in many other countries.

3. Third, there is a technical factor: the capital lumpiness of some of the new technology. For example expensive, large and fast sizing machines can hardly get the through-put necessary to make them profitable within a single firm. Inter-firm specialization becomes the best way of realizing economies of scale.
4. Fourth, much higher levels of numeracy and literacy mean a much wider diffusion of the accounting and managerial skills necessary to run a small business, the prudent ability to calculate the rentability of investments, etc.

These are all features common to societies other than Japan and may well be part of the explanation why the woollen industry of Prato has also moved to a fragmented structure in recent years. But there is another factor which applies especially in Japan. The reason why the dominant trend in the west seems to be in the reverse direction – away from co-ordination through the market towards co-ordination through the hierarchy of a vertically integrated firm – is, as Oliver Williamson is never tired of telling us, because of the transaction costs entailed, the costs arising from the imperfections of markets with small numbers of buyers and sellers in which the bargaining transactions are made difficult by what the jargon calls 'impacted information'. These features so enhance the bargaining power of each party that, when there are no significant economies of scale to be gained by their mutual independence one party (usually the stronger one) buys out the other to put a stop to his 'opportunism' (rapid response not only to price signals – which of course is always admirable – but also to information about vulnerable weaknesses of the other party.)

RELATIONAL CONTRACTING

Here is another of those timeless generalizations about 'capitalist economies' about which Japan gives pause. Transaction costs for large Japanese firms may well be lower than elsewhere. 'Opportunism' may be a lesser danger in Japan because of the explicit encouragement, and actual prevalence, in the Japanese economy of what one might call moralized trading relationships of mutual goodwill.

The stability of the relationship is the key. Both sides recognize an obligation to try to maintain it. If a finisher re-equips with a new and more efficient dyeing process which gives him a cost advantage and the opportunity of offering discounts on the going contract price he does not immediately get all the business. He may win business from one or two converters if they had some *other* reason for being dissatisfied with their own finisher. But the more common consequence is that the other merchant-converters go to their finishers and say: 'Look how X has got his price down. We hope you can do the same because we really would have to reconsider our position if the price difference goes on for months. If you need bank finance to get the new type of vat we can probably help by guaranteeing the loan.'

It is a system, to use a distinction common in the Williamson school, of relational contracting rather than spot-contracting[6] — or to use Williamson's more recent phrase[7] 'obligational contracting'. More like a marriage than a one-night stand as Robert Solow has said about the modern employment relation.[8] The rules of chastity vary. As is commonly the case, for those at the lower end of the scale, monogamy is the rule. A weaver with a couple of dozen automatic looms in a back garden shed will usually weave for only one converter, so that there should be no dispute about prior rights to the fruits of his looms — no clash of loyalties. Specialists with faster, larger volume, through-puts, like beamers — scarcer, more attractive, more in demand, therefore — may have a relation *à trois* or *à quatre*. For the converters themselves, at the top of the local hierarchy, there have grown up curious conventions rather like polyandrous concubinage. The Japan Spinners Association is dominated by the so-called Big Nine firms. None of the Big Nine will tolerate one of its converters taking cotton yarn from *another* of the Big Nine. However, one rank below the Big Nine are the so called New Spinners, and below them the post-war upstarts, the New New Spinners. A Big Nine spinner will tolerate its converters having relations with them, though, of course a New Spinner will not tolerate a relation with another New Spinner. So the converter can end up with one of each — a first husband and a number two and a number three husband as it were.

As in nearly all systems of marriage, divorce also happens. That is why I said that a finisher with a cost advantage could attract other converters who happen for other reasons to be dissatisfied with their finisher. When I use the analogy of divorce, I mean traditional divorce in obligation-conscious societies, rather than the 'sorry I like someone else better: let's be friends' divorce of modern California. That is to say, the break usually involves recrimination and some bitterness, because it usually has to be justified by accusing the partner of some failure of goodwill, some lack of benevolence — or, as the Japanese phrase is more often translated, 'lack of sincerity'. It is not enough that some external circumstances keep his prices high.

I have made these relations sound like the kinship system of a Himalayan village, but of course the specific patterns of who may trade with whom are of very recent origin. What are entirely traditional, however, are, first, the basic pattern of treating trading relations as particularistic personal relations; second, the values and sentiments which sustain the obligations involved, and third such things as the pattern of mid-summer and year-end gift exchange which symbolizes recognition of those obligations.

But how on earth, the economist will want to know, do the prices and ordered quantities get fixed? The answer seems to be that, once established, prices can be re-negotiated at the initiative of either party on the grounds either of cost changes affecting either party, or else of changes in the competitive conditions in the final market in which the brand cloth is sold. There are also fringe spot-markets for cotton yarn and grey cloth, and the prices ruling in these markets and reported in the daily textile press provide guides. To further complicate the issue there is some collective bargaining. Both the weavers and the converters in Nishiwaki have their own co-operative union and guide prices may be agreed between them; alternatively, in some other textile areas, the weavers co-op sets a minimum contract price which its members are not supposed to undercut, though there is general scepticism about the effectiveness of such an agreement.

RELATIONAL CONTRACTING BETWEEN UNEQUALS

The basic principles on which these price and quantity negotiations rest appear to be three-fold. First that the losses of the bad times and the gains of the good times should be shared. Second, that in recognition of the hierarchical nature of the relationship — of the fact that weavers are more dependent on converters than converters are on weavers — a fair sharing of a fall in the market may well involve the weaker weaver suffering more than the converter — having his profits squeezed harder. But, third, the stronger converter should not use his bargaining superiority in recession times, and the competition between his weavers to have their orders cut as little as possible, to drive them over, or even to, the edge of bankruptcy.

It is in the interpretation of these principles, of course, that ambiguity enters. Benevolence all too easily shades into exploitation when the divorce option — the option of breaking off the relationship — is more costlessly available to one party than to the other. There is, even, an officially-sponsored Association for the Promotion of the Modernization of Trading Relations in the Textile Industry in Japan which urges the use of written rather than verbal contracts in these relationships and is devoted to strengthening moral constraints on what it calls the abuse — but our economic textbooks would presumably call the legitimate full use — of market power. As for the nature of such abuse, surveys conducted by the Association show that suppliers with verbal contracts are more likely to have goods returned for quality deficiencies than those with proper written contracts.[9] Weavers will wryly remark that returns become strangely more common when the price is falling (and a rejected lot contracted at a higher price can be replaced by a newly contracted cheaper lot).

The work of the Association is an interesting illustration of the formal institutionalization of the ethics of relational contracting — doing, perhaps, for contracting what the post-war labour reform did to transform the employment system of large firms from manipulative paternalism into something less exploitative and better described as welfare corporatism.[10] All one can say about the contemporary trading reality is that those ethics appear to be sufficiently institutionalized, to be sufficiently constraining on a sufficient number of the firms and families in Nishiwaki textiles, for the pattern of trading I have described to be a stable and viable one.

That pattern is repeated in many other areas of the Japanese economy — between, for example, an automobile firm like Toyota and its sub-contractors. Here again, the obligations of the relationship are unequal; the sub-contractor has to show more earnest goodwill, more 'sincerity', to keep its orders than the parent company to keep its supplies. But equally the obligatedness is not entirely one-sided, and it does limit the extent to which the parent company can, for example, end its contracts with a sub-contractor in a recession in order to bring the work into its own factory and keep its own workforce employed.

I have been taken to task by Okumura, the Japanese economist who has written most interestingly about these relationships, for speaking of the 'obligatedness' of a firm like Toyota as if a corporation was, or behaved like, a natural person.[11] But I still think the term is apt. The mechanisms are easy to intuit, if ponderous to spell out. First of all, there are *real* personal relations between the purchasing manager of Toyota and the manager or owner-manager of a sub-contracting firm. But, of course, managers change frequently, particularly in firms with a bureaucratic career-promotion structure like Toyota. It is part of the commitment of such managers, however, that they identify with their firm and their department. If it were said, therefore, in the world outside, that Toyota, or its purchasing department in particular, had behaved badly by playing fast and loose with its sub-contractors, the manager responsible would feel that he had let his firm down. If the accountants in the costing department urge a tough line with sub-contractors, he may well tell them that they are short-sighted and even disloyal to the firm in under-estimating the importance of its reputation. These seem to me readily understandable mechanisms by which the patterns of obligation between individual owner-managing converters and weavers in Nishiwaki can be duplicated between corporations.

I have discussed two cases of obligated trading relationships which are explicitly hierarchical. If there is any doubt as to who pecks whom in the pecking order look at the mid-summer and year-end gifts. Although it may vary depending on the precise nature of the concessions sought or granted in the previous six months or anticipated in the next, the weaver's gift to the converter will usually cost more than vice versa — unless, that is, either of them miscalculates the gift inflation rate, the point of transition, say, from Black Label against Suntory Old to Napoleon brandy against Dimple Haig.

RELATIONAL CONTRACTING BETWEEN EQUALS

But these relations are not confined to the hierarchical case. Even between firms of relatively equal strength the same forms of obligated relational contracting exist. Competition between Japanese firms is intense, but only in markets which are (a) consumer markets and (b) expanding. In consumer markets which are not expanding cartelization sets in rather rapidly, but that is a rather different story which does not concern us here. What does concern us here are markets in producers' goods, in intermediates. And for many such commodities markets can hardly be said to exist. Take steel, for instance, and one of its major uses for automobiles. The seven car firms buy their steel through trading companies, each from two or three of the major steel companies, in proportions which vary little from year to year. Prices, in this market, are set by the annual contract between the champions — Toyota on the one side, New Japan Steel on the other.

It is the concentration of such relationships which is the dominant characteristic of the famous large enterprise groups, known to Japanese as *grūpu*, and to foreigners, usually, as *zaibatsu* or *keiretsu*. There are six main ones of which the two best known are Mitsui and Mitsubishi. These groups are quite distinct from the hierarchical groupings of affiliates and subsidiaries around some of the giant individual firms like Hitachi or Matsushita or MHI. The Mitsubishi group, for example, has no clear hierarchical structure. In its core membership of 28 firms, there is a certain amount of intra-group share ownership — on average about 26 per cent of total equity widely dispersed throughout the group in three or four per cent shares. There is a tiny amount of interlocking directorships — about three per cent of all directors' seats. And most of the firms have the group bank as their lead bank, and bank of last pleading resort, but that bank provides on average less than 20 per cent of all loan finance to group firms. The only thing which formally defines the identity of the group is the lunch on the last Friday of the month when the Presidents of every company in the group get together, often to listen to a lecture on, say, the oil market in the 1990s, to discuss matters like political party contributions, sometimes to hear news of, or give blessings to, some new joint venture started up by two or more member firms, or a rescue operation for a member firm in trouble.[12]

But the main *raison d'etre* of these groups is as networks of preferential, stable, obligated *bilateral* trading relationships, networks of relational contracting. They are not conglomerates because they have no central board or holding company. They are not cartels because they are all in diverse lines of business. Each group has a bank and a trading company, a steel firm, an automobile firm, a major chemical firm, a shipbuilding and plant engineering firm and so on – and, except by awkward accident, not more than one of each. (The 'one set' principle, as the Japanese say.) Hence, trade in producer goods within the group can be brisk. To extend earlier analogies; it is a bit like an extended family grouping, where business is kept as much as possible within the family, and a certain degree of give and take is expected to modify the adversarial pursuit of market advantage – a willingness, say, to pay above the market price for a while to help one's trading partner out of deep trouble.

THE PREFERENCE FOR RELATIONAL CONTRACTING: CULTURAL SOURCES?

The starting point of this discussion of relational contracting was the search for reasons to explain why it made sense for the spinning firms producing brand cloth to co-ordinate production neither through hierarchy in the usual Williamson sense of full vertical integration, nor through the market in the normal sense of continuously pursuing the best buy, but through 'relational contracting'. It was, I said, because such arrangements could be *relied on* in Japan more than in most other economies. There is one striking statistic which illustrates the extent to which it is in fact relied on. The volume of wholesale transactions in Japan is no less than four times as great as the volume of retail transactions. For France the multiple is not four but 1.2; for Britain, West Germany and the USA the figure is between 1.6 and 1.9.[13]

How does one explain the difference between Japan and other capitalist economies? Williamson has 'theorized' these 'obligational relationships' and explained the circumstances in which they will occur – when the extent to which the commodities traded are idiosyncratically specific (such that the economies of scale can be as easily appropriated by buyer or by seller), and the extent to which either party has invested in equipment or specialized knowledge for the trading relationship, are not quite such that vertical integration

Goodwill and the spirit of market capitalism   **469**

makes sense, but almost so. He also asserts that in such relationships quantity adjustments will be preferred to price adjustments
and price adjustments will be pegged to objective exogenous indi-
cators (though he allows, in passing, for the not very 'relevant' or
'interesting' possibility that 'ad hoc price relief' might be given as
an act of kindness by one party to the other.)[14]

Perhaps Williamson has evidence that that is the way it is in
America and the fact that his argument is couched in the terms of
a timeless generalization merely reflects the tendency of American
economists to write as if all the world were America. (Just as British
economists write micro-economics as if all the world were America,
and macro-economics as if all the world were Britain.) Or perhaps
he does not have much evidence about America either, and just
assumes that 'Man' is a hard-nosed short-run profit-maximizer
suspicious of everyone he deals with, and allows everything else to
follow from that. At any rate Williamson's account does not provide
the tools for explaining the difference between the Japanese and
the British or American economies. There is nothing particularly
idiosyncratic about the steel or cloth traded in many of the obligated
relationships, little specialized assets involved (though there are in
automobile sub-contracting). Nor is there clear avoidance of price
adjustments – weaving contract prices, in fact, look like graphs of
nineteenth century business cycles.

Clearly we have to look elsewhere for an explanation. Try as one
might to avoid terms like 'national character' which came naturally
to Hobhouse, in favour of the scientific pretensions of, say, 'modal
behavioural dispositions', it is clearly national differences in value
preferences, or dispositions to action, with which we are concerned.
And, as Macfarlane showed when he looked into the origins of
English individualism,[15] to attempt to explain *those* takes one on a
long speculative journey – at least into distant ill-recorded history,
even if, for ideological reasons, one wishes to rule out genes. But it
is legitimate and useful to ask: what are the concomitants of these
dispositions? What do they correlate with? Are they an expression
of more general traits?

One candidate explanation is that the Japanese are generally very
long-term-future-oriented. At this moment, for example, the Japanese
Industry Ministry's Industrial Structure Council is already com-
posing what it calls a 'vision' of the shape of the world economy in
the mid-1990s. The economist is likely to seize on this explanation
with relief, because it will allow him to ignore all dangerous thoughts
about benevolence, and accommodate the relational contracting
phenomenon in the conventional micro-economics of risk aversion
and low time-discounts. Any sacrifice of short-run market advantage
is just an insurance premium for more long-term gains.

And he would find some good evidence. Nakatani has recently

470   *Ronald Dore*

done an interesting calculation comparing 42 large firms inside one
of the large kinship groupings like Mitsui and Mitsubishi which I have
just described and a matched sample of 42 loners. The loners had
higher average profit levels and higher growth rates in the 1970s.
But they also had a considerably higher dispersal around the means.
The group firms were much more homogeneous in growth and profit
levels. What went on in the groups, he concluded, was an overall
sacrifice of efficiency in the interests of risk-sharing and greater
equality.[16]

Relational contracts, in this interpretation, are just a way of trading
off the short term loss involved in sacrificing a price advantage,
against the insurance that one day you can 'call off' the same type of
help from your trading partner if you are in trouble yourself. It is a
calculation, perhaps, which comes naturally to a population which
until recently was predominantly living in tightly nucleated hamlet
communities in a land ravished by earthquake and typhoon. Traditionally, you set to, to help your neighbour rebuild his house
after a fire, even though it might be two or three generations before
yours was burnt down and your grandson needed the help returned.

But you could be *sure* that the help *would* be returned. And this
is where we come back to Adam Smith. The Japanese, in spite of
what their political leaders say at summit conferences about the
glories of free enterprise in the Free World, and in spite of the fact
that a British publisher with a new book about Adam Smith can
expect to sell half the edition in Japan, have never really caught up
with Adam Smith. They have never managed actually to bring
themselves to *believe* in the invisible hand. They have always insisted
— and teach in their schools and their 'how to get on' books of
popular morality — that the butcher and the baker and the brewer
need to be benevolent as well as self-interested. They need to be
able to take some personal pleasure in the satisfaction of the diners
quite over and above any expectation of future orders. It is not just
that benevolence is the best policy — much as we say, rather more
minimally, that honesty is the best policy. They do not doubt that
it is — that it is not a matter of being played for a sucker, but actually
the best way to material success. But that is not what they most
commonly say. They most commonly say: benevolence is a duty.
Full stop. It is that sense of duty — a duty over and above the terms
of written contract — which gives the assurance of the pay-off which
makes relational contracting viable.

Note that this is a little different from what Durkheim had in
mind when he was talking about the non-contractual elements in
contract and refuting Spencer's claim that modern societies were
held together solely by an organic web of individualistic contracts.[17]
Durkheim was talking about the intervention of *society* both in
enforcing the basic principles of honesty and the keeping of promises,

and in regulating the content of contracts, deciding what was admissible and what offended social decency or basic human rights. And in Durkheim's book it is the consciousness of an obligation imposed by society as a whole — or, on its members, by an occupational group of professional practitioners — which enforces those rules. Hobhouse, likewise, in his brisker and more historically rooted discussion of the way freedom of contract and the rights of private property come to be curtailed by, for example, redistributive welfare measures, stressed the benefits the individual receives from society and the corresponding obligations to society.[18] In Japanese relational contracting, by contrast, it is a particular sense of diffuse obligation to the individual trading partner, not to society, which is at issue. To put the matter in Parson's terms, relational contracting is to be understood in the universalism/particularism dimension, whereas the Durkheim point relates to the fifth dichotomy that Parsons later lost from sight: collective-orientation versus individual-orientation. To put it another way, the Japanese share with Durkheim the perception that contract, far from being fundamentally integrative, is basically a marker for conflict. Every harmonization of interest in a contract simply conceals a conflict either latent or adjourned, as Durkheim said.[19] The Durkheim solution is to have universalistic social institutions contain the conflict — an engine-cooling system to take away the heat. The Japanese prefer particularistically to reduce the friction in all the moving parts with the emollient lubrication of mutual consideration.

Perhaps one should not overdraw the contrast, however, in view of the empirical fact that the Japanese, who stand out among other capitalist societies for their addiction to relational contracts, also stand out as the nation whose businessmen and trade unionists seem to have a more lively sense of their obligated membership in the national community than those of other nations. Japan has fewer free-rider problems in the management of the national economy; patriotism seems to supplement profit-seeking more substantially in, say, the search for export markets, and so on. Perhaps the common syndrome is a generalized dutifulness, or to put it in negative form, a relatively low level of individualistic self-assertion. I am reminded of the Japanese scholar and publicist, Nitobe. In his lectures in the USA in the 1930s he used to tell the national character story about the international prize competition for an essay about the elephant. In his version the Japanese entry was entitled 'The duties and domestication of the elephant'.

But there is, it seems to me, a third element in the Japanese preference for relational contracting besides risk sharing and long-term advantage on the one hand and dutifulness on the other. That is the element, to go back to Parsons' variables again, best analysed in his affectivity/affective-neutrality dimension. People born and brought up in Japanese society do not much *like* openly adversarial bargaining relationships — which are inevitably low-trust relationships because information is hoarded for bargaining advantage and each tries to manipulate the responses of the other in his own interest. Poker is not a favourite Japanese game. Most Japanese feel more comfortable in high-trust relations of friendly give-and-take in which each side recognizes that he also has some stake in the satisfaction of the other.

All of which, of course, is not necessarily to say that the affect is geniune. Pecksniffs can do rather well in exploiting these relationships when they are in a stronger bargaining position — the point made earlier about the ambiguities of these relationships.

EMPLOYMENT PRACTICES AND RELATIONAL CONTRACTS

The discussion so far has centred on markets in intermediates and capital goods, and about relational contracting between enterprises. I have not so far mentioned labour markets, though the predominance of relational contracting in Japanese labour markets is, of course, much more widely known than its predominance in inter-firm trading. By now every television viewer has heard of the life-time commitment pattern — the transformation of the employment contract from a short-term spot contract agreement to provide specific services for a specific wage (termination by one week or one month's notice on either side), into a long-term commitment to serve as needs may from time-to-time dictate, with wages negotiated according to criteria of fairness which have precious little to do with any notion of a market rate-for-the-job. The contract is seen, in fact, less as any kind of bilateral bargain, than as an act of admission to an enterprise community wherein benevolence, goodwill and sincerity are explicitly expected to temper the pursuit of self-interest. The parallel between relational contracting in the intermediates market and in the labour market is obvious. There can be little doubt that the same cultural values explain the preferred patterns in both fields.

RELATIONAL CONTRACTING AND EFFICIENCY

But anyone looking at the competitive strength of the Japanese economy today must also wonder whether this institutionalization of relational contracting, as well as serving the values of risk-sharing security, dutifulness and friendliness *also* conduces to a fourth valued end — namely economic efficiency. Any economist, at least any economist worth his neo-classical salt, would be likely to scoff

Goodwill and the spirit of market capitalism   473

at the idea. Just think, he would say, of the market imperfections, of the misallocation and loss of efficiency involved. Think how many inefficient producers are kept out of the bankruptcy courts by all this give-and-take at the expense of the consuming public. Think of the additional barriers to entry against new, more efficient, producers. Gary Becker, in a lecture at the LSE a couple of years ago, claimed that give-and-take trading was even an inefficient way of being altruistic. In the end, he said, through greater survival power, you get more dollars-worth of altruism by playing the market game and then using the profits to endow a charitable foundation like Rockefeller — which I suppose is true and would even be significant. if 'altruism' were a homogeneous commodity indifferently produced either by being friendly to your suppliers or by posthumously endowing scholarship.[20]

But that apart, the main point about sub-optimality is well-taken. The Japanese economy is riddled with misallocation. A lot of the international dispute about non-tariff barriers, for example, has its origin in relational contracting. Take the market for steel which I mentioned earlier. Brazil and Korea can now land some kinds of steel in Japan more cheaply than Japanese producers can supply it. But very little of it is sold. Japan can remain as pure as the driven snow in GATT terms — no trigger prices, minimal tariffs, no quotas — and still have a kind of natural immunity to steel imports which Mr. MacGregor would envy. None of the major trading companies would touch Brazilian or Korean steel, especially now that things are going so badly for their customers, the Japanese steel companies. Small importers are willing to handle modest lots. But they will insist on their being landed at backwater warehouses away from where any domestic steel is going out, so that the incoming steel is not seen by a steel company employee. If that happens, the lorries taking the steel out might be followed to their destination. And the purchaser, if he turned out to be a disloyal customer, would be marked down for less than friendly treatment next time a boom brings a seller's market. What distortions, an economist would say. What a conspiracy against the consumer! What a welfare loss involved in sacrificing the benefits of comparative advantage! If the Japanese economy has a good growth record, that can only be *in spite of* relational contracting and the consequent loss of efficiency.

And yet there are some good reasons for thinking that it might be *because of*, and not *in spite of* relational contracting that Japan has a better growth performance than the rest of us. There is undoubtedly a loss of allocative efficiency. But the countervailing forces which more than outweigh that loss can *also* be traced to relational contracting. Those countervailing forces are those which conduce to, not allocative efficiency, but what Harvey Leibenstein calls X-efficiency — those abilities to plan and programme, to

cooperate without bitchiness in production, to avoid waste of time
or of materials, capacities which Leibenstein tries systematically to
resolve into the constituent elements of selective degrees of rationality
and of effort.[21] We have recently been told by a solemn defender of
the neo-classical paradigm that we need not bother about Leibenstein
and X-efficiency because he is only reformulating the utility-maximiz-
ing paradigm of the generalized equilibrium theory as developed by
the Williamson school (i.e. that which incorporates transaction costs,
property-right constraints, etc.)[22] To argue thus is not only to destroy
the usefulness of 'utility-maximization' for any precise calculations,
it is also to ignore the achievement of Leibenstein in actually noticing
(a) that individuals, firms and nations differ greatly in degrees of
generalized *sloppiness*, and (b) that other kinds of sloppiness are
far more important for output growth and welfare than that involved
in failing to fine-tune economic behaviour in response to changes in
price signals – or *even* in failing to calculate the relative transaction
costs of internal and external procurement.

In his book Leibenstein tries a rough comparison between the
estimated welfare loss from tariffs and price distortions in a number
of empirical cases, and that implied by the 'inefficiency' of business
firms inferrable from the range in outputs with similar inputs as
between 'best practice' and 'worst practice' firms. His evidence that
for most economies for most of the time the latter vastly exceeds
the former is of crucial policy importance, and any theory which
succeeds in assimilating both phenomena within the same umbrella
framework is, like unisex fashions, less an achievement than a
distraction. The distinction between allocative efficiency which
has to do with rational responses to price signals and all those other
kinds of efficiency which raise the productivity of inputs in a business
organization is an extremely useful one, and X-efficiency is as good
a catch-all term for the second bundle of qualities as any other.

It is in the second dimension, in its effect in making 'best practice'
better and more widely diffused, that the Japanese system of
relational contracting has merits which, I suggest, more than compensate for its price-distorting consequences. To take the case of
employment and the life-time commitment first, the compensatory
advantages which go with the disadvantage of inflexible wage costs,
are reasonably well known. In a career employment system people
accept that they have continually to be learning new jobs; there can
be great flexibility, it makes more sense for firms to invest in training, the organization generally is more likely to be a learning environment open to new ideas. If a firm's market is declining, it is less
likely to respond simply by cutting costs to keep profits up, more
likely to search desperately for new product lines to keep busy the
workers it is committed to employing anyway. Hence a strong
growth dynamism. And so on.

Goodwill and the spirit of market capitalism **475**

As for relational contracting between enterprises, there are three things to be said. First, the relative security of such relations encourages investment in supplying firms. The spread of robots has been especially rapid in Japan's engineering sub-contracting firms in recent years, for example. Second, the relationships of trust and mutual dependency make for a more rapid flow of information. In the textile industry, for example, news of impending changes in final consumer markets is passed more rapidly upstream to weavers and yarn dyers; technical information about the appropriate sizing or finishing for new chemical fibres is passed down more systematically from the fibre firms to the beamers and dyers. Third, a by-product of the system is a general emphasis on quality. What holds the relation together is the sense of mutual obligation. The butcher shows his benevolence by never taking advantage of the fact that the customer doesn't know rump from sirloin. If one side fails to live up to his obligations, the other side is released from his. According to the relational contract ethic, it may be difficult to ditch a supplier because, for circumstances for the moment beyond his control, he is not giving you the best buy. It is perfectly proper to ditch him if he is not giving the best buy and not *even trying* to match the best buy. The single most obvious indicator of effort is product quality. A supplier who consistently fails to meet quality requirements is in danger of losing even an established relational contract. I know that even sociologists should beware of anecodotal evidence, but single incidents can often illustrate national norms and I make no apology for offering two.

1. The manager of an automobile parts supplier said that it was not uncommon for him to be rung up at home in the middle of the night by the night-shift supervisor of the car factory 60 miles away. He might be told that they had already found two defective parts in the latest batch, and unless he could get someone over by dawn they were sorry, but they'd have to send the whole lot back. And he would then have to find a foreman whom he could knock up and send off into the night.

2. The manager of a pump firm walking me round his factory explains that it is difficult to diagnose defects in the pump-castings before machining though the founders are often aware when things might have gone wrong. 'I suspect', he said cheerfully, 'our supplier keeps a little pile of defective castings in the corner of his workshop, and when he's got a good batch that he thinks could stand a bit of rubbish he throws one or two in'.

I leave the reader to guess which is the Japanese and which the British story.

HOW *UNIQUELY* JAPANESE?

So if it is the case that relational contracting has some X-efficiency advantages which compensate for allocative inefficiencies, what lessons should we draw from all this about how to run an efficient economy and build a decent society? The first thing to do is to look around at our economies and take stock of the ways in which benevolence/goodwill actually modify the workings of the profit motive in daily practice. So far I have referred to relational contracting as something the Japanese have an *unusual* preference for. But that is far from saying that they are *uniquely* susceptible to it. If we look around us we will find far more evidence of relational contracting than we think. This is so even in America where capitalism seems generally to be more hard-nosed than in Europe. In an interesting article written 20 years ago, Stewart Macaulay examined the relative importance of personal trust and enforceable legal obligation in business contracts in the USA. He found many businessmen talking of the need for give-and-take, for keeping accountants and lawyers, with their determination to press every advantage, out of direct dealings with other firms.[23] Among those with experience of large projects in the civil construction industry it is a truism that successful work requires a bond of trust between client and contractor. Engineers, as fellow-professionals, sharing a commitment to the project's success, can create that trust. Their firms' lawyers can endanger it by the confrontational stance with which they approach all potential conflicts of interest. Recently I got a simple questionnaire answered by seven managers or owner-managers of weaving mills in Blackburn asking them about their trading practices, and found a strong preference for stable long-term relationships with give-and-take on the price, and a claim that, on average, two-thirds of their business already was that way. In the British textile trade, of course, Marks and Spencers is well known for its relational contracting, squeezing suppliers a bit in times of trouble but not ditching them as long as they are maintaining quality standards, and accepting some responsibility for helping them technically. In the supermarket world, Sainsbury's have the same reputation, supposedly very different from that of Tesco's which believes that frequent switching of suppliers encourages the others to keep the price down.

QUALITY, AFFLUENCE AND RELATIONAL CONTRACTING

There may be something very significant in the nature of these examples. Try adding together the following thoughts.

1. Marks and Spencers is well known for one thing besides

Goodwill and the spirit of market capitalism 477

    relational contracting, namely that it bases its appeal on product quality more than on price.

2. There is also an apparent relation between a quality emphasis and relational contracting in Japan.
3. Sainsburys is up-market compared with Tesco which is for keen pricers.
4. Japan's consumer markets are *generally* reckoned to be more middle-class, more quality sensitive and less price sensitive than Britain's. (Textile people, for instance, have given me rough estimates that if one divides the clothing market crudely into the AB groups, fastidious about quality and not too conscious of price, and the rest who look at price and superficial smartness rather than the neatness of the stitching, in Britain the proportions are: 25:75; in Japan 60:40.)
5. Japan of the 1920s, and again in the post-war period, was much more of a cut-throat jungle than it is today. Not the ethics of relational contracting nor the emphasis on product quality nor the life-time employment system, seem to have been at all characteristic of earlier periods of Japanese industrialization.

Add all these fragments together and an obvious hypothesis emerges that relational contracting is a phenomenon of affluence, a product, Hobhouse would say, of moral evolution. It is when people become better off and the market-stall haggle gives way to the world of *Which*, where best buys are defined more by quality than by price criteria, that relational contracting comes into its own.

It does so for two reasons: first because quality assurance has to depend more on trust. You always *know* whether the butcher is charging you sixpence or sevenpence. But if you don't know the difference between sirloin and rump, and you think your guests might, then you *have* to trust your butcher: you have to depend on his benevolence. Also, I suspect, when affluence reduces price pressures, any tendencies to prefer a relationship of friendly stability to the poker-game pleasures of adversarial bargaining – tendencies which might have been formerly suppressed by the anxious concern not to lose a precious penny – are able to assert themselves. Japan's difference from Britain, then, is explained both by the fact that the cultural preferences, the suppressed tendencies, are stronger *and* by the fact that the price pressures have been more reduced by a much more rapid arrival at affluence, and consequently a greater subjective sense of affluence.

The fragmentary evidence about relational contracting in inter-firm trading relations in Britain, is much more easily complemented by evidence of its growth in the labour market. Not only Britain, but Europe in general – even the USA to a lesser extent – are no longer countries where employers hire and fire without compunction. Statutory periods of notice gradually lengthen. National redundancy payment schemes recognize the expectation of continuance of an employment contract as a property right. In industries like steel, job tenures are valued at well over a year's wages. More generally, labour mobility has been falling for 15 years. Factory flexibility agreements take the employment contract further away from the original rate-for-the-specific-job basis. More attention to career-promotion systems within the firm, managerial doctrines about 'worker involvement' in the affairs of the enterprise and, inter-mittently, talk of, and even occasional moves towards, enterprise-based industrial democracy all exemplify the transformation of the employment contract into a more long-term, more diffuse commitment.

RELATIONAL CONTRACTING, RIGIDITIES AND ECONOMIC POLICY

Economists have occasionally noted these trends, but have generally treated them as market imperfections, basically lag problems of the long and the short run — for in the end, habit always succumbs to the pursuit of profit. And among imperfection problems they have found them less interesting to analyse than other kinds like monopoly. And those bold souls among them who *have* taken aboard the new phenomenon of stagflation, and tried to explain the tendency for contraction in demand to lead to a contraction in output not a fall in price, to increased unemployment but only slow, delayed and hesitant deceleration in the rate of wage increase, have rarely recognized the importance of a general growth in relational con-tracting — of the effects on the effectiveness of fiscal and monetary regulators of the fact that more and more deals are being set by criteria of fairness not by market power. More commonly, they speak of the growth of oligopoly on the one hand and on the other of trade union monopoly consequent on statutory job protection and higher welfare benefits. They have explained stagflation, in other words, not as the result of creeping benevolence — the diffusion of goodwill and mutual consideration through the economy — but as the result of creeping malevolence, increasing abuse of monopoly power. And the cure which our modern believers in the supreme virtues of the market have for these 'rigidities', is a deflation stiff enough to restore the discipline of market forces, to make firms competitive again and force the inefficient out of business, to weaken trade union monopolies and get firms hiring and firing according to their real needs.

A few people have given relational contracting and its growth the importance it is due. Albert Hirschman, first in this as in so many things, described the general syndrome of voice and loyalty taking over from exit and entry as the characteristic disciplining force of advanced capitalism.[24] More recently Arthur Okun developed before his untimely death a similarly comprehensive view of relational contracting and, moreover, explained in his *Prices and Quantities* its connection to worsening stagflation.[25] He wrote of the tendency in capital goods and intermediate markets, and to some extent in consumer markets, for what he called 'customer markets', to grow at the expense of 'auction markets', and of the corresponding growth of 'career labour markets' — employment characterized by an implicit contract of quasi-permanence — the invisible handshake is one of his phrases — all adding up to what he called a 'price-tag economy' as opposed to the 'auction economy' of orthodox text books. What I do not think he fully took aboard is the way in which social relations in customer markets and career-labour markets take on a moral quality and become regulated by criteria of fairness. Consequently, his remedies, apart from being far more imaginatively interventionist, are not so very different in kind from the more common marketist prescriptions for dealing with the rigidities of stagflation. That is to say, he also concentrates on devices to change (a) incentives and (b) expectations under the unchanged assumption that economic behaviour will continue to be guided solely by short-run income-maximizing considerations.

There is no mention of Japan in his index, and none that I have discovered in his book. But if we do think of Japan, a society which has far more developed forms of relational contracting than ours and glories in it, *and* achieves high growth and technical progress, we might think of a different prescription.

It would run something like this. First, recognize that the growth of relational contracting can provide a very real enhancement of the quality of life. Not many of us who work in a tenured job in the academic career market, for example, would relish a switch to freelance status. I hear few academics offering to surrender their basic salary for the freedom to negotiate their own price for every lecture, or even demanding personally negotiated annual salaries in exchange for tenure and incremental scales. And if you overhear a weaving mill manager on the telephone, in a relaxed friendly joking negotiation with one of his long-standing customers, you may well wonder how much more than the modest profits he expects would be required to tempt him into the more impersonal cut-and-thrust of keen auction-market-type competition.

But the second point is this. Having recognized that relational contracting is something that we cannot expect to go away, and that inevitably a lot of allocative efficiency is going to be lost, try to achieve the advantages of X-efficiency which can compensate for the loss.

This prescription has a macro-part and a micro-part. The macro-part includes, first of all, maintaining the conditions for free competition in the one set of markets which remain impersonally competitive – the markets for final consumer goods. This is necessary to provide the external stimulus for the competing chains or pyramids of relational-contract-bound producers to improve their own internal efficiency. It means on the one hand an active competition policy, and on the other, where monopoly is inevitable, the organization of countervailing consumer watchdog groups. Also included in the macro-part are first, an incomes policy, since if it *is* now criteria of fairness rather than the forces of supply and demand which determine wages in career labour markets, those fairness criteria had better be institutionalized. Second it means an attempt, if you like, to tip the ideology towards benevolence; in Fred Hirsch's terms, to try to revive an 'ethos of social obligation' to replenish the 'depleting moral legacy' which capitalism inherited from an earlier more solidary age[26], not least by stressing the importance of quality and honest thoughtful service, the personal satisfactions of doing a good job well as a source of pride and self-respect – letting profits be their own reward, not treated as if they were a proxy measure of social worth. The Department of Industry's recent announcement of an £8 million programme of subsidies for improvement in quality assurance systems in British factories is at least a recognition of the enhanced importance of quality in the modern world, even if there are no signs of a recognition that this might entail new attitudes and values (or a new affirmation of old ones now lost), a move away from the spirit of *caveat emptor*.

The micro-part of the prescription involves a better specification of the ethics of relational contracting; perhaps, as the French have been contemplating, criteria for deciding what constitutes unfair dismissal of a sub-contractor, parallel to those for employees, with protection depending on performance, including quality criteria and conscientious timing of deliveries. Second, at the enterprise level, it means taking the growth of job tenure rights not just as an unfortunate rigidity, but as an opportunity for developing a sense of community in business enterprises. It means, that is to say, reaping the production advantages which can come from a shared interest in the firm's success, from co-operation and free flow of information and a flexible willingness not to insist on narrow occupational roles. What those advantages can be we can see in Japan, but in Britain, where attitudes to authority are very different from those of Japan, the prescription probably means not manipulative policies of worker 'involvement' in existing hierarchies, but some real moves towards constitutional management, industrial democracy or what you will – anything *except* the extension of traditional forms of collective bargaining made for, and growing out of, the era of auction markets for labour.

Goodwill and the spirit of market capitalism 481

I think Hobhouse would not have objected to a lecture in his honour being used as an occasion for preaching, though I am not sure that he would have approved of the contents. I am enough of an old-fashioned liberal, however, to hope that he might.

Ronald Dore

NOTES

1. A. Smith, *The Wealth of Nations*, London, J. M. Dent, 1910, p. 13.

2. R. H. I. Palgrave, *Dictionary of Political Economy*, ed. H. Higgs, London, Macmillan, 1923-6.

3. D. Greenwald, *McGraw-Hill Dictionary of Modern Economics*, New York, McGraw-Hill, 1973.

4. P. A. Samuelson, *Economics*, Eleventh Edition, New York, London, McGraw-Hill, 1980, pp. 121-2.

5. O. E. Williamson, 'The modern corporation: Origins, evolution, attributes', *Journal of Economic Literature*, vol. 19, no. iv, December 1981.

6. V. P. Goldberg, 'A relational exchange perspective on the employment relationship', Paper for SSRC Conference, York, 1981.

7. O. E. Williamson, 'Transaction-cost economics: the governance of contractual relations', *Journal of Law and Economics*, vol. 22, no. ii, 1979, pp. 233-61.

8. R. M. Solow, 'On theories of unemployment', *American Economic Review*, vol. 70, i, 1980.

9. Seni Torihiki Kindaika Suishin Kyogikai (Association for the Promotion of the Modernization of Trading Relations in the Textile Industry), *Nenji Hōkoku* (Annual Report), 1980.

10. R. Dore, *British factory: Japanese Factory: The Origins of National Diversity in Industrial Relations*, Berkeley, University of California Press, 1973, pp. 269 ff.

11. H. Okumura, 'Masatsu o umu Nihonteki keiei no heisa-sei' (The closed nature of Japanese corporate management as a source of international friction), *Ekonomisuto*, 6 July

1982. H. Okumura, 'The closed nature of Japanese intercorporate relations', *Japan Echo*, vol. 9, no. iii, 1982.

12. H. Okumura, 'Interfirm relations in an enterprise group: The case of Mitsubishi', *Japanese Economic Studies*, Summer 1982. H. Okumura, *Shin Nihon no Rokudai-kigyō-shūdan. (A new view of Japan's six great enterprise groups)*, Tokyo, Diamond, 1983.

13. Okumura in *Japan Echo*, 1982.

14. O. E. Williamson, 'Transaction-cost economics: the governance of contractual relations', *Journal of Law and Economics*, vol. 22, no. ii, 1979, pp. 233-261.

15. A. Macfarlane, *The Origins of English Individualism*, Oxford, Basil Blackwell, 1978.

16. I. Nakatani, *The Role of Intermarket keiretsu Business Groups in Japan*, Australia-Japan Research Centre, Research Paper, no. 97, Canberra, ANU. I. Nakatani, Risuku-shearingu kara mita Nihon Keizai, ('Risk-sharing in the Japanese economy'), 'Osaka-daigaku Keizaigaku', col. 32, nos. ii-iii, December 1982.

17. E. Durkheim, *De la Division du travail social*, Paris, Felix Alcan, 1893, tr. G. Simpson, *The Division of Labour in Society*, 1960.

18. L. T. Hobhouse, *Morals in Evolution*, London, Chapman & Hall, 1908, 7th ed., 1951.

19. Durkheim, op. cit., p. 222.

20. G. Becker, *Altruism in the Family and Selfishness in the Market Place*, Centre for Labour Economics, LSE, Discussion Paper No. 73, 1980.

21. H. Leibenstein, *Beyond Economic Man: A New Foundation for Micro Economics*, Cambridge, Mass., Harvard University Press, 1976.

22. L. De Alessi, 'Property rights transaction costs and X-efficiency: An essay in economic theory', *American Economic Review*, vol. 73, no. i, March, 1983.

23. S. Macaulay, 'Non-contractual relations in business: a preliminary study', *American Sociological Review*, vol. 28, no. i, February, 1963.

24. A. O. Hirschman, *Exit, Voice and Loyalty: Responses to Decline in Firms, Organizations and States*, Cambridge, Mass., Harvard University Press, 1970.

25. A. Okun, *Prices and Quantities*, Oxford, Basil Blackwell, 1981.

26. F. Hirsch, *Social Limits to Growth*, London, Routledge & Kegan Paul, 1977.

[12]

Networks as the Pipes and Prisms of the Market[1]

Joel M. Podolny
Stanford University

This article draws an analytical distinction between two types of market uncertainty: egocentric, which refers to a focal actor's uncertainty regarding the best way to convert a set of inputs to an output desired by a potential exchange partner, and altercentric, which denotes the uncertainty confronted by a focal actor's exchange partners regarding the quality of the output that the focal actor brings to the market. Given this distinction, the article considers how the value of "structural holes" and market status vary with these two types of uncertainty. The article proposes that the value of structural holes increases with egocentric uncertainty, but not with altercentric uncertainty. In contrast, the value of status increases with altercentric uncertainty, but declines with egocentric uncertainty. Thus actors with networks rich in structural holes should sort into markets or market segments that are high in egocentric uncertainty; high-status actors should sort into markets that are low in egocentric uncertainty. Support for this claim is found in an examination of the venture capital markets.

INTRODUCTION

Economic sociologists and organizational scholars have traditionally regarded networks as the "plumbing" of the market. In this view, networks are the channels or conduits through which "market stuff" flows, where "market stuff" encompasses information about exchange opportunities as

[1] I wish to thank Jim Baron, David Brady, Fabrizio Castellucci, Mike Hannan, Greta Hsu, Ezra Zuckerman, and two *AJS* reviewers for their helpful comments on an earlier draft of this article. I also wish to thank Andrew Feldman for assistance in the collection of the data employed in the analyses in this article. Earlier versions were presented at the Sloan School of Management, the Department of Social and Decision Sciences at Carnegie Mellon University, and the 2000 Sunbelt Social Network Conference in Vancouver. Direct correspondence to Joel Podolny, Graduate School of Business, Stanford University, 518 Memorial Way, Stanford, California, 94305-5015. E-mail: podolny_joel@gsb.stanford.edu

American Journal of Sociology

well as the actual goods, services, and payments that are transferred between buyer and seller. Research emphasizing the role of networks in job search (Granovetter 1974; Fernandez and Weinberg 1997), the significance of interlocking directorates in corporate decision making (Davis 1991; Haunschild 1993), and the importance of the pattern of intersectoral flows for firm profitability (Burt 1992) are all exemplary of this particular perspective.

Given an understanding of networks as pipes, one of the central analytic questions becomes: What network position is most beneficial? In his answer to this question, Granovetter (1974) emphasized the importance of a position characterized by weak, bridging ties. Burt (1992) refined the argument, decoupling the benefits of bridging ties from the average strength of those ties. As Burt writes, tie weakness is a correlate rather than a cause of the value deriving from bridging ties. In fact, controlling for the extent to which a tie serves as a bridge to distinctive sources of information, stronger ties are actually more beneficial than weak ties since they allow a greater volume of resources to move between actors. Such an argument is complemented by an ever-larger volume of research on buyer–supplier relations that emphasizes the relative advantages of more intensive, long-term relations over weaker, short-term market transactions (Dore 1983; Uzzi 1996). The principle of nonredundancy or, to use Burt's terminology, the cultivation of structural holes emerges as the fundamental principle guiding the formation of ties. When "ego" is tied to a large number of "alters" who themselves are not tied to one another, then ego has a network rich in structural holes.

More recently, a second view of networks has arisen in the sociological research on markets. In this second view, a tie between two market actors is not only to be understood as a pipe conveying resources between those two actors; in addition, the presence (or absence) of a tie between two market actors is an informational cue on which others rely to make inferences about the underlying quality of one or both of the market actors. For example, Baum and Oliver (1992) show that day care centers can enhance their legitimacy in the eyes of potential consumers by establishing ties to prominent organizations in the community, such as governmental agencies or church groups. Similarly, in a study of investment banks (Podolny 1993), I argue that the syndicate relations between investment banks are important not only because these syndicate relations imply the transfer of resources between banks but also because these syndicate relations provide the basis for a status ordering that corporate issuers and investors use to make inferences about the quality of the banks. Indeed, an increasingly broad array of work highlights how an actor's pattern of market relations are informational cues on which other market actors rely

34

Pipes and Prisms

to make inferences about the quality of that actor (Han 1994; Stuart, Hoang, and Hybels 1999).

One particularly distinct but nonetheless related piece of research within this second view is Zuckerman's (1999, 2000) research on firm valuation. Zuckerman examines the extent to which a firm's valuation and divestment activities are driven by the cognitive classifications employed by the financial analysts of the major securities firms. A financial analyst at a major securities firm does not track and aim to predict the performance of all firms; rather, he or she focuses on some particular subset of firms. Zuckerman argues that the choice of subset is strongly informed by institutionalized cognitive categories that permeate the profession. A category such as health care might be institutionalized, but a category like entertainment might not. Zuckerman then contends that analysts are less likely to track firms whose portfolio of business lines does not conform neatly to these institutionalized categories. Since a lack of attention from analysts raises a firm's costs of capital, a firm has a strong incentive to divest those businesses that make it difficult for analysts to assign firms to one of the categories. As with these other examples, the pattern of exchange relations in which a firm engages (i.e., its pattern of acquisitions and divestments) is not only relevant because of the resources that flow between firms but also because of how the pattern of those resource flows affect the perceptions of third parties.

Stated generally, this second view posits that a market relation between A and B is not only relevant to market outcomes as a conduit of resources or information passed between A and B. The relation is also relevant because it affects some third actor's perceptions of the relative quality of the product services that A and B offer in the market. Raised to a level of metaphorical abstraction, networks are not only pipes carrying the stuff of the market; they are prisms, splitting out and inducing differentiation among actors on at least one side of a market.

When work emphasizing the perceptual consequences of exchange relations is set alongside the structural hole argument, an interesting tension emerges. Whereas the structural hole logic pushes actors to develop expansive networks, stretching beyond the boundaries of their current set of ties, the work emphasizing the perceptual externalities of tie formation highlights negative consequences that derive from this expansion. For example, elsewhere I have demonstrated the negative perceptual consequences that accrue to an actor who engages in an exchange relation with others that are significantly lower in status (Podolny 1994; Podolny and Phillips 1996). Similarly, Zuckerman (1999, 2000) suggests strong negative consequences of engaging in merger and acquisition (M&A) activity that expands a firm's identity beyond the bounds of the categories employed by the analysts. In the work on status, the bounds on expansion are

35

American Journal of Sociology

vertical in nature; in Zuckerman's work on firm boundaries, the bounds on expansion are horizontal. Yet in both cases, there are clear negative consequences that derive from a lack of bounds on bridges that an actor may build to different segments of the market or economy.

How do we reconcile these principles of network expansion and exclusion? One way is to assert simply that the status orderings and cognitive categories set the bounds within which actors are able to cultivate structural holes. In effect, perceptual orderings set a landscape for the formation of structural holes; the gradient of the landscape rises at the bounds of status positions and cognitive categories, greatly inhibiting the formation of ties to actors that may lie on the other side of these perceptually defined hills. In this view, the pursuit of structural holes and the avoidance of perceptual boundaries are countervailing principles that have roughly equally relevance in all markets.

Another way to reconcile the principles is to argue that the relevance of each principle is contingent on certain features of the market. There is increasing evidence that the rewards of status are contingent on the uncertainty that buyers face (Podolny 1993; Podolny, Stuart, and Hannan 1996, Stuart et al. 1999). While few contingent effects of structural holes have been identified in the market, some work on intraorganizational mobility has sought to identify the contingent effects of structural holes within organizations (e.g., Burt 1992, 1997; Gabbay and Zuckerman 1998; Podolny and Baron 1997). Some of the findings of this research have relevance in the market context. For example, Burt (1997) demonstrates that the more that an actor is surrounded by structurally equivalent others, the less benefit that the actor receives from structural holes in his or her network. Gabbay and Zuckerman (1998) find that structural holes are more beneficial when the overall network of ties is less dense. The market-related implication of both pieces of research is that structural holes are less beneficial in more crowded, interconnected markets.

While some work has identified the contingent effects of status and other work has identified the contingent effects of structural holes, no work has sought to enumerate boundary conditions that determine whether an exclusive or expansionary network is more advantageous. Though a complete enumeration of such boundary conditions is beyond the scope of this article, it is possible to take some initial steps in that direction by focusing on a more specific question: How does market uncertainty affect the relative advantage of a high-status position versus a position characterized by numerous structural holes? This is the central question that is addressed in the theory section of this article. Consideration of this question in turn gives rise to specific hypotheses regarding how a firm's network position affects its relative participation in a given

Pipes and Prisms

market or market segment, where markets and market segments can be characterized in terms of the uncertainty underlying actors' decisions.

THEORY

In order to answer how market uncertainty affects the relative advantages of a high-status network versus a network with considerable structural holes, it is first necessary to adopt the perspective of a focal producer and distinguish two types of market uncertainty. The first type is the uncertainty that the producer has regarding market opportunities and the set of resource allocation decisions that will best enable the producer to realize those opportunities. An automobile producer, for example, faces some uncertainty in deciding which hiring decisions, supplier relations, and production choices will result in a vehicle that is perceived by some set of buyers to provide considerable value. This type of uncertainty can be labeled "egocentric uncertainty" since the focal producer is the actor who is uncertain. The second type is the uncertainty that consumers or possibly other constituencies, such as potential alliance partners, have about the quality of goods or services that the producer presents to them in the market. In the automobile example, potential purchasers of automobiles face considerable uncertainty regarding which vehicle will provide them with the most value. This type of uncertainty can be labeled "altercentric uncertainty" because the producer's alters—the consumers or potential alliance partners—are the actors who are uncertain.[2]

A market or market segment can rate highly on one type of uncertainty without rating highly on the other. For instance, consider the four markets represented in figure 1, beginning with the market for a particular vaccine, such as polio or smallpox, in the upper left-hand quadrant. The most salient source of uncertainty in this market is in that which underlies the development of the vaccine. Once the vaccine is developed and is given regulatory approval, there is little uncertainty on the part of consumers

---

[2] Given a highly reified market in which there are consumers on one side and producers on another side, one could perhaps label egocentric uncertainty as producer uncertainty and altercentric uncertainty as consumer or market uncertainty. However, there are three reasons that I prefer this particular nomenclature. First, in most markets, consumers are not the only actors evaluating producers as a potential exchange partner. In a large number of markets, producers are also evaluated by potential alliance partners or by intermediaries between consumer and producers, such as distributors or retailers. Second, a nomenclature based on the terms ego and alter is quite consistent with the network literature's focus on exchange relations (see Burt 1992). Finally, as I discuss in the conclusion, the arguments developed in this article potentially apply in domains outside the market. As a result, it seems reasonable to use language that is not specific to the market context.

37

American Journal of Sociology

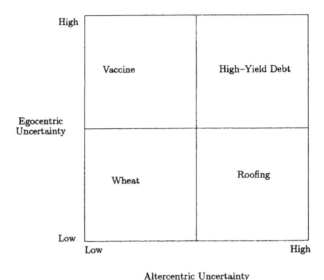

FIG. 1.—Illustrative markets arrayed by altercentric and egocentric uncertainty

as to whether they will benefit from the innovation. Accordingly, a market for a vaccine is a market that rates high on egocentric uncertainty, but low on altercentric uncertainty. Alternatively, consider the market in the lower right-hand corner, a regional market for roofers. "Roofing technology" is relatively well understood, and while roofers may face some uncertainty as to who needs a roof in any particular year, they can be confident that every homeowner will need repair work or a replacement every 20 years or so. By sending out fliers or advertising in the yellow pages, they can be assured of reaching a constituency with a demand for their service. However, because an individual consumer only infrequently enters the market, the consumer is generally unaware of quality-based distinctions among roofers. The consumer may be able to alleviate some of this uncertainty through consultation with others who have recently had roof repairs; however, the need for such consultation is an illustration of the basic point. Only through such search and consultation can the consumer's relatively high level of uncertainty be reduced. Accordingly, this is a market that is comparatively low in terms of egocentric uncertainty, but relatively high in terms of altercentric uncertainty. Many of the standard "asymmetric information" models in economics—like reputation models or signaling models—assume market conditions that are implicitly high on altercentric uncertainty and low on egocentric uncer-

Pipes and Prisms

tainty. However, such asymmetric information is not the only condition that would imply this combination of altercentric and egocentric uncertainty. Another instance of this combination is "conspicuous consumption" markets, in which buyers purchase goods not so much for their inherent quality but in order to demonstrate that they are part of an elite that consumes a particular brand. In this case, the uncertainty of the buyers is less about the inherent quality of the good and more about the trends in tastes and fashion that will lead one brand or style to become identified with elite status.

Finally, there are some markets that may be high or low on both egocentric and altercentric uncertainty. Particularly during the time of its emergence, the market for noninvestment grade, or "junk" debt, rated high on both types (Podolny 1994). Conversely, the market for wheat can be characterized as low on both. The technology and demand for wheat is generally well understood by wheat farmers, and the standardization of the product means that buyers face relatively little uncertainty about the quality of the product.

The distinction between egocentric and altercentric uncertainty is important because it lays a conceptual foundation for an important difference between the pipes and prism perspectives. Whereas the pipes/structural holes perspective has generally concerned itself with the usefulness of networks in reducing egocentric uncertainty, the prismatic/status perspective has focused on how networks reduce altercentric uncertainty.

Structural Holes and Egocentric Uncertainty

Burt (1992) argues that structural holes yield both information benefits and control benefits. For the purposes of this discussion, I set aside consideration of the control benefits because there is as yet no theoretical or empirical basis for asserting that they vary with egocentric or altercentric uncertainty. Focusing on the information benefits, it is clear that a network position with many structural holes is beneficial primarily because it resolves ego's uncertainty about the market decisions that ego needs to make. Again, to return to Granovetter's example of job search, bridging ties are valuable primarily because they increase ego's (i.e., the job searcher's) information about the breadth of opportunities that are presented in the market. If the job searcher had complete information on all job opportunities, then structural holes would be of no value. In the interorganizational context, ties between corporate actors on one side of a market take numerous forms, such as alliances, syndicate relations, interlocking directorate ties, or simply personal relations among the leaders within an industry. The basic claim is that the more structural holes that exist in a firm's network of relations with other firms, the greater

39

American Journal of Sociology

the information that the focal firm has about a wide range of market opportunities and the greater the information about how to fill those opportunities.[3]

This observation that structural holes reduce egocentric uncertainty has important implications for a firm's choice of markets and market segments because related markets or market segments frequently vary in terms of their egocentric uncertainty. For example, consider cultural organizations, such as a film studio, record company, or art gallery. Such cultural organizations must make decisions about the genres or styles that they will produce and/or broker to the broader public. Often these genres can be ranked in terms of the uncertainty around standards of quality (e.g., Greenfeld 1989). Or, consider the primary securities markets. These markets can at least sometimes be distinguished in terms of uncertainty confronting investment banks (e.g., Podolny 1994).

Because structural holes help reduce egocentric uncertainty, firms possessing many structural holes in their network should seek out markets and market segments that are characterized by this type of uncertainty. Conversely, firms possessing few structural holes in their network should avoid such contexts since the lack of structural holes is most disadvantageous when there is much to learn. Or, stated in the form of a hypothesis:

HYPOTHESIS 1.—*The more (fewer) structural holes in a producer's net-*

---

[3] In the earliest formulation of his structural hole argument, Burt (1992) also suggested that structural holes in ego's network might be valuable in establishing a broad, positive reputation. If ego is only connected to a small, tightly bound clique of individuals, then there are at most only a small group of individuals who will be exposed to ego's reputation. Conversely, if ego is connected to a large number of individuals who are themselves disconnected, then ego can more easily establish a broad, positive reputation. If this relationship between structural holes and reputation exists, then the value of structural holes would also be enhanced by altercentric uncertainty. When altercentric uncertainty is high, those with many structural holes in their network would have a reputational advantage over those with few structural holes in their network. However, research by Burt and Knez (1995) finds that a broad, expansive network is not more conducive to a positive reputation. A broad, expansive network reduces the variance in an actor's reputation across a set of alters, but it does not improve the mean reputation across those alters. That is, actors with many structural holes in their network are less likely to have a very negative reputation, but they are also less likely to have a very positive reputation. As the number of structural holes in an actor's network increases, so does the probability that the actor will have a middle-of-the-road reputation. Since structural holes do not have a positive effect on an actor's reputation, the value of structural holes is enhanced only by egocentric uncertainty and not by altercentric uncertainty.

Pipes and Prisms

work, the more that it will sort into (away from) market segments that are high in egocentric uncertainty.[4]

Status and Egocentric Uncertainty

The value of status varies with these two types of uncertainty in a different way. As noted above, previous research has shown that the value of a producer's status in the market hinges on the uncertainty that the producer's constituencies have about the quality of the good or service that the producer and its competitors offer on the market. If consumers face little or no uncertainty about the quality of the goods that confront them, then the value of status as a signal of quality is essentially zero. Accordingly, for status to be of some value, there must be some minimal level of altercentric uncertainty. However, as suggested in figure 1, given some minimal level of altercentric uncertainty in a market, it is possible for egocentric uncertainty to vary somewhat independently of the level of altercentric uncertainty. What is the effect of varying egocentric uncertainty on the value of status?

In order to answer this question, it is helpful to remember that the advantage of status rests at least in part on the fact that potential exchange partners would rather enter into an exchange relation with a high-status rather than a low-status producer if only because high status is a signal of quality (Podolny 1993). To oversimplify somewhat, ceteris paribus, the highest-status producer should essentially have its choice of exchange partner. To be sure, the highest-status producer may have reason to avoid entering into exchange relations with some potential exchange partners. For example, the highest-status producer may wish to avoid exchange relations with a low-status actor either because the producer believes the low-status actor to be of low quality or because the producer is simply concerned that the affiliation with a low-status actor will lower the producer's own status. Yet, what is important for our purposes is that the highest-status producer has greater discretion than other producers in choosing an exchange partner. While the highest-status producer may generally wish to avoid entering an exchange relation with low-status

---

[4] In this hypothesis as well as the one developed in the next section, I use the term "sort" intentionally to reflect the fact that the matching of network to segment can result both from strategic action and constraint. As I discuss further below, it is possible to exploit some features of the data to provide some insight into the mechanism underlying the sorting process in the particular context being analyzed. However, it should be clear that at a general level, sorting could result either from strategic anticipation of the advantages or disadvantages of a particular network configuration or from external environmental pressures.

41

American Journal of Sociology

others, the highest-status producer may also decide on occasion that the potential benefits of such a relation outweigh the potential costs.

The value of such enhanced access is contingent on the extent to which the high-status producer is able to ascertain what combination of exchange relations will actually result in a superior quality product or service. A higher-status producer may have greater access to upstream suppliers, providers of financial capital, human capital, and alliance partners, but unless the producer knows what combination of those relations will result in a higher-quality product, the enhanced access is of little value.

Since a market segment that is high in egocentric uncertainty is by definition one in which the producer is not certain what combination of inputs is likely to result in the most desirable output, status is of little value in such a context. When egocentric uncertainty is low, a producer does not know how it should best use the enhanced access that status provides.

This observation is perhaps best captured by framing the matching process in markets in terms of a queuing imagery. Imagine that producers queue up for whatever exchange opportunities they would like to pursue, and their position in the queue is a function of their desireability as an exchange partner. To the extent that others prefer to enter into an exchange relation with a higher-status producer than a lower-status producer, then ceteris paribus the highest-status producer should be at the front of the queue, the second highest-status producer should be next in line, and so on. However, when egocentric uncertainty is high, the highest-status producer does not know for which exchange opportunities it should queue up. As a result, in the high egocentric uncertainty context, its status is of little value; in contrast, in the low egocentric uncertainty context, there is tremendous benefit in being able to be at the front of the queue. This reasoning gives rise to the following hypothesis:

HYPOTHESIS 2.—*The higher (lower) a producer's status, the more likely it will sort into (away from) market segments that are low in egocentric uncertainty.*

Once again, it is important to reemphasize that hypothesis 2 is premised on the assumption that there is some basic level of altercentric uncertainty ensuring the relevance of status in a market. If consumers and other relevant constituencies have no uncertainty about the quality or value of what is offered by producers in the market, then status is of essentially no value. However, in a market in which consumers face some minimum level of uncertainty as to the quality differences of producers, then producers should attempt to shift to those segments of the market where the distinguishing features of their networks are of the greatest value.

Before moving to the empirical analysis, a simple example should help to illustrate the joint implications of these two hypotheses. Consider a

Pipes and Prisms

college or university department making decisions about the hiring of faculty. The college or university department enters into exchange relations in the academic labor market with the hope of offering some combination of research and teaching excellence that is valued by the various constituencies that provides the larger institution of which it is a part with funds (i.e., incoming students, alumni, grantmaking institutions, etc.).

With some oversimplification, one can think about the department's hiring decisions as taking place in one of two market segments: a junior segment, consisting of newly minted Ph.D.'s, and a senior segment, consisting of those who have held an academic position for a number of years and most likely have tenure at their current institution. Since more information is known about the individuals in the senior segment than in the junior segment, the junior segment is obviously one that is relatively high in egocentric uncertainty, and the senior segment is obviously one that is relatively low.

We can now think about the personal ties of a department into its field as constituting the network of that department. The information provided by these ties can be used in evaluating the candidates in their respective market segments, and the network position of the department within the broader discipline can be characterized in terms of the volume of structural holes and status. A department with a network that is rich in structural holes is one in which the members of that department are connected to a large number of disconnected others within the field. A department with a high-status network is one in which the ties of its faculty members are primarily to (other) high-status departments.

Hypothesis 1 implies that the more structural holes in the department's joint personal network, the better that department will be in making hiring decisions in the junior segment. The personal information yielded by such a network will be helpful in this context in which there is typically little tangible information on which to make a hiring decision. In contrast, a network laden with structural holes will be of comparatively little value in the senior segment since there exists a detailed research and teaching history on which to base evaluations that is independent of the personal information yielded through the network. Hypothesis 2 implies that the greater the status of the department, the more that the department will be at an advantage in bidding for talent in the senior segment. While status may also be of some advantage in the junior segment, the high-status department faces much greater uncertainty as to who it should use its status to attract. The joint implication of the two hypotheses is therefore that departments with networks possessing numerous structural holes will tend to shift more of their hiring to the junior market, and high-status departments will tend to shift more of their hiring to the senior segment.

A reader familiar with the network conceptions of status and structural

43

American Journal of Sociology

holes might reasonably ask whether status and structural holes could have these apparently opposite effects on selection of market segments. It seems reasonable to anticipate a high correlation between an actor's status and the presence of structural holes in the actor's network. An actor with many structural holes in his or her network of exchange relations is, by definition, an actor that is quite prominent in the larger network of relationships—serving as a bridge and boundary spanner across numerous diverse cliques within the larger structure.

However, even if one expects that high-status actors will have a disproportionate number of holes in their network or that Burt's entrepreneurs will generally be high-status actors, the conceptual difference between a high-status network position and a position with many structural holes is sufficient for there to often exist a real trade-off between the formation of ties that will add structural holes to the network and ties that will augment the actor's status. Consider again the example of the high-status academic department. To the extent that the focal department has ties primarily to other high-status departments, the members of the focal department can maintain or perhaps even increase the department's status by building ties to another high-status department that is tied to other departments to whom the focal department is tied. Alternatively, the focal department could attempt to build ties to a middle-status or perhaps lower-status department to which no member of the focal department is currently tied. The first would be the more status-enhancing or status-maintaining option; the second option would be more consistent with maximizing the number of structural holes.

It is important to note that, in asserting that actors possessing networks with considerable structural holes will sort into market segments that are high in egocentric uncertainty and that high-status actors will shift into segments that are low in this type of uncertainty, I do not need to assume that market actors are cognizant of how the features of their network allow them to confront the problems of egocentric uncertainty. The linkage between network pattern and market segment requires only that firms respond to reinforcement of poor or strong performance across various segments. For example, a high-status firm need only be aware that its activities in a high-egocentric uncertainty segment are yielding a comparatively low return and that it therefore should direct resources toward the low-egocentric uncertainty segment. The firm does not need to be aware that its status is of less use in a high-egocentric uncertainty segment.

Notably, if such reinforcement is the primary driver behind the shift in segment, there is value in empirically distinguishing "focused" firms, whose fate is determined primarily by their performance in closely related markets or market segments from diversified firms, whose fate is determined by performance across a broad array of relatively distinct markets.

44

Pipes and Prisms

The business units of diversified firms will be relatively insulated from the costs of a mismatch between network and market segment since the continued viability of the unit depends not simply on its own actions but on the actions of other business units within the firm (Milgrom and Roberts 1992). This observation leads naturally to the empirical analysis.

To test these basic claims regarding the contingent effects of status and structural holes, I focus on the venture capital market, a market in which there is considerable altercentric uncertainty across all market segments and considerable variance in egocentric uncertainty between markets segments. This variation in egocentric uncertainty allows for a test of the basic hypotheses. While the vast majority of "producers" in this market are venture capitalists, there are a significant number of other entities—companies, investment banks, diversified financial firms—that try to decide which entrepreneurial firms they should fund and which they should not. As a consequence, in conducting the analysis, it will be important to attend to whether the hypotheses apply primarily to the venture capital firms or to these more diversified institutions.

THE EMPIRICAL CONTEXT: VENTURE CAPITAL

In venture capital markets, venture capitalists occupy an intermediary or broker role between investors and entrepreneurial companies in need of financial capital.[5] A venture capital firm enacts this brokerage role by first raising money from the investors and placing the raised money into a fund. The fund is organized as a partnership, with the senior members of the venture capital firm serving as general partners and the investors as limited partners. The venture capital firm invests the fund's money in entrepreneurial companies in exchange for an ownership stake. At the end of a fixed period of time, usually 7–10 years, the fund is dissolved. The venture capital firm takes a fraction of the proceeds, usually about 20%, and distributes the remainder to the limited partners in proportion to their original investment in the fund.

Venture capital firms are evaluated on their ability to generate high returns for their limited partners by successfully investing the fund's resources. A venture capital firm may be managing more than one fund at a time, but the returns to the limited partner are based solely on the performance of the fund in which she or he invested. The more successful a fund, that is, the higher the return on investment paid to the limited partners at liquidation, the easier it is for a venture capitalist to raise

---

[5] This section draws heavily on the description of the venture capital industry in Podolny and Feldman (1997).

45

American Journal of Sociology

money for subsequent funds. Moreover, venture capital firms with a history of delivering extraordinary returns on investment to their limited partners not only find it easier to raise funds but also can increase the fraction of the proceeds that they keep for themselves.

For the purpose of this analysis, I regard investors as "consumers" and venture capital firms as "producers." From the perspective of the venture capitalist, the venture capital markets are characterized by both high egocentric uncertainty and high altercentric uncertainty, where investors constitute the critical "alters." Neither the investors nor the venture capitalists are highly certain of the benefit that they will derive from any particular investment. Even though some of the uncertainty associated with investments in this market can be "priced away" and thus transformed into risk, there remains considerable uncertainty in these markets that is difficult if not impossible to price. Venture capital emerged as an institution largely because traditional financing institutions were unwilling to invest in entrepreneurial firms lacking collateral. The origins of venture capital are thus indicative of the generally high level of egocentric and altercentric uncertainty in this particular market. In background interviews for this article, venture capitalists were quite open about the fact that there exist no reliable quantitative formulas for evaluating the risk associated with their investments.

A venture capital firm's quality is determined by its ability to make superior investment decisions in the context of this uncertainty. The venture capital firm must learn to identify characteristics of an entrepreneurial firm that increase the likelihood that the start-up will emerge as a success. In evaluating an entrepreneurial firm's chances for success, the venture capitalist will typically consider numerous factors. For example, the venture capital firm must assess the entrepreneurial firm's technology, the managerial ability of the firm's founders, the dynamics of the market(s) in which the entrepreneurial firm hopes to compete, and the potential responsiveness of the financial markets to a public offering of the entrepreneurial firm's equity.

While it should now be clear that the venture capital markets are characterized by a high level of altercentric and egocentric uncertainty, it is equally important to note that there is variance in the level of egocentric uncertainty across investments. To understand the basis for this variance, it is necessary to review in somewhat more detail how start-ups raise capital from venture capitalists. Entrepreneurial firms generally raise money in "rounds." That is, entrepreneurial companies do not receive a continuous flow of payments from venture capitalists. Rather, they seek financing over some discrete time period. At the end of the time period, the process is then repeated. In some rounds, a firm may require more

Pipes and Prisms

money than any one venture capital firm is willing to invest. In these cases, multiple firms may invest in a given round.

Rounds can be categorized into stages. For the purpose of this analysis, I divide rounds into three stages. Start-ups that do not have a viable product are regarded as being in the first stage. At this stage, the entrepreneurial firm may have little more than an idea or concept for a product. At least some of the financing in this stage is referred to as "seed" or "start-up" financing. Once an entrepreneurial firm establishes the viability of its product, that firm may pursue financing for the commercial manufacturing and sales of its product. I denote such financing as second-stage financing. Second-stage financing takes place after a company has initiated production but typically before the company has become profitable. Finally, the company enters third-stage financing when it is profitable and is pursuing capital for further expansion. As a company progresses through the various stages, its value increases. From the perspective of the venture capital firm, that is, from the perspective of an investor purchasing equity in a company, the highest returns are to be found when a company that was financed in the early stage proves to be successful. Because there is less uncertainty in the later stages, the returns from a successful late-stage investment are smaller.

An entrepreneurial company does not necessarily begin to receive financing in a seed or a start-up round, and a company need not go through all stages of financing before being acquired or going public. For example, because they have high capital needs in the product development stage, biotechnology firms typically go public long before they have a marketable product.

On the other side of the market, a venture capital firm need not invest in a firm in the earliest stage in order to make an investment in a later stage. However, once a firm makes its initial investment, it obviously has privileged access to information about the firm and accordingly the uncertainty around a reinvestment decision is very different than the uncertainty around an initial investment decision. This fact has important implications for the empirical analysis. In examining the investment patterns of venture capital firms, I will only focus on initial investments made in a start-up since the initial investment generally implies a high likelihood that the firm will invest if and when others make subsequent investments in the firm.

More generally, for the purposes of this article, what is important about these stages is that they provide a basis for categorizing investments in terms of the egocentric uncertainty faced by the venture capitalist at the time of the resource allocation decision. The later the stage of the investment at which a venture capitalist first becomes involved with a start-

47

American Journal of Sociology

up, the less uncertainty that the venture capital firm confronts regarding the outcome of an investment decision.

MODEL

To test the hypotheses elaborated above, I propose the following model:

$$\overline{R}_{i,t+1} = \alpha H_{i,t} + \beta S_{i,t} + \sum_{k=1}^{n} \gamma_k + \sigma_i + \tau_t + \epsilon_{i,t+1},$$

where $\overline{R}_{i,t+1}$ denotes the average stage of firm i's initial investments in year $t + 1$, $H_{i,t}$ denotes a measure of the structural holes in firm i's network in year t, $S_{i,t}$ signifies the status of venture capitalist i in year t, $\gamma_1 - \gamma_n$ represents a set of control variables, σ_i indicates a firm-specific effect for venture capital firm i, and τ_t reflects a time-specific effect for year t. The central hypotheses are that $a < 0$ and $\beta > 0$. That is, the more structural holes in a firm's network, the earlier the stage in which the firm first invests in a start-up. Conversely, the higher a firm's status, the later the stage in which the firm invests.

The model can be estimated using conventional ordinary least squares (OLS) techniques for the analysis of panel data. The firm-specific effect σ_i absorbs all of the between-firm variance in the model estimation. As a consequence, the estimates of the other terms are not confounded by any unobserved variables that are time-invariant. Moreover, the absorption of between-firm variance with these firm effects gives us greater confidence that the changes in the values of the independent variables at time t are temporally followed by a change in the outcome measure at time $t + 1$. Absent these firm-specific effects, one might worry that there is some unobserved attribute that varies across firms and leads firms with a disproportionate number of structural holes (at time t) to also have a disproportionate number of early-stage investments (at time $t + 1$). However, because only within-firm variance is used in the estimation of the network effects, we can rule out the confounding effects of any unobserved variables that systematically differ across firms.

DATA AND MEASUREMENT

The data for this examination were obtained from the Securities Data Corporation's (SDC) Venture Economics database. The SDC collects information on numerous financial markets and then sells this information to the various financial communities. The SDC assimilates the information

Pipes and Prisms

in the Venture Economics database from both public and private sources. Venture capitalists use this data to obtain benchmarks for their perform- ance, and entrepreneurs use this data to better understand venture cap- italists' investment preferences.

Though the SDC has information on entrepreneurial start-ups dating back to the early 1970s, data from the 1970s is extremely scant, raising the possibility that much of the data from this time period is missing. Because of concerns about the scantness of the data during the early period, I limit the analysis to the time period between 1981 and 1996, inclusive, though I also use data from 1980 for the purpose of constructing independent variables that rely on a one-year historical "window."

In addition to deciding on an appropriate time period for the analysis, one also needs to decide which actors to include in the population of "producers" making resource allocation decisions. The SDC venture cap- ital database includes information on the investments of venture capital firms as well as information on the investments of diversified financial institutions, nonprofit organizations such as governments and universities, and wealthy individuals. Some of these entities only make episodic in- vestments and accordingly appear in the data only a few times. Since the network and identity of an actor making only infrequent investments is not meaningfully bound to the venture capital community, it seems im- portant to exclude those actors who make only infrequent investments in this market. As a selection rule, I require that an actor make at least five investments in year t (i.e., the lagged year) to be included in the population for that particular year. Such a selection threshold seems conservative; that is, I am including actors for whom venture capital is most likely not a principal form of economic activity. However, it seemed preferable to err on the side of inclusion than exclusion.

Even with this selection rule, one ends up with a number of actors in the analysis that are not venture capital firms. Using a variety of archival sources, I categorized entities investing in start-ups into seven categories: venture capital firms, consumer banks (e.g., First Boston), investment banks (e.g., Goldman Sachs), nonbank financial institutions such as in- surance companies or investment funds (e.g., Fidelity, Allstate Insurance), nonfinancial firms (e.g., Apple Computer, Raytheon Corporation), non- profit institutions such as governmental organizations or universities, and, finally, individual investors. For the sake of exposition, I will refer to all of the actors as venture capitalists insofar as they are all making decisions about which start-ups to fund. However, being a venture capitalist ob- viously does not imply that an actor is a venture capital firm.

Table 1 reports the distribution of actors across the various categories. Despite consulting a number of sources, I could not classify approximately 12% of the investing entities. The first column lists the number of actors

American Journal of Sociology

TABLE 1
CATEGORIES OF FINANCIAL SUPPORTERS OF START-UPS

Financial Supporters	N	$N \times T$	N of Investments
Venture capitalist	248	1,788	9,853
Investment bank	13	126	1,129
Diversified financial	18	101	670
Consumer bank	7	41	204
Governmental organization ...	2	5	26
Nonfinancial firm	28	163	1,607
Individuals	10	57	262
Uncertain	50	204	770
Total N	387	2,485	13,547

in each category. The second column lists the number of actor-years in each category, and the third column lists the number of investments with each category. (The actor-years need not be consecutive, but for the vast majority of actors, they are consecutive.) As noted above, one would expect the theory discussed above to apply most strongly to those entities whose primary form of economic activity is venture capital. The more that a decision-making entity is subject to competitive stimuli from outside of the venture capital markets, the less that the competitive dynamics within this market should lead to the sorting processes specified in the hypotheses. Accordingly, I will conduct the analyses with the population of investing entities defined in three ways: (1) only U.S.-based venture capital firms ($N = 248$), (2) U.S.-based venture capital firms and other U.S.-based financial institutions ($N = 238 + 13 + 18 + 7 = 276$), and (3) all entities making more than five investments in year t ($N = 387$). If reinforcement-based learning is the driving mechanism behind the sorting process, one would expect the strongest effects of network on sorting in the subsample of dedicated venture capital firms, somewhat weaker effects in the sample that includes all financial firms, and the weakest effects in the full population.[6]

Dependent Variable: Average Investment Stage

Measuring the average stage of a venture capitalist's investments is straightforward. The SDC Venture Economics database categorizes investments into the three investment stages discussed above. To reiterate,

---

[6] One might reasonably ask why I do not simply construct interaction effects by type of firm. The reason is that the inclusion of firm-specific effects precludes the estimation of such interaction effects.

Pipes and Prisms

TABLE 2

DISTRIBUTION OF FUNDING BY
STAGE

Stage	N of Investments
1	7,525
2	4,706
3	1,300
Total ...	13,531

NOTE.—Total number of investments
for this table is 16 less than the total number of investments in table 1 due to missing
data on investment stage for 16
investments.

an entrepreneurial firm is considered a first-stage investment when it does
not yet have a viable product. It is identified as a second-stage investment
when it has a viable product but is not yet able to profitably manufacture
and distribute the product. Finally, the entrepreneurial firm is categorized
as a third-stage investment when it is generating a profit. Table 2 reports
the distribution of investments across the stages. As should be clear, there
is a strong decline in the number of stage 3 investments. This implies
that the vast majority of firms either go public or fail before becoming
profitable.

I assign first-stage investments a value of 1, second-stage investments
a value of 2, and third-stage investments a value of 3. I then add up the
values associated with a firm's investments in a given year and divide
by the total number of investments. The range of this variable is accordingly 1–3.

There are two concerns that one can have about this dependent variable. First, because the stages are simply ordinal, there is an obvious
arbitrariness in assuming that the interval distance between the values
for stage 1 and 2 is identical to the interval distance between the values
for stage 2 and stage 3. That is, one could just as easily assign stage 1
investments a value of 0.5 rather than a value of 1, and such a change
would obviously affect the value of the dependent variable and accordingly the point estimates in the analysis. Second, because the dependent
variable is bounded at one and three, heteroscedasticity is a concern. On
account of these two issues, I will conduct the analyses with a second
dependent variable—the proportion of investments that are *not* in stage
1.[7] Because this variable is a proportion, heteroscedasticity is less of a

[7] I used the proportion *not* in stage 1, rather than proportion in stage 1, as the dependent
variable so that the hypothesized coefficients are in the same direction as when the
dependent variable is average investment stage. With both dependent variables, a
higher value means that the firm has a portfolio of investments that is more shifted
to the later rounds.

American Journal of Sociology

concern, and because the proportion implicitly dichotomizes the coding of investments into those that are in stage 1 and those that are not in this stage, interval distance is not a concern. Of course, this outcome measure is not as sensitive to stratification in the later rounds. However, to the extent that the results are robust across both outcome measures, we can be relatively confident in the analyses.

Independent Variables

Structural holes.—To measure the structural holes in a venture capitalist's network, I rely on Burt's (1992) measure of autonomy. Formally, Burt (1992) defines actor i's autonomy as follows:

$$H_i = 1 - \sum_{i'} (p_{ii'} + \sum_q p_{iq} p_{qi'})^2, i \neq i' \neq q,$$

where $p_{ii'}$ denotes the proportion of i's network that is invested in the relation with i', $p_{qi'}$ indicates the proportion of q's network that is invested in its relation with i'.[8] H_i can range from 0 to 1. As i is connected to an infinite number of others who are themselves disconnected, H_i approaches 1. If i is connected to only one other actor, $H_i = 0$. For the purposes of this analysis, I identify a venture capitalist's network from the venture capitalist's joint involvement in financing entrepreneurial start-ups. That is, when venture capitalist i invests in the same start-up as venture capitalist i', I code that joint participation as a tie between i and i'. Therefore, H_i is a positive function of the number of different venture capitalists with which i is involved and the extent to which those other venture capitalists themselves invest in numerous, different start-ups. Conversely, if i makes a small number of investments, and the other venture capitalists in these investments constitute a clique with identical investment patterns, then H_i will be relatively low.

Because I am examining changes in the stage in which venture capital firms invest over time, I allow the venture capitalist's network to vary over time and identify the structural holes in actor i's network at time t as H_{it}. I use a moving "one-year window" to identify ties among venture capitalists. That is, venture capitalist i and venture capitalist i have a tie if they jointly financed a start-up in the same year. Burt's autonomy measure allows for a continuous measure of tie strength. For the purpose of the analysis, I weight a tie between two venture capitalists by the number of deals that they jointly finance.

Status.—To measure the status of the venture capital firms in year t,

[8] Burt uses A_i as the notation to represent the autonomy of actor i; however, I use H_i to make it clear that this is the indicator of the extent of holes in an actor's network.

Pipes and Prisms

I construct a matrix based on the joint involvement of venture capitalists in financing entrepreneurial start-ups. That is, I construct a matrix R_t in which cell $R_{ii't}$ denotes the number of times that venture capitalist i and i' jointly financed a start-up in year t. Given R_t, I then calculate status scores based on Bonacich's (1987) measure:

$$s_t(a,B) = \sum_{\kappa=0}^{\infty} aB^\kappa R_t^{\kappa+1} \mathbf{1}.$$

In this expression, a is an arbitrary scaling coefficient, B is a weighting parameter that can range between zero and the absolute value of the inverse of the value of the maximum eigenvalue of the matrix R_t, $\mathbf{1}$ is a column vector where each element has the value "1," and s_t is also a column vector where element $S_{i,t}$ denotes the status of venture capitalist i. Given this specification, a venture capitalist's status is a function of the number and status of the firms with which it jointly finances start-ups; the status of these financing partners is in turn a function of the number and status of their syndicate partners, and so on. Particularly given that I include the number of deals in which a venture capitalist has participated as a control variable in the analysis (see below), this status measure reflects the extent to which a firm has financing partners who are "players." Status scores are standardized such that the highest status firm in any given year has a status of "1." The B parameter is set equal to the reciprocal of the maximum eigenvalue, though there is an extremely high correlation among status scores for different values of this parameter. The distribution is skewed, with many more low-status firms than high-status firms. This skewed distribution is consistent with the status distributions observed in other industries, such as investment banking (Podolny 1993) and wine (Benjamin and Podolny 1999). Descriptive information reported in table 3 provides more information on the distribution of the status score.

Conversations with those in the industry provide at least anecdotal support for the use of this particular measure. Lower-status venture capitalists express a strong desire to be included on deals financed primarily by higher-status firms, and higher-status venture capitalists occasionally refuse to finance a venture if that venture is receiving financing from a lower-status venture capitalist. In effect, to be high-status is to be an insider; to be a low-status actor is to be an outsider, and joint financing constitutes a symmetrical form of deference in which each venture capitalist acknowledges the standing of the others that are included in the deal.

Control variables.—I include two control variables in the analysis. First, I include the number of investments made by the venture capitalist in

American Journal of Sociology

year *t*. There are several reasons to include this variable as a control variable. First, to the extent that there is evidence consistent with the elaborated hypotheses, I would like to disentangle the effects of status and structural holes from the volume of activity in which a venture capitalist is engaged. It is possible that at least some observed network effects could be the spurious consequence of the volume of activity in which a venture capitalist participates. Second, the number of deals in which an actor is engaged is a measure of an actor's experience, and to the extent that the actor learns from experience, an actor's total amount of investments should reduce the uncertainty that it confronts in making subsequent investment decisions. Since there is more egocentric uncertainty and thus more to learn about investing in the early stages than in the late stages, I would expect that such learning from experience would have a greater effect on a firm's ability to make judicious early-stage investments than judicious late-stage investments. In effect, whereas status should push firms to make more late-stage investments, experience—like structural holes—should push actors to engage in a high proportion of early round investments.

A second control variable is the number of funds from which a venture capital firm makes investments in year *t*. As noted above, a venture capital firm can have more than one fund from which it makes investments at any particular time. There are three reasons for including this control variable. The first two reasons are similar to the reasons for including the lagged number of deals as a control variable. As with number of deals, lagged number of funds is likely to be an indicator of both size and experience. To the extent that the number of funds is an indicator of size, I want to distinguish any potential structural hole and status effects from a possible size effect. To the extent that number of funds is an indicator of experience, number of funds should have a negative effect on the average stage of a venture capital firm's investment. The third reason for including this control variable is to rule out an alternative explanation for the hypothesized effect of status. I have argued that high-status firms should be more likely to make late-stage investments because status is most valuable in those market segments in which a firm knows how to best leverage its status in forming exchange relations. However, if higher-status firms generally have access to more financial resources than lower-status firms, high-status firms may be forced to make more late-stage investments because—with the notable exception of biotechnology start-ups—early-stage investments generally have small capital requirements. For example, the capital requirements for a first-stage software company, which is engaged in the development of a product, are typically much less than the capital requirements of a second- or third-stage software company, which must either put together or at least outsource manufac-

Pipes and Prisms

TABLE 3
DESCRIPTIVE STATISTICS

| | MEAN | | | |
VARIABLE	25th Percentile	Median	75th Percentile	Average Investment
Stage	1.56 (.46)	1.20	1.50	1.90
Structural holes ...	.83 (.17)	.81	.88	.93
Status	.11 (.16)	.01	.04	.13
N of deals	34.79 (39.83)	11	22	43
N of funds	2.24 (1.74)	1	2	3

NOTE.—$N \times T = 2,470$. Total $N \times T$(investor-years) for this table is 15 less than the corresponding total in table 1 due to missing data on average investment stage for 15 investor-years. Numbers in parentheses are SDs.

turing and distribution functions. Put simply, the high-status firms may simply have too much money to invest in early-stage firms. In short, there are at least two reasons to expect that the effect of number of funds will be positive and at least one reason to expect that the effect will be negative. Since I include this variable only as a control, I do not hypothesize as to whether the negative or positive effect should be stronger.

Finally, in addition to these two control variables, I include firm-specific effects, σ_i, and period-specific effects, τ_t. These effects simply control for unobserved heterogeneity that would be common either to all of the observations drawn from a particular firm or all of the observations drawn from a particular year.

RESULTS

Table 3 presents the descriptive statistics for both the dependent and explanatory variables. Table 4 reports the bivariate correlations between the main explanatory variables in the analysis. It is noteworthy that the correlation between structural holes and status is 0.23. While the correlation is statistically significant, it should be clear that the two measures are empirically distinguishable.

Table 5 depicts the regression results when the population includes only identified venture capital firms. Models 1 and 2 respectively exclude either status or structural holes; models 3 and 4 represent the complete model. The difference between models 3 and 4 is in the dependent variable. In model 3, the dependent variable is average investment stage. In model 4, the dependent variable is proportion of investments not in stage 1.

Looking first at the control variables, number of deals done over the last year does not have a significant effect on average round of investment. Number of funds does have a significant negative effect in the first column,

American Journal of Sociology

TABLE 4
CORRELATIONS OF EXPLANATORY VARIABLES

Variables	Status	N	N of Funds
Structural holes ...	.23	.26	.19
Status	...	.71	.55
N of deals	...	...	.75
N of funds	...	...	...

NOTE.—All correlations are statistically significant at the $P < .05$ level.

when status is excluded from the analysis. However, the variable becomes marginally insignificant when status is included.

Turning to the main effects, the results are consistent with the basic hypotheses. The fact that these results are based on within-firm variance is especially noteworthy. Because all cross-sectional variation is removed due to the inclusion of the fixed-effects for each firm, the results show how a firm's investment decisions change as the firm's network changes. As a venture capital firm acquires a "deal-flow" network that is characterized by numerous structural holes, the firm makes a greater proportion of its investments in the earlier stages. As the firm acquires a network that is indicative of greater status, it makes a greater proportion of its investments in the later round. Notably, the results are robust with respect to the different operationalizations of the dependent variable.

However, because both operationalizations of the dependent variable are ratio variables, there is some ambiguity in how to interpret shifts in the variable. A positive shift could imply an increase in the numerator, a decrease in the denominator, or both. For example, simply by looking at the dependent variable, we cannot tell if high-status firms are undertaking less early-stage investments, more late-stage investments, or both. However, the control variable for number of deals helps to resolve this ambiguity. Because number of deals is not significantly related to average investment stage, those firms that add late-stage investments must be reducing their early-stage investments. Similarly, those firms that are increasing their number of early-stage investments are reducing the number of late-stage investments. Thus, the structural hole effect implies a true shift from late stage to early stage, and the status effect implies a true shift from early stage to late stage.[9]

---

[9] To the extent that there is reason to worry about reverse causality, it is possible to provide a check by repeating the analysis, but rearranging the temporal sequencing of the variables. Specifically, one can perform the analysis with average investment stage at time t and the network variables measured at $t + 1$. The coefficients associated with the network variables are insignificant, with both t-ratios less than 1. This check provides some added confidence that the causality flows in the hypothesized direction.

56

Pipes and Prisms

TABLE 5
EFFECT OF EXPLANATORY VARIABLES ON INVESTMENT ROUND DISTRIBUTION WITH
ONLY VENTURE CAPITAL FIRMS INCLUDED IN POPULATION

	MODEL			
VARIABLE	1	2	3	4
Structural holes ...	$-.14^+$	...	$-.14^+$	$-.12^+$
	(0.07)		(0.07)	(.05)
Status	...	$.22^+$	$.22^+$	$.13^+$
		(.10)	(0.11)	(.08)
N of deals	2.9e−4	4.5e−4	3.23e−4	4.9e−4
	(5.8e−4)	(6.5e−4)	(6.5e−4)	(4.9−4)
N of funds	−.02*	−.02	−.02	−.014
	(.01)	(−0.012)	(−0.012)	(.009)

NOTE.—$N = 1,783$. Dependent variable for cols. 1–3 is average investment round. Dependent variable for col. 4 is proportion of investments not in round 1. Indicator variables for years are not reported, but are included in all models. SEs are reported in parentheses.
  $^+$ $P < .05$, one-tailed test.
  $*$ $P < .05$, two-tailed test.

Table 6 reports the results for the full model with average investment stage as the dependent variable. However, the population is defined in three different ways. For the results in column 1, the population is defined only as venture capital firms. Accordingly, the results in this column are identical to the results in column 3 in table 6. Column 2 reports results when the population is defined as all financial institutions making investments in start-ups, and column 3 reports the results when the population is defined to include all actors making investments in start-ups. The effects are weaker—indeed, they are not statistically significant—when the population is defined to include all actors. The results are significant when the population is defined as all financial institutions, but the positive effect of status nonetheless declines. As noted earlier, such a pattern of results is consistent with a reinforcement-based mechanism. Relatively diversified actors, whose financial success is not strongly linked to their financial investments, are not nearly as responsive to the pressures to sort into a market niche in which their network fits the level of egocentric uncertainty.[10]

[10] While the results in table 5 are consistent with the hypotheses, one might still question why high-status venture capitalists move to the later stages. One's argument might go something like the following: while there is less egocentric uncertainty in the later stages than in the earlier stages, there is presumably also less altercentric uncertainty. Accordingly, while the ability of high-status venture capitalists to discriminate good from bad investments goes up in the later stages, the ability of investors to discriminate between good and bad investments presumably also increases. Investors therefore do not need to rely on the signal of status as much when they invest in late-stage investments as when they invest in early-stage investments. Thus, even if a high-status

57

American Journal of Sociology

TABLE 6
EFFECT OF EXPLANATORY VARIABLES ON INVESTMENT ROUND DISTRIBUTION WITH
DIFFERENT POPULATION DEFINITIONS

Variables	Venture Capital Firms (1)	All Financial Firms (2)	All Firms (3)
Structural holes ...	$-.14^+$	$-.14^+$	$-.06$
	(.07)	(.06)	(.06)
Status	$.22^+$	$.15^+$	$.11$
	(.11)	(.09)	(.08)
N of deals	$3.23e-4$	$-1.9e-4$	$-1.5e-4$
	$(6.5e-4)$	$(4.4e.4)$	$(4.7e-4)$
N of funds	$-.02$	$-.016$	$-.015$
	$(-.012)$	$(.01)$	$(.010)$
$N \times T$	1,783	2,046	2,470

$^+ P < .05$, one-tailed test.

CONCLUSION

At a specific level, this article has highlighted how structural holes and status represent assets for addressing different types of market uncertainty. Whereas previous research has highlighted the utility of status for reducing altercentric uncertainty, this article shows that status leads a focal firm to avoid segments that are high in egocentric uncertainty. In direct contrast, a network position with many structural holes leads a firm to select market segments that are characterized by this latter type of uncertainty.

At a broader level, this article has drawn attention to two alternative ways in which network scholars have conceptualized networks in markets. One is as a conduit or pipe for information and resources. The second is as a lens or prism through which the qualities of actors are inferred by potential exchange partners. While this first view has been well-developed

---

venture capitalist has a better understanding as to where to "spend" its status in the later stages, the high-status venture capitalist cannot as easily capture the rents from that status. An increment in status accordingly would seem to have an indeterminate effect on average investment stage. However, such a concern is based on a false premise: as noted above, whereas venture capitalists make investments in individual start-ups, the investors who provide financial capital to the venture capitalists generally do not. Rather, they put their money into a venture fund, and the venture capitalist managing that fund will distribute the financial capital across a range of companies. Because investors typically put their money into this fund before they know which companies at which stages will be financed and because the fund is aggregated across multiple investments, the investor is not nearly as sensitive to shifts in uncertainty across investments as the venture capitalist. So, while egocentric uncertainty—the uncertainty of the venture capitalist—varies considerably from the early stage to the last stage, altercentric uncertainty can generally be regarded as constant. There is then no countervailing uncertainty-induced cause for high-status firms to shift to the early stages.

58

Pipes and Prisms

over the last decade or so, this second view has only recently been a defining orientation for network research.

In my view, a particularly important direction for future research will be to consider the macrolevel implications of these results. For example, if egocentric uncertainty undercuts a high-status firm's ability to sustain its status, one would expect much less stable status orderings in high egocentric uncertainty markets. Another direction for further research would be to apply the conceptual distinctions and test the basic hypotheses in other domains. For example, consider a political arena, like a legislature. Each politician within the legislature has bills that she wishes to pass, but in order to win approval, she must win the support of a majority of her colleagues. Just as one can apply the concepts of egocentric and altercentric uncertainty to the market, so one could apply egocentric and altercentric uncertainty to this domain. For example, in putting forward a bill on some complex topic like health care, the legislator putting forward the bill may face considerable egocentric uncertainty in trying to design a bill that will yield the outcome that she desires. There is also altercentric uncertainty; the colleagues of the legislator proposing the bill may have doubts as to the "quality" of the bill (i.e., whether the bill's espoused potential will be realized). As in the market, these types of uncertainty are analytically distinguishable. For example, the legislator may have no uncertainty about the the actual impact of the bill either because the bill is not very complex or because the legislator has considerable knowledge of the issue area. However, if the legislative arena is characterized by considerable mistrust, there may nonetheless be considerable altercentric uncertainty. As in the market case, one would expect that a network rich in structural holes would be especially helpful in resolving egocentric uncertainty, whereas a high-status network would be especially helpful in overcoming the doubts of colleagues that would arise in a situation of high altercentric uncertainty. In short, regardless of whether one focuses on the macrolevel implications of this research within the market context or considers the applicability of the concepts and arguments in other contexts, the findings of this article lay a foundation for further research.

REFERENCES

Baum, Joel A. C., and Christine Oliver. 1992. "Institutional Embeddedness and the Dynamics of Organizational Populations." *American Sociological Review* 57 (4): 540–59.

Benjamin, Beth A., and Joel M. Podolny. 1999. "Status and Social Order in the California Wine Industry." *Administrative Science Quarterly* 44 (3): 563–89.

Bonacich, Philip. 1987. "Power and Centrality: A Family of Measures." *American Journal of Sociology* 92 (5): 1170–82.

Burt, Ronald S. 1992. *Structural Holes: The Social Structure of Competition.* Cambridge, Mass.: Harvard University Press.

American Journal of Sociology

————. 1997. "The Contingent Effects of Social Capital." *Administrative Science Quarterly* 42: (2) 339–65.

Burt, Ronald S., and Mark Knez. 1995. "Kinds of Third-Oarty Effects on Trust." *Rationality and Society* 7:255–92.

Davis, Gerald F. 1991. "Agents without Principles? The Spread of the Poison Pill through the Intercorporate Network." *Administrative Science Quarterly* 36:583–613.

Dore, Ronald S. 1983. "Goodwill and the Spirit of Market Capitalism." *British Journal of Sociology* 34:459–82.

Fernandez, Roberto, and Nancy Weinberg. 1997. "Sifting and Sorting: Personal Contacts and Hiring in a Retail Bank." *American Sociological Review* 62 (6): 883–902.

Gabbay, Shaul M., and Ezra W. Zuckerman. 1998. "Social Capital and Opportunity in Corporate R & D: The Contingent Effect of Contact Density on Mobility Expectations." *Social Science Research* 27:189–217.

Granovetter, Mark S. 1974. *Getting a Job: A Study of Contacts and Careers.* Cambridge, Mass.: Harvard University Press.

Greenfeld, Liah. 1989. *Different Worlds: A Sociological Study of Taste, Choice, and Success in Art.* New York: Cambridge University Press.

Han, Shin-Kap. 1994. "Mimetic Isomorphism and Its Effect on the Audit Services Market." *Social Forces* 73 (2): 637–63.

Haunschild, Pamela R. 1993. "Interoganization Imitation: The Impact of Interlocks on Corporate Acquisition Activity." *Administrative Science Quarterly* 38:564–92.

Milgrom, Paul R., and John Roberts. 1992. *Economics, Organization, and Management* Englewood Cliffs, N.J.: Prentice Hall.

Podolny, Joel M. 1993. "A Status-Based Model of Market Competition." *American Journal of Sociology* 98:829–72.

————. 1994. "Market Uncertainty and the Social Character of Economic Exchange." *Administrative Science Quarterly* 39 (3): 458–83.

Podolny, Joel M., and James N. Baron. 1997. "Resources and Relationships: Social Networks and Mobility in the Workplace." *American Sociological Review* 62: 673–93.

Podolny, Joel M., and Andrew Feldman. 1997. "Choosing Ties from the Inside of a Prism: Egocentric Uncertainty and Status in the Venture Capital Markets." Working paper. Stanford University, Graduate School of Business:

Podolny Joel M., and Damon J. Phillips. 1996. "The Dynamics of Organizational Status."*Industrial and Corporate Change* 5:453–72.

Podolny, Joel M., Toby E. Stuart, and Michael T. Hannan. 1996. "Networks, Knowledge, and Niches." *American Journal of Sociology* 102:659–89.

Stuart Toby E., H. Hoang, and Ralph Hybels. 1999. "Interorganizational Endorsements and the Performance of Entrepreneurial Ventures." *Administrative Science Quarterly* 44 (2): 315–49.

Uzzi, Brian. 1996. "The Sources and Consequences of Embeddedness for the Economic Performance of Organizations: The Network Effect." *American Sociological Review* 61:674–98.

Zuckerman, Ezra W. 1999. "The Categorical Imperative: Securities Analysts and the Legitimacy Discount." *American Journal of Sociology* 104 (5): 1398–1438.

————. 2000. "Focusing the Corporate Product: Securities Analysts and De-diversification." *Administrative Science Quarterly* 45: 59–619.

D
Power and Control

[13]

Restricted Access in Networks and Models of Power[1]

Peter V. Marsden
University of North Carolina at Chapel Hill

This paper modifies the model of purposive action proposed by Coleman to encompass circumstances in which actors have imperfect access to one another. An access network indicating the available channels for exchange is introduced; it creates discrepancies in the number of alternative exchange relationships available to different actors. The connection of two ideas—Emerson's notion that dependency of one actor on another is inversely related to the first actor's number of alternative exchange relationships and Coleman's conception of dependency in terms of the control of one actor's interests by another—permits the introduction of what is termed "price-making behavior." This allows actors favorably situated in the access network to inflate the exchange value of their resources in transactions with peripheral actors. Effects of the modifications are investigated by means of artificial data; the effects include shifts in the equilibrium distribution of power among actors, in the levels of resource transfer among actors in a given time period, in the outcomes of events, and in the interest satisfaction of actors.

The idea that dependency is the source of an actor's power over others has been a central theme in the study of power over the past two decades. Since the publication of Emerson's (1962) seminal paper on power-dependence relations and Blau's (1964) related discussion of tactics for balancing dependency relations (and hence equalizing power relations), it has become commonplace to assert that power is less an attribute of an actor than of a relationship between actors. Thus, to speak of "the power of actor A" in an undifferentiated manner has been seen as misleading, in that one should specify the actors B, C, and so on that are dependent on A and should also consider the reciprocal dependence of A on these actors in describing power relations.

This relational conception of power has seen application at virtually all levels of analysis. Research at the social psychological level (e.g., Cook and

[1] A previous version of this paper was presented at a conference on Contributions of Networks Analysis to Structural Sociology, sponsored by the Department of Sociology of the State University of New York, Albany, in April 1981. For helpful comments on previous versions of the paper before it was submitted to the *AJS*, I am grateful to Ronald S. Burt, Glenn R. Carroll, James S. Coleman, David Knoke, and Edward O. Laumann. I am also indebted to Peter Kappelhoff and an anonymous referee. Requests for reprints should be sent to Peter V. Marsden, Department of Sociology, University of North Carolina at Chapel Hill, Hamilton Hall 070A, Chapel Hill, North Carolina 27514.

Networks

Emerson 1978) has made use of the power-dependence framework. In the study of complex organizations, substantial literatures consistent with this approach have been produced for the study of both intraorganizational power relations (e.g., Hickson et al. 1971; Pfeffer and Salanick 1974; Kanter 1977; Bacharach and Lawler 1980; Pfeffer 1981) and interorganizational relations (e.g., Jacobs 1974; Mindlin and Aldrich 1975; Cook 1977; Pfeffer and Salanick 1978). The general approach and the notion that dependency begets power, while not always derived from Emerson's work, have stimulated research on communities and decision making (e.g., Marsden and Laumann 1977) as well as theorizing about international relations (e.g., Roxborough 1979).

In this paper I seek to develop a connection between Emerson's power-dependence framework and the model of power and collective decision making developed by Coleman (1973; see also Coleman 1977; Marsden and Laumann 1977; Marsden 1981). I am particularly concerned with integrating into Coleman's model the idea, given by Emerson, that dependency is inversely related to the number of alternative relationships an actor may choose among in attempting to realize interests. I propose that one useful way of doing this is to view differences in alternatives as a result of the different positions of individuals within a network of access relationships. The fact that individuals may differ greatly in their centrality and accessibility to others in such networks is offered as a partial explanation for the fact that centrally positioned actors appear to possess a special prominence in most empirical studies of social networks.

In the following section I shall state some elementary foundations of the Emerson model of power relations and of Coleman's model of purposive action. I then develop a dynamic version of the latter model, as a preliminary to modifying it to take account of restricted access in networks. Effects of introducing the modification are illustrated with the use of artificial data.

POWER-DEPENDENCE RELATIONS AND COLEMAN'S
MODEL OF PURPOSIVE ACTION

The idea proposed by Emerson (1962) is that the power relationship between actors A and B is defined by the relative dependence of the actors on one another. Power is defined as the inverse of dependence, that is,

$$P_{AB} = D_{BA} , \qquad (1)$$

where P_{AB} is the power of actor A over actor B and D_{BA} is the dependency of actor B on actor A. The question of what produces power then becomes a question of what factors create dependence of actor B on actor A. Emerson specifies two such factors: the motivational investment of actor B in outcomes controlled by actor A and the number of alternative sources available

American Journal of Sociology

to B for the outcomes controlled by A. Dependency of B on A is said to be directly related to motivational investment and inversely related to the number of alternative sources of outcomes accessible to B.

The basic concepts in Coleman's model of purposive action are *interest* and *control;* each refers to a relationship between two sets of units of analysis, *actors* and *events*. The magnitude of actor j's interest in event i, x_{ji}, is conceived as the proportion of the variability in actor j's well-being that is related to the outcome of event i; thus

$$\sum_{i=1}^{m} x_{ji} = 1.0 , \tag{2}$$

where m is the number of events. Interests may be signed according to outcome preference, in which case they are symbolized by y_{ji}, but my primary concern here is with their magnitude.

The control of actor j over event i is symbolized by c_{ij}. For divisible events, c_{ij} is conceived to be the proportion of event i controlled by actor j. For indivisible events or collective decisions, c_{ij} is conceived as the probability that actor j alone can determine the outcome of event i; thus

$$\sum_{j=1}^{n} c_{ij} = 1.0 , \tag{3}$$

where n is the number of actors. The concept of control may be decomposed in various ways: see Coleman (1977), Feld (1977), or Marsden and Laumann (1977). Here, a concept of direct control by actors over events is sufficient. For further discussion of the concepts of interest and control, see Coleman (1973, 1977) or Marsden (1979).

Given these elementary concepts, it is possible to capture explicitly the dependence of an actor j on a second actor k, z_{jk}. Coleman defines the dependency of actor j on actor k as the extent to which events in which actor j is interested are controlled by actor k:

$$z_{jk} = \sum_{i=1}^{m} x_{ji} c_{ik} . \tag{4}$$

Note that the definition of dependency in (4) refers to only one aspect of Emerson's definition of dependency, the aspect parallel to "motivational investment of actor j in goals controlled by actor k." The definition in (4) does not refer to the number of alternative sources for those outcomes outside this relationship, a central determinant of dependency for Emerson. Below, I shall introduce modifications of Coleman's model designed to incorporate this additional aspect of dependency.

Given, for the present, the definition of dependency in (4), it becomes possible to describe the power relationship between actors j and k by comparing z_{jk} with z_{kj}. Coleman, in fact, suggests that it is possible to think of the power of an actor in an undifferentiated way (i.e., without referring to the other actors in a power relationship) if we make the assumption that actors may exchange their control over events by trading control over ones in which they have little interest for control over ones in which they are interested. The "terms of trade" between pairs of actors are defined by ratios of dependencies z_{jk}. If z_{jk} exceeds z_{kj}, then k is in a position of power over j and receives a proportion z_{jk} of j's resources in exchange for a proportion z_{kj} of his or her resources; the relative dependencies determine the exchange ratio between the actors.

If exchange is unrestricted and is permitted to continue until an equilibrium point is reached, then the power of actors can be defined as follows:

$$p_j = \sum_{k=1}^{n} p_k z_{kj} , \qquad (5)$$

where p_j is the power of actor j. Actor j's power, then, is defined as the sum of the dependencies of other actors k on j, weighted by their power. Actors with many favorable exchange ratios will have high overall power, while those with unfavorable ratios will have lower power. Power advantages or disadvantages are, of course, ultimately rooted in the patterns of interest and control. Coleman (1973, 1977) gives additional details.

A system of n equations like (5) can be written in matrix form as follows:

$$P = PXC , \qquad (6)$$

where P is a row vector of n elements containing the p_j, X is a matrix of order $n \times m$ containing the interest magnitudes x_{ji}, and C is a matrix of order $m \times n$ containing the proportions of control c_{ij}. The system of equations (6) can be solved as an eigenvalue/eigenvector problem, subject to the constraint

$$\sum_j p_j = 1.0 , \qquad (7)$$

which implies that the power of an actor is the proportion of generalized control over resources into which his or her initial control may be converted (see Marsden and Laumann [1977] for details on the solution).

BASES OF RESTRICTED ACCESS

It is clear that there are important points of convergence between the Coleman model and Emerson's power-dependence scheme. Nonetheless, they differ in a basic way: Emerson's model considers the number of alternative relationships available to an actor as an element defining dependency, while Coleman ignores this factor implicitly by assuming that it is possible for any pair of actors to exchange resources with one another.

There is reason to expect, however, that unrestricted access may not be a

American Journal of Sociology

reasonable assumption with which to work. Many social circumstances may impose limits on the set of other actors a focal actor may contact in efforts to conclude bargains. If access is limited, then the "market" for control specified by Coleman is restricted; no longer is it possible for an actor to conclude all "rational" transactions, because the set of actors that he or she can contact may not always include those with complementary patterns of interest and control. Mechanisms limiting contact of actors with one another create a network of access relationships, and an actor's position in such a network defines a set of potential exchange partners. This set of partners constitutes both the set of "suppliers" from whom needed resources may be obtained and the set of "consumers" to whom resources can be traded.

There are many mechanisms which might generate networks of restricted access. Two mechanisms of particular importance are *ideological similarity* and *embeddedness*. The notion of ideological similarity reflects the fact that actors may be unwilling to form even ephemeral coalitions with others to whom they are ideologically opposed, even if their interest and control patterns suggest that an exchange would be mutually beneficial. This notion is derived from "ideological distance" models of coalition formation (see Bacharach and Lawler 1980), and it suggests that two actors will be accessible to one another for exchange only if their interests are tolerably consistent with one another. Formally, it might be suggested that the members of a pair are accessible to each other only if

$$f\left(\sum_{i=1}^{m} |y_{ji} - y_{ki}|\right) < \alpha, \tag{8}$$

where f is some function of the interest discrepancy and α is some criterion level. Given that on an ideological spectrum "centrist" actors are by definition the most similar to all other actors, such restrictions on exchange might lead to a bias toward middle-of-the-road policy outcomes.[2]

Embeddedness of actors in preexisting social networks (Marsden and Laumann 1977, pp. 235–37) is also an important basis for access limitations. It is axiomatic (Blau 1977) that social relations depend on opportunities for contact. Actors in geographically dispersed systems of action may have limited access to one another because of their positions in communication or transportation networks. Likewise, the formal structure of organizations serves to provide opportunities for contacts between actors, making the use of particular relationships for coalition formation more likely. Generally, preexisting network structures can be expected to create a sort of "social inertia" or "commitment" (Cook and Emerson 1978) analogous to "brand

[2] The use of the term "centrist" here refers to the middle position on the ideological distribution within the system of action under analysis and not to any substantive ideology.

Networks

loyalty" in which a focal actor considers only certain other actors as possible exchange or coalition partners (see, e.g., Laumann and Marsden 1979).

A key to understanding the rationale for such network-induced restrictions on exchange is the fact that mutual trust is a precondition for exchange in political systems. Generating such trust can be extremely problematic (Kanter 1977, chap. 3). In political systems, a formally institutionalized medium of exchange comparable to money has not evolved (see Parsons and Smelser 1956; Parsons 1963a, 1963b; Coleman 1970). Two properties of money as a medium of exchange are of particular importance in this connection. First, its worth is more or less effectively guaranteed by central banking authorities, so that an actor exchanging something of concrete economic value for the symbolic currency of money may be reasonably confident of recovering that economic value in some subsequent transaction, probably with a third actor. Second, money is physically alienable: it is embodied in physical proxies, so that an actor possessing these proxies is capable of exercising direct control over the economic value represented by the money. The actor relinquishing control over this value retains no capacity to use, control, or dispose of it. Together, these two features of money serve to provide trust in the operation of the system of economic exchange; trust in the value and alienability of currency is essential to the ongoing operation of such a system.

The nature of a political exchange process is quite different. Here, the absence of a physical currency and the existence of laws or norms governing the formal alienability of certain resources such as official decision-making authority mean that trust in the operation of political exchange must be guaranteed in a manner distinct from that used in economic exchange. Bargains struck may involve one actor using resources in the interest of another at one time in exchange for a promised reciprocation by the other actor. These bargains are different from economic exchanges because the actor receiving political value does not surrender constitutional control over an equivalent amount of value at the time it is received. Instead, a promise is made concerning the disposition of equivalent value at a future time. But no mechanism such as money is available to insure that the promised future action will indeed be forthcoming. This may inhibit mutually beneficial exchanges, as it would clearly be irrational for an actor to use control in a direction contrary to his interest on an issue (even if that interest were of very low magnitude) if the probability that the transaction partner would later renege on the other end of the bargain were sufficiently high.

In legislative bodies, physical copresence and tradition may give rise to informal norms guaranteeing the value of exchanges made in the absence of currency. When such environing features are absent, as they often are for decision-making processes in communities or organizations, the problem of

American Journal of Sociology

maintaining trust may be especially severe. In such situations actors may attempt to guarantee value in their political exchanges by restricting the set of other actors with whom transactions are made. These restrictions may be based on some shared characteristic such as race, sex, or social status (Kanter 1977, esp. chap. 3) or on preexisting network relationships, most often involving positive affect of some type, in social networks.[3] Features of the social relationship between a pair of actors, then, serve as an imperfect substitute for the assurances provided by money in an economic system.

Several consequences can be expected when exchange is conducted subject to the limitations of a network of restricted access. First, exchange among actors in the Coleman model need not reach the equilibrium point defined by the interactor dependency relations z_{jk}; the formalization of the model must be modified to permit a partial approach to this equilibrium point. Only some of the objectively rational exchanges of control will actually take place, and actors may retain control over more of the resources they initially hold, even when these resources are of little relevance to the events in which they have a strong interest, because they are unable directly to access those interested in such resources.[4]

A second consequence of network restrictions follows as a result of the fact that the variance among actors in the number of contacts in the network defining a restricted market may be considerable. Often, some actors will have more alternative channels through which exchanges can be conducted than others and will thus have relatively many suppliers of control among whom to choose and relatively many potential consumers to whom they can transfer their unwanted resources. Those consumers, however, may be insulated from many other potential sources of supply. When an actor with many contacts exchanges with an actor having few alternatives, the one with many contacts may engage in "price-making" behavior. He may be able to influence the terms of trade between himself and other actors having a more restricted range of potential exchange partners. If this type of behavior occurs, it will force the system of exchange toward an equilibrium different from the one defined previously.

A third possible result of market restrictions concerns the optimality of the decisions or outputs generated by the system of action. The question of system optimality is a difficult one because it may involve explicit and somewhat problematic comparisons of the interest satisfaction of different

[3] Additionally, in circumstances where a focal actor is unable for some reason to conclude an exchange with a direct network contact, he may target an actor structurally equivalent to the direct contact (Burt 1977). Structural equivalence, then, may also serve as a basis for the generation of trust in exchange relationships.

[4] Some transfers of resources between unconnected actors may occur if they are mediated by intervening linkages. The implicit exchange rates involved will be determined, not by the dependencies on one another of the actors involved, but by their exchange rates with the mediating actor(s).

Networks

actors. Nonetheless, if exchanges are conducted on the basis of the self-interest of the parties involved, it is intuitive that restrictions preventing a pair of actors from concluding a mutually advantageous exchange should result in lower interest satisfaction for them than that provided by an unrestricted market. If this is the case, it seems equally clear that virtually any scheme of aggregating individual interest satisfactions into a measure of system performance should indicate that the restricted market performs poorly in comparison with a system involving unrestricted access.

Three steps are involved in the development of a restricted exchange model. I shall first introduce a dynamic version of the Coleman model described above and a procedure for restricting the aggregate rates of resource flow between pairs of actors. I do not, in this step, consider the composition of these resource flows, that is, the specific amount of control over each event involved in these aggregate flows. Results of this modification should indicate reduced overall levels of exchange during a given interval of time and may result in some redistribution of power measured against an open market standard. Second, I make a provision for "price-making" behavior in the market, giving some actors the capacity to affect their terms of exchange with others. Here, a redistribution of power toward those actors well situated in the network of relations defining the restricted market should be observed. Third, I explore the effects of market restrictions on interest satisfaction and system efficacy; this requires that the aggregate flows of generalized resources in the restricted market be decomposed into transfers of control over specific events.

CONSTRAINING RESOURCE FLOWS BETWEEN ACTORS

Above, it was suggested that there are several sorts of social circumstances which might require actors to conclude transactions only by way of certain network relationships. Certain flows of resources will *not* occur, then, despite the presence of a configuration of interest dependency which might encourage them. This fact requires that a distinction be made between two interpretations of the interactor dependency relations z_{jk} given in (4). These are interpretable both as objective interest dependencies and as reflections of the terms of trade between actors; results for the unrestricted exchange model indicate that, at market equilibrium, the balance of trade between a pair of actors will reflect their dependencies on one another. This means that the proportion of a focal actor's generalized resources reaching another actor through the market equals the proportion of the focal actor's interest realization controlled by the other actor (see eq. [5] above).

In a system of exchange in which actors limit their potential exchange partners, however, trade need not reach the equilibrium point defined by interest dependency. It will approach this point only as closely as market restrictions permit. Some actors may be unable to exploit their favorable

American Journal of Sociology

exchange ratios with others, and power in the system may be realigned accordingly.

To facilitate the introduction of access limitations into the formal structure of the exchange model, I will develop a dynamic model of the approach to equilibrium in the system. Once that model has been outlined, it can be modified by introducing constraints on rates of resource flow which limit the approach to the equilibrium defined by interest dependencies.

This development requires a strong and possibly problematic assumption concerning the information available to actors. Though access is not assumed to be perfect, it is assumed that actors know the extent to which their interests depend on resources at all points in the system. It can therefore be suggested that exchange behavior in the restricted market will reflect the interest dependencies, subject to the constraints on resource flow.

Because the proposed modification imposes restrictions on transactions between actors, it is useful to begin by conceiving of the market as one in which the power, or "price," of actors is determined, rather than making the value of events drive the system toward equilibrium as Coleman (1973, 1977) does. The development here of this process for the unrestricted market follows a parallel derivation for the value of events given by Coleman (1973, pp. 131–33). In this process the power of an actor is determined by weighing the supply of generalized resources held by that actor against other actors' demands for those resources. If there is a discrepancy between supply and demand, the actor's power will be adjusted toward a point at which supply and demand are equivalent. The rate of adjustment is specified as a linear function of the discrepancy between supply and demand:

$$\frac{dp_j}{dt} = h(d_j - s_j) \,, \tag{9}$$

where d_j is the demand for resources held by actor j, s_j is the supply of resources held by that actor, and h is an arbitrary positive constant.[5]

The supply of resources or power held by actor j at time t is simply the value of the control j holds, aggregated over all events:

$$s_j = \sum_{i=1}^{m} v_i(t) c_{ij} = p_j(t) \,, \tag{10}$$

where $v_i(t)$ is the relative value or price of control over event i at time t (see Coleman 1973, p. 95). The effective demand for resources held by actor j, aggregated over all actors, is given by:

$$d_j = \sum_{k=1}^{n} p_k(t) \sum_{i=1}^{m} x_{ki} c_{ij} \,. \tag{11}$$

[5] Parameter h governs the speed at which the equilibrium distribution of power is reached (Nielsen and Rosenfeld 1981); this distribution is reached more rapidly for higher values of h. Here the value of h will be fixed arbitrarily at 1.0.

694

Networks

Substitution of (10) and (11) into (9) yields an expanded differential equation for the rate at which an actor's power is adjusted:

$$\frac{dp_j}{dt} = h\left[\sum_{k=1}^{n} p_k(t) \sum_{i=1}^{m} x_{ki}c_{ij} - p_j(t)\right].$$ (12)

The set of n equations like (12) may be written compactly in matrix form as

$$\dot{P}(t) = h^*P(t)(XC - I) = P(t)G,$$ (13)

where $P(t)$ is a vector giving the power of each actor at time t, $\dot{P}(t)$ is a vector giving the derivatives with respect to time for the elements of $P(t)$, I is an identity matrix of order n, and a new matrix G is defined as h^* $(XC - I)$.

The solution of the system of equations (13) is given as (Coleman 1964, p. 178):

$$P(t) = P(0)e^{Gt},$$ (14)

where $P(0)$ is a vector giving the relative power of actors at time 0, before initiation of the exchange process. This means that

$$P(1) = P(0)e^G, \quad P(2) = P(0)e^{2G} = P(1)e^G, \quad \text{etc.}$$ (15)

Since at the equilibrium point $P(t_e + 1) = P(t_e)$, induction gives the result that

$$P(t_e) = P(t_e)e^G,$$ (16)

where $P(t_e)$ is a vector giving the power of actors at the equilibrium point eventually reached by the system. This result is the dynamic equivalent of equation (6), and it can be solved in a manner similar to that used to solve (6).

It is useful at this point to explore equation (12) in greater detail. Expanding and substituting, we obtain[6]

$$\frac{dp_j}{dt} = h\left[p_1(t)\sum_{i=1}^{m} x_{1i}c_{ij} + \ldots + p_n(t)\sum_{i=1}^{m} x_{ni}c_{ij}\right.$$

$$\left. - \left(\sum_{l=1}^{n}\sum_{i=1}^{m} x_{ji}c_{il}\right)p_j(t)\right].$$ (17)

Further manipulation of (17) yields[7]

$$\frac{dp_j}{dt} = h\left[\sum_{\substack{k=1 \\ (k\neq j)}}^{n} p_k(t)\sum_{i=1}^{m} x_{ki}c_{ij} - \left(\sum_{\substack{l=1 \\ (l\neq j)}}^{n}\sum_{i=1}^{m} x_{ji}c_{il}\right)p_j(t)\right]$$ (18)

$$= h\left[\binom{\text{resources transferred}}{\text{to actor } j} - \binom{\text{resources transferred}}{\text{from actor } j}\right].$$

[6] The substitution in the last term of (17) is possible because the sum of the elements in the jth row of the dependency matrix $Z = XC$ equals 1.0; this follows from constraints (2) and (3).

[7] The terms pertaining to actor j in the two summations in eq. (18) are equivalent and thus vanish from the equation.

American Journal of Sociology

This equation gives the change in power for an actor during a time period as a function of his overall balance of resource exchange during that time period. If inflows exceed outflows, the actor's power rises; if outflows exceed inflows, it falls.

This formulation permits an analogy to be drawn between the process of approaching the equilibrium distribution of power among actors in the unrestricted exchange model and a continuous-time Markov chain process with n states. In this analogy the unknown values p_j for the relative amounts of power held by actors correspond to equilibrium state probabilities in the Markov chain, while quantities

$$g_{kj} = \sum_{i=1}^{m} x_{ki} c_{ij} \tag{19}$$

correspond to continuous-time transition rates between states in the Markov chain. The g_{kj} are off-diagonal elements of the matrix G defined in connection with equation (13) above, taking the constant h to be 1 (see n. 5).

This analogy between the two types of processes is useful because it suggests a strategy by which restrictions on resource transfer may be introduced into the model. Thus far, all the results given in this section are merely a dynamic restatement of the equilibrium results given earlier. Coleman (1964, pp. 177–81) suggests a method by which a priori knowledge that direct movements between certain pairs of states do not occur may be incorporated within the continuous-time Markov chain model. A similar approach can be used for imposing restrictions on exchange within the model for the power of actors.

The analogy between the two types of processes breaks down, however, when the differing purposes for the imposition of restrictions are considered. In the Markov chain model with restricted transition rates, the imposition of restrictions constitutes an attempt to obtain a parsimonious description of a complex pattern of observed movements between states (see Coleman 1964, pp. 459–65). If the overall pattern of movement between states predicted by the restricted model does not correspond well with the observed pattern of movement, a given restricted model is discarded in favor of a more complicated explanation.

The analog in the exchange model of the observed pattern of movement between states is the pattern of interactor interest dependency. This pattern of dependency is also the pattern of aggregate resource transfer when all trading routes are available, and it constitutes a "target" which will be approached by exchanges in the restricted market. Typically, however, the imposition of restrictions on exchange will result in a pattern of resource transfer that is different from the pattern of interest dependency. Such a discrepancy, though, does not provide cause for discarding the restricted market model; in fact, it is precisely the discrepancy between dependency and exchange, and the effect of this discrepancy on the distribution of power among actors and on other results of the model, that is of concern here.

When there are restrictions on resource exchange, rates of resource transfer g_{kj} can be estimated by defining an $n \times n$ binary symmetric matrix, as follows:

$$a_{ij} = a_{ji} = \begin{cases} 1 \text{ if } i \neq j \text{ and transactions are possible} \\ \quad \text{between actors } i \text{ and } j; \\ \\ 0 \text{ if } i \neq j \text{ and transactions are not possible} \\ \quad \text{between actors } i \text{ and } j; \\ \\ 1 \text{ if } i = j. \end{cases} \quad (20)$$

Matrix A defines the alternatives available to actors in their efforts to realize interests. The only restriction placed on A is a condition that A^{n-1} contain all positive entries; if this condition does not hold, then there exist within the system at least two disjoint subsets of actors who can exchange only with other members of their subset (Harary, Norman, and Cartwright 1965, p. 68). It is clearly impossible to maintain an exchange market involving both sets of actors if it is impossible for them to access one another at all. The rates of resource transfer are then defined as follows:

$$g_{kj} = \begin{cases} a_{kj} \sum_{i=1}^{m} x_{ki} c_{ij} & \text{if} \quad k \neq j; \quad \text{and} \\ \\ -\sum_{\substack{j=1 \\ (k \neq j)}}^{n} g_{kj} & \text{if} \quad k = j. \end{cases} \quad (21)$$

These rates of resource flow in matrix G are of little intrinsic concern. They are important, though, because they permit the estimation of the aggregate levels of resource transfer that occur during some time period. The resource movements between actors during t units of time are obtained by computing

$$e^{Gt} = \sum_{l=0}^{\infty} \frac{1}{l!} G^l t^l , \quad (22)$$

where higher terms in the infinite series are neglected when they contribute increments predefined as negligible.

To obtain the levels of exchange occurring in the restricted market in a single time unit via process (9), we can use the special case of (22) in which $t = 1$. Substituting this result in turn into equation (16) provides a measure

American Journal of Sociology

of the equilibrium power of actors in the presence of restrictions on exchange.[8]

RESTRICTED ACCESS: EFFECTS ON POWER AND EXCHANGE

To illustrate the effects of the modifications introduced, two hypothetical action systems will be analyzed. Table 1 displays basic data on these systems. The first system, for which the interest matrix is shown in panel A of table 1, involves 10 actors and two events, on which there is substantial conflict of interest, as indicated by the signs in the interest distribution. The control structure (not shown) is a very simple one, in which each actor possesses an equal proportion of control over each of the events; this means that, in the unrestricted model, the actors necessarily have equal power, as panel C shows.

The interest distribution for the second system to be analyzed is shown in panel B of table 1. This system involves five actors and five events. Again, the actors have conflicting preferences on the events; but in this case, the control structure is one in which each actor holds total control over one of the events, and none over the other events. Because actors have comparatively little interest in the events they control, this distribution of control is far from the equilibrium distribution. Panel C shows the equilibrium distribution of power in this system.

To see the way in which restricted access alters the operation of these action systems, assume that, for whatever reasons, exchanges in the two hypothetical systems can occur only through the linkages between actors shown in the diagrams in figure 1. The network of restrictions for system 1 exhibits a "star" pattern centered on actor 10, while that for system 2 forms a "chain" pattern.

The network of restrictions shown in figure 1*A*, for system 1, is of some interest because it has been studied in experimental exchange studies (see Cook and Emerson 1978; Cook 1982; Cook et al. 1980). Results from these studies suggest that this network will transfer power toward actors 7, 8, and 9, who occupy a position of intermediate centrality in the network. This is in contrast to the predictions which might be made on the basis of network concepts of centrality (e.g., Freeman 1977), which would imply that actor 10 would be the most powerful actor.

In contrast to both of these views, results presented in table 2 for the modified model from the preceding section indicate *no* redistribution of equilibrium power when restrictions on exchange are imposed for system 1.

---

[8] The choice of the value of t to substitute into eq. (22) will affect the estimated levels of resource transfer, higher values of t resulting in greater movements of resources. The choice of t does not affect estimates of equilibrium actor power in the restricted system, however. This is the case because all nonzero powers of e^{G} have the same eigenvectors (see, e.g., Van de Geer 1971, p. 69).

698

TABLE 1
DATA ON HYPOTHETICAL ACTION SYSTEMS
A. SYSTEM 1: INTEREST DISTRIBUTION*

EVENT	Actor									
	1	2	3	4	5	6	7	8	9	10
1	.400	.400	.400	.400	.400	.400	−.700	−.700	−.700	.500
2	−.600	−.600	−.600	−.600	−.600	−.600	.300	.300	.300	.500

B. SYSTEM 2: INTEREST DISTRIBUTION†

EVENT	Actor				
	1	2	3	4	5
1	.050	−.250	−.150	.350	.200
2	.350	.050	.250	.200	.250
3	−.250	−.200	.050	.250	.350
4	−.200	−.350	.200	.050	.150
5	−.150	−.150	.350	.150	.050

C. EQUILIBRIUM DISTRIBUTIONS OF POWER, UNRESTRICTED MODEL

SYSTEM	Actor									
	1	2	3	4	5	6	7	8	9	10
1	.100	.100	.100	.100	.100	.100	.100	.100	.100	.100
2	.199	.217	.214	.195	.175	...	...	...	...	...

* For system 1, the control structure is such that each actor has equal control over each event, i.e., $c_{ij} = 0.100$ ($i = 1, 2; j = 1, \ldots, 10$).

† For system 2, the control structure is such that each actor has total control over a single event, i.e., $c_{ij} = 1.000$ if $i = j$ and $c_{ij} = 0.000$ if $i \neq j$.

American Journal of Sociology

A. Pattern of Available Alternatives, Hypothetical Action System 1

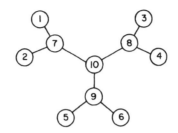

B. Pattern of Available Alternatives, Hypothetical Action System 2

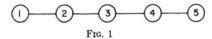

FIG. 1

In panel A, it can be seen that all actors in system 1 have equal power, as they did when there were no limits on access. In contrast, for system 2, the imposition of restrictions does redistribute equilibrium power: actor 2 gains substantially, while the remaining actors (particularly actor 4) lose power.

To understand these results, it is useful to inspect panels B and C of table 2. These report the transfers of generalized resources that take place in the first time unit between pairs of actors, for the models without and with restrictions on access. Contrasting the patterns of resource movement shows that the unrestricted systems move toward equilibrium more rapidly than the restricted ones. For instance, in system 1 (panel B), each actor retains only .431 of his or her initial resources after one time unit in the absence of restrictions; but when the "star" restrictions are present, all actors retain .752 or more of their initial resources after a single time unit. Similar results are exhibited for system 2 in panel C of table 2; here, it is notable that virtually no indirect transfers of resources occur between actors at opposite ends of the chain of access restrictions during the first time unit.

These differences in resource transfer mask an underlying similarity. The exchange ratios linking pairs of actors having access to one another are identical to the ratios of interest dependencies (see eq. [4]) that define the relative power of actors in the unrestricted market. Thus, for system 1, all actors exchange on equal terms in the unrestricted market, and all *connected* pairs of actors exchange on equal terms in the restricted market. In system 2, the ratios of resource transfer z_{jk}/z_{kj} that describe unrestricted power relations are matched by ratios of rates g_{jk}/g_{kj} in the presence of restrictions

TABLE 2

POWER AND RESOURCE MOVEMENT WITH EXCHANGE CONSTRAINED BY NETWORKS IN FIGURE 1

A. POWER OF ACTORS

SYSTEM	\multicolumn{10}{c}{ACTOR}									
	1	2	3	4	5	6	7	8	9	10
1	.100	.100	.100	.100	.100	.100	.100	.100	.100	.100
2	.187	.262	.211	.170	.171	...	...	...	...	...

B. RESOURCE MOVEMENT IN ONE UNIT OF TIME—SYSTEM 1

ACTOR	\multicolumn{10}{c}{ACTOR}									
	1	2	3	4	5	6	7	8	9	10
Unrestricted transfers:										
1	.431	.063	.063	.063	.063	.063	.063	.063	.063	.063
2	.063	.431	.063	.063	.063	.063	.063	.063	.063	.063
3	.063	.063	.431	.063	.063	.063	.063	.063	.063	.063
4	.063	.063	.063	.431	.063	.063	.063	.063	.063	.063
5	.063	.063	.063	.063	.431	.063	.063	.063	.063	.063
6	.063	.063	.063	.063	.063	.431	.063	.063	.063	.063
7	.063	.063	.063	.063	.063	.063	.431	.063	.063	.063
8	.063	.063	.063	.063	.063	.063	.063	.431	.063	.063
9	.063	.063	.063	.063	.063	.063	.063	.063	.431	.063
10	.063	.063	.063	.063	.063	.063	.063	.063	.063	.431
Restricted transfers:										
1	.909	.004	.000	.000	.000	.000	.082	.000	.000	.004
2	.004	.909	.000	.000	.000	.000	.082	.000	.000	.004
3	.000	.000	.909	.004	.000	.000	.000	.082	.000	.004
4	.000	.000	.004	.909	.000	.000	.000	.082	.000	.004
5	.000	.000	.000	.000	.909	.004	.000	.000	.082	.004
6	.000	.000	.000	.000	.004	.909	.000	.000	.082	.004
7	.082	.082	.000	.000	.000	.000	.752	.004	.000	.075
8	.000	.000	.082	.082	.000	.000	.004	.752	.004	.075
9	.000	.000	.000	.000	.082	.082	.000	.004	.752	.075
10	.004	.004	.004	.004	.004	.004	.075	.075	.075	.752

American Journal of Sociology

TABLE 2 (*Continued*)

C. RESOURCE MOVEMENT IN ONE UNIT OF TIME—SYSTEM 2

ACTOR	ACTOR				
	1	2	3	4	5
Unrestricted transfers:					
1...........	.444	.179	.146	.128	.103
2...........	.146	.449	.131	.172	.102
3...........	.111	.147	.451	.124	.167
4...........	.174	.135	.147	.441	.103
5...........	.124	.148	.178	.110	.439
Restricted transfers:					
1...........	.735	.240	.023	.002	.000
2...........	.171	.683	.132	.013	.001
3...........	.021	.165	.670	.133	.011
4...........	.002	.021	.167	.695	.116
5...........	.000	.001	.014	.116	.870

on resource transfer. This similarity is not difficult to understand, when it is noted that the estimates of the rates g_{jk} are based on the dependencies z_{jk} (see eq. [21]); connected pairs of actors in the restricted market exchange on the basis of their relative self-interest, as defined by their dependencies on one another.

The reason power is redistributed in system 2 but not in system 1, then, is not to be found in the way the modified model affects relations between pairs of actors having direct access to one another. Redistribution of power is instead a result of what happens to resource exchanges between pairs of actors without direct connections. These are determined, not by the self-interest of the two actors involved, but by the chain(s) of transactions mediated by the self-interest of intervening actors. In system 1, all indirect exchanges in the presence of restrictions involve equal terms, as they do in the unrestricted version of the model. This, together with the equal exchange ratios involving connected pairs of actors, means that there is no shift in the distribution of equilibrium power.

For system 2, the implicit indirect exchange ratios in the restricted market are not the same as the corresponding ratios in the absence of restrictions. For instance, in the open market, actor 2 is disadvantaged in exchanges with actor 4: the dependency ratio is $z_{24}/z_{42} = 0.35/0.20 = 1.75$. In the presence of restrictions, though, actor 4 cannot exploit this favorable situation, for lack of direct access to actor 2. Exchanges between these two actors are mediated by actor 3 and are governed by the reciprocal dependencies of these actors with actor 3. Thus, in the presence of restrictions, panel C of table 2 shows that the implicitly established exchange ratio between actors 2 and 4 has changed to $0.013/0.021 = 0.62$, a situation far more favorable to actor 2 than the open market is. Thus, the bias in implicit exchange ratios introduced by restrictions in system 2 (and the lack of such bias in system 1) explains the way in which the modifications introduced above affect the distribution of equilibrium power among actors.

The possible shifts in the distribution of power on the basis of implicit exchange ratios may be interesting, but they are somewhat idiosyncratic. The modifications above continue to conceive of dependency only in terms of interest and control; no explicit account is taken of the fact that some actors may have more alternative exchange relationships than others, and no purposive action is taken by actors in response to discrepancies in alternatives. I now introduce a further modification which permits such action.

PRICE-MAKING BEHAVIOR

As the preceding illustrations show, imposition of restrictions on resource flow does not influence the relative power of actors in a connected dyad, as far as their transactions with one another are concerned. That is, the procedure introduced for estimating resource flow and power in the presence of a network of access restrictions (see above, eqq. [20]–[22]) does not change the exchange ratios

$$R_{jl} = \frac{g_{lj}}{g_{jl}} \tag{23}$$

between actors having direct access to one another from the values these ratios assume in the absence of restrictions.

The exchange ratios in connected dyads remain constant because actors in the restricted market are treated as "price takers," accepting the terms of trade dictated by interest dependency and exchanging accordingly. Stratification in the relative numbers of alternative exchange relationships for actors, however, introduces a new feature to be taken into account. Some actors may have relatively many sources of supply for needed control and relatively many potential consumers for resources they wish to trade. Other actors may be forced to use one of a very small number of linkages if they wish to be involved in any exchange at all.

When an actor with many linkages in the restricted market confronts one with relatively few, it is plausible to suggest that the former actor will no longer have to be a price taker; instead, he may be able to alter the terms of exchange in the dyad, causing the other's dependency—and resource flow—to rise as a result of the discrepancy in alternatives. The well-connected actor in the presence of restrictions, then, will possess an element of what Lipsey and Steiner (1969, p. 297) term "monopoly power." They state that "monopoly power exists when a firm is at least to some extent insulated from loss of customers to other sellers." Note that this definition does not require that an actor possessing monopoly power be the *sole*

American Journal of Sociology

supplier of a commodity or resource; it involves only the condition that the range of choice for some actors be relatively restricted (see Burt's [1980] discussion of autonomy). The latter actors can be forced to exchange resources at a price less than their open market value because of their lack of alternatives.

What this suggests is that an actor's position in the network A defined in equation (20) may influence the value that resources possessed by that actor can obtain. The position is not valuable in and of itself; it signifies no direct control over events. By virtue of occupancy of a dominant position in the access network, however, an actor may inflate the price of his resources as against those held by others. In this way, the network distorts the operation of the resource-pricing mechanism of the market, imputing a higher exchange value to resources controlled by well-connected actors than they would draw under conditions of unrestricted access.

To incorporate price-making behavior within the modified exchange model, it is necessary to assume a specific mathematical form showing how discrepancies in alternatives transform the exchange ratios in (23). Some analysis by Coleman (1981) suggests that this form should exhibit several properties. First, it should be such that there are definite upper and lower limits to the modified exchange rate; beyond these limits, one party would withdraw from the exchange relation. Second, the exchange ratio in (23) should become larger—and thus more favorable to actor j—as the ratio of alternatives a_{j+}/a_{l+} increases, where a_{j+} is the total number of alternatives available to actor j. Third, the limits between which the modified rate varies should become narrower as the minimum number of alternatives available to either party in the relationship rises; if an actor has no alternative to a particular relationship, the amount of distortion of the open market exchange rate he will be forced to accept will be larger than if one or more alternative relationships are available. When the absolute number of alternatives for either party in the exchange is reasonably large, the limits should converge upon the open-market exchange ratio, and the ratio of alternatives a_{j+}/a_{l+} should have little effect on the terms of trade.

A function that appears to have all the properties required is the function

$$F_{jl} = e^{-(2\gamma Q)^{-1} + [\gamma Q(1 + e^{-\beta \log \omega})]^{-1}}, \tag{24}$$

where e is the base of the natural logarithm, Q is the minimum of a_{j+} and a_{l+}, ω is the ratio a_{j+}/a_{l+}, γ is a parameter (assumed to be greater than zero) governing the speed at which limits on the alteration of the exchange rate shrink with increases in the minimum number of alternatives Q, and β is a parameter (also assumed to be positive) governing the speed at which these limits are approached with increases or decreases in the ratio of alternatives ω. As the ratio of alternatives ω becomes large, F_{jl} tends to $e^{(2\gamma Q)^{-1}}$; when $\omega = 1$, F_{jl} is also 1, indicating no alteration in terms of exchange; and when ω approaches zero, F_{jl} approaches the lower limit of $e^{-(2\gamma Q)^{-1}}$. Clearly the limits $e^{(2\gamma Q)^{-1}}$ and $e^{-(2\gamma Q)^{-1}}$ approach one another as γQ increases.

With this form for the way in which discrepancies in alternatives affect the open market exchange ratio involving a pair of actors, the revised ratio can be defined as

$$R_{jl}F_{jl} . \qquad (25)$$

This modified exchange ratio varies between limits of $R_{jl}e^{(2\gamma Q)^{-1}}$ and $R_{jl}e^{-(2\gamma Q)^{-1}}$.

The adjustment (25) in the exchange ratio between j and l must next be translated into an adjustment of the rates of resource flow themselves. This can be accomplished by using the following:

$$
*_{lj} = \begin{cases} g_{lj}\sqrt{F_{jl}} & \text{if} \quad j \neq l \\ -\sum_{\substack{k=1 \\ (k \neq l)}}^{n} g^{*}_{lk} & \text{if} \quad j = l . \end{cases} \qquad (26)
$$

The matrix G^{*} of these revised rates of resource flow may then be substituted into equation (22) to give the interactor balance of trade during some time period. The equilibrium power of actors in the restricted market with price-making behavior will be given by equation (16).

It may be objected that the adjusted terms of trade specified by equations (25) and (26) are inequitable and will not be accepted by an actor in an unfavorable market position. Assessing equity in exchange is relative, of course, to some subjectively determined standard; an "operational" standard of equity is given by the ratio of resource flows in equation (23), which is based on exogenously determined distributions of interest and control. By this standard, the adjusted exchange ratio of equation (25) is obviously inequitable.

Disadvantaged actors will not necessarily reject the inequitable terms of trade, however; in fact, Emerson's use of discrepancies in alternatives as components of dependency implies that actors do accept such terms. Moreover, Burgess and Nielson (1974) present experimental evidence indicating that actors will engage in inequitable exchanges rather than withhold their resources *when they lack valuable alternatives to an exchange relation.*[9] There are, of course, likely to be limits on the degree of inequity an actor will accept ˈrather than withdraw from the relationship (cf. Bacharach and

[9] Burgess and Nielson (1974) note that another determinant of what they term "inequity" in exchange is the relative value of the resources being exchanged. This evidently equates equity with equality (see Bonacich and Light 1978); presumably, though, the value of a resource is conditioned on the distributions of control and interest. Thus, discrepancies in resource flow between actors that are traceable to disparities in resource value are presumed to be part of an operational definition of equity as the ratio of interest dependencies (see eq. [23]).

American Journal of Sociology

Lawler 1980), and the function (eq. [24]) used to modify the exchange ratios and rates of resource flow includes such limits.

Obviously, the primary effect of permitting well-connected actors to influence their terms of exchange with poorly connected actors should be an increased flow of power toward the well-connected actors. To see this, let us consider the results shown in table 3 for the two hypothetical systems of action.[10]

Panel A of table 3 shows that centrally positioned actors do indeed gain power when price-making behavior is permitted. Actors 7–10 in system 1 all gain power, as do actors 2–4 in system 2. Note, for system 2, that part of the shift in the distribution of power comes by virtue of changes in implicit exchange ratios involving indirectly connected actors (compare panel A of table 2 with panel C of table 1), while the remainder of the shift occurs because actors 2 and 4 (and, indirectly, actor 3) are able to capitalize on their superior numbers of alternatives in exchanges with actors 1 and 5.[11]

The results for system 1 and the "star" pattern of access restrictions do not agree completely with the experimental results reported by Cook et al. (1980); results here indicate that actors 7–10 have equal power, while results of the experiments conducted by Cook et al. suggest that actors 7–9 (of intermediate centrality) have more power than the central actor in the star, actor 10. The special control structure for system 1 (see table 1, asterisked n.) permits us to analyze this system in more detail. Since all actors have equal control over each event here, it is reasonable to assume that the initial distribution of power, $P(0)$, is also equal across actors. Equation (14) can then be used to trace the way in which this initial distribution changes as the system moves toward equilibrium.

Relevant results appear in panel B of table 3. They show that, in the initial time periods, actors 7–9 gain power rapidly, because they are able to exploit their favorable positions in the access network when dealing with the peripheral actors 1–6. On the other hand, the power of actor 10, who exchanges on equal terms with the intermediately central actors 7–9, rises only slightly. The gap between actor 10 and the intermediately central actors 7–9 is maximal at times 3 and 4 and shrinks thereafter, vanishing at equilibrium. This happens because dependency relations between actor 10 and actors 7–9 are balanced. This balance eventually transfers some of the advantages obtained by actors 7–9 in their relations with actors 1–6 to actor 10.

The point on which the results reported here differ from those of Cook

[10] In obtaining the results shown in table 3, I set parameters γ and β in eq. (24) at the values 0.5 and 2.0, respectively.

[11] Results (not shown) for the model with price-making behavior also illustrate reduced levels of exchange in a given time period, in comparison with the unrestricted exchange model (see panels B and C of table 2).

TABLE 3
POWER DISTRIBUTIONS FOR CONSTRAINED EXCHANGES WITH PRICE-MAKING BEHAVIOR

A. EQUILIBRIUM POWER OF ACTORS

SYSTEM	Actor									
	1	2	3	4	5	6	7	8	9	10
1	.067	.067	.067	.067	.067	.067	.149	.149	.149	.149
2	.122	.313	.251	.202	.112	...	...	...	...	...

B. POWER OF ACTORS AT SELECTED TIME POINTS: SYSTEM 1

TIME	Actor									
	1	2	3	4	5	6	7	8	9	10
0	.100	.100	.100	.100	.100	.100	.100	.100	.100	.100
1	.093	.093	.093	.093	.093	.093	.114	.114	.114	.102
2	.087	.087	.087	.087	.087	.087	.123	.123	.123	.106
3	.083	.083	.083	.083	.083	.083	.130	.130	.130	.111
4	.080	.080	.080	.080	.080	.080	.134	.134	.134	.117
5	.078	.078	.078	.078	.078	.078	.138	.138	.138	.122
10	.071	.071	.071	.071	.071	.071	.146	.146	.146	.138
∞	.067	.067	.067	.067	.067	.067	.149	.149	.149	.149

American Journal of Sociology

et al. (1980) concerns the power of the most central actor, actor 10. In these results, the power of actor 10 rises toward the power of the intermediately central actors 7–9, while the experimental results of Cook et al. indicate that the power of actor 10 at equilibrium declines toward that of the peripheral actors 1–6. Both sets of results are contrary to what would be expected if the mechanisms transforming network position into power advantages were based on "betweenness" (Freeman 1977). The results suggest that the feature of a network position creating gains in power is not overall communication centrality but a configuration of relations permitting an actor to exploit relations with exchange partners, particularly those with direct control over events. It is possible that the reason for the difference between the results here and those of the experiments of Cook et al. lies in the fact that the experiments assume "negatively connected" exchange relations, in which an actor's decision to exchange with one partner precludes exchange with other partners. No such contingency between different exchange relations is assumed here, and the presence of such a contingency may alter the balance in the dependency relations between actors 7–9 and actor 10. Cook (1982) indicates that new experiments that do not assume negatively connected relations are under way.

EVENT OUTCOMES AND SYSTEM PERFORMANCE

To move beyond an illustration of the way in which restricted access affects the distribution of power to consideration of the way collective decisions and interest satisfaction are altered, it is necessary to know the composition of the generalized resources transferred between actors. In particular, the way in which control is distributed when exchange reaches the equilibrium point is of concern. Coleman (1973) shows that actor j's control over event i at the equilibrium point for the unrestricted exchange model, c^*_{ij}, is given by the equation

$$c^*_{ij} = \frac{x_{ji}}{v} p_j. \tag{27}$$

This equation can also be used for the model adding restrictions on access developed here.[12]

---

[12] It might seem that eq. (27) would be inapplicable to the model with access restrictions, in that the scope of the relevant market, or "opportunity structure" for exchange (Laumann, Galaskiewicz, and Marsden 1978, p. 471), differs from the viewpoint of each actor. For instance, in hypothetical action system 2, actor 4, with a substantial interest in event 1, has no direct access to control over that event (all of which is initially held by actor 1) when exchange commences. As long as the condition on A^{n-1} stated in connection with eq. (20) holds, however, actors will have indirect access to all control at the equilibrium point. The problem of allocating final control over events at nonequilibrium points is both difficult and fascinating. Some informal exploration of this problem for the model with restrictions on access suggests that network proximity to relevant

With (27), the outcomes of events are defined under Coleman's probabilistic rule. This rule balances against one another applications of control
by actors toward the two outcomes of each event, yielding the probability
of a positive outcome for event i, r_i:

$$r_i = 0.5 + 0.5 \sum_{j=1}^{n} c^*_{ij} \ \text{sign} \ (y_{ji}) = 0.5 + 0.5 \sum_{j=1}^{n} \frac{y_{ji}}{v_i} p_j \ . \qquad (28)$$

Also of concern here is the extent to which each actor can expect his interests to be satisfied by the outcomes (28). This may be viewed as measuring
each actor's probable welfare given the distributions of interest and power.
Such a measure for actor j, w_j, can be defined as

$$w_j = 0.5 + 0.5 \, Y_j V_{\text{diag}}^{-1} Y' P' \ , \qquad (29)$$

where Y_j is a row vector of n elements containing the directed interests of
actor j in events, Y is an $n \times m$ matrix containing the directed interests of
all actors, V_{diag} is a diagonal matrix in which the elements v_i of the value
vector V appear on the diagonal, and the prime denotes transposition.
Further, if one is willing to compare the welfare of different actors—a
comparison many are unwilling to accept as a meaningful operation—it is
possible to evaluate overall system performance by aggregating the w_j
from equation (29) using some weights for each actor. Coleman suggests
the use of weights based on the operational standard of an actor's open
market power, which results in the following measure W of overall system
efficacy:

$$W = 0.5 + 0.5 P^* Y V_{\text{diag}}^{-1} Y' P' \ , \qquad (30)$$

where P^* is a row vector giving the distribution of power to actors at open
market equilibrium (see eq. [6]). Since the value of events can be defined in
terms of the power and interests of actors (see Feld 1977)

$$V = PX \ , \qquad (31)$$

equation (30) suggests that the efficacious allocation of power in a given
system of action is given by that vector P which maximizes W for a given
distribution of interests Y.

Table 4 presents the results of computations based on equations (28)–(30)
for the two hypothetical action systems analyzed here. In view of the
results on redistribution of power found above in tables 2 and 3, the results
in panels A and B of table 4 are not especially surprising. Event outcomes
change toward the ones favored by those gaining power. For instance, in
system 1, the more central actors for the most part favor a negative out-

---

control, rather than equilibrium power, is the pivotal factor affecting event outcomes
and interest satisfaction at nonequilibrium points. The present discussion is concerned,
however, only with equilibrium results.

TABLE 4
EVENT OUTCOMES AND INTEREST SATISFACTION
A. OUTCOMES OF EVENTS (r_i)

SYSTEM	Event 1	2	3	4	5
System 1:					
Unrestricted exchange	.580	.280	...	...	...
Restricted access, no price making	.580	.280	...	...	...
Restricted access, with price making	.430	.462	...	...	...
System 2:					
Unrestricted exchange	.567	.432	.564	.405	.644
Restricted access, no price making	.514	.432	.532	.371	.615
Restricted access, with price making	.462	.443	.524	.366	.655

B. INTEREST SATISFACTION OF ACTORS (w_j)

SYSTEM	Actor 1	2	3	4	5	6	7	8	9	10
System 1:										
Unrestricted exchange	.664	.664	.664	.664	.664	.664	.378	.378	.378	.430
Restricted access, no price making	.664	.664	.664	.664	.664	.664	.378	.378	.378	.430
Restricted access, with price making	.495	.495	.495	.495	.495	.495	.538	.538	.538	.446
System 2:										
Unrestricted exchange	.509	.479	.542	.543	.512	...	...	...	...	...
Restricted access, no price making	.525	.515	.531	.510	.483	...	...	...	...	...
Restricted access, with price making	.516	.526	.549	.498	.474	...	...	...	...	...

C. AGGREGATE INTEREST SATISFACTION (W)

System	Unrestricted Exchange	Restricted Access, No Price Making	Restricted Access, with Price Making
1	.555	.555	.503
2	.516	.514	.515

come on event 1 and a positive outcome on event 2; and as these actors gain power when restrictions on access (with price-making behavior) are imposed, these outcomes become more likely than was expected in the absence of restrictions on access. Similarly, it can be seen in panel B of table 4 that most actors gaining power in the context of restrictions on access also gain in expected interest satisfaction.

In panel C of table 4 it can be observed that the measure of weighted interest satisfaction given by equation (30) is lower for these systems of action when the restrictions of figure 1 are imposed. This is an interesting result, in that it squares with the intuition that restrictions reduce welfare, but it is of little generality. An interesting and important question is whether the imposition of restrictions altering the equilibrium distribution of power will always reduce the measure of efficacy defined in (30).

The answer to this question is no. I cannot state an analytic solution for the value of P that will maximize (30), subject to (7), (31), and the restriction that the power of an actor is nonnegative.[13] It is possible, though, to show that, for the specific systems analyzed here, there exist values of P that give higher values of W than those obtained when $P = P^*$. In system 1, for example, if all power is allocated to actors 1–6 while none is held by actors 7–10, the measure of weighted interest satisfaction rises to .650: event 1 has a 1.0 probability of a positive outcome and event 2 has a 1.0 probability of a negative outcome, which means that all interests of actors 1–6, half of the interests of actor 10, and none of the interests of actors 7–9 are satisfied. Restrictions on access that transfer power to actors 1–6, then, would raise the measure of aggregate interest satisfaction above the level it assumes in the absence of access restrictions. Similarly, for system 2, restrictions on access that increase the power of actor 4 and, to a more limited extent, actor 1 serve to increase the measure W defined in (30) above the level obtained when the power distribution is given by the unrestricted exchange equilibrium.[14]

It is possible that a case can be made for the optimality of the open market distribution of power on grounds other than those given in (30). For instance, if interactor comparisons of interest satisfaction are not made,

[13] The matrix expression in (30) cannot be differentiated using available formulas for matrix differentiation (Goldberger 1964). Differentiation of the expression in (30) using scalars for the simplest case of interest, in which there are two actors and two events, yields a quartic equation in terms of the power of one of the actors. Lacking a general formula for the roots of a quartic equation, it is impossible to state an analytic solution even for this special case. I therefore resorted to the numerical approach discussed in n. 14 below.

[14] The results reported in this paragraph were obtained numerically, by inspecting the values taken by eq. (30) in a grid search procedure over values of P satisfying (7) and the nonnegativity constraint. It is possible that the procedure used did not locate an absolute maximum for (30), but the procedure does establish that such a maximum does not necessarily occur at $P = P^*$.

American Journal of Sociology

one might define an optimal allocation of power as one giving a distribution of interest satisfaction such that any shift in the distribution of power that improves the satisfaction of one actor will lower that of another. My search for a maximal value of (30) (see n. 14) suggests that the open market power distribution may be optimal in this sense for these two systems of action, but I am unable to generalize this result beyond the systems inspected. Moreover, the same search revealed other power distributions that also appear to satisfy the criterion stated in this paragraph. The primary basis for choosing the power distribution of the unrestricted market over these other distributions would be that it is the distribution resulting when actors allocate their resources on the basis of a certain standard of individually rational action (see Coleman 1973, pp. 82–88).

SUMMARY AND DISCUSSION

In this paper I have continued the effort, initiated earlier (Marsden 1981), to incorporate social structural restrictions in the form of social networks into Coleman's exchange model. My concerns here have been directed toward introducing the consequences of restricted access and discrepancies in alternative relationships into the exchange process; I have argued that, just as geographical or other barriers limit access of consumers to producers in economic markets, social barriers, ideological discrepancies, the lack of a generalized currency, and other social circumstances may prevent systems of political exchange from reaching an unrestricted market equilibrium. Limited physical access, for spatially differentiated systems of action, or limited social access imposed by the formal authority structure or the informal social structure of an organization might serve to create restrictions on potential exchanges. To recapitulate, the three main effects of restricted access were shown to be a reduction in the levels of resource exchange among actors, a redistribution of open market power toward actors well situated in the network of relations defining the restricted market, and a possible shift in the level of system efficacy as measured by an aggregation of individual interest satisfaction.

These results make some progress toward taking effects of network structures on exchange processes into account. It would be comforting, of course, to have some additional evidence about the operation of a restricted exchange process to replace the contrived examples used here as illustrations. Michener, Cohen, and Sorensen (1977; see also Bonacich and Light 1978) report experimental evidence tending to confirm predictions of Coleman's basic exchange model. It would be useful to have similar studies of the operation of systems subject to access restrictions of the type considered in this paper. Studies of cooperative groups in which restrictions are imposed on communication flows (Bavelas 1950; Guetzkow 1960) indicate

712

that the configuration of restrictions influences both a group's response to a problem-solving task and the individual behavior of group members. The situations discussed here are ones in which collective actions involve conflict rather than cooperation; also, the network linkages of concern here pertain to bargaining and resource exchange rather than communication. Nonetheless, the results here suggest that both collective and individual actions are affected by access restrictions, and it would be useful to have empirical studies of these effects. Among other things, such studies could yield estimates of the degree to which actors in favorable network positions (e.g., actors 7–9 in system 1) are able to inflate the exchange value of resources they control initially (see eqq. [24]–[26]). The experimental studies of restricted access networks reported by Cook and Emerson (1978), Cook et al. (1980), and Cook (1982) constitute a promising beginning in this direction.

Efforts here and elsewhere (Marsden 1981; Marsden and Laumann 1977) have attempted to specify biases in the operation of exchange systems that occur as a result of constraints imposed by interactor social networks. The results, however, help to provide an explanation for one feature of these networks themselves. A common finding in studies of social networks is that the actors most centrally located in such structures have a special prominence. Occupancy of a central position is regularly associated with assumption of leadership roles, possession of a reputation as an influential actor, participation in collective action, and other dependent variables. Findings of this type have been reported for networks in diverse types of systems: small, task-oriented work groups (Bavelas 1950), interorganizational resource networks (Galaskiewicz 1979), professional communities (Coleman, Katz, and Menzel 1966; Breiger 1976), and community elites (Laumann and Pappi 1976). These associations of network centrality with other attributes do not appear to be due to the mere fact that central actors are also those who are most likely to control many resources; structural position itself appears to have an independent effect (Galaskiewicz 1979; Burt 1977). The usual rationale given for such effects of central position is based on control of communication channels; many graph-theoretic measures of centrality are based on an actor's "betweenness" in a social network (Harary et al. 1965, pp. 185–91; Nieminen 1973; Freeman 1977).

In modifying the unrestricted exchange model to encompass interactor social structures, different mechanisms by which effects of centrality emerge in systems of social exchange involving at least potential conflict of interest have been specified. One modification, developed in Marsden (1981), permits actors to affect the outcomes of events by shaping the interests pursued by other actors. Clearly, actors centrally located in an influence network will be those who exert many influences on others but

713

American Journal of Sociology

are subject to few. Under certain conditions, this means that collective actions will be biased toward the preferences of these central actors; the degree of bias is contingent on the pattern of interest differentiation, the degree to which the influence network is centralized, and the way in which the interest and influence patterns are articulated. This paper introduces a network effect into the process of exchange itself instead of modifying one of the inputs to that process, as the influence network does. The imposition of restrictions on rates of resource transfer means that transfers of resources between unconnected actors can take place only through more central, intervening actors, and this can alter the implicit exchange ratios between the unconnected actors. The result is some bias in the equilibrium distribution of system power among actors, but such bias does not involve purposive action by actors in favorable network positions. Permitting price-making behavior by such actors, however, allows them to inflate the price of their resources by capitalizing on the fact that their trading partners lack valuable alternatives to an exchange relationship. One result of this modification, as we have seen, is an increased concentration of power to control event outcomes in the more central nodes of the network.

An interesting direction for future work would be the introduction of additional types of purposive action in the context of access restrictions. Here, actors exchange on a dyadic basis, trading resources on the basis of their relative self-interest and alternatives only. A second sort of mechanism that could be operative in a system of exchange with access restrictions might be "middleman" behavior in which central actors facilitate exchanges between unconnected peripheral actors, extracting of course a "commission" or "fee" in the process.

Taken together, the modifications that have been introduced permit actors to affect the outcomes of events in three distinct ways. The first is through the direct control of events or resources with high impact on events, as discussed by Coleman (1973). A second form of control is indirect; it involves the use of social status or control over information to persuade actors in possession of the first type of control to pursue interests consonant with those of the actor exerting the influence (see Marsden 1981). The final form of control arises as a result of an actor's occupancy of a nodal position in a network of potential transaction routes; this allows such an actor to affect the exchange value of resources he controls. The two latter forms of control, then, arise as a result of position in a network, and more central actors are most likely to have access to them. It seems plausible that these forms of control are responsible for some of the unique effects of network positions cited above.

The three forms of control discussed in the preceding paragraph are related to the three conceptions of power discussed by Burt (1977). The first type of control is identical to Burt's concept of "power as control

Networks

over valuable resources via possession." The second, the capacity to influence interest formation, is related to Burt's idea of "power as influence." The third, the ability to alter terms of trade between actors, in some ways parallels Burt's notion of "power as control over valuable resources via possession and constraint." I have attempted to move beyond Burt's analysis, however, by describing the mechanisms through which these forms of control operate and by incorporating all three of them within a model describing issue resolution processes. I have also pointed to some system-level effects—on system levels of resource mobilization, on the degree of consensus on issue outcomes, and on system efficacy—that occur when these market imperfections are taken into account.

These modifications begin to integrate social structural constraints into the framework of the basic exchange model and to show how networks constrain individual and collective actions. Furthermore, the modified exchange model can aid in explaining some of the features found in static analyses of social networks by providing a description of the processes involved in the generation of such networks.

REFERENCES

Bacharach, Samuel B., and Edward J. Lawler. 1980. *Power and Politics in Organizations.* San Francisco: Jossey-Bass.
Bavelas, Alex. 1950. "Communication Patterns in Task-oriented Groups." *Journal of the Acoustical Society of America* 22:725–30.
Blau, Peter M. 1964. *Exchange and Power in Social Life.* New York: Wiley.
———. 1977. *Inequality and Heterogeneity.* New York: Free Press.
Bonacich, Philip, and John Light. 1978. "Laboratory Experimentation in Sociology." Pp. 145–70 in *Annual Review of Sociology*, edited by Alex Inkeles. Vol. 4. Palo Alto, Calif.: Annual Reviews.
Breiger, Ronald L. 1976. "Career Attributes and Network Structure: A Blockmodel Study of a Biomedical Research Specialty." *American Sociological Review* 41:117–35.
Burgess, Robert L., and Joyce McCarl Nielson. 1974. "An Experimental Analysis of Some Structural Determinants of Equitable and Inequitable Exchange Relations." *American Sociological Review* 39:427–43.
Burt, Ronald S. 1977. "Power in a Social Topology." *Social Science Research* 6:1–83.
———. 1980. "Autonomy in a Social Topology." *American Journal of Sociology* 85: 892–925.
Coleman, James S. 1964. *Introduction to Mathematical Sociology.* New York: Free Press.
———. 1970. "Political Money." *American Political Science Review* 64:1074–87.
———. 1973. *The Mathematics of Collective Action.* Chicago: Aldine.
———. 1977. "Social Action Systems." Pp. 11–50 in *Problems of Formalization in the Social Sciences*, edited by Klemens Szaniawski. Wroclaw: Polskiej Akademii Nauk.
———. 1981. "Systems of Action with Few Actors." Unpublished manuscript. Chicago: University of Chicago, Department of Sociology.
Coleman, James S., Elihu Katz, and Herbert Menzel. 1966. *Medical Innovation: A Diffusion Study.* Indianapolis: Bobbs-Merrill.
Cook, Karen S. 1977. "Exchange and Power in Networks of Interorganizational Relations." *Sociological Quarterly* 18:64–84.
———. 1982. "Network Structures from an Exchange Perspective." In *Social Structure and Network Analysis*, edited by Peter V. Marsden and Nan Lin. Beverly Hills, Calif.: Sage.

American Journal of Sociology

Cook, Karen S., and Richard M. Emerson. 1978. "Power, Equity, and Commitment in Exchange Networks." *American Sociological Review* 43:721–39.
Cook, Karen S., Richard M. Emerson, Mary R. Gillmore, and Toshio Yamagishi. 1980. "Power, Dependency and Collective Action in Exchange Networks." Technical report. Seattle: University of Washington, Institute for Sociological Research.
Emerson, Richard M. 1962. "Power-dependence Relations." *American Sociological Review* 27:31–41.
Feld, Scott. 1977. "A Reconceptualization of the Problem of Collective Decisions." *Journal of Mathematical Sociology* 5:257–71.
Freeman, Linton C. 1977. "A Set of Measures of Centrality Based on Betweenness." *Sociometry* 40:35–41.
Galaskiewicz, Joseph. 1979. *Exchange Networks and Community Politics.* Beverly Hills, Calif.: Sage.
Goldberger, Arthur S. 1964. *Econometric Theory.* New York: Wiley.
Guetzkow, Harold. 1960. "Differentiation of Roles in Task-oriented Groups." Pp. 683–704 in *Group Dynamics: Research and Theory*, edited by Dorwin Cartwright and Alvin Zander. 2d ed. New York: Harper & Row.
Harary, Frank, Dorwin Cartwright, and Robert Z. Norman. 1965. *Structural Models: An Introduction to the Theory of Directed Graphs.* New York: Wiley.
Hickson, D. J., C. R. Hinings, C. A. Lee, R. H. Schneck, and J. M. Pennings. 1971. "A Strategic Contingencies' Theory of Intraorganizational Power." *Administrative Science Quarterly* 16:216–29.
Jacobs, David. 1974. "Dependency and Vulnerability: An Exchange Approach to the Control of Organizations." *Administrative Science Quarterly* 19:45–59.
Kanter, Rosabeth M. 1977. *Men and Women of the Corporation.* New York: Basic.
Laumann, Edward O., Joseph Galaskiewicz, and Peter V. Marsden. 1978. "Community Structure as Interorganizational Linkages." Pp. 455–84 in *Annual Review of Sociology*, edited by Alex Inkeles. Vol. 4. Palo Alto, Calif.: Annual Reviews.
Laumann, Edward O., and Peter V. Marsden. 1979. "The Analysis of Oppositional Structures in Political Elites: Identifying Collective Actors." *American Sociological Review* 44:713–32.
Laumann, Edward O., and Franz U. Pappi. 1976. *Networks of Collective Action: A Perspective on Community Influence Systems.* New York: Academic Press.
Lipsey, Richard G., and Peter O. Steiner. 1969. *Economics.* 2d ed. New York: Harper & Row.
Marsden, Peter V. 1979. "Community Leadership and Social Structure: Bargaining and Opposition." Ph.D. dissertation, University of Chicago.
———. 1981. "Introducing Influence Processes into a System of Collective Decisions." *American Journal of Sociology* 86:1203–35.
Marsden, Peter V., and Edward O. Laumann. 1977. "Collective Action in a Community Elite: Exchange, Influence Resources, and Issue Resolution." Pp. 199–250 in *Power, Paradigms, and Community Research*, edited by Roland J. Liebert and Allen Imershein. London: ISA/Sage.
Michener, H. Andrew, Eugene D. Cohen, and Aage B. Sorensen. 1977. "Social Exchange: Predicting Transactional Outcomes in Five-Event, Four-Person Systems." *American Sociological Review* 42:522–35.
Mindlin, Sergio E., and Howard Aldrich. 1975. "Interorganizational Dependence: A Review of the Concept and a Reexamination of the Findings of the Aston Group." *Administrative Science Quarterly* 20:382–92.
Nielsen, François, and Rachel A. Rosenfeld. 1981. "Substantive Interpretations of Differential Equation Models." *American Sociological Review* 46:159–74.
Nieminen, Juhari. 1973. "On the Centrality in a Directed Graph." *Social Science Research* 2:371–78.
Parsons, Talcott. 1963a. "On the Concept of Influence." *Public Opinion Quarterly* 27:37–62.
———. 1963b. "On the Concept of Political Power." *Proceedings of the American Philosophical Society* 107:232–63.

Networks I

Parsons, Talcott, and Neil J. Smelser. 1956. *Economy and Society.* New York: Free Press.
Pfeffer, Jeffrey. 1981. *Power in Organizations.* Marshfield, Mass.: Pitman.
Pfeffer, Jeffrey, and Gerald R. Salancik. 1974. "Organizational Decision Making as a Political Process: The Case of a University Budget." *Administrative Science Quarterly* 19:135–51.
———. 1978. *The External Control of Organizations: A Resource Dependence Perspective.* New York: Harper & Row.
Roxborough, Ian. 1979. *Theories of Underdevelopment.* London: Macmillan.
Van de Geer, John P. 1971. *Introduction to Multivariate Analysis for the Social Sciences.* San Francisco: W. H. Freeman.

[14]

Markets, Networks and Control

HARRISON C. WHITE[1]

Any market of significance operates itself and reproduces itself without external planning or auctioneer.[2] It is a social mechanism, which is to say it is an institution and cannot be installed to order, by decree, at least also because it is sustained in part by competing attempts at control. Furthermore, in the longer run a market continues only because and as it is caught up in ties among some larger networks of markets. Call the whole a system an economy or sector of an economy. Such a system supports and is supported by shared terminology and conventions across a population. Such a system entails networks of tangible flows among specific markets.

The general question of this paper is how to conceive of markets effectively within networks of flows and attempts at control which generate and which in turn are generated by and around those markets. Prices and allocations are central to markets and their systems. Also central are flexibilities in choice of whom to deal with and in what particular variety of goods. But then some form of mutually-enforced commitment is also central to sustaining a given market. There are great differences between individual markets in these respects, as there can be major differences among systems.

Two species should be distinguished among individual markets. In exchange markets, ranging from lawn sales or county fairs on through international trade,[3] selling and buying are roles for

[1]Center for the Social Sciences and Department of Sociology Columbia University. *Author's note:* An early version of this paper was also given at a Moscow seminar of young Soviet social scientists. The author is grateful to Seweryn Bialer and Lynn A. Cooper for suggesting changes there, and also to comments from Eric Leifer, Siegwart Lindenberg and Ilan Talmud. I am indebted to the Netherlands Institute for Advanced Study, Wassenaar, for support during the period of preparation for the conference which engendered this volume.
[2]If some auctioneer core is crucial, then that, not the market dress, is the source of control for terms of trade and their evolution.
[3]The range can be extended to cover Coleman's (1990) schoolboys trading cards picturing professional sports players, and the New York Stock Exchange (Baker,

actors rather than positions necessarily fixed with respect to a
given sort of product. In this species of markets, the notion
of product is labile. A second species, the production market,
is the main transducer mechanisms within Western economies.
These markets as institutions shape an array of products together
with a population of producers as formal organizations. A market
is committed to a product. Development paths of markets and
networks interact. Exchange markets have generated and nested
in mercantile networks for millennia, as portrayed, for example,
by Braudel (1982) and Polanyi et al. (1957). Various sorts of
partnerships and leagues come to be important actors in such
economies. Production markets and networks are also evolved
together, along lines sketched, for example, by Bythel (1978) and
Kriedte et al. (1981), into the distinctive pattern which we observe
today as a manufacturing economy. Each production market ties to
other markets in a network of flows, in an input–output network,
which can be further dissected into many subsidiary networks of
specialized flows.

Just as markets of this second species build up around participation by large producer firms, the networks among these markets
embody the actions of producer firms. Yet flows in these networks
are subject to pressures from transactions through exchange markets,
markets of the first species that are neither localized nor tied down
within the input–output network of manufacturing economy. There
is a bewildering profusion of levels and locales, as long ago noted
by Marshall (1891) and Jevons (1875), such that the species of
market and network are sometimes observed as concrete types but
sometimes are best seen as analytic abstractions. Control efforts by
participants will repeatedly attempt to cross-cut the species.

Current developments in Eastern Europe and elsewhere may be
giving rise to new subspecies of markets and networks, and certainly
to new configurations and mixes, as, for example, Granick (1972,
1975) and Hamilton and Biggart (1985) have long been suggesting.
Fresh ideas are needed in any case to develop for the current
Organization of European Economic Cooperation (OEEC) context
more adequate theories of markets, networks and their system of
organizations and products.

In the following, we begin with phenomenology for networks of
markets. Then we turn to individual markets, for which later an

---

1984), and also New Guinea kula rings (Strathern, 1971). This illustrates the
extraordinary scope in exchange markets, which are markets of the episode rather
than markets of reproduction.

explicit and testable model is proposed, a model of production markets as a group of peers signalling by a self-reproducing schedule. Finally, among discussion of predictions and conjectures, a central conundrum is identified and a resolution suggested.

Origins and Self-Similarity

A set of actors can become comparable, become peers, through jostling to join in production on comparable terms. They commit by joining together to pump downstream versions of a common product, which are subjected by both themselves and downstream actors to invidious comparison. Children competing in hopscotch or reciting for a teacher, mathematicians in a test for a prize, actors in a play—and manufacturers of recreational aircraft for the U.S. market—are all examples of this basic social formation. The production market is a special case of this social formation, call it the commit interface.

Each production economy is the result of a historical evolution in which market and firm and network and product change together, usually slowly, from a base system of markets in long-distance trade and exchange, markets of the first species. The process began independently many times in Europe, as putting-out systems evolved in tandem with marketing networks. Input–output networks build historically within and into a given economy.

For example, in Florence and other Italian cities of the early Renaissance, production of cloth induced networks for "putting-out" the production of parts of the initial product, such as fustian, and each of these parts could itself become established as the product of a separate market (e.g., Lachmann and Peltersen, 1988). The pattern was heralded earlier in the painful forging of *verlager* and *kaufmann* systems by entrepreneurs in late medieval Europe (Kriedte et al., 1981), in the hinterlands of medieval networks of German cities: early entrepreneurs "put out" raw materials and/or tools cottagers and then "marketed" the resulting production which they collected. And the process was elaborated further in "out-work" patterns of subsequent periods and locales (e.g., Bythell, 1978, on London in the industrial revolution).

Slow change on the surface does not contradict intense social pressures to compete for and to sustain a distinct position. In addition, attempts to assert a new kind of control flair up continuously. Effects of introducing a new technology can partially reroute the input–output networks, and wholly new markets can appear in various ways.

Besides introducing hysteresis and other complexities of analysis,

226   *Harrison C. White*

this historicity suggests the possibility of self-similarity. That is, the forms of networks within an industry—itself embracing scores of actual production markets—may resemble the forms of local networks (for example, the *verlager* networks in one sort of cloth among a few cities) and, in turn, both may be homomorphic to input–output networks across a whole industrial sector or national economy.[4] Failing some such cross-level similarity, there is indeed little prospect for effective analysis of economies, and in fact most economic constructs used today rely implicitly on self-similarity.

Products and Production Markets

The producer firms can be seen as pumps expensively committed to spouting continuing flows of products. The set of pumps acting together form the market as superpump in interaction with, and with confidence in, provision of an orderly and continuing social setting with buyers. To the buyers, the array of pumps is a menu of terms of trade. It is this social process which induces a definition of "product" from the common properties of the flows, rather than the product being some pre-existing given.

Thus markets and their products emerge and evolve in a symbiotic process of definition and recognition by suitable clienteles and producers. And here producers typically are large compound actors, firms or other organizations. Equipment and expertise commit them over long terms, as just one "side" to a given market. A product also becomes publicly defined as buyers settle down with the producers across terms of trade.[5] The terms of trade settle into a schedule which becomes the interface between the two sides.

[4]Alfred Marshall before 1900 seemed well aware of this. Other levels are required for a full theory of economy: for example, the internal constitution of firms. See Williamson (1975) for one attempt to integrate this level with that of exchange markets. See Eccles and White (1985) for one attempt to integrate the level of firms with that of production markets.

Self-similarity can extend down through persons. Recent surveys of social network analysis construed primarily around individuals can be found in Wellman and Berkowitz (1988), which also contains applications to business at several different scales, which latter are the focus in Burt (1990), and in Mizruchi and Schwartz (1988).

[5]Various of these producers also come to be, simultaneously, members of other production markets (see Baumol et al., 1988). And of course the buyers are in many other markets so that there is an intricate structure of mappings and correspondences required to read input–output networks accurately.

Markets, networks and control 227

Begin from the individual positions of production firms within a market. For example, in some market for rubber used to manufacture tires,[6] one firm becomes known for producing lower-quality but cheap rubber, another for higher-cost rubber of high durability but low flexibility, and so on. Within a market, each producer is committed for a substantial period, given immobile investment in physical and social machinery. Each producer becomes specialized with a view to maximum net return given the constraints of the structure of competition imposed in that market.

Each producer has established a position on a schedule of terms of trade, in a space with dimensions for producers' volumes and revenues. This schedule is observable from information available to every producer, and it is reproduced by the actions of the "other side" of the market.[7] The producers do not bounce in and out of a market, as they can in the exchange market of economic theory. Each producer is also a consumer of inputs from other markets; so that each market presupposes a continuing network of flows from and among specific other markets (cf. Leontief, 1965). The production economy consists of overlapping networks of procurement and supply among firms in markets (e.g., Corey, 1978).

This view contrasts with and supplements the account of a market as an abstract category that suits the Pure Theory of Exchange (e.g., Newman, 1965; Arrow and Hahn, 1975). Discussions of supply-and-demand also recede into the background, along with money supply and other macro-institutional features. Producers' basic concerns are to hold on to distinctive positions in their markets. They adapt their current outputs to fluctuations in the economy by layoffs and the like without any necessary change in market positions as producers.

Production Network Economies

There are levels in network economies, but they are not discrete hierarchical levels. A given firm may have a position in each of

---

[6]It depends in part on incident and chance—on history—whether the market boundaries are of all tires, or only auto tires, or only in a region, or whether, for example, a separate market develops, permanently or temporarily, around a technological innovation such as radial tires. Or rubber markets may not partition according to end use in vehicles at all.

[7]For simplicity, the "other side" is assumed to be the buyers; but a dual form (White, 1988) of the same model holds when the other side are suppliers of a dominant input, say skilled labor.

228   *Harrison C. White*

several distinct production markets, and the firm may exceed in total size each of the markets it is "in". While there must be at least several firms to structure any given market mechanism, this mechanism usually cannot sustain participation by more than say a score of producers. One can by contrast discriminate hundreds and more markets in a production network.[8]

Terms of trade establish themselves as an interface *within* a given market very differently than do terms of trade *between* markets in production networks. In the latter, entirely different features emerge. Social discipline and the competitive pressures underlying it are no less real, but these pressures are changeable and variegated so that the discipline is of a system within which commitments can be changed. Efforts at control, especially of engrossment of stocks, that is to say of speculation, are important along with strivings for profit from routine mark-ups. Gross profits depend on network possibilities for autonomy and control. Autonomy is possible to the extent there are alternative market sources and destinations for various products as conceived and packaged by a given actor, whereas constraint comes via the actor's lack of alternatives within the established network of markets. Attempts at control can be predicted from reading the converse sides to others' autonomies.

Sense can be made of observations of a production economy only by modeling how all these different attempts fit together over time. This is not easy, since framing of inter-market theory is incompatible with the framing of intra-market theory. One can attempt to stuff the entire picture into one or the other frame. Arrow and Hahn (1973) represent the high-water mark of attempts to make the Pure Theory of Exchange serve as a general theory of a whole economy.[9] Leontief's input–output model is the high-water mark of attempts by economists to stuff an entire economy into the ecological niche suitable to intra-market structure.

A different approach is worth exploring. In this approach we focus on how production markets resemble other social formations, rather than on how they are different. We bring out the abstract parallels between economic and other institutional realms, rather

[8]The assertions of my model, like assertions in micro-economic textbooks, require imposition of sharp boundaries upon blurry situations. For example, producers may string out geographically such that the buyers from one producer overlap but do not coincide with buyers of even nearest neighbor producers. The vision of a neat partition among separate markets is an idealization for the purpose of obtaining useable predictions and insights.
[9]A convenient overview of the Pure Theory of Exchange at an intermediate level of technical detail is Newman (1965).

Markets, networks and control 229

than emphasizing their differences. This amounts to developing a theory of a general social discipline of which one of the species of markets above is a special case. Repeat this for the other species of markets. Then develop and deploy similar theories for still other species of social discipline, whether or not they have a known economic representative. Observations can suggest how such disciplines cumulate and grow into broader social institutions.[10]

Let me rephrase the matter. It aids comprehension to show how the production market, under its particular institutional dress, is an example of a very widespread social formation. This can lead into a formulation of how networks of such markets are special cases of social networks in general. I draw upon models of networks and of control interactions from Burt (1990), which he also applies to systems of other actors besides markets, in order to develop an explanation of aggregate volumes and payments from markets across a production network.

First, I embody my view of the production market in an explicit model, the mathematical formulae and equations for which can be found in White (1988). The main result is that the average price in a production market is arbitrary; only relative prices among producers matter in its construction. The conception behind this model derives from Chamberlin (1933),[11] but its implementation was developed from the mechanism proposed by Spence (1974) for market signalling.

Second, I sketch how one might extend these results so as to embed them in a broader view of an economic system, be that a sector or some more inclusive level. In doing so I shall be guided by sociological theory of how institutional forms in general emerge out of network cumulation. The contrast with extrapolation of the Pure Theory of Exchange to the level of economy should be instructive, as should the contrasts and parallels to the Leontief line.

Terms of Trade in Production

To begin with, in a given market, each producer firm will have a position which is entirely relative to the positions of other producers in that market. So this production market can be conceived as an interface, as terms-of-trade which are a schedule,

---

[10]I offer such a theory elsewhere (White, 1992); here I sketch applications to an economy.
[11]Subsequent microeconomics proved unable to assimilate Chamberlin's seminal analysis of monopolistic competition, and Joan Robinson's parallel discovery (1933), which each brought into focus the vision sketched by Marshall (1891).

230   *Harrison C. White*

say of volume versus price, a schedule in which each producer firm has a distinctive position. This schedule will not reproduce itself unless the specialized product varieties from the various producer firms come to seem to the other side to be equivalent tradeoffs of quality for price at observed total volumes. A handful of producers is sufficient to sustain a market, which cannot support the very large number of producers envisioned in the pure competitive markets of microeconomic textbooks.

The key point is that the terms of trade and the choices of position within this schedule can be estimated by businessmen using ordinary calculations from just the tangible signals that each can garner in the course of business, together with the practical knowledge of one's own cost-of-production schedule. No auctioneer need be hypothesized; instead the practical activities generate the signals needed. Thus the concrete market composes itself as some definite mesh between array of values seen by buyers and array of costs; without such meshing it does not reproduce itself.

Gossip can supply to each producer an estimate of most of the terms achieved by peers. The production market consists of the observable spread of terms of trade being achieved by various producers with their distinctive flows. At the simplest, these terms are revenue for volume shipped.[12] For the market to reproduce itself, each producer must continue to see its pair, revenue and volume, as its optimal choice from the menu of observed terms of trade; only this menu is known to be sustainable by the buyers, who themselves are comparison shopping.

Terms of trade are a commonly observable shape which cues actors into niches by their own preferences which yet are agreeable across the interface. This is an interpolation across revenue and volume pairs observed for the various producers.[13] The terms of trade must be accepted by the purchaser side, which is the arbiter of the competition, the judge of relative performances. The ironic implication is that production markets generate only the relative sizes of differentiated flows, not the aggregate size of flow.

Market outcomes and their correlates. Market stability proves to come from having *unequal* shares held by the different producers, while, sadly for them, cash flows—price less cost—tend to be larger

---

[12]Leave aside for more detailed modeling the line of related products which any given producer may supply.
[13]For illustration see figs. 3.1–3.3 in Leifer and White (1988). The mathematical model is worked out in White (1988).

Markets, networks and control 231

the more nearly equal are the market shares. Increasing returns to scale, which in microeconomics textbooks bar market formation, can be accommodated by the market mechanism as modeled here.

Supply equals demand as a tautology, each time after the fact. It is the variation among producers in qualities, and the difficulties each confronts in production, that shape the interface which motivates and sets the terms of trade which reproduce themselves. But actors ordinarily do not conceive and relate to higher-order measures like variances, and they may tell stories in stylized terms of supply and demand. The production market mechanism, like any commit interface, must be realized through forms which are perceived and estimated directly in everyday terms.

Control and Network Averages

There is a central conundrum to be resolved: A production market builds itself out of dispersions so that it is variances rather than means of outputs that are controlled. And control is the primary concern in network ties. Yet a network of flows *among* markets must primarily deal with and respond to averages, to what we call "supply and demand".

Control struggles in the network of production markets account for the form for any particular market. No firm likes to depend on a single supplier or a single customer firm or market. So it is hard for firms to survive as isolates, against the pressures from others' desires to have multiple partners for trades. Firms find it necessary to push into a niche among peers in a market, simply in order to gain standing with possible buyers.[14]

Struggles for control and autonomy accompany every tie between markets in the network of a production economy. A market's terms-of-trade schedule can be pushed up or down in these struggles, although the relative positions of producers within the market need not change. The preceding model for a single market leaves arbitrary its exact overall size—in physical volume and in cash flow. It also shows how the sizes of buyer surplus and producer profit, the respective aggregate payoffs for the two sides, follow from the aggregate size, and move in opposite directions with respect to it.

Location in the network determines how much autonomy can

[14]This profile of evolution in Western production markets, and their network economies, may suggest leads for conversion of Soviet ones (Podolny, 1990).

232   *Harrison C. White*

accrue to a given market through efforts of producers in it *vis-à-vis*
other markets located upstream, downstream and parallel—how
much choice it has among other markets for supplying and being
supplied with components. Burt has systematically developed this
thesis and applied it to interrelations among industries in the U.S.
He shows (1983; 1992, ch. 4) that profit margins correlate with
network measures of autonomy. If entrepreneurs within a market
exploit autonomy and constraint, they increase control and can
obtain higher average returns.

Two complementary sorts of regularity can be predicted from
Burt's vision. One concerns how individual firms exploit within
a market their degree of autonomy across markets. The other
regularity is the longer term impact of all these autonomy maneuvers
on the relative price levels of different markets. This second
regularity can be seen as a new specification or operationalization
of actual mechanisms for the Pure Theory of Exchange (Newman,
1965).

The first regularity is exactly that there should be more deviations
away from terms-of-trade schedules when more of the producers
in a market have high autonomy. There are no such comparative
data now available across a population of production markets.
But we can rely on self-similarity to argue for a correlation of
higher standard deviations in pricing for industrial sectors which
have higher degrees of autonomy. Burt has found exactly such to
be the case (Burt, 1992).

Average price levels, and thus profits, come from ties between
whole markets and not from relative positions of producer firms
within a market, which are a profile that shapes only relative prices.
But the longer-term effect of the first regularity—the outcomes
of individual producer's efforts to exploit autonomy—will tend
to move other producers in a given market back into line, or
rather into profile, with the achievements of the more autonomous
ones.[15] Profits of producers in different markets can be expected
to correlate with the objective measures of autonomy in their
production network, an autonomy that frees action of executives
from external constraints. Substitution is the key in the network
of markets. It follows that autonomies and constraints suffered by

---

[15]The more autonomous producers' interests are not served by disappearance of
less autonomous peers. The whole point of a market, as discussed before, is
to induce custom by having enough similar producers to attract buyers from
other markets' substitutable goods—and to reassure such buyers that they are
not entering a situation offering no autonomy to them.

Markets, networks and control 233

neighbor markets also should be taken into account, since they will indirectly influence the autonomy achievable in a given market.

Interfaces

A supplementary goal of this paper is to show how analysis of economies of markets and networks can and should be fitted in as a special case of a more general analysis of social structure. This enriches the latter and ensures the former against divorce from reality, which is a social reality. The component processes of markets can be seen as examples of more general processes with other embodiments more widely familiar in all societies.

In a time when attempts are being made to change whole economies toward a form closer to the Western ones, it is especially instructive to be explicit about how capitalist forms can be understood as particular cases of more general social processes. The aura of magic which at present surrounds "the market" in discussions within formerly state socialist societies should be dissipated. Western economic institutions are robust and effective, but academic economic analysis of them has little correspondence to their realities.[16]

The focus of the study of interfaces, and of markets in particular, should be how separate actors embed into a joint formation and induce a new identity.

Material production of all sorts tends to come from commit interfaces. Here the "receivers" are a distinct set and the context is neither relaxed nor social. The hunting or gathering groups described for tribal contexts (Firth, 1957; Lee, 1979; Rose, 1960; Udy, 1959) are early realizations which have analogues today in sports teams (Leifer, 1990) and in children's games (Fine, 1983; Opie and Opie, 1969). The basic mechanism does not require or presuppose distinct roles among the producers along with explicit cues and assignments. Rather, a spread of performances is induced by attention of producers to differential preferences by the other side, who can turn off their attention (or more tangible payments for production).

Interfaces do not build from a concern with ecology. In shaping structures of importance, it is control projects that compete, and they only peripherally attend to effectiveness of physical work.

---

[16]This is evidenced by the disdain of business executives, both Western and Japanese, for academic micro-economics. The abstract and hypothetical nature of modern micro-economic theory unfortunately contributes to a magical cast of thinking by inexperienced reformers in the Eastern bloc.

234   *Harrison C. White*

Social life is about actors' importance within social settings; so these settings cannot be shaped primarily to effective joint operations on physical settings. As Udy (1970) was among the first to say explicitly, production in the ordinary sense of practical work is difficult to reconcile with the universal tendencies of elaboration and embedding which come with the ongoing process of social structuring.[17]

Asymmetry underlies all the variations of the commit interface. Embedding is built into the form. On one side, individual flows are being induced amid jockeying for relative position, or niche; the other side is (possibly disparate) receivers appropriating the aggregate flow. The flow is always from the one, disaggregate side to the other. The social perceptions that discipline producers into order come from both sides, but behavioral cues to specific niches are on one side only. Producers are choosing what flows to offer. The commit interface presupposed and requires unremitting attention to the flows and the interface by the producers.

Underlying this mechanism is a matching of variances. Producers differ in various combinations of abilities, and so are differentially attractive to receivers. The mechanism sustaining a commit interface continues only if relative recognition of producers can be mapped to their spread on actual productivity. This mapping must emerge and reproduce itself, which happens only when the producer set is arrayed in reward in the same order in which their productions are discriminated. Only if there is variance in abilities across producers, correlated with variance in their receptions, can the commit interface reproduce itself.

Reference group theory long ago came to the view that it was dispersions among actors in rewards, not averages, that drove any organized system. The classic formulation came from the Stouffer (1948) study of World War II military: anticipation over time was equally important with dispersion. Tversky and Kahneman (Kahneman, Slovic and Tversky, 1982), and recently Lindenberg

---

[17]Udy worked out his argument from an extensive cross-cultural canvass of detailed forms of hunting, gathering, agriculture, craft, manufacturing and other contexts for work. The problem of succession to social positions is one major exemplification of this tension between work and the social. Performance in a work team can be seen as dependent on succession, day-by-day, to tasks of work. And the same issue recurs at larger scopes and periods. Solutions of social equations of balance deliver the successors and thereby impinge on technical equations of physical production. Udy's theorem is that the longer and more fully developed the social context of production is, the less effective and efficient the work process: Hunting and gathering, he argues, dominates settled agriculture in efficiency.

(Lindenberg, 1989) have revived this notion. By my different route through study of production markets, I have come to a clipped version of the same general view: species of interfaces disciplined by quality orderings, but only them, survive or not according to, and only to, matchings of variances among the constituent actors.

Industrial production markets of this century are the exemplars of commit interfaces. A production market must induce distinctive flows, at the same time as it renders them comparable, from a to-be-determined set of producers and into the hands of an array of buyers becoming accustomed and committed to that market. Some agreed framing as a linear ordering—which acquires the connotations of a valuation—can provide a scaffolding. Within this scaffolding, dispersions across observed quantities can array in social formations that then prove able to reproduce themselves. "Quality" captures the connotations of the invidious transitive order induced to form this mechanism of commitment. This is the market as interface, the production market induced from quality valuation. Valuations need not find their source in the induction and routing of average flows![18]

Conclusion

A combination of control struggles over time generates the production market as a social category, distinct from the exchange market. The evolution has continued further, as large firms diversify by buying positions in production markets for other products, in an effort to enhance their overall autonomy (Vancil, 1979). But the production market remains the social construction for what "a product" is, overriding engineering and cultural preconceptions.

The commit interface comes in many other varieties than production market, other institutional embodiments. "Star" systems, in entertainment and elsewhere, grow out of interfaces where embedding induces perceptions of events which are greatly exaggerated from the view of actors producing them (Faulkner, 1983). Even where the differentiation or dependence is limited, as among starlets in entertainment, there is the same pressure to generate events sufficient to embed them with a skew distribution of fame despite undetectable differences as judged within the interface. These star systems can be seen as closely analogous to the industrial markets, where some firms or other are forced into leading roles willy-nilly by the enormous social pressures of contention.

[18]This is just as the economist Frank Knight long ago intuited (1921).

236   *Harrison C. White*

Competition within any commit interface is about the importance of doing slightly better than your peers who in the larger context are so very similar to oneself. What is not necessarily signified explicitly is the strength of the new joint identity being created by the competition. The interface, in particular the production market, functions as a strong identity. Interjections of manipulations as attempts at control from within, by assembling peers or receivers, find hard going. The equivalency in peer positions subjects insiders to very strong discipline by the comparable others. Effective discipline comes from those similarly located, and thus conversant with the information and perspective the subject brings. Yet interjections by outsiders also find the commit interface difficult to disrupt. The commit interface is robust to both external and internal control projects.

Commit interfaces by their construction do not control for averages, cannot be programmed to yield prespecified flows. Instead commit interfaces build their dynamics around the spread of contributions across the comparable set. The commit interface is best portrayed as a curvature or response across the variation in members' properties. Mutual attention of peers is directed toward jockeying for relative positions which yield each a distinctive niche.

It follows, however, that the commit interface can become a profile subject to higher-level control, conditional on skills in manipulation of multiple rhetorics. A whole new level of sophistication opens up. Only variances and their ratios constrain the shape and positioning of the interface when it is operating autonomously. But rewards, severally and in aggregate, depend upon means, so that there is a latent motivation to try to shift interface in concert. The shift can be accomplished only if the acceptable shapes of profile are retained; so they become envelopes for achieving control. Participants can make systematic use of these facts. For example, Eccles (1985) showed how chief executive officers make use of these interfaces in achieving control over leading subordinates. The executive perspective on markets is to use markets to enhance control within the firm.[19]

Given all these considerations, it is possible to see how networks among markets can come to seem as live actors on their own. The situation is strikingly akin to that in the neural networks of the brain as envisioned in models of parallel distributed processing (McClelland and Rumelhart, 1986). Nonlinearities in synapses, firings of ties, sustain evolution of self-reproducing patterns: what

---

[19]Tendencies toward this have been observed in large Soviet as well as American firms in a recent comparative field study by Vlachoutsicos and Lawrence (1990).

Markets, networks and control   237

we call memories for brains and faction fights in networks. But these outcomes presuppose the continuation of the substrate of cells and production market interfaces, respectively. An argument can be made that the origin of production firms themselves can be seen as just such nonlinearities or memories in earlier and smaller networks among production interfaces.

References

Arrow, Kenneth J. and Hahn, Frank H. (1971) *General Competitive Analysis*. San Francisco: Holden-Day.

Baumol, William J., Panzar John C. and Willig R. D. (1988) *Contestable Markets and the Theory of Industry Structure*. San Diego, CA: Harcourt Brace Jovanovich.

Baker, Wayne (1984) The social structure of a national securities market. *American Journal of Sociology*, 89 775–811.

Burt, Ronald S. (1983) *Corporate Profits and Cooptation: Networks of Market Constraints and Directorate Ties in the American Economy*. New York: Academic Press.

Burt, Ronald S. (1992) *Structural Holes, The Social Structure of Competition*. Cambridge, MA: Harvard University Press.

Braudel, Ferdinand (1982) *The Wheels of Commerce*. Translated by S. Reynolds. Harper & Row.

Bythell, Duncan (1978) *The Sweated Trades: Outwork in Nineteenth Century Britain*. London: St. Martin's.

Chamberlin, E. H. (1933) *The Theory of Monopolistic Competition*. Cambridge, MA: Harvard University Press.

Coleman, James S. (1990) *Foundations of Social Theory*. Cambridge, MA: Harvard University Press.

Corey, E. Raymond (1978) *Procurement Management*. Boston: CBI.

Dehez, Pierre and Dreze, Jacques (1987) Competitive equilibria with increasing returns. European University Institute, Florence, Working Paper no. 86/243.

Eccles, Robert G. (1981a) Bureaucratic versus craft administration: the relationship of market structure to the construction firm. *Administrative Science Quarterly*, 26 449–469.

Eccles, Robert G. (1981b) *VISA International: The Management Change*. Case 0–482–022, HBS Case Services, Harvard Graduate School of Business Administration, Boston, MA.

Eccles, Robert G. (1981c) The quasifirm in the construction industry. *Journal of Economic Behavior and Organization*, 2 335–57.

Eccles, Robert G. (1985) *The Transfer Pricing Problem: A Theory for Practice*. Lexington, MA: Lexington Books.

Faulkner, Robert R. (1983) *Music on Demand: Composers and Careers in the Hollywood Film Industry*. New Brunswick: Transaction Books.

Fine, Gary A. (1983) *Shared Fantasies: Role Play Games as Social Worlds*. Chicago: University of Chicago Press.

Firth, Raymond (1957) *We, The Tikopia*. London: Allen & Unwin.

Granick, David (1972) *Managerial Comparisons of Four Developed Countries*. Cambridge, MA: MIT Press.

238   *Harrison C. White*

Granick, David (1975) *Enterprise Guidance in Eastern Europe: A Comparison of Four Socialist Economies*. Princeton, NJ: Princeton University Press.

Hamilton, Gary G. and Biggart, Nicole W. (1985) Why people obey. *Sociological Perspectives*, 28 3–28.

Jevons (1875) *Money and the Mechanism of Exchange*. London: Appleton.

Kahneman, D., Slovic, P. and Tversky, A. (eds.) (1982) *Judgment under Uncertainty: Heuristics and Decisions*. Cambridge: Cambridge University Press.

Knight, Frank (1921) *Risk, Uncertainty and Profit*. Cambridge, MA: Houghton Mifflin.

Kriedte, Peter, Medick, Hans and Shlumbohm, Jurgen (1981) *Industrialization Before Industrialisation*. Cambridge: Cambridge University Press.

Lachmann, Richard and Pelterson, Stephen (1988) *Rationality and Structure in the "Failed" Capitalism of Renaissance Italy*. Department of Sociology, University of Wisconsin, Madison.

Lee, Richard B. (1979) *The !Kung San*. Cambridge: Cambridge University Press.

Leifer, Eric M. (1990) Inequality among equals: performance inequalities in league sports. *American Journal of Sociology*.

Leifer, Eric M. and White, Harrison C. (1988) A structural approach to markets. In Mizruchi and Schwartz, eds.

Leontief, Wassily W. (1966) *Input–Output Economics*. New York: Oxford University Press.

Lindenberg, Siegwart (1989) Choice and culture: the behavioral basis of cultural impact on transactions. In *Social Structure and Culture Berlin*, pp. 175–200, edited by Hans Haferkamp. De Gruyter.

Mansfield, Edwin (1975) *Microeconomics: Theory and Applications*, 2nd ed. New York: Norton.

Marshall, Alfred (1891, 1920) *Principles of Economics*, 8th edition. London: Macmillan.

McClelland, James L., Rumelhart, David E. and others (1986) *Parallel Distributed Processing*, Vols. 1 and 2. Cambridge, MA: MIT Press.

Mizruchi, Mark S. and Schwartz, Michael (eds.) (1988) *Intercorporate Relations: The Structural Analysis of Business*. Cambridge University Press.

Newman, Peter (1965) *The Theory of Exchange*. Englewood Cliffs, NJ: Prentice-Hall.

Opie, Peter and Opie, Iona (1969) *Children's Games in Street and Playground: Chasing, Catching, Seeking, Hunting, Racing, Duelling, Exerting, Daring, Guessing, Acting, Pretending*. Oxford: Clarendon Press.

Polanyi, Karl, Arensberg, Conrad M. and Pearson, Harry W. (1957) *Trade and Market in the Early Empires*. Glencoe, IL: Free Press.

Podolny, Joel (1990) *A Sociologically Informed View of the Market*. Harvard University: William James Hall.

Robinson, Joan (1933) *The Economics of Imperfect Competition*. London: Macmillan.

Rose, F. G. G. (1960) *Classification of Kin, Age Structure, and Marriage amongst the Groote Eylandt Aborigines*. Berlin: Akademie-Verlag.

Spence, A. Michael (1974) *Market Signalling*. Cambridge, MA: Harvard University Press.

Stouffer, Samuel A. (1948) *The American Soldier*. Princeton, NJ: Princeton University Press.

Strathern, Andrew (1971) *The Rope of Moka*. Cambridge: Cambridge University Press.

Markets, networks and control 239

Udy, Stanley (1959) *Organization of Work*. Human Relations Area Files.

Udy, Stanley (1970) *Work in Traditional and Modern Society*. NJ: Prentice-Hall.

Vancil, Richard F. (1979) *Decentralization: Managerial Ambiguity by Design*. Honewood, IL: Dow-Jones.

Vlachoutsicos, C. and Lawrence, Paul (1990) What we don't know about Soviet management. *Harvard Business Review*, pp. 50–64.

Wellman, Barry and Berkowitz, S. D. (eds.) (1988) *Social Structures: A Network Approach*. New York: Cambridge University Press.

White, Harrison C. (1988) Varieties of markets. In Wellman and Berkowitz (eds.), *Social Structures. A Network Approach*. Cambridge: Cambridge University Press.

White, Harrison C. (1992) *Identity and Control*. Princeton: Princeton University Press.

Williamson, Oliver E. (1975) *Market and Hierarchies*. New York: Free Press.

[15]

Robust Action and the Rise of the Medici, 1400–1434[1]

John F. Padgett and Christopher K. Ansell
University of Chicago

We analyze the centralization of political parties and elite networks that underlay the birth of the Renaissance state in Florence. Class revolt and fiscal crisis were the ultimate causes of elite consolidation, but Medicean political control was produced by means of network disjunctures within the elite, which the Medici alone spanned. Cosimo de' Medici's multivocal identity as sphinx harnessed the power available in these network holes and resolved the contradiction between judge and boss inherent in all organizations. Methodologically, we argue that to understand state formation one must penetrate beneath the veneer of formal institutions, groups, and goals down to the relational substrata of peoples' actual lives. Ambiguity and heterogeneity, not planning and self-interest, are the raw materials of which powerful states and persons are constructed.

INTRODUCTION

Regardless of time or place, political centralization lies at the heart of state building. Less widely appreciated is the fact that the process of centralization is contradictory: its agents are forced to seek both reproduction and control. Centralization occurs, often abruptly, when founders emerge out of the soup of contending actors to establish (perhaps unintentionally) new rules for others' interaction. Reproduction ensues when rules induce roles, which induce interests, which induce strategic exchanges, which lock in patterns of collective action that depend on the

[1] Our colleague Paul McLean is a full joint participant in the larger project out of which this paper has been drawn. His help has been invaluable. We would also like to thank Wayne Baker, Ronald Breiger, Gene Brucker, Michael Cohen, Samuel Cohn, Walter Fontana, Mark Granovetter, the late David Greenstone, Wendy Griswold, the late David Herlihy, Alex Hicks, Ian Lustick, Charles Perrow, Tony Tam, Charles Tilly, and participants in the University of Chicago's Organizations and State-Building Workshop, the New School's "think and drink" seminar, and the Santa Fe Institute's Adaptive Organizations Conference for their many helpful comments. This article is dedicated to the memory of David Herlihy, whose quantitative research on Renaissance Florence made work like this possible.

American Journal of Sociology

rules.[2] Control is when others' locked-in interactions generate a flow of collective behavior that just happens to serve one's interests.

The contradiction, in state building or in any organization, is between judge and boss: founders cannot be both at once. Stable self-regulating maintenance of rules (i.e., legitimacy) hinges on contending actors' conviction that judges and rules are not motivated by self-interest (Elster 1983; Padgett 1986; Douglas 1986). At the same time, the nightmare of all founders is that their organizational creation will walk away from them. As Weber recognized long ago, in crisis (sooner or later inevitable), direct intervention in or overt domination of locked-in interactions is a sure sign of control's absence, not of its presence. Tactical tinkering to maintain fleeting control sucks in founders to locked-in role frames, thereby inducing attributions of self-interest and undermining their judicial perch above the fray.

This article analyzes one historical resolution of this state-building contradiction: the early 15th-century rise of Cosimo de' Medici in Renaissance Florence. We focus in particular on analyzing the structure and the sequential emergence of the marriage, economic, and patronage networks that constituted the Medicean political party, used by Cosimo in 1434 to take over the budding Florentine Renaissance state.

The historical case is exemplary in numerous ways. From a state centralization perspective, the period marks the abrupt transition from the late medieval pattern of fluid urban factionalism to the birth of a regionally consolidated Renaissance state (Baron 1966).[3] Before the advent of the Medici, two centuries of late medieval Florentine politics could be characterized by a cyclic alternation between guild corporatism and warring urban feudal factions, as is implied by figure 1. Originally, the Medici partook of this ancient rhythm, which became puzzlingly muted thereby. After the rise of the Medici, the periodic explosion of the system, under the pressure of "new men" families surging from below, abruptly stopped, never to be renewed.[4]

---

[2] Feedback dependence is not necessarily of the form of everyone's obeying the rules. More common is when rules structure the patterned process of subverting themselves, thereby sustaining a mutual symbiosis between subversion and rules. See Padgett (1990) for an example in the domain of courts.

[3] The oligarchic regime of Maso degli Albizzi and Niccolo da Uzzano (1382–1433) was significant in effecting this transition, as well as Cosimo's regime (1434–1464). The oligarchic regime spawned the formally democratic institutions that newly constituted "the consensual state" (Najemy 1982). Through political party networks, the Medicean regime learned how to use these institutions for purposes of control (Rubinstein 1966).

[4] "New men" (*novi cives*) refers to families only "recently" admitted to legal participation in the state. See fig. 1.

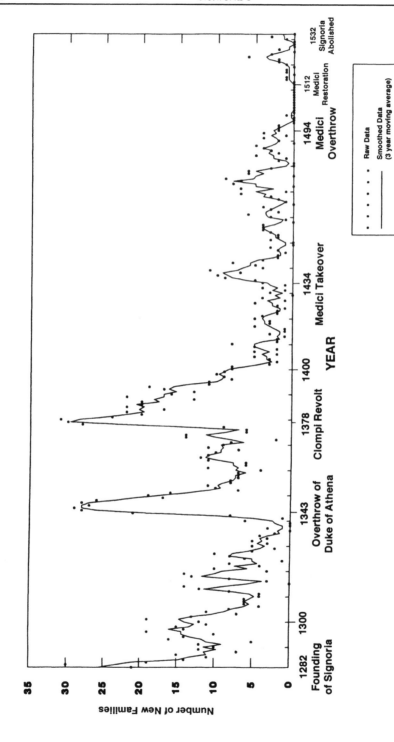

FIG. 1.—New families admitted to the Signoria, 1282–1532 (Source: Najemy 1982, pp. 320–22).

American Journal of Sociology

The dynamic underlying Florentine state centralization, we shall show, was this: unsuccessful class revolt (1378–82) and fiscal catastrophe due to wars (1424–33) were the ultimate causes, but these shocks were transmitted through the ratchet mechanism of elite network transformation. A citywide oligarchy, cemented through marriage, first emerged from a quasi-feudal federation of patrician neighborhood hierarchies. The very process of oligarchic consolidation, however, also produced the agent of its own destruction: the Medici party. The Medici party was a heterogeneous mixture of contradictory interests and crosscutting networks. In stark contrast to this fact, contemporaries perceived the Medici categorically as "heroes of the new men." The Medici's contradictory agglomeration exhibited great cohesion and capacity for sustained collective action. But what the Medici stood for is unclear to this day.

On the surface, it seems obvious that Cosimo de' Medici (1389–1464) did it all. Cosimo de' Medici was multiply embedded in complicated and sprawling Florentine marriage, economic, and patronage elite networks. And he was riding herd on vast macropolitical and macroeconomic forces far beyond his control. Yet he founded a dynasty that dominated Florence for three centuries. He consolidated a Europe-wide banking network that helped induce both international trade and state making elsewhere (de Roover 1966). And he oversaw and sponsored the Florentine intellectual and artistic efflorescence that we now call "the Renaissance."

Contemporaries deeply appreciated Cosimo's power. Foreign princes after 1434 flocked to Cosimo's private palazzo to work out international relations, much to the consternation of bypassed Florentine officials. Cosimo was legally enshrined on his death as the father of his country—no mean recognition from citizens as cynical and suspicious as the Florentines. Machiavelli ([1525] 1988), almost a full century later, still held Cosimo and his family in awe—attributing both all good and all evil in recent Florentine history to Cosimo's deep and ruthless machinations.[5]

Yet the puzzle about Cosimo's control is this: totally contrary to Machiavelli's portrait in *The Prince* of effective leaders as decisive and goal oriented, eyewitness accounts describe Cosimo de' Medici as an indecipherable sphinx (Brown 1961, p. 186). "Cosimo was anxious to remain in the background, hiding his great influence, and acting, when need arose, through a deputy. As a result, very little is known of the measures for which he was directly responsible" (Gutkind 1938, p. 124). Despite almost complete domination of the state, Cosimo never assumed lasting

---

[5] This is not entirely surprising, since Niccolo Machiavelli enjoyed the freedom to write in the first place because he had been outmaneuvered into exile by his boyhood friends, the Medici. Only their memory of his childhood saved Machiavelli from summary execution, a fact that probably focused his gaze.

Robust Action

public office.[6] And he hardly ever gave a public speech.[7] Lest one conclude that this implies only savvy back-room dealing, extant accounts of private meetings with Cosimo emphasize the same odd passivity.[8] After passionate pleas by supplicants for action of some sort, Cosimo typically would terminate a meeting graciously but icily, with little more commitment than "Yes my son, I shall look into that" (cf. Vespasiano 1963, pp. 223, 226).

Moreover, especially after 1434, all action by Cosimo (never explained or rationalized) appeared extraordinarily reactive in character. Everything was done in response to a flow of requests that, somehow or other, "just so happened" to serve Cosimo's extremely multiple interests.

We use the term "robust action" to refer to Cosimo's style of control. The key to understanding Cosimo's sphinxlike character, and the judge/boss contradiction thereby, we argue, is multivocality—the fact that single actions can be interpreted coherently from multiple perspectives simultaneously, the fact that single actions can be moves in many games at once, and the fact that public and private motivations cannot be parsed. Multivocal action leads to Rorschach blot identities, with all alters constructing their own distinctive attribution of the identity of ego. The "only" point of this, from the perspective of ego, is flexible opportunism—maintaining discretionary options across unforeseeable futures in the face of hostile attempts by others to narrow those options.

---

[6] The only state offices Cosimo ever held were short-term: three two-month terms as Gonfalonier of Justice (Gutkind 1938, p. 123), a one-year stint as one of the Ufficiali del Banco in 1428 (Molho 1971, p. 218), and a few martial and Monte commissions.
[7] We know of Cosimo's reticence because Florentine verbatim documentation of Consulte e Pratiche (an informal "inner elite" advisory body) and other speeches is very extensive. Two rare exceptions were a 1446 debate about potential electoral reforms (Rubinstein 1966, p. 24) and a vigorous public debate with Neri Capponi in 1450 about whether Florence should realign from Venice to Milan (Gutkind 1938, p. 110).
[8] Contemporaneous reports of Cosimo's personal style are as follows: "He acted privately with the greatest discretion in order to safeguard himself, and whenever he sought to attain an object he contrived to let it appear that the matter had been set in motion by someone other than himself. . . . He replies were brief and sometimes obscure, so that they might be made to bear a double sense" (Vespasiano [ca. 1495] 1963, p. 223). "In 1432, just before his exile and triumphant return, a political opponent, Francesco Filefo, described in a letter how Cosimo, in contrast to his 'open and lighthearted' brother, Lorenzo, 'is, I notice, despite appearing devoted to me, the kind of man who feigns and dissembles everything. He is so taciturn that he can scarcely be understood even by his intimates and servants in his family circle' " (Brown 1992, p. 106). "Said Neri di Gino [Capponi] to Cosimo: I would like for you to say things clearly to me, so that I can understand you. He replied: Learn my language!" (Poliziano [ca. 1478] 1985, p. 57). Cosimo's speech, when it occurred, was often Delphic in form. "As Gutkind has suggested, in this situation Cosimo's use of proverbs and fables served a useful political purpose—in delivering messages 'in such a way that no one noticed,' as Vespasiano put it" (Brown 1992, p. 106).

American Journal of Sociology

Crucial for maintaining discretion is *not* to pursue any specific goals. For in nasty strategic games, like Florence or like chess, positional play is the maneuvering of opponents into the forced clarification of their (but not your) tactical lines of action.[9] Locked-in commitment to lines of action, and thence to goals, is the product not of individual choice but at least as much of others' successful "ecological control" over you (Padgett 1981). Victory, in Florence, in chess, or in *go* means locking in others, but not yourself, to goal-oriented sequences of strategic play that become predictable thereby.[10]

Robust action resolves the contradiction between judge and boss because at the center there are no unequivocal self-interests. Cosimo, after all, "merely" responded graciously to the flow of requests. Because requests had to flow to him, others, not Cosimo himself, struggled to infer and then to serve Cosimo's inscrutable interests. Control was diffused throughout the structure of others' self-fashionings.

Of course, robust action will not work for just anyone. For the flow of requests to be channeled, only some network structures will do. And for the resolution of judge and boss to be credible, coherent interests must remain opaque as far down as it is conceivable to peer.[11] Contra Machiavelli, even Cosimo himself did not set out with a grand design to take over the state: this assumption reads history backward. As this article will show, Cosimo's political party first emerged around him. Only later, during the Milan war, did Cosimo suddenly apprehend the political capacity of the social network machine that lay at his fingertips.

[9] Our original inspiration for the robust action idea was the research of Eric Leifer (1991; this is a revised version of his 1985 Harvard University dissertation), who studied chess. While skill, not identity, was Leifer's main focus, he did point out that experts' moves in chess and in dyadic roles often are directed toward maintaining multiple lines of play, especially in balanced situations. Of course, one difference between Florence and chess is that the multiple networks of Florence constituted an entire linked ecology of games, each game layered on top of another. One single action, therefore, might be a move in multiple games simultaneously.

[10] Harrison C. White (1992) argues along similar lines. John Holland was the one who informed us that locking in others but not yourself to clear lines of play is also the secret to victory in the Japanese game *go*.

[11] Of course, Cosimo had goals tied to specific roles—to make money as a banker, to increase family prestige through marriage, to maintain power as leader of Florence— but the points here are three: (1) goals are properties of roles, not of persons, (2) no overarching trade-off or utility function existed for Cosimo that could prioritize these possibly conflicting role-based goals, and (3) once he was in structural position, success in attaining these goals flowed to him without tactical intervention or even effort on his part. In Cosimo's special position, indeed, which role was in play at which time was not transparent. Therefore, whether Cosimo de' Medici was really a person, as conceived by modern liberalism, is undecidable by any means available to us, or to them (cf. Goffman 1974, pp. 293–300; Foucault 1975).

Robust Action

The bulk of this article is an archaeological dig for the structural preconditions of that learning and of that success.

These arguments will be developed in the following stages: after a brief
summary of data, we will analyze first the attributional composition and
then the social network structure of the Medici party, during the period
1427–34, as compared with those of their opponents, the "oligarchs."
After this cross-sectional anatomy, we will sketch the long-term historical
dynamic—the emergence first of the marriage and second of the economic
patronage halves of the Medici party as a function of ongoing transformations within the Florentine elite. At the end, we will show how contradictory networks induced both robust action in Cosimo and political legitimacy in the Medicean state.

DATA SOURCES AND SELECTION

This article is empirically possible because of the thorough and impressive work of many historians of Florence. In particular, we build on the
work of Dale Kent, whose book, *The Rise of the Medici* (1978), in the
tradition of Lewis Namier (1929), is an intimate prosopographical description of the network foundations both of the Medici party, or faction,
and of the looser alliance system of their opponents.[12] From the detailed
text of this account, we coded a core network data set, which consists of
information on the following nine types of relations among early 15th-
century Florentine elite families: (*a*) one type of kinship relation—
intermarriage ties,[13] (*b*) four types of economic relations—trading or business ties, joint ownerships or partnerships, bank employment, and real
estate ties,[14] (*c*) two types of "political" relations—patronage and per-

[12] Some may question whether the term "party" is apt for such an early time period.
If presentist definitions, which include reference to mass electorates, are insisted on,
then of course the Medici did not organize a party. But the Medicean organization
was mobilized, in part, in order to influence the outcomes of popular elections (called
"scrutinies") for government office, albeit in a restricted electorate. This certainly fits
dictionary meanings of the term.

[13] At the valuable suggestion of Ronald Breiger, we took care in the second round of
our coding to distinguish the family that provided the marrying male from the family
that provided the marrying female. Hence, unlike the data provided to Breiger and
Pattison (1986), the interfamily marriage relations analyzed here are asymmetric. Only
marriages occurring in the time period 1394–1434 were coded. The modern reader
may need reminding that all of the elite marriages recorded here were arranged by
patriarchs (or their equivalents) in the two families. Intraelite marriages were conceived of partially in political alliance terms. Hence, there is little doubt that, in this
time and place, marriage relations were interfamily, not interpersonal, relations.

[14] Kent's sources for all these different types of economic relations (except bank employment) were the 1427 and 1433 *catasti*, which are registers of tax reports. Trading
and partnership data were symmetric, by definition, since information on directional-

American Journal of Sociology

sonal loans,[15] and (d) two types of personal friendship relations—personal friends and *mallevadori*, or surety, ties.[16] Social network ties were constituents of, as well as backdrops to, Florentine political party formation.

These network data, coded from Kent, were supplemented with attributional data coded from a variety of sources: (a) economic wealth was obtained from the computer tape of the 1427 *catasto,* coded and generously made available for public access by the late David Herlihy and Christiane Klapisch-Zuber (1981);[17] (b) "date of first Prior," the Florentine measure of family social status, was obtained from Najemy (1982) and Kent (1975);[18] (c) neighborhood residence, at both the ward (*gonfalone*) and the quarter levels, was obtained from Herlihy and Klapisch-Zuber's tape (1981) and from Kent (1975); and (d) 1403 tax assessments, for the richest 600 households in the city, were obtained from Martines (1963). In addition, for interpretative purposes, systematic data over time on factional memberships, bank employment, city finances, and rates of neighborhood exogamy were obtained from Brucker (1962, 1977), de Roover (1966), Molho (1971), and Cohn (1980), respectively.

All in all, the unusual richness of these data, from such a distant time, bear witness to the impressive creativity and industry both of the original

---

ity of trade and magnitude of partnership investment was not provided by Kent. Kent's asymmetric bank employment data were coded mostly from de Roover (1966). Real estate ties were coded as symmetric when they referred to joint ownership of property, and as asymmetric when they referred to rental relations.

[15] "Political" is in quotations here because the motivations underlying these relations may be complicated: a mixture of political aid, economic exchange, personal friendship, and unspecified "building up of credits." Such mixtures of motives are typical of multifaceted patron-client relations.

[16] Personal friends were coded conservatively as such only when Kent seemed to indicate, on the basis of surviving letters, that the relationship had no political content. This coding rule keeps "friendship" from being confounded by our dependent variable, membership in political faction. *Mallevadori* are friends who put up surety, or bond, to guarantee the good behavior of an exile. "Citizens who helped relatives or friends accused of political crimes were motivated by a strong sense of obligation, for they were risking not only money, but their reputations and status" (Brucker 1977, p. 29).

[17] Household economic wealth was aggregated to the clan or "common last name" level of aggregation, to be consistent with other attributional data. Some small amount of error is inevitable in this procedure (Kent 1978, p. 119).

[18] The Priorate (or city council), first created in 1282, was Florence's governing body. This board was almost sacred in its ritual construction (Trexler 1980); membership, on a randomly rotating (within a select circle) two-month-term basis, was public confirmation of one's family's and one's own highest status and honor, in peers' eyes (Martines 1963). Hence, the date of first Prior measures how old and dignified one's family was. Consciousness of their family's date of entry into the elite, relative to other families' dates of entry, was acute among Florentines.

Robust Action

Florentine scribes and of the modern historians who labor in the Florentine field.

Two matters are important to clarify at the outset, in order to frame
the universe of this study—the definition of "family" and the definition
of "elite."

Operationally, "family" here means "people with a common last
name." Hence, it is more equivalent to clan than to household.[19] This
level of aggregation is forced on us by the nature of some of our data
(particularly, date of first Prior and neighborhood).[20] However, F. W.
Kent (1977) provides strong substantive justification for this coding. Relations between distant lineages in an elite clan were less solidary during
the Renaissance than they had been in medieval *consorteria* times. But,
contra Burckhardt (1860) and Goldthwaite (1968), the Renaissance in
Florence was not an era of individualism. Relations among households
in a clan were typically, although not universally, very strong (see also
Brucker 1977, pp. 18–19). The turbulence of the times reinforced defensive cohesion (Brucker 1977, pp. 19–21; Kent and Kent 1981). And communal citizenship and office-holding regulations during the early 15th-
century placed more emphasis on the unitary legal character of clans
than before (Witt 1976, p. 262; Najemy 1982, chap. 8). In other words,
while the clan level of data aggregation is indeed a data convenience, it
was also a Florentine social reality.

The definition of "elite" is more complicated. The Florentine political
elite (called the *reggimento*) was in no way identical to the Florentine
economic elite, in part because of volatility in international markets. In
our definition, which emphasizes political practice, we follow the lead of
Kent (1975), who in turn follows the practice of Brucker (1977).

For us, a Florentine family is politically elite if it satisfies any of the
following criteria: (*a*) it had two or more members who spoke in the
Consulte e Pratiche three or more times between January 1429 and December 1434, (*b*) it had three or more members who qualified in 1433 for
scrutiny, or election to the leading public offices in Florence,[21] or (*c*) it
was a magnate clan.[22] Information on the former two criteria is contained

---

[19] The median number of households in the 92 elite families studied here is nine. One
household, in turn, may contain a number of politically active brothers, in addition
to the patriarch father. (See Herlihy and Klapisch-Zuber [1985] for more information
on elite vs. nonelite household composition.)

[20] But also Kent and Brucker, following the practice of Florentine chroniclers, frequently report alliances and ties by family name only.

[21] In particular, the so-called Tre Maggiori: the Signoria (or Priorate) and the Dodici
and Sedici (auxiliary colleges to the Signoria).

[22] Magnate clans were old, previously powerful and violent noble families that had
misbehaved politically in the past. They and their offspring were punished by the

American Journal of Sociology

in Kent (1975); information on the last criterion (added because of the political importance of this legally excluded group) is contained in Becker (1965) and Lansing (1991). Since official Florentine political participation was comparatively broad, this liberal definition of the ruling elite contains more parvenu new men and upper middle classes than one might expect.

In all, 215 Florentine families (i.e., clans) satisfied one or more of these criteria. Attributes of these 215 families are analyzed in the following section. Kent's book (1978) contains information on at least one marriage or economic relation for 92 of these 215 families. These 92 families are the basis for the network analysis contained herein.

By intention, Kent's book is a comparative study of the Medici party and its oligarch opponents. Hence, the 92-family "sample" is skewed, relative to the 215-family elite "universe," toward active participation in factions and away from political neutrals.[23] We are not aware of any sample bias in Kent's selection of network data *among* partisans.[24]

NETWORK STRUCTURE

Attributional Analyses of Florentine Partisanship

Let us begin our analysis in the traditional way: namely, let us ask, Who exactly were the Mediceans and their oligarch opponents? And what social interests did they represent? Four hypotheses (not necessarily mutually exclusive) have been presented in the literature, all built around a common assumption that politics fundamentally means a struggle between self-interested groups.

---

victorious *popolani* in 1293, and occasionally thereafter, by being excluded legally from high public office (Becker 1965; Lansing 1991). They were politically defanged, however, only in this formal sense.

[23] This fact means that it is difficult, with these data, to study factional participation—only factional membership, given participation, can be studied. As will be seen in the attributional analyses below, however, "factional participation" included virtually all of the economically and socially important families in Florence. Nonparticipation was more an issue for the politically active, but not factional, middle classes. We are currently working to expand our network data set with primary materials, in part in order to evaluate potential sample selection problems. Padgett has been coding original Carte dell'Ancisa marriage records in the Florentine archives, covering the *longue durée* period 1300–1500. Our colleague, Paul McLean, likewise has been coding original 1427 and 1433 *catasti* tax records in order to assemble a broader cross-section of economic relations in the Florentine elite. Analyses of these primary materials will be reported in future publications.

[24] In particular, residential distribution of marriage dyads (possibly relevant for bias in estimated exogamy rates, calculated below) is not seriously skewed. The slight overrepresentation of San Giovanni families if anything works against the Medici neighborhood exogamy finding reported below.

Robust Action

An older economic class hypothesis is that the oligarchs were rich, and the Mediceans were of the middling sort. Prominent recent exponents of the class perspective, albeit not explicitly applied to the Medici, include Martines (1963) and Cohn (1980). An important variant of the economic class hypothesis applies not to volume of wealth but to its change: the Mediceans were rising economic parvenus, while oligarchs were "old money," generally on the decline.[25]

Tables 1–4 present distributional data on these two economic class hypotheses for the entire 215-family universe of elite. Distributions of wealth and of change in wealth are tabulated for Medici partisan families, for oligarchic partisan families, and for neutral families. Party memberships were taken, here and throughout this paper, from the two lists published as appendices to Kent (1978).[26]

Both economic class hypotheses are false. While both the Mediceans and the oligarchs were significantly more wealthy than the neutrals, the two parties' wealth distributions were statistically identical to each other. Moreover, the elite was not split into partisan rich and neutral poor; both parties were extremely heterogeneous in their wealth composition. A similar story holds for change in wealth, as measured relative to a 1403 base. A Marxist class struggle this was not.

Correlated with but not identical to the economic class view is the social class (or prestige) argument: the oligarch party was recruited from older patricians, whereas the Mediceans were new men—defined not in terms of wealth, but rather in terms of the political age of their families. Brucker (1962, 1977) and Becker (1962) are the most prominent exponents of the view that broad stretches of Florentine history should be analyzed primarily as a conflict between old and new family political cohorts. Bolstering this interpretation is the fact that numerous contemporaries, such as (pseudo) Niccolo da Uzzano (Kent 1978, pp. 212–14) and the chronicler Cavalcanti, forcefully analyzed the conflict in class terms, without always distinguishing between economic and social versions.

As presented in tables 5 and 6, evidence for the social class hypothesis is mixed. The oligarchs were indeed more skewed toward patricians than were the Mediceans, but this was due to the relative absence of new men

---

[25] Logically, a third variant might be occupational in focus: the Mediceans were bankers, and the oligarchs rentiers. However, no one in the literature has, to our knowledge, seriously proffered this view, for the simple reason that Florentine economic elites are well-known to have been extremely multifaceted and nonspecialized in their money-making activities.

[26] Kent identified Medicean partisans primarily from private letters to and from the Medici. She identified oligarch partisans from lists of those exiled when the Medici took over.

American Journal of Sociology

TABLE 1

REGGIMENTO FAMILY DISTRIBUTIONS OF WEALTH IN 1427

Gross Wealth (1,000 florins)	No. of Oligarch Families	No. of Medicean Families	No. of Neutral Families	Total No. of Families	Proportion Partisan
More than 100	4	2	0	6	1.000
50–100	7	7	6	21	.714
10–50........................	16	23	44	86	.488
0–10	14	10	58	83	.301
Missing	0	0	18	19	.053
Total	41	42	126	215	.414

NOTE.—Median gross wealth (in florins) was, for oligarch families, 21,053; for Medicean families, 20,874; for neutral families, 9,052; for total families, 12,414. The source for the data in this table is Herlihy and Klapisch-Zuber (1981). "Family" is operationally defined by common last name. Hence, the gross family wealth reported here is sums of the prededuction wealth of all households that shared last names in the 1427 *catasto*, according to Herlihy's computerized coding. Numbers do not add perfectly because of families whose partisan loyalties were split. When split families had a majority on one partisan side or the other, they were allocated to the majority side for purposes of the attributional analyses here. However, six families were tied, and excluded from all tabular breakdowns (but not from proportion partisan calculations).

TABLE 2

KOLMOGOROV-SMIRNOV TESTS FOR DISTRIBUTIONAL DIFFERENCE IN FAMILY WEALTH

	Kolmogorov-Smirnov Statistic	One-tailed P
Mediceans vs. oligarchs	.1051	.632
Mediceans vs. neutrals	.3942	.000
Oligarchs vs. neutrals..	.3202	.002

NOTE.—Here and in tables 4 and 6, Kolmogorov-Smirnov statistics were calculated on the basis of underlying continuous distributions, not on the basis of the summary tables 1, 3, and 5, in which the data have been made ordinal through cut points. Stricter one-tailed tests which use the chi-square approximation, not the more usual two-tailed Kolmogorov-Smirnov tests, are applied in tables 2, 4, and 6 since the literature implies the following expectations: Mediceans were on average less wealthy, more recently wealthy, and newer (in terms of first Prior) than oligarchs. See Blalock (1972, p. 264) for this one-tailed chi-square approximation procedure, which makes it harder to reject the hypothesis that parties are different. (I thank Ed Laumann for this suggestion.)

from the oligarch party, not to the absence of patricians from the Medicean side. Mediceans were not more new men than the oligarchs; they simply were more socially heterogeneous. Relative to political neutrals as a control group, the Mediceans were distinctly old-guard patrician in cast.

Finally, both Dale Kent herself (1978; Kent and Kent 1982) and F. W.

Robust Action

TABLE 3

Reggimento Family Distributions of Relative Wealth Change, 1403–27

Estimated Change in Relative Wealth	No. of Oligarch Families	No. of Medicean Families	No. of Neutral Families	Total No. of Families	Proportion Partisan
More than 100%......	2	7	7	17	.588
0% to 100%...........	15	11	19	46	.587
0% to −50%.........	8	7	17	34	.500
−50% to −100%	4	8	17	29	.414
Missing.................	12	9	66	89	.258
Total.................	41	42	126	215	.414

Note.—Median tax in 1403 was 24 florins; median wealth in 1427 was 22,500 florins. The sources for the data in this table are Herlihy and Klapisch-Zuber (1981) and Martines (1963). Since systematic data on wealth do not exist before the 1427 *catasto*, this table is based on the tax tables of 1403 *prestanza* (or forced loans) found in Martines (1963, pp. 353–65). These tables report tax data only on the 150 wealthiest households in each of the four quarters—that is, 600 households in all. Thus, the 1403 *prestanza* information used here is a truncated data set. *Prestanza* tax data of course are not comparable to gross wealth data, so both data sets were standardized by their medians before estimated change was calculated—that is, estimated change = [(1427 wealth/wealth median) − (1403 tax/tax median)]/(1403 tax/tax median). Because of this standardization, "estimated change" refers not to absolute change in florins, which is impossible to know, but rather to relative change, in ranked comparison to peers. Data in the above table (and associated medians) include only those families with nonmissing data in both 1403 and 1427. Missing data is a serious problem here because of the truncated nature of Martines's 1403 "wealthiest" data set.

TABLE 4

Kolmogorov-Smirnov Tests for Distributional Difference in (Estimated) Relative Wealth Change

	Kolmogorov-Smirnov Statistic	One-tailed *P*
Mediceans vs. oligarchs	.1735	.395
Mediceans vs. neutrals	.1606	.333
Oligarchs vs. neutrals..	.2954	.033

Note.—For an explanation of the statistics used, see table 2.

Kent (1977, 1987; Kent and Kent 1982), without directly disagreeing with either class view, distinctively emphasize the importance of neighborhood: The Medici party was rooted in the San Giovanni quarter, particularly the Medici's home ward of Lion d'oro, whereas their opponents were centered in the Santa Croce quarter.

Tables 7 and 8 show that there was no statistically significant difference between the two parties by neighborhood. This does not mean that

American Journal of Sociology

TABLE 5

REGGIMENTO FAMILY DISTRIBUTIONS OF SOCIAL PRESTIGE

Date of First Prior	No. of Oligarch Families	No. of Medicean Families	No. of Neutral Families	Total No. of families	Proportion Partisan
1282–1299...............	24	19	26	72	.639
1300–1342...............	10	7	30	48	.375
1343–1377...............	5	9	31	45	.311
1378–1434...............	2	7	33	44	.250
Missing	0	0	6	6	.000
Total	41	42	126	215	.414

NOTE.—Median date of first Prior is, for oligarch families, 1289; for Medicean families, 1318.5; for neutral families, 1349; for total families, 1327. The source for the data in this table is Najemy (1982, 323–27). Except for the arbitrary date of 1300, the intervals in dates reported here are defined by major revolutions in the history of Florence: 1282, 1343, and 1378. Since large waves of new families were admitted to eligibility in the priorate during these revolutions, the historical periodization in table 5 corresponds to discrete political cohorts. Old magnates either have no date of first Prior, by virtue of never being legally eligible for this office, or have a misleadingly recent date of first Prior, if they were reinstated as *popolani* somewhere along the line. Therefore, most magnates were coded as having a date of 1284, essentially the oldest possible. There are 21 magnate families in this data set.

TABLE 6

KOLMOGOROV-SMIRNOV TESTS OF DISTRIBUTIONAL DIFFERENCE IN SOCIAL PRESTIGE

	Kolmogorov-Smirnov Statistic	One-tailed *P*
Mediceans vs. oligarchs	.2968	.026
Mediceans vs. neutrals	.2619	.014
Oligarchs vs. neutrals...	.4477	.000

NOTE.—For an explanation of the statistics used, see table 2.

geography was irrelevant: the two parties mirrored each other in geographical concentration, especially relative to neutrals. The Mediceans were indeed overrepresented in San Giovanni, but then again so were the oligarchs. San Giovanni was the most polarized of quarters; Santa Croce was a distant second.

The main theme that comes through these attributional analyses is similarity, not difference. With the important exception of the absence of new men from the oligarch side, the Mediceans and oligarchs were mirror images of each other. The elite as a whole appears to have fractured in two, with no underlying social group basis.

A deep historical enigma remains. Contrary to these heterogeneous

Robust Action

TABLE 7

REGGIMENTO FAMILY DISTRIBUTIONS OF NEIGHBORHOOD RESIDENCE

Quarter of City	No. of Oligarch Families	No. of Medicean Families	No. of Neutral Families	Total No. of Families	Proportion Partisan
Santo Spirito................	7	8	36	52	.308
Santa Croce.................	14	6	33	55	.400
Santa Maria Novella......	9	7	29	46	.370
San Giovanni	11	21	27	61	.557
Missing.......................	0	0	1	1	.000
Total......................	41	42	126	215	.414

NOTE.—The source for these data, both for the four quarters and for the 16 *gonfaloni* (or wards), is Kent (1975, pp. 624–32).

TABLE 8

CHI-SQUARE TESTS OF DISTRIBUTIONAL DIFFERENCE IN RESIDENCE

	ACROSS QUARTERS $(df = 3)$		ACROSS GONFALONI $(df = 15)$	
	χ^2	P	χ^2	P
Mediceans vs. oligarchs	6.629	.084	17.806	.273
Mediceans vs. neutrals	12.554	.006	29.567	.014
Oligarchs vs. neutrals................	2.683	.443	19.660	.185

membership statistics, contemporaries had a perfectly clear, almost po-lemical, understanding of what was at stake. Virtually all recorded par-ticipants interpreted the partisan conflict in traditional economic and/or social class terms: the oligarchs were considered to be the conservative party of old, wealthy, and threatened patricians, and the Mediceans were considered to be the heroes of the economically rising new men (Brucker 1977; Kent 1978). This in spite of the fact that it does not objectively appear to be true.[27] A puzzling structural mismatch existed between clear cognitive typifications of social groups at the level of culture and extreme heterogeneity and overlap of social groups at the level of behavioral action.

This puzzle about mismatch between cognition and behavior remains

[27] Moreover, even if the difference were one of policy, not one of membership, fig. 1 shows clearly that the Medici did not in fact represent the interests of the new men once they assumed office.

American Journal of Sociology

to be solved, but even at this point we can conclude that tables 1–8 provide prima facie evidence against classical group theories of parties, of either the pluralist or the neo-Marxist varieties. These theories assume that parties represent coalitions of groups. But political "groups" in the sense of sets of attributionally similar individuals who solve collective action problems in order to coordinate action on common (latent) interests simply did not exist in Renaissance Florence. Indeed, as we shall show below, the more homogeneous the attributes, the less coherent the collective action. We do not argue thereby that social attributes and groups are irrelevant to party formation; merely that their role needs to be understood within a deeper relational context. There is no simple mapping of groups or spatial dimensions onto parties; social attributes and group interests are "merely" *cognitive* categories, which party mobilization, networks, and action crosscut.

Social Structure: Blockmodel Analysis

We now look more directly at this mobilization, through an analysis of our nine microstructural networks. Party organization was not reflective of any one of these networks, taken alone, but Kent has already demonstrated persuasively the fact that both parties were constructed from differing concatenations of preexisting social networks. We will return in subsequent sections to examine the consequences of these patterns of micromobilization for the aggregate social characteristics (or "interests") that they organized.

The essential step in this task is to derive an overall relational picture of Florence's social structure, within the 92-family ruling elite. For the purposes of this article, we define "social structure" to be marriage and economic networks, which we take to be "strong ties" in Granovetter's (1973) sense.[28] Figure 2a presents, in graphical form, the result of our

[28] This distinction between "strong tie" marriage and economic networks and "weak tie" political and friendship networks was to some extent arrived at inductively. We were concerned from the beginning with excluding patronage and friendship networks from this particular analysis, because these might be too close to our dependent variable, political partisanship, to be considered legitimate independent predictors. Marriage and economic networks, on the other hand, are driven primarily by nonpartisan calculations. It goes against the whole thrust of our article to assert that these networks were independent of politics, but the first-order consideration in economic relations was making money, while the first-order consideration in marriage was hierarchical status. Furthermore, partisan politics operated on a higher-frequency temporal pulse than did the more glacially changing marriage and economic structures. Personal loans and *mallevadori* ties, however, were ambiguous in our minds. We ran the blockmodel analyses both including and excluding these networks and examined the robustness of the resulting partitions as well as the goodness of fit (see below). Includ-

Robust Action

analyses: an aggregate blockmodel image of the marriage and economic networks, obtained by methods described in Appendix A. Figure 2b presents the parallel blockmodel image of "weak tie" political and friendship networks, based on the family clusters generated by the analysis of marriage and economic data. Appendix B lists the cluster memberships of those families that are contained in the various structural blocks graphed in figures 2a and 2b, along with those families' partisan affiliations and social attributes.

Methodological and goodness-of-fit issues are addressed in Appendix A. Suffice it to say here that the structuralist research style embedded in blockmodeling aggregates actors into structurally equivalent sets, or "blocks," in accordance with their common *external* ties with outsiders, rather than in accordance with dense internal relations with each other (as in cliques). The sets of families observed in Appendix B, in other words, were clustered or "thrust together" by common third-party relations to outside families; the blocks need not (and usually do not) contain any ties within themselves.[29]

Three graphical points need to be borne in mind in order to interpret the figures: (1) Family labels in figures 2a and 2b do not indicate solo families; they encode the most prominent family in that structurally equivalent block of families (App. B gives details). (2) An image line or "bond" in this global portrait corresponds to at least two underlying ties between families in the linked blocks, of the graphically indicated type. (3) The triangulated circle superimposed onto the blockmodel diagram contains the dependent variable, Medici party membership. The bulk of oligarchic partisans are contained in the rectangular set of intermarrying blocks, directly beneath the Medicean party.

The first thing to observe about figure 2a is that the capacity of marriage and economic blockmodels to predict political partisanship is remarkable, especially given the virtual attributional identity of the two parties. The partisanship of the Medici family itself is impossible to predict from social structure alone, since the Medici family was deeply tied to both sides. But given the Medici split from the lower set of blocks, prediction of Medicean followers is obvious: the enclosed circle of blocks

---

ing these two networks did not improve goodness of fit but did have the effect of breaking up the oligarch blocks into smaller "globules," an indicator of ties that cut across rather than reinforce the existing system. Figure 2b illustrates this graphically: Personal loans and *mallevadori* ties were sent not only to structural intimates, but also to families far distant in the social structure. Perhaps these were the "bridges" to future structural change, as elite families attempted to reach to new partners, just as Granovetter's weak tie image conveys.

[29] If they do, this is indicated in the figures by a circle around the block name.

American Journal of Sociology

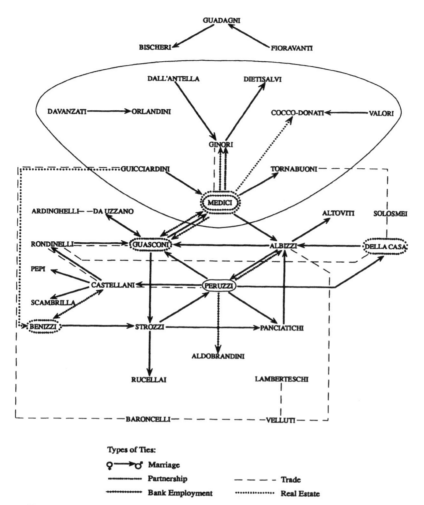

Types of Ties:

♀———♂ Marriage

············· Partnership   — — — — Trade

············· Bank Employment   ··············· Real Estate

Fig. 2a.—Marriage and economic blockmodel structure (92 elite families)

contains families that had systematic access to the rest of the elite only through the Medici.

More specifically, 93% of the families within the triangulated circle were mobilized actively into the Medici party. Fifty-nine percent of all other families, including neutrals, were organized actively into the oligarch party. Excluding neutrals, 82% of all other partisan families joined the oligarch side (see App. A, tables A1 and A2, for details). Even errors in partisanship prediction here are a bit overstated: in fact, we would predict families in the cross-pressured Guasconi and Albizzi blocks to be

Robust Action

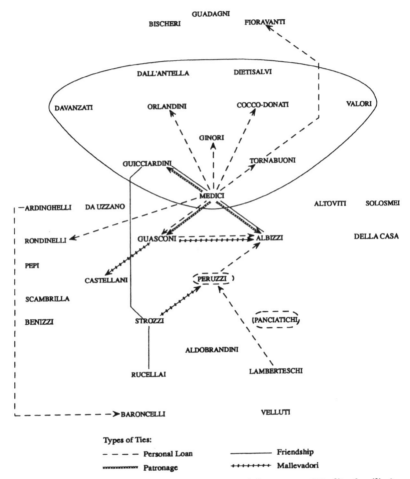

GUADAGNI
BISCHERI   FIORAVANTI

DALL'ANTELLA   DIETISALVI

DAVANZATI   ORLANDINI   COCCO-DONATI   VALORI

GINORI

GUICCIARDINI   TORNABUONI

MEDICI

—ARDINGHELLI   DA UZZANO   ALTOVITI   SOLOSMEI

RONDINELLI   ←   GUASCONI +++++++++ ALBIZZI   DELLA CASA

PEPI

CASTELLANI   PERUZZI

SCAMBRILLA

BENIZZI   STROZZI   (PANCIATICHI)

ALDOBRANDINI

RUCELLAI   LAMBERTESCHI

BARONCELLI   VELLUTI

Types of Ties:

– – – – Personal Loan   ———— Friendship

⌁⌁⌁⌁⌁⌁ Patronage   +++++++ Mallevadori

FIG. 2b.—"Political" and friendship blockmodel structure (92 elite families)

split in their partisan loyalties, which for the most part they were. Truly, the microstructure of marriage and economics was central to the formation of parties in Florence.[30] Rather than parties being generated by social

[30] The lack of congruence between patronage (fig. 2b) and the rest of the social structure (fig. 2a) is worthy of note. A standard image is that patronage is the glue that binds parties together internally. Here, however, this is not particularly true. Elites did tax, job-hunting, court, and miscellaneous favors for other elites, almost regardless of partisanship, as much as they did favors for their client followers. Even though patronage was pervasive, in Renaissance Florence party was far more deeply embedded in marriage and economic relations than it was in patronage relations.

American Journal of Sociology

groups, we argue, both parties and social groups were induced conjointly by underlying networks.

We will return in a later section to a causal discussion of the exact temporal unfolding of this intimate connection between social networks and party membership. For now, however, we discuss only the consequences of this social structure for political control.

Contemporaries and historians have long known that the Medici party was far more cohesive and tightly centralized than was the looser and more cross-pressured oligarch faction. With the aid of figure 2a, it is easy to see why.

The Medici party was an extraordinarily centralized, and simple, "star" or "spoke" network system, with very few relations among Medici followers: the party consisted almost entirely of direct ties to the Medici family.[31] One important consequence for central control was that Medici partisans were connected to other Medici partisans almost solely through the Medici themselves. In addition, Medici partisans were connected to the rest of the oligarchic elite only through the intermediation of the Medici family. Medici partisans in general possessed remarkably few intraelite network ties; compared to oligarchs, they were structurally impoverished.[32] In such an impoverished network context, it is easy to understand how a solo dependence on a powerful family would loom very large indeed (Emerson 1962).

---

[31] Graph centralization can be measured with the network betweenness statistic (C_B) of Freeman (1979, p. 230), usually interpreted as intensity of concentration of resource or information flows. Among Medicean families, marriage relations were concentrated at the level $C_B = .362$. Among oligarch partisans, marriage $C_B = .184$. On the economic front, $C_B = .429$ among Mediceans, compared to $C_B = .198$ among oligarchs. (Economic ties, including personal loans, were pooled for the latter calculations. Personal loans were included because otherwise the density of intra-Medicean ties was too low. All data were binarized and symmetrized for these calculations, as required by the Freeman measure.) We thank an *AJS* referee for the suggestion of calculating these statistics.

[32] Statistics on two-step ties—the number of families that families tied to the Medici were tied to (by marriage or economic relations)—demonstrate this clearly, especially for the case of marriage. Within this 92-family data set, Medici marriage partners were married, on median, to only 2 other families. (According to blockmodel analysis, these two ties were structurally incoherent.) In contrast, the median number of marriage partners for two oligarch control groups (see below for description) were as follows: 6.5 for Santa Croce faction leader families and 4.5 for oligarchic superelite families. Data on "political" and friendship partners show the same pattern less dramatically: The median numbers of (marriage or economic) partners of Medici "political" or friendship partners were 2 and 3, respectively. This compares with the control groups' partners: 5.5 and 6.5 for the Santa Croce leaders, and 4 and 4 for the superelite. For economic partners, on the other hand, there was little difference: 3.5 for the Medici's partners versus 5 for Santa Croce partners, and only 3 for the partners of the superelite.

Robust Action

Conversely, the oligarch side was densely interconnected, especially through marriage. Dense structural interconnection, however, did not lead to cohesive collective action. The oligarchs were composed of too many status equals, each with plausible network claims to leadership. In dense networks in times of crisis, cacophony ensued, as each family conspired privately with other families to which they were tied about the proper course of action. Simultaneous and contradictory conversations redounded through ambagious private network channels, generating cross-pressure on each family instead of collective convergence.

A concrete behavioral example, the final "military" showdown between the two sides, will illustrate this point. On the morning of September 26, 1433, Rinaldo Albizzi, titular leader of the oligarchs, passed the word to his supporters to assemble their troops at a certain piazza in order forcibly to seize the city hall and the government (Kent 1978, pp. 332–34). At the appointed hour, only a portion of his supporters appeared. Each supporter looked around at, and no doubt consulted with, other supporters, and a stochastic threshold equilibrium ensued, in which repeated efforts by Rinaldo to assemble more troops (especially from Palla Strozzi) were offset by other supporters' changing their mind and drifting away.

In contrast, while the oligarchs dithered, the Medici immediately and decisively mobilized their supporters to join the Priors in the embattled Palazzo Vecchio. The clarity of this coordinated response was astonishing, given the fact that Cosimo and Lorenzo de' Medici were in Venice at the time.[33] As a result of this Medicean mobilization, no military engagement actually ensued, since it became clear to Albizzi supporters, if not to Rinaldo himself, that they had no chance. At this point, popular opinion swung massively behind the Medici, Cosimo was recalled from Venice in triumph, and Cosimo's oligarchic enemies were exiled, this time for good.

Kent (1978, pp. 228–34) also gives examples, less dramatic than this, of the greater cohesion of the Medici side during 1427–28 electoral maneuvering.

Even granted this explanation of the greater cohesion of the Medici side, an equilibrium puzzle remains: How could such a centralized spoke system maintain itself? Florentine clientage systems historically had been notoriously fluid. And the oligarchs had a clear incentive to marry into or do business with Medici supporters, thereby inducing cross-pressure and sowing dissent. The Medici supporters would appear to have had

---

[33] Temporarily, the Medici brothers had been exiled. They were not, however, successfully cut off from secretly communicating with and issuing standing orders to their supporters.

American Journal of Sociology

an equally clear incentive to respond, in order to alleviate their extreme dependence. At the very least, one would assume Medicean supporters would want to interbreed among themselves, for defensive if no other purposes, for only then would they have the organizational capacity to resist Medici domination, should they ever choose to do so. Structural isolation among Medici partisans would seem to have been in the long-term self-interest only of the Medici.

This structural atomization puzzle is only deepened through closer inspection of figures 2a and 2b. Two large blocks of Medici supporters were connected to the Medici essentially through marriage alone. Other blocks of Medici supporters were connected to the Medici solely by economic or by personal loan relations. The Medici had strongly multiplex ties with the oligarch Guasconi block,[34] but, within their own party, the Medici did not marry those families with whom they engaged in economic relations, nor did they do business with those whom they married.[35]

This is in sharp contrast to the greater multiplexity of relations on the oligarch side: core oligarch families, the superelite and the Santa Croce faction leaders (see below), married into 40% and 38%, respectively, of the clans with whom they did business.

Most sociologists' Durkheimian presumptions are that the more overlapping ties one has with another, the more closely and holistically bound the other is to you. Obligations from one sphere spill over into another. The Medici, however, apparently believed the opposite: to control followers politically, segregate one's social relations with them. On the whole, multiplex ties (across marriage and economics) were discouraged. Thus, structural isolation operated in two ways: the marriage and economic isolation of partisans from all others (including other partisans), and the segregation of types of ties with the Medici themselves.

Comparative Statics of Attributes with Networks

The beginnings of an understanding of stability can be gained from a reexamination of the social attributes listed in Appendix B. The large Guicciardini and Tornabuoni blocks, with whom the Medici were intermarried, were composed virtually entirely of patricians (i.e., date of first Prior before 1343) who also had substantial wealth. In sharp contrast, the Ginori, the Orlandini, and the Cocco-Donati blocks, to whom the Medici were connected through economic or personal loan ties, were

[34] The Medici bank was a primary source of these exceptional multiplex ties. Often such multiply tied exceptions did not politically support the Medici in the end—e.g., two prominent families in the Guasconi block: the Bardi and the Guasconi themselves.
[35] There was only one exception to this rule: the Tornabuoni.

Robust Action

composed almost entirely of new men (date of first Prior after 1343). The remaining Medicean blocks—the Davanzati, the dall'Antella, the Dietisalvi, and the Valori blocks—were for the most part patricians of only modest wealth. These blocks of families were connected to the Medici indirectly, via intermarriage with economically connected new men.

The hybrid social class character of the Mediceans, revealed in tables 5 and 6, has now been clarified: actually, the Medici party was an agglomeration of structurally disjoint patrician and new men components. Different social class interests were embodied in the Medici party; (social) class contradiction was quite real. Not only that, but within the party these elements were separately clustered by Medici ties and then kept rigidly segregated from each other, to be connected indirectly only through the Medici themselves.

Given this, there is no particular mystery about the low intermarriage rate among Mediceans: patrician and new men supporters despised each other. Status-conscious patricians (Medici included) usually would not dream of sullying their own honor by marrying into new men families; such would be a downward-mobility admission of status equality. Part of the distinctive Medicean party organization, in other words, was simply leveraged off and sustained by the ordinary cognitive classifications and social marriage rules of Florentine elites.

A close reexamination of Appendix B also reveals a second striking attributional cleavage between these Medicean social class segments, this time on the dimension of neighborhood. Almost none of the patricians in the Guicciardini and Tornabuoni blocks came from the San Giovanni quarter, where the Medici resided. The Medici, in other words, did not marry those with whom they lived.[36] However, 10 of the 14 families in the other Medici blocks—both new men and the indirectly tied patricians, married to new men—resided in San Giovanni. The Medici, in other words, did a great deal of business (plus personal loans) with those with whom they lived. In addition, they somehow induced local San Giovanni patrician supporters to marry into the families of their economic partners, rather than into their own.

Thus, the Medicean supporters were deeply cleaved on two attributional dimensions simultaneously—social class (i.e., prestige) and neighborhood. Not only did the various components despise each other; they did not run into each other much either. Only the Medici family itself linked the segments.

To give a more precise sense of the distinctiveness of this Medici agglomeration, we present table 9. The upper panels of the three parts

[36] Weissman (1982) makes vivid the dense piazza-oriented street life of Renaissance Florence, in which one constantly mingled with (or at least ran into) one's neighbors.

TABLE 9

SOCIAL ATTRIBUTES AND PARTISANSHIP OF TIES: MEDICI VERSUS SUPERELITE VERSUS SANTA CROCE FACTION LEADERS

SOCIAL PRESTIGE: DATE OF FIRST PRIOR

	Medici			Superelite			Santa Croce Faction Leaders		
	Pre-1343	Post-1343	*n*	Pre-1343	Post-1343	*n*	Pre-1343	Post-1343	*n*
Allocation of types of ties:									
Marriage (M)	.93	.07	28	.93	.07	58	.87	.13	30
Friendship (F + M)	1.00	.00	9	.87	.13	31	.79	.21	14
"Political" (L + P)	.62	.38	45	.86	.14	21	.69	.31	16
Economic (T + P + B + R)	.44	.56	27	.88	.12	16	.86	.14	21
Total	.69	.31	109	.90	.10	126	.81	.19	81
Political support consequences of ties:*									
Marriage (M)	.71	1.0		.73	.31		.85	.37	
Friendship (F + M)	.76	...		.57	.00		.84	.00	
"Political" (L + P)	.58	.97		.42	.17		.82	.20	
Economic (T + P + B + R)	.55	.90		.81	..		.85	.50	
Total	.64	.94		.65	.25		.84	.27	

ECONOMIC CLASS: WEALTH (in 1,000 Florins)

	Medici			Superelite			Santa Croce Faction Leaders		
	More than 25	0–25	*n*	More than 25	0–25	*n*	More than 25	0–25	*n*
Allocation of types of ties:									
Marriage (M)	.82	.18	28	.79	.21	58	.83	.17	30
Friendship (F + M)	.89	.11	9	.81	.19	31	.86	.14	14

(table continued from previous page)

	Medici			Superelite			Santa Croce Faction Leaders		
	San Giovanni	Outside Quarter	n	In Quarter	Outside Quarter	n	Santa Croce	Outside Quarter	n
"Political" (L + P)	.51	.49	45	.71	.29	21	.94	.06	16
Economic (T + P + B + R)	.56	.44	27	.50	.50	16	.52	.48	21
Total	.63	.37	109	.75	.25	126	.78	.22	81
Political support consequences of ties:*									
Marriage (M)	.72	.80		.72	.64		.74	1.0	
Friendship (F + M)	.73	...		.54	.33		.61	...	
"Political" (L + P)	.67	.74		.47	.17		.60	...	
Economic (T + P + B + R)	.61	.92		.79	.81		.76	.85	
Total	.68	.78		.63	.54		.69	.92	

NEIGHBORHOOD: CITY QUARTER

	Medici			Superelite			Santa Croce Faction Leaders		
	San Giovanni	Outside Quarter	n	In Quarter	Outside Quarter	n	Santa Croce	Outside Quarter	n
Allocation of types of ties:									
Marriage (M)	.14	.86	28	.36	.64	58	.33	.67	30
Friendship (F + M)	.33	.67	9	.29	.71	31	.36	.64	14
"Political" (L + P)	.40	.60	45	.48	.52	21	.50	.50	16
Economic (T + P + B + R)	.59	.41	27	.31	.69	16	.43	.57	21
Total	.38	.62	110	.36	.64	126	.39	.61	81
Political support consequences of ties:*									
Marriage (M)	.58	.76		.65	.73		.80	.77	
Friendship (F + M)	.78	.76		.33	.57		.70	.64	
"Political" (L + P)	.82	.62		.60	.18		.75	.50	
Economic (T + P + B + R)	.84	.60		.80	.80		.78	.82	
Total	.80	.68		.61	.62		.76	.72	

NOTE.—Superelite families are Peruzzi, Albizzi, Strozzi, and Gianfigliazzi. Santa Croce faction leaders of the oligarch side are Peruzzi, Ricasoli, and Castellani. Amount shown, except for n's, are proportions.

* Political support consequences of ties = (no. of ties to fellow partisans)/(total no. of ties), with split families allocated proportionately. A tie to a neutral family is treated the same here as a tie to an enemy.

American Journal of Sociology

tabulate prestige, wealth, and neighborhood endogamy rates for the Medici and for two comparable oligarch reference groups: a set of superelite families—the Peruzzi, the Strozzi, the Albizzi, and the Gianfigliazzi—and a set of Santa Croce faction leaders—the Peruzzi, the Ricasoli, and the Castellani families. The lower panels of the three parts give the partisanship consequences of the network mobilization ties tabulated in the upper panels.

We begin by discussing the first control group, the superelite. Table 9, part A, on prestige, shows that the Peruzzi, Strozzi, Albizzi, and Gianfigliazzi families were patrician to the core. It mattered not what the type of network relation was—marriage, economic, "political," or friendship; across the board, these families directed about 90% of their ties to fellow patricians. New men were snubbed in all spheres.

Table 9, part B, on wealth, tells a similar story, with one exception: the superelite did business with many less well off families. But this was just another sign of their exclusivity on prestige. Even though many patricians had fallen on hard times, the superelite stuck with them in their economic relations, rather than switch to wealthier new men.

Santa Croce factional leaders behaved little differently, except of course that their degree of social exclusivity was slightly less than that of the superelite, since their own status was slightly lower.

Compared to these reference groups, the Medici's own network strategies were, as already argued, more differentiated. In marriage and friendship, the Medici were even more snobbish than the superelite, if that were possible. However, in the economic sphere, the Medici associated heavily with the new men, quite unlike their elite counterparts. "Political" ties (i.e., personal loans and patronage) were intermediate in social class endogamy; the Medici established such relations with both their economic and marriage partners. The Medici's distinctiveness within the elite, in other words, was not that they represented new men; their distinctiveness was that they associated with them at all.

The political responsiveness of those new men with whom the Medici chose to associate was breathtaking: 90% and 96% of those new men tied to the Medici through economic or "political" relations became active Medici partisans. This rate of response was so overwhelming, indeed, that the fact that the Medici did not associate with more new men shows that party building was not the only thing on their minds. New men not explicitly mobilized through Medici ties showed no great enthusiasm for the Medici cause (see tables 5, 6).

Thus, we have an important insight into the reason for the strong contemporary image of the Medicean party affair as a social class struggle. It was not that the Medici did all that much actively to mobilize new men. It was that the oligarchs did so extraordinarily little. In as deeply elitist a context as Florence, a mere pittance thrown the new men's way, even by such an archpatrician family as the Medici, could generate overwhelming response. Parvenu new men, anxious for inclusion but long barred from entry, were structurally available, awaiting mobilization, for reasons that had nothing to do with the Medici per se. The Medici opened the door just a crack, and for that they were polemically tarred by their enemies with the rhetorical brush of class traitor: the label "heroes of the new men" connoted contempt. *Cognitive classification of Medici group identity, both by contemporaries and by historians, was the product not of Medici action but of vitriolic oligarch polemics* (supported, no doubt, by wishful thinking among new men). Inscrutable Cosimo of course did nothing to deny it.

Table 9, part C, demonstrates statistically what we have already asserted about neighborhood. Both the superelite and the Santa Croce faction leaders were citywide in their networks, regardless of type of tie.[37] In contrast, the Medici's relations geographically were quite differentiated: only 14% of Medici marriages were within their home quarter, compared with 36% for the superelite. Yet 59% of Medici economic ties were within San Giovanni, compared with 31% for the superelite.

We now have a clear picture of the structure of the Medici party and of its roots in elite network strategies. The Medici party was an agglomeration of doubly disarticulated parts: structurally isolated new men living within San Giovanni, whom the Medici mobilized directly through economic relations, and structurally isolated patricians residing outside San Giovanni, whom the Medici mobilized directly through marriage. Conscious residential segregation, as well as "natural" social class segregation, were keys to the inhibition both of independent ties among followers and of multiplex ties with the Medici themselves. The result was an awesomely centralized patrimonial machine, capable of great discipline and "top down" control because the Medici themselves were the only bridge holding this contradictory agglomeration together.[38]

---

[37] Perhaps an exception could be argued for the cases of loans and patronage.

[38] Our general position on the interrelation of social attributes and social networks can now be clarified. Obviously (contra some occasionally overstated polemics by network aficionados) we do not believe that social attributes are irrelevant: the particular way in which the Medici recombined social attributes through networks is the heart of the story here. What we object to is the arraying of attributes discretely as groups or spatially as grids—a procedure that presumes attributes to be behaviorally meaningful in a network vacuum. Of course, actors in the system, as well as researchers, do exactly these clustering procedures mentally when they analyze their own social structure; this is what "boundedly rational" cognitive classifications are all about. But there is a widely underappreciated gap between these macrocognitive (or "cultural") operations and microbehavioral "local action" taken by concrete individuals in very particular, heterogeneous, and often cross-pressured circumstances. Sim-

American Journal of Sociology

The specific micromechanisms that translated this network structure into Medici control were as follows:

1. Spoke structure induced common dependence of partisans on the Medici for access to the rest of the elite, and it forced any sensitive intraparty communication that required tie-enforced trust to be channeled through the Medici (cf. Molho 1979, p. 19).

2. Double segregation of attributes inhibited defensive counteralliance among mutually suspicious partisans: no "revolt of the colonels" was possible.[39]

3. Interactionally, marrying geographically distant patricians, whom the Medici met casually only rarely, kept affine relations socially proper and formal—thereby inhibiting unwanted presumptions of familiarity and status equality. In contrast, doing business with new men inside the neighborhood engendered motivationally useful friendliness. The status gap between Medici and new men was so enormous that the Medici did not need to fear any slackening of their abject deference.

4. The attributional heterogeneity of the party made the Medici party a swing vote, potent beyond its numbers, in Florentine legislative politics. The reason, explained below, was the bitter class polarization that was reviving in Florence.

Thus, attributional heterogeneity and contradiction of group interests were not a problem for Medici party control. Quite the contrary, they were the keys to Medici control. For this result to be generally true, however, surrounding cognitive group identities (and animosities) must be intense. Stable monopoly of broker position is leveraged off this, and practical political organization becomes cognitively invisible (or at least murky) to the outside world precisely when it cuts across strong identities.

NETWORK DYNAMICS

The Dynamics of Party Formation: Patrician Marriage

We have insufficient space in this article to show how figure 2a emerged historically in detail, but in the next two sections we shall sketch the

---

plifying social reality into homogeneous subsets "with common interests" rips individuals out of their (often contradictory) multiple network contexts and obscures the very heterogeneity and complexity of which organizations like the Medici party are constructed.

[39] A "revolt of the colonels" requires more than just comparing dissatisfactions. Colonels have to have confidence that other colonels are not just stabbing them in the back. There has to be an organizational infrastructure, independent of the boss, through which they can coordinate. And there has to be something they are offering to each other that is better than their current state. Crosscutting Medici networks inhibited each of these preconditions.

driving dynamic: elite marriage and economic networks were reconfigured by working-class revolt and wartime fiscal crisis, respectively. Elite
reconfiguration explains why oligarchs would not marry Medicean patricians.

Our core conclusion regarding party formation will be simple: Cosimo
de' Medici did *not* design his centralized party, nor did he intend (until
the very end) to take over the state. The network patterns of figure 2a
were produced by oligarchs' earlier successful reassertions of their own
control. The Medici party grew up around Cosimo and Lorenzo from
raw network material unintentionally channeled to them by the oligarchs'
previous smashing both of the wool workers known as *ciompi* (1378) and
of the new men's challenge during the Milan and Lucca wars (1424–33).
Only very late in the game, we shall argue, did the Medici adaptively
learn of the political potential of the social network machine that lay at
their fingertips. In almost Hegelian fashion, oligarchs crafted the networks of their own destruction.

Historical trends in neighborhood exogamy.—The first thing to appreciate in any dynamic analysis of Medicean marriage strategy is the
fact, uncovered by Cohn (1980), that increasing rates of neighborhood
exogamy were a historical trend in Florentine elite marriage behavior.
The Medici were not tactical revolutionaries; they were simply the leading edge of an ongoing transformation in the network structure of the
Florentine elite.

Table 10 presents a recalculated version of Cohn's neighborhood data,
along with our own data for historical comparison. By coincidence, Cohn
studied the mid-14th- and late 15th-century periods, which bracket the
early 15th-century focus of this study. Since Cohn's primary focus was
on changing marriage patterns within the lower classes, the volume of
elite marriages is lower than that which was extracted from Kent.[40]
Cohn's listing of his late 15th-century data permitted a further breakdown into "state marriages" and others—a concept that has no real
meaning for the period before the Medici changed the republic into a
de facto principality.[41] It is reassuring, given different operational defini-

---

[40] For the lower classes, or *popolo minuto,* Cohn found a trend just the opposite of
that of the elite: increasing rates of marriage *within* neighborhoods. Some portion,
but not all, of this trend was due to growing immigrant ethnic enclaves, organized
around the silk industry. Cohn argues forcefully that new administrative methods of
lower-class control (containment within parishes) during the late 15th century inhibited cross-neighborhood contact and organization among workers. A recurrence of the
Ciompi revolt became well-nigh impossible (cf. Molho 1979).

[41] We label as "state marriages" those marriages registered by Lorenzo de' Medici's
personal secretary. "The majority of these marriages were celebrated at the Medici
palace and were witnessed by Lorenzo. In several instances Lorenzo even provided

TABLE 10

HISTORICAL TRENDS IN ELITE MARRIAGE

	No. within Parish	No. within Gonfalone	No. within Quarter	No. across Quarter	Total
I. Fourteenth-century elite marriages (1340–83)*	5	8.5	12	13	25
	(20)	(34)	(48)	(52)	
II. Early 15th-century elite marriages (1395–1434):†					
Patrician-patrician		16	37	92	129
		(12)	(29)	(71)	
Patrician–new man		8	17	13	30
		(27)	(57)	(43)	
New man–new man		1	1	1	2
Total		25	55	106	161
		(16)	(34)	(66)	
III. Late 15th-century elite marriages (1450–1530):‡					
State marriages:††					
Patrician-patrician		0	1	11	12
		(0)	(8)	(92)	
Patrician–new man		1	1	1	2
New man–new man		0	0	0	0
Total		1	2	12	14
		(7)	(14)	(86)	
Other elite marriages:					
Patrician-patrician		0	2	5	7
		(0)	(29)	(71)	
Patrician–new man		1	4	3	7
		(17)	(57)	(43)	
New man–new man		0	2	3	5
		(0)	(40)	(60)	
Total		1	8	11	19
		(5)	(42)	(58)	

NOTE.—Numbers in parentheses are percentages.

* "Elite" is defined by family name plus a dowry of at least 400 florins. Data are from Cohn (1980, p. 52). To make the data comparable with others in this table, we report the number of marriages rather than Cohn's "number of marriage relations," which, for Cohn, equaled two times the number of marriages, i.e., one for each partner.

† "Elite" is defined by political participation (see text). Data are from this article. Except for "Total" in this category, entries refer to marriages between a patrician and a patrician within the political elite, to marriages between a patrician and a new man within the political elite, etc.

‡ "Elite" is defined by having passed scrutiny plus a dowry of at least 600 forins. Figures are from marriage data listed in Cohn (1980, pp. 54–56.) Due to the passage of time, "new men" is defined here as post-Ciompi (post-1383), rather than post-1343 as in the rest of this paper.

†† These are marriages notarized by Lorenzo de' Medici's personal secretary (see Cohn 1980, p. 53).

tions of the elite, that neighborhood endogamy/exogamy estimates are perfectly consistent between our two studies.

These aggregate statistics demonstrate what has already been asserted—that rates of elite marriage outside neighborhood quarter increased progressively over the course of the 14th and 15th centuries. Cohn's elite marriage data are too scanty to disaggregate reliably by decade, but the combined data give the impression that the bulk of change occurred between 1383 and about 1420—namely, precisely at the time when the patrician elite reconsolidated its control after the disastrous (from their perspective) Ciompi revolution.

Cross-sectional estimates are also consistent: for both 15th-century periods, the higher the position in the elite hierarchy, the higher the rate of marriage outside neighborhood. Patricians married other patricians at higher exogamous rates than they married new men. And, most striking in spite of the low numbers, 92% of state marriages in the late 15th century were arranged across rather than within neighborhoods. In other words, what in the early 15th century was an innovative Medici strategy of partisan control, applicable only to their own marriages, later appears to have become official state policy, applicable to all their top supporters.

This trend is better interpreted from the perspective of its origin than from knowledge of its final result: patrician neighborhood clusters based on marriage gradually dissolved. The Peruzzi-Ricasoli-Castellani clique in Santa Croce, the Albizzi and Guadagni blocs in San Giovanni, and the Strozzi group in Santa Maria Novella indicate clearly that this process was hardly complete during our period (if indeed it ever was).[42] But this "neighborhood solidarity" mode of elite organization, which linked patricians of different stature, was a residue of the past.

In particular, this mode historically descended from feudalism. Florentine neighborhoods originally (in the 1200s) were settled by immigration from contiguous regions of the surrounding rural countryside. Urbanizing feudal lords brought their hierarchical retinues with them, thereby creating self-sufficient neighborhood pockets with stronger ties to the rural homeland than to other parts of Florence (Weissman 1983, pp. 7–9). By the 15th century, "feudalism" is hardly an apt description of Florentine

---

the dowry. We find the state, in effect, taking an active role in the structuring of marriage relations, which were at the same time political alliances" (Cohn 1980, p. 53).

[42] Given the vigor of F. W. Kent's recent defense (1987) of the continuing importance of neighborhood in quattrocento Florence, a clarification is in order. We are not arguing that the importance of neighborhood for patricians declined, in some totalistic sense. In fact, we agree with Kent's emphasis on neighborhood patronage (and, we would add, neighborhood economics). However, marriage was no longer the primary basis of elite consolidation within quarter.

American Journal of Sociology

neighborhoods, but hierarchical intraneighborhood marriage among patricians persisted.

As neighborhood marriage solidarity disintegrated roughly around the turn of the century, however, patricians may have been almost forced to reach outside the comfortable (and essentially defensive) shells of their own wards, parishes, and piazzas. Later, such marriage outreach would provide the organizational infrastructure to undergird the emergence of a self-consciously "city" elite, psychologically (though not materially) decoupled from its original neighborhood base.[43]

The question therefore arises: What forces led to this widespread corrosion of elite neighborhood solidarity and to its replacement by elite neighborhood exogamy? The answer to this question will take us far toward understanding the historical roots of the Medici's own innovative marriage strategy.

Political vulnerability among Medicean patricians.—The mid-14th-century, pre-Ciompi story is best told by Brucker (1962). Progressive waves of new men were economically thrust up by the internationalization of trade and finance. Without aristocratic sponsorship, such mercantile new men (hardly radicals in any event) were doomed to political ostracism and frustration. However, this upward thrust often coincided with intraelite factional cleavage. The Albizzi-Ricci factions were the most important such split in the mid-14th century, with the Ricci garnering more new men's support. Intense politics ensued from 1343 to 1378 about who was to be eligible for election to the Signoria. The new men (with artisan support) took the tack of trying to label their opponents officially as lawless magnates, and the old guard countered by trying to get their opponents designated as traitorous antipapal Ghibellines.

Eventually, such aristocratic-mercantile feuding got out of hand, and the Ciompi rose up in alliance with the artisans to take over the state for two months in 1378. Through their major guilds, the merchants quickly realigned with artisans in minor guilds to reestablish control, but in 1382 this alliance in turn was overthrown by an embittered patrician elite (which included earlier cohorts of now old "new men" merchants). These "oligarchs" excluded the artisans and ruled Florence until the Medici took over in 1434.[44]

[43] This extrapolation into psychology is not fanciful. Without much commentary, Cohn reports (1980, p. 37) that he had much trouble reconstructing the neighborhood residences of his late 15th-century families, because notaries of the time, who registered the marriage deeds, recorded these families only as *cives Florentinis* (citizens of Florence). In contrast, in the 14th century, residence down to the level of parish was routinely recorded, irrespective of status.

[44] In the field of Florentine studies, Brucker represents the highest quality of history written with groups as the primary agents. While I disagree with his group-based approach, I have nothing but the highest respect for his pathbreaking research.

Robust Action

For us, the clue in this account is to understand how first the Albizzi-Ricci factional feuds and then the searing revolt of the Ciompi placed strain on neighborhood solidarities. Could it be that intraelite factional struggles of the 14th century were so intense that, first following medieval patterns, they polarized each neighborhood into competing patrician clusters (cf. Barth 1959), but then, because of Ciompi escalation, they pulverized the losing patrician side into structural isolates, which the Medici much later exploited? If so, this would account in part for the increasing rate of neighborhood exogamy, as the winners and, even more, the losers had fewer compatible intraneighborhood marriage options to choose from. Assuming social class endogamy, Florentine patrician marriages would be forced outward because of neighborhood blockage, or structural "holes," within.

We will test the plausibility of this account in pieces. One observable corollary of the hypothesis is that Medicean patrician support derived disproportionately from losers of earlier factional struggles. We have gathered evidence from secondary sources (a) about patrician family membership in the mid-14th century Albizzi and Ricci factions and (b) about patrician support for the 1378–82 Ciompi/artisan regime. We also have very limited information about the Alberti faction (a transformed descendant of the Ricci) of 1385–1400.

From the detailed text of Brucker (1962), we could identify 39 14th-century families from the Albizzi or Ricci factions that also appeared in Dale Kent's (1978) list of 1434 partisans. The relationship between these two lists of partisans is shown in table 11. The evidence is much stronger for the historical continuity of the winning oligarchic side than it is for the losing "liberal" Ricci. The Medici did indeed gain some support from families of the old 14th-century Ricci faction, but this support is not a major factor in Medicean mobilization.[45]

More convincing evidence of historical continuity dates from the 1378–82 period. Najemy (1982, p. 260) has published a list of families from "traditional inner elite" families that were members of the governing Signoria during the 1378–82 corporatist guild regime. This list of 15 "collaborator" patrician families is as follows: Alberti, Aldobrandini, Ardinghelli, del Bene, Corbinelli, Corsini, Davanzati, Medici, Pitti, Rinuccini, Salimbeni, Salviati, Scali, Strozzi, and Vecchietti.

Six of these families were unequivocal Medici supporters in 1434. Moreover, the split Salviati family leaned strongly to the Medici side

---

[45] In hindsight, perhaps we should not have expected much from such a lengthy time-lagged effect. Not only did much transpire between the Ricci and the Medici, but the leaders of the Ricci and Alberti factions were not just ostracized; their participation, and even life, in the regime was completely obliterated.

American Journal of Sociology

TABLE 11

LEGACY OF MID-14TH CENTURY PARTISANSHIP

1360 PARTISAN FAMILIES*	1434 PARTISAN FAMILIES[†]		
	Medici	Split	Oligarch
Albizzi faction	4	3	12
Split loyalties	4	4	2
Ricci faction	5	2	3
Not mentioned in Brucker	44	3	34

* Brucker (1962).
† Kent (1978).

(Kent 1978, p. 55), and the technically neutral Corsini were in the process of joining the Medici when 1434 arrived (Kent 1978, p. 53). Only three collaborator families supported the oligarchs in 1434.[46]

The Alberti faction of 1385–1400 was the last barrier of opposition to the revived patrician oligarchy (Brucker 1977, p. 75–102). However, apart from descriptions of the extremely wealthy Alberti themselves, who were papal bankers before the Medici replaced them as a result of the Alberti's 1393 exile (Holmes 1968; Foster 1985), almost no published information exists on the composition of this faction. We do know, however, that Acciaiuoli support for the Medici dated from the exile of Alberti supporter Donato Acciaiuoli (Brucker 1977, p. 97; Kent 1978, p. 59).[47] In addition, the close friends of Acciaiuoli who put up 20,000 florins as security for his exile included three Cavalcanti, Luigi Guicciardini, and Nicola di Vieri de' Medici (Brucker 1977, p. 29)—all later patrician supporters of the Medici.

In sum, while the evidence that historical continuity among Medicean patricians went back as far as the mid-14th century is very weak, the evidence for grounding our understanding of patrician support for the Medici in the events of the Ciompi revolution and its immediate aftermath is quite strong (albeit still only suggestive). Our data, merged with Cohn's, on neighborhood exogamy support the view that elite neighborhood solidarity dissolved in the decades following the Ciompi revolution;

[46] The Rinuccini and Salimbeni, along with the exiled del Bene and Scali, no longer figured prominently in Florentine politics.

[47] A close relationship between the Acciaiuoli and the Medici families, however, predated this period. In the mid- to late 14th century, an important client of the banker Vieri di Cambio de' Medici was Bishop Angelo Acciaiuoli, who played a major role in Florentine politics while occupying the city's episcopal see (Brucker 1977, p. 10). A marriage around 1405 consolidated this family relationship.

Robust Action

the data on patrician factional continuity supports the further view that structural isolation among Medicean patricians dates from this period as well.

Oligarchic elite closure.—Establishing the existence of historical continuity, however important, is not the same thing as establishing the mechanism through which such continuity was created. A priori, there is no obvious reason that factional wounds could not have been gradually healed (perhaps under the goad of a massive external threat, like the Milanese war), that disaffected elites could not have been reabsorbed (under careful controls), or that the political system could not therefore have returned to its routinely tumultuous stochastic equilibrium. In reality, however, an irreversible "ratchet effect" appears to have occurred, which we need to explain.

In particular, we argue, elite marriage networks shifted permanently during the period from 1385 to about 1420 from a quasi-feudal pattern of parallel, intraneighborhood marriage hierarchies, which had incorporated most patrician families, toward a citywide elitist pattern of cross-neighborhood marriage cycles, which co-opted "politically correct" patrician families while structurally isolating patrician "class traitors" who had collaborated with the Ciompi and artisan guilds. The folding of a dense oligarchic core into itself (the rectangular set of blocks in fig. 2a) and the segregation of patrician Medici supporters from this core (the Guicciardini and Tornabuoni blocks in fig. 2a), in other words, were two sides of the same elite reconsolidation process.[48] The effect of this marriage transformation was to keep Ciompi-type challenges from ever arising again; no longer were there fluid elite factions to play off one another.

The process is illustrated graphically in figure 3. The solid lines give a stylized portrait of the quasi-feudal pattern of parallel neighborhood hierarchies before the Ciompi.[49] As mentioned above, this marriage pattern originally derived, centuries before, from rural lord-retinue hierarchies transplanted to local city neighborhoods. During the late medieval interim, however, neighborhood hierarchies were sustained by a logic of status: enshrouded within overtly symmetric political alliance marriages,

---

[48] The shift from neighborhood to citywide patrician elites is exemplified in fig. 2a by the contrast between, on the one hand, the old Santa Croce hierarchical organization of Peruzzi→Castellani→Pepi and, on the other hand, the newer self-encapsulating organization of Guasconi→Strozzi→Panciatichi→Albizzi→Guasconi (and similar cycles).

[49] This portrait may conflate prematurely the Albizzi-Ricci factional underpinnings with earlier Guelf-Ghibelline and Black-White Guelf marriage structures, but no data exist at present to trace medieval stages of transformation, if any. With the new Carte dell'Ancisa marriage information currently being processed, we will be able to investigate this further.

American Journal of Sociology

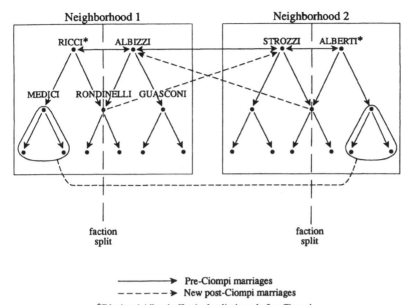

Neighborhood 1   Neighborhood 2

faction
split

faction
split

————————▶ Pre-Ciompi marriages
- - - - - - ▶ New post-Ciompi marriages
*Ricci and Alberti effectively eliminated after Ciompi.

FIG. 3.—Mechanics of elite closure (1380–1420)

arranged by Florentine patriarchs,[50] was an implicit claim on the part of
the family giving the dowried wife to be superior in status to the family
receiving the dowried wife.[51] The reasons for this were two: (*a*) culturally,
in all ceremonial exchange or gift-giving systems, prestige accrues to
the more (competitively) generous (Mauss [1925] 1967);[52] (*b*) structurally,
son-in-law relations often were the raw material for constructing political
lieutenants (Kent 1978, p. 55).[53]

[50] Needless to say, modern conceptions of romance are anachronistic in this deeply
sexist context. Patrician fathers arranged marriages between sons around 35 years old
and daughters in their teens (Herlihy and Klapisch-Zuber 1985).

[51] This combination of implicit domination enshrouded in a cultural veneer of friendship is typical of patron-client relations.

[52] This also fits with the Catholic principle of plenitude, or grace—the ideological
foundation for European nobility (Lovejoy 1936; Duby 1980).

[53] This potential could be actualized most easily in two circumstances: (*a*) when the
son-in-law came from a small disorganized clan, in which therefore the potentially
countervailing father of the son was weak, or (*b*) when the son-in-law was a "black
sheep" for whatever reason. Examples of both cases can easily be found in the Medici
party.

Because of intense status competition, wife-giving families could not take back daughters from their wife-receiving affines without thereby relinquishing their claim to superiority. *Gonfaloni* neighborhoods in particular were strongly bounded hothouses, in which frequencies of both interaction and status rivalry were high (Weissman 1982; Kent 1977). Add asymmetric marriage to bounded neighborhoods, and the result is the network pattern drawn in figure 3: hierarchical linear trees or "pecking orders."[54]

Medieval factions were driven by local neighborhood antagonisms at their root, even when they aggregated under broader pope-versus-emperor banners (Waley 1969, p. 203). This is shown in figure 3 by factional splits between rival lords within each neighborhood. The factions link up, in geographical checkerboard fashion, across neighborhoods (cf. Barth 1959).[55] The medieval dynamic at this point was that things eventually would explode, with top leaders of the losing side suffering exile, expropriation of wealth, and burning of homes. After a rocky period of probation, however, losing lieutenants and those lower down slowly would be reabsorbed back into the system through asymmetric marriage (since new local challengers in the old winning faction reached to them for support).

The Albizzi-Ricci feuds of the mid-14th century, we argue, were just this sort of traditional medieval factional affair, except for one catastrophic complication: The Ciompi working-class revolt threatened the elite in toto, which suddenly was confronted with mass exile. Ricci partisans and, even more, patrician sympathizers with the Ciompi (like the Medici) now were not just normal elite from a losing faction; they were class traitors in a very direct and deep sense. Resurgent oligarch consciousness was seared by the Ciompi event to a degree that it structured both polemics and virtually every domestic institutional reform for decades (Brucker 1977; Najemy 1982).

After the oligarchs' return to power in 1382, the reverberating consequences for intraelite marriage networks were profound.

1. Class traitor patrician sympathizers with the Ciompi were shunned in marriage by victorious oligarch families. This is the source of the

---

[54] Of course, top-level lords also had to get wives from somewhere. Inability to accept daughters from below, within their neighborhood, forced them to trade among themselves, across neighborhoods, but only at the very top. Some neighborhood bosses were prestigious enough to obtain wives from outside the city.

[55] That is, each local faction was surrounded by its enemies. The aggregation logic here is balance theory: "[neighboring] enemies of my [neighboring] enemies are my friends."

American Journal of Sociology

structural barrier to marriage between the oligarchs and the Guicciardini and Tornabuoni Medicean blocks, observed in figure 2a. To see the dynamic of how this came to be, refer again to figure 3: (*a*) Ricci and Alberti families were effectively expunged from the diagram, the normal consequence of being leaders of losing medieval factions. (*b*) This left losing and now leaderless lieutenant families, such as the Medici, structurally isolated and cut off from their victorious neighbors. (*c*) Cross-pressured "swing-vote" families, such as the Rondinelli, who might be potential bridges for reintegrating the losers, were temporarily left hanging. But (*d*) marriage ostracism of patrician losers by victorious oligarchs was exceedingly intense and vengeful.

This last assertion is not mere hypothesis. When the Alberti males were finally banished in 1397, virtually no one would marry them (Foster 1985, p. 321). Before that, in 1394, the very prestigious moderate, Filippo Bastari, was sentenced to perpetual exile merely for trying to talk Rinaldo Gianfigliazzi into changing his mind about withdrawing from a marriage agreement with the Alberti. Gianfigliazzi had withdrawn from the Alberti agreement in the first place because of pressure he had received from Maso degli Albizzi (Brucker 1977, pp. 95–96).[56] This prominent example apparently was taken to heart, and routinized into marriage maxims, by the patrician rank and file desirous of advancement within the new regime.[57]

2. Not only were Ciompi sympathizers shunned, however, but oligarchs themselves were restructured by their vengeful ostracism: cross-

---

[56] Such cross-family consultations about politically significant marriages involving only one of them may have been common. Kent (1978, p. 130) cites a much later 1431 case of Almanno Salviati's consulting Averardo de' Medici, his father-in-law, about the proposed marriage of Salviati's daughter to a Frescobaldi. (Averardo apparently okayed the deal.)

[57] In the early 15th century, Giovanni Morelli wrote as follows in his memoirs, intended as posthumous instruction for his sons: "[When you decide to marry] think of this first of all: don't demean yourself with an inferior person; try instead to improve your condition, though not to such an extent that she would want to be the husband and make you the wife. . . . Aside from being of old stock in the city, they should also be Guelfs who are honored by the Commune and who are free of all stains, such as those associated with treason. . . . In marriage, connect yourself with a Guelf family in government; it ought to be a powerful and trusted family, free of all scandal" (cited in Martines 1963, pp. 58–59). According to Martines, Morelli was particularly sensitive about this subject because he himself had made the mistake of marrying into the Alberti. "According to Morelli's testimony, this marriage hurt his career in public life, undermined his contacts, and left him exposed, during a period of twenty years, to tax rates aimed at his ruin" (Martines 1963, p. 59; we thank Samuel Cohn for suggesting the relevance of Morelli's memoirs).

Robust Action

neighborhood marriage cycles began to form.[58] A dense, citywide elite was created thereby, which transcended its earlier neighborhood base.[59]

The short-term motivation for cross-neighborhood marriage cycles, we argue, was co-optation, especially of potentially bridging swing-vote families, such as the Rondinelli in figure 3. Oligarchs wanted the doors completely slammed in traitors' faces, without leaving open the traditional route for rehabilitation. And they certainly did not want to give patrician outcasts any network room to pluck away wavering supporters from themselves.

The complication was the status implications of intermarriage, mentioned above. "Big cheese" families could not reach down to, and accept daughters from, middling swing-vote patricians in the same neighborhood, without at the same time jeopardizing their own status positions in the local pecking order.But other prominent oligarch families, outside the neighborhood, could do so without disrupting either local neighborhood order. Given the decline in neighborhood intermarriage because of the ostracism, moreover, there was a demographic push to do just that. Cross-neighborhood co-optative daughter flows are illustrated as dotted lines in figure 3. Marriage cycles are the straightforward, even if unintended, result.

Since this co-optation process was occurring in all neighborhoods simultaneously (the consequence of the checkerboard pattern), the oligarchic elite as a whole closed in on itself: given the unexpected windfall of exogamous marriage into the truly elite, patricians of moderate position had fewer daughters available to send down. But this new cross-neighborhood elite was far more expansive and inclusive in status than had been the earlier medieval pattern of a federated alliance of neighborhood bosses: because of co-optation, the truly elite had fewer sons available to trade among themselves. The net result was the rectangular clique of oligarch blocks in figure 2a.

3. A final consequence was cross-neighborhood intermarriage among structurally isolated class traitor patricians. Given successful co-optation of swing votes into the reconsolidated elite and their own geographical scatter, outcast patricians were left with very few status-appropriate mar-

---

[58] From a network perspective, triadic cycles cause networks to fold into themselves, thereby creating clear "group" boundaries. Understanding how cyclic marriage triads formed, therefore, is the microbehavioral essence of understanding how the reconstituted patrician elite congealed.

[59] Civic humanism, a 1400–1430 ideology of citywide elites, arguably was built on top of this new elite marriage network foundation, even as it was catalyzed more proximately by 1390–1402 wars with Milan (Baron 1966).

American Journal of Sociology

riage options in their own neighborhoods. (We have argued, of course, that that was precisely the point.)

This left such patricians with two marriage options. (*a*) They could start to accept daughters from lower social groups. But this moved patricians down to the new men's status level, in other patricians' eyes.[60] (*b*) Alternatively, they could start to marry fellow isolates outside the neighborhood. This at least preserved their claim to status, even if it did nothing to restore power. For outcasts who wanted to remain patricians, this extraneighborhood marriage game was the only game in town. Hence, even though exogamy rates were increasing for all, intrapatrician exogamy rates were higher among outcasts than among oligarchs: Oligarchs married both outside and inside the neighborhood.

In short, this is how we claim the outcast Medici discovered their "leading edge" and highly consequential marriage strategy. Near exclusive intermarriage with patricians outside their own neighborhood was a network strategy forced on the Medici by the resurgent oligarchs' successful blockage of Medici marriage with their San Giovanni patrician neighbors. The half of the Medici party that was based on marriage was "chosen" by the Medici family only in the sense of positional chess: oligarchs structurally induced their choice.

Thus, the oligarchic clique and the Medicean spoke marriage networks were not two separate party organizations, later to butt heads as autonomous units. They emerged in tandem, as a single network, each reflexively and asymmetrically structuring the other.[61]

Data on change in elite marriage strategy over time.—We still have not shown how the Medici themselves, alone among patrician outcasts, eventually came to marry into the oligarchy. But before we solve this final puzzle, let us present evidence in support of the above account.

We have attempted to date the 162 marriages in our data set, which span the period from about 1395 to 1434. Fifty-three of these marriages are precisely dated by Kent in her book. For 84 of the remaining 109 marriages, we have been able to estimate the decade of the marriage, usually through triangulating the known dates of relatives with genealogical information contained in Florentine names.[62] Because of this estima-

---

[60] This is not to say that patricians never would do this—say, for money. But wealthy dowries from new men daughters were always implicitly purchased at the cost of lowered prestige. The dowry money was tainted, a sign of patricians on hard times.

[61] Padgett (1990, p. 450) develops a similar "reflexive structuring through mutual contestation" argument in a totally different empirical context, that of professionalism and plea bargaining in U.S. criminal courts.

[62] Florentine names usually include the father, and frequently the grandfather, in them—e.g., Cosimo di Giovanni di Bicci de' Medici. This is yet another indicator of the Florentine concern with patrilineage.

Robust Action

TABLE 12

ELITE MARRIAGES OVER TIME

Neighborhood by Estimated Date of Marriage	Overall	1395–1410	1411–20	1421–29	1430–34	No Date
Medici marriage strategies:						
San Giovanni............	4 (.143)	0	0	3	0	1
Santo Spirito	10 (.357)	1	2	3	4	0
Santa Maria Novella	9 (.321)	2	4	2	0	1
Santa Croce...............	5 (.179)	2	1	2	0	0
Total	28					
Peruzzi + Ricasoli + Castellani marriage strategies:						
San Giovanni............	10 (.345)	2	3	1	3	1
Santo Spirito	5 (.172)	0	1	0	4	0
Santa Maria Novella	6 (.207)	3	1	1	1	0
Santa Croce...............	8 (.276)	4	0	1	3	0
Total	29					
Strozzi + Gianfigliazzi marriage strategies:						
San Giovanni............	11 (.344)	4	2	1	2	2
Santo Spirito	6 (.188)	2	0	0	3	1
Santa Maria Novella	9 (.281)	4	2	1	1	1
Santa Croce...............	6 (.188)	3	1	0	2	0
Total	32					
Albizzi + Guadagni marriage strategies:						
San Giovanni............	13 (.591)	2	5	5	0	1
Santo Spirito	4 (.182)	2	0	1	1	0
Santa Maria Novella	3 (.136)	3	0	0	0	0
Santa Croce...............	2 (.091)	0	1	0	0	1
Total	22					

NOTE.—Values in parentheses are percentages of total.

tion procedure, table 12 contains measurement error, which will be reduced through ongoing archival work. For our purposes, however, these
best estimates are sufficient to reveal broad trends in strategic behavior
of the elite.

Table 12 presents, for the leading elite families in various quarters,
the number of their marriages into families in all other quarters (including
their own), broken down by decade. The Medici lived in the western
portion of San Giovanni; the rival but intimately connected Albizzi and
Guadagni lived in the eastern half. The Peruzzi, Ricasoli, and Castellani
were leaders of Santa Croce, as already mentioned. And the Strozzi and

American Journal of Sociology

Gianfigliazzi were the most prominent families in Santa Maria Novella. No family in Santo Spirito had a volume of marriages high enough to warrant inclusion in this table.

If one looks first at the overall figures, what is most striking about these data is the fact that all of the most prestigious oligarch families intermarried at the highest rate with patrician families in San Giovanni— the Medici's own homeland. We have already established that the Medici themselves married at very low rates into their own neighborhood. We now have a better sense of why: they were surrounded by patrician enemies (Kent 1978, p. 170) whom the oligarchs already had successfully wired into themselves. The more detailed timing data also support this conclusion: the oligarchs were active in the 1395–1420 period in establishing marriage links with San Giovanni, during which time the Medici made not a single marriage (in our data set at least). Apparently, the oligarchs were quite aware of the potential for trouble from this quarter (also home to the Ricci) and took active steps to contain it at its source.

The case of the Rondinelli, mentioned above as a swing vote, illustrates the oligarchs' strategy more precisely. In the 1340s the Medici, the Rondinelli, and the della Stufa had formed a San Giovanni clique, apparently of the traditional sort (Kent 1978, p. 65). As late as the 1370s, the Rondinelli were active, along with a portion of the Medici, in the Ricci's San Giovanni faction (Brucker 1977, pp. 34, 125). Hence, the Rondinelli were prime candidates for neighborhood intermarriage with the Medici and for pariah status. However, an early wife-giving marriage with the Strozzi (themselves split between Albizzi and Ricci factions), followed by both types of marriage with the Guasconi (who themselves furnished an early wife to the Strozzi) apparently saved them from ostracism and turned them into avid oligarchs. In this manner, the Strozzi dissolved the Medici's local patrician clique.

In addition to such innovative cross-neighborhood raiding into the Medici's base by the Santa Maria Novella and the Santa Croce elites, the data reveal that the Medici's San Giovanni heartland was being squeezed in a traditional way. For reasons we do not know, from 1410 on, the old-line Albizzi and Guadagni retreated to an old-fashioned but successful neighborhood consolidation strategy. This retreat made them less integrated into the elite than one might suspect from their stature (cf. Kent 1978, p. 177). But it also made it harder for the Medici to rebuild their own local patrician base.

So far, the data are consistent with our expectations. In addition to this (albeit loose) confirmation, however, the data contain a surprise. The oligarchy worked so hard on controlling San Giovanni that they apparently overlooked the "older suburb" quarter of Santo Spirito (that

Robust Action

is, until the 1430s). Perhaps this was a simple and traditional oversight on their part, based on the slightly less prestigious character of this district; but we suspect that the overemphasis on San Giovanni, relative to Santo Spirito, was at least partly a conscious allocation of scarce marriage resources.[63]

In any event, this oversight represented a clear "structural hole" within the oligarchic marriage network, which the data reveal the Medici to have exploited—at first gradually, but then with a vengeance, as they incrementally but clearly learned about the political potential in Santo Spirito: by the early 1430s, 100% of the Medici's own marriages were directed to this quarter. Three of every four of these late Medici marriages were wife-receiving rather than wife-giving—an indication that the Medici by this point were not particularly picky about relative status claims. One of these wife-receiving marriages was with the Guicciardini, a family fairly well integrated into the elite, in order to reinforce an old marriage alliance under siege.[64] But all the others (with the Corbinelli, the Corsini, and the Ridolfi) fit the classic Medicean pattern of marriage to patrician structural isolates.

The oligarch families apparently were not fools, and so moved quite late to repair this breach in their own defenses. As was the oligarchs' wont, all of these Santo Spirito marriages in the 1430s were to old-line families, already well integrated into the Florentine marriage network, albeit not at the highest levels. Thus, the late but intense mobilization of Santo Spirito patricians, by both sides, followed in microcosm the same pattern as that found in the global blockmodel—successful Medicean mobilization of structurally isolated patricians, and successful oligarchic co-optation of fairly well integrated patricians.

It may be of more general interest to pause here for an observation about the apparent microbehavioral decision processes revealed in these data. This sequence of structural holes, created in the first place by active elite attention focused elsewhere and then exploited gradually but surely by opponents, suggests more than anything that elite tactics evolve not as part of interacting sets of omniscient "grand strategies," à la game

[63] Santo Spirito, located across the Arno river (on the "other side of the tracks"), originally was more like an old suburb than a part of the city's geographical core (Weissman 1982, p. 6). It was the heart of the Ciompi wool workers' district. This hardly implied that the quarter contained nothing but workers and new men—after all, many old magnate families resided there. But it does imply that the elite of this quarter were somewhat less densely integrated by marriage (though not economics) into themselves and into other neighborhood elites.

[64] The Peruzzi also arranged a marriage with the Guicciardini, in 1434, in an apparent effort to induce the Guicciardini to switch sides. The net effect of these offsetting moves was a Guicciardini family split in its partisan loyalties.

American Journal of Sociology

theory, but rather as a mutually adaptive learning process (Lave and March 1975).

Florentine families were extremely shrewd and opportunistic, but nonetheless they were always engaged in boundedly rational local action dictated by their own deep embedding through networks in localistic and highly idiosyncratic circumstances. Any complicated and endogenous marriage system presents each actor with narrow and changing opportunities, derived like vacancy chains (White 1970) from the actions and inactions of others in other arenas. Yet no one, not even Cosimo de' Medici, possessed the clear global overview of figure 2a. Everyone looked out at elite structure egocentrically from the vantage point of his or her own network location. This conclusion is not to doubt that families learned, and often shrewdly so, but to question the plausibility of historical explanations that place much weight on Machiavellian foresight and planning, especially in tumultuous times (cf. Skocpol 1979, pp. 14–18).

The Medici's own structurally anomalous position.—Finally, we need to explain: Given a global predisposition to form parties, why the Medici in particular as leaders of that party? After all, given the success of their opponents' control strategy against them, and especially given the depth of their involvement in previous discredited regimes,[65] the Medici emergence to take over the state in 1434 would seem, from the perspective of 1400, to be little short of miraculous.

One possible explanation might be the Medici bank, founded on ties with the pope. But this is not convincing. As a "cash cow" generator of personal wealth, which the Medici used both for personal patronage (Molho 1979) and for city loans (Molho 1971, p. 168), the role of the bank is clear. However, an identical economic position did not save the Alberti, who were the pope's primary bankers before their exile. And the Medici bank as an institution (not just as a generator of wealth) was useless for political mobilization: apart from the fact that not many fami-

---

[65] Salvestro di Alamanno de' Medici was the forceful, and somewhat demagogic, leader of the campaign against the Parte Guelfa that triggered the Ciompi revolution (Brucker 1962, chap. 8). For this role, and his subsequent leadership, he was the Ciompi's hero. On the very day of their street triumph, as patrician houses burned, the Ciompi "mob" knighted Salvestro for his services to the *popolo*. Other Medici followed in Salvestro's footsteps, through their heavy involvement with the Alberti faction. In 1397, shortly after the 1393 downfall of the Alberti, Bastardino de' Medici (along with Maso de' Ricci) was executed for attempting to assassinate Maso degli Albizzi and Rinaldo Gianfigliazzi and thereby to overthrow the regime (Brucker 1977, p. 100). In 1400, the Medici were involved in another such conspiracy and assassination attempt, with the result that the entire Medici family (along with the Alberti and Ricci) were excluded from holding public office for 20 years. Actions more anathema to the oligarch regime can hardly be imagined.

lies were involved, the bank was heavily infiltrated with oligarchic partners and employees (particularly the Bardi, but also the Guasconi and
della Casa), later purged (de Roover 1966, p. 56).

A better answer, we believe, has to do with the Medici's own anomalous or structurally contradictory position in the patrician networks. They
were the only major Florentine family to span the structural chasm created by elite closure and to participate simultaneously in the two disarticulated patrician worlds. (Refer to Medici links to the Guasconi and Albizzi blocks in figure 2a.) To understand this oddity, we need more
information on the Medici's own, rather peculiar, family history.

Brucker's article (1957) on the 14th-century Medici makes it clear that
the Medici were hardly a mercantile banking family throughout most
of their history. On the whole, they were a rather violent and lawless
bunch—*popolani* imitating magnates. Only Vieri di Cambio engaged in
banking, and even then the Medici economic fortunes did not really begin
to rise until Giovanni de' Medici used the remnants of Vieri's firm to
capture the pope's business from the discredited Alberti (Holmes 1968).
Perhaps in part because of his relative Salvestro's Ciompi exploits (see n.
65), Giovanni himself assiduously avoided politics throughout his lifetime
(1360–1429) and tried to talk his sons, Cosimo and Lorenzo, into the
same course (Machiavelli 1988, p. 161).

More particularly, Machiavelli describes (on the basis of earlier chroni-
cles) two incidents that may account for how the Medici avoided utter,
rather than just heavy, ostracism after 1382.

In 1393, immediately after the Alberti were finally banished by the
Albizzi oligarchs, a crowd of guildsmen and *popolo minuto* ran to the
house of Vieri di Cambio, who was left head of the Medici clan after
the death of Salvestro in exile in 1388. According to Machiavelli (1988,
pp. 139–140), this crowd implored Vieri in the name of Salvestro to
lead a pro-Alberti revolt to topple the oligarchic regime. Vieri's kinsman
Antonio also urged Vieri to commit the Medici to immediate revolt.
However,

> Going among them in the piazza and from there into the palace, he said
> before the Signoria that he could not in any mode regret having lived in
> such a manner that the people of Florence loved him, but that he regretted
> very much the judgment that had been made of him, which his past life
> did not deserve. . . . He therefore begged the Signoria that the ignorance
> of the multitude not be imputed to his sin because, as far as he was con-
> cerned, as soon as he could he had put himself in [the Signoria's] power. . . .
> After these words, Messer Veri returned to the piazza and joined his follow-
> ers with those who had been led by Messer Rinaldo [Gianfigliazzi] and
> Messer Donato [Acciaiuoli]. . . . He begged [the mob] to put down their
> arms and obey the Signoria [which they did]. [Machiavelli 1988, p. 140]

American Journal of Sociology

Much later, in 1426, Giovanni de' Medici behaved in much the same way, although a change in who initiated the action reveals how far roles had altered in the interval. Rinaldo Albizzi came to Giovanni to ask him to join his faction of oligarchs in their efforts to disenfranchise new men (about which more below). He refused, saying that he opposed factions of any sort.

> These things, so dealt with, were learned of outside and brought more reputation to Giovanni and hatred to the other citizens. But Giovanni sought to detach himself from this so as to give less spirit to those who might plan new things under the cover of his favor. . . . Many of those who followed his part were malcontent at this because they would have liked him to show himself more active in things. Among these was Alamanno de' Medici [son of Salvestro], who was fierce by nature and did not cease inciting him for his coldness and for his mode of proceeding slowly, which, he said, was the cause of his enemies' dealing against him without respect. . . . Inspiring him also in the same way was his son Cosimo. Nonetheless, Giovanni . . . did not budge from his position. [Machiavelli 1988, p. 156]

In other words, throughout the decades following the Ciompi revolt, the leaders of the Medici clan tried hard to distance themselves from their more fractious relatives and to reestablish their family within the conservative oligarchic regime. Not only that, they went out of their way to keep the lid on trouble. As the Machiavelli accounts make clear (see also Martines 1963, p. 55), this docile political behavior did not expunge the pro-new-men image that the Medici name had in the popular mind. But, for their role in squelching discontent, the oligarchs apparently were begrudgingly grateful.

Even so, it was not until the 1420s that the oligarchs relented and began to co-opt the Medici through marriage cycles. Except for marriages with the Bardi, all of the marriages between the Medici and the oligarch blocks in figure 2a were recent.[66] This readmission of the Medici into elite circles was just what the cautious Giovanni had struggled for all his life. But what would have worked splendidly with the older generation of Vieri and Giovanni was too late for the fractious Young Turks Cosimo and Lorenzo di Giovanni and their cousin Averardo di Francesco. Events sketched in the next section led the die to be cast.

Thus, we lay at Vieri di Cambio's doorstep the explanation of the structurally anomalous position that the Medici house held in 15th-

---

[66] The early 1420s period of this co-optative marriage behavior is quite narrow, so the volume of evidence is not overwhelming. But what we have in mind here are the 1420s wife-giving marriages with Luca di Maso Albizzi (after the death of his father), with the Gianfigliazzi, and with the Barbadori—in other words, with the Albizzi block of figure 2a. In addition, there was a wife-receiving marriage with the Guasconi.

century patrician marriage networks. Giovanni followed up Vieri's abject plea with exemplary circumspection, but it was the defusion of popular rebellion by Vieri di Cambio, we argue, that saved the Medici name in oligarch eyes.[67]

Even so, oligarchic acceptance of Giovanni de' Medici, however delimited, suspicious, and constrained, did not occur without a debate. "Niccolo da Uzzano did not fail to alert the other citizens [about the political inclusion of Giovanni di Bicci] by pointing out how dangerous it was to foster one who had such a reputation in the generality of people, and how easy it was to oppose disorders in their beginnings, but how difficult it was to remedy them when they were left alone to increase; and he recognized in Giovanni many parts superior to those of Messer Salvestro. Niccolo was not heeded by his peers because they were envious of his reputation and desired to have partners in defeating him" (Machiavelli 1988, p. 148).

The Dynamics of Party Formation: New Men Economic Ties

We shall now sketch, in exceedingly brief compass because of space limitations, the 1420s and 1430s Medici mobilization, through economic ties, of the second half of their party—the San Giovanni new men. In this reconstruction, we rely heavily on hard-earned data and interpretation in Molho (1971), Brucker (1977), and Kent (1978). The Milan and Lucca wars of 1424–33, we shall argue, were the short-term catalysts that galvanized San Giovanni new men into support and triggered, thereby, selfconsciousness of the Medici as party. The argument in brief is as follows:[68]

The Milan and Lucca wars triggered tax extraction of such magnitude that entire family patrimonies, both of patricians and of new men, were being destroyed. This set off a frantic scramble, among everyone, to escape ruinous tax assessment.

Taxes were levied administratively by neighborhood; thus, fiscal crisis revived the politics of neighborhood. Neighbors looked to neighbors to gain leverage on other neighbors who allocated assessments through rotating offices.

---

[67] Further evidence of this is the fact that only the descendants of Vieri were exempted from the oligarchs' blanket proscription of the Medici clan in 1433 (Kent 1978, p. 295).

[68] Readers interested in documentation of the claims herein can write the authors for an earlier draft of this paper. We have chosen to respond to page limitations by drastically shortening this section on new men, because the argument in this section is primarily a synthesis of secondary sources.

American Journal of Sociology

Administrative assessment procedures could more easily uncover fixed assets like real estate than liquid assets like cash and business investments. Patricians went on the legislative offensive to squeeze more offices and taxes out of mercantile new men.

New men responded initially by banding together in parish-based secret societies: the religious confraternities. While not class homogeneous, this corporate form was a first step toward organized class solidarity and resistance.

Oligarchs responded with vicious and successful repression. Abolition of confraternities left new men bereft of coordinated local neighborhood support from each other.

New men responded in the only way left: supplication of local neighborhood patrician patrons for help. But successful mobilization of patricians for class repression had locked in most oligarchs against responding to appeals from below. The enforcement mechanism behind this coordinated class rejection of new men was the dense marriage network analyzed above.

The Medici were the only exception: their structurally contradictory position within elite marriage networks gave Giovanni and Cosimo the truly discretionary choice of responding or not to pleas from San Giovanni new men. Giovanni de' Medici, late in his life, responded to Rinaldo Albizzi's explicit request to join him in repression in the manner described in the quotation from Machiavelli above. In the sharply polarized context of the time, the hotheaded Rinaldo probably took Giovanni's equivocal response as throwing down the Ciompi (or at least new men) gauntlet. Henceforth (after 1426), the Medici family was severed from budding oligarchic co-optation and was now afloat as a distinct political faction.

San Giovanni new men received patronage, through economic ties, from their neighbors the Medici, but other new men did not, from the Medici or any other source.[69]

Therefore, we believe that the surge of supplication from San Giovanni new men during the Milan war is what triggered Medici self-consciousness of themselves as a political party (as opposed to just an outcast family struggling desperately to regain admittance to the club). Oligarchs funneled new men's support to them and then cut off any possibility of equivocating response. Certainly, the first evidence of intentional and coordinated Medici manipulation of elections dates from 1427, right after this period.

[69] Hence, the 1434 peak of newly admitted families is only one-fourth as large as the historical average. See fig. 1.

1306

NETWORK IDENTITIES

Robust Action

With these analyses of Medicean party dynamics in hand, we are now in position to understand the structural preconditions for robust action. We can only assume that Cosimo learned sphinxlike behavior at his father Giovanni's knee, and then adapted that to revolutionary circumstances. The strategy certainly was not unknown in Florence (Weissman 1989). But robust action is not just a matter of behaving ambiguously. Others are too shrewd not to see through behavioral facades down to presumed self-interested motivations. To act credibly in a multivocal fashion, one's attributed interests must themselves be multivocal.

Within the Medici party itself, the structural underpinnings for contradictory attributions of "Medici self-interest" are clear. The Medici were heroes of the new men not just because they inherited the historical legacy of Salvestro d'Alamanno. They did sponsor a few San Giovanni families of new men, quite unlike their oligarch opponents. And, after Giovanni spurned Rinaldo Albizzi's class alliance request, oligarchs heaped the scornful opprobrium of that label on Medici heads in a polemical effort to whip up patrician fury. At the same time, the Medici's deep patrician roots were clear enough to those whom they married. One can easily imagine Medicean patrician supporters knowingly winking at each other on hearing the public charges of favoring the new men that swirled around their in-laws. Such patricians' hatred of the oligarchs ran deep, and "everyone knows that tactical alliances are sometimes necessary to reestablish an old regime." After all, it would not be the first or last time in Florentine history that the new men had been sold down the river.

Which attribution was true? Plausible evidence could be assembled for either view, but new men and patrician supporters of the Medici hardly ever had the opportunity to get together privately to compare contradictory notes. Even if they had, trust between them was so low that neither should have believed a word of the other. Robust action by the Medici was credible precisely because of the contradictory character of their base of support.

Descending to more micro levels does not help to clarify attributions. Everyone knew that the Medici wanted, as bankers, to make money; as families, to increase prestige; as neighborhood patrons, to amass power. But which of the goals (which really are roles) was in play when? Given fixed role frames, self-interests (and attributions) are clear, but in complicated chaos like the Milan and Lucca wars the games themselves are all up for grabs. Rational choice requires a common metric of utility for

American Journal of Sociology

footing, but revealed preferences (the basis for inferring trade-offs across goals/roles) only exist post hoc.

A Medicean goal of taking over the state can be inferred from the historical record, but only after their choice already had been narrowed to that or exile. Before that, the Medici appear to have been traditional incrementalists, trying only to worm their way back into oligarchs' good graces. Yet, at the level of sphinxlike style, it is not at all clear that Cosimo and Giovanni were any different. Both were shrewd and multi-vocal opportunists, pursuing openings whenever they presented themselves. Clear goals of self-interest, we conclude, are not really features of people; they are Florentine (and our) interpretations of varying structures of games.

Legitimacy

Besides multivocal placement in contemporary conflict, however, there was a second dimension to Medicean robust action. Not only has Cosimo been remembered in history as a Machiavellian deep thinker, but also at his death he was legally enshrined as *pater patriae,* father of his country, by his contemporaries (cf. Schwartz 1983). The very ambiguity of his placement in self-interest somehow became elevated, in the public mind, into the essence of public interest.

This transposition from hero of the new men to Solomonic sage, we believe, can be understood by returning to those Florentines who have remained on the margins of our account so far—the political neutrals. Cosimo never beat the oligarchs in pitched battle; he was recalled from Venetian exile in public triumph, as savior of the republic.[70]

The key is the cognitive category "oligarch." After all, when the oligarchs were firmly in control, they were not labeled "oligarchs"; they were republican "public citizens of the state." Loss of legitimacy and Medici victory are what got them their pejorative tag. No longer public-spirited and selfless in attribution, they came to epitomize class self-interest in Florentine eyes.

How did this delegitimizing change in attribution come to pass? Our answer, basically, is positional chess. The Medici themselves never slung "oligarch" mud back into oligarch eyes. As mentioned in the introduction, Cosimo never said a clear word in his life. Instead, others—new men and eventually political neutrals—were the agents of active tactical slashing.

The sequence went like this: As already described, the fiscal crisis of

---

[70] The irony, of course, is that most historians regard Cosimo as the destroyer of republicanism (Rubinstein 1966).

the wars repolarized social classes and tempted oligarchs into a successful (in the short run) repression campaign. This campaign earned them their label in new men's eyes. However, as Kent (1978) makes clear, the oligarchs' attack was not just a rash tilt at windmills, based on lack of sophisticated foresight. Oligarchs' ability to control the legislative process (especially the colleges), and therefore to attain their goals peacefully, had been hindered recently by the network tentacles of the duplicitous Medici faction. Medicean latent appeal to new men and heterogenous control of some offices gave them swing-vote influence out of proportion to their numbers—even though legislatively all they did was block. In the context of vanishing patrician patrimonies, however, mere blockage was sufficient to force oligarchs onto the offensive. Either they purged the opposition or else all their wealth would be gone.

Cosimo, in contrast, behaved in his typically reactive fashion of only responding to requests. He funneled a sizable portion of the assets of his bank into funding the state's short-term debt, for which he was rewarded with brief public office—member of the Ufficiali del Banco, from November 1427 to December 1428.[71] The monetary catch was this: as incentive to grant such emergency loans, the state offered above-average short-term returns. Thus, while his opponents faced financial catastrophe, Cosimo actually may have made money.[72] More to the point here, once Florence survived, Cosimo de' Medici took on the appearance of financial savior of the city (Molho 1971).

Knowing this, once the Lucca war had ended, the oligarchs moved quickly to send Cosimo, Lorenzo, and other Medici and lieutenants into exile in Venice (and elsewhere). In anticipation of this very move, Cosimo had shifted much of his wealth out of the city, away from potential expropriation, and used it to cultivate Venetian support (de Roover 1966, p. 54; Kent 1978, pp. 304–8). Oligarchic legitimacy was now in deep trouble. They still did not have enough control to purge sufficiently the Signoria electoral bags,[73] so, when the lottery randomly produced too many Medicean officeholders (Kent 1978, p. 328), the oligarchy was forced to take desperate action. Rinaldo Albizzi sent out the word to

---

[71] Even after Cosimo left this post, his supporters continued to dominate this financial nerve center (Molho 1971).

[72] A number of oligarchs possessed as much, or almost as much, raw wealth as did Cosimo, but theirs often was not as liquid as his—a consequence of Cosimo's special ties to the pope.

[73] The Florentines had an elaborate electoral system that involved electing candidates to bags, one bag for every class of offices. Offices were filled every two months by randomly drawing names from the bags and checking these against various legal restrictions. The whole republican purpose of the system was to make it hard for any one faction to consolidate control. See Najemy (1982).

assemble the troops in order forcibly to seize the Signoria, with the stochastic turnout consequences described above. Political neutrals joined the cry for Medici return, and Cosimo became in public acclamation the political as well as financial savior of Florence.

War of course was the sine qua non, but note that at each step of the way Cosimo's careful positional maneuvering forced or enticed oligarchs into offensive lines of action, which connoted private self-interest. These were clear, irrevocable, and hence foreseeable. The reactive character of his robust and multivocal actions gained for Cosimo the revolutionary the legitimizing aureole of protector of the status quo. Party transmuted into state.

CONCLUSION

We shall not summarize the arguments in this paper, except for this: state centralization and the Renaissance emerged from the grinding of tumultuous historical events, as these were filtered through elite transformation. Cosimo did not create the Medici party, but he did shrewdly learn the rules of the networks around him. Rather than dissipate this power through forceful command, Cosimo retreated behind a shroud of multiple identities, impenetrable to this day. These credibly imparted multivocal meanings to all his reactive actions. Robust discretion, in the face of unpredictably hostile futures, and Solomonic legitimacy, above the self-interested fray, were the intended or unintended (who knows?) consequences.

We close on this methodological note: to understand state building, we have argued, one needs to penetrate beneath the veneer of formal institutions and apparently clear goals, down to the relational substratum of people's actual lives. Studying "social embeddedness," we claim, means not the denial of agency, or even groups, but rather an appreciation for the localized, ambiguous, and contradictory character of these lives. Heterogeneity of localized actions, networks, and identities explains both why aggregation is predictable only in hindsight and how political power is born.

APPENDIX A

Blockmodeling Methods

We adopt correlation as our operational measure of structural equivalence, just as in CONCOR (White, Boorman, and Breiger 1976). A frequently used alternative measure, Euclidean distance (Burt 1976), gives weight to volume of ties as well as to pattern of ties (Faust and Romney

1985). In the current context, in which parties and class crosscut, this weighting unhelpfully differentiates elite from nonelite rather than one party from another. Unlike CONCOR, however, we prefer agglomerative to divisive clustering.[74]

Thus, our method is to correlate columns of "stacked" matrices (and transposes), across all strong tie networks, and then to input the resulting correlation matrix into the standard Johnson's complete-link clustering algorithm.[75] This produced the partition of families given in Appendix B. To get the structural portraits of figures 2a and 2b, blockmodel images of social bonds among clusters were generated by (a) aggregating each raw network matrix according to Appendix B's clustering of families and then (b) defining and drawing a social "bond" whenever the number of raw network ties between clusters equaled or exceeded two.[76]

Tables A1 and A2 address goodness-of-fit issues. There are two such issues: How well do the simplified blockmodels represent the more complex actual network data? How well does the blockmodel partition predict actual party memberships, as recorded in Kent? The first issue is assessed, in table A1, in two ways: (a) by the percentage of actual ties among families represented in figure 2's image bonds among blocks and (b) by correlations between raw data matrices and block mean densities, based on the partitions in Appendix B (Noma and Smith 1985).

All correlations in tables A1 and A2 are significant at the $P < .001$ level, according to the QAP procedure of Baker and Hubert (1981).[77]

---

[74] The reason is the two procedures' differing treatments of structural isolates. We prefer to inhibit these "irrelevant" actors from contaminating our structural picture of relations within the core. (This does not mean that information on ties between central and isolated families is ignored in the discovery of the core. Such information already has been incorporated into the original correlation measure.)

[75] In addition to this computer output, we did one manual correction: we merged the Capponi/Busini block with the Strozzi solo block. This merger improved (marginally) goodness of fit. More important, Kent (1978, p. 184) makes a strong case for the structural equivalence of Strozzi and Capponi. In addition, it was clear (from comparing D. Kent [1978] to F. W. Kent [1977]) that we possessed only limited marriage and economic data on Capponi.

[76] Often, density percentages are used as cutoff criteria, instead of raw number of ties, as is the case here. The reason for our approach is that, with small block sizes, percentages are not robust: a single actual tie can mean as much as a 50% density.

[77] In the nonparametric QAP procedure (Baker and Hubert 1981), an empirical distribution of random correlations is generated by repeatedly permuting rows and columns of the raw data matrix and then correlating this with the fixed image matrix. In no case, out of about 1,000 trials, did any of our own simulated random correlations exceed .10. More formal parametric significance tests are rarely possible with network data, since the data grossly violate the "independent observations" assumptions of traditional tests.

TABLE A1

GOODNESS OF FIT OF BLOCKMODEL IMAGE TO RAW NETWORK DATA

TYPE OF RELATION	OVERALL			MEDICI	
	No. of Ties	Proportion of Ties in Image	Correlation with Block Means	No. of Ties	Proportion of Ties in Image
Marriage	161	.646	.492	28	.964
Trade	92	.674	.561	10	.800
Partnership	45	.556	.513	13	.846
Bank	13	.769	.415	10	.800
Real estate	22	.091	.378	5	.400
Subtotal*	333	.610		66	.848
Mallevadori	31	.194	.338	3	.000
Friendship	50	.360	.381	14	.714
Personal loan.........	89	.404	.408	25	.840
Patronage	36	.222	.389	21	.381
Subtotal*	206	.330		63	.619
Total	539	.503		129	.736

* The blockmodel partitions were derived from data on the first five of these relations only. Goodness-of-fit measures for the last four relations derive from the superposition of best-fitting partitions from the first five relations. All correlations are significant at the $P < .001$ level, according to the nonparametric QAP procedure (Baker and Hubert 1981), implemented in UCINET.

TABLE A2

GOODNESS OF FIT OF BLOCKMODEL PARTITIONS TO PARTY MEMBERSHIP

No. of Families	Medici Blocks	All Other Blocks	Elite Blocks	Nonelite Blocks
Mediceans............................	26	4	2	2
Split loyalty...........................	2	10	6	4
Oligarchs..............................	0	31	8	23
Neutrals	1	18	2	16
Proportion mobilized*	.966	.714	.889	.644
Proportion own party†.............	.958	.823	.737	.871

* % Mobilized measures relative recruitment of blocked families into any party; i.e., proportion mobilized = (no. of families − no. of neutral families)/(no. of families).

† % Own party measures relative partisanship of activists; i.e., proportion own party = (no. of families in own party)/(no. of families − no. of neutral families), with split families allocated proportionately.

Robust Action

Moreover, 50% of the total volume of ties,[78] 61% of marriage and economic ties (fig. 2a), and 33% of "political" and friendship ties (fig. 2b) are captured by the central tendencies in the blockmodel. Given that the blockmodel was derived from the strong tie marriage and economic relations alone, we were pleasantly surprised by the weak tie performance.

More particularly, it is clear that marriage and trading relationships are the primary driving forces behind this blockmodel portrait of the Florentine elite. In part, this is because of their high rates of inclusive success, but it is also due to the higher volume of data. Partnerships and especially bank employment relations were very important when they appeared, but they do not span much of the elite. Real estate relations essentially were irrelevant.

On the weak tie side, personal friendships and personal loans operated in large part within the framework of marriage and economic relations. *Mallevadori* and patronage relations, however, were not well predicted by marriage and economic ties.

The success with which the blockmodel predicts political partisanship, in the table A2, speaks for itself. Ninety-three percent of the families in the Medicean blocks were mobilized into the Medici party. Fifty-nine percent of the families in the non-Medicean blocks were mobilized into the oligarch party.

---

[78] Considering that this blockmodel has been disaggregated to an average of 2.7 families per block, and considering that the average overall density of the nine historical networks here is an extremely sparse 0.7%, this is excellent performance.

APPENDIX B

TABLE B1

BLOCK MEMBERSHIPS: CLUSTERING OF CORRELATIONS OF MARRIAGE, TRADE,
PARTNERSHIP, BANK, AND REAL ESTATE RELATIONS

Reggimento Family	Party*	Gross Wealth (Florins)	Date of First Prior	Neighborhood (*Gonfalone*)†
Medicean blocks:				
MEDICI:				
Medici....................	Medici (5)	199,672	1291	41
Carnesecchi............	Medici	42,316	1297	42
Berlinghieri	Medici	6,117	1365	22
TORNABUONI:				
Tornabuoni/				
Tornaquinci	Medici	121,310	Magnate	34
Salviati...................	Split loyalties (1/1)	29,964	1297	24
Serristori................	Medici	56,675	1392	23
Giugni....................	Medici (3)	41,086	1291	24
Pecori	Medici	17,244	1284	42
Corsini		16,387	1290	13
Vecchietti................	Medici	17,212	Magnate	34
GUICCIARDINI:				
Acciaiuoli................	Medici	28,200	1282	31
Guicciardini	Medici	60,060	1302	12
Ridolfi....................	Medici	46,196	1290	13
Pitti........................	Medici (2)	9,676	1283	12
Corbinelli................	Medici	58,955	1286	12
GINORI:				
Ginori	Medici (3)	34,831	1344	41
Martelli	Medici (8)	7,502	1343	41
DIETISALVI:				
Dietisalvi	Medici (2)	3,943	1291	41
Ciai	Medici	22,331	1389	41
DALL'ANTELLA:				
dall'Antella	Split loyalties (1/2)	18,437	1282	21
Bartolini.................	Medici	19,477	1299	42
ORLANDINI:				
Orlandini................	Medici	11,012	1420	42
Lapi	Medici	5,303	1394	44
DAVANZATI:				
Davanzati	Medici (2)	19,887	1320	32
COCCO-DONATI:				
Cocco-Donati...........	Medici (2)	2,580	1376	22
Arnolfi	Medici	4,160	1318	42
Pandolfini	Medici	30,520	1381	43
VALORI:				
Valori	Medici	15,213	1322	43
del Benino	Medici	22,629	1345	13
Non-Medicean blocks:				
ARDINGHELLI:				
Ardinghelli..............	Oligarch	57,596	1282	32
da Panzano	Split loyalties (1/1)	. . .	1312	22

1314

continued overleaf

TABLE B1 *(Continued)*

Reggimento Family	Party*	Gross Wealth (Florins)	Date of First Prior	Neighborhood *(Gonfalone)*†
DA UZZANO:				
da Uzzano..............		75,737	1363	11
Bucelli	Oligarch	20,394	1284	22
GUASCONI:				
Guasconi	Oligarch (3)	29,074	1314	41
Bardi	Split loyalties (3/5)	189,452	Magnate	11
Cavalcanti	Split loyalties (1/1)	50,122	Magnate	31
Pazzi......................	Medici	72,550	Magnate	43
RONDINELLI:				
Rondinelli	Oligarch	21,053	1296	41
Brancacci...............	Oligarch (4)	15,697	1317	14
Mancini..................		6,838	1284	22
ALDOBRANDINI:				
Aldobrandini	Oligarch	7,171	1307	34
Raugi.....................	Oligarch	3,634	1304	21
PERUZZI:				
Peruzzi	Oligarch (8)	104,795	1283	23
Ricasoli	Oligarch (2)	36,178	Magnate	21
degli Agli...............		9,402	Magnate	42
CASTELLANI:				
Castellani...............	Oligarch (5)	61,696	1326	21
Spini......................	Oligarch	39,553	Magnate	32
Fagni		10,106	1295	23
PEPI:				
Pepi.......................	Oligarch	2,865	1301	23
Doffi......................	Oligarch	12,700	1393	22
Morelli		27,535	1387	23
SCAMBRILLA:				
Scambrilla..............	Oligarch (2)	148	1387	21
Sertini...................		. . .	1376	34
BENIZZI:				
Benizzi...................	Oligarch (2)	9,672	1301	12
Manelli..................		16,421	Magnate	12
STROZZI:				
Strozzi...................	Oligarch (4)	296,250	1283	33
Capponi	Medici	54,027	1287	12
Busini....................		57,019	1345	23
RUCELLAI:				
Rucellai		54,968	1302	33
Baldovinetti	Oligarch (2)	9,831	1287	31
Sacchetti................		29,092	1335	22
PANCIATICHI:				
Frescobaldi	Oligarch	28,898	Magnate	12
Panciatichi.............	Oligarch	151,542	Consular	42
Manovelli	Oligarch	13,438	1283	42
ALBIZZI:				
Albizzi	Split loyalties (1/2)	92,599	1282	43
Gianfigliazzi	Split loyalties (1/5)	47,853	Magnate	32
Barbadori	Split loyalties (1/2)	98,663	1295	12
Belfradelli..............	Oligarch (2)	9,014	1321	12
Bencivenni..............	Split loyalties (1/1)	1,811	1389	43

TABLE B1 (*Continued*)

Reggimento Family	Party*	Gross Wealth (Florins)	Date of First Prior	Neighborhood (*Gonfalone*)†
ALTOVITI:				
Altoviti..................	Oligarch (2)	42,357	1282	31
del Palagio..............		8,676	1328	43
Corsi......................	Split loyalties (1/3)	26,588	1354	23
DELLA CASA:				
della Casa...............	Split loyalties (1/1)	31,069	1393	42
Adimari.................		45,689	Magnate	44
Serragli		63,866	1325	14
SOLOSMEI:				
Solosmei	Oligarch (2)	5,757	1364	41
LAMBERTESCHI:				
Lamberteschi..........	Oligarch (2)	52,524	Consular	21
Baronci	Oligarch	12,251	1330	42
VELLUTI:				
Velluti...................	Split loyalties (1/1)	22,372	1283	12
Arrigucci	Oligarch	5,736	Magnate	42
BARONCELLI:				
Baroncelli		67,966	1287	21
Rossi......................	Oligarch	24,649	Magnate	44
GUADAGNI:				
Guadagni...............	Oligarch (5)	25,179	1289	43
BISCHERI:				
Bischeri.................	Oligarch	55,230	1309	44
Arrighi..................		23,499	1373	43
FIORAVANTI:				
Donati...................		26,099	Magnate	43
Scolari...................		12,074	Magnate	43
Fioravanti...............	Medici	19,501	1344	43
Miscellaneous (unblocked):				
Carducci.................	Medici (2)	28,909	1380	31
Fortini		30,645	1386	43
del Forese..............	Oligarch	4,220	1296	24
Bartoli	Oligarch	54,956	1345	32

* For Medici and oligarch parties, numbers in parentheses are numbers active, if more than one. For split loyalties, numbers in parentheses are, first, number of Mediceans and, second, number of oligarchs. Blank spaces indicate that there were no active partisans.

† For Santo Spirito quarter, 11 = Scala *gonfalone*, 12 = Nicchio *gonfalone*, 13 = Ferza *gonfalone*, 14 = Drago Verde *gonfalone*. For Santa Croce quarter, 21 = Carro *gonfalone*, 22 = Bue *gonfalone*, 23 = Lion Nero *gonfalone*, 24 = Ruote *gonfalone*. For Santa Maria Novella quarter, 31 = Vipera *gonfalone*, 32 = Unicorno *gonfalone*, 33 = Lion Rosso *gonfalone*, 34 = Lion Bianco *gonfalone*. For San Giovanni quarter, 41 = Lion d'oro *gonfalone*, 42 = Drago San Giovanni *gonfalone*, 43 = Chiavi *gonfalone*, 44 = Vaio *gonfalone*.

Robust Action

REFERENCES

Baker, Frank B., and J. Lawrence Hubert. 1981. "The Analysis of Social Interaction Data: A Nonparametric Technique." *Sociological Methods and Research* 9:339–61.
Baron, Hans. 1966. *The Crisis of the Early Italian Renaissance*. Princeton, N.J.: Princeton University Press.
Barth, Fredrik. 1959. *Political Leadership among Swat Pathans*. London: Athlone.
Becker, Marvin. 1962. "An Essay on the 'Novi Cives' and Florentine Politics, 1343–1382." *Mediaeval Studies* 24:35–82.
———. 1965. "A Study in Political Failure, the Florentine Magnates: 1280–1343." *Mediaeval Studies* 27:246–308.
Blalock, Hubert. 1972. *Social Statistics*. New York: McGraw-Hill.
Breiger, Ronald L., and Philippa E. Pattison. 1986. "Cumulated Social Roles: The Duality of Persons and Their Algebras." *Social Networks* 8:215–56.
Brown, Allison. 1961. "The Humanist Portrait of Cosimo de' Medici, Pater Patriae." *Journal of the Warburg and Courtauld Institutes* 26:186–221.
———. 1992. "Cosimo de' Medici's Wit and Wisdom." Pp. 95–113 in *Cosimo "il Vecchio" de' Medici, 1389–1464*, edited by Francis Ames-Lewis. Oxford: Clarendon.
Brucker, Gene A. 1957. "The Medici in the Fourteenth Century." *Speculum* 32:1–26.
———. 1962. *Florentine Politics and Society, 1343–78*. Princeton, N.J.: Princeton University Press.
———. 1977. *The Civic World of Early Renaissance Florence*. Princeton, N.J.: Princeton University Press.
Burckhardt, Jacob. 1860. *The Civilization of the Renaissance in Italy*, translated by S. G. C. Middlemore. London: Phaidon.
Burt, Ronald. 1976. "Positions in Networks." *Social Forces* 55:93–122.
Cohn, Samuel Kline. 1980. *The Laboring Classes in Renaissance Florence*. New York: Academic.
De Roover, Raymond. 1966. *The Rise and Decline of the Medici Bank*. New York: Norton.
Douglas, Mary. 1986. *How Institutions Think*. Syracuse, N.Y.: Syracuse University Press.
Duby, Georges. 1980. *The Three Orders: Feudal Society Imagined*. Chicago: University of Chicago Press.
Elster, Jon. 1983. *Sour Grapes: Studies in the Subversion of Rationality*. Cambridge: Cambridge University Press.
Emerson, Richard M. 1962. "Power-Dependence Relations." *American Sociological Review* 27:31–40.
Faust, Katherine, and A. Kimball Romney. 1985. "Does STRUCTURE Find Structure? A Critique of Burt's Use of Distance as a Measure of Structural Equivalence." *Social Networks* 7:77–103.
Foster, Susannah. 1985. *The Ties That Bind: Kinship Association and Marriage in the Alberti Family, 1378–1428*. Ph.D. dissertation. Cornell University, Ithaca, N.Y.
Foucault, Michel. 1975. "What Is an Author?" *Partisan Review* 42:603–14.
Freeman, Linton C. 1979. "Centrality in Social Networks: Conceptual Clarification." *Social Networks* 1:215–39.
Granovetter, Mark S. 1973. "The Strength of Weak Ties." *American Journal of Sociology* 78:1360–80.
Goffman, Erving. 1975. *Frame Analysis*. Boston: Northeastern University Press.
Goldthwaite, Richard A. 1968. *Private Wealth in Renaissance Florence: A Study of Four Families*. Princeton, N.J.: Princeton University Press.

American Journal of Sociology

Gutkind, Curt S. 1938. *Cosimo de' Medici: Pater patriae, 1389–1464.* Oxford: Oxford University Press.

Herlihy, David, and Christiane Klapisch-Zuber. 1981. *Census and Property Survey of Florentine Domains in the Province of Tuscany, 1427–1480.* Madison: University of Wisconsin, Data and Program Library Service.

———. 1985. *Tuscans and Their Families: A Study of the Florentine Catasto of 1427.* New Haven, Conn.: Yale University Press.

Holmes, George. 1968. "How the Medici Became the Pope's Bankers." Pp. 357–80. In *Florentine Studies,* edited by Nicolai Rubinstein. Evanston, Ill.: Northwestern University Press.

Kent, Dale. 1975. "The Florentine Reggimento in the Fifteenth Century." *Renaissance Quarterly* 28:575–638.

———. 1978. *The Rise of the Medici: Faction in Florence, 1426–1434.* Oxford: Oxford University Press.

Kent, D. V., and F. W. Kent. 1981. "A Self-disciplining Pact Made by the Peruzzi Family of Florence (June 1433)." *Renaissance Quarterly* 34:337–55.

———. 1982. *Neighbours and Neighbourhood in Renaissance Florence: The District of the Red Lion in the Fifteenth Century.* Locust Valley, N.Y.: Augustin.

Kent, F. W. 1977. *Household and Lineage in Renaissance Florence.* Princeton, N.J.: Princeton University Press.

———. 1987. "Ties of Neighborhood and Patronage in Quattrocento Florence." Pp. 79–98 in *Patronage, Art, and Society in Renaissance Italy,* edited by F. W. Kent and Patricia Simons. Oxford: Clarendon.

Lansing, Carol. 1991. *The Florentine Magnates: Lineage and Faction in a Medieval Commune.* Princeton, N.J.: Princeton University Press.

Lave, Charles A., and James G. March. 1975. *An Introduction to Models in the Social Sciences.* New York: Harper & Row.

Leifer, Eric. 1988. "Interaction Preludes to Role Setting: Exploratory Local Action." *American Sociological Review* 53:865–78.

———. 1991. *Actors as Observers: A Theory of Skill in Social Relationships.* New York: Garland.

Lovejoy, Arthur O. 1936. *The Great Chain of Being.* Cambridge, Mass.: Harvard University Press.

Machiavelli, Niccolo. (1525) 1988. *Florentine Histories,* translated by Laura F. Banfield and Harvey Mansfield, Jr. Princeton, N.J.: Princeton University Press.

Martines, Lauro. 1963. *The Social World of the Florentine Humanists, 1390–1460.* Princeton, N.J.: Princeton University Press.

Mauss, Marcel. (1925) 1967. *The Gift: Forms and Functions of Exchange in Archaic Societies.* New York: Norton.

Molho, Anthony. 1971. *Florentine Public Finances in the Early Renaissance, 1400–1433.* Cambridge, Mass.: Harvard University Press.

———. 1979. "Cosimo de' Medici: Pater Patriae or Padrino?" *Stanford Italian Review* 1:5–33.

Najemy, John M. 1982. *Corporation and Consensus in Florentine Electoral Politics.* Chapel Hill: University of North Carolina Press.

Namier, Lewis. 1929. *The Structure of Politics at the Accession of George III.* New York: Macmillan.

Noma, Elliot, and D. Randall Smith. 1985. "Benchmark for the Blocking of Sociometric Data." *Psychological Bulletin* 97:583–91.

Padgett, John F. 1981. "Hierarchy and Ecological Control in Federal Budgetary Decision Making." *American Journal of Sociology* 87:75–129.

———. 1986. "Rationally Inaccessible Rationality." *Contemporary Sociology* 15:26–28.

Robust Action

————. 1990. "Plea Bargaining and Prohibition in the Federal Courts, 1908–1934."
  Law and Society Review 24:413–50
Poliziano, Angelo. (Ca. 1478) 1985. *I detti piacevoli,* edited by Mariano Fresta. Siena:
  Editori del Grifo.
Rubinstein, Nicolai. 1966. *The Government of Florence under the Medici (1434–
  1494).* Oxford: Clarendon.
Schwartz, Barry. 1983. "George Washington and the Whig Conception of Heroic
  Leadership." *American Sociological Review* 48:18–33.
Skocpol, Theda. 1979. *States and Social Revolutions.* Cambridge: Cambridge Univer-
  sity Press.
Trexler, Richard C. 1980. *Public Life in Renaissance Florence.* New York: Academic.
Vespasiano da Bisticci. (Ca. 1495) 1963. *Renaissance Princes, Popes, and Prelates:
  The Vespasiano Memoirs,* edited by Myron P. Gilmore. New York: Harper & Row.
Waley, Daniel. 1969. *The Italian City-Republics.* New York: McGraw-Hill.
Weissman, Ronald F. E. 1982. *Ritual Brotherhood in Renaissance Florence.* New
  York: Academic.
————. 1989. "The Importance of Being Ambiguous: Social Relations, Individualism,
  and Identity in Renaissance Florence." Pp. 269–80 In *Urban Life in the Renais-
  sance,* edited by Susan Zimmerman and Ronald Weissman. Dover: University of
  Delaware Press.
White, Harrison C. 1970. *Chains of Opportunity.* Cambridge, Mass.: Harvard Univer-
  sity Press.
————. 1992. *Identity and Control: A Structural Theory of Social Action.* Princeton,
  N.J.: Princeton University Press.
White, Harrison C., Scott A. Boorman, and Ronald L. Breiger. 1976. "Social Structure from Multiple Networks. I. Blockmodels of Roles and Positions." *American
  Journal of Sociology* 81:730–50.
Witt, Ronald G. 1976. "Florentine Politics and the Ruling Class, 1382–1407." *Journal of Medieval and Renaissance Studies* 6:243–67.

E
Cohesion

[16]

An Experimental Study of the Small World Problem*

JEFFREY TRAVERS

Harvard University

AND

STANLEY MILGRAM

The City University of New York

Arbitrarily selected individuals (N=296) in Nebraska and Boston are asked to generate acquaintance chains to a target person in Massachusetts, employing "the small world method" (Milgram, 1967). Sixty-four chains reach the target person. Within this group the mean number of intermediaries between starters and targets is 5.2. Boston starting chains reach the target person with fewer intermediaries than those starting in Nebraska; subpopulations in the Nebraska group do not differ among themselves. The funneling of chains through sociometric "stars" is noted, with 48 per cent of the chains passing through three persons before reaching the target. Applications of the method to studies of large scale social structure are discussed.

The simplest way of formulating the small world problem is "what is the probability that any two people, selected arbitrarily from a large population, such as that of the United States, will know each other?" A more interesting formulation, however, takes account of the fact that, while persons a and z may not know each other directly, they may share one or more mutual acquaintances; that is, there may exist a set of individuals, B, (consisting of individuals $b_1, b_2 \ldots b_n$) who know both a and z and thus link them to one another. More generally, a and z may be connected not by any single common acquaintance, but by a series of such intermediaries, $a\text{-}b\text{-}c\text{-}\ldots\text{-}y\text{-}z$; i.e., a knows b (and no one else in the chain); b knows a and in addition knows c, c in turn knows d, etc.

To elaborate the problem somewhat further, let us represent the popula-

---

* The study was carried out while both authors were at Harvard University, and was financed by grants from the Milton Fund and from the Harvard Laboratory of Social Relations. Mr. Joseph Gerver provided invaluable assistance in summarizing and criticizing the mathematical work discussed in this paper.

425

tion of the United States by a partially connected set of points. Let each point represent a person, and let a line connecting two points signify that the two individuals know each other. (Knowing is here assumed to be symmetric: if *a* knows *b* then *b* knows *a*. Substantively, "knowing" is used to denote a mutual relationship; other senses of the verb, e.g. knowing about a famous person, are excluded.) The structure takes the form of a cluster of roughly 200 million points with a complex web of connections among them. The acquaintance chains described above appear as pathways along connected line segments. Unless some portion of the population is totally isolated from the rest, such that no one in that subgroup knows anyone outside it, there must be at least one chain connecting any two people in the population. In general there will be many such pathways, of various lengths, between any two individuals.

In view of such a structure, one way of refining our statement of the small world problem is the following: given two individuals selected randomly from the population, what is the probability that the minimum number of intermediaries required to link them is 0, 1, 2, . . . *k*? (Alternatively, one might ask not about the minimum chains between pairs of people, but mean chain lengths, median chain lengths, etc.)

Perhaps the most direct way of attacking the small world problem is to trace a number of real acquaintance chains in a large population. This is the technique of the study reported in this paper. The phrase "small world" suggests that social networks are in some sense tightly woven, full of unexpected strands linking individuals seemingly far removed from one another in physical or social space. The principal question of the present investigation was whether such interconnectedness could be demonstrated experimentally.

The only example of mathematical treatment dealing directly with the small world problem is the model provided by Ithiel Pool and Manfred Kochen (unpublished manuscript). Pool and Kochen assume a population of N individuals, each of whom knows, on the average, n others in the population. They attempt to calculate P_k, the probability that two persons chosen randomly from the group can be linked by a chain of k intermediaries. Their basic model takes the form of a "tree" or geometric progression. Using an estimate of average acquaintance volume provided by Gurevitch (1961), they deduce that two intermediaries will be required to link typical pairs of individuals in a population of 200 million. Their model does not take account of social structure. Instead of allowing acquaintance nets to define the boundaries of functioning social groups, Pool and Kochen must, for the purposes of their model, conceive of society as being partitioned into a number of hypothetical groups, each with identical populations. They are then able to devise a way to predict chain lengths within and between such hypothesized groups.

In an empirical study related to the small world problem Rapoport and Horvath (1961) examined sociometric nets in a junior high school of 861 students. The authors asked students to name in order their eight best friends within the school. They then traced the acquaintance chains created by the students' choices. Rapoport was interested in connectivity, i.e. the fraction of the total population that would be contacted by tracing friendship choices from an arbitrary starting population of nine individuals. Rapoport and his associates (Rapoport and Horvath, 1961; Foster et al., 1963; Rapoport, 1953; 1963) have developed a mathematical model to describe this tracing procedure. The model takes as a point of departure random nets constructed in the following manner: a small number of points is chosen from a larger population and a fixed number of "axones" is extended from each of these points to a set of target points chosen at random from the population. The same fixed number of axones is then extended from each of the target points to a set of second generation target points, and the process is repeated indefinitely. A target point is said to be of the tth remove if it is of the tth generation and no lower generation. Rapoport then suggests a formula for calculating the fraction, P_t, of the population points which are targets of the tth remove. He is also able to extend the formula to nonrandom nets, such as those created in the Rapoport and Horvath empirical study, by introducing a number of "biases" into the random net model. Rapoport shows that two parameters, obtainable from the data, are sufficient to produce a close fit between the predictions of the model and the empirical outcome of the trace procedure.[1]

Rapoport's model was designed to describe a trace procedure quite different from the one employed in the present study; however, it has some relation to the small world problem. If we set the number of axones traced from a given individual equal to the total number of acquaintances of an average person, the Rapoport model predicts the total fraction of the population potentially traceable at each remove from the start, serving precisely the aims of the model of Pool and Kochen. (It should, however, be noted that Rapoport's model deals with asymmetric nets, and it would be difficult to modify the model to deal with general symmetric nets, which characterize the small world phenomenon.)

Despite the goodness of fit between Rapoport's model and the data from

---

[1] There is additional empirical evidence (Fararo and Sunshine, 1964) and theoretical support (Abelson, 1967) for the assumption that two parameters are sufficient to describe the Rapoport tracing procedure, i.e. that more complex biases have minimal effects on connectivity in friendship nets.

two large sociograms, there are unsolved problems in the model, as Rapoport himself and others (Fararo and Sunshine, 1964) have pointed out. The Pool-Kochen model involves assumptions difficult for an empirically oriented social scientist to accept, such as the assumption that society may be partitioned into a set of groups alike in size and in internal and external connectedness. In the absence of empirical data, it is difficult to know which simplifying assumptions are likely to be fruitful. On the other hand, with regard to the empirical study of Rapoport and Horvath, the fact that the total population employed was small, well-defined, and homogeneous leaves open many questions about the nature of acquaintance nets in the larger society.[2] An empirical study of American society as a whole may well uncover phenomena of interest both in their own right and as constraints on the nature of any correct mathematical model of the structure of large-scale acquaintanceship nets.

PROCEDURE

This paper follows the procedure for tracing acquaintance chains devised and first tested by Milgram (1967). The present paper introduces an experimental variation in this procedure, by varying "starting populations"; it also constitutes a first technical report on the small world method.

The procedure may be summarized as follows: an arbitrary "target person" and a group of "starting persons" were selected, and an attempt was made to generate an acquaintance chain from each starter to the target. Each starter was provided with a document and asked to begin moving it by mail toward the target The document described the study, named the target, and asked the recipient to become a participant by sending the document on. It was stipulated that the document could be sent only to a first-name acquaintance of the sender. The sender was urged to choose the recipient in such a way as to advance the progress of the document toward the target; several items of information about the target were provided to guide each new sender in his choice of recipient. Thus, each document made its way along an acquaintance chain of indefinite length, a chain which would end only when it reached the target or when someone along the way declined to participate. Certain basic information, such as age, sex and occupation, was collected for each participant.

---

[2] In addition to the Pool-Kochen and Rapoport work, there are numerous other studies of social network phenomena tangentially related to the small-world problem. Two well-known examples are Bailey's *The Mathematical Theory of Epidemics* and Coleman, Katz and Menzel's *Medical Innovation*. Bailey's work deals with diffusion from a structured source, rather than with convergence on a target from a set of scattered sources, as in the present study. The Coleman, Katz and Menzel study deals with an important substantive correlate of acquaintance nets, namely information diffusion.

We were interested in discovering some of the internal structural features of chains and in making comparisons across chains as well. Among the questions we hoped to answer were the following: How many of the starters —if any—would be able to establish contact with the target through a chain of acquaintances? How many intermediaries would be required to link the ends of the chains? What form would the distribution of chain lengths take? What degree of homogeneity in age, sex, occupation, and other characteristics of participants would be observed within chains? How would complete chains differ from incomplete on these and other dimensions?

An additional comparison was set up by using three distinct starting subpopulations. The target person was a Boston stockbroker; two of the starting populations were geographically removed from him, selected from the state of Nebraska. A third population was selected from the Boston area. One of the Nebraska groups consisted of bluechip stockholders, while the second Nebraska group and the Boston group were "randomly" selected and had no special access to the investment business. By comparisons across these groups we hoped to assess the relative effects of geographical distance and of contact with the target's occupational group. Moreover we hoped to establish a strategy for future experimental extensions of the procedure, in which the sociological characteristics of the starting and target populations would be systematically varied in order to expose features of social structure.

The primary research questions, then, involved a test of the feasibility and fruitfulness of the method as well as an attempt to discover some elementary features of real social nets. Several experimental extensions of the procedure are already underway. A more detailed description of the current method is given in the following sections.

PARTICIPANTS. *Starting Population.* The starting population for the study was comprised of 296 volunteers. Of these, 196 were residents of the state of Nebraska, solicited by mail. Within this group, 100 were systematically chosen owners of blue-chip stocks; these will be designated "Nebraska stockholders" throughout this paper. The rest were chosen from the population at large; these will be termed the "Nebraska random" group. In addition to the two Nebraska groups, 100 volunteers were solicited through an advertisement in a Boston newspaper (the "Boston random" group). Each member of the starting population became the first link in a chain of acquaintances directed at the target person.

Intermediaries. The remaining participants in the study, who numbered 453 in all, were in effect solicited by other participants; they were acquaintances selected by previous participants as people likely to extend the chain toward the target. Participation was voluntary. Participants were not paid, nor was money or other reward offered as incentive for completion of chains.

THE DOCUMENT. The 296 initial volunteers were sent a document which was the principal tool of the investigation.[3] The document contained:

a. a description of the study, a request that the recipient become a participant, and a set of rules for participation;
b. the name of the target person and selected information concerning him;
c. a roster, to which each participant was asked to affix his name;
d. a stack of fifteen business reply cards asking information about each participant.

Rules for Participation. The document contained the following specific instructions to participants:

a. Add your name to the roster so that the next person who receives this folder will know whom it came from.
b. Detach one postcard from the bottom of this folder. Fill it out and return it to Harvard University. No stamp is needed. The postcard is very important. It allows us to keep track of the progress of the folder as it moves toward the target person.
c. If you know the target person on a personal basis, mail this folder directly to him (her). Do this only if you have previously met the target person and know each other on a first name basis.
d. If you do not know the target person on a personal basis, do not try to contact him directly. Instead, mail this folder to a personal acquaintance who is more likely than you to know the target person. You may send the booklet on to a friend, relative, or acquaintance, but it must be someone you know personally.

Target Person. The target person was a stockholder who lives in Sharon, Massachusetts, a suburb of Boston, and who works in Boston proper. In addition to his name, address, occupation and place of employment, participants were told his college and year of graduation, his military service dates, and his wife's maiden name and hometown. One question under investigation was the type of information which people would use in reaching the target.

Roster. The primary function of the roster was to prevent "looping," i.e., to prevent people from sending the document to someone who had already received it and sent it on. An additional function of the roster was to motivate people to continue the chains. It was hoped that a list of prior participants, including a personal acquaintance who had sent the document to

[3] A photographic reproduction of this experimental document appears in Milgram, 1969: 110-11.

the recipient, would create willingness on the part of those who received the document to send it on.

Tracer Cards. Each participant was asked to return to us a business reply card giving certain information about himself and about the person to whom he sent the document. The name, address, age sex and occupation of the sender and sender's spouse were requested, as were the name, address, sex and age of the recipient. In addition, the nature of the relationship between sender and recipient—whether they were friends, relatives, business associates, etc.—was asked. Finally, participants were asked why they had selected the particular recipient of the folder.

The business reply cards enabled us to keep running track of the progress of each chain. Moreover, they assured us of getting information even from chains which were not completed, allowing us to make comparisons between complete and incomplete chains.

RESULTS

COMPLETIONS. 217 of the 296 starting persons actually sent the document on to friends. Any one of the documents could reach the target person only if the following conditions were met: 1) recipients were sufficiently motivated to send the document on to the next link in the chain; 2) participants were able to adopt some strategy for moving the documents closer to the target (this condition further required that the given information allow them to select the next recipient in a manner that increased the probability of contacting the target); 3) relatively short paths were in fact required to link starters and target (otherwise few chains would remain active long enough to reach completion). Given these contingencies, there was serious doubt in the mind of the investigators whether any of the documents, particularly those starting in an area remote from the target person, could move through interlocking acquaintance networks and converge on him. The actual outcome was that 64 of the folders, or 29 per cent of those sent out by starting persons, eventually reached the target.

DISTRIBUTION OF CHAIN LENGTHS. *Complete Chains.* Figure 1 shows the frequency distribution of lengths of the completed chains. "Chain length" is here defined as the number of intermediaries required to link starters and target. The mean of the distribution is 5.2 links.

It was unclear on first inspection whether the apparent drop in frequency at the median length of five links was a statistical accident, or whether the distribution was actually bimodal. Further investigation revealed that the summary relation graphed in Figure 1 concealed two underlying distributions: when the completed chains were divided into those which approached the target through his hometown and those which approached him via

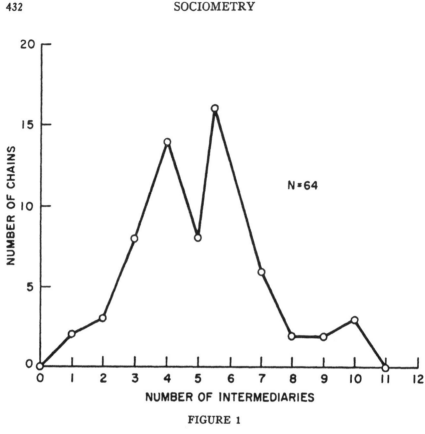

FIGURE 1

Lengths of Completed Chains

Boston business contracts, two distinguishable distributions emerged. The mean of the Sharon distribution is 6.1 links, and that of the Boston distribution is 4.6. The difference is significant at a level better than .0005, as assessed by the distribution-free Mann-Whitney U test. (Note that more powerful statistical tests of the significance of differences between means cannot be applied to these data, since those tests assume normality of underlying distributions. The shape of the true or theoretical distribution of lengths of acquaintance chains is precisely what we do not know.)

Qualitatively, what seems to occur is this. Chains which converge on the target principally by using geographic information reach his hometown or the surrounding areas readily, but once there often circulate before entering the target's circle of acquaintances. There is no available information to narrow the field of potential contacts which an individual might have within the town. Such additional information as a list of local organizations

STUDY OF THE SMALL WORLD PROBLEM   **433**

of which the target is a member might have provided a natural funnel, facilitating the progress of the document from town to target person. By contrast, those chains which approach the target through occupational channels can take advantage of just such a funnel, zeroing in on him first through the brokerage business, then through his firm.

Incomplete Chains. Chains terminate either through completion or dropout: each dropout results in an incomplete chain. Figure 2 shows the number of chains which dropped out at each "remove" from the starting population. The "0th remove" represents the starting population itself: the "first remove" designates the set of people who received the document directly from members of the starting population. The "second remove" received the document from the starters via one intermediary, the third through two intermediaries, etc. The length of an incomplete chain may be defined as the number of removes from the start at which dropout occurs, or, equivalently, as the number of transmissions of the folder which precede dropout. By this definition, Figure 2 represents a frequency distribution of the lengths of incomplete chains. The mean of the distribution is 2.6 links.

The proportion of chains which drop out at each remove declines as

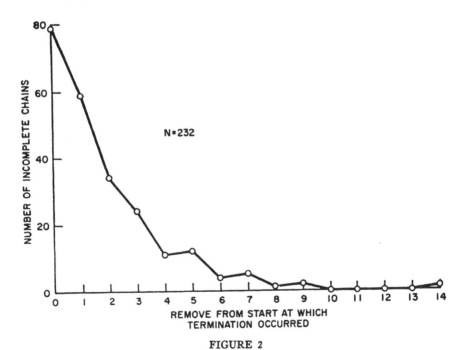

FIGURE 2

Lengths of Incomplete Chains

chains grow in length, if that proportion is based on all chains active at each remove (those destined for completion as well as incompletion). About 27 per cent of the 296 folders sent to the starting population are not sent on. Similarly, 27 per cent of the 217 chains actually initiated by the starters die at the first remove. The percentage of dropouts then appears to fall. It also begins to fluctuate, as the total number of chains in circulation grows small, and an increasing proportion of completions further complicates the picture.

It was argued earlier that, in theory, any two people can be linked by at least one acquaintance chain of finite length, barring the existence of totally isolated cliques within the population under study. Yet, incomplete chains are found in our empirical tracing procedure because a certain proportion of those who receive the document do not send it on. It is likely that this occurs for one of two major reasons: 1) individuals are not motivated to participate in the study; 2) they do not know to whom to send the document in order to advance it toward the target.

For purposes of gauging the significance of our numerical results, it would be useful to know whether the dropouts are random or systematic, i.e., whether or not they are related to a chain's prognosis for rapid completion. It seems possible, for example, that dropouts are precisely those people who are least likely to be able to advance the document toward the target. If so, the distribution of actual lengths of completed chains would understate the true social distance between starters and target by an unknown amount. (Even if dropouts are random, the observed distribution understates the true distribution, but by a potentially calculable amount.) We can offer some evidence, however, that this effect is not powerful.

First, it should be clear that, though people may drop out because they see little possibility that any of their acquaintances can advance the folder toward the target, their subjective estimates are irrelevant to the question just raised. Such subjective estimates may account for individual decisions not to participate; they do not tell us whether chains that die in fact would have been longer than others had they gone to completion. People have poor intuitions concerning the lengths of acquaintance chains. Moreover, people can rarely see beyond their own acquaintances; it is hard to guess the circles in which friends of friends—not to mention people even more remotely connected to oneself—may move.

More direct evidence that dropouts may be treated as "random" can be gleaned from the tracer cards. It will be recalled that each participant was asked for information not only about himself but also about the person to whom he sent the document. Thus some data were available even for dropouts, namely age, sex, the nature of their relationship to the people

STUDY OF THE SMALL WORLD PROBLEM 435

TABLE 1

Activity of Chains at Each Remove

	All Chains					Incomplete Chains Only		
Remove	Chains Reaching this Remove	Completions at this Remove	Dropouts at this Remove	Per cent Dropouts	Remove	Chains Reaching this Remove	Dropouts at this Remove	Per cent Dropouts
0	296	0	79	27	0	232	79	34
1	217	0	59	27	1	153	59	39
2	158	2	34	22	2	94	34	36
3	122	3	24	20	3	60	24	40
4	95	8	11	12	4	36	11	31
5	76	14	12	16	5	25	12	48
6	50	8	4	8	6	13	4	31
7	38	16	5	13	7	9	5	55
8	17	6	1	6	8	4	1	25
9	10	2	2	20	9	3	2	67
10	6	2	0	0	10	1	0	0
11	4	3	0	0	11	1	0	0
12	1	0	0	0	12	1	0	0
13	1	0	0	0	13	1	0	0
14	1	0	1	100	14	1	1	100

436   SOCIOMETRY

preceding them in the chain, and the reason the dropout had been selected to receive the document. These four variables were tabulated for dropouts versus non-dropouts. None of the resulting contingency tables achieved the .05 level of statistical significance by chi-square test; we are therefore led to accept the null hypothesis of no difference between the two groups, at least on this limited set of variables. Of course, a definitive answer to the question of whether dropouts are really random must wait until the determinants of chain length are understood, or until a way is found to force all chains to completion.[4]

SUBPOPULATION COMPARISONS. A possible paradigm for future research using the tracing procedure described here involves systematic variation of the relationship between the starting and target populations. One such study, using Negro and White starting and target groups, has already been completed by Korte and Milgram (in press). In the present study, which involved only a single target person, three starting populations were used (Nebraska random, Nebraska stockholders, and Boston random.) The relevant experimental questions were whether the proportion of completed chains or mean chain lengths would vary as a function of starting population.

Chain Length. Letters from the Nebraska subpopulations had to cover a geographic distance of about 1300 miles in order to reach the target, whereas letters originating in the Boston group almost all started within 25 miles of his home and/or place of work. Since social proximity depends in part on geographic proximity, one might readily predict that complete chains originating in the Boston area would be shorter than those originating in Nebraska. This presumption was confirmed by the data. As Table 2 shows, chains originating with the Boston random group showed a mean length of 4.4 intermediaries between starters and target, as opposed to a mean length of 5.7 intermediaries for the Nebraska random group. ($p \leqslant .001$ by

---

[4] Professor Harrison White of Harvard University has developed a technique for adjusting raw chain length data to take account of the dropout problem. His method assumes that dropouts are "random," in the following sense. An intermediary who knows the target sends him the folder, completing the chain, with probability 1. Otherwise, an intermediary throws away the folder with fixed probability 1-a, or sends it on with probability a. If sent on, there is a probability Q_1 (which depends on number of removes from the origin) that the next intermediary knows the target. The data is consistent with a value for a of approximately 0.75, independent of remove from the origin, and hence with a "random" dropout rate of 25 per cent. The limited data further suggest that Q_1 grows in a "staircase" pattern from zero (at zero removes from the starting population) to approximately one-third at six removes, remaining constant thereafter. Based on these values, the hypothetical curve of completions with no dropouts resembles the observed curve shifted upward; the median length of completed chains rises from 5 to 7, but no substantial alteration is required in conclusions drawn from the raw data.

STUDY OF THE SMALL WORLD PROBLEM 437

TABLE 2

Lengths of Completed Chains

Population	Frequency Distribution — Number of Intermediaries													Means	
	0	1	2	3	4	5	6	7	8	9	10	11	Total	Starting Population	Mean Chain Length
Nebraska Random	0	0	0	1	4	3	6	2	0	1	1	0	18	Nebraska Random	5.7
Nebraska Stock	0	0	0	3	6	4	6	2	1	1	1	0	24	Nebraska Stockholders	5.4
Boston Random	0	2	3	4	4	1	4	2	1	0	1	0	22	All Nebraska	5.5
All	0	2	3	8	14	8	16	6	2	2	3	0	64	Boston Random	4.4
														All	5.2

438   SOCIOMETRY

a one-tailed Mann-Whitney U test.) Chain length thus proved sensitive to one demographic variable—place of residence of starters and target.

The Nebraska stockholder group was presumed to have easy access to contacts in the brokerage business. Because the target person was a stock-broker, chains originating in this group were expected to reach the target more efficiently than chains from the Nebraska random group. The chain-length means for the two groups, 5.7 intermediaries for the random sample and 5.4 for the stockholders, differed in the expected direction, but the difference was not statistically significant by the Mann-Whitney test. The stockholders used the brokerage business as a communication channel more often than did the random group; 60.7 per cent of all the participants in chains originating with the stockholder group reported occupations connected with finance, while 31.8 per cent of participants in chains originating in the Nebraska random group were so classified.

Proportion of Completions. As indicated in Table 3, the proportions of chains completed for the Nebraska random, Nebraska stockholder, and Boston subpopulations were 24 per cent, 31 per cent and 35 per cent, respectively. Although the differences are not statistically significant, there is a weak tendency for higher completion rates to occur in groups where mean length of completed chains is shorter. This result deserves brief discussion.

Let us assume that the dropout rate is constant at each remove from the start. If, for example, the dropout rate were 25 per cent then any chain would have a 75 per cent probability of reaching one link, $(.75)^2$ of reaching two links, etc. Thus, the longer a chain needed to be in order to reach completion, the less likely that the chain would survive long enough to run its full course. In this case, however, chain-length differences among the three groups were not sufficiently large to produce significant differences in completion rate. Moreover, if the dropout rate declines as chains grow long, such a decrease would off-set the effect just discussed and weaken the observed inverse relation between chain length and proportion of completions.

TABLE 3

Proportion of Completions for Three Starting Populations

	Starting Population							
	Nebraska Random		Nebraska Stock.		Boston		Total	
Complete	18	(24%)	24	(31%)	22	(35%)	64	(29%)
Incomplete	58	(76%)	54	(69%)	41	(65%)	153	(71%)
	76	(100%)	78	(100%)	63	(100%)	217	(100%)

$\chi^2 = 2.17$, df. $= 2$, $p > .3$, N.S.

STUDY OF THE SMALL WORLD PROBLEM 439

COMMON CHANNELS. As chains converge on the target, common channels appear—that is, some intermediaries appear in more than one chain. Figure 3 shows the pattern of convergence. The 64 letters which reached the target were sent by a total of 26 people. Sixteen, fully 25 per cent, reached the target through a single neighbor. Another 10 made contact through a single business associate, and 5 through a second business associate. These three "penultimate links" together accounted for 48 per cent of the total completions. Among the three, an interesting division of labor appears. Mr. G,

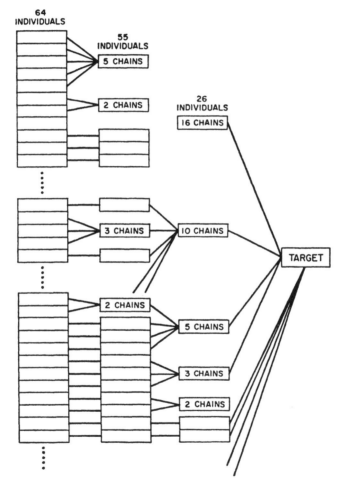

FIGURE 3

Common Paths Appear as Chains Converge on the Target

who accounted for 16 completions, is a clothing merchant in the target's hometown of Sharon; Mr. G funnelled toward the target those chains which were advancing on the basis of the target's place of residence. Twenty-four chains reached the target from his hometown; Mr. G accounted for ⅔ of those completions. All the letters which reached Mr. G came from residents of Sharon. By contrast, Mr. D and Mr. P, who accounted for 10 and 5 completions, respectively, were contacted by people scattered around the Boston area, and in several cases, by people living in other cities entirely. On the other hand, whereas Mr. G received the folder from Sharon residents in a wide variety of occupations, D and P received it almost always from stockbrokers. A scattering of names appear two or three times on the list of penultimate links; seventeen names appear once each.

Convergence appeared even before the penultimate link. Going one step further back, to people two removes from the target, we find that the 64 chains passed through 55 individuals. One man, Mr. B, appeared 5 times, and on all occasions sent the document to Mr. G. Other individuals appeared two or three times each.

ADDITIONAL CHARACTERISTICS OF CHAINS. Eighty-six per cent of the participants sent the folder to persons they described as friends and acquaintances; 14 per cent sent it to relatives. The same percentages had been observed in an earlier pilot study.

Data on patterns of age, sex and occupation support the plausible hypothesis that participants select recipients from a pool of individuals similar to themselves. The data on age support the hypothesis unequivocally; the data on sex and occupation are complicated by the characteristics of the target and the special requirement of establishing contact with him.

Age was bracketed into ten-year categories and the ages of those who sent the document tabled against the ages of those to whom they sent it. On inspection the table showed a strong tendency to cluster around the diagonal, and a chi-square test showed the association to be significant at better than the .001 level.

Similarly, the sex of each sender was tabled against the sex of the corresponding recipient. Men were ten times more likely to send the document to other men than to women, while women were equally likely to send the folder to males as to females ($p < .001$). These results were affected by the fact that the target was male. In an earlier pilot study using a female target, both men and women were three times as likely to send the document to members of the same sex as to members of the opposite sex. Thus there appear to be three tendencies governing the sex of the recipient: (1) there is a tendency to send the document to someone of one's own sex, but (2) women are more likely to cross sex lines than men, and (3) there is a tendency to send the document to someone of the same sex as the target person.

The occupations reported by participants were rated on two components—one of social status and one of "industry" affiliation, that is, the subsector of the economy with which the individual would be likely to deal. The coding system was *ad hoc,* designed to fit the occupational titles supplied by participants. Tabling the status and "industry" ratings for all senders of the document against those of respective recipients, we observed a strong tendency for people to select recipients similar to themselves on both measures ($p < .001$ for both tables). However, the strength of the relationship for industry seemed to be largely due to a tendency for the folder to stay within the finance field once it arrived there, obviously because the target was affiliated with that field. Moreover, the participants in the study were a heavily middle-class sample, and the target was himself a member of that class. Thus there was no need for the document to leave middle-class circles in progressing from starters to target.

When separate contingency tables were constructed for complete and incomplete chains, the above results were obtained for both tables. Similarly, when separate tables were constructed for chains originating in the 3 starting populations, the findings held up in all 3 tables. Thus, controlling for completion of chains or for starting population did not affect the finding of demographic homogeneity within chains.

CONCLUSIONS

The contribution of the study lies in the use of acquaintance chains to extend an individual's contacts to a geographically and socially remote target, and in the sheer size of the population from which members of the chains were drawn. The study demonstrated the feasibility of the "small world" technique, and took a step toward demonstrating, defining and measuring inter-connectedness in a large society.

The theoretical machinery needed to deal with social networks is still in its infancy. The empirical technique of this research has two major contributions to make to the development of that theory. First, it sets an upper bound on the minimum number of intermediaries required to link widely separated Americans. Since subjects cannot always foresee the most efficient path to a target, our trace procedure must inevitably produce chains longer than those generated by an accurate theoretical model which takes full account of all paths emanating from an individual. The mean number of intermediaries observed in this study was somewhat greater than five;

442   SOCIOMETRY

additional research (by Korte and Milgram) indicates that this value is quite stable, even when racial crossover is introduced. Both the magnitude and stability of the parameter need to be accounted for. Second, the study has uncovered several phenomena which future models should explain. In particular, the convergence of communication chains through common individuals is an important feature of small world nets, and it should be accounted for theoretically.

There are many additional lines of empirical research that may be examined with the small world method. As suggested earlier, one general paradigm for research is to vary the characteristics of the starting person and the target. Further, one might systematically vary the information provided about the target in order to determine, on the psychological side, what strategies people employ in reaching a distant target, and on the sociological side, what specific variables are critical for establishing contact between people of given characteristics.

REFERENCES

Abelson, R. P.
    1967   "Mathematical models in social psychology." Pp. 1–54 in L. Berkowitz (ed.) Advances in Experimental Social Psychology, Vol. III. New York: Academic Press.
Bailey, N. T. J.
    1957   The Mathematical Theory of Epidemics. New York: Hafner.
Coleman, J. S., E. Katz and H. Menzel
    1966   Medical Innovation: A Diffusion Study. Indianapolis: Bobbs-Merrill.
Fararo, T. J. and M. H. Sunshine
    1964   A Study of a Biased Friendship Net. Syracuse: Youth Development Center, Syracuse University.
Foster, C. C., A. Rapoport and C. J. Orwant
    1963   "A study of a large sociogram II. Elimination of free parameters." Behavioral Science 8(January):56–65.
Gurevitch, M.
    1961   The Social Structure of Acquaintanceship Networks. Unpublished doctoral dissertation, Cambridge: M.I.T.
Korte, C. and S. Milgram
        Acquaintance Links Between White and Negro Populations: Application of the Small World Method. Journal of Personality and Social Psychology (in press).
Milgram, S.
    1967   "The small world problem." Psychology Today 1(May):61–67.
    1969   "Interdisciplinary thinking and the small world problem." Pp. 103–120 in Muzafer Sherif and Carolyn W. Sherif (eds.) Interdisciplinary Relationships in the Social Sciences. Chicago: Aldine Publishing Company.

STUDY OF THE SMALL WORLD PROBLEM 443

Pool, I. and M. Kochen
>   A Non-Mathematical Introduction to a Mathematical Model. Undated mimeo. Cambridge: M.I.T.

Rapoport, A.
>   1953 "Spread of information through a population with socio-structural bias." Bulletin of Mathematical Biophysics 15(December):523–543.
>
>   1963 "Mathematical models of social interaction." Pp. 493–579 in R. D. Luce, R. R. Bush and E. Galanter (eds.) Handbook of Mathematical Psychology, Vol. II. New York: John Wiley and Sons.

Rapoport, A. and W. J. Horvath
>   1961 "A study of a large sociogram." Behavioral Science 6(October):279–291.

[17]

The Strength of Weak Ties[1]

Mark S. Granovetter
Johns Hopkins University

Analysis of social networks is suggested as a tool for linking micro and macro levels of sociological theory. The procedure is illustrated by elaboration of the macro implications of one aspect of small-scale interaction: the strength of dyadic ties. It is argued that the degree of overlap of two individuals' friendship networks varies directly with the strength of their tie to one another. The impact of this principle on diffusion of influence and information, mobility opportunity, and community organization is explored. Stress is laid on the cohesive power of weak ties. Most network models deal, implicitly, with strong ties, thus confining their applicability to small, well-defined groups. Emphasis on weak ties lends itself to discussion of relations *between* groups and to analysis of segments of social structure not easily defined in terms of primary groups.

A fundamental weakness of current sociological theory is that it does not relate micro-level interactions to macro-level patterns in any convincing way. Large-scale statistical, as well as qualitative, studies offer a good deal of insight into such macro phenomena as social mobility, community organization, and political structure. At the micro level, a large and increasing body of data and theory offers useful and illuminating ideas about what transpires within the confines of the small group. But how interaction in small groups aggregates to form large-scale patterns eludes us in most cases.

I will argue, in this paper, that the analysis of processes in interpersonal networks provides the most fruitful micro-macro bridge. In one way or another, it is through these networks that small-scale interaction becomes translated into large-scale patterns, and that these, in turn, feed back into small groups.

Sociometry, the precursor of network analysis, has always been curiously peripheral—invisible, really—in sociological theory. This is partly because it has usually been studied and applied only as a branch of social psychology; it is also because of the inherent complexities of precise network analysis. We have had neither the theory nor the measurement and sampling techniques to move sociometry from the usual small-group level to that of larger structures. While a number of stimulating and suggestive

[1] This paper originated in discussions with Harrison White, to whom I am indebted for many suggestions and ideas. Earlier drafts were read by Ivan Chase, James Davis, William Michelson, Nancy Lee, Peter Rossi, Charles Tilly, and an anonymous referee; their criticisms resulted in significant improvements.

The Strength of Weak Ties

studies have recently moved in this direction (Bott 1957; Mayer 1961; Milgram 1967; Boissevain 1968; Mitchell 1969), they do not treat structural issues in much theoretical detail. Studies which do so usually involve a level of technical complexity appropriate to such forbidding sources as the *Bulletin of Mathematical Biophysics,* where the original motivation for the study of networks was that of developing a theory of neural, rather than social, interaction (see the useful review of this literature by Coleman [1960]; also Rapoport [1963]).

The strategy of the present paper is to choose a rather limited aspect of small-scale interaction—the strength of interpersonal ties—and to show, in some detail, how the use of network analysis can relate this aspect to such varied macro phenomena as diffusion, social mobility, political organization, and social cohesion in general. While the analysis is essentially qualitative, a mathematically inclined reader will recognize the potential for models; mathematical arguments, leads, and references are suggested mostly in footnotes.

THE STRENGTH OF TIES

Most intuitive notions of the "strength" of an interpersonal tie should be satisfied by the following definition: the strength of a tie is a (probably linear) combination of the amount of time, the emotional intensity, the intimacy (mutual confiding), and the reciprocal services which characterize the tie.[2] Each of these is somewhat independent of the other, though the set is obviously highly intracorrelated. Discussion of operational measures of and weights attaching to each of the four elements is postponed to future empirical studies.[3] It is sufficient for the present purpose if most of us can agree, on a rough intuitive basis, whether a given tie is strong, weak, or absent.[4]

---

[2] Ties discussed in this paper are assumed to be positive and symmetric; a comprehensive theory might require discussion of negative and/or asymmetric ties, but this would add unnecessary complexity to the present, exploratory comments.

[3] Some anthropologists suggest "multiplexity," that is, multiple contents in a relationship, as indicating a strong tie (Kapferer 1969, p. 213). While this may be accurate in some circumstances, ties with only one content or with diffuse content may be strong as well (Simmel 1950, pp. 317–29). The present definition would show most multiplex ties to be strong but also allow for other possibilities.

[4] Included in "absent" are both the lack of any relationship and ties without substantial significance, such as a "nodding" relationship between people living on the same street, or the "tie" to the vendor from whom one customarily buys a morning newspaper. That two people "know" each other by name need not move their relation out of this category if their interaction is negligible. In some contexts, however (disasters, for example), such "negligible" ties might usefully be distinguished from the absence of one. This is an ambiguity caused by substitution, for convenience of exposition, of discrete values for an underlying continuous variable.

American Journal of Sociology

Consider, now, any two arbitrarily selected individuals—call them A and B—and the set, $S = C, D, E, \ldots$, of all persons with ties to either *or* both of them.[5] The hypothesis which enables us to relate dyadic ties to larger structures is: the stronger the tie between A and B, the larger the proportion of individuals in S to whom they will *both* be tied, that is, connected by a weak or strong tie. This overlap in their friendship circles is predicted to be least when their tie is absent, most when it is strong, and intermediate when it is weak.

The proposed relationship results, first, from the tendency (by definition) of stronger ties to involve larger time commitments. If A-B and A-C ties exist, then the amount of time C spends with B depends (in part) on the amount A spends with B and C, respectively. (If the events "A is with B" and "A is with C" were independent, then the event "C is with A and B" would have probability equal to the product of their probabilities. For example, if A and B are together 60% of the time, and A and C 40%, then C, A, and B would be together 24% of the time. Such independence would be less likely after than before B and C became acquainted.) If C and B have no relationship, common strong ties to A will probably bring them into interaction and generate one. Implicit here is Homans's idea that "the more frequently persons interact with one another, the stronger their sentiments of friendship for one another are apt to be" (1950, p. 133).

The hypothesis is made plausible also by empirical evidence that the stronger the tie connecting two individuals, the more similar they are, in various ways (Berscheid and Walster 1969, pp. 69–91; Bramel 1969, pp. 9–16; Brown 1965, pp. 71–90; Laumann 1968; Newcomb 1961, chap. 5; Precker 1952). Thus, if strong ties connect A to B and A to C, both C and B, being similar to A, are probably similar to one another, increasing the likelihood of a friendship once they have met. Applied in reverse, these two factors—time and similarity—indicate why weaker A-B and A-C ties make a C-B tie less likely than strong ones: C and B are less likely to interact and less likely to be compatible if they do.

The theory of cognitive balance, as formulated by Heider (1958) and especially by Newcomb (1961, pp. 4–23), also predicts this result. If strong ties A-B and A-C exist, and if B and C are aware of one another, anything short of a positive tie would introduce a "psychological strain" into the situation since C will want his own feelings to be congruent with those of his good friend, A, and similarly, for B and *his* friend, A. Where the ties are weak, however, such consistency is psychologically less crucial. (On this point see also Homans [1950, p. 255] and Davis [1963, p. 448].)

Some direct evidence for the basic hypothesis exists (Kapferer 1969, p. 229 n.; Laumann and Schuman 1967; Rapoport and Horvath 1961;

---

[5] In Barnes's terminology, the union of their respective primary stars (1969, p. 58).

The Strength of Weak Ties

Rapoport 1963).[6] This evidence is less comprehensive than one might hope. In addition, however, certain inferences from the hypothesis have received empirical support. Description of these inferences will suggest some of the substantive implications of the above argument.

WEAK TIES IN DIFFUSION PROCESSES

To derive implications for large networks of relations, it is necessary to frame the basic hypothesis more precisely. This can be done by investigating the possible triads consisting of strong, weak, or absent ties among *A*, *B*, and any arbitrarily chosen friend of either or both (i.e., some member of the set *S*, described above). A thorough mathematical model would do this in some detail, suggesting probabilities for various types. This analysis becomes rather involved, however, and it is sufficient for my purpose in this paper to say that the triad which is most *unlikely* to occur, under the hypothesis stated above, is that in which *A* and *B* are strongly linked, *A* has a strong tie to some friend *C*, but the tie between *C* and *B* is absent. This triad is shown in figure 1. To see the consequences of this assertion,

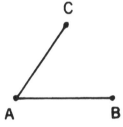

FIG. 1.—Forbidden triad

I will exaggerate it in what follows by supposing that the triad shown *never* occurs—that is, that the *B-C* tie is always present (whether weak or strong), given the other two strong ties. Whatever results are inferred from this supposition should tend to occur in the degree that the triad in question tends to be absent.

[6] The models and experiments of Rapoport and his associates have been a major stimulus to this paper. In 1954 he commented on the "well-known fact that the likely contacts of two individuals who are closely acquainted tend to be more overlapping than those of two arbitrarily selected individuals" (p. 75). His and Horvath's 1961 hypothesis is even closer to mine: "one would expect the friendship relations, and therefore the overlap bias of the acquaintance circles, to become less tight with increasing numerical rank-order" (p. 290). (I.e., best friend, second-best friend, third-best, etc.) Their development of this hypothesis, however, is quite different, substantively and mathematically, from mine (Rapoport 1953*a*, 1953*b*, 1954, 1963; Rapoport and Horvath 1961).

American Journal of Sociology

Some evidence exists for this absence. Analyzing 651 sociograms, Davis (1970, p. 845) found that in 90% of them triads consisting of two mutual choices and one nonchoice occurred less than the expected random number of times. If we assume that mutual choice indicates a strong tie, this is strong evidence in the direction of my argument.[7] Newcomb (1961, pp. 160–65) reports that in triads consisting of dyads expressing mutual "high attraction," the configuration of three strong ties became increasingly frequent as people knew one another longer and better; the frequency of the triad pictured in figure 1 is not analyzed, but it is implied that processes of cognitive balance tended to eliminate it.

The significance of this triad's absence can be shown by using the concept of a "bridge"; this is a line in a network which provides the *only* path between two points (Harary, Norman, and Cartwright 1965, p. 198). Since, in general, each person has a great many contacts, a bridge between A and B provides the only route along which information or influence can flow from any contact of A to any contact of B, and, consequently, from anyone connected *indirectly* to A to anyone connected indirectly to B. Thus, in the study of diffusion, we can expect bridges to assume an important role.

Now, if the stipulated triad is absent, it follows that, except under unlikely conditions, *no strong tie is a bridge*. Consider the strong tie A-B: if A has another strong tie to C, then forbidding the triad of figure 1 implies that a tie exists between C and B, so that the path A-C-B exists between A and B; hence, A-B is not a bridge. A strong tie can be a bridge, therefore, *only if* neither party to it has any *other* strong ties, unlikely in a social network of any size (though possible in a small group). Weak ties suffer no such restriction, though they are certainly not automatically bridges. What is important, rather, is that all bridges are weak ties.

In large networks it probably happens only rarely, in practice, that a specific tie provides the *only* path between two points. The bridging function may nevertheless be served *locally*. In figure 2*a*, for example, the tie A-B is not strictly a bridge, since one can construct the path A-E-I-B (and others). Yet, A-B *is* the shortest route to B for F, D, and C. This function is clearer in figure 2*b*. Here, A-B is, for C, D, and others, not only a local bridge to B, but, in most real instances of diffusion, a much more likely and efficient path. Harary et al. point out that "there may be a distance [length of path] beyond which it is not feasible for u to communicate with

[7] This assumption is suggested by one of Davis's models (1970, p. 846) and made explicitly by Mazur (1971). It is not obvious, however. In a free-choice sociometric test or a fixed-choice one with a large number of choices, most strong ties would probably result in mutual choice, but some weak ones might as well. With a small, fixed number of choices, most mutual choices should be strong ties, but some strong ties might show up as asymmetric. For a general discussion of the biases introduced by sociometric procedures, see Holland and Leinhardt (1971*b*).

The Strength of Weak Ties

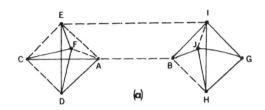

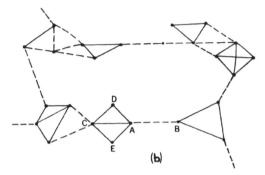

FIG. 2.—Local bridges. *a*, Degree 3; *b*, Degree 13. ——— = strong tie; — — — = weak tie.

v because of costs or distortions entailed in each act of transmission. If *v* does not lie within this critical distance, then he will not receive messages originating with *u*" (1965, p. 159). I will refer to a tie as a "local bridge of degree *n*" if *n* represents the shortest path between its two points (other than itself), and *n* > 2. In figure 2*a*, *A-B* is a local bridge of degree 3, in 2*b*, of degree 13. As with bridges in a highway system, a local bridge in a social network will be more significant as a connection between two sectors to the extent that it is the only alternative for many people—that is, as its degree increases. A bridge in the absolute sense is a local one of infinite degree. By the same logic used above, only weak ties may be local bridges.

Suppose, now, that we adopt Davis's suggestion that "in interpersonal flows of most any sort the probability that 'whatever it is' will flow from person *i* to person *j* is (*a*) directly proportional to the number of all-positive (friendship) paths connecting *i* and *j*; and (*b*) inversely proportional to the length of such paths" (1969, p. 549).[8] The significance of weak ties, then, would be that those which are local bridges create more, and shorter, paths. Any given tie may, hypothetically, be removed from a network; the number of paths broken and the changes in average path length resulting

[8] Though this assumption seems plausible, it is by no means self-evident. Surprisingly little empirical evidence exists to support or refute it.

American Journal of Sociology

between arbitrary pairs of points (with some limitation on length of path considered) can then be computed. The contention here is that removal of the average weak tie would do more "damage" to transmission probabilities than would that of the average strong one.[9]

Intuitively speaking, this means that whatever is to be diffused can reach a larger number of people, and traverse greater social distance (i.e., path length),[10] when passed through weak ties rather than strong. If one tells a rumor to all his close friends, and they do likewise, many will hear the rumor a second and third time, since those linked by strong ties tend to share friends. If the motivation to spread the rumor is dampened a bit on each wave of retelling, then the rumor moving through strong ties is much more likely to be limited to a few cliques than that going via weak ones; bridges will not be crossed.[11]

Since sociologists and anthropologists have carried out many hundreds of diffusion studies—Rogers's 1962 review dealt with 506—one might suppose that the above claims could easily be put to test. But this is not so, for several reasons. To begin with, though most diffusion studies find that personal contacts are crucial, many undertake no sociometric investigation. (Rogers [1962] discusses this point.) When sociometric techniques *are* used, they tend to discourage the naming of those weakly tied to the respondent by sharply limiting the numbers of choices allowed. Hence, the proposed importance of weak ties in diffusion is not measured. Even when more sociometric information is collected there is almost never an attempt to directly retrace the exact interpersonal paths traversed by an (idea, rumor, or) innovation. More commonly, the time when each individual adopted the innovation is recorded, as is the number of sociometric choices he received from others in the study. Those receiving many choices are characterized as "central," those with few as "marginal"; this variable is then correlated with time of adoption and inferences made about what paths were probably followed by the innovation.

[9] In a more comprehensive treatment it would be useful to consider to what extent a *set* of weak ties may be considered to have bridging functions. This generalization requires a long, complex discussion and is not attempted here (see Harary et al. 1965, pp. 211–16).

[10] We may define the "social distance" between two individuals in a network as the number of lines in the shortest path from one to another. This is the same as the definition of "distance" between points in graph theory (Harary et al. 1965, pp. 32–33, 138–41). The exact role of this quantity in diffusion and epidemic theory is discussed by Solomonoff and Rapoport (1951).

[11] If a damping effect is not specified, the whole population would hear the rumor after a sufficiently large number of retellings, since few real networks include totally self-contained cliques. The effective difference between using weak and strong ties, then, is one of people reached per unit of (ordinal) time. This could be called "velocity" of transmission. I am indebted to Scott Feld for this point.

The Strength of Weak Ties

One point of controversy in diffusion studies can be related to my argument. Some have indicated that early innovators are marginal, that they "underconform to norms to such a degree that they are perceived as highly deviant" (Rogers 1962, p. 197). Others (e.g., Coleman, Katz, and Menzel [1966] on the adoption of a new drug by doctors) find that those named more frequently adopt an innovation substantially earlier. Becker (1970) tries to resolve the question of whether early innovators are "central" or "marginal" by referring to the "perceived risks of adoption of a given innovation." His study of public health innovations shows that when a new program is thought relatively safe and uncontroversial (as with the drug of Coleman et al.), central figures lead in its adoption; otherwise, marginal ones do (p. 273). He explains the difference in terms of a greater desire of "central" figures to protect their professional reputation.

Kerckhoff, Back, and Miller (1965) reach a similar conclusion in a different type of study. A Southern textile plant had been swept by "hysterical contagion": a few, then more and more workers, claiming bites from a mysterious "insect," became nauseous, numb, and weak, leading to a plant shutdown. When the affected workers were asked to name their three best friends, many named one another, but the very *earliest* to be stricken were social isolates, receiving almost no choices. An explanation, compatible with Becker's, is offered: since the symptoms might be thought odd, early "adopters" were likely to be found among the marginal, those less subject to social pressures. Later, "it is increasingly likely that some persons who are socially integrated will be affected. . . . The contagion enters social networks and is disseminated with increasing rapidity" (p. 13). This is consistent with Rogers's comment that while the *first* adopters of innovations are marginal, the next group, "early adopters," "are a more integrated part of the local social system than the innovators" (1962, p. 183).

"Central" and "marginal" individuals may well be motivated as claimed; but if the marginal are genuinely so, it is difficult to see how they can ever spread innovations successfully. We may surmise that since the resistance to a risky or deviant activity is greater than to a safe or normal one, a larger number of people will have to be exposed to it and adopt it, in the early stages, before it will spread in a chain reaction. Individuals with many weak ties are, by my arguments, best placed to diffuse such a difficult innovation, since some of those ties will be local bridges.[12] An initially un-

---

[12] These individuals are what is often called, in organizational analysis, "liaison persons," though their role here is different from the one usually discussed. (Cf. the concept in graph theory of a "cut point"—one which, if removed from a graph, disconnects one part from another [Harary 1965].) In general, a bridge has one liaison person on each side, but the existence of a liaison person does not imply that of a bridge. For local

American Journal of Sociology

popular innovation spread by those with *few* weak ties is more likely to be confined to a few cliques, thus being stillborn and never finding its way into a diffusion study.

That the "marginal" innovators of diffusion studies might actually be rich in *weak* ties is possible, given the usual sociometric technique, but in most cases this is purely speculative. Kerckhoff and Back, however, in a later more detailed analysis of the hysteria incident, indicate that besides asking about one's "three best friends," they also asked with whom workers ate, worked, shared car pools, etc. They report that five of the six workers earliest affected "are social isolates when friendship choices are used as the basis of analysis. Only 1 of the 6 is mentioned as a friend by *anyone* in our sample. This is made even more striking when we note that these 6 women are mentioned with considerable frequency when other bases for choice are used. In fact, they are chosen more frequently on a 'non-friendship' basis than are the women in any of the other categories" (1968, p. 112).

This finding lends credence to the weak-tie argument, but is inconclusive. A somewhat different kind of diffusion study offers more direct support: the "small-world" investigations of Milgram and his associates. The name of these studies stems from the typical comment of newly introduced individuals who discover some common acquaintance; this situation is generalized in an attempt to measure, for arbitrarily chosen pairs of individuals in the United States, how long a path of personal contacts would be needed to connect them. A booklet is given to randomly designated senders who are asked to forward it toward some named target person, via someone the sender knows personally who would be more likely than himself to know the target. The new recipient then advances the booklet similarly; eventually it reaches the target or someone fails to send it on. The proportion of such chains completed has ranged from 12% to 33% in different studies, and the number of links in completed chains has ranged from two to 10, averaging between five and eight (Milgram 1967; Travers and Milgram 1969; Korte and Milgram 1970).

Each time someone forwards a booklet he also sends a postcard to the researchers, indicating, among other things, the relationship between himself and the next receiver. Two of the categories which can be chosen are "friend" and "acquaintance." I will assume that this corresponds to "strong" and "weak" ties. In one of the studies, white senders were asked to forward the booklet to a target who was Negro. In such chains, a crucial point was the *first* sending of the booklet from a white to a Negro. In 50%

bridges, the concept of local liaisons could be developed. In a more microscopically oriented discussion I would devote more time to the liaison role. For now, I only point out that, under the present assumptions, one can be a liaison between two network sectors *only* if all his ties into one or both are weak.

The Strength of Weak Ties

of the instances where the white described this Negro as an "acquaintance," the chain was ultimately completed; completion rate fell to 26%, however, when the white sent the booklet to a Negro "friend." (My computation, based on unpublished data kindly supplied by Charles Korte. See Korte [1967] and Korte and Milgram [1970].) Thus, weaker interracial ties can be seen to be more effective in bridging social distance.

Another relevant study, by Rapoport and Horvath (1961), is not exactly one of diffusion but is closely related in that it traces out paths along which diffusion *could* take place. They asked each individual in a Michigan junior high school ($N = 851$) to list his eight best friends in order of preference. Then, taking a number of random samples from the group (sample size, an arbitrary number, was nine), they traced out, for each sample, and averaged over all the samples, the total number of people reached by following along the network of first and second choices. That is, the first and second choices of each sample member were tabulated, then the first and second choices of *these* people were added in, etc., counting, at each remove, *only* names not previously chosen, and continuing until no new people were reached. The same procedure was followed using second and third choices, third and fourth, etc., up to seventh and eighth. (The theoretical connection of this tracing procedure to diffusion is discussed by Rapoport [1953a, 1953b, and especially 1954].)

The smallest total number of people were reached through the networks generated by first and second choices—presumably the strongest ties—and the largest number through seventh and eighth choices. This corresponds to my assertion that more people can be reached through weak ties. A parameter in their mathematical model of the sociogram, designed to measure, approximately, the overlap of acquaintance circles, declined monotonically with increasing rank order of friends.[18]

WEAK TIES IN EGOCENTRIC NETWORKS

In this section and the next, I want to discuss the general significance of the above findings and arguments at two levels: first that of individuals, then that of communities. These discussions make no pretense of being comprehensive; they are meant only to illustrate possible applications.

In recent years, a great deal of literature has appeared analyzing the impact on the behavior of individuals of the social networks in which they are imbedded. Some of the studies have emphasized the ways in which

---

[18] This parameter, θ, measures such overlap in the following sense: it is zero in a random net—one in which individuals choose others at random—and is one in a net made up entirely of cliques disconnected each from every other. Intermediate values of θ, however, do not have a good intuitive interpretation in terms of individuals, but only with reference to the particular mathematical model defining the parameter; thus it does not correspond precisely to my arguments about friendship overlap.

American Journal of Sociology

behavior is shaped and constrained by one's network (Bott 1957; Mayer 1961; Frankenberg 1965), others the ways in which individuals can manipulate these networks to achieve specific goals (Mayer 1966; Boissevain 1968; Kapferer 1969). Both facets are generally supposed to be affected by the structure of one's network. Bott argued that the crucial variable is that of whether one's friends tend to know one another ("close-knit" network) or not ("loose-knit" network). Barnes makes this dichotomy into a continuous variable by counting the number of ties observed in the network formed by ego and his friends and dividing it by the ratio of possible ones; this then corresponds to what is often called network "density" (Barnes 1969; Tilly 1969).[14]

Epstein (1969) points out, however, that different *parts* of ego's network may have different density. He calls those with whom one "interacts most intensely and most regularly, and who are therefore also likely to come to know one another," the "effective network"; the "remainder constitute the *extended* network" (pp. 110–11). This is close to saying, in my terms, that one's strong ties form a dense network, one's weak ties a less dense one. I would add that one's weak ties which are not local bridges might as well be counted with the strong ties, to maximize separation of the dense from the less dense network sectors.

One point on which there is no general agreement is whether ego's network should be treated as composed only of those to whom he is tied directly, or should include the contacts of his contacts, and/or others. Analyses stressing encapsulation of an individual by his network tend to take the former position, those stressing manipulation of networks, the latter, since information or favors available through direct contacts may depend on who *their* contacts are. I would argue that by dividing ego's network into that part made up of strong and nonbridging weak ties on the one hand, and that of bridging weak ties on the other, both orientations can be dealt with. Ties in the former part should tend to be to people who not only know one another, but who also have few contacts not tied to ego as well. In the "weak" sector, however, not only will ego's contacts not be tied to one another, but they *will* be tied to individuals not tied to ego. Indirect contacts are thus typically reached through ties in this sector; such ties are then of importance not only in ego's manipulation of networks, but also in that they are the channels through which ideas, influences, or

---

14 But if the crucial question is really whether ego's *friends* know each other, this measure should probably be computed after ego and his ties have been subtracted from the network; distortions caused by failure to do so will be especially great in small networks. It is important to note, also, that in *non*egocentric networks, there is no simple correspondence between density and any "average" measure of the extent to which the various egos have friends who know one another. "Density," as used here, should not be confused with the "axone density" of Rapoport's models—the number of choices issuing from each node of a network.

The Strength of Weak Ties

information socially distant from ego may reach him. The fewer indirect contacts one has the more encapsulated he will be in terms of knowledge of the world beyond his own friendship circle; thus, bridging weak ties (and the consequent indirect contacts) are important in both ways.

I will develop this point empirically by citing some results from a labor-market study I have recently completed. Labor economists have long been aware that American blue-collar workers find out about new jobs more through personal contacts than by any other method. (Many studies are reviewed by Parnes 1954, chap. 5.) Recent studies suggest that this is also true for those in professional, technical, and managerial positions (Shapero, Howell, and Tombaugh 1965; Brown 1967; Granovetter 1970). My study of this question laid special emphasis on the nature of the *tie* between the job changer and the contact person who provided the necessary information.

In a random sample of recent professional, technical, and managerial job changers living in a Boston suburb, I asked those who found a new job through contacts how often they *saw* the contact around the time that he passed on job information to them. I will use this as a measure of tie strength.[15] A natural a priori idea is that those with whom one has strong ties are more motivated to help with job information. Opposed to this greater motivation are the structural arguments I have been making: those to whom we are weakly tied are more likely to move in circles different from our own and will thus have access to information different from that which we receive.

I have used the following categories for frequency of contact: often = at least twice a week; occasionally = more than once a year but less than twice a week; rarely = once a year or less. Of those finding a job through contacts, 16.7% reported that they saw their contact often at the time, 55.6% said occasionally, and 27.8% rarely ($N = 54$).[16] The skew is clearly to the weak end of the continuum, suggesting the primacy of structure over motivation.

In many cases, the contact was someone only marginally included in the current network of contacts, such as an old college friend or a former work-mate or employer, with whom sporadic contact had been maintained

[15] Although this corresponds only to the first of the four dimensions in my definition, supplementary anecdotal evidence from interviews makes it likely that, in this case, the entire definition is satisfied by this measure. At the time of research, it had not occurred to me that tie strength would be a useful variable.

[16] The numbers reported are small because they represent a random subsample of 100, who were interviewed personally, of the total sample of 282. The personal interview allowed more detailed questioning. Comparisons between the mail sample and the interview sample on the large number of items which were put to both show almost no significant differences; this suggests that results observed in the smaller sample on those items put to it alone would not be much different in the mail sample.

American Journal of Sociology

(Granovetter 1970, pp. 76–80). Usually such ties had not even been very strong when first forged. For work-related ties, respondents almost invariably said that they never saw the person in a nonwork context.[17] Chance meetings or mutual friends operated to reactivate such ties. It is remarkable that people receive crucial information from individuals whose very existence they have forgotten.[18]

I also asked respondents where their contacts *got* the information they transmitted. In most cases, I traced the information to its initial source. I had expected that, as in the diffusion of rumors or diseases, long paths would be involved. But in 39.1% of the cases information came directly from the prospective employer, whom the respondent already knew; 45.3% said that there was one intermediary between himself and the employer; 12.5% reported two; and 3.1% more than two ($N = 64$). This suggests that for some important purposes it may be sufficient to discuss, as I have, the egocentric network made up of ego, his contacts, and *their* contacts. Had long information paths been involved, large numbers might have found out about any given job, and no particular tie would have been crucial. Such a model of job-information flow actually does correspond to the economists' model of a "perfect" labor market. But those few who did acquire information through paths with more than one intermediary tended to be young and under the threat of unemployment; influence was much less likely to have been exerted by their contact on their behalf. These respondents were, in fact, more similar to those using *formal* intermediaries (agencies, advertisements) than to those hearing through short paths: both of the former are badly placed and dissatisfied in the labor market, and both receive information without influence. Just as reading about a job in the newspaper affords one no recommendation in applying for it, neither does it to have heard about it fifth hand.

The usual dichotomy between "formal" or mass procedures and diffusion through personal contacts may thus be invalid in some cases where, instead, the former may be seen as a limiting case of long diffusion chains. This is

---

[17] Often when I asked respondents whether a friend had told them about their current job, they said, "Not a friend, an acquaintance." It was the frequency of this comment which suggested this section of the paper to me.

[18] Donald Light has suggested to me an alternative reason to expect predominance of weak ties in transfer of job information. He reasons that most of any given person's ties are weak, so that we should expect, on a "random" model, that most ties through which job information flows should be weak. Since baseline data on acquaintance networks are lacking, this objection remains inconclusive. Even if the premise were correct, however, one might still expect that greater motivation of close friends would overcome their being outnumbered. Different assumptions yield different "random" models; it is not clear which one should be accepted as a starting point. One plausible such model would expect information to flow through ties in proportion to the time expended in interaction; this model would predict much more information via strong ties than one which merely counted all ties equally.

The Strength of Weak Ties

especially likely where information of instrumental significance is involved. Such information is most valuable when earmarked for one person.

From the individual's point of view, then, weak ties are an important resource in making possible mobility opportunity. Seen from a more macroscopic vantage, weak ties play a role in effecting social cohesion. When a man changes jobs, he is not only moving from one network of ties to another, but also establishing a link between these. Such a link is often of the same kind which facilitated his own movement. Especially within professional and technical specialties which are well defined and limited in size, this mobility sets up elaborate structures of bridging weak ties between the more coherent clusters that constitute operative networks in particular locations. Information and ideas thus flow more easily through the specialty, giving it some "sense of community," activated at meetings and conventions. Maintenance of weak ties may well be the most important consequence of such meetings.

WEAK TIES AND COMMUNITY ORGANIZATION

These comments about sense of community may remind us that in many cases it is desirable to deal with a unit of analysis larger than a single individual. I would like to develop my argument further by analyzing, in this section, why some communities organize for common goals easily and effectively whereas others seem unable to mobilize resources, even against dire threats. The Italian community of Boston's West End, for example, was unable to even *form* an organization to fight against the "urban renewal" which ultimately destroyed it. This seems especially anomalous in view of Gans's description of West End social structure as cohesive (1962).

Variations in culture and personality are often cited to explain such anomalies. Gans contrasts "lower"-, "working"-, and "middle"-class subcultures, concluding that only the last provides sufficient trust in leaders and practice in working toward common goals to enable formation of an effective organization. Thus, the working-class West End could not resist urban renewal (pp. 229–304). Yet, numerous well-documented cases show that *some* working-class communities have mobilized quite successfully against comparable or lesser threats (Dahl 1961, pp. 192–99; Keyes 1969; Davies 1966, chap. 4).[19] I would suggest, as a sharper analytical tool, examination of the network of ties comprising a community to see whether aspects of its structure might facilitate or block organization.

Imagine, to begin with, a community completely partitioned into cliques, such that each person is tied to every other in his clique and to none outside. Community organization would be severely inhibited. Leafletting, radio announcements, or other methods could insure that everyone was *aware* of

[19] This point was brought to my attention by Richard Wolfe.

American Journal of Sociology

some nascent organization; but studies of diffusion and mass communication have shown that people rarely *act* on mass-media information unless it is also transmitted through personal ties (Katz and Lazarsfeld 1955; Rogers 1962); otherwise one has no particular reason to think that an advertised product or an organization should be taken seriously. Enthusiasm for an organization in one clique, then, would not spread to others but would have to develop independently in *each one* to insure success.

The problem of trust is closely related. I would propose that whether a person trusts a given leader depends heavily on whether there exist intermediary personal contacts who can, from their own knowledge, assure him that the leader is trustworthy, and who can, if necessary, intercede with the leader or his lieutenants on his behalf. Trust in leaders is integrally related to the *capacity to predict and affect their behavior*. Leaders, for their part, have little motivation to be responsive or even trustworthy toward those to whom they have no direct or indirect connection. Thus, network fragmentation, by reducing drastically the number of paths from any leader to his potential followers, would inhibit trust in such leaders. This inhibition, furthermore, would not be entirely irrational.

Could the West End's social structure really have been of this kind? Note first that while the structure hypothesized is, by definition, extremely fragmented, this is evident only at a macroscopic level—from an "aerial view" of the network. The local phenomenon is cohesion. (Davis [1967] also noted this paradox, in a related context.) An analyst studying such a group by participant observation might never see the extent of fragmentation, especially if the cliques were not earmarked by ethnic, cultural, or other visible differences. In the nature of participant observation, one is likely to get caught up in a fairly restricted circle; a few useful contacts are acquired and relied on for introduction to others. The "problem of entry into West End society was particularly vexing," Gans writes. But eventually, he and his wife "were welcomed by one of our neighbors and became friends with them. As a result they invited us to many of their evening gatherings and introduced us to other neighbors, relatives and friends. . . . As time went on . . . other West Enders . . . introduced me to relatives and friends, although *most* of the social gatherings at which I participated were those of our *first* contact and their circle" (1962, pp. 340–41; emphasis supplied). Thus, his account of cohesive groups is not *inconsistent* with overall fragmentation.

Now, suppose that all ties in the West End were either strong or absent, and that the triad of figure 1 did not occur. Then, for any ego, all his friends were friends of one another, and all their friends were ego's friends as well. Unless each person was strongly tied to *all* others in the community, network structure did indeed break down into the isolated cliques posited above. (In terms of Davis's mathematical treatment, the overall network

The Strength of Weak Ties

was "clusterable," with unique clusters [1967, p. 186].) Since it is unlikely that anyone could sustain more than a few dozen strong ties, this would, in fact, have been the result.

Did strong ties take up enough of the West Enders' social time to make this analysis even approximately applicable? Gans reported that "sociability is a routinized gathering of a relatively unchanging peer group of family members and friends that takes place several times a week." Some "participate in informal cliques and in clubs made up of unrelated people. . . . In number, and in the amount of time devoted to them, however, these groups are much less important than the family circle" (1962, pp. 74, 80). Moreover, two common sources of weak ties, formal organizations and work settings, did not provide them for the West End; organization membership was almost nil (pp. 104–7) and few worked within the area itself, so that ties formed at work were not relevant to the community (p. 122).

Nevertheless, in a community marked by geographic immobility and lifelong friendships (p. 19) it strains credulity to suppose that each person would not have known a great many others, so that there would have been *some* weak ties. The question is whether such ties were bridges.[20] If *none* were, then the community would be fragmented in exactly the same way as described above, except that the cliques would then contain weak as well as strong ties. (This follows, again, from Davis's analysis of "clusterability," with strong and weak ties called "positive" and absent ones "negative" [1967].) Such a pattern is made plausible by the lack of ways in the West End to *develop* weak ties other than by meeting friends of friends (where "friend" includes relatives)—in which case the new tie is automatically not a bridge. It is suggested, then, that for a community to have many weak ties which bridge, there must be several distinct ways or contexts in which people may form them. The case of Charlestown, a working-class community which successfully organized against the urban renewal plan of the same city (Boston) against which the West End was powerless, is instructive in this respect: unlike the West End, it had a rich organizational life, and most male residents worked within the area (Keyes 1969, chap. 4).

In the absence of actual network data, all this is speculation. The hard information needed to show either that the West End was fragmented or that communities which organized successfully were not, and that both patterns were due to the strategic role of weak ties, is not at hand and would not have been simple to collect. Nor has comparable information been collected in *any* context. But a theoretical framework has, at least, been suggested, with which one could not only carry out analyses post hoc, but also *predict* differential capacity of communities to act toward common

[20] See Jane Jacobs's excellent, intuitive, discussion of bridging ties ("hop-skip links") in community organization (1961, chap. 6.)

American Journal of Sociology

goals. A rough principle with which to begin such an investigation might be: the more local bridges (per person?) in a community and the greater their degree, the more cohesive the community and the more capable of acting in concert. Study of the origins and nature (strength and content, for example) of such bridging ties would then offer unusual insight into the social dynamics of the community.

MICRO AND MACRO NETWORK MODELS

Unlike most models of interpersonal networks, the one presented here is not meant primarily for application to small, face-to-face groups or to groups in confined institutional or organizational settings. Rather, it is meant for linkage of such small-scale levels with one another and with larger, more amorphous ones. This is why emphasis here has been placed more on weak ties than on strong. Weak ties are more likely to link members of *different* small groups than are strong ones, which tend to be concentrated within particular groups.

For this reason, my discussion does not lend itself to elucidation of the internal structure of small groups. This point can be made more clearly by contrasting the model of this paper to one with which it shares many similarities, that of James Davis, Paul Holland, and Samuel Leinhardt (hereafter, the DHL model) (Davis 1970; Davis and Leinhardt 1971; Holland and Leinhardt 1970, 1971a, 1971b; Davis, Holland, and Leinhardt 1971; Leinhardt 1972). The authors, inspired by certain propositions in George Homans's *The Human Group* (1950), argue that "the central proposition in structural sociometry is this: *Interpersonal choices tend to be transitive—if P chooses O and O chooses X, then P is likely to choose X*" (Davis et al. 1971, p. 309). When this is true without exception, a sociogram can be divided into cliques in which every individual chooses every other; any asymmetric choices or nonchoices are *between* such cliques, and asymmetry, if present, runs only in one direction. A partial ordering of cliques may thus be inferred. If mutual choice implies equal, and asymmetric choice unequal, status, then this ordering reflects the stratification structure of the group (Holland and Leinhardt 1971a, pp. 107–14).

One immediate difference between this model and mine is that it is cast in terms of "choices" rather than ties. Most sociometric tests ask people whom they *like* best or would *prefer* to do something with, rather than with whom they actually spend time. If transitivity is built more into our cognitive than our social structure, this method might overstate its prevalence. But since the DHL model could recast in terms of ties, this is not a conclusive difference.

More significant is the difference in the application of my argument to transitivity. Let P choose O and O choose X (or equivalently, let X choose

The Strength of Weak Ties

O and *O* choose *P*): then I assert that transitivity—*P* choosing *X* (or *X*, *P*)—is most likely when both ties—*P-O* and *O-X*—are strong, least likely when both are weak, and of intermediate probability if one is strong and one weak. Transitivity, then, is claimed to be a function of the strength of ties, rather than a general feature of social structure.

The justification of this assertion is, in part, identical with that offered earlier for the triad designated *A-B-C*. In addition, it is important to point out here that the DHL model was designed for small groups, and with increasing size of the group considered the rationale for transitivity weakens. If *P* chooses *O* and *O* chooses *X*, *P* should choose *X* out of consistency; but if *P* does not *know* or barely knows *X*, nonchoice implies no inconsistency. For the logic of transitivity to apply, a group must be small enough so that any person knows enough about every other person to be able to decide whether to "choose" him, and encounters him often enough that he feels the need for such a decision. Including weak ties in my model, then, lessens the expectation of transitivity and permits analysis of intergroup relationships and also of amorphous chunks of social structure which an analyst may ferret out as being of interest, but which are not easily defined in terms of face-to-face groups. Anthropologists have recently referred to such chunks as "quasi-groups" (Mayer 1966; Boissevain 1968).

Since, as I have argued above, weak ties are poorly represented in sociograms, there is little in the DHL empirical studies—which apply statistical tests to sociometric data—to confirm or disconfirm my argument on transitivity. One finding does lend itself to speculation, however. Leinhardt (1972) shows that the sociograms of schoolchildren conform more and more closely to the transitive model as they become older, sixth graders being the oldest tested. He interprets this as reflecting cognitive development—increasing capacity to make use of transitive logic. If my assertion is correct, an alternative possibility would be that children develop stronger ties with increasing age. This is consistent with some theories of child development (see especially Sullivan 1953, chap. 16) and would imply, on my argument, greater transitivity of structure. Some support for this explanation comes from Leinhardt's finding that proportion of choices which were mutual was positively correlated with both grade level and degree of transitivity. In these sociograms, with an average of only about four choices per child, it seems likely that most mutual choices reflected strong ties (see n. 7, above).

CONCLUSION

The major implication intended by this paper is that the personal experience of individuals is closely bound up with larger-scale aspects of social structure, well beyond the purview or control of particular individuals.

American Journal of Sociology

Linkage of micro and macro levels is thus no luxury but of central importance to the development of sociological theory. Such linkage generates
paradoxes: weak ties, often denounced as generative of alienation (Wirth
1938) are here seen as indispensable to individuals' opportunities and to
their integration into communities; strong ties, breeding local cohesion,
lead to overall fragmentation. Paradoxes are a welcome antidote to theories
which explain everything all too neatly.

The model offered here is a very limited step in the linking of levels; it
is a fragment of a theory. Treating only the *strength* of ties ignores, for
instance, all the important issues involving their content. What is the relation between strength and degree of specialization of ties, or between
strength and hierarchical structure? How can "negative" ties be handled?
Should tie strength be developed as a continuous variable? What is the
developmental sequence of network structure over time?

As such questions are resolved, others will arise. Demography, coalition
structure, and mobility are just a few of the variables which would be of
special importance in developing micro-macro linkage with the help of
network analysis; how these are related to the present discussion needs
specification. My contribution here is mainly, then, exploratory and programmatic, its primary purpose being to generate interest in the proposed
program of theory and research.

REFERENCES

Barnes, J. A. 1969. "Networks and Political Process." In *Social Networks in Urban
    Situations,* edited by J. C. Mitchell. Manchester: Manchester University Press.
Becker, Marshall. 1970. "Sociometric Location and Innovativeness." *American Socio-
    logical Review* 35 (April): 267–82.
Berscheid, E., and E. Walster. 1969. *Interpersonal Attraction.* Reading, Mass.: Addison-
    Wesley.
Boissevain, J. 1968. "The Place of Non-Groups in the Social Sciences." *Man* 3
    (December): 542–56.
Bott, Elizabeth. 1957. *Family and Social Network.* London: Tavistock.
Bramel, D. 1969. "Interpersonal Attraction, Hostility and Perception." In *Experimental
    Social Psychology,* edited by Judson Mills. New York: Macmillan.
Brown, David. 1967. *The Mobile Professors.* Washington, D.C.: American Council
    on Education.
Brown, Roger. 1965. *Social Psychology.* New York: Free Press.
Coleman, J. S. 1960. "The Mathematical Study of Small Groups." In *Mathematical
    Thinking in the Measurement of Behavior,* edited by H. Solomon. Glencoe: Free
    Press.
Coleman, J. S., E. Katz, and H. Menzel. 1966. *Medical Innovation: A Diffusion Study.*
    Indianapolis: Bobbs-Merrill.
Dahl, Robert. 1961. *Who Governs?* New Haven, Conn.: Yale University Press.
Davies, J. C. 1966. *Neighborhood Groups and Urban Renewal.* New York: Columbia
    University Press.
Davis, James A. 1963. "Structural Balance, Mechanical Solidarity and Interpersonal
    Relations." *American Journal of Sociology* 68 (January): 444–62.
———. 1967. "Clustering and Structural Balance in Graphs." *Human Relations* 20
    (May): 181–87.

The Strength of Weak Ties

——. 1969. "Social Structures and Cognitive Structures." In R. P. Abelson et al., *Theories of Cognitive Consistency*. Chicago: Rand McNally.

——. 1970. "Clustering and Hierarchy in Interpersonal Relations." *American Sociological Review* 35 (October): 843–52.

Davis, James A., P. Holland, and S. Leinhardt. 1971. "Comment." *American Sociological Review* 36 (April): 309–11.

Davis, James A., and S. Leinhardt. 1971. "The Structure of Positive Interpersonal Relations in Small Groups." In *Sociological Theories in Progress*. Vol. 2, edited by J. Berger, M. Zelditch, and B. Anderson. Boston: Houghton-Mifflin.

Epstein, A. 1969. "The Network and Urban Social Organization." In *Social Networks in Urban Situations*, edited by J. C. Mitchell. Manchester: Manchester University Press.

Frankenberg, R. 1965. *Communities in Britain*. Baltimore: Penguin.

Gans, Herbert. 1962. *The Urban Villagers*. New York: Free Press.

Granovetter, M. S. 1970. "Changing Jobs: Channels of Mobility Information in a Suburban Community." Doctoral dissertation, Harvard University.

Harary, F. 1965. "Graph Theory and Group Structure." In *Readings in Mathematical Psychology*. Vol. 2, edited by R. Luce, R. Bush, and E. Galanter. New York: Wiley.

Harary, F., R. Norman, and D. Cartwright. 1965. *Structural Models*. New York: Wiley.

Heider, F. 1958. *The Psychology of Interpersonal Relations*. New York: Wiley.

Holland, Paul, and S. Leinhardt. 1970. "Detecting Structure in Sociometric Data." *American Journal of Sociology* 76 (November): 492–513.

——. 1971a. "Transitivity in Structural Models of Small Groups." *Comparative Group Studies* 2:107–24.

——. 1971b. "Masking: The Structural Implications of Measurement Error in Sociometry." Mimeographed. Pittsburgh: Carnegie-Mellon University.

Homans, George. 1950. *The Human Group*. New York: Harcourt, Brace & World.

Jacobs, Jane. 1961. *The Death and Life of Great American Cities*. New York: Random House.

Kapferer, B. 1969. "Norms and the Manipulation of Relationships in a Work Context." In *Social Networks in Urban Situations*, edited by J. C. Mitchell. Manchester: Manchester University Press.

Katz, E., and P. Lazarsfeld. 1955. *Personal Influence*. New York: Free Press.

Kerckhoff, A., and K. Back. 1968. *The June Bug: A Study of Hysterical Contagion*. New York: Appleton-Century-Crofts.

Kerckhoff, A., K. Back, and N. Miller. 1965. "Sociometric Patterns in Hysterical Contagion." *Sociometry* 28 (March): 2–15.

Keyes, L. C. 1969. *The Rehabilitation Planning Game*. Cambridge, Mass.: M.I.T. Press.

Korte, Charles. 1967. "Small-World Study (Los Angeles): Data Analysis." Mimeographed. Poughkeepsie, N.Y.: Vassar College.

Korte, Charles, and Stanley Milgram. 1970. "Acquaintance Networks between Racial Groups." *Journal of Personality and Social Psychology* 15 (June): 101–8.

Laumann, Edward. 1968. "Interlocking and Radial Friendship Networks: A Cross-sectional Analysis." Mimeographed. Ann Arbor: University of Michigan.

Laumann, Edward, and H. Schuman. 1967. "Open and Closed Structures." Paper prepared for the 1967 ASA meeting. Mimeographed.

Leinhardt, Samuel. 1972. "Developmental Change in the Sentiment Structure of Childrens' Groups." *American Sociological Review* 37 (April): 202–12.

Mayer, Adrian. 1966. "The Significance of Quasi-Groups in the Study of Complex Societies." In *The Social Anthropology of Complex Societies*, edited by M. Banton. New York: Praeger.

Mayer, Phillip. 1961. *Townsmen or Tribesmen?* Capetown: Oxford.

Mazur, B. 1971. "Comment." *American Sociological Review* 36 (April): 308–9.

Milgram, Stanley. 1967. "The Small-World Problem." *Psychology Today* 1 (May): 62–67.

Mitchell, J. Clyde. 1969. *Social Networks in Urban Situations*. Manchester: Manchester University Press.

American Journal of Sociology

Newcomb, T. M. 1961. *The Acquaintance Process.* New York: Holt, Rinehart & Winston.
Parnes, Herbert. 1954. *Research on Labor Mobility.* New York: Social Science Research Council.
Precker, Joseph. 1952. "Similarity of Valuings as a Factor in Selection of Peers and Near-Authority Figures." *Journal of Abnormal and Social Psychology* 47, suppl. (April): 406–14.
Rapoport, Anatol. 1953a. "Spread of Information through a Population with Socio-Structural Bias. I. Assumption of Transitivity." *Bulletin of Mathematical Biophysics* 15 (December): 523–33.
———. 1953b. "Spread of Information through a Population with Socio-Structural Bias. II. Various Models with Partial Transitivity." *Bulletin of Mathematical Biophysics* 15 (December): 535–46.
———. 1954. "Spread of Information through a Population with Socio-Structural Bias. III. Suggested Experimental Procedures." *Bulletin of Mathematical Biophysics* 16 (March): 75–81.
———. 1963. "Mathematical Models of Social Interaction." In *Handbook of Mathematical Psychology.* Vol. 2, edited by R. Luce, R. Bush, and E. Galanter. New York: Wiley.
Rapoport, A., and W. Horvath. 1961. "A Study of a Large Sociogram." *Behavioral Science* 6:279–91.
Rogers, Everett. 1962. *Diffusion of Innovations.* New York: Free Press.
Shapero, Albert, Richard Howell, and James Tombaugh. 1965. *The Structure and Dynamics of the Defense R & D Industry.* Menlo Park, Calif.: Stanford Research Institute.
Simmel, Georg. 1950. *The Sociology of Georg Simmel.* New York: Free Press.
Solomonoff, Ray, and A. Rapoport. 1951. "Connectivity of Random Nets." *Bulletin of Mathematical Biophysics* 13 (June): 107–17.
Sullivan, Harry Stack. 1953. *The Interpersonal Theory of Psychiatry.* New York: Norton.
Tilly, Charles. 1969. "Community:City:Urbanization." Mimeographed. Ann Arbor: University of Michigan.
Travers, Jeffrey, and S. Milgram. 1969. "An Experimental Study of the 'Small-World' Problem." *Sociometry* 32 (December): 425–43.
Wirth, Louis. 1938. "Urbanism as a Way of Life." *American Journal of Sociology* 44 (July): 1–24.

[18]

Networks, Dynamics, and the Small-World Phenomenon[1]

Duncan J. Watts
Santa Fe Institute

The small-world phenomenon formalized in this article as the coincidence of high local clustering and short global separation, is shown to be a general feature of sparse, decentralized networks that are neither completely ordered nor completely random. Networks of this kind have received little attention, yet they appear to be widespread in the social and natural sciences, as is indicated here by three distinct examples. Furthermore, small admixtures of randomness to an otherwise ordered network can have a dramatic impact on its dynamical, as well as structural, properties—a feature illustrated by a simple model of disease transmission.

INTRODUCTION

The small-world phenomenon (Milgram 1967; Pool and Kochen 1978) has long been an object of popular fascination and anecdotal report. The experience of meeting a complete stranger with whom we have apparently little in common and finding unexpectedly that we share a mutual acquaintance is one with which most of us are familiar—"It's a small world!" we say. More generally, most people have at least heard of the idea that any two individuals, selected randomly from almost anywhere on the planet, are "connected" via a chain of no more than six intermediate acquaintances, a notion made popular by the Broadway play (and later movie) *Six Degrees of Separation* (Guare 1990).

But is this phenomenon merely the confluence of unlikely coincidence and curious anecdote, or is it actually indicative of the underlying structure of modern social networks and, hence, not unlikely at all? Furthermore, if the small-world phenomenon does turn out to be a deep feature

[1] The author gratefully acknowledges the guidance of Steven Strogatz during the period in which this research was conducted and the extensive comments of Harrison White on an earlier draft of this article. Research was supported in part by the National Science Foundation through a grant to Steven Strogatz. Direct correspondence to Duncan Watts, Santa Fe Institute, 1399 Hyde Park Road, Santa Fe, New Mexico 87501. E-mail: duncan@santafe.edu

American Journal of Sociology

of the social world, in what other contexts can it arise (such as telecommunications and neural networks), and what mechanism drives it? Finally, does its presence in the real world have any implications for the dynamical properties of the networks in which it occurs?

An explanation of the phenomenon, and more generally, a framework for examining the properties of networks consisting of very many components, is of general sociological interest: Many social metrics, such as status (Harary 1959; Burt 1982) and power (Coleman 1973), and social processes, such as the diffusion of innovations (Rogers 1995) and transmission of influence (Friedkin 1990), are usefully represented in terms of networks of relationships between social actors, be they individuals, organizations, or nations. Indeed, the theory of social networks is one that has seen extensive development over the past three decades, yielding multiple measures both of individual significance, such as centrality (Freeman 1979, 1982; Friedkin 1991), and of network efficiency (Yamaguchi 1994*a*), which may elucidate nonobvious phenomena such as "key players" in an organization or its optimal structure for, say, information diffusion. Frequently, however, this research assumes linear models of social processes,[2] such as Markov models of diffusion, and is generally applied to networks that consist of a relatively small number of components.[3] While many of the measures defined in the literature can in principle be applied to networks of arbitrary size and structure, the computational costs of doing so may be prohibitive (such as for Freeman's [1979] betweenness centrality), and the benefits are at any rate unclear if the process of interest is inherently *nonlinear*, as is the case for information (or disease) contagion models involving threshold (Granovetter 1978; Arthur and Lane 1993) or refractory (Murray 1993, chap. 19) effects. Hence, the problem of analyzing efficiently the structure of extremely large networks (in which components may easily number in the hundreds of thousands, or more), and modeling the effects of structure on nonlinear dynamical processes, remains relatively unexplored. This article presents one possible approach to these very general problems by postulating a model of network formation that is sufficiently flexible to account for a wide variety of interesting cases (although not all cases, by any means, as will be pointed out) and that,

---

[2] "Social process" here refers to the person-to-person dynamics occurring on the network. Such *local* dynamical models are thus distinct from *global* models, such as classical homogeneous mixing models of diffusion, which are generally nonlinear (see e.g., Yamaguchi 1994*b*), but which do not model the underlying network explicitly.

[3] Test cases appearing in the literature typically use small numbers for ease of computation (e.g., Friedkin [1991] and Yamaguchi [1994*a*, 1994*b*] consider networks of five and seven elements respectively) and documented empirical examples rarely exceed $O(100)$ nodes.

Small-World Phenomenon

in turn, suggests which structural parameters are the appropriate ones to study.

The problem of relating network structure to dynamics is then illustrated with a very simple model of disease spreading, which implies that the specified structural parameters are significant in determining the dynamics (usually in a highly nonlinear fashion), although probably insufficient to describe it completely. It should be pointed out that networks can affect a system's dynamical behavior in what might be termed an active and a passive sense; and that it is the passive sense that is investigated here. Active implies that the network is a device to be manipulated consciously for an actor's own ends; passive implies that the network connections themselves, in concert with blind dynamical rules, determine the global behavior of the system. The active sense has been investigated, for example, by Granovetter (1973, 1974) in the context of finding a job and Burt (1992) for maximizing social capital. The passive sense—with which this article is concerned—has been explored in systems as varied as biological oscillators (Strogatz and Stewart 1993), neural networks (Crick and Koch 1998), genetic-control networks (Kauffman 1969), epidemiology (Hess 1996*a*, 1996*b*; Longini 1988; Kretzschmar and Morris 1996), and game theory (Nowak and May 1993; Herz 1994; Cohen, Riolo, and Axelrod 1999). Before addressing any of these questions, however, it is necessary to agree on precisely what is meant by the small-world phenomenon, what is already known about it, and why such a thing should be surprising in the first place.

PROPERTIES OF RANDOM-CLUSTERED NETWORKS

What Is the Small-World Phenomenon?

What do we mean when we say the world is "small"? In general, there is no precise answer, but in this article, "small" means that almost every element of the network is somehow "close" to almost every other element, even those that are perceived as likely to be far away.[4] This disjuncture between reality and perception is what makes the small-world phenomenon surprising to us. But why should we perceive the world to be anything other than small in the first place? The answer to this is fourfold:

1. The network is numerically large in the sense that the world contains $n \gg 1$ people. In the real world, n is on the order of billions.
2. The network is sparse in the sense that each person is connected to an average of only k other people, which is, at most, on the order of thou-

---

[4] Precise definitions of "small" and "far away" require some additional terminology that is developed below.

American Journal of Sociology

sands (Kochen 1989)—hundreds of thousands of times smaller than the population of the planet.

3. The network is decentralized in that there is no dominant central vertex to which most other vertices are directly connected. This implies a stronger condition than sparseness: not only must the average degree k be much less than n, but the *maximal* degree k_{max} over all vertices must also be much less than n.

4. The network is highly clustered, in that most friendship circles are strongly overlapping. That is, we expect that many of our friends are friends also of each other.

All four criteria are necessary for the small-world phenomenon to be remarkable. If the world did not contain many people, then it would not be surprising if they were all closely associated (as in a small town). If most people knew most other people then, once again, it would not be surprising to find that two strangers had an acquaintance in common. If the network were highly centralized—say a star—then an obvious short path would exist through the center of the star between all pairs of vertices. Finally, if the network were not clustered—that is, if each person chose their friends independently of any of their friends' choices—then it follows from random-graph theory (Bollobás 1985) that most people would be only a few degrees of separation apart even for very large n.[5]

But are these criteria satisfied by the real world? Given that the population of the planet is several billion and that even the most generous estimates of how many acquaintances an average person can have (Kochen 1989) is only a few thousand, then the first two criteria are likely to be satisfied. The last two conditions are harder to be sure of and certainly harder to measure, but they also seem quite reasonable in the light of everyday experience. Some people are clearly more significant players than others, but even the most gregarious individuals are constrained by time and energy to know only a tiny fraction of the entire population. What significance these individuals have must be due to other more subtle and interesting reasons. Finally, while it might be difficult to determine in practice how many of a given person's friends are also friends with each other, and even more difficult to measure this for a large population, common sense tells us that whatever this fraction is, it is much larger than that which we would expect for a randomly connected network.[6]

The first evidence that the world might indeed be small was presented over 30 years ago by the psychologist Stanley Milgram (1967). Milgram

---

[5] In fact, a random graph is a close approximation to the *smallest possible* graph for any given n and k (where $k_{max} \ll n$ and the variance in k is not too large).

[6] To be more explicit, if the world *were* randomly connected, then one's acquaintances would be just as likely to come from a different country, occupation, and socioeconomic class as one's own. Clearly this is not the case in real life.

Small-World Phenomenon

initiated a number of chain letters with sources in Kansas and Nebraska, to be sent to one of two targets in Boston. Each source was given the name of the target and some demographic information about them but was instructed that they could only send the letter to someone they knew by first name. If they did not know the target directly (a remote possibility), the idea was to send it to whichever of their friends they considered was most likely to. This procedure was then to be repeated, generating a chain of recipients that either reached the target or else petered out due to apathy. Of the chains that did complete, Milgram found that the median number of links in the chain was about six, thus giving rise to the famous phrase, "six degrees of separation." A later work of Milgram's (Korte and Milgram 1970) found similar results for senders and recipients in different racial subgroups, thus bolstering the claim that the world was not just small within particular socioeconomic categories but was, perhaps, small universally.

Although the first theoretical examination of the small-world phenomenon, by Pool and Kochen (1978), did not appear in published form until well after Milgram's experiment, the ideas had been in circulation for some 10 years beforehand. Pool and Kochen posed the problem in terms of the probability (p_i) that two randomly selected elements of a network would be connected via a shortest path consisting of i intermediaries. They calculated expected values of p_i under a variety of assumptions about local network structure and stratification. They concluded, as had Milgram, that the world was probably a small one, in the sense that randomly selected pairs could generally be connected by chains of only a few intermediaries. However, their assumptions concerning network structure and the independence of connections were so restrictive that they declined to place much weight on their hypothesis. Little progress has been made on this work since, and Pool and Kochen's conclusions remain essentially unchanged (Kochen 1989).

Another starting point for theoretical investigation of the small-world phenomenon was the study of random-biased nets, developed in the 1950s and 1960s by Anotol Rapoport and his colleagues at the University of Chicago. Motivated by the desire to understand the spread of infectious diseases, Solomonoff and Rapoport (1951) calculated the expected fraction of a randomly mixed population to be infected by a small initially infected seed. Rapoport then determined the corresponding fractions to be infected in populations where network connections exhibited increasing levels of local redundancy due to effects such as homophily, symmetry of edges, and triad-closure bias (Rapoport 1953*a*, 1953*b*, 1957, 1963; Foster, Rapoport, and Orwant 1963). More sophisticated approximations were developed subsequently by Fararo and Sunshine (1964) and, later, Skvoretz (1985) to account for differentiation of ties as well as vertices. However,

American Journal of Sociology

as was the case with Pool and Kochen, all these approximations focused on altering the *local structure* of the network and so showed only that significant changes in global structure will result from correspondingly significant changes in local structure. This statement is not contradicted here. Rather, what is new is that equally significant changes in global structure can result from changes in local structure that are so minute as to be effectively undetectable at the local level. This is an important distinction, as it is at the local level—and only at the local level—that individuals in a network make measurements.

Formalization of the Small-World Phenomenon

In order to make the requisite notions precise, some definitions are borrowed from graph theory. For simplicity, the networks considered here will be represented as connected graphs, consisting solely of undifferentiated vertices and unweighted, undirected edges.[7] All graphs must also satisfy the sparseness conditions specified above.

The first statistic of interest, for a given graph, is the *characteristic path length* (L), defined here as the average number of edges that must be traversed in the shortest path between any two pairs of vertices in the graph.[8] In terms of Milgram's experiment, L would be the chain length averaged over all possible sources in the network *and* all possible targets. L then is a measure of the global structure of the graph (because, in general, determining the shortest path length between any two vertices requires information about the entire graph). By contrast, the *clustering coefficient* (C) is a measure of the local graph structure. Specifically, if a vertex v has k_v immediate neighbors, then this neighborhood defines a subgraph in which at most $k_v(k_v - 1)/2$ edges can exist (if the neighborhood is fully connected). C_v is then the fraction of this maximum that is realized in v's actual neighborhood, and C is this fraction averaged over all vertices in the graph.[9] Equivalently, C can be regarded as the probabil-

---

[7] These assumptions are unrealistic in general, as many networks of interest in both the social and natural sciences are composed of weighted and directed relationships. However, generalizations of the resulting graph statistics to account for these added complexities—although straightforward in principle—may depend on the particular application at hand. Therefore, for the purpose of constructing a broadly relevant framework, undirected, unweighted graphs are the natural starting point.

[8] Variants of L have appeared in other contexts as diverse as the status of individuals in an organization (Harary 1959), the floor plans of buildings (March and Steadman 1971), the efficiency of communications networks (Chung 1986), and even the properties of chemical compounds (Wiener 1947; Rouvray 1986).

[9] Local clustering, or variants thereof, has also appeared in the literature as a measure of network structure, originally in Davis (1967).

Small-World Phenomenon

ity that two vertices (u, v) will be connected, given that each is also connected to a "mutual friend" (w).

All the graphs considered in this article will be characterized in terms of these two statistics. But in order to contextualize the results—to decide, in effect, what is "small" and what is "large," what counts as "clustered" and what does not—it is necessary to determine the *ranges* over which L and C can vary. Three constraints are imposed upon this exercise:

1. The population size (n) is fixed.
2. The average degree k of the vertices is also fixed such that the graph is sparse $(k \ll n)$ but sufficiently dense to have a wide range of possible structures $(k \gg 1)$.[10]
3. The graph must be *connected* in the sense that any vertex can be reached from any other vertex by traversing a finite number of edges.

Fixing n and k enables valid comparisons to be made between many different graph structures. Clearly, the largest value that C can attain for *any* connected graph is $C = 1$, for a *complete graph* $(k = n - 1)$. Conversely, the minimum conceivable value of C is $C = 0$ for an *empty graph* $(k = 0)$. These two graphs also have extremal length properties. This, however, is not a very instructive comparison, as it is obvious that clustering and length will change as more and more edges are added to any graph. A more interesting question is how these statistics can change simply by rearranging a fixed number of edges among a fixed number of vertices. The sparseness conditions focus our attention on the most interesting terrain from the perspective of a wide range of applications in both the social and natural sciences. That is, the network is sufficiently well connected to admit rich structure, yet each element is confined to operate within a local environment that encompasses only a tiny fraction of the entire system. Finally, by insisting that all graphs be connected, L is guaranteed to be a truly global statistic. Hence, comparisons of characteristic path length are valid comparisons of global structure. Bearing in mind these conditions, the following questions present themselves:

1. What is the most clustered graph possible, and what is its characteristic path length?

---

[10] Because, in the models considered here, fluctuations in vertex degree (k_v) are roughly normally distributed around k, this condition becomes in practice the more strict condition mentioned earlier: $(k_{max} \ll n)$. This is a qualitatively stronger constraint than $k \ll n$ because it precludes not only densely connected graphs, but also star-like graphs, which have $L \approx 2$, regardless of n, by virtue of one (or a few) highly centralized vertices. That star graphs are ignored in this analysis is not to imply that they are uninteresting, simply that our concern here is with *decentralized* graphs—a reasonable restriction if one considers large enough n (where no one member could possibly know all others).

American Journal of Sociology

2. What graph has the lowest possible characteristic path length, and what
   is its clustering coefficient?
3. What do these results imply about the relationship between the clustering
   coefficient and characteristic path length of a sparse graph?

Turning first to clustering, a significant insight is that, although a connected graph can only attain the maximal value of $C = 1$ when $k = (n -
1)$, even a very sparse graph may have a clustering coefficient that is, in
practice, indistinguishable from the complete case. The most clustered,
sparse graph possible is what might be termed the *caveman graph*, which
consists of $n/(k + 1)$ isolated cliques or "caves": that is, clusters of $(k +
1)$ vertices within which all vertices are connected to all others but be-
tween which no edges exist at all. It is easy to see that this graph has $C
= 1$, on a par with a complete graph. However, it fails another required
condition—that all graphs must be *connected*. Fortunately, global connectivity is an easy property to achieve in this case, simply by extracting one
edge from each clique and using it to connect to a neighboring clique such
that all cliques eventually form a single, unbroken loop. This *connected
caveman graph* (fig. 1) can be shown to have a clustering coefficient of

$$C_{caveman} \approx 1 - \frac{6}{(k^2 - 1)}, \tag{1}$$

which approaches 1 as k becomes sufficiently large (without violating $k \ll
n$; a detailed derivation of equation 1 is given in Watts [1999, chap. 4]).[11]
    One can also calculate the corresponding characteristic path length for
large n and k (see Watts 1999, chap. 4):

$$L_{caveman} \approx \frac{n}{2(k + 1)}. \tag{2}$$

Note that, for $n \gg k$, L must necessarily be large and also increases linearly with increasing n. Hence, the connected caveman graph can be used
as a benchmark for a "large, highly clustered graph."[12]

---

[11] The connected caveman graph does not, in fact, have the highest possible clustering
coefficient for fixed n and k. For instance, the last edge required to complete the ring in
figure 1 is not required for connectivity and so can remain in its clique, thus marginally
increasing C. Other even more clustered constructions may also be possible. Nevertheless, no graph can be constructed whose clustering exceeds that of the connected caveman graph by more than $O(1/k^2)$, which becomes vanishingly small as k increases.
[12] Of course, sparse, connected networks with larger L can be constructed (trivially,
by severing one of the between-cluster edges to form a line of clusters instead of a
ring). Such changes, however, do not affect the essential structural properties of the
network—that is, its linear scaling properties—and so are not of concern here. Other,
more elaborate constructions (such as a large, dense cluster trailed by a long line of
vertices) are ruled out by the same regularity requirement that excluded star-like
graphs from consideration. Hence, within the bounds of the model, the connected
caveman graph is a plausible (albeit approximate) upper limit for L.

Small-World Phenomenon

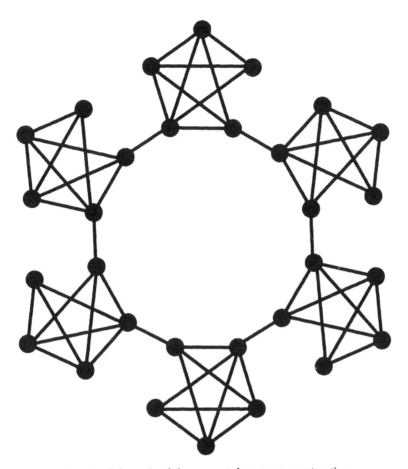

FIG. 1.—Schematic of the connected caveman construction

At the other extreme, no general, realizable structure can be shown to exhibit minimal characteristic path length for arbitrary n and k (Cerf et al. 1974; Bollobás 1985), but a good approximation to the theoretical lower bound is realized by a random graph (Bollobás 1985), where $kn/2$ out of all possible $n(n-1)/2$, edges are chosen at random and with equal probability. Precise formulas do not exist for L and C of a random graph, but in the limits of large n and k, the corresponding asymptotic approximations are[13]

[13] For an argument justifying the approximation for L, see Bollobás (1985) and Bollobás and Chung (1988). The asymptotic expression for C_{random} can easily be derived by

American Journal of Sociology

$$L_{random} \sim \frac{\ln(n)}{\ln(k)}, \tag{3}$$

and

$$C_{random} \sim \frac{k}{n}. \tag{4}$$

Note that not only is $L_{random} \ll L_{caveman}$ for any $n \gg 1$, but that the scaling of L_{random} is logarithmic with respect to n instead of linear. Hence, as n becomes larger, the discrepancy between the two extremes in length becomes increasingly pronounced (linearly in n). Note also that the sparse-graph condition ($k \ll n$) implies that C_{random} is very small. Hence (recalling the probabilistic interpretation of the clustering coefficient), C can be thought of as a simple measure of *order* in a graph—graphs with $C \gg k/n$ (like the connected caveman graph) are considered *locally ordered* (in the sense that vertices with at least one mutually adjacent vertex are likely to be themselves adjacent), and random graphs are, naturally, disordered.

The intuition that one might draw from these results is that highly clustered or locally ordered graphs necessarily have long characteristic path lengths, and conversely, graphs with short characteristic path lengths have clustering that is vanishingly small in the limit of large n. This is a reasonable intuition but is at odds with the (so far anecdotal) claim that the world can be small and still be highly clustered. In the absence of definitive data for the whole world, an alternative test of the small-world problem is to determine the minimum conditions that are both necessary and sufficient for the world to be small. The approach adopted here is to introduce a family of graphs that interpolates approximately between the two extremes discussed above and then to examine the intermediate region for evidence of small-world effects.

A Theory of Length Contraction in Sparse Networks

For this purpose, it is natural to consider a model that captures, in some abstract sense, the formation of social connections. A number of social network theorists have utilized the concept of a "social space" in which people exist as points separated by distances that can be measured according to some appropriately defined metric (see, e.g., Davidson 1983). Unfortunately, this approach often runs into treacherous waters due to

---

considering that a neighbor of any given vertex (v) has an expected probability ($k_v -$ 1)/n of being adjacent to another vertex (u) in v's neighborhood.

Small-World Phenomenon

the inherent difficulty both of characterizing the space (which is all but unknown) and defining the metric (equally so). The following three assumptions avoid these difficulties:

1. All networks can be represented solely in terms of the connections between their elements, assuming that whatever combination of factors makes people more or less likely to associate with each other is accounted for by the distribution of those associations that actually form.
2. All connections are symmetric and of equal significance. That is, a definition of what is required in order to "know" someone is defined such that either two people know each other or they do not.[14]
3. The likelihood of a new connection being created is determined, to some variable extent, by the already existing pattern of connections.

Exactly how existing connections determine new ones is a big part of the mystery. One might imagine a world in which people only become acquainted through introduction by one or more mutual friends. It is easy to see that a mechanism such as this leads inevitably to a locally ordered world (in the sense of $C \gg k/n$), the extreme case being the caveman world. At the other extreme, one might also imagine a world in which new friendships are made autonomously and at random, without regard for current friendships.[15] The end product of this tie formation process is naturally a random graph. Of course, the real world lies somewhere between these two extremes but precisely where is anybody's guess. Hence, rather than assuming some specific functional relationship between current and future friendships, let us examine a whole universe of possible "worlds" that lie between the ordered and random extremes. One way to do this in a precise and explicit fashion is through a graph construction algorithm that embodies the following features (also shown graphically in fig. 2):

1. At the ordered extreme, the propensity of two unrelated people (meaning they share no mutual friends) to be connected is very small. Once they have just one friend in common, however, their propensity to be acquainted immediately becomes very high and stays that way regardless of how many additional mutual friends they may have. In worlds like this one, it is almost a certainty that the only people anyone will ever connect to are those with whom they share at least one mutual friend. So, plotting "propensity to become friends" against "fraction of current mutual friends," the propensity starts near zero, rises very rapidly to some relatively large number (which can be normalized to one), and then plateaus.

[14] Unlike the one-way connection that often exists between, e.g., a professor and a student, or a celebrity and a fan.

[15] We may be seeing the beginnings of such a world already in the proliferation of Internet "chat lines," where complete strangers can meet, interact, and sometimes even end up marrying.

American Journal of Sociology

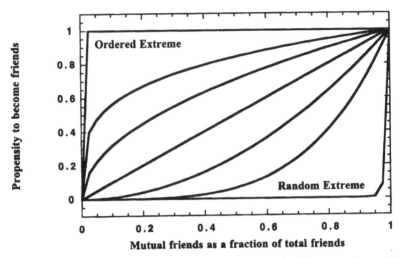

FIG. 2.—Family of functions representing the propensity of strangers to meet, given the fraction of the friends that they currently share.

2. At the random extreme, no one has much propensity to connect to anyone in particular. In this sort of world, the "propensity versus mutual friends" curve remains near zero up until the point where all friends are mutual friends.[16]
3. In between these two extremes, the propensity curve can take any one of an infinite number of intermediate forms, specified by a single, tunable parameter, where it is important only that the dependency be smooth and monotonically increasing with respect to increasing mutual friends. These conditions are satisfied by the following construction:

$$R_{i,j} = \begin{cases} 1 & m_{i,j} \geq k \\ \left[\dfrac{m_{i,j}}{k}\right]^{\alpha}(1-p)+p & k > m_{i,j} > 0, \\ p & m_{i,j} = 0 \end{cases} \quad (5)$$

where $R_{i,j}$ is a measure of vertex i's propensity to connect to vertex j (zero if they are already connected), $m_{i,j}$ is the number of vertices that are adjacent both to i and j, k is the average degree of the graph, p is a baseline

---

[16] The rapid jump from near zero to near one in fig. 2 is necessitated by continuity conditions but can be rationalized in modeling terms by considering that in such a situation the two parties must have *all* their friends in common, in which case it is reasonable to assume that they cannot avoid meeting.

504

Small-World Phenomenon

propensity for an edge (i, j) to exist (set at $p = 10^{-10}$),[17] and α is a tunable parameter, $0 \leq \alpha \leq \infty$.[18]

Numerical simulation.—Equation (5) is, in principle, an abstract representation of a graph or rather, for each value of α, an enormous (but finite) number of *potential* graphs that share certain statistical characteristics. However, it seems unlikely that the properties of these graphs, and how those properties vary with α, can be derived in any precise analytical sense. This is an important point, because a great deal of work in graph theory is analytical. However, analytical approaches are generally confined to cases where either n is small and the rules for constructing the graph are strictly deterministic or n is so large that it can be treated as infinite and the rules are strictly random. Both of these extremes exhibit certain properties that simplify the situation, thus enabling analytical descriptions. The case presented by equation (5), however, falls squarely into the messy no-man's-land between these two extremes: n is large but not infinite, and the rule for constructing edges is partly deterministic and partly random, where even the balance between determinism and randomness varies as α changes. The only manner in which such a model can be analyzed is through a rigorous process of computer-based, numerical simulation.[19] Adopting this approach, equation (5) now forms the basis for a construction algorithm,[20] which builds a graph of specified n, k, and α.[21]

A problem that immediately rises with this "α-model" is that, for small α, the resulting graphs tend overwhelmingly to consist of small, isolated, and densely internally connected components. This results from a *start-up problem*—initially no edges exist in the graph, so p dominates $R_{i,j}$ in equation (5), and edges form randomly until, by chance, two edges share a vertex in common. At this point, because α is small, the two vertices that share a mutual "friend" will almost certainly become connected at the expense of expanding their friendship networks into new territory. The fraction of pairs of vertices that are members of the same connected component grows only linearly with k, so connected graphs cannot be

---

[17] The actual value of p is not important so long as it is small enough that no random edges can be expected for $\alpha = 0$ (i.e., $p \ll 2/n[n - 1]$). More specifically, the numerical results with respect to α do change as p changes, but this dependency disappears when the model is recast in terms of the model-independent parameter ϕ, introduced below. That is, $\phi(\alpha)$ varies with p, but $L(\phi)$ and $C(\phi)$ do not.

[18] Note that α has no physical or social significance—it is simply a parameter that enables the model to generate graphs ranging from highly ordered to highly random.

[19] All work described was conducted on either a SUN\ Sparc 20 or a DEC\ alpha 500 running C under a UNIX operating system.

[20] The technical details of the algorithm are provided in the appendix.

[21] Unless otherwise stated, the parameters used to generate the results presented here are: $n = 1,000$, $k = 10$.

American Journal of Sociology

generated for small α without violating the sparse graph condition. Disconnected graphs pose a problem because they necessarily have $L = \infty$, and this makes them hard to compare with connected graphs or even each other. One way to resolve this dilemma is to build in a connected substrate before commencing the algorithm, thus ensuring that all subsequently constructed graphs will be connected. A potentially serious objection to such a step is that the properties of the resulting graphs may be so dominated by the presence of the substrate that any conclusions drawn from the model will fail to be sufficiently general to be of interest. The following constraints on the choice of substrate minimize (although do not remove) this concern:

1. It must exhibit *minimal structure*, in that no vertices are to be identified as special. This eliminates structures like stars, trees, and chains, which have centers, roots, and end-points, respectively.
2. It must be *minimally connected*. That is, it must contain no more edges than necessary to connect the graph in a manner consistent with condition 1.

The only structure that satisfies both these criteria is a topological ring. One advantage of this choice of substrate is that for sufficiently small α, it results in graphs that resemble the connected caveman limit described above; that is, densely intraconnected clusters strung loosely together in a ring (with its attendant linear length-scaling properties). It is less obvious that the random limit also can be attained with this additional structure built in. Nevertheless, numerical evidence suggests that this is precisely the case. Hence, the ring substrate not only ensures connectivity, but also allows the model to interpolate between roughly the desired limits. More important, we will see that the results generated by the corresponding model exhibit sufficiently generic features in the intermediate regime that quite general conditions can be specified under which small-world networks should arise.

The clearest way to see this is to measure L and C for the α-model, for fixed n and k, over a range of $0 \leq \alpha \leq 20$. The following functional similarities between $L(\alpha)$ and $C(\alpha)$ are revealed (figs. 3 and 4):[22]

1. For large α, both statistics approach their expected random-graph values.
2. At $\alpha = 0$, both L and C are high relative to their random-graph limits and increase (as α increases) to a distinct maximum at small α.
3. Both statistics exhibit a sharp transition from their maximum values to their large-α limits.

[22] Each of the points in fig. 5 is the average value of the relevant statistic over 100 random realizations of the construction algorithm for the corresponding value of α.

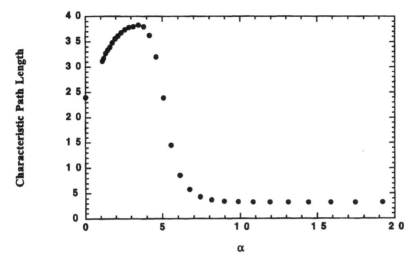

FIG. 3.—Characteristic path length (L) as a function of α for the α-model defined by equation 5 ($n = 1,000$, $k = 10$).

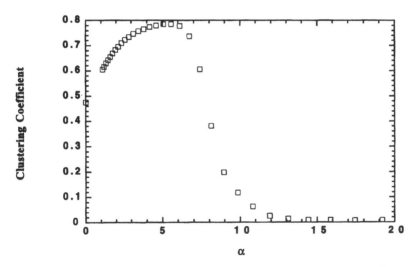

FIG. 4.—Clustering coefficient (C) as a function of α for the α-model defined by equation 5 ($n = 1,000$, $k = 10$).

American Journal of Sociology

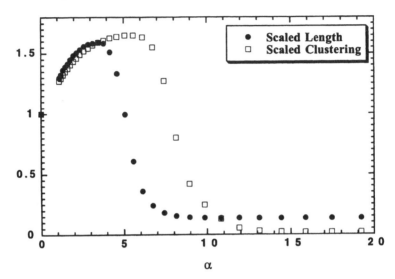

FIG. 5.—Comparison of $L(\alpha)$ and $C(\alpha)$, scaled by their corresponding values at $\alpha = 0$.

So far, the model appears to conform to the earlier statement that highly clustered graphs have large characteristic path lengths and, conversely, that graphs with short characteristic path lengths are necessarily poorly clustered.[23] However, as figure 5 indicates, $L(\alpha)$ and $C(\alpha)$ exhibit one important functional difference: the transition from large to small clustering coefficients occurs at a larger value of α than the equivalent length transition. The upshot of this disparity is that there exists a class of graphs in this region of α for which characteristic path length is small but clustering is high.[24] Thus the small-world phenomenon can be cast in graph-theoretic terms as the *coexistence* of high clustering and small characteristic path length.

DEFINITION 1.—*A small-world graph is a large-*n, *sparsely connected, decentralized graph* (n $\gg$ k$_{max}$ $\gg$ 1) *that exhibits a characteristic path*

[23] This conclusion is bolstered by the additional observation that, in the small-α regime, L scales linearly with respect to n and logarithmically with respect to n for large α, in correspondence with eqq. (2) and (3).

[24] These results remain qualitatively the same for a wide range of n and k, strongly suggesting that they are true for *all* n and k, with the usual caveat $n \gg k \gg 1$. Of course, in practice, these inequalities are imprecise, the effective limits being: if k is too small (in this case $k \to 2$), the substrate *will* dominate the results; and if k is too large ($k \to n$), then all topologies will be equivalent.

Small-World Phenomenon

length close to that of an equivalent random graph ($L \approx L_{random}$), *yet with a clustering coefficient much greater* ($C \gg C_{random}$).

This definition does not depend on the specifics of the graph-construction algorithm—in fact, it can be applied to any graph regardless of its construction. Nevertheless, the definition is only *interesting* if the phenomenon it describes can also be shown to be independent of the specifics of the model—in particular, the substrate. The reason for this is obvious: networks in the real world are no more likely to be constructed on ring substrates than they are to be completely ordered or completely random. This potential shortfall in the theory can be addressed in two ways. First, a variety of different substrates can be tested and their results compared with those generated above. If small-world graphs are still attainable over a significant interval of α values, then there is reason to think that they constitute a robust class of graphs. Second, a theoretical understanding of length contraction in partly ordered, partly random graphs may shed some light on the existence of small-world graphs and help to specify *model-independent* conditions that, if satisfied, will yield small-world graphs.

The first approach is straightforward but tedious. The same model has been tested with a number of other substrates—a two-dimensional lattice, a Cayley tree, and a random substrate. All the substrates surveyed exhibit qualitatively different properties from those of a ring, and also each other, yet α-graphs based on all substrates invariably yield small-world graphs over an extended interval of α.[25] The second approach—a theoretical explanation of small-world graphs—is presented in the next section.

Shortcuts and contractions.—Drawing intuition from the results of the α-model, it is now possible to develop an explanation of small-world graphs in terms of a parameter that is independent of the particular model used to construct them. To motivate this approach, note that, according to equation (5) for $\alpha = 0$, newly created edges are virtually guaranteed to complete at least one triad.[26] Two vertices connected by any such edge must necessarily have been separated by a path of length two, prior to the addition of the new edge. Hence, the addition of a new edge to an α-graph at $\alpha = 0$ contributes little in the way of length contractions, as it can connect only pairs of vertices that are already "close." In random graphs, however, this condition no longer applies, and vertices that are widely separated are as likely to become connected as those that are near neighbors. These observations lead to the following definitions:

---

[25] A detailed description of these substrates and the corresponding model properties is presented in Watts (1999, chap. 3).

[26] This is aside from the negligible propensity p to make a random connection.

American Journal of Sociology

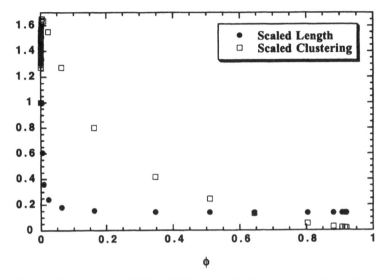

FIG. 6.—Comparison of $L(\phi)$ and $C(\phi)$, scaled by their corresponding values at $\phi_0 = \phi(\alpha = 0) = 0$.

DEFINITION 2.—*The range* r *of an edge is the distance between the two vertices that the edge in question connects when the edge itself has been deleted. Equivalently, range can be thought of as the second-shortest path length between two connected vertices (where the shortest path length is necessarily one).*

DEFINITION 3.—*A shortcut is any edge with a range* r > 2.

DEFINITION 4.—*The parameter* ϕ *is the fraction of all edges in the graph that are shortcuts.*

Figure 5 can now be replotted against ϕ instead of α. The result, in figure 6, demonstrates not only the previous result that it is possible for highly clustered graphs to have small characteristic path lengths, but also that this happens principally for small ϕ.[27]

---

[27] For very small ϕ (too small to resolve on the linear scale of fig. 6), there is an apparent increase in both L and C as ϕ increases—analogous to the humps in fig. 5. The basis of this effect is that, for small but nonzero α, an increase in α results in higher local clustering, and so previously overlapping neighborhoods can become distinct, yielding edges with $r > 2$ that do not connect previously distant parts of the graph. This is indeed a practical problem with detecting shortcuts for this particular construction algorithm, but it occurs only at very small ϕ—below the value at which the small-world phenomenon is relevant. Hence, it does not affect any of the results stated here.

510

Small-World Phenomenon

The intuitive explanation for this additional observation is that, for small ϕ, the characteristic path length of the graph is large. Hence, the introduction of a single shortcut is likely to connect vertices that were previously widely separated. This shortcut then contracts the distance not only between that pair of vertices, but also between their immediate neighborhoods, their neighborhoods' neighborhoods, and so on. Thus, one single shortcut can potentially have a highly nonlinear impact on L. By contrast, the clustering coefficient C is only reduced in a single neighborhood—as the result of one less triad being formed—and so the decrease in C can be at most linear in ϕ. This nonlinear (global) versus linear (local) impact of shortcuts enables large C to coexist with small L at small values of ϕ. But once ϕ becomes large, L has already decreased to a small value, and so subsequent shortcuts can do little to reduce it further. Thus $L(\phi)$ must approach its random graph limit asymptotically, as shown in figure 6.

The parameter ϕ turns out to have explanatory power even beyond the specific construction presented above. Other models of graphs that interpolate between ordered and random limits also exhibit length and clustering properties that can be understood in terms of shortcuts, the key requirement being that shortcuts be permitted to connect vertices that are separated by distances on the order of the size of the entire graph. Thus, it can be conjectured that any graph with the property $n \gg k_{max} \gg 1$, which exhibits (a) a clustering coefficient $C \gg k/n$ and (b) a small fraction of long-range shortcuts, will be a small-world graph.

If this conjecture is true, then small-world graphs can be realized by a great many construction algorithms, of which the α-model is but one. However, it also suggests that there are many kinds of partly ordered, partly random graphs in which the small-world phenomenon will not occur. The key criterion that the small fraction of introduced shortcuts be "long range" is really equivalent to the statement that new connections be determined without regard to any kind of *external length scale* imposed upon the graph (such as by explicitly disallowing connections to be made between vertices that are separated by greater than a certain physical distance). It is the independence of any external length scale that enables a tiny fraction of shortcuts to collapse the characteristic path length of the system to near its asymptotic, random-graph value, without significantly reducing the corresponding clustering coefficient. This constraint implies that the small-world phenomenon is unlikely to be exhibited by networks whose connectivity is determined solely by physical forces, which imply corresponding length scales.

Although the above conjecture appears to be a sufficient condition for the existence of small-world networks, it turns out that it is not necessary. In other words, it is possible to contract distances in large graphs with a

American Journal of Sociology

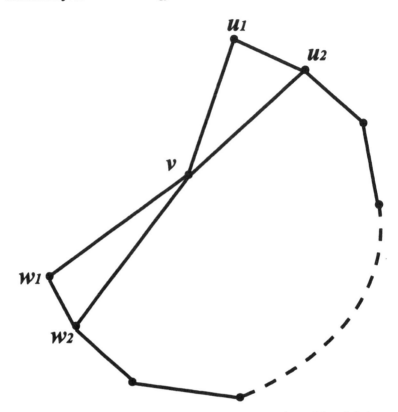

FIG. 7.—Schematic of a contraction: vertex v contracts the path length between groups u and w, but no edges are shortcuts.

negligible effect on the clustering, without using any shortcuts at all. The simplest example of such a situation is detailed in figure 7, from which it is obvious that groups of vertices are being brought closer together by virtue of a single common *member* but that none of the edges involved is a shortcut. Fortunately, a simple modification of the definition of a short-cut is adequate to capture this new scenario:

DEFINITION 5.—*A contraction occurs when the second-shortest path length between two vertices, sharing a common neighbor, is greater than two. In other words, a contraction is a pair of vertices that share one and only one common neighbor.*

DEFINITION 6.—*By extension, ψ can be defined as the fraction of pairs of vertices with common neighbors that are contractions.*

The results displayed in figure 7 can be expressed in terms of ψ (see

Small-World Phenomenon

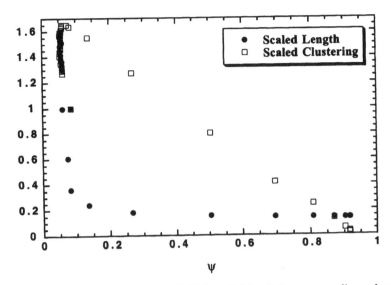

FIG. 8.—Comparison of $L(\psi)$ and $C(\psi)$, scaled by their corresponding values at $\psi_0 = \psi(\alpha = 0) \approx .08$.

fig. 8), which again shows the coexistence of small L and large C over a large range of ψ.[28] It follows from these definitions that a shortcut is simply a special case of a contraction in which one (or both) of the "groups" consists of a single vertex. Long-range contractions are thus a more general mechanism than shortcuts for generating small-world networks. In principle though, both shortcuts and contractions achieve essentially the same end—to connect what would otherwise be distant parts of a large, sparse graph with a large characteristic path length. Hence, because shortcuts are conceptually simpler and require less computational effort, all results in this article are stated in terms of ϕ, bearing in mind that they can be recast in terms of ψ if necessary.

Evidence of the Small-World Phenomenon in Real Networks

Milgram's experiment suggested that the idea of the small-world phenomenon is at least plausible for a real social network the size of the U.S. population. But the precise mapping out of social networks of this magnitude is a practical impossibility, due to the ambiguities inherent in defining

[28] Note that, unlike ϕ, ψ is never zero, even for the most clustered graphs.

American Journal of Sociology

both a member of the network and also what constitutes a friendship. Furthermore, tracing experiments like Milgram's face a number of technical obstacles, which he outlines (Milgram 1967); the main problem being that one can never be sure that the chain of intermediaries actually traced between two people is the shortest one possible.[29] We can now understand, in terms of shortcuts, at least one reason why this may be so. As noted in the previous section, small-world graphs occur for values of ϕ at which most vertices have no shortcuts at all. For example, for $n = 1,000$ and $k = 10$, $\phi = .01$ is sufficient for L to be indistinguishable from that of a random graph. If only one in a hundred edges is a shortcut, however, then (for $k = 10$) about 90% of all vertices will have no shortcuts in their local neighborhood. This absence of global information at the local scale poses significant problems for effective tracing of shortest path lengths in a network, as such an exercise requires knowledge not just of one's friends, but of one's friends' friends, and so on. If shortcuts exist, but only outside of one's local network vicinity, it becomes extremely difficult to utilize them consciously and thus construct an optimal path.

For these reasons, along with the practical difficulty associated with the empirical estimation of even local parameters like k and C (Kochen 1989), direct resolution of the small-world phenomenon in the actual social world seems unlikely. However, there is nothing about the small-world graph definition above that demands the graph in question represent a social network. In fact, one of the useful aspects of the corresponding conjecture is that it is quite general, specifying neither the nature of the vertices and edges, nor a particular construction algorithm required to build the graph. If it is true, then many real networks, satisfying the required n and k conditions, should turn out to be small-world networks. Examples of large, sparse graphs are easy to think of (neural networks, large organizations, citation databases, etc.) but difficult to obtain in the required format where both vertex and edge sets are precisely defined and completely documented. Nevertheless, three scientifically interesting examples are presented below.

The first example is the collaboration graph of feature-film actors. In the *actor collaboration graph* (Tjaden 1997), a vertex is defined as a cast member of any feature film registered on the Internet movie database,[30]

---

[29] On the other hand, as White (1970) points out, longer chains tend not to complete, biasing the sample toward shorter chains and leading to a corresponding underestimate of length.

[30] The Internet Movie Database (http://www.us.imdb.com) lists the cast members of all films, of all nationalities, since 1898. The graph studied in this article is actually the largest connected compenent of the entire graph, consisting of about 90% of all actors listed in the IMDB as of April 1997.

Small-World Phenomenon

TABLE 1

CHARACTERISTIC PATH LENGTH (L) AND CLUSTERING
COEFFICIENT (C) FOR THREE REAL NETWORKS

	L_{Actual}	L_{Random}	C_{Actual}	C_{Random}
Movie actors	3.65	2.99	.79	.00027
Power grid	18.7	12.4	.080	.005
C. elegans	2.65	2.25	.28	.05

and an edge represents two actors appearing in the same movie. This structure is interesting, as it is a simple case of a large (n = 226,000), sparse (k = 61) social network. It is also reminiscent of the collaboration graph of mathematicians that is traditionally centered on Paul Erdös (Grossman and Ion 1995).[31] The second example—the *western states power graph* (n = 4,941, k = 2.94)—represents the power-transmission grid of the western United States and is relevant to the efficiency and robustness of power networks (Phadke and Thorp 1988). Vertices represent generators, transformers, and substations, and edges represent high-voltage transmission lines between them. The final example is that of the neural network of the nematode *C. elegans* (White, Thompson, and Brenner 1986; Achacoso and Yamamoto 1992)—the sole example of a completely mapped neural network. For the *C. elegans graph* (n = 282; k = 14), an edge joins two neurons if they are connected by either a synapse or a gap junction. All edges are treated as undirected, and all vertices as identical, recognizing that these are crude approximations from a biological perspective.

Table 1 shows a comparison between L and C for each of these graphs and also L and C for random graphs with the same n and k. Note that, in each case, the characteristic path length is close to that of the equivalent random graph, yet the clustering coefficient is consistently much greater. A graphical way to view the same relationship is presented in figure 9. Here, L is plotted versus C for the three real graphs, and also for equivalent (that is, with same n and k) connected caveman graphs, where in each case, the statistics have been normalized by their corresponding random-graph values. From this picture, it is clear that not only are the real networks statistically distinct from both their random and caveman equivalents, but they are all distinct in the *same way*. Furthermore, their

[31] This collaboration graph would also be an interesting case to examine. Unfortunately, the only data available is that in the immediate neighborhood of Paul Erdös, and this is not sufficient to draw any conclusions about its global structure.

American Journal of Sociology

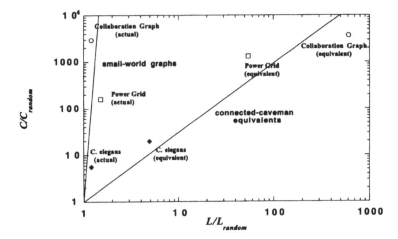

FIG. 9.—L and C statistics for the three real networks (the actor collaboration graph, the western states power graph, and the *C. elegans* graph) and their connected caveman equivalents (same n and k), scaled by their values for equivalent random graphs.

combination of small L and large C cannot be explained as a linear interpolation between the two extremes—in other words, clustering and length do not vary in a commensurate fashion. As figure 10 shows, however, this combination of properties can be replicated by the α-model. It is clear that, as α increases, the α-statistics remain at first clustered along the (high-L, high-C) diagonal and then sharply depart from the diagonal to become small-world graphs, decreasing rapidly in characteristic path length while remaining almost constant in terms of the clustering coefficient. As α increases to reach the clustering transition, C decreases rapidly for L fixed near its asymptotic limit, until the random limit is reached at large α. These results indicate that the small-world phenomenon is not just a property of an abstract class of hypothetical graphs, but arises in real networks. Furthermore, it is not specific to a particular kind of network or restricted to a certain size range. The three graphs examined span a range of three orders of magnitude in n and represent completely different actual networks, yet all are small-world graphs in the sense defined above. Finally, not only are all three graphs small-world graphs in the broad sense of high clustering coexisting with small characteristic path length, but the relationship between L and C in the real graphs is consistent with the corresponding statistics of the α-graph model.

Small-World Phenomenon

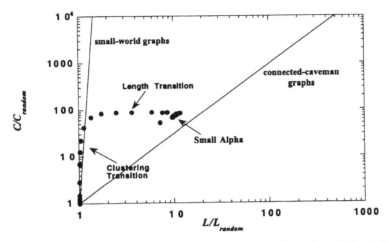

FIG. 10.—*L* and *C* statistics for the α-model ($n = 1,000$, $k = 10$), scaled by their values at the random-graph limit (in practice, this is taken as α = 20).

DYNAMICAL SYSTEMS ON SMALL-WORLD GRAPHS

Having established that a set of relatively tiny perturbations to the local structure of a highly clustered graph can have a dramatic impact upon its global structural properties, it is natural to ask whether or not the same changes can also affect the behavior of dynamical systems that are coupled according to such a graph. This is a topic that is directly relevant to the social sciences: the role of social structure in generating globally observable, dynamical features. So far, structure has been treated as an autonomous feature of networks and defined narrowly in terms of sparse, undirected graphs. This has paid off by yielding some robust statements about the small-world properties of a general class of graphs that are partly ordered and partly random, and that seem to reflect some of the features of real networks. However, a greater issue is to understand the relationship between structure and dynamics.

As such, the following discussion builds not only on issues of network structure, but also upon a whole literature of distributed dynamical systems, in which systems are often assumed to be completely connected (the most tractable case). Where sparsely coupled systems are considered, the relevant coupling topology is usually assumed to be either completely ordered (e.g., a low-dimensional cubic lattice) or completely random. As emphasized earlier, real networks are likely to be sparse and may combine significant elements both of order and randomness, with resultant proper-

American Journal of Sociology

ties, like the small-world phenomenon, that cannot be captured by either of these approximations. Whether or not this structural oversight turns out also to be an oversight from the perspective of dynamical systems is not obvious. This article offers a more specific way to cast the issue at hand: do significant new phenomena emerge when the connectivity of distributed dynamical systems are modeled on the graphs presented earlier?

Disease Spreading in Structured Populations

A simple case of a dynamical system is that of a disease spreading from a small seed of initiators into a much larger population whose structure is prescribed by some underlying graph.[32] The bulk of previous work on the spread of diseases focuses on populations in which uniform mixing is assumed between elements (see, e.g., Murray 1991). This is an important assumption because it enables population structure to be ignored, thus greatly simplifying the analysis. Some work, however, has grappled with the issue of population structure. Kareiva (1990) reviews a number of such attempts (which he calls "stepping-stone" models), and May and colleagues (Hassell, Comins, and May 1994; May 1995) have considered various parasite-host problems on two-dimensional grids of discrete but homogeneous patches. Both Kareiva and May conclude that the introduction of spatial structure can significantly affect both the population size and its susceptibility to parasites and disease. A similar approach has been used by Hess (1996*a*, 1996*b*) to compare virus transmission among subpopulations that are connected according to various simple topologies such as a ring and a star. Also, Sattenspiel and Simon (1988) have considered a detailed model of the spread of an infectious disease in a structured population in which different connective arrangements between the subpopulations are compared. Finally, Longini (1988) has utilized real airline network data in order to model the 1968 global outbreak of influenza. None of this work, however, goes on to treat the global dynamical properties of the system explicitly as a function of the structure. The models of Sattenspiel, Simon, and also Hess do consider different types of connectivity between subpopulations, but they consider isolated topologies, as opposed to a continuum, and their choices reflect those cases which, in the context of this article, are extremal (such as a ring versus a random graph). Extremal cases are certainly natural to consider, but if it is true that real

---

[32] Here I discuss disease spreading because of its obvious public health relevance, but qualitatively similar dynamics could describe the spread of other kinds of contagion such as ideas, rumors, fashion, or even crime (Gladwell 1996).

Small-World Phenomenon

networks exhibit important properties of both ordered and random networks, then it is important to consider the intermediate regime as well.

Dynamics as a function of structure.—In this sense, the work most closely related to the approach taken here is that by Kretzschmar and Morris (1996), who analyze the spread of a disease—both in terms of extent and time scale—as a function of the overall concurrency of relationships in the population. Roughly speaking, they examine a family of graphs that interpolates between a world of exclusively monogamous (but randomly formed) relationships and an unconstrained random graph, in which concurrent relationships are likely to form. They determine that increased concurrency of relationships significantly increases the extent of the disease and its rate of spread, even when the total number of relationships in the population is held constant. Essentially, this result stems from the increasing connectedness of extremely sparse ($k = 1$) graphs: serial monogamy yields almost completely disconnected graphs (in the sense that no connected components larger than dyads can exist), but random graphs with the same number of edges exhibit relatively large connected components. Hence, as Kretzschmar and Morris conclude, it is the size of the largest connected component that drives the spread of disease across the population. The approach here also examines the effects on disease spread of changing the distribution of a fixed number of edges over a fixed number of vertices. It is different, however, in that Morris and Kretschmar consider changing concurrency in an otherwise randomly mixing population with $k = 1$, while here the amount of randomness is varied in a connected population with $k \gg 1$. Hence, any observed differences in the dynamical properties of the system must be driven by more subtle features of the topology than connectedness. In fact, as we shall see, there is much about the system that cannot be reduced to any single structural characteristic of the underlying graphs—a warning signal for dealing with any more complicated dynamics.

In order to emphasize the role of population structure, the subsequent analysis is restricted to a simplified model of disease spreading in which each element of the population is in one of three states: *susceptible, infected,* or *removed.* At each discrete point in time (t), every infected element can infect each one of its neighbors with probability (p), the *infectiousness.* Any newly infected elements remain infected for one time step,[33]

---

[33] The time period (τ) for which an infected agent remains infectious can be set to one without loss of generality. The reason is that p and τ do not vary independently. In fact, the dynamics for any given τ can be reproduced with $\tau = 1$ merely by rescaling p. In other words, there is complete equivalence (in this model) between being exposed to a more infectious disease for a short period of time and a less infectious disease for a long period of time. This feature of the model greatly simplifies its analysis.

American Journal of Sociology

after which they are removed permanently from the population (presumably by immunity or death) and so play no further part in proceedings. Hence, if at $t = 0$ a single element is infected (by some external influence), then at some later time, one of two things must have happened:

1. The disease will have run its course and died out, infecting some fraction of the population and leaving the remaining fraction F_s uninfected,

or

2. The whole population will have been infected ($F_s = 0$) in some characteristic time T.

The natural question to ask then is whether or not the structure of the population, expressed in terms of the α-graph model presented earlier, has any effect on F_s and T of the related system. Furthermore, if so, can the functional forms of $F_s(\phi)$ and $T(\phi)$ be understood in terms of our structural statistics $L(\phi)$ and $C(\phi)$?

Results.—The model has two parameters that can vary independently of each other: the infectiousness p, which determines the local dynamics; and the fraction of shortcuts ϕ. We are now in a position to compare some results for an entire range of topologies as a means of answering the two questions stated above within the very narrow context of this specific dynamical system. Figure 11 shows the steady-state fraction of susceptibles F_s versus p for the two extreme values of ϕ, where graphs of parameters $n = 1,000$, $k = 10$ have been used to determine the couplings of the system. Three distinct regions are apparent:

1. For $p \lesssim 1/(k - 1) \approx .11$ all topologies (i.e., all values of ϕ) yield the same result: the disease infects only a negligible fraction of the population before dying out. This is a *trivial* steady state, because nothing happens that can distinguish between different topologies.
2. For $.11 \lesssim p \lesssim .5$ different topologies yield different F_s.
3. For $p \gtrsim .5$, all topologies once again yield the same end result, only this time it is a *nontrivial* steady state because the disease has taken over the entire population.

There is nothing more to say about region 1, but regions 2 and 3 deserve some extra attention. Region 2 is confusing: there appears to be some significant relationship between structure and dynamics, but its mechanism is not transparent. Figure 11 suggests that in region 2 the fraction of the population that will become infected with a disease of some specified p depends significantly on ϕ, and this is shown more explicitly in figure 12 for a particular value of p. In epidemiological terms, this dependence on ϕ is equivalent to the statement that the impact of a disease depends not just on how infectious it is, but also on the connective topology of the population. This message is not new in the epidemiological literature, es-

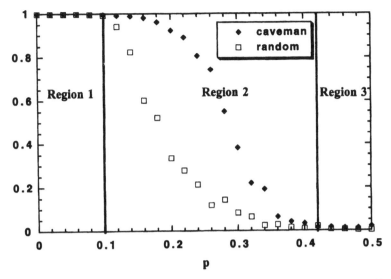

FIG. 11.—Fraction of uninfected survivors (F_s) versus infectiousness (p) for disease spreading dynamics on a network generated by the α-model at clustered and random extremes.

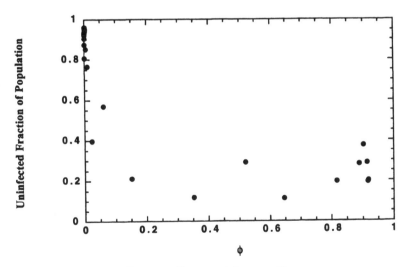

FIG. 12.—F_s versus ϕ for $p = .24$

American Journal of Sociology

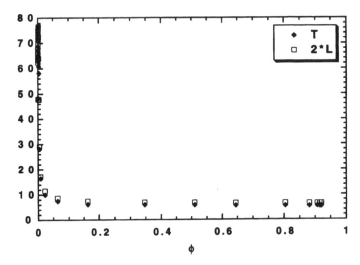

FIG. 13.—Time taken to reach a steady state (T) versus fraction of shortcuts (ϕ) in the underlying α-graph for the disease spreading model.

pecially that of sexually transmitted diseases. What is new is the idea that the structural changes required can be very subtle. Unlike the difference between a chain and a star graph or a ring lattice and a random graph, the difference between a big- and a small-world graph can be a matter of only a few randomly rewired edges—a change that is effectively undetectable at the level of individual vertices. Unfortunately, it is difficult to be any more precise than this, as the functional form of $F_s(\phi)$ is not clear. Nevertheless, even this broad-brush observation has implications for the way we think about social diseases, which are often perceived as confined to isolated subgroups of a population. The message here is that the highly clustered nature of small-world graphs can lead to the intuition that a given disease is "far away" when, on the contrary, it is effectively very close.

Region 3 is a simpler matter to examine, as the disease always takes over the entire population regardless of its connective topology. It is merely a question of how long this takes. However, figure 13 shows that in this region the time taken to reach the steady-state $F_s = 0$ varies dramatically as a function of ϕ and that disease can spread on a small-world graph far more rapidly than in a connected caveman graph and almost as fast as in a random graph. In fact, figure 13 also shows that when $p = 1$, $T(\phi)$ bears a close functional relationship to $L(\phi)$.[34] Hence, in this parameter

[34] For $p = 1$, this functional similarity might be expected, as T is just the maximum distance from the initially infected vertex to any other vertex in the graph. For a

Small-World Phenomenon

regime at least, the transient time for the dynamics to reach the same, nontrivial steady state bears a simple and obvious relationship to the structure of the underlying graph. That is, shorter characteristic path length implies faster spreading of the disease. In a real-world scenario, where an epidemic can be responded to, the time scale on which it spreads becomes a crucial factor. A striking consequence of this result is that, in a small-world graph, the characteristic time scale has become very small, but the clustering C is still large. As with the extent of disease spread in region 2, the change in structure in region 3 that causes the disease to spread much faster may not be observable at a local level.

Although the relationship between population structure and disease dynamics is not always clear, even for this simple model, it does appear as if the gross features of the dynamics are dominated by the characteristic path length of the underlying graph. This is by no means universally true of dynamical systems on graphs. For instance, when the transmission of a behavioral trait exacts a cost, such as for a prisoner's dilemma model of cooperation, a high degree of reciprocity may be necessary for the trait to survive in the population (Axelrod 1984; Boyd and Richerson 1988; Cohen, Riolo, and Axelrod 1999). In the case of small groups of cooperators struggling for survival in a sea of defectors, Axelrod (1984) notes that cooperators must interact preferentially, which in network terms is equivalent to high local clustering. In a highly clustered graph, cooperators located in the same cluster can survive—even thrive—in the midst of a noncooperative majority. Conversely, in a random graph (with negligible clustering), any small group of initial cooperators will be eroded from the periphery, as each peripheral cooperator will be interacting predominantly with defectors, thus failing to reap the benefits of reciprocity. As with disease spreading, there is a transition between these two extremes, but in this case, the dynamics tend to be dominated by the clustering coefficient rather than by the characteristic path length.[35]

This result suggests an interesting role for small-world architectures, which by virtue of their short characteristic path length and high cluster-

---

perfect ring structure $T = D$, where D is the diameter of the graph and $D = 2L$. Hence, for even the approximate ring structure generated for an α-graph with $\phi = 0$, we could expect that $T \approx 2L$. Furthermore, for *any* graph, it is necessarily true that $L \leq T \leq D$. For random graphs, where the number of vertices at a distance d from any vertex generally grows exponentially (Bollobás 1985), $D < 2L$ so we could also expect that $L \leq T \leq 2L$ for *any* value of ϕ. Thus T should be related to L through nothing more than a multiplicative factor $1 \leq c(\phi) \leq 2$, which is not significant on the scale of the changes occuring in both statistics as a function of ϕ. Hence, the two curves in figure 13 might be expected to look very much alike, as they do.

[35] There are a number of subtleties to this result which are explained more completely in Watts (1999, chap. 8).

American Journal of Sociology

ing coefficient, can support the rapid dissemination of information without necessarily compromising behavior that is individually costly but beneficial when reciprocated. Furthermore, the more general idea of optimizing an architecture to satisfy two or more opposing constraints may prove a useful concept in the design or modification of large networks such as organizations.

SUMMARY

This article examines a particular class of graphs that interpolates between highly ordered and highly random limits. A significant feature of these graphs is that the presence of a very small fraction of long-range shortcuts can lead to the coexistence of high local clustering and a small global length scale. The superposition of these apparently contradictory properties is a graph-theoretic formalization of the small-world phenomenon. The motivation for the small-world phenomenon comes from social networks, but it turns out to be a much more general effect that arises under quite weak conditions in large, sparse, partly ordered and partly random networks. Its existence is not predicted by current network theories, yet it seems likely to arise in a wide variety of real networks, especially in social, biological, and technological systems. One consequence of this result is that it is highly likely that the phenomenon exists in the real social world—a notion currently supported by only limited data but consistent with anecdotal experience.

In addition to their interesting structural properties, small-world graphs are also relevant to the social and natural sciences through their effect on the globally emergent features of dynamical systems. Specifically, distributed dynamical systems can exhibit dramatically different behavior on small-world networks—an effect that may have implications in fields as diverse as public health and organizational behavior and design.

APPENDIX

The algorithm for constructing a graph according to equation (5) proceeds as follows:

1. Fix a vertex i.
2. For every other vertex j, compute $R_{i,j}$ according to equation (5), with the additional constraint that $R_{i,j} = 0$ if i and j are already connected.
3. Sum the $R_{i,j}$ over all j, and normalize each to obtain variables $P_{i,j} = R_{i,j}/(\sum_{l \neq i} R_{i,l})$. Then, since $\sum_j P_{i,j} = 1$, we can interpret $P_{i,j}$ as the probability that i will connect to j. Furthermore, we can interpret $P_{i,j}$ geometrically as follows: divide the unit interval $(0, 1)$ into $n - 1$ half-open subintervals with length $P_{i,j} \ \forall \ j \neq i$.

Small-World Phenomenon

4. A uniform random variable is then generated on (0, 1). It must fall into one of the subintervals, say the one corresponding to j_*.
5. Connect i to j_*.

This procedure is then repeated until the predetermined number of edges ($M = kn/2$) has been constructed. The vertices i are chosen in random order, but once a vertex has been allowed to "choose" a new neighbor, it may not choose again until all other vertices have taken their turn. However, vertices may be "chosen" arbitrarily often, and this leads to a nonzero variance in the degree k. But the fact that all vertices are forced to make one new connection before any others are allowed to choose a second time ensures at least that no vertices will be isolated (as long as $k \geq 2$).

REFERENCES

Achacoso, T. B., and W. S. Yamamoto. 1992. *AY's Neuroanatomy of* C. elegans *for Computation*. Boca Raton, Fla.: CRC Press.
Arthur, W. Brian, and David Lane. 1993. "Information Contagion." *Structural Change and Economic Dynamics* 4 (1): 81–104.
Axelrod, Robert. 1984. *The Evolution of Cooperation*. New York: Basic Books.
Bollobás, Bela. 1985. *Random Graphs*. London: Academic Press.
Bollobás, Bela, and Fan R. K. Chung. 1988. "The Diameter of a Cycle Plus a Random Matching." *SIAM Journal of Discrete Mathematics* 1 (3): 328–33.
Boyd, Robert, and Peter J. Richerson. 1988. "The Evolution of Reciprocity in Sizable Groups." *Journal of Theoretical Biology* 132:337–56.
Burt, Ronald S. 1982. *Toward a Structural Theory of Action*. New York: Academic Press.
———. 1992. *Structural Holes: The Social Structure of Competition*. Cambridge, Mass.: Harvard University Press.
Cerf, V. G., D. D. Cowan, R. C. Mullin, and R. G. Stanton. 1974. "A Lower Bound on the Average Shortest Path Length in Regular Graphs." *Networks* 4:335–42.
Cohen, Michael D., Rick L. Riolo, and Robert Axelrod. 1999. "The Emergence of Social Organization in the Prisoner's Dilemma: How Context-Preservation and Other Factors Promote Cooperation." Working Paper 99-01-002. Santa Fe Institute.
Coleman, James S. 1973. *The Mathematics of Collective Action*. Chicago: Aldine.
Chung, Fan R. K. 1986. "Diameters of Communications Networks." Pp. 1–18 in *Mathematics of Information Processing*, vol. 34 in Proceedings of Symposia in Applied Mathematics. Providence, R.I.: American Mathematical Society.
Crick, Francis, and Christof Koch. 1998. "Constraints on Cortical and Thalamic Projections: The No-Strong-Loops Hypothesis." *Nature* 391:245–50.
Davidson, Mark L. 1983. *Multidimensional Scaling*. New York: Wiley.
Davis, James A. 1967. "Clustering and Structural Balance in Graphs." *Human Relations* 20:181–87.
Fararo, Thomas J., and M. Sunshine. 1964. *A Study of a Biased Friendship Net.* Syracuse, N.Y.: Syracuse University Press.
Foster, Caxton C., Anatol Rapoport, and Carol J. Orwant. 1963. "A Study of Large Sociogram: Estimation of Free Parameters." *Behavioral Science* 8:56–65.
Freeman, Linton C. 1979. "Centrality in Social Networks: Conceptual Clarification." *Social Networks* 1:215–39.

American Journal of Sociology

———. 1982. "Centered Graphs and the Structure of Ego Networks." *Mathematical Social Sciences* 3:291–304.
Friedkin, Noah E. 1990. "Social Networks in Structural Equation Models." *Social Psychology Quarterly* 53 (4): 316–28.
———. 1991. "Theoretical Foundations for Centrality Measures." *American Journal of Sociology* 96 (6): 1478–1504.
Gladwell, Malcolm. 1996. "The Tipping Point." *New Yorker*, June 3, pp. 32–38.
Granovetter, Mark S. 1973. "The Strength of Weak Ties." *American Journal of Sociology* 78 (6): 1360–80.
———. 1974. *Getting a Job: A Study of Contacts and Careers.* Cambridge, Mass.: Harvard University Press.
———. 1978. "Threshold Models of Collective Behavior." *American Journal of Sociology* 83 (6): 1420–43.
Grossman, Jerry W., and Patrick D. F. Ion. 1995. "On a Portion of the Well-Known Collaboration Graph." *Congressus Numeratium* 108:129–31.
Guare, John. 1990. *Six Degrees of Separation: A Play.* New York: Vintage Books.
Harary, Frank. 1959. "Status and Contrastatus." *Sociometry* 22:23–43.
Hassell, Michael P., Hugh N. Comins, and Robert M. May. 1994. "Species Coexistence and Self-Organizing Spatial Dynamics." *Nature* 370:290–92.
Herz, Andreas V. 1994. "Collective Phenomena in Spatially-Extended Evolutionary Games." *Journal of Theoretical Biology* 169:65–87.
Hess, George. 1996a. "Disease in Metapopulation Models: Implications for Conservation." *Ecology* 77 (5): 1617–32.
———. 1996b. "Linking Extinction to Connectivity and Habitat Destruction in Metapopulation Models." *American Naturalist* 148 (1): 226–36.
Kareiva, Peter. 1990. "Population Dynamics in Spatially Complex Environments: Theory and Data." *Philosophical Transactions of the Royal Society of London* 330: 175–90.
Kauffman, Stuart A. 1969. "Metabolic Stability and Epigenesis in Randomly Constructed Genetic Nets." *Journal of Theoretical Biology* 22:437–67.
Kochen, Manfred. 1989. "Toward Structural Sociodynamics." Pp. 52–64 in *The Small World*, edited by Manfred Kochen. Norwood N.J.: Ablex.
Korte, Charles, and Stanley Milgram. 1970. "Acquaintance Linking between White and Negro Populations: Application of the Small World Problem." *Journal of Personality and Social Psychology* 15:101–18.
Kretzschmar, Mirjam, and Martina Morris. 1996. "Measures of Concurrency in Networks and the Spread of Infectious Disease." *Mathematical Biosciences* 133:165–95.
Longini, Ira M., Jr. 1988. "A Mathematical Model for Predicting the Geographic Spread of New Infectious Agents." *Mathematical Biosciences* 90:367–83.
March, L., and P. Steadman. 1971. Chapter 14 in *The Geometry of Environment.* London: RIBA Publications.
May, Robert M. 1995. "Necessity and Chance: Deterministic Chaos in Ecology and Evolution." *Bulletin of the American Mathematical Society* 32:291–308.
Milgram, Stanley. 1967. "The Small World Problem." *Psychology Today* 2:60–67.
Murray, James D. 1991. *Mathematical Biology*, 2d ed. Berlin: Springer Verlag.
———. 1993. *Mathematical Biology*, 2d ed. Berlin: Springer Verlag.
Nowak, Martin A., and Robert M. May. 1993. "The Spatial Dilemmas of Evolution." *International Journal of Bifurcations and Chaos* 3 (1): 35–78.
Phadke, Arun G., and James S. Thorp. 1988. *Computer Relaying for Power Systems.* New York: John Wiley.
Pool, Ithiel de Sola, and Manfred Kochen. 1978. "Contacts and Influence." *Social Networks* 1:1–48.
Rapoport, Anatol. 1953a. "Spread of Information through a Population with Socio-

Small-World Phenomenon

Structural Bias: I. Assumption of Transitivity." *Bulletin of Mathematical Biophysics* 15:523–33.

————. 1953*b*. "Spread of Information through a Population with Socio-Structural Bias: II. Various Model with Partial Transitivity." *Bulletin of Mathematical Biophysics* 15:535–46.

————. 1957. "A Contribution to the Theory of Random and Biased Nets." *Bulletin of Mathematical Biophysics* 19:257–71.

————. 1963. "Mathematical Models of Social Interaction." Pp. 493–579 in *Handbook of Mathematical Psychology*, vol. 2. Edited by R. R. Bush, R. D. Luce, and E. Galanter. New York: Wiley.

Rouvray, Dennis H. 1986. "Predicting Chemistry from Topology." *Scientific American* (September): 40–47.

Sattenspiel, Lisa, and Carl P. Simon. 1988. "The Spread and Persistence of Infectious Diseases in Structured Populations." *Mathematical Biosciences* 90:341–66.

Skvoretz, John. 1985. "Random and Biased Networks: Simulations and Approximations." *Social Networks* 7:225–61.

Solmonoff, Ray, and Anatol Rapoport. 1951. "Connectivity of Random Nets." *Bulletin of Mathematical Biophysics* 13:107–17.

Strogatz, Steven H., and Ian Stewart. 1993. "Coupled Oscillators and Biological Synchronization." *Scientific American* 269 (6): 102–9.

Tjaden, Brett. 1997. E-mail to author, May 14.

Watts, D. J. 1999. *Small Worlds: The Dynamics of Networks between Order and Randomness*. Princeton, N.J.: Princeton University Press.

White, Harrison. 1970. "Search Parameters for the Small World Problem." *Social Forces* 49:259–64.

White, J., E. Southgate, J. N. Thompson, and S. Brenner. 1986. "The Structure of the Nervous System of the Nematode *Caenorhabditis elegans.*"*Philosophical Transactions of the Royal Society of London,* Series B, 314:1–340.

Wiener, Harry. 1947. "Structural Determination of Paraffin Boiling Points." *Journal of the American Chemistry Society* 69:17–20.

Yamaguchi, Kazuo. 1994*a.* "The Flow of Information through Social Networks Diagonal-Free Measures of Inefficiency and the Structural Determinants of Inefficiency." *Social Networks* 16:57–86.

————. 1994*b.* "Some Accelerated Failure-Time Regressive Models Derived from Diffusion Process Models: An Application to Network Diffusion Analysis." *Sociological Methodology* 24:267–300.

F

Lock-in and Vulnerability

[19]

The weakness of strong ties

The lock-in of regional development in the Ruhr area[1]

Gernot Grabher

The glorious history of the Ruhr, the industrial heartland of West Germany, could be written as the success story of an industrial district. At a glance at least, the prosperous Ruhr industry of former decades corresponds with the prosperous industrial districts of today. Highly specialized regional industry was effectively supported by a developed infrastructure of supplier firms and regional institutions which tailored their services to the specific needs of regional industry. The agglomeration of industry facilitated personal communication and exchange of ideas and generated a process of mutual training and learning by doing. Marshall's metaphor of 'industrial atmosphere' certainly applied to the culture of the Ruhr:

> It is to be remembered that a man can generally pass easily from one machine to another; but that the manual handling of a material often requires a fine skill that is not easily acquired in middle age: for that is characteristic of a special industrial atmosphere.
>
> (Marshall 1919/1927: 287)

Especially in the steel industry of the Ruhr, the 'fine skills' to run a furnace were provided by a long-term process of mutual training. In essence, the production of steel used to be less a rational technology than a culinary art that required a fine flair for the different ingredients.

Apparently, the systemic and agglomerative character of the Ruhr justified the label 'industrial district'.

> The conditions of population density, presence of infrastructure, industrial atmosphere, which are both the source and the result, the cause and the effect, of that part of returns which cannot be explained either by internal economies of scale or by R&D, apply to the industrial district. It is this extra-element of productivity which made

256   *Limits of networks*

> Lancashire, the Ruhr and Lombardy yesterday, and the so-called
> Third Italy today, stand out against the rest.
>
> (Becattini 1989: 132)

According to this analogy, however, the future of the industrial districts
of today will eventually resemble the present conditions of the
industrial districts of the past. Given the decline of the latter, that future
is not very reassuring. The initial strengths of the industrial districts of
the past – their industrial atmosphere, highly developed and specialized
infrastructure, the close interfirm linkages, and strong political support
by regional institutions – turned into stubborn obstacles to innovation.
Regional development became 'locked in' by the very socioeconomic
conditions that once made these regions 'stand out against the rest'. In
other words, they fell into the trap of 'rigid specialization'.

The arguments in this chapter are not directed against the concept of
industrial districts. Rather, the attempt is made to move beyond the
tautological circle according to which 'industrial districts are successful
economies, and they are successful because they are industrial districts'.
This tautology idealizes industrial districts as a new master paradigm
and a universally applicable blueprint for regional regeneration. Numerous success stories fuse description, prediction, and prescription
towards a self-fulfilling prophecy, rendering assessments of the potential of industrial districts for regional regeneration superfluous (Amin
and Robins 1990). The heroic intention of this chapter is to protect the
concept of industrial districts against hasty political conclusions by
elucidating the ambivalence of their basic features: intense interfirm
linkages and close relations between leading industry and politics. The
first section of this chapter deals with the decline of the Ruhr. The
purpose, however, is not to offer a comprehensive theory of old
industrial areas but to elaborate the significance of interfirm cooperation and regional politics in the decline of the Ruhr during the
1970s. The second section is focused on the role of interfirm cooperation in reorganizing the Ruhr during the 1980s. I describe the
troublesome attempts to transform the close interfirm linkages into
loosely coupled networks. Finally, I speculate on policies that could
support this change of the industrial core of the Ruhr yet avoid the trap
of rigid specialization.

DECLINE: REGIONAL OR SECTORAL?

The Ruhr, a polycentric urban agglomeration of more than 5 million
inhabitants, was the motor driving the 'industrial takeoff' of Germany.

The coal, iron, and steel complex of the Ruhr was considered a major growth pole of national economic development. At the end of the 1950s, approximately 13 per cent of the country's gross domestic product was still attributed to the Ruhr, which accounts for 8 per cent of the population of West Germany (Müller 1989). At the end of the 1970s, however, spectacular plant closures, radical drops in production, and mass dismissals indicated a severe crisis in the Ruhr. To be sure, the decline of the Ruhr had already begun in the 1960s. First, the period of reconstruction, with its enormous demand for basic materials and capital goods, came to an end. Second, the income elasticity of demand for iron and steel – main products of the Ruhr – dropped from 1.8 in 1950 to 0.9 in 1964 (Schlieper 1986: 178). In other words, in the mid-1960s the amount of iron and steel required to produce an additional unit of gross domestic product was only half what had been needed one and a half decades earlier. Third, the old industrial areas were faced with increasing competition, especially from the newly industrializing countries, which had comparative advantages in producing homogeneous mass goods. As a result, the iron and steel industry reduced employment between 1977 and 1986 by 23.2%. In the first half of the 1980s, the Ruhr lost more than 100,000 jobs in industry. The unemployment rate in the Ruhr amounted in September 1988 to 15.1 per cent as compared to 8.1 per cent in West Germany as a whole. In addition, the average duration of unemployment in the Ruhr (40 weeks) was significantly above the national average of 31 weeks (Landesarbeitsamt Nordrhein-Westfalen).

The decline of the Ruhr, however, cannot be traced back simply to the dominance of a few industries that faced dramatic decreases in demand. A purely demand-side approach is inadequate for at least two reasons. First, on a theoretical level, a demand-side approach does not explain why regional redeployment of the productive resources that were set free by the decreases in demand did not occur. Second, as empirical analysis has pointed out, it is not just a few traditional industries that have been affected by crisis. Even high-technology industries and the service sector are growing at below-average rates (Junkernheinrich 1989: 31). While the production of high-technology products (according to the OECD categorization) in West Germany grew between 1977 and 1983 by 39 per cent, the Ruhr's growth in production was just 25 per cent. The machine-building and steel construction industry of the Ruhr fell far behind the development of these industries at the national level (see Figure 12.1).

An essential reason for the poor performance of these industries, which do not belong to the traditional core of the Ruhr, are the specific

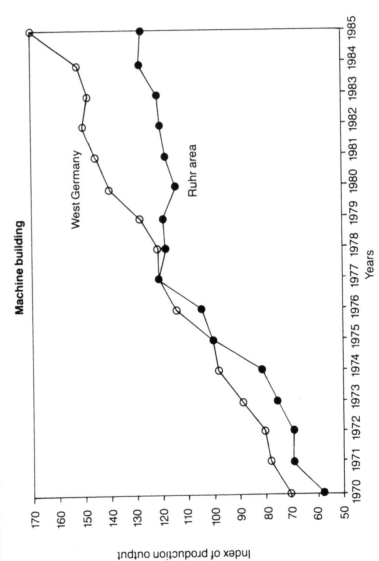

Figure 12.1   Development of the machine-building and steel construction industries, 1970–85 (index of production output)
Source: GEWOS, GfAH, and WSI (1988: 92)

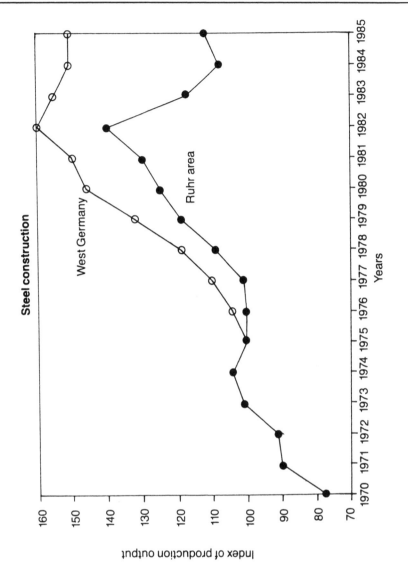

Steel construction

West Germany

Ruhr area

Index of production output

Years

1970 1971 1972 1973 1974 1975 1976 1977 1978 1979 1980 1981 1982 1983 1984 1985

70 80 90 100 110 120 130 140 150 160

260 *Limits of networks*

interfirm linkages shaping the development of the region. The regional core firms were established in locations that allowed a profitable exploitation of natural resources but that frequently lacked a well-developed handicraft infrastructure (Herrigel 1989). Although the missing infrastructure forced industrial enterprises initially to provide supplies to a large extent on their own, regional industry became involved in an increasing division of labour during subsequent periods of development. On the one hand, individual steel producers specialized in different product areas, such as Thyssen in high-grade steel and Mannesmann in pipes, whereas raw materials and crude steel were provided cooperatively. On the other hand, an industrial infrastructure of suppliers emerged that amounted to approximately 190,000 jobs in 1976, including, above all, the machine-building industry, electronics industry, and commercial services (Schröter 1986: 381). The close intraregional interdependence, which is what constituted the coal, iron, and steel complex, had disastrous long-term consequences for the region's adaptability.

THE RIGID SPECIALIZATION TRAP: THE THREEFOLD LOCK-IN OF REGIONAL DEVELOPMENT

'Functional lock-in'

The long-term stability and predictability of demand for iron and steel favoured close and stable linkages between the regional core firms and the supplier sector. Investments in the stability of interfirm relations and mutual adaptations promised to reduce transaction costs. The close intraregional relations embedded in long-standing personal connections resulted in serious shortcomings in so-called boundary-spanning functions, which are of utmost importance in scanning the economic environment and in making external information relevant for the firm. Moreover, they are concerned with identifying and mobilizing external resources (Aldrich 1979: 248–55).

First, knowledge of the long-term investment plans of the core firms made it possible for the suppliers largely to dispense with their own long-term R&D aimed at developing new products for a new clientele. The still strong orientation of development and innovation activities to regional core firms has been confirmed in a recent analysis of machine-building firms supplying the coal industry of the Ruhr. Of the machine-building firms supplying the coal industry, 57 per cent developed new products in close cooperation with their main customers; 33 per cent cooperated solely with their single most important customer. This cooperation proved to be of crucial importance for the success of product innovations: just 9 per cent of the machine-building firms supplying the coal industry would have been able to innovate without their cooperating partners. Furthermore, 35 per cent of these machine-building firms drew innovation ideas from their main customers. By comparison, innovation ideas of machine-building firms that do not supply the coal industry stem primarily from observations made of the competitive environment (43 per cent) and from these firms' own R&D departments (20 per cent). Acting on innovative ideas, these firms draw resources from a wider network of cooperating partners, including suppliers, universities, and professional associations (Lehner, Nordhause-Janz, and Schubert 1990: 44–7).

Second, well-developed personal connections with the middle management of core firms quite often took the place of the suppliers' own marketing. Personal ties to a few client firms were given preference over the development of a firm's own channels of distribution. Consequently, the distribution departments of supplier firms within the coal, iron, and steel complex are generally of little significance. The qualifications of distribution personnel in machine-building firms supplying the coal industry, for example, are considerably below the industrial average (Lehner, Nordhause-Janz, and Schubert 1990: 18).

These empirical findings cannot simply be traced back to the 'dependent supplier syndrome'. Shortcomings in boundary-spanning functions do not apply solely to small sweatshops run by structurally overloaded artisans; they apply equally to technologically advanced, medium-sized and even large firms with developed organizational and management systems. Consequently, functional shortcomings characterizing the core of the Ruhr industry cannot be explained exclusively in terms of the structural dependence of small suppliers. Those shortcomings must also be considered as outcomes of long-term adaptations and explicit strategies to facilitate interfirm cooperation and reduce transaction costs. At least in the case of the larger firms, the high risks of low investments in boundary-spanning functions and high investments in transaction-specific personal relations seemed to be justified by the continuity of interfirm relations. The common interest in continuity, in turn, favoured transaction-specific investments, thereby setting up a vicious circle locking firms into specific exchange relations. This vicious circle, caused by and resulting in functional shortcomings, was reinforced by a 'cognitive lock-in'.

262   *Limits of networks*

'Cognitive lock-in'

Personal ties of long standing resulted in mutual orientations involving a common language regarding technical matters, contracting rules, and knowledge on which the parties could draw in communicating with one another. Common orientation was reinforced by social processes such as 'groupthink' (Morgan 1986: 91). That is, within the coal, iron, and steel complex a specific world view was developed on the basis of social reinforcement. This world view determined which phenomena were perceived and which phenomena were ignored. Then, when events and signals were perceived, the world view determined how they had to be interpreted. Above all, this world view referred to the long-term development of demand for the main product of the Ruhr: steel. Particularly on account of the long-term continuity in demand trends (see Figure 12.2), the slumps in the early 1970s were at first interpreted as breaks in a growth path that was stable in the long run. In other words, the idea of a 'cycle' was rediscovered (Pichierri 1986: 10). In this light, the sharp downturns in demand were interpreted as a phase in a business cycle, not as the beginning of long-term decline. This unchallenged groupthink interpretation prevented a reorganization of the regional economy in an early period of decline, when the region was still well equipped with resources for innovation (Schlieper 1986).

Personal cohesiveness and well-established relations within the coal, iron, and steel complex turned out to be another trap. Intensive internal relations limited the perception of innovation opportunities and left no

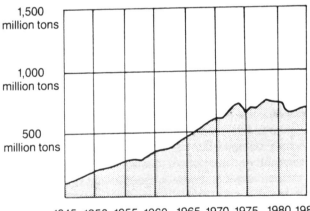

Figure 12.2 Development of world crude steel production, 1945–85
Source: Grabher (1988: 35)

room for 'bridging relationships' – those that transcend a firm's own narrowly circumscribed group and bring together information from different sources (Wegener 1987: 28). This handicap is the weakness of strong ties, to paraphrase Granovetter (1973). Personal cohesiveness and groupthink favoured 'parametric rationality', as opposed to 'strategic rationality' (Elster 1979), and resulted in 'overcompensatory response'. Increasing the quantity of the same prescription was given preference over trying a new one. In the Ruhr, overcompensatory response was reflected in huge investments in existing technology and a marked predilection for process innovations. The physical investments of the West German steel industry, for example, amounted in 1976 to DM2.7b as compared to DM2.1b in 1970, when demand for steel was still growing (Schröter 1986: 370). The machine-building firms of the coal, iron, and steel complex adopted CNC, CAD, computer-aided quality control (CAQ), and flexible manufacturing systems (FMS) significantly earlier than the machine-building firms outside the coal, iron, and steel complex, and are at present leading with respect to the computer integration of manufacturing (CIM). However, shortcomings in boundary-spanning functions prevent these firms from leaving the technological trajectory of the coal, iron, and steel complex and from shifting to more promising markets (Lehner, Nordhause-Janz, and Schubert 1990: 34). Functional lock-in and cognitive lock-in resulted inevitably in the 'sailing-ship effect' (Rothwell and Zegveld 1985: 41). The sailing-ship effect refers to the fact that most important improvements to the sailing ship occurred after the introduction of the steamship. As Rothwell and Zegveld emphasize,

> it illustrates how established companies can become locked into existing technological trajectories. Rather than attempting to capitalize on the possibilities offered by the emergence of a superior new substitute technology, they vigorously defend their position through the accelerated improvement of the old technology.
>
> (Rothwell and Zegveld 1985: 41)

'Political lock-in'

The economic development of the Ruhr along its historical trajectory was effectively supported by cooperative relations between industry, the government of the federal state (*Land*) of North Rhine-Westphalia, regional and local planning authorities, unions, and professional associations. The politico-administrative system kept the region effectively on course, even when this course became a dead-end. This

264   *Limits of networks*

political support had been mainly related to physical infrastructure. During the 1970s, however, several programmes were launched to support the coal, iron, and steel complex directly. The programme for North Rhine-Westphalia (*Nordrhein-Westfalen-Programm*, 1975), as well as highly endowed technology programmes (*Technologieprogramm Bergbau*, *Technologieprogramm Energie*, and *Technologieprogrammem Stahl*) were focused primarily on subsidies for the coal, iron, and steel complex. Altogether, these programmes supplied to R&D projects on core technologies of the coal, iron, and steel complex approximately DM2.6b (Simonis 1989: 356).

The highly cooperative relations between industry and the politico-administrative system petrified to a pre-*perestroika* culture of consensus. For decades, this culture, shaped by rather conservative social democrats, conservative unions, and patriarchal industrialists, remained unchallenged. The close formal and informal relations among these groups, which were colloquially labelled *Filz* (venality), led to a strong alliance supporting the coal, iron, and steel complex. The cohesiveness of this alliance was reinforced by emphatic appeals to the specific 'production mission' of the Ruhr within the national economy (Heinze, Hilbert, and Voelzkow 1989: 79). The specific regional 'production mission' also provided the ideological background for blocking the settlement of new industries. While the leading industrialists aimed at protecting their monopsony position on the regional labour market, the unions and the social democrats tried to maintain the cultural coherence and homogeneity that produced 'resonance' among workers – a basis for solidarity (Friedman 1977: 53). For both the unions and the social democrats, support of the coal, iron, and steel complex during the 1970s turned more and more into a desperate defence of their political base, for which they had pushed through high wages and high labour standards. Certainly, this is not to blame them for pursuing their policy but to indicate how the symbiotic relations between the politico-administrative system and industry obstructed a timely reorganization of the Ruhr and paralysed political innovation (Kunzmann 1986: 413).

THE DIALECTICS OF ADAPTATION AND ADAPTABILITY: A THEORETICAL CONCLUSION

The production pattern of close interfirm linkages embedded in strong personal relations and supported by a tightly knit politico-administrative system reflected the perfect adaptation of the Ruhr to a specific economic environment. The crisis of the Ruhr, however, illustrates how perfect adaptation to a specific economic environment may undermine a region's adaptability. If adaptation and adaptability are not necessarily positively correlated, the success stories of today's industrial districts could also indicate the challenges they may face in the future. In any case, the relevance of the dialectics of adaptation and adaptability for the successful industrial districts of today cannot simply be neglected by saying that the Ruhr never has been nor ever will be an industrial district in the Marshallian sense (which is claimed in this chapter only for polemic purposes). In the case of the Italian industrial districts, however, some rather superficial observations could be interpreted as potential threats to the regional adaptability. First, innovation in the industrial districts seems to be concerned mainly with improvements of the production process rather than with major product developments (Bianchi, forthcoming). Second, at least in the less urbanized industrial districts such as Marche and Abruzzi, the firms often produce for a few, large subcontractors or wholesalers and, consequently, lack boundary-spanning functions (Amin and Robins 1990: 199). Finally, cultural coherence and corporatist relations at the local level (Trigilia 1989) may also give rise to inertia that restricts regional adaptability.

Adaptation endangers adaptability through processes of 'involution'. Adaptation leads to an increasing specialization of resources and a pronounced preference for innovations that reproduce existing structures. And while the system optimizes the 'fit' into its environment, it loses its adaptability. Ultimately, the internal coherence of the system results in a 'pathological homeostasis'. The system loses its ability to reorganize its internal structure in order to cope with unpredictable changes in the environment (Maruyama 1963). Adaptability crucially depends on the availability of unspecific and uncommitted capacities that can be put to a variety of unforeseeable uses: redundancy. Redundancy enables social systems not just to adapt to specific environmental changes but to question the appropriateness of adaptation. It is this kind of self-questioning ability that underpins the activities of systems capable of learning to learn and self-organize (Bateson 1972). The essential difference between the adaptive type and self-organizing type of learning is sometimes identified in terms of a distinction between 'single-loop' and 'double-loop' learning (Argyris and Schon 1978). Single-loop learning allows systems

1 to scan and monitor significant aspects of the environment;
2 to compare this information against operating norms; and
3 to initiate corrective actions when discrepancies are detected.

Single-loop learning is essentially the intelligence of a thermostat.

266   *Limits of networks*

However, the learning abilities thus defined are limited in that the system can maintain only the course of action determined by the operating norms and standards guiding it. This is fine as long as the action defined by those standards is appropriate for dealing with the changes encountered. But when this is not the case, the process of negative feedback eventually promotes an inappropriate pattern of behaviour. This is the story of the overcompensatory response to the decline of the Ruhr. In a sense, this story demonstrates 'that highly sophisticated single-loop learning systems may actually serve to keep the organization on the wrong course, since people are not prepared to challenge underlying assumptions' (Morgan 1986: 90). It is the ability to question the appropriateness of behaviour that distinguishes double-loop from single-loop learning systems. The self-questioning and self-organizing ability of the coal, iron, and steel complex of the Ruhr was restricted by a production pattern of rigid and intensive interfirm linkages. The more this production pattern adapted to its specific environment, the more redundancy was eliminated on the regional level. Analogously, the coherence of the political alliance supporting the coal, iron, and steel complex prevented constructive conflict and debate over the pursued strategy.

REORGANIZATION: CONVERSION OR SUBSTITUTION?

The lock-in of the coal, iron, and steel complex prevented an appropriate and timely reorganization of the Ruhr. The dramatic aggravation of the crisis in the early 1980s, however, broke this lock-in. Plant closures and a shift of economic activities to the prosperous south of West Germany were the most obvious signs of an incipient reorganization triggered by repeated sharp downturns in demand for steel. For example, the oldest firm of the coal, iron, and steel complex of the Ruhr, Gutehoffnungshütte (founded in 1758) transferred its headquarters and R&D department from the Ruhr town of Oberhausen to one of the major centres of Germany's electronics industry, Munich. In all, the old steel firms have cut more than 60,000 jobs since 1980 (Heinze, Hilbert, and Voelzkow 1989: 33). Symptomatically, the historically dominant interpretations and world views were not modified gradually; they were abruptly replaced by new world views. All of a sudden, the short cyclical fluctuations in demand in the 1970s were recognized as structural changes. Firms of the Ruhr considered themselves no longer part of the coal, iron, and steel complex but as 'technology firms'. Although the billboard jargon of business reports and political rhetoric overstated the factual extent of innovation, leading Ruhr firms made considerable progress in reorganizing their business and their interfirm relations. They began to reduce the 'steel' divisions in favour of new fields of production with a significantly higher value-added component. The strategic reorientation of former steel companies towards new markets can be observed especially in the development of revenue shares accounted for by the 'processing' divisions (see Table 12.1).

Table 12.1 Shares of central divisions in total sales of the five most important steel enterprises in western Germany (in percentages)

		1970	1980	1986
Thyssen[1]	Steel	60.3	37.8	35.9
	Nonsteel	39.7	62.2·	64.1
	of which processing	4.2	22.5	23.7
Krupp[2]	Steel	31.9	36.3	27.6
	Nonsteel	68.1	63.7	72.2
	of which processing	34.0	36.5	47.0
Mannesmann[3]	Steel	43.9	30.4	25.1
	Nonsteel	56.1	69.4	74.9
	of which processing	23.8	43.9	53.8
Klöckner	Steel	60.7	60.8	49.5
	Nonsteel	39.3	39.2	50.5
	of which processing	28.3	38.8	49.5
Hoesch[4]	Steel		40.5	40.9
	Nonsteel		59.5	59.1
	of which processing		33.3	38.4

Source: Grabher (1991: 68)
Notes:
1   Until 30 September 1975, Thyssen-Gruppe; thereafter Thyssen-Welt.
2   Steel, including about 50 per cent high-grade steel.
3   Only pipes to be subsumed under steel; 1970: domestic corporation; as of 1975: global corporation.
4   Until 1981, together with Estel.

Thus, Thyssen alone, the largest of the former steel companies, increased the revenue share of its processing division from 4.2 per cent to 23.7 per cent between 1970 and 1986. During the same period, the steel division was reduced from 60.3 per cent to 35.9 per cent. Another firm of the coal, iron, and steel complex, Mannesmann, increased its processing division between 1970 and 1986 from 23.8 per cent to 53.8 per cent. Of course, the situation varied from company to company, but

268   Limits of networks

plant engineering, environmental technology, mechanical engineering, and electronics were the sectors at the centre of the strategic reorientation. Plant engineering, in particular, was traditionally part of the production range of large steel enterprises, though initially it was limited to serving the needs of the maintenance and repair departments within the enterprise. With the reduction of steel capacity to a level that no longer allowed the full utilization of these maintenance and repair departments, companies began marketing their plant-engineering know-how externally (Geer 1985: 86). This led to an organizational differentiation and decentralization that was oriented to product markets rather than to internal production processes.

The steel companies did not enter the field of environmental technology primarily on the basis of an explicit marketing strategy. Rather, the plant-engineering divisions were confronted by the requirements of customers who had to adhere to new environment regulations. These customers figured large as 'lead users' (Von Hippel 1988). Their experience with the operation of pilot plants directly flew in the face of research and development process of the producer. The exchange of ideas between user and producer contributed considerably to the final design of the plants. Although this 'user-producer interaction' (Lundvall 1988) triggered innovation, it reinforced a concentration of resources upon specific problems of the coal, iron, and steel complex. The cooperation with the traditional clientele resulted repeatedly in products based on 'end-of-pipe technologies' aimed at mitigating already existing environmental problems. Cases in point are filtration plants and decontamination plants designed by Ruhr firms to repair environmental damage caused by Ruhr firms. To give an impression, in North Rhine-Westphalia, the *Land* in which the Ruhr is located, more than 8,500 areas are laden with noxious substances. These areas consist mainly of former mining and steel mill sites that are concentrated in the Ruhr. More than 80 per cent of all sites of the regional real estate pool of the Ruhr (*Grundstücksfond Ruhr*) are suspected of containing noxious substances (Minister für Wirtschaft, Mittelstand und Technologie des Landes Nordrhein-Westfalen 1988: 7).

Doubtless, environmental regulations such as the new water and soil protection regulations will transform these environmental problems too into effective demand for the end-of-pipe technologies supplied by the Ruhr firms. Investment in end-of-pipe technologies, however, is generally considered a transition stage. In the long run, the costly *ex-post* reduction of pollution with end-of-pipe technologies will be replaced by production processes that prevent environmental pollution in the first place. This bias towards end-of-pipe technologies refers primarily to the reorganizing of old steel companies. The environmental technology complex of the Ruhr, however, is not confined to reorganizing old firms. About half of the firms that have entered the market for environmental technology since 1981 are newly founded firms. And most important, more than 50 per cent of the firms founded since 1987 are mainly concerned with pollution-preventing technologies (IFO 1988: 5). Thus, the end-of-pipe technology bias of the reorganizing old firms is partially offset by newly founded firms.

In all, the environmental technology complex of North Rhine-Westphalia accounts for more than 600 firms, totalling about 100,000 jobs, as compared to approximately 300,000 jobs in the coal, iron, and steel complex, which still represents about 40 per cent of all industrial jobs (GEWOS, GfAH, and WSI 1988). However, more essential than the sheer size of the environmental technology complex is its internal structure. According to the diagnosis of the lock-in of the coal, iron, and steel complex, regional adaptability depends basically on the redundancy embedded in the regional production pattern. In fact, as preliminary empirical evidence suggests (IFO 1988; Heinze, Hilbert, and Voelzkow 1989; Grabher 1991), the environmental technology complex seems to be less prone to lock-in effects than the coal, iron, and steel complex is, because redundancy is provided by loosely coupled networks of relatively autonomous firms.

LOOSENING TIES: REDUNDANCY WITHIN NETWORKS

Redundancy on the firm level: relative autonomy

Cooperation in plant engineering and environmental technology is typically arranged as consortia. Large firms act as 'general contractors' that offer integrated system solutions, from the conception of plants and equipment to their maintenance and servicing. Since plant engineering and environmental technology are customized individual production, it would not be rational from the point of view of the general contractor to maintain resources for solving clients' specific problems. Rather, general contractors attempt to deal with their clients' widely varying demands, such as those in the areas of control systems and complex plant components, by cooperating with specialized firms. The strategic know-how of plant engineers, as a Krupp manager has put it, consists precisely in 'knowing the right project partner for each problem'. The general contractors are responsible for the financial expenditure connected with the planning and management of large projects, costs that would pose an insuperable barrier to market entry

270   *Limits of networks*

No. of firms

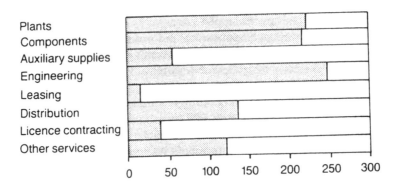

Figure 12.3   Profile of suppliers of environmental technology in North Rhine-
Westphalia
Source: IFO (Institut für Wirtschaftsforschung) (1988: 3)

for single firms, especially small ones. The cooperating partners of the
general contractors add their highly specialized competence to the
planning and realization of the projects. In North Rhine-Westphalia,
approximately 220 firms of the environmental technology complex are
suppliers of special components (see Figure 12.3).

  In contrast to the coal, iron, and steel complex, the cooperating firms
of the general contractors have to be well equipped with their own
boundary-spanning and strategic entrepreneurial functions, that is,
R&D and marketing. The role of cooperating firms consists not simply
of supplying components produced according to the blueprints of the
general contractors: it is also to develop solutions for problems that are
only roughly specified by the general contractors and that evolve only
in the course of the planning and production phase. Obviously, only
firms with their own research and engineering capacities are able to
meet this high demand for flexibility. This applies especially with
respect to mechanical engineering of high complexity and microelec-
tronic control systems, areas that account for about 50 per cent of the
orders in plant engineering (see Table 12.2). The relative functional
autonomy and broad problem-solving capacities of the cooperating
firms provide redundancy on the firm level. The relative functional
autonomy of individual firms, especially with regard to the boundary-
spanning functions R&D and marketing, encourages the openness and

reflectivity of the entire network since information stemming from different sources and evaluated against different backgrounds flow together.

Table 12.2 Structure of orders in plant engineering (shares in total volume of orders)

(a)	30% plant infrastructure
(b)	20% steel engineering and machine components of low complexity
(c)	20% mechanical engineering of high complexity
(d)	30% control systems and system know-how

Source: Expert interview at Krupp, 23 May 1988

Redundancy on the regional level: loose coupling

Cooperation in the environmental technology complex differs in a second important aspect from cooperation in the coal, iron, and steel complex. The specific characteristics of plant engineering and environmental technology do not allow for the intensive and rigid interfirm linkages that characterize the coal, iron, and steel complex. Rather, firms are 'loosely coupled' in networks. From the perspective of the general contractors, there are several arguments against having highly dependent project partners.

First, such partners will be threatened in their existence as soon as cooperative relations are interrupted, even if this is only for a short time. Interruptions, however, are characteristic of plant engineering because demand is rather discontinuous. Yet the loss of project partners entails high costs in searching for new partners for cooperation.

Second, the general contractors offer their clients not only hardware but also 'co-specialized assets' permitting the greatest possible degree of utilization of the capital-intensive plants (Teece 1986). Above all, these co-specialized assets include training of the plant operators, maintenance services, and spare-part guarantees. Since these co-specialized assets would also have to be provided by the project partners, the interest that general contractors have in the stability of their cooperation partners becomes understandable.

Finally, if project partners cooperate with several partners, it will allow general contractors to realize economies of scale. Individual system components can be offered at a cheaper rate if utilized repeatedly.

Loosely coupled networks create opportunities for sharing the learning experience of cooperating partners that results from their exchange relations with third parties. Loose coupling thus increases the

272   *Limits of networks*

learning capacity of networks: 'The premise that all economic exchanges must also be occasions for reciprocal learning implies that the
parties anticipate problems, and that the problems will be solved
jointly' (Sabel, Herrigel, Deeg, and Kazis 1989: 389). Moreover, one of
the key advantages of loosely coupled networks is their ability to
disseminate and interpret new information. Information passed through
networks is 'thicker' than information obtained in the market, and
'freer' than information communicated in a hierarchy (Kaneko and
Imai 1987). An innovation 'can reach a larger number of people, and
traverse greater social distance . . . when passed through weak ties
rather than strong' (Granovetter 1973: 1366). Loosely coupled networks are particularly adept at generating new interpretations. It is this
ability to generate new interpretations that is essential to the region's
capacity for self-organization and learning to learn.

RESISTING ECONOMISTIC TEMPTATIONS: A POLITICAL CONCLUSION

As Weick emphasizes,

> loosely coupled systems may be elegant solutions to the problem that
> adaptation can preclude adaptability. . . . In loosely coupled systems
> where the identity, uniqueness, and separateness of elements is
> preserved, the system potentially can retain a greater number of
> mutations and novel solutions than would be the case with a tightly
> coupled system. A loosely coupled system could preserve more
> 'cultural insurance' to be drawn upon in times of radical change than
> in the case for more tightly coupled systems.
>
> (Weick 1976: 7)

This cultural insurance is provided by investments in redundancy.
However, purely market-oriented considerations will most probably
result in low investment in redundancy because of the difficulties of
calculating their future returns: 'the economistic temptation'.

> Redundant capacities are difficult to build in markets and through, or
> against, hierarchies, even if investing in them would open up
> superior market opportunities. . . . To the extent that indiv-
> idual interests are not sufficiently instructive for investment in
> redundant capacities, following such interests may be the same as
> violating them – by letting present, short-term, defensive oppor-
> tunism deprive actors of their capacity for future, long-term, offensive
> opportunism.
>
> (Streeck 1991: 36)

In the absence of conclusive market signals as to where redundant capacities are best developed, their generation calls for regional policy that redefines incentives and disincentives of regional actors and actively provides redundancy.

At least two decisive steps towards the encouragement of redundancy have been taken by the Ruhr and the *Land* North Rhine-Westphalia in the last few years. First, Ruhr politics traditionally focused on a single target. For decades, politics for the coal, iron, and steel complex reflected the self-conception of the dominant coalition that the Ruhr had a special 'production mission' within the national economy. This ideology gave way to an increasing differentiation of political targets. This reorientation was first indicated by the Ruhr programme (*Aktions-programm Ruhr*) and later deepened by a further technology pro-gramme (*Technologieprogramm Wirtschaft*) and the *Land* initiative for future technologies (*Landesinitiative Zukunftstechnologien*). These programmes are not simply aimed at substituting the support of environmental technologies for the support of the coal, iron, and steel complex; they also cover a broad range of related technology areas. Second, the new Ruhr programmes reveal a shift from a centralized approach based on financial transfer to a decentralized approach including real transfer. The future initiative for the coal, iron, and steel region (*Zukunftsinitiative Montanregion*) marked this shift in instrum-ental design clearly. Achievement of this initiative's aims – support of innovation and qualification, modernization of infrastructure, and improvement of environmental conditions – is left to the local level. Political and financial support is thus no longer allocated to specific programmes but to specific projects that involve a rather broad range of actors at the local and regional level.

Whereas the traditional attitude was to produce master plans with a single clear-cut target, the new programmes focus on 'enabling con-ditions'. Above all, this orientation is manifested in the attempts to improve the regional infrastructure supporting institutions involved in the transfer of information and know-how. In fact, the Ruhr has made considerable headway in developing its support infrastructure in recent years. Information and innovative services are provided by the Centre for Innovation and Technology in North Rhine-Westphalia (*ZENIT*), community-owned technology centres such as the *Technologiezentrum Dortmund*, information centres of trade associations such as the Chambers of Commerce and Industry (*Industrie-und Handelskammer*) and the Chambers of Crafts (*Handwerkskammer*), information centres of the unions, and the transfer institutions of the universities.

However, a transformation of this infrastructure into an effective

274   *Limits of networks*

support system for loosely coupled networks seems to depend on two
basic conditions. First, the efficacy and efficiency of this support
infrastructure is not determined by the mere number and variety of
institutions providing innovative services. In other words, the performance of the regional support infrastructure cannot simply be
improved through the continued formation of new institutions. Only
when these institutions are linked together do their individual information supplies and problem-solving capacities add up to a support
infrastructure with a high level of redundancy. After all, connectivity
creates a much greater degree of cross-connection and exchange of
information than may be needed at any given time. It is exactly this
kind of redundant institutional infrastructure that seems appropriate for
the initiation and support of loosely coupled networks. Linking together these institutions increases the knowledge about complementarities in regional industry, for these institutions are mostly concerned with a specific clientele. The association of the Chambers of
Crafts, for example, is by definition assigned to serve small craft firms.
Thus, linking different institutions may uncover potentials for cooperation between firms of different size and technological specialization. Bringing together firms with complementary resources and
abilities seems to be especially important in the area of environmental
technology and plant engineering:

> They come closest to representing a production type of the future
> which brings together components of different sectors and contribu-
> tions from various areas of technology in an interdisciplinary fashion
> and further develops them into tailor-made applied solutions.
>   (GEWOS, GfAH, and WSI 1988: 151)

Second, the formation of new regional institutions and the thickening of
the regional infrastructure have cast doubts on its efficiency. These
doubts underlie the recommendations to streamline the regional infrastructure in order to reduce overlapping responsibilities and problem-
solving capacities. However, streamlining the infrastructure according
to a narrow economistic logic of efficiency may have counterproductive
effects because 'the fragmented, overlapping and seemingly redundant
character of the public and private institutional network . . . is, paradoxically, the most efficient way to provide services to decentralized
production', as Herrigel (chapter 11: 232) concludes from his analysis of
Germany's most successful regional economy, Baden-Württemberg.

   Probably one of the major challenges for the long-term future of the
Ruhr is to resist the economistic temptation of rigidly streamlining
industry and the politico-administrative system in order to optimize the

fit to a specific economic environment. As the decline of the coal, iron, and steel complex has demonstrated, adaptation may lock a region into its trajectory and undermine its ability to learn and self-organize, that is, it may lead that region into the trap of rigid specialization. The Ruhr did not suffer from a lack of external adaptation, nor of internal coherence. On the contrary, it suffered from a pre-*perestroika* consensus culture, from a lack of constructive conflict, and creative chaos. Perhaps one should bear this in mind when reading accounts that stress the superior adaptation and internal coherence of the successful regional economies of today.

NOTE

I would like to thank Peter Auer, Michael Best, Egon Matzner, Michael Piore, Woody Powell, and Günther Schmid for their suggestions and warnings.

REFERENCES

Aldrich, H. E. (1979) *Organizations and Environments*, Englewood Cliffs, NJ: Prentice-Hall.

Amin, A. (1989) 'Specialization without growth: small footwear firms in Naples', in E. Goodman, J. Bamford, and P. Saynor (eds) *Small Firms and Industrial Districts in Italy*, London: Routledge, 239–59.

Amin, A. and Robins, K. (1990) 'Industrial districts and regional development: limits and possibilities', in F. Pyke, W. Sengenberger, and G. Becattini (eds) *Industrial Districts and Inter-Firm Cooperation in Italy*, Geneva: International Institute for Labour Studies, 185–220.

Argyris, C. and Schon, D. A. (1978) *Organizational Learning: A Theory of Action Perspective*, Reading, MA: Addison-Wesley.

Bateson, G. (1972) *Steps to an Ecology of Mind*, New York: Ballantine Books.

Becattini, G. (1989) 'Sectors and/or districts: some remarks on the conceptual foundations of industrial economics', in E. Goodman, J. Bamford, and P. Saynor (eds) *Small Firms and Industrial Districts in Italy*, London: Routledge, 123–36.

Bianchi, G. (forthcoming) 'Innovation and spatial systems of small and medium-sized enterprises', in G. Sweeny (ed.) *Strategies for Local Economic Development*, London: Taylor & Francis.

Elster, J. (1979) *Ulysses and the Sirens*, Cambridge: Cambridge University Press.

Friedman, A. (1977) *Industry and Labour: Class Struggle at Work and Monopoly Capitalism*, London: Macmillan.

Geer, T. (1985) 'Internationaler Wettbewerb und regionale Entwicklung: Preisunempfindliche Branchen', *Nordrhein-Westfalen in der Krise – Krise in Nordrhein-Westfalen?* Schriftenreihe des Rheinisch-Westfälischen Instituts für Wirtschaftsforschung Essen, Neue Folge 46, Berlin: Duncker & Humblot, 83–99.

GEWOS, GfAH, and WSI (1988) 'Strukturwandel und Beschäftigungs-

276   *Limits of networks*

perspektiven der Metallindustrie an der Ruhr', final report, Hamburg.

Grabher, G. (1988) *De-Industrialisierung oder Neo-Industrialisierung? Innovationsprozesse und Innovationspolitik in traditionellen Industrieregionen*, Berlin: Edition Sigma.

—— (1991) 'Against de-industrialization: a strategy for old industrial areas', in E. Matzner and W. Streeck (eds) *Beyond Keynesianism: The Socio-Economics of Production and Full Employment*, Aldershot: Edward Elgar, 62–81.

Granovetter, M. (1973) 'The strength of weak ties', *American Journal of Sociology* 78, 6: 1360–80.

—— (1985) 'Economic action and social structure: the problem of embeddedness', *American Journal of Sociology* 91, 8: 481–510.

—— (1990) 'Entrepreneurship, development, and the emergence of firms', Discussion Paper FS I-90-2, Wissenschaftszentrum Berlin für Sozialforschung.

Heinze, R. G., Hilbert, J., and Voelzkow, H. (1989) 'Strukturwandel und Strukturpolitik in Nordrhein-Westfalen', unpublished manuscript, Institut Arbeit und Technik, Wissenschaftszentrum Nordrhein-Westfalen, Gelsenkirchen.

Herrigel, G. B. (1989) 'Industrial order and the politics of industrial change: mechanical engineering in the Federal Republic of Germany', in P. Katzenstein (ed.) *Industry and Politics in West Germany. Toward the Third Republic*, Ithaca, NY: Cornell University Press, 185–221.

IFO (Institut für Wirtschaftsforschung) (1988) 'Das Angebot der nordrhein-westfälischen Wirtschaft auf dem Umweltschutzmarkt. Ausgewählte Ergebnisse einer schriftlichen Erhebung vom Frühjahr 1988', unpublished manuscript, Munich.

Junkernheinrich, M. (1989) 'Ökonomische Erneuerung alter Industrieregionen: Das Beispiel Ruhrgebiet', *Wirtschaftsdienst* 69, 1: 28–35.

Kaneko, I., and Imai, K. (1987) 'A network view of the firm', paper presented at the 1st Hitotsubashi-Stanford Conference, Hitotsubashi University, Tokyo.

Kunzmann, K. R. (1986) 'Structural problems of an old industrial area: the case of the Ruhr district', in W. H. Goldberg (ed.) *Ailing Steel: The Transoceanic Quarrel*, Aldershot: Gower, 409–37.

Lehner, F., Nordhause-Janz, J., and Schubert, K. (1990) 'Probleme und Perspektiven des Strukturwandels der Bergbau-Zulieferindustrie', unpublished manuscript, Institut Arbeit und Technik, Wissenschaftszentrum Nordrhein-Westfalen, Gelsenkirchen.

Lundvall, B.-A. (1988) 'Innovation as an interactive process: from user–producer interaction to the national system of innovation', in G. Dosi, C. Freeman, R. Nelson, G. Silverberg, and L. Soete (eds) *Technical Change and Economic Theory*, London: Pinter, 349–70.

Marshall, A. (1927) (1st edn 1919) *Industry and Trade*, London: Macmillan.

—— (1986) (1st edn 1890) *Principles of Economics*, London: Macmillan.

Maruyama, M. (1963) 'The second cybernetics: deviation-amplifying mutual causal process', *American Scientist* 51: 164–79.

Minister für Wirtschaft, Mittelstand und Technologie des Landes Nordrhein-Wesfalen (1988) *Neues im Westen: Stellenwert der Umwelttechnologien in der NRW-Wirtschaftsstruktur*, Düsseldorf.

Morgan, G. (1986) *Images of Organization*, Beverly Hills, CA: Sage.

The weakness of strong ties 277

Müller, G. (1989) 'Strukturwandel und Beschäftigungsperspektiven an der Ruhr', *WSI-Mitteilungen* 4: 188–97.

Pezzini, M. (1989) 'The small-firm economy's odd man out: the case of Ravenna', in E. Goodman, J. Bamford, and P. Saynor (eds) *Small Firms and Industrial Districts in Italy*, London: Routledge, 223–39.

Pichierri, A. (1986) 'Diagnosis and strategy in the decline of the European steel industry', Discussion Paper IIM/LMP 86–22, Forschungsschwerpunkt Arbeitsmarkt und Beschäftigung, Wissenschaftszentrum Berlin für Sozialforschung.

Rothwell, R. and Zegveld, W. (1985) *Reindustrialization and Technology*, Harlow: Longman.

Sabel, C. F., Herrigel, G. B., Deeg, R., and Kazis, R. (1989) 'Regional prosperities compared: Massachusetts and Baden-Württemberg in the 1980's', *Economy and Society* 18, 4: 374–405.

Schlieper, A. (1986) *150 Jahre Ruhrgebiet – Ein Kapitel deutscher Wirtschaftsgeschichte*, Düsseldorf: Schwann.

Schröter, L. (1986) '"Steelworks now!" The conflicting character of modernisation: a case study of Hoesch in Dortmund', in W. H. Goldberg (ed.) *Ailing Steel: The Transoceanic Quarrel*, Aldershot: Gower, 361–409.

Simonis, G. (1989) 'Modernisierungspolitik in Nordrhein-Westfalen: Vollbeschäftigung als Vision', in J. Hucke and H. Wollmann (eds) *Dezentrale Technologiepolitik?* Basel: Birkhäuser, 348–77.

Streeck, W. (1991) 'On the social and political conditions of diversified quality production', in E. Matzner and W. Streeck (eds) *Beyond Keynesianism: The Socio-Economics of Production and Full Employment*, Aldershot: Edward Elgar, 21–62.

Teece, D. (1986) 'Firm boundaries, technological innovation, and strategic management', in L. G. Thomas (ed.) *The Economics of Strategic Planning*, Lexington, MA: Lexington Books, 187–201.

Trigilia, C. (1989) 'Small firm development and political subcultures in Italy', in E. Goodman, J. Bamford, and P. Saynor (eds) *Small Firms and Industrial Districts in Italy*, London: Routledge, 174–98.

Von Hippel, E. (1988) *The Sources of Innovation*, Oxford: Oxford University Press.

Wegener, B. (1987) 'Vom Nutzen entfernter Bekannter', *Kölner Zeitschrift für Soziologie und Sozialpsychologie* 39: 278–301.

Weick, K. E. (1976) 'Educational organizations as loosely coupled systems', *Administrative Science Quarterly* 21: 1–26.

[20]

Social Structure and
Competition in Interfirm
Networks: The Paradox
of Embeddedness

Brian Uzzi
Northwestern University

The purpose of this work is to develop a systematic
understanding of embeddedness and organization
networks. Drawing on ethnographic fieldwork conducted
at 23 entrepreneurial firms, I identify the components of
embedded relationships and explicate the devices by
which embeddedness shapes organizational and economic outcomes. The findings suggest that embeddedness is a logic of exchange that promotes economies of
time, integrative agreements, Pareto improvements in
allocative efficiency, and complex adaptation. These
positive effects rise up to a threshold, however, after
which embeddedness can derail economic performance
by making firms vulnerable to exogenous shocks or
insulating them from information that exists beyond their
network. A framework is proposed that explains how
these properties vary with the quality of social ties, the
structure of the organization network, and an organization's structural position in the network.[•]

Research on embeddedness is an exciting area in sociology
and economics because it advances our understanding of
how social structure affects economic life. Polanyi (1957)
used the concept of embeddedness to describe the social
structure of modern markets, while Schumpeter (1950) and
Granovetter (1985) revealed its robust effect on economic
action, particularly in the context of interfirm networks,
stimulating research on industrial districts (Leung, 1993;
Lazerson, 1995), marketing channels (Moorman, Zaltman,
and Deshponde, 1992), immigrant enterprise (Portes and
Sensenbrenner, 1993), entrepreneurship (Larson, 1992),
lending relationships (Podolny, 1994; Sterns and Mizruchi,
1993; Abolafia, 1996), location decisions (Romo and
Schwartz, 1995), acquisitions (Palmer et al., 1995), and organizational adaptation (Baum and Oliver, 1992; Uzzi, 1996).

The notion that economic action is embedded in social
structure has revived debates about the positive and
negative effects of social relations on economic behavior.
While most organization theorists hold that social structure
plays a significant role in economic behavior, many economic
theorists maintain that social relations minimally affect
economic transacting or create inefficiencies by shielding the
transaction from the market (Peterson and Rajan, 1994).
These conflicting views indicate a need for more research on
how social structure facilitates or derails economic action. In
this regard, Granovetter's (1985) embeddedness argument
has emerged as a potential theory for joining economic and
sociological approaches to organization theory. As presently
developed, however, Granovetter's argument usefully
explicates the differences between economic and sociological schemes of economic behavior but lacks its own concrete account of how social relations affect economic
exchange. The fundamental statement that economic action
is embedded in ongoing social ties that at times facilitate
and at times derail exchange suffers from a theoretical
indefiniteness. Thus, although embeddedness purports to
explain some forms of economic action better than do pure
economic accounts, its implications are indeterminate
because of the imbalance between the relatively specific
propositions of economic theories and the broad statements

© 1997 by Cornell University.
0001-8392/97/4201-0035/$1.00.

•

Financial assistance from the NSF (Grants
SES-9200960 and SES-9348848), the
Sigma Xi Scientific Research Society, and
the Institute of Social Analysis—SUNY at
Stony Brook made this research possible.
Unpublished portions of this paper have
been awarded the 1991 American
Sociological Association's James D.
Thompson Award, the 1993 Society for
the Advancement of Socio-Economics
Best Paper Prize, and the 1994 Academy
of Management's Louis Pondy Dissertation Prize. I thank Jerry Davis, James
Gillespie, Mark Lazerson, Marika Lind-
holm, Willie Ocasio, Michael Schwartz,
Frank Romo, Marc Ventresca, the *ASQ*
editors and anonymous reviewers, and
especially Roberto Fernandez for helpful
comments on earlier drafts of this paper.

about how social ties shape economic and collective action.

This work aims to develop one of perhaps multiple specifications of embeddedness, a concept that has been used to refer broadly to the contingent nature of economic action with respect to cognition, social structure, institutions, and culture. Zukin and DiMaggio (1990) classified embeddedness into four forms: structural, cognitive, political, and cultural. The last three domains of embeddedness primarily reflect social constructionist perspectives on embeddedness, whereas structural embeddedness is principally concerned with how the quality and network architecture of material exchange relationships influence economic activity. In this paper, I limit my analysis to the concept of structural embeddedness.

THE PROBLEM OF EMBEDDEDNESS AND ECONOMIC ACTION

Powell's (1990) analysis of the sociological and economic literatures on exchange suggests that transactions can take place through loose collections of individuals who maintain impersonal and constantly shifting exchange ties, as in markets, or through stable networks of exchange partners who maintain close social relationships. The key distinction between these systems is the structure and quality of exchange ties, because these factors shape expectations and opportunities.

The neoclassical formulation is often taken as the baseline theory for the study of interfirm relationships because it embodies the core principles of most economic approaches (Wilson, 1989). In the ideal-type atomistic market, exchange partners are linked by arm's-length ties. Self-interest motivates action, and actors regularly switch to new buyers and sellers to take advantage of new entrants or avoid dependence. The exchange itself is limited to price data, which supposedly distill all the information needed to make efficient decisions, especially when there are many buyers and sellers or transactions are nonspecific. Personal relationships are cool and atomistic; if ongoing ties or implicit contracts exist between parties, it is believed to be more a matter of self-interested, profit-seeking behavior than willful commitment or altruistic attachment (Macneil, 1978). Accordingly, arm's-length ties facilitate performance because firms disperse their business among many competitors, widely sampling prices and avoiding small-numbers bargaining situations that can entrap them in inefficient relationships (Hirschman, 1970). Although some economists have recognized that the conclusion that markets are efficient becomes suspect when the idealization of theoretical cases is abandoned, they nonetheless have tended to regard the idealized model as giving a basically correct view and have paid scant attention to instances that diverge from the ideal (Krugman, 1986).

At the other end of the exchange continuum are embedded relationships, and here a well-defined theory of embeddedness and interfirm networks has yet to emerge. Instead, findings from numerous empirical studies suggest that embedded exchanges have several distinctive features. Research has shown that network relationships in the

Paradox of Embeddedness

Japanese auto and Italian knitwear industries are characterized by trust and personal ties, rather than explicit contracts,
and that these features make expectations more predictable
and reduce monitoring costs (Dore, 1983; Asanuma, 1985;
Smitka, 1991; Gerlach, 1992). Helper (1990) found that close
supplier-manufacturer relationships in the auto industry are
distinctive for their "thick" information exchange of tacit and
proprietary know-how, while Larson (1992) and Lazerson
(1995) found that successful entrepreneurial business
networks are typified by coordination devices that promote
knowledge transfer and learning. Romo and Schwartz's
(1995) and Dore's (1983) findings concerning the embeddedness of firms in regional production networks suggest that
embedded actors satisfice rather than maximize on price and
shift their focus from the narrow economically rational goal
of winning immediate gain and exploiting dependency to
cultivating long-term, cooperative ties. The basic conjecture
of this literature is that embeddedness creates economic
opportunities that are difficult to replicate via markets,
contracts, or vertical integration.

To a limited degree, revisionist economic frameworks have
attempted to explain the above outcomes by redefining
embeddedness in terms of transaction cost, agency, or
game theory concepts. Like their neoclassical parent,
however, these schemes do not explicitly recognize or
model social structure but, rather, apply conventional
economic constructs to organizational behavior, bypassing
the issues central to organization theorists.[1] Transaction cost
economics, for example, has usefully revised our understanding of when nonmarket transactions will arise, yet
because its focus is on dyadic relations, network dynamics
"are given short shrift" (Williamson, 1994: 85). Transaction
cost economics also displays a bias toward describing
opportunistic rather than cooperative relations in its assumption that, irrespective of the social relationship between a
buyer and seller, if the transaction degenerates into a
small-numbers bargaining situation, then the buyer or seller
will opportunistically squeeze above-market rents or shirk,
whichever is in his or her self-interest (Ghoshal and Moran,
1996).

Agency theory also focuses mainly on self-interested human
nature, dyadic principal-agent ties, and the use of formal
controls to explain exchange, rather than on an account of
embeddedness. For example, Larson's (1992) study of
interfirm exchange relationships revealed agency theory's
limited ability to explain network forms of organization when
she showed that there is a lack of control and monitoring
devices between firms, that the roles of principal and agent
blur and shift, and that incentives are jointly set. Similarly,
team theory is pressed to explain interfirm exchange
relations because of its assumption that group members
have identical interests, an unrealistic assumption when
formal rule structures (a hierarchy) do not exist or group
members both cooperate and compete for resources, as in
the case of manufacturer-supplier networks (Cyert and
March, 1992).

Game theory can accommodate *N*-person, network-like
structures, yet the core argument—that selfish players will

1
My intent is not to critique revisionist
economic approaches or contrast all their
similarities and differences with network
perspectives (see Burt, 1992; Zajac and
Olsen, 1993; Ghoshal and Moran, 1996).
Rather, I review the main points of
existing critiques to show that the
features of embeddedness cannot be
adequately explained by these approaches.

defect from cooperation when the endgame ensues even if
they have had on-going social ties and like each other well
(Jackson and Wolinsky, 1996)—fits poorly with the empirical
regularities of networks. Padgett and Ansell (1993: 1308)
found in their network analysis of fifteenth-century Medici
trading companies that "clear goals of self-interest . . . are
not really features of people; they are . . . varying structures
of games." In cases in which game theory concedes
outcomes to social structure, it tends to do so after the fact,
to align predictions and empirical results, but continues to
ignore sociological questions on the origin of expectations,
why people interpret rules similarly, or why actors cooperate
when it contradicts self-interest (Kreps, 1990).

Thus, while revisionist economic schemes advance our
understanding of the economic details of transacting, they
faintly recognize the influence of social structure on economic life. Similarly, theory about the properties and process
by which embeddedness affects economic action remains
nascent in the organizations literature. Below, I report results
and formulate arguments that attempt to flesh out the
concept of embeddedness and its implications for the
competitive advantage of network organizations.

RESEARCH METHODOLOGY

I conducted field and ethnographic analysis at 23 women's
better-dress firms in the New York City apparel industry, a
model competitive market with intense international competition, thousands of local shops, and low barriers to entry,
start-up costs, and search costs. In this type of industrial
setting economic theory makes strong predictions that social
ties should play a minimal role in economic performance
(Hirschman, 1970), and this is thus a conservative setting in
which to examine conjectures about embeddedness. Field
methods are advantageous here because they provided rich
data for theorizing and conducting a detailed analysis of the
dynamics of interfirm ties, even though the 23 cases
examined here can have but moderate generalizability.

I interviewed the chief executive officers (CEOs) and
selected staff of 23 apparel organizations with sales ranging
from $500,000 to $1,000,000,000. An advantage of studying
firms of this type is that the senior managers are involved in
all key aspects of the business and consequently have
firsthand knowledge of the firm's strategy and administrative
activities. I selected firms that varied in age, sales, employment, location, type, and the CEO's gender and ethnicity to
insure proper industry representation and to minimize the
likelihood that interfirm cooperation could be attributed to
ethnic homogeneity or size (Portes and Sensenbrenner,
1993). The sample was drawn from a register that listed all
the firms operating in the better-dress sector of the New
York apparel industry. Table 1 provides a descriptive summary of the sample. This register and other data on firm
attributes came from the International Ladies' Garment
Workers' Union (ILGWU, now called UNITE), which organizes 87 percent of the industry (Waldinger, 1989) and which
helped me identify representative firms from their data base.
Union records indicate that there were 89 unionized manufacturers and 484 unionized contractors in the better-dress

Paradox of Embeddedness

Table 1

Summary of Ethnographic Interviews and Organizational Characteristics of the Sample*

Type of firm	Firm's birth year	Size	Number of employees	HQ or factory location	CEO demographics	Number of interviews	Number of interview hours
Converter	1962	Medium	22	Midtown	Jewish female	1	2
Designer	1986	Small	3	Midtown	Jewish female	2	4
Designer	1980	Small	3	Midtown	Swedish male	2	6
Manufacturer	1951	Large	182	Midtown	Jewish male	1	2
Manufacturer	1950	Large	30	Midtown	Jewish male	1	2
Manufacturer	1986	Large	6	Midtown	Anglo male	1	3
Manufacturer	1974	Large	153	Brooklyn	Anglo male	2	2
Manufacturer	1985	Large	16	Midtown	Jewish male	3	15
Manufacturer (Pilot study)	1954	Large	7	Denver	Jewish male	1	2
Manufacturer	1941	Medium	51	Midtown	Arab male	1	2
Manufacturer	1939	Medium	75	Midtown	Jewish female	1	3
Manufacturer	1977	Medium	10	Midtown	Jewish female	7	35
Manufacturer (Pilot study)	1970	Small	2	Midtown	Jewish male	1	3
Manufacturer	1930	Small	7	Midtown	Jewish male	1	2
Manufacturer	1989	Small	3	Midtown	Jewish male	1	2
Manufacturer	1973	Small	4	Midtown	Anglo female	2	2
Contractor–Cutting	1962	Large	40	Midtown	Jewish male	1	2
Contractor–Sewing	1976	Large	72	Chinatown	Chinese female	1	4
Contractor–Sewing	1982	Large	150	Chinatown	Chinese male	1	6
Contractor–Sewing	1989	Medium	85	Chinatown	Chinese female	2	2
Contractor–Pleating	1972	Small	31	Midtown	Hispanic male	2	2
Contractor–Sewing	1986	Small	46	Chinatown	Chinese female	4	8
Trucking company	1956	Small	45	Brooklyn	Italian male	3	2
Total						42	113

* Size in sales: small = $500,000–$3 million; medium = $3–10 million; large = $10–35 million. (One large firm had sales of $1 billion.) Mean number of ties/contractor = 4.33; embedded ties = 1–2, or 61–76% of total business. Mean number of ties/manufacturer = 12; embedded ties = 2, or 42% of total business. Source is ILGWU records. Sample and population means do not significantly differ.

sector at the time of the study. The unit of analysis was the interfirm relationship.

My analysis focused on the women's better-dress sector to control for the differences that exist across industry sectors (other sectors include menswear, fantasywear, etc.). Better dresswear is a midscale market (retails for $80–$180), comprises off-the-rack dresses, skirts, and jackets, typically sells in department stores and chains, and tends to be price, quality, and fashion sensitive.

Figure 1 depicts a typical organizational network in this sector. Production revolves around manufacturers (called "jobbers") that normally fabricate no part of the garment; instead, they design and market it. The first step in the production process of a garment entails a manufacturer making a "collection" of sample garment designs in-house or with freelance designers and then showing its collection to retail buyers, who place orders. The jobber then "manu-factures" the designs selected by the retail buyers by managing a network of grading, cutting, and sewing con-tracting firms that produce in volume the selected designs in their respective shops. Jobbers also link to textile mills that take raw materials such as cottons and plant linens and make them into griege goods—cloth that has no texture, color, or patterns. Converters buy griege goods from textile mills and transform them into fabrics (cloth that has color and patterns). The fabric is then sold to jobbers who use it in their clothing designs.

Figure 1. Typical interfirm network in the apparel industry's better-dress sector.

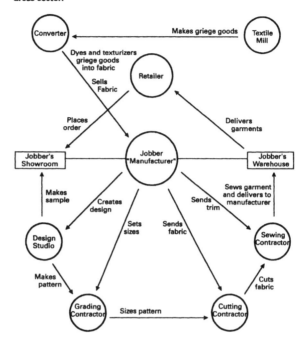

Data collection and analysis followed grounded theory building techniques (Glaser and Strauss, 1967; Miles and Huberman, 1984). I contacted each CEO by phone and introduced myself as a student doing a doctoral dissertation on the management practices of garment firms. In-depth interviews were open-ended, lasted two to six hours, and were carried out over a five-month period. In eight cases I was invited to tour the firm and interview and observe employees freely, and in fourteen cases I was invited for a follow-up visit. At three firms I passed several days interviewing and observing personnel. In these cases and others, I accompanied production managers when they visited their network contacts. These trips enabled me to gather first-hand ethnographic data on exchange dynamics and to compare actors' declared motives and accounts with direct observations. I recorded interviews and field observations in a hand-size spiral notebook, creating a record for each firm. I augmented these data with company and ILGWU data on the characteristics of the sampled firms.

I conducted the study in four phases. A pre-study phase consisted of two pilot interviews that I used to learn how the interview materials, my self-presentation, and the frequency or salience of an event such as price negotiation, tie formation, or problem solving affected the accuracy of reporting. Phase one involved open-ended, moderately directive interviews, and direct field observations. I con-

Paradox of Embeddedness

ducted interviews carefully so that economic explanations were adequately examined during discussions. If an interviewee spoke only of the relationship between trust and opportunism, I asked how she or he differentiated trust and risk or why hostage taking or information asymmetry could not explain an action he or she attributed to social ties. I stressed accuracy in reporting and used nondirective items to probe sensitive issues, for example, "Can you tell me more about that," "Is there anything else," or "I am interested in details like that." The Appendix lists the interview items. In phase two, I formed an organized interpretation of the data. I first developed a working framework based on extant theory and then traveled back and forth between the data and my working framework. As evidence amassed, expectations from the literature were retained, revised, removed, or added to my framework. In this stage, I also did a formal analysis of the data using a "cross-site display," shown in Table 2 below, that indicates the frequency and weighting of data across cases and how well my framework was rooted in each data source (Miles and Huberman, 1984). Like all data reduction methods, however, it cannot display the full richness of the data, just as statistical routines don't explain all the variance. Phase three focused on gaining construct validity by conferring with over a half-dozen industry experts at the ILGWU, the Fashion Institute of New York, and the Garment Industry Development Corporation. These discussions revealed few demand characteristics or recording errors in my data. Thus I believe the chance of response bias is low, given the sample's breadth, the cross-checking of interview and archival data, and the formalization of the analysis.

FEATURES AND FUNCTIONS OF EMBEDDED TIES

Table 2 summarizes the evidence for the features and functions of embedded ties. One important initial finding is that the different accounts of transacting can be accurately summarized by two forms of exchange: arm's-length ties, referred to by interviewees as "market relationships," and embedded ties, which they called "close or special relationships." These data and the literature on organization networks form the basis for my analysis and the framework developed in this paper.

I found that market ties conformed closely to the concept of an arm's-length relationship as commonly specified in the economic literature. These relationships were described in the sharp, detached language that reflected the nature of the transaction. Typical characterizations focused on the lack of reciprocity between exchange partners, the non-repeated nature of the interaction, and narrow economic matters: "It's the opposite [of a close tie], one hand doesn't wash the other." "They're the one-shot deals." "A deal in which costs are everything." Other interviews also focused on the lack of social content in these relationships: "They're relationships that are like far away. They don't consider the feeling for the human being." "You discuss only money."

An examination of close relationships suggested that they reflected the concept of embeddedness (Granovetter, 1985). These relationships were distinguished by the personal

Table 2

Summary of Cross-Site Ethnographic Evidence for Features and Functions of Embeddedness in 21 Firms*

				Source of Evidence		
		Arm's-length Ties			Embedded Ties	
Features and Functions of Exchange	CEO	Product manager	Direct observation	CEO	Product manager	Direct observation
Uses written contracts	2	5	2			
Personal relationship with partner matters	2	2		18	7	11
Trust is major aspect of relationship				14	7	5
Reputation of a potential partner matters	1	2		2	2	2
Reciprocity and favors are important	4	2		10	4	3
Small-numbers bargaining is risky	11	5	4	2	1	
Monitor partner for opportunism	13	7	4	3	1	
Thick information sharing				17	7	4
Use exit to solve problems	13	5				
Joint problem solving				15	5	3
Concentrated exchange with partner matters	1	1		10	7	
Push for lowest price possible	7	4	2	2		
Promotes shared investment				9	4	
Shortens response time to market	3	1		8	5	2
Promotes innovation	2			4	5	2
Strong incentives for quality	2			10	5	1
Increases fit with market demand	4	1		7	4	
Source of novel ideas	5	3	1	1	2	

* Numbers in cells represent frequency of responses by interviewees aggregated across person-cases. Empty cells indicate that no responses were made by interviewees in that category. Multiple and unambiguous examples across cases and sources constitute strong evidence for an element of the framework. An unambiguous example across a single case constitutes modest evidence.

nature of the business relationship and their effect on economic process. One CEO distinguished close ties from arm's-length ties by their socially constructed character: "It is hard to see for an outsider that you become friends with these people—business friends. You trust them and their work. You have an interest in what they're doing outside of business." Another interviewee said, "They know that they're like part of the company. They're part of the family."

All interviewees described dealings with arm's-length ties and reported using them regularly. Most of their interfirm relationships were arm's-length ties, but "special relations," which were fewer in number, characterized critical exchanges (Uzzi, 1996). This suggested that (a) arm's-length ties may be greater in frequency but of lesser significance than close ties in terms of company success and overall business volume and that (b) stringent assumptions about individuals being either innately self-interested or cooperative are too simplistic, because the same individuals simultaneously acted "selfishly" and cooperatively with different actors in their network—an orientation that was shown to be an emergent property of the quality of the social tie and the structure of the network in which the actors were embedded. Finer analyses showed that embedded relationships have three main components that regulate the expectations and behaviors of exchange partners: trust, fine-grained information transfer, and joint problem-solving arrangements. The components are conceptually independent, though related because they are all elements of social structure.

Paradox of Embeddedness

Trust

Respondents viewed trust as an explicit and primary feature of their embedded ties. It was expressed as the belief that an exchange partner would not act in self-interest at another's expense and appeared to operate not like calculated risk but like a heuristic—a predilection to assume the best when interpreting another's motives and actions. This heuristic quality is important because it speeds up decision making and conserves cognitive resources, a point I return to below. Typical statements about trust were, "Trust is the distinguishing characteristic of a personal relationship"; "It's a personal feeling"; and "Trust means he's not going to find a way to take advantage of me. You are not selfish for your own self. The partnership [between firms] comes first."

Trust developed when extra effort was voluntarily given and reciprocated. These efforts, often called "favors," might entail giving an exchange partner preferred treatment in a job queue, offering overtime on a last-minute rush job, or placing an order before it was needed to help a network partner through a slow period. These exchanges are noteworthy because no formal devices were used to enforce reciprocation (e.g., contracts, fines, overt sanctions), and there was no clear metric of conversion to the measuring rod of money. The primary outcome of governance by trust was that it promoted access to privileged and difficult-to-price resources that enhance competitiveness but that are difficult to exchange in arm's-length ties. One contractor explained it this way, "With people you trust, you know that if they have a problem with a fabric they're just not going to say, 'I won't pay' or 'take it back'. If they did then we would have to pay for the loss. This way maybe the manufacturer will say, 'OK so I'll make a dress out of it or I can cut it and make a short jacket instead of a long jacket'." In contrast, these types of voluntary and mutually beneficial exchanges were unlikely in arm's-length relationships. A production manager said, "They [arm's-length ties] go only by the letter and don't recognize my extra effort. I may come down to their factory on Saturday or Sunday if there is a problem . . . I don't mean recognize with money. I mean with working things out to both our satisfaction." Trust promoted the exchange of a range of assets that were difficult to put a price on but that enriched the organization's ability to compete and overcome problems, especially when firms cooperatively traded resources that produced integrative agreements.

An analysis of the distinction between trust and risk is useful in explicating the nature of trust in embedded ties (Williamson, 1994). I found that trust in embedded ties is unlike the calculated risk of arm's-length transacting in two ways. First, the distributional information needed to compute the risk (i.e., the expected value) of an action was not culled by trusting parties. Rather, in embedded ties, there was an absence of monitoring devices designed to catch a thief. Second, the decision-making psychology of trust appeared to conform more closely to heuristic-based processing than to the calculativeness that underlies risk-based decision making (Williamson, 1994). Interviewees reported that among embedded ties the information needed to make risk-based decisions was not systematically compiled, nor were base rates closely attended to, underscoring the heuristic processing associated with trust. Moreover, the calculative stance of risk-based judgments, denoted by the skeptical interpretation of another's motives when credible data are absent, was replaced by favorable interpretations of another's unmonitored activities. One CEO said, "You may ship fabric for 500 garments and get only 480 back. So what happened to the other 20? Twenty may not seem like a lot, but 20 from me and 20 from another manufacturer and so on and the contractor has a nice little business on the side. Of course you can say to the contractor, 'What happened to the 20?' But he can get out of it if he wants. 'Was it the trucker that stole the fabric?' he might ask. He can also say he was shorted in the original shipment from us. So, there's no way of knowing who's to blame for sure. That's why trust is so important." This interviewee's statement that he trusts his exchange partner is also not equivalent to his saying that the probability of my exchange partner skimming off 20 garments is very small, because that interpretation cannot explain interviewees' investments in trust if calculations using base-rate data on shrinkage could supply sufficient motives for action.

These observations are also consistent with the psychology of heuristics in several other ways. Although my intention here is not to explain social structural outcomes via psychological reductionism, I mention these links because they help distinguish the psychology of embeddedness from that of atomistic transacting. By the term "heuristic," I refer to the decision-making processes that economize on cognitive resources, time, and attention processes but do not necessarily jeopardize the quality of decisions (Aumann and Sorin, 1989). In making this argument, I draw on the literature that shows that heuristics can help people make quick decisions and process more complex information than would be possible without heuristics, especially when uncertainty is high and decision cues are socially defined. In such contexts, heuristics have been shown to produce quality decisions that have cognitive economy, speed, and accuracy (Messick, 1993). Thus, the research that shows that heuristic processing is most likely when the problem is unique or decision-making speed is beneficial (Kahneman and Tversky, 1982) is consistent with how embedded ties particularize the features of the exchange relationship, how information is attended to, gathered, and processed, and my finding that decision-making speed is advantageous among network partners.

The heuristic character of trust also permits actors to be responsive to stimuli. If it didn't, actors relying on trust would be injured systematically by exchange partners that feign trust and then defect before reciprocating (Burt, Knez, and Powell, 1997). I found that trust can break down after repeated abuses, because its heuristic quality enables actors to continue to recognize nontrivial mistreatments that can change trust to mistrust over time, a finding consonant with research on keiretsu ties (Smitka, 1991). Two CEOs described how repeated abuse of trust can corrode a close tie: "Sometimes they ask a favor for a lower price and I'll do it.

Paradox of Embeddedness

But if they always do that, they're ripping me off." "If the other firm's busy he'll stay with us and vice versa. If he switches to a new contractor then I won't work with that manufacturer again."

Unlike governance structures in atomistic markets, which are manifested in intense calculativeness, monitoring devices, and impersonal contractual ties, trust is a governance structure that resides in the social relationship between and among individuals and cognitively is based on heuristic rather than calculative processing. In this sense, trust is fundamentally a social process, since these psychological mechanisms and expectations are emergent features of a social structure that creates and reproduces them through time. This component of the exchange relationship is important because it enriches the firm's opportunities, access to resources, and flexibility in ways that are difficult to emulate using arm's-length ties.

Fine-grained Information Transfer

I found that information exchange in embedded relationships was more proprietary and tacit than the price and quantity data that were traded in arm's-length ties. Consistent with Larson's (1992) findings, it includes information on strategy and profit margins, as well as tacit information acquired through learning by doing. The CEO of a pleating firm described how exchange of nonprice and proprietary information is a main feature of his embedded ties: "Constant communication is the difference. It's just something you know. It's like having a friend. The small details really help in a crunch. They know we're thinking about them. And I feel free to ask, 'How are things going on your end, when will you have work for us?'"

Relative to price data, fine-grained information transfer is not only more detailed and tacit but has a holistic rather than a divisible structure that is difficult to communicate through market ties. In the context of the fashion industry, I found that this information structure is manifested as a particular "style," which is the fusion of components from different fashions, materials, nomenclatures, and production techniques. Because a style tends to be forbidding and time consuming even for experts to articulate and separate into discrete component parts, it was difficult to codify into a pattern or to convey via arm's-length ties without the loss of information. For example, a designer showed me a defective pleated skirt and described how only his embedded ties would be likely to catch the problem. His demonstration of how different fabrics are meant to "fall," "run," "catch light," and "forgive stitching" made it clear that information transfer with his close ties is a composite of "chunks" of information that are not only more detailed than price data but more implied than overtly expressed in conversation. It also appeared that the transfer of fine-grained information between embedded ties is consistent with Herbert Simon's notions of chunking and expert rationality, in that even though the information exchanged is more intricate than price data, it is at the same time more fully understood because it is processed as composite chunks of information (a style) rather than as sequential pieces of dissimilar data.[2] A designer explained how these factors improve a firm's ability to bring products to market quickly and to reduce errors: "If we have a factory that is used to making our stuff, they know how it's supposed to look. They know a particular style. It is not always easy to make a garment just from the pattern. Especially if we rushed the pattern. But a factory that we have a relationship with will see the problem when the garment starts to go together. They will know how to work the fabric to make it look the way we intended. A factory that is new will just go ahead and make it. They won't know any better."

Fine-grained information transfer benefits networked firms by increasing the breadth and ordering of their behavioral options and the accuracy of their long-run forecasts. A typical example of how this occurs was described by a manufacturer who stated that he passes on critical information about "hot selling items" to his embedded ties before the other firms in the market know about it, giving his close ties an advantage in meeting the future demand: "I get on the phone and say to a buyer, 'this group's on fire' [i.e., many orders are being placed on it by retail buyers]. But she'll buy it only as long as she believes me. Other manufacturers can say, 'It's hot as a pistol,' but she knows me. If she wants it she can come down and get it. The feedback gives her an advantage."

These cases demonstrate that fine-grained information transfer is also more than a matter of asset-specific know-how or reducing information asymmetry between parties, because the social relationship imbues information with veracity and meaning beyond its face value. An illustrative case involved a manufacturer who explained how social ties are critical for evaluating information even when one has access to an exchange partner's confidential data. In such a case, one would imagine that this access would make the quality of the social relationship unimportant because the information asymmetry that existed between the buyer and seller has been overcome. This interviewee argued, however, that while he could demand that the accounting records of a contractor be made available to him so that he might check how the contractor arrived at a price, the records would be difficult to agree upon in the absence of a relationship that takes for granted the integrity of the source. The manufacturer said, "If we don't like the price a contractor gives us, I say, 'So let's sit down and discuss the costing numbers.' But there are all these 'funny numbers' in the contractor's books and so we argue over what they mean. We disagree . . . and in the end the contractor says, 'We don't have a markup,' and then he looks at you like you have three heads for asking . . . because he knows we don't know each other well enough to agree on the numbers in the first place."

Thus, information exchange in embedded ties is more tacit and holistic in nature than the price and quantity data exchanged in arm's-length ties. The valuation of this information has its basis in the social identities of the exchange partners and in the manner in which it is processed, via

---

2
I owe the insightful observation about chunking and expert rationality to an anonymous reviewer, who helped me fine-tune my analysis and who also suggested a more radical implication of my findings—that embeddedness can overcome bounded rationality altogether—an interpretation I am more reluctant to endorse. Although embedded ties appear to reduce bounded rationality by expanding the range of data attended to and the speed of processing, I would argue that this expansion does not constitute full rationality. I am more confident in concluding at this point that embedded ties reflect "expert rationality," a third kind of rationality that exists between pure and bounded rationality (Prietula and Simon, 1989). Many points in Prietula and Simon's (1989) discussion of the organizational implications of expert rationality support and extend the arguments made here.

chunking, even though it is intricate and detailed. These features help to convey the preferences and range of strategic options available to exchange partners, increasing effective interfirm coordination.

Joint Problem-solving Arrangements

The use of social arrangements to coordinate market transactions is supposedly inefficient because the price system most efficiently coordinates transactions, except under conditions of bilateral monopoly or market imperfection (Hirschman, 1982: 1473). In contrast, I found that embedded ties entail problem-solving mechanisms that enable actors to coordinate functions and work out problems "on the fly." These arrangements typically consist of routines of negotiation and mutual adjustment that flexibly resolve problems (see also Larson, 1992). For example, a contractor showed me a dress that he had to cut to different sizes depending on the dye color used because the dye color affected the fabric's stretching. The manufacturer who put in the order didn't know that the dress sizes had to be cut differently to compensate for the dyeing. If the contractor had not taken the initiative to research the fabric's qualities, he would have cut all the dresses the same way—a costly mistake for the manufacturer and one for which the contractor could not be held responsible. Both the manufacturer and the contractor reported that this type of integration existed only in their embedded ties, because their work routines facilitated troubleshooting and their "business friendship" motivated expectations of doing more than the letter of a "contract." The manufacturer explained: "When you deal with a guy you don't have a close relationship with, it can be a big problem. Things go wrong and there's no telling what will happen. With my guys [his key contractors], if something goes wrong, I know we'll be able to work it out. I know his business and he knows mine."

These arrangements are special, relative to market-based mechanisms of alignment, such as exit (Hirschman, 1970), because learning is explicit rather than extrapolated from another firm's actions. Hirschman (1970) showed that a firm receives no direct feedback if it loses a customer through exit; the reasons must be inferred. In embedded relationships, firms work through problems and get direct feedback, increasing learning and the discovery of new combinations, as Helper (1990) showed in her study of automaker-supplier relationships. In contrast, one informant said about market ties, "They don't want to work with the problem. They just want to say, 'This is how it must be.' Then they switch [to a new firm] again and again." In this way, joint problem-solving arrangements improve organization responses by reducing production errors and the number of development cycles. Joint problem-solving arrangements are mechanisms of voice. They replace the simplistic exit-or-stay response of the market and enrich the network, because working through problems promotes learning and innovation.

A Note on the Formation of Embedded Ties and Networks

Although a full discussion of network formation exceeds this paper's scope, I can summarize my findings on this process to establish the link between embedded ties and the structure of organization networks (Uzzi, 1996). I found that embedded ties primarily develop out of third-party referral networks and previous personal relations. In these cases, one actor with an embedded tie to two unconnected actors acts as their "go-between." The go-between performs two functions: He or she rolls over expectations of behavior from the existing embedded relationship to the newly matched firms and "calls on" the reciprocity owed him or her by one exchange partner and transfers it to the other. In essence, the go-between transfers the expectations and opportunities of an existing embedded social structure to a newly formed one, furnishing a basis for trust and subsequent commitments to be offered and discharged. As exchange is reciprocated, trust forms, and a basis for fine-grained information transfer and joint problem solving is set in place (Larson, 1992). This formation process exposes network partners to aspects of their social and economic lives that are outside the narrow economic concerns of the exchange but that provide adaptive resources, embedding the economic exchange in a multiplex relationship made up of economic investments, friendship, and altruistic attachments.

The significant structural consequence of the formation of dyadic embedded ties is that the original market of impersonal transactions becomes concentrated and exclusive in partner dyads. Since an exchange between dyads has repercussions for the other network members through transitivity, the embedded ties assemble into extended networks of such relations. The ties of each firm, as well as the ties of their ties, generate a network of organizations that becomes a repository for the accumulated benefits of embedded exchanges. Thus the level of embeddedness in a network increases with the density of embedded ties. Conversely, networks with a high density of arm's-length ties have low embeddedness and resemble an atomistic market. The extended network of ties has a profound effect on a firm's performance, even though the extended network may be unknown or beyond the firm's control (Uzzi, 1996).

EMBEDDEDNESS, INTERFIRM NETWORKS, AND PERFORMANCE

Embeddedness is of slight theoretical and practical value if more parsimonious accounts of exchange can explain as much. As Friedman (1953) argued, it doesn't matter if reality is not as the economic model purports so long as the model's forecasts agree with empirical observation. In response to this argument and the need to specify the mechanisms of embeddedness, I show in this section how embeddedness advances our understanding of key economic and social outcomes. For each outcome, I specify propositions about the operation and outcomes of interfirm networks that are guided implicitly by ceteris paribus assumptions. My goal is not to model a specific outcome, such as profitability, but to show how social structure governs the intervening processes that regulate key performance outcomes, both positive and negative.

Economies of Time and Allocative Efficiency

Economists have argued that people's time is the scarcest resource in the economy and that how it is allocated has a

Paradox of Embeddedness

profound economic effect (Juster and Stafford, 1991). I
found that embeddedness promotes economies of time (the
ability to capitalize quickly on market opportunities), because
the transactional details normally worked out to protect
against opportunism (contracts, price negotiations, schedul-
ing) in arm's-length relationships prior to production are
negotiated on the fly or after production is completed.
Contracting costs are avoided, because firms trust that
payoffs will be divided equitably, even when comparative
market transactions do not exist. In addition, fine-grained
information transfer speeds data exchange and helps firms
understand each other's production methods so that
decision making can be quickened. Joint problem-solving
arrangements also increase the speed at which products are
brought to market by resolving problems in real time during
production. "Bud," the CEO of a large dress firm, explained
how embeddedness economizes on time in a way that is
unachievable using arm's-length contacts: "We have to go to
market fast. Bids take too long. He [the contractor] knows
he can trust us because he's part of the 'family.' Sometimes
we get hurt [referring to a contractor that takes too long to
do a job] and we pay more than we want to. Sometimes we
think the contractor could have done it quicker and he takes
less than he wants. But everything is negotiated and it saves
us both from being killed from a poor estimate. We do first
and fix price after."

While economies of time due to embeddedness have
obvious benefits for the individual firm, they also have
important implications for allocative efficiency and the
determination of prices. This is because embeddedness
helps solve the allocation problem by enabling firms to
match product designs and production levels more closely to
consumer preferences than is possible in an atomized
market governed by the price system. When the price
system operates, there is a lag between the market's
response and producers' adjustments to it. The longer the
lag, the longer the market is in disequilibrium, and the longer
resources are suboptimally allocated. Underproduced items
cause shortages and a rise in prices, while overproduced
items are sold at a discount. This is especially true when
goods are fashion-sensitive or when long lead times exist
between design and production, because producers are
more likely to guess inaccurately the future demands of the
market. They may devote excess resources to goods that do
not sell as expected and too few resources to goods that
are in higher demand than expected. Consumers can also
gain increased access to goods that best meet their needs,
while the production of low-demand goods is minimized
before prices react.

Consequently, the allocative efficiency of the market
improves as waste is reduced (fewer products are discounted), and fast-selling items do not run out of stock. In
this way, embedded ties offer an alternative to the price
system for allocating resources, especially under conditions
of rapid product innovation and mercurial consumer preferences. While these findings are not meant to imply that
prices offer no valuable information for making adjustments,
they do suggest that they are a limited device when adjust-

ment must be timely and coordinated. Under these conditions, as Hirschman (1970) conjectured, both organizational and interfirm adaptation appears less effectively coordinated by prices than by embeddedness. These observations can be summarized in the following propositions:

Proposition 1a: The weaker the ability of prices to distill information, the more organizations will form embedded ties.

Proposition 1b: The greater the level of embeddedness in an organization's network, the greater its economies of time.

Proposition 1c: The greater the competitive advantage of achieving real-time change to environmental shifts or fashion-sensitive markets, the more network forms of organization will dominate competitive processes and produce allocative efficiencies relative to other forms of organization.

Search and Integrative Agreements

In the neoclassical model, efficiency and profit maximization depend on individual search behavior. Search is needed to identify a set of alternatives that are then ranked according to a preference function. If there is no search behavior, there can be no ranking of alternatives and therefore no maximization. This suggests that search procedures are a primary building block of economic effectiveness and therefore are of great theoretical and practical importance to the study of the competitiveness of organizations.

In the neoclassical model, search ends when the marginal cost of search and the expected marginal gain of a set of alternatives is equal to zero. "In a satisficing model search terminates when the best offer exceeds an aspiration level that itself adjusts gradually to the value of the offers received so far" (Simon, 1978: 10). The above statements by "Bud" that "everything is negotiated" and that "Sometimes . . . we pay more than we want to," or "Sometimes we think the contractor could have done it quicker and he takes less than he wants," suggest that each firm satisfices rather than maximizes on price in embedded relationships. Moreover, Bud's statements that "we need to go to market fast" and "We do first and fix price after" demonstrate that in contrast to arm's-length market exchange, firms linked through embedded ties routinely do not search for competitive prices first but, rather, negotiate key agreements afterwards.

To Simon's (1978) model of search I add the following qualification: *search procedures depend on the types of social ties maintained by the actor, not just the cognitive limits of the decision maker.* I found that embedded ties shape expectations of fairness and aspiration levels, such that actors search "deeply" for solutions within a relationship rather than "widely" for solutions across relationships. A reasonable first conjecture of how this network phenomenon operates is that multiplex links among actors enable assets and interests that are not easily communicated across market ties to enter negotiations, increasing the likelihood of integrative agreements that pool resources and promote mutually beneficial solutions, rather than distributive agreements that aim for zero-sum solutions. Solutions are resolved within the relationship, on integrative rather than distributed grounds, where integrative agreements are

Paradox of Embeddedness

themselves made possible because multiplex ties among network partners (e.g., supplier, friend, community member) reveal interests and enlarge the pie of negotiable outcomes (Bazerman and Neale, 1992). For example, when the above-described contractor incorrectly cut a jobber's garment, the jobber searched for a solution within the relationship (i.e., making a short jacket instead of the planned long jacket) based on the expectation that the contractor would voluntarily reciprocate in the future and prefer to solve the problem within the relationship rather than through exit. An interviewee explained this logic: "I'd rather business go to a friend, not an enemy. My theory is it is not competition. Problems are always happening in production. I always tell the manufacturer that 'it's not my problem, it's not his.' I call to always solve the problem, not to get out of fixing the problem. We are all in the same boat." Another said succinctly, "Win-win situations definitely help firms survive. The contractors know that they will not lose."

My findings also suggest that embeddedness operates under microbehavioral decision processes that promote a qualitative analysis of discrete categories (high vs. low quality), rather than continuous amounts (quantities and prices), as in the neoclassical approach. This point is illustrated by a CEO's ranking of embedded ties as more effective enablers of quality production than arm's-length ties: "Any firm, any good firm that's been around, whether it's Italian, Japanese, or German, and I've been there because we've been around for four generations, does business like we do. I have a guy who has been with me 22 years. We all keep long-term relationships with our contractors. That's the only way you become important to them. And if you're not important, you won't get quality." Embedded ties promote each party's commitment to exceed willingly the letter of a contract, to contribute more to the relationship than is specified, and solve problems such that categorical limits are sufficient to motivate a high level of quality in production. In arm's-length ties, by contrast, target outcomes must be contractually detailed at the outset because there are no incentives to motivate positive contributions afterwards, a condition that also limits the search for and recognition of potential problems.

These findings suggest that it is of theoretical and practical import to assess the economic development potential of different search procedures. Hence, I offer the following propositions:

Proposition 2a: Search procedures depend on the type of exchange tie. The width of search across relationships increases with the number of arm's-length ties in the network and decreases with the number of embedded ties in the network. The depth of search within a relationship increases with the strength of the embedded tie.

Proposition 2b: The greater the level of embeddedness in a network, the more likely it is that integrative rather than distributive agreements will be reached.

Proposition 2c: The more competitive advantage depends on reaching positive-sum solutions to interfirm coordination problems, the more organization networks, rather than other forms of organization, will dominate competitive processes.

Risk Taking and Investment

The level of investment in an economy promotes positive changes in productivity, standards of living, mobility, and wealth generation. Economic theory credits investment activity primarily to tax and interest-rate policies that influence the level, pattern, and timing of investments. I found that in the apparel industry embeddedness enables investments beyond the level that would be generated alone by the modern capital and factor markets. Embeddedness creates economic opportunities because it exists prior to the individuals who occupy competitive positions in a network of exchange and defines how traits that signal reliability and competence are interpreted by potential exchange partners, for three reasons. First, it increases expectations that noncontractual, nonbinding exchanges will be reciprocated (Portes and Sensenbrenner, 1993). Second, social networks reduce the complexity of risk taking by providing a structure that matches known investors. Third, network ties link actors in multiple ways (as business partners, friends, agents, mentors), providing a means by which resources from one relationship can be engaged for another. In risky investment situations, these factors increase an actor's capacity to access resources, adjust to unforeseen events, and take risks.

Interviewees argued that the unique expectations of reciprocity and cooperative resource sharing of embedded ties generate investments that cannot be achieved through arm's-length ties that are based on immediate gain. The importance of these consequences of embeddedness seemed particularly meaningful for investments in intellectual property or cultural products (i.e., an original style), which are difficult to value by conventional means but important for economic development in information economies. On the nature of this process of valuation through embedded ties, a characteristic response was, "If someone needs advertising money, or returns, or a special style for windows—it will be like any relationship. You'll do things for friends. You'll go to the bank on their orders. The idea that 'they buy and we sell' is no good. Friends will be there with you through the bad times and good."

The role of embeddedness in matching investors and investment opportunities was exemplified by the CEO of a trucking and manufacturing firm who explained the conditions under which his firm helps contractors who need capital to expand. Consistent with Macaulay's (1963) findings, both parties independently said that they signed no contracts because of their long-term fair play. The CEO stated, "We never make gifts [i.e., sewing machines, hangers, racks, new lighting] to potential startups unless there is a history of personal contact. Never for a stranger. Only for people we have a rapport with. So, if Elaine [CEO of a contracting firm] wanted to start her own shop I would make her a gift. But for some stranger—never. Why should I invest my money on a guy I may never see again?" In contrast, interviewees believed that few firms use arm's-length ties to find investment partners. On this point, a CEO said, "I will give a firm a chance based on Dun and Bradstreet data. I call the bank and get a financial report on

Paradox of Embeddedness

the firm's size. I know this is 'marketing' but most contractors don't do marketing [they mainly use firms they know]."

I observed a similar pattern for investment in special-purpose technology. The added risk of special-purpose technology, however, meant that firms wanted assurances that usually consisted of a joint-equity stake in the technology. Interestingly, the demand for shared equity was not viewed as distrust but as a deepening of trust and a symbol of risk sharing. This was demonstrated by the fact that CEOs most often approached another firm about joint investments when a close tie existed prior to the planned investment. The president of a dress company described how prior social relations shape investment behavior in specialized technology, in this case a $20,000 stitching machine: "Say we want to do a special stitch. So we go to the contractor and ask him to buy the machine to do the job. But he says that he wants us to buy it. But, he has money for this machine like you have money for bubble gum. He's been with us for 25 years. You see, we might not like the way the dress looks with the special stitch. Then we won't use the machine, so he's stuck. The reason he wants us to buy it is that he wants to know that we're not committed to bullshit—we're committed to using it."

This kind of joint equity sharing is only partly consistent with the transaction cost economic notion of credible commitments, since the equity ties symbolize trust, not protection against perfidy—a finding consistent with the Japanese supplier model (Smitka, 1991; Gerlach, 1992). Since both parties had money for the machine, the co-equity stake was not a significant enough sum to be a reliable hostage for either firm. Moreover, since both firms had the money to buy the machine unilaterally and auction it to the lowest-bidding shop if they wanted, the transaction costs of monitoring a joint investment and haggling with a known individual could have been avoided altogether.

My analysis suggests that in these situations, the equity investment acted primarily as a backup—a redundant structural tie that reinforced the firms' attachments to each other. Just as engineers overbuild structures such as bridges to withstand supernormal stress when the cost of a failure is high but the chance of failure is low, these actors appear to overbuild the structures of important exchanges even though the risk of failure due to opportunism may be low, perhaps because the cost of random mishaps is high. The mechanism guiding this process, like that of integrative bargaining, appears to be multiplexity. In risky situations, multiplexity enables resource pooling and adaptation to random events. This implies that multiplex ties may develop because of the riskiness of exchanges. The action of taking risks, however, is a consequence of having multiplex ties at one's disposal. Cyert and March (1992: 228) discussed a similar association between risk taking and physical assets in the form of slack. The contribution here is that a portfolio of social ties can perform the same function slack does in boosting risk taking, especially when actors are in resource-scarce, competitive environments. The key implication is that firms would be less likely to make investments and take risks in the absence of embeddedness. These observations suggest the following propositions:

Proposition 3a: The greater the level of embeddedness in an organization's network, the greater an organization's investment activity and risk taking and the lower its level of resource commitment to hostage taking.

Proposition 3b: The more competitive advantage depends on the ability to reduce product development risk or investment uncertainty, the more organizational networks, rather than other forms of organizations, will dominate competitive processes.

Complex Adaptation and Pareto Improvements

Neoclassicists argue that social arrangements of coordination among firms are unnecessary because the price system directs self-interested maximizers to choose optimally adaptive responses. A related approach held in game theory, agency theory, and evolutionary economics predicts that actors will coordinate only as long as the expected payoffs of cooperation exceed those of selfish behavior (Simon, 1991).

Contrary to these arguments, I found that embeddedness assists adaptation because actors can better identify and execute coordinated solutions to organizational problems. Similar to mechanisms identified by Dore (1983) and Lincoln, Gerlach, and Ahmadjian (1996) on the duration of Japanese interfirm ties, these solutions stem from the willingness of firms to forego immediate economic gain and the ability to pool resources across firms. In embedded relationships, it was typical for exchange partners to inform one another in advance of future work slowdowns or to contract early for services to help out an exchange partner whose business was slow. These actions improve forecasts and adaptation to market changes in ways that cannot be achieved through prices or the narrow pursuit of self-interest. A production manager explained to me how her firm foregoes immediate self-gain in embedded relationships to benefit the adaptation of her exchange partners. In this case, she could not predict if the aided contractor would regain profitability or how long a recovery might take, but she knew that another contractor could offer high volume discounts and a better immediate payoff. She said, "I tell them [key contractors] that in two weeks I won't have much work. You better start to find other work. [At other times] when we are not so busy, we try to find work for that time for our key contractors. We will put a dress into work to keep the contractor going. We'll then store the dress in the warehouse. Where we put work all depends on the factory. If it's very busy I'll go to another factory that needs the work to get by in the short run."

In contrast, these behaviors were virtually nonexistent in arm's-length ties because information about the need for work was used opportunistically to drive price down, a finding consistent with traditional U.S. automaker-supplier relationships (Helper, 1990). Moreover, price is too unresponsive and noisy a signal of organizational effectiveness to foster interfirm coordination or adaptation (Hirschman, 1970). A contractor illustrated why price is a poor signal for organizational adaptation and how it can be used opportunistically to mask problems: "In close relationships we work together.

Paradox of Embeddedness

I handle their last-minute garment changes and ship fast and jobbers help me expand and solve production problems. . . . [Other] jobbers push the price down when the contractor tells his production problems. Eventually the contractor wants to leave the manufacturer because he doesn't pay enough next time [to make up for earlier price concessions]. But in the time a good contractor needs to find a new jobber to replace their business they lose their best workers and then they go out of business."

The implications of these findings are revealing when contrasted with game theoretic predictions that rely on self-interested motives to explain cooperation. A core prediction of game theory is that players will switch from cooperative to self-interested behavior when the end game is revealed—when players know the end of the game is near and therefore should end cooperative play because it yields lower payoffs than unilateral self-interest (Murnighan, 1994). Contrary to this prediction, I found that embedded firms continue to cooperate even after the end of the game is apparent. An illustrative case concerned a manufacturer that was permanently moving all its production to Asia and thus had begun its end game with its New York contractors. As a result, this manufacturer had strong incentives not to tell its contractors that it intended to leave. Doing so put it at risk of receiving low-quality goods from contractors who now saw the account as temporary and had to redirect their efforts to new manufacturers who could replace the lost business. Yet the CEO of this manufacturer personally notified his embedded ties, because his relationships with them obliged him to help them adapt to the closing of his business, and his trust in them led him to believe that they would not shirk on quality. Consistent with his account, one of his contractors said that the jobber's personal visit to his shop reaffirmed their relationship, which he repaid with quality goods. The same manufacturer, however, did not inform those contractors with which it had arm's-length ties.

These findings thus suggest another important outcome of embedded networks: They generate Pareto improvements, promoting a reallocation of resources that makes at least one person better off without making anyone worse off. In the above case, the jobber's embedded ties were made better off by receiving information that enabled them to adapt to the loss of his business. By contrast, in the baseline system of market exchange, the jobber's arm's-length ties were denied access to critical information and thus found the manufacturer's departure debilitating.

This behavior is difficult to explain as rational reputation maintenance. The manufacturer's New York reputation was irrelevant to its future success in Asia. Likewise, it would not have hurt the contractors' reputations to shirk, since the manufacturer was "deserting" them, not the reverse. As a rule, I found that in a large market like New York's, general-ized reputations are surprisingly weak control devices because firms can easily escape their bad reputations, while positive information is often hoarded in the open "market." One contractor said, "Manufacturers can play hit and run for years before their reputation catches up with them." Another added, "I hear 'This one is very picky' or 'This guy is really bad trouble.' But firms I do all the business for, I don't tell a word about to others. I don't want the competition.''

Such acts of nondefection raise an interesting question: Why don't actors defect when it serves their self-interest to do so? One possibility is that embedded social structures entail expectations that either change more slowly than or remain resistant to changes in the purely economic features of the exchange. This enables the logic of embedded ties to extend to subsequent transactions, even those subject to different incentive structures, at least in the near term. In the above case, the manufacturer's visit to the contractor's factory continued their reciprocal indebtedness even though the incentive systems for both firms were radically transformed at the instant the manufacturer revealed his preference to migrate offshore.

Although a conclusive account of such non-self-interested behavior calls for more than ethnographic analysis, one explanation is that, with the blending of the social and economic lives of actors, relationships take on an existence of their own that remains after the economic transaction ends (Granovetter, 1993). Collective successes ("We had a hit season"), common experiences ("I went to her daughter's wedding"), and shared symbols (plaques of appreciation from exchange partners) vividly and enduringly influence actions to furnish resources for which no future gain can be expected. These causal mechanisms are buttressed by ample psychological research that shows that close personal ties heighten empathy, which increases altruistic behavior (Batson, 1990). One manufacturer explicitly displayed this reasoning in discussing the main issues affecting his decision not to move to Taiwan, "You have a heart and a soul here with the people you work with. I don't want to pick up my family either. So, I'll try to make it work here. Not everything in business works by the economic model. You act like a schmuck sometimes." This suggests that the motivation to cooperate when it is not in an individual's self-interest occurs because the expectations of embedded ties lag changes in economic incentives or persist against them, an outcome that is itself sustained by psychological processes that are set in motion by embedded ties.

This altruistic behavior appears irrational only in the narrow economic sense, in that actors forego purely self-seeking behavior (Simon, 1978). These actors are conscious nonetheless of the fact that they are in business to make a return and that big returns are better than small ones. What distinguishes this rationality from formal economic rationality is not just satisficing and heuristics, but the fact that self-interest gives way to altruism: Actors strategically cooperate and equitably distribute both positive and negative outcomes. Thus, contrary to Adam Smith's quip that individuals do best for others by doing selfishly for themselves, the above evidence suggests that firms that act in the interest of others (and against their short-term interests) may do more for the collective economy and society than if they had followed purely selfish pursuits. Hence, I offer the following propositions:

Paradox of Embeddedness

Proposition 4a: The weaker the ability of generalized reputation or prices to provide reliable information about products or exchange partners' characteristics, the more organizations will form embedded rather than arm's-length ties.

Proposition 4b: The greater the level of embeddedness in an organization's network, the more likely are Pareto-improved solutions to coordination problems.

Proposition 4c: The more competitive advantage depends on complex adaptation, the more network forms of organization, rather than other forms, will dominate competition.

PARADOXES OF EMBEDDEDNESS

If a firm becomes too embedded, does adaptation become more difficult as network relationships are tuned to specific trading partners, isomorphism within the network decreases diversity, and a concentrated level of exchange with only a few network partners reduces nonredundant information and access to new opportunities (Burt, 1992)? This question suggests a paradox of theoretical significance: The same processes by which embeddedness creates a requisite fit with the current environment can paradoxically reduce an organization's ability to adapt. In this section I explicate three conditions that turn embeddedness into a liability: (1) there is an unforeseeable exit of a core network player, (2) institutional forces rationalize markets, or (3) overembeddedness characterizes the network.

The unexpected loss of a network's core organization, or more generally, a deep and sudden structural change in resource flows can cause embeddedness to shift from an asset to a liability. Under these conditions, social processes that increase integration combine with resource dependency problems to increase the vulnerability of networked organizations. For example, a contractor may become highly skilled at working with a manufacturer's fabric, production schedule, and design specifications. If that manufacturer closes shop or migrates offshore, then the embedded relationship that had originally benefited the contractor may now put it at a higher risk of failure than if it had diversified its ties, because it is likely to lack the resources needed to transition to a replacement partner (Romo and Schwartz, 1995).

The problem is the opposite of the free-rider problem: diligent commitment, backed by expectations of reciprocity and social pressure to perform, intensifies an organization's involvement with certain network partners while raising the concomitant costs of keeping ties to extra-network partners that can provide a safety net for unexpected or random fluctuations. Portes and Sensenbrenner (1993: 1340) drew attention to this phenomenon in their study of entrepreneurs, whose socially embedded relationships gave them access to resources but restricted their actions outside their network. In the apparel industry, the unexpected failure of Leslie Fay, Inc., a manufacturer at the center of a large network, was most debilitating for the primary contractors that had benefited from their close tie to Leslie Fay, Inc. which, before falling victim to a few unscrupulous top executives, had sheltered them from a glut of low-cost competitors and downturns in the economy (Uzzi, 1997). The above arguments suggest the following propositions:

Proposition 5a: The loss of a core organization in a network will have a large negative effect on the viability of the network as a whole.

Proposition 5b: The intensity of the effects of the loss of a core organization increases with its size and the level of embeddedness in the network such that, at the limit, an "extinction effect" will occur, as the deleterious effect of destabilized economic transactions ripples through the network and causes widespread failure of even healthy firms in the network.

Institutional arrangements that "rationalize" markets or fracture social ties can also cause instability. If changes to the system rupture social ties, then the benefits of embeddedness generated by the ties can be lost. Ironically, this can place firms that invested heavily in networks at a higher risk of failure than market-oriented firms because the social relationships that created and supported competitive advantages no longer exist, and the distinctive competencies of managing network relationships may not translate well to other modes of exchange. An example of this type of breakdown occurred in the apparel retail trade in the 1980s. Prior to that time, retail buyers maintained embedded relationships with clothing manufacturers. During the '80s these longstanding ties were broken when many of the giant retailers (e.g., Macy's, Bullocks, A&S) were bought by corporate conglomerates (e.g., Federated, Inc.) that imposed a shift from "relationship buying" to "numbers buying" among their retail buyers. Numbers buying emphasizes short-term profits, one-shot relationships, and whipsaw-like competitive bidding. A manufacturer with 30 years of experience explained how a shift toward impersonal market exchange destabilized embedded ties and permanently affected organizational outcomes:

A symbolic relationship developed into a one-sided relationship. The big stores got accounting running the store. You didn't have fashion-sensitive people running the store any longer. The fashion-sensitive people had great fashion sense. They couldn't read a balance sheet [but] they developed merchants and buyers in the stores. If there was a problem you knew you'd work it out and they'd help you. There was a personal rapport with buyers. We'd say to one another "Let's work it out." It happened in lots of situations—promotions, joint advertising, in seeing what's in for next year. Then everyone became cautious [post buyout]. There was no longer a good dialogue. Ultimately we walked away from the department stores. The relationship became very impersonal and the manufacturers got squeezed. The corpses [of failed manufacturers] littered 7th Avenue.

These observations suggest another proposition:

Proposition 6: Organizations that build their competitive advantage on the use of embedded ties will be at a high risk of failure if institutional changes fundamentally rationalize the basis of, or preclude the formation of, new embedded ties.

The third instability results from overembeddedness, when all firms in a network are connected through embedded ties. This can reduce the flow of new or novel information into the network because redundant ties to the same network partners mean that there are few or no links to outside members who can potentially contribute innovative ideas (Burt, 1992). Under these conditions, the network becomes

Paradox of Embeddedness

ossified and out of step with the demands of its environment, ultimately leading to decline.

Overembeddedness can also stifle effective economic action if the social aspects of exchange supersede the economic imperatives. Feelings of obligation and friendship may be so great between transactors that a firm becomes a "relief organization" for the other firms in its network. The stronger firms in the network may dedicate resources to weaker members at a rate that outpaces their capacity to rejuvenate their own resources, an argument that is consistent with Portes and Sensenbrenner's (1993: 1339) finding that networks of exclusive ties "turn promising enterprises into welfare hotels, checking economic expansion."

Overembedded networks can sometimes release intense negative emotions of spite and revenge that trap firms in self-defeating cycles of behavior. For example, Axelrod (1984) found that defection, even in simple tit-for-tat games, can cause feuding when it is perceived as illicit or violates an implicit understanding between players to cooperate. I found that if the strong assumptions of trust and cooperation are exploited in embedded ties, vendettas and endless feuds can arise. Over time these actions can prevail against rational action and reduce the firm's ability to meet the economic demands of the market place. A CEO put it simply, "If you screw a guy like that [a close tie] he'll stay in business just long enough to get even."

How can these results be reconciled with the finding that embeddedness is an enabling feature of organizational efficacy? My argument has been that organizations gain access to special opportunities when connected to their exchange partners through embedded ties, such that the opportunity level is positively related to the degree to which a firm's network partners use embedded ties—at least up to some threshold. These relationships suggest that the effect of embeddedness and network structure on economic action depends on two variables: (1) how a firm links to its network and (2) the composition of the network that a firm is linked to. The best way for an organization to link to its network is by means of embedded ties, which provide better access to the benefits circulating in the network than arm's-length ties. The optimal network structure to link to is a mix of arm's-length and embedded ties, because each type of tie performs different functions: Embedded ties enrich the network, while arm's-length ties prevent the complete insulation of the network from market demands and new possibilities. This suggests two propositions:

Proposition 7a: Organizational performance increases with the use of embedded ties to link to network partners.

Proposition 7b: Network structures that integrate arm's-length and embedded ties optimize an organization's performance potential; network structures comprising only arm's-length ties or embedded ties decrease organizational performance potential.

In a study of the New York apparel industry, I found plausible evidence for propositions 7a and 7b using data on the network ties among contractors and manufacturers in the better-dress sector of the New York apparel industry over an 18-month period (Uzzi, 1996). I found that contractors had a

Figure 2. Network structure and embeddedness from a focal firm's perspective.

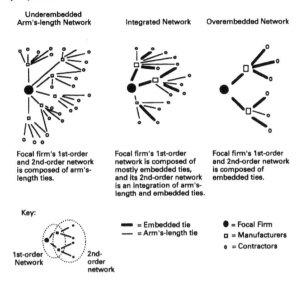

Underembedded Arm's-length Network Integrated Network Overembedded Network

Focal firm's 1st-order and 2nd-order network is composed of arm's-length ties.

Focal firm's 1st-order network is composed of mostly embedded ties, and its 2nd-order network is an integration of arm's-length and embedded ties.

Focal firm's 1st-order and 2nd-order network is composed of embedded ties.

Key:

1st-order Network   2nd-order network

━━ = Embedded tie
── = Arm's-length tie

● = Focal Firm
□ = Manufacturers
○ = Contractors

significantly lower failure rate when linked by embedded ties to their network partners and that being connected to a network comprising an integration of embedded ties and arm's-length ties, rather than a network comprising either embedded ties or arm's-length ties, significantly decreased the failure rate even further. Figure 2 summarizes this theoretical argument and the types of network structures a firm could be linked to. For illustrative purposes, each network is composed of contractors (circles) and manufacturers (squares) and has a first-order network made up of an actor's ties to its exchange partners and a second-order network made up of an actor's exchange partners' ties to their trading partners. Exchange relationships also vary in quality—thick lines and thin lines represent embedded ties and arm's-length ties, respectively. The underembedded network structure has first- and second-order networks that both comprise arm's-length ties. In this type of network, all ties are arm's-length: A contractor uses arm's-length ties to link to its manufacturers, who also use arm's-length ties to transact with their contractors. This network has low embeddedness and approximates an atomistic market (Baker, 1990). The overembedded network structure has first- and second-order networks that comprise embedded ties: The contractor uses embedded ties to transact with its manufacturers, who also use embedded ties to transact with their contractors. The integrated network structure exemplifies the hypothesized optimal, integrated structure. The focal firm's first-order network comprises embedded ties, and its second-order network is an integration of embedded and arm's-length ties. The conjecture drawn from these patterns is that the degree to which embeddedness facilitates economic action depends on the quality of interfirm ties, network position, and network architecture.

DISCUSSION

If economic action is embedded in networks of relations (Granovetter, 1985), then a logical first step is to specify the dimensions of embedded relationships and the mechanisms by which they influence economic action. This undertaking builds on the work of others who have launched the important enterprise of reintroducing social structure into the analysis of economic phenomena. In trying to demonstrate the unique organizational and market processes that follow from an understanding of social structure and economic performance, I analyzed the properties of embedded relations and how they create competitive advantages for firms and networks of firms.

While these processes and outcomes are not quickly summarized, Figure 3 diagrams the propositions and logic presented in the preceding sections into their antecedents and consequences. The figure lays out, from left to right, the social structural antecedents of embedded ties, the components of embedded ties, the positive outcomes of an integrated network structure, and the negative outcomes of overembedded networks. The plausibility of these propositions has been partly established in the empirical research analyzed here. Testing and refinement await future research.

The programmatic implication of this work is that embeddedness is a unique logic of exchange that results from the distinct social structure of organization networks and the microbehavioral decision-making processes they promote. In an embedded logic of exchange, trust acts as the primary governance structure. Calculative risk and monitoring systems play a secondary role. Information transfer is more fine-grained, tacit, and holistic than the typical price data of pure market exchanges, and joint problem-solving arrangements promote voice rather than exit. On a microbehavioral level, actors follow heuristic and qualitative decision rules, rather than intensely calculative ones, and they cultivate long-term cooperative ties rather than narrowly pursue self-interest. These factors furnish an alternative mechanism for coordinating adaptation, speeding products to market, and matching consumer demand to production.

This paper offers an explanation of the links between social structure, microbehavioral decision-making processes, and economic outcomes within the context of organizational networks. At the same time, it adds complexity to models of exchange such as game theory, agency theory, and transaction costs economics. Typical classification schemes differentiate these theories according to an actor's motivation (selfish or cooperative) and rationality (pure or bounded) (Williamson, 1985: 50). But I found that in embedded ties, an actor's motivation and rationality resist characterization within these distinctions, thereby demonstrating the unique logic of embeddedness. My findings suggest that in networks of close ties, motivation is neither purely selfish or cooperative but an emergent property of the social structure within which actors are embedded and that rationality is neither purely rational or boundedly rational, but expert. Thus embeddedness broadens the typical typology of exchange theories to include a new categorization for motives (emer-

Figure 3. Antecedents and consequences of embeddedness and interfirm network structure.

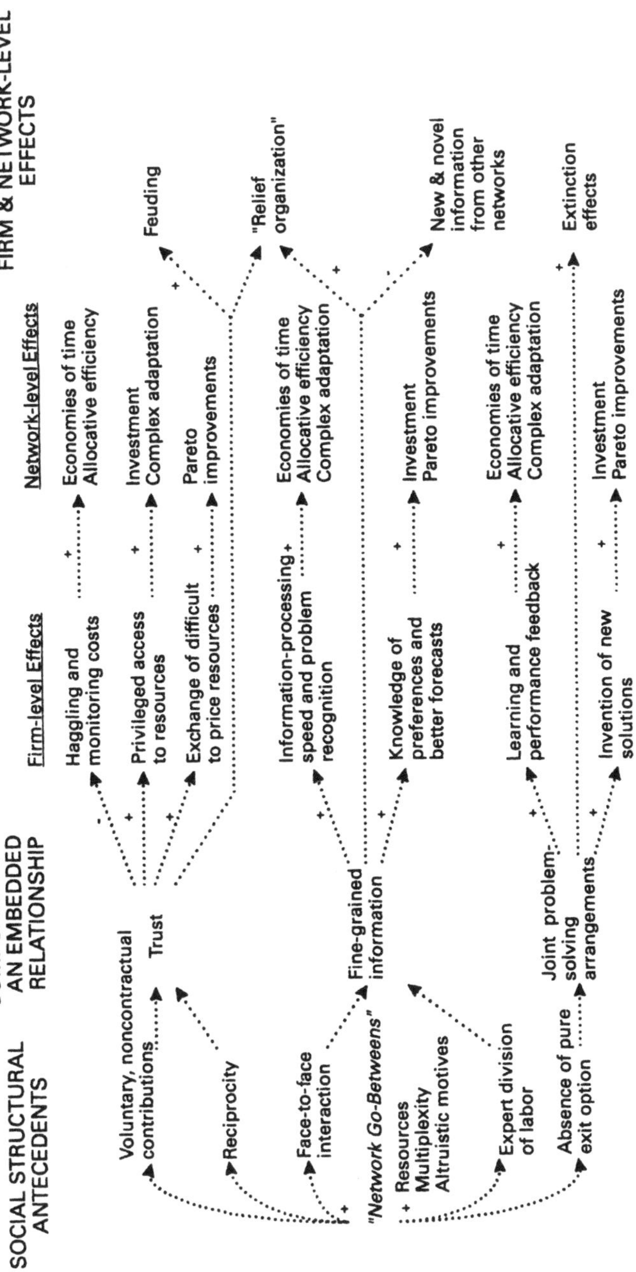

Paradox of Embeddedness

gent rationality) and for rationality (expert rationality). Together, the emergent character of motives and the expanded
nature of information processing sets embeddedness apart
from other logics of exchange and situates social structure
as a precondition to these psychological processes.

While structural embeddedness rests on different behavioral
assumptions than revisionary economic accounts, it also
shares commonalities and differences with these frameworks that have implications for future research. A key
difference is that the unit of analysis is the relationship
between and among actors. This unit of analysis shifts the
focus of inquiry from the qualities of the transaction to the
qualities of the relationship. Another difference is how
structuration influences economic action. The cooperative
behaviors that follow from an organization network are
significant because networks are the sociological analogue of
the type of small-numbers bargaining situations that in
transaction cost, game, and agency theories are a fundamental source of opportunism and inefficiency (Harrison, 1994).
In contrast, I have shown that firms in networks cooperate
under ostensible small-numbers bargaining situations and
end-game conditions. These differences suggest that future
research might examine how different interfirm relationships
affect the development of different types of transactions,
inverting the logic of transaction costs economics. If embeddedness encourages firms to *increase* their asset specificity
or to engage in repeated transactions that have uncertain
future states, then there are significant implications for how
learning and technology transfer are promoted in alliances.
Future research might also examine when embeddedness
can solve coordination problems without the need to
integrate vertically or erect costly monitoring systems.

My finding that actors acknowledge differences between
arm's-length and embedded ties and designedly use them
has implications for research in network analysis, where it is
often proposed that network structure alone virtually
determines action (Emirbayer and Goodwin, 1994). Burt's
(1992) foundational work takes this structural approach to its
most natural conclusion: A network structure rich in structural holes is virtually all that is needed to induce information
and resources to flow through the network like electric
current through a circuit board. Understanding the difference
between embedded and arm's-length ties can add to these
theories by specifying how an actor's ability to access the
opportunities of a contact or network strategically depends
on the quality of the relationship that connects them and
how it is managed.

This research extends classic statements of embeddedness.
Polanyi (1957: 43–68) argued that the embeddedness of
economic action in preindustrial societies was for all intents
and purposes supplanted in modern life by the logic of
efficient markets. Elaborating on this view, Granovetter
(1985) argued that virtually all economic behavior in modern
life is embedded in networks of social relations that condition economic processes in ways that Polanyi and neoclassicists only faintly recognized. My work adds complexity to
both of these views. Like Polanyi, I found that in the apparel
industry at least, atomistic relations govern some transac-

tions. Yet, consistent with Granovetter, I found that atomistic relations occupy a confined area of economic life and that the critical transactions on which firms depend most are embedded in networks of social relationships that produce positive and unique outcomes that are difficult to imitate via other means.

Granovetter (1985) also argued that institutional economics overly emphasizes the selection mechanism of efficiency in explaining the existence of organizational forms. I found that the functioning of organization networks depends in part on historical and institutional factors, as well as their ability to satisfy non-efficiency-based selection mechanisms. Like Schumpeter (1950), I found that organization performance can depend on the ability to service niche markets, which requires that the firm bring products to market quickly and adapt rapidly, rather than to optimize cost efficiency. Embedded networks offer competitive advantages of precisely the type Schumpeter conjectured: entrepreneurial firms adept at innovating and organizing a shifting network of talent, products, and resources. This implies that future research might examine how markets function and competitive dynamics unfold when organizations compete on the basis of their ability to access and reconfigure an external pool of resources and partners rather than firm-based competencies.

Finally, some caveats may be in order, given that my argument is grounded in observations from one industry. First, because I focused on fleshing out the concept of structural embeddedness, I necessarily neglected other types of embeddedness that affect organizations, including cognitive, institutional, and political embeddedness (Zukin and DiMaggio, 1990; Oliver, 1996). Second, the small employment size of these firms and the personal nature of interfirm ties in this industry may provide an especially fertile ground for embeddedness that might not exist for larger firms. As firms grow, ties among individuals may become insufficient sources of embeddedness, and other social mechanisms such as interlocks or shared equity may then be needed. Studies of large Japanese firms show, however, that the critical factor may be organizational form rather than size (Dore, 1983; Gerlach, 1992). If this is true, and the trend toward smaller, flatter, more connected organizations continues, networks could become an important mode of organizing. Third, the fashion- and quality-sensitive nature of better-dress firms may make economies of time, allocative efficiency, and complex adaptation more competitive advantages in this industry than in others.

Embeddedness is a puzzle that, once understood, can furnish tools for explicating not only organizational puzzles but market processes such as allocative efficiency, economies of time, Pareto-improvements, investment, and complex adaptation. While these processes are sociological, they have needlessly been the subject of only economics, both because of a historical division of labor between the disciplines and because organization theorists have been reluctant to study problems that are not within the boundary of the firm (Swedberg, 1994). As economists pay greater attention to organizational issues and the field of organization

Paradox of Embeddedness

theory matures, this division of labor appears outmoded. The interconnected and institutional character of the world economy denotes an opportune time for economic sociology to contribute to the theory of markets in a way that connects organization theory with an understanding of the social mechanisms that underlie market allocation processes.

REFERENCES

Abolafia, Mitchell Y.
1996 Taming the Market. Chicago: University of Chicago Press.

Asanuma, Banri
1985 "The organization of parts purchases in the Japanese automotive industry." Japanese Economic Studies, Summer: 32–53.

Aumann, Robert, and S. Sorin
1989 "Cooperation and bounded recall." Games and Economic Behavior, 1: 5–39.

Axelrod, Robert
1984 The Evolution of Cooperation. New York: Basic Books.

Baker, Wayne E.
1990 "Market networks and corporate behavior." American Journal of Sociology, 6: 589–625.

Batson, Daniel C.
1990 "How social an animal: The human capacity for caring." American Psychologist, 45: 336–346.

Baum, Joel A. C., and Christine Oliver
1992 "Institutional embeddedness and the dynamics of organizational populations." American Sociological Review, 57: 540–559.

Bazerman, Max, and Margaret Neale
1992 Negotiating Rationally. New York: Free Press.

Burt, Ronald
1992 Structural Holes: The Social Structure of Competition. Cambridge, MA: Harvard University Press.

Burt, Ronald, Marc Knez, and Walter W. Powell
1997 "Trust and third-party ties." Unpublished manuscript, Graduate School of Business, University of Chicago.

Cyert, Richard, and James G. March
1992 A Behavioral Theory of the Firm, 2d ed. New York: Blackwell.

Dore, Ronald
1983 "Goodwill and the spirit of market capitalism." British Journal of Sociology, 34: 459–482.

Emirbayer, Mustafa, and Jeff Goodwin
1994 "Network analysis, culture, and the problem of agency." American Journal of Sociology, 99: 1411–1454.

Friedman, Milton
1953 Essays in Positive Economics. Chicago: University of Chicago Press.

Gerlach, Michael L.
1992 Alliance Capitalism: The Social Organization of Japanese Business. Berkeley, CA: University of California Press.

Ghoshal, Sumantra, and Peter Moran
1996 "Bad for practice: A critique of the transaction cost theory." Academy of Management Review, 21: 13–47.

Glaser, Barney G., and Anselm Strauss
1967 The Discovery of Grounded Theory: Strategies for Qualitative Research. New York: Aldine.

Granovetter, Mark
1985 "Economic action and social structure: The problem of embeddedness." American Journal of Sociology, 91: 481–510.
1993 "The nature of economic relationships." In Richard Swedberg (ed.), Exploration in Economic Sociology: 3–41. New York: Russell Sage.

Harrison, Bennett
1994 Lean and Mean: The Changing Landscape of Corporate Power in the Age of Flexibility. New York: Basic Books.

Helper, Susan
1990 "Comparative supplier relations in the U.S. and Japanese auto industries: An exit voice approach." Business Economic History, 19: 153–162.

Hirschman, Albert O.
1970 Exit, Voice and Loyalty: Responses of Decline in Firms, Organizations, and States. Cambridge, MA: Harvard University Press.
1982 "Rival interpretation of market society: Civilizing, destructive or feeble?" Journal of Economic Literature, 20: 1463–1484.

Jackson, Matthew O., and Asher Wolinsky
1996 "A strategic model of social and economic networks." Journal of Economic Theory, 71: 44–74.

Juster, Thomas F., and Frank Stafford
1991 "The allocation of time: Empirical findings, behavioral models, and problems of measurement." Journal of Economic Literature, 29: 471–522.

Kahneman, Daniel, and Amos Tversky
1982 "The psychology of preferences." Scientific American, 246: 161–173.

Kreps, David
1990 Game Theory and Economic Modeling. New York: Oxford University Press.

Krugman, Paul R.
1986 Strategic Trade Policy and the New International Economics. Cambridge, MA: MIT Press.

Larson, Andrea
1992 "Network dyads in entrepreneurial settings: A study of the governance of exchange processes." Administrative Science Quarterly, 37: 76–104.

Lazerson, Mark
1995 "A new phoenix: Modern putting-out in the Modena knitwear industry." Administrative Science Quarterly, 40: 34–59.

Leung, Chi Kin
1993 "Personal contacts, subcontracting linkages, and development in the Hong Kong-Zhuiang Delta Region." Annals of the Association of American Geographers, 83: 272–302.

Lincoln, James R., Michael L. Gerlach, and Christina L. Ahmadjian
1996 "Keiretsu networks and corporate performance in Japan." American Sociological Review, 61: 67–88.

Macaulay, Stuart
1963 "Non-contractual relations in business: A preliminary study." American Sociological Review, 28: 53–67.

Macneil, Ian R.
1978 "Contracts: Adjustment of long-term economic relations under classical, neoclassical, and relational contract law." Northwestern University Law Review, 72: 854–905.

Messick, David
1993 "Equality as a decision heuristic." In Barbara A. Mellers and Jonathan Baron (eds.), Psychological Perspectives on Justice: Theory and Applications: 11–31. New York: Cambridge University Press.

Miles, Matthew, and Michael Huberman
1984 Qualitative Data Analysis. Newbury Park, CA: Sage.

Moorman, Christine, Gerald Zaltman, and Rohit Deshponde
1992 "Relationships between providers and users of market research: The dynamics of trust within and between organizations." Journal of Marketing Research, 29: 314–328.

Murnighan, Keith J.
1994 "Game theory and organizational behavior." Research in Organizational Behavior, 16: 83–123.

Oliver, Christine
1996 "The institutional embeddedness of economic activity." In Jane Dutton and Joel Baum (eds.), The Embeddedness of Strategy: Advances in Strategic Management: 163–186. Greenwich, CT: JAI Press.

Padgett, John F., and Christopher K. Ansell
1993 "Robust action and the rise of the Medici, 1400–1434." American Journal of Sociology, 98: 1259–1319.

Palmer, Donald, Brad Barber, Xueguang Zhou, and Yasemin Soysal
1995 "The friendly and predatory acquisition of large U.S. corporations in the 1960s." American Sociological Review, 60: 469–500.

Peterson, Mitchell, and Raghu Rajan
1994 "The benefits of lending relationships: Evidence from small business data." Journal of Finance, 49: 3–37.

Podolny, Joel
1994 "Market uncertainty and the social character of economic exchange." Administrative Science Quarterly, 39: 458–483.

Polanyi, Karl
1957 The Great Transformation. Boston: Beacon Press.

Portes, Alejandro, and Julia Sensenbrenner
1993 "Embeddedness and immigration: Notes on the social determinants of economic action." American Journal of Sociology, 98: 1320–1350.

Powell, Walter W.
1990 "Neither market nor hierarchy: Network forms of organization." In Barry Staw and L.L. Cummings (eds.), Research in Organizational Behavior, 12: 295–336. Greenwich, CT: JAI Press.

Prietula, Michael J., and Herbert Simon
1989 "The experts in your midst." Harvard Business Review, Jan.–Feb.: 120–124.

Romo, Frank P., and Michael Schwartz
1995 "Structural embeddedness of business decisions: A sociological assessment of the migration behavior of plants in New York State between 1960 and 1985." American Sociological Review, 60: 874–907.

Schumpeter, Joseph A.
1950 Capitalism, Socialism and Democracy. New York: Harper Collins.

Simon, Herbert A.
1978 "Rationality as process and as product of thought." American Economic Review, 68: 1–16.
1991 "Organizations and markets." Journal of Economic Perspectives, 5: 24–44.

Smitka, Michael
1991 Competitive Ties: Subcontracting in the Japanese Automotive Industry. New York: Columbia University Press.

Sterns, Linda Brewster, and Mark Mizruchi
1993 "Corporate financing: Social and economic determinants." In Richard Swedberg (ed.), Explorations in Economic Sociology: 279–308. New York: Russell Sage.

Swedberg, Richard
1994 "Markets as social structures." In Neil J. Smelser and Richard Swedberg (eds.), The Handbook of Economic Sociology: 255–282. Princeton, NJ: Princeton University Press.

Uzzi, Brian
1996 "The sources and consequences of embeddedness for the economic performance of organizations." American Sociological Review, 61: 674–698.
1997 "A network perspective on organizational decline and deindustrialization." International Journal of Sociology and Social Policy (forthcoming).

Waldinger, Roger D.
1989 Through the Eye of the Needle: Immigrants and Enterprise in New York's Garment Trades. New York: New York University Press.

Williamson, Oliver E.
1985 The Economic Institutions of Capitalism. New York: Free Press.
1994 "Transaction cost economics and organization theory." In Neil J. Smelser and Richard Swedberg (eds.), The Handbook of Economic Sociology: 77–107. Princeton, NJ: Princeton University Press.

Wilson, Robert B.
1989 "Exchange." In John Eatwell, Murray Milgate, and Peter Newman (eds.), Allocation, Information, and Markets, The New Palgrave: A Dictionary of Economics: 83–93. New York: W. W. Norton.

Zajac, Edward J., and Cyrus Olsen
1993 "From transaction cost to transactional value analysis: Implications for the study of interorganizational strategies." Journal of Management Studies, 30: 132–145.

Zukin, Sharon, and Paul DiMaggio
1990 Structures of Capital: The Social Organization of the Economy. New York: Cambridge University Press.

Paradox of Embeddedness

APPENDIX: Open-ended Interview Items

Because many of the data were collected ethnographically, these items summarize the questions but only partly convey the nuances and details of the lengthy, interactive, and face-to-face discussions reported in the text.

Internal organization:

Is this a proprietorship, partnership, or corporation?
How many years of industry experience do the principals have?
Do you produce any products in-house?
Why do you contract instead of produce in-house?
Do you outsource work that was done in-house?
Is the decision to produce in-house primarily financial, organizational, or historic?
How many firms work for you per year?
How many retailers do you typically sell to in a year?

Market and product characteristics:

What are the characteristics of your product?
How is your production organized?
How sensitive is your product's demand to quality, price, and fashion trends?
How has your market changed in the last 5 years?
How has the firm adapted to these changes?
What does it take to succeed in this business?

Forming interfirm contacts:

How do you contact new contractors?
When will you use new contractors?
What role does reputation play?
How does the typical relationship begin and develop over time?
Are written contracts used and when?

Interfirm interaction:

What kinds of relationships do you form with contractors?
Is opportunism a problem?
How do you protect yourself?
How are disagreements resolved?
How do you manage the tradeoffs?
In what ways is power gained in a relationship?
When are you most vulnerable in a relationship?
How do you respond to poor performance?
How do you react to a contractor that passes on his price increases?
What happens when a new contractor offers you a lower price than your present contractor(s)? Do you visit your contractor's shop?
In what way do you reward good performance?

Network outcomes:

What benefits do you get from each type of relationship?
What are the downsides?
How do you set prices for goods and services?
What kind of information is shared in different relationships?
Please describe your contractual agreements with regard to setting performance and price.
How are new products created and test marketed?
How are investments in new equipment made?
How do firms borrow money or get loans?
How do you increase your ability to respond to the market?
What promotes innovation?
What events or conditions lead to close business relationships?
What mechanisms are effective in reducing costs?
Do you attempt to attain a specific mix of relationships?
What prevents you from attaining the mix you want?

[21]

Error and attack tolerance of complex networks

Réka Albert, Hawoong Jeong & Albert-László Barabási

Department of Physics, 225 Nieuwland Science Hall, University of Notre Dame, Notre Dame, Indiana 46556, USA

Many complex systems display a surprising degree of tolerance against errors. For example, relatively simple organisms grow, persist and reproduce despite drastic pharmaceutical or environmental interventions, an error tolerance attributed to the robustness of the underlying metabolic network[1]. Complex communication networks[2] display a surprising degree of robustness: although key components regularly malfunction, local failures rarely lead to the loss of the global information-carrying ability of the network. The stability of these and other complex systems is often attributed to the redundant wiring of the functional web defined by the systems' components. Here we demonstrate that error tolerance is not shared by all redundant systems: it is displayed only by a class of inhomogeneously wired networks,

letters to nature

called scale-free networks, which include the World-Wide Web[3-5], the Internet[6], social networks[7] and cells[8]. We find that such networks display an unexpected degree of robustness, the ability of their nodes to communicate being unaffected even by unrealistically high failure rates. However, error tolerance comes at a high price in that these networks are extremely vulnerable to attacks (that is, to the selection and removal of a few nodes that play a vital role in maintaining the network's connectivity). Such error tolerance and attack vulnerability are generic properties of communication networks.

The increasing availability of topological data on large networks, aided by the computerization of data acquisition, had led to great advances in our understanding of the generic aspects of network structure and development[9-16]. The existing empirical and theoretical results indicate that complex networks can be divided into two major classes based on their connectivity distribution $P(k)$, giving the probability that a node in the network is connected to k other nodes. The first class of networks is characterized by a $P(k)$ that peaks at an average $\langle k \rangle$ and decays exponentially for large k. The most investigated examples of such exponential networks are the random graph model of Erdős and Rényi[9,10] and the small-world model of Watts and Strogatz[11], both leading to a fairly homogeneous network, in which each node has approximately the same number of links, $k \approx \langle k \rangle$. In contrast, results on the World-Wide Web (WWW)[3-5], the Internet[6] and other large networks[17-19] indicate that many systems belong to a class of inhomogeneous networks, called scale-free networks, for which $P(k)$ decays as a power-law, that is $P(k) \sim k^{-\gamma}$, free of a characteristic scale. Whereas the probability that a node has a very large number of connections ($k \gg \langle k \rangle$) is practically prohibited in exponential networks, highly connected nodes are statistically significant in scale-free networks (Fig. 1).

We start by investigating the robustness of the two basic connectivity distribution models, the Erdős–Rényi (ER) model[9,10] that produces a network with an exponential tail, and the scale-free model[17] with a power-law tail. In the ER model we first define the N nodes, and then connect each pair of nodes with probability p. This algorithm generates a homogeneous network (Fig. 1), whose connectivity follows a Poisson distribution peaked at $\langle k \rangle$ and decaying exponentially for $k \gg \langle k \rangle$.

The inhomogeneous connectivity distribution of many real networks is reproduced by the scale-free model[17,18] that incorporates two ingredients common to real networks: growth and preferential attachment. The model starts with m_0 nodes. At every time step t a new node is introduced, which is connected to m of the already-existing nodes. The probability Π_i that the new node is connected to node i depends on the connectivity k_i of node i such that $\Pi_i = k_i/\Sigma_j k_j$. For large t the connectivity distribution is a power-law following $P(k) = 2m^2/k^3$.

The interconnectedness of a network is described by its diameter d, defined as the average length of the shortest paths between any two nodes in the network. The diameter characterizes the ability of two nodes to communicate with each other: the smaller d is, the shorter is the expected path between them. Networks with a very large number of nodes can have quite a small diameter; for example, the diameter of the WWW, with over 800 million nodes[20], is around 19 (ref. 3), whereas social networks with over six billion individuals

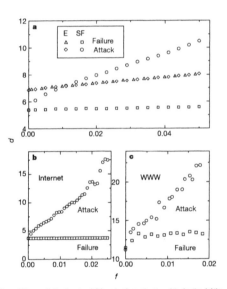

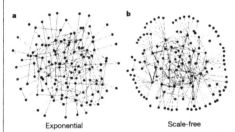

Exponential   Scale-free

Figure 1 Visual illustration of the difference between an exponential and a scale-free network. **a**, The exponential network is homogeneous: most nodes have approximately the same number of links. **b**, The scale-free network is inhomogeneous: the majority of the nodes have one or two links but a few nodes have a large number of links, guaranteeing that the system is fully connected. Red, the five nodes with the highest number of links; green, their first neighbours. Although in the exponential network only 27% of the nodes are reached by the five most connected nodes, in the scale-free network more than 60% are reached, demonstrating the importance of the connected nodes in the scale-free network Both networks contain 130 nodes and 215 links ($\langle k \rangle = 3.3$). The network visualization was done using the Pajek program for large network analysis: ⟨http://vlado.fmf.uni-lj.si/pub/networks/pajek/pajekman.htm⟩.

Figure 2 Changes in the diameter d of the network as a function of the fraction f of the removed nodes. **a**, Comparison between the exponential (E) and scale-free (SF) network models, each containing $N = 10,000$ nodes and 20,000 links (that is, $\langle k \rangle = 4$). The blue symbols correspond to the diameter of the exponential (triangles) and the scale-free (squares) networks when a fraction f of the nodes are removed randomly (error tolerance). Red symbols show the response of the exponential (diamonds) and the scale-free (circles) networks to attacks, when the most connected nodes are removed. We determined the f dependence of the diameter for different system sizes ($N = 1,000; 5,000; 20,000$) and found that the obtained curves, apart from a logarithmic size correction, overlap with those shown in **a**, indicating that the results are independent of the size of the system. We note that the diameter of the unperturbed ($f = 0$) scale-free network is smaller than that of the exponential network, indicating that scale-free networks use the links available to them more efficiently, generating a more interconnected web. **b**, The changes in the diameter of the Internet under random failures (squares) or attacks (circles). We used the topological map of the Internet, containing 6,209 nodes and 12,200 links ($\langle k \rangle = 3.4$), collected by the National Laboratory for Applied Network Research ⟨http://moat.nlanr.net/Routing/rawdata/⟩. **c**, Error (squares) and attack (circles) survivability of the World-Wide Web, measured on a sample containing 325,729 nodes and 1,498,353 links[3], such that $\langle k \rangle = 4.59$.

letters to nature

are believed to have a diameter of around six[21]. To compare the two network models properly, we generated networks that have the same number of nodes and links, such that $P(k)$ follows a Poisson distribution for the exponential network, and a power law for the scale-free network.

To address the error tolerance of the networks, we study the changes in diameter when a small fraction f of the nodes is removed. The malfunctioning (absence) of any node in general increases the distance between the remaining nodes, as it can eliminate some paths that contribute to the system's interconnectedness. Indeed, for the exponential network the diameter increases monotonically with f (Fig. 2a); thus, despite its redundant wiring (Fig. 1), it is increasingly difficult for the remaining nodes to communicate with each other. This behaviour is rooted in the homogeneity of the network: since all nodes have approximately the same number of links, they all contribute equally to the network's diameter, thus the removal of each node causes the same amount of damage. In contrast, we observe a drastically different and surprising behaviour for the scale-free network (Fig. 2a): the diameter remains unchanged under an increasing level of errors. Thus even when as many as 5% of

the nodes fail, the communication between the remaining nodes in the network is unaffected. This robustness of scale-free networks is rooted in their extremely inhomogeneous connectivity distribution: because the power-law distribution implies that the majority of nodes have only a few links, nodes with small connectivity will be selected with much higher probability. The removal of these 'small' nodes does not alter the path structure of the remaining nodes, and thus has no impact on the overall network topology.

An informed agent that attempts to deliberately damage a network will not eliminate the nodes randomly, but will preferentially target the most connected nodes. To simulate an attack we first remove the most connected node, and continue selecting and removing nodes in decreasing order of their connectivity k. Measuring the diameter of an exponential network under attack, we find that, owing to the homogeneity of the network, there is no substantial difference whether the nodes are selected randomly or in decreasing order of connectivity (Fig. 2a). On the other hand, a drastically different behaviour is observed for scale-free networks. When the most connected nodes are eliminated, the diameter of the scale-free network increases rapidly, doubling its original value if 5% of the nodes are removed. This vulnerability to attacks is rooted in the inhomogeneity of the connectivity distribution: the connectivity is maintained by a few highly connected nodes (Fig. 1b), whose removal drastically alters the network's topology, and

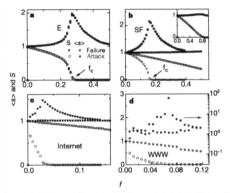

Figure 3 Network fragmentation under random failures and attacks. The relative size of the largest cluster S (open symbols) and the average size of the isolated clusters $\langle s \rangle$ (filled symbols) as a function of the fraction of removed nodes f for the same systems as in Fig. 2. The size S is defined as the fraction of nodes contained in the largest cluster (that is, $S = 1$ for $f = 0$). **a**, Fragmentation of the exponential network under random failures (squares) and attacks (circles). **b**, Fragmentation of the scale-free network under random failures (blue squares) and attacks (red circles). The inset shows the error tolerance curves for the whole range of f, indicating that the main cluster falls apart only after it has been completely deflated. We note that the behaviour of the scale-free network under errors is consistent with an extremely delayed percolation transition: at unrealistically high error rates ($f_{max} \simeq 0.75$) we do observe a very small peak in $\langle s \rangle$ ($\langle s_{max} \rangle \simeq 1.06$) even in the case of random failures, indicating the existence of a critical point. For **a** and **b** we repeated the analysis for systems of sizes $N = 1,000, 5,000$ and $20,000$, finding that the obtained S and $\langle s \rangle$ curves overlap with the one shown here, indicating that the overall clustering scenario and the value of the critical point is independent of the size of the system. **c**, **d**, Fragmentation of the Internet (**c**) and WWW (**d**), using the topological data described in Fig. 2. The symbols are the same as in **b**. $\langle s \rangle$ in **d** in the case of attack is shown on a different scale, drawn in the right side of the frame. Whereas for small f we have $\langle s \rangle \simeq 1.5$, at $f_c^w = 0.067$ the average fragment size abruptly increases, peaking at $\langle s_{max} \rangle \simeq 60$, then decays rapidly. For the attack curve in **d** we ordered the nodes as a function of the number of outgoing links, k_{out}. We note that while the three studied networks, the scale-free model, the Internet and the WWW have different γ, $\langle k \rangle$ and clustering coefficient[11], their response to attacks and errors is identical. Indeed, we find that the difference between these quantities changes only f_c and the magnitude of d, S and $\langle s \rangle$, but not the nature of the response of these networks to perturbations.

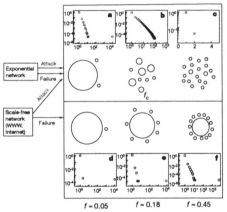

Figure 4 Summary of the response of a network to failures or attacks. **a–f**, The cluster size distribution for various values of f when a scale-free network of parameters given in Fig. 3b is subject to random failures (**a–c**) or attacks (**d–f**). Upper panels, exponential networks under random failures and attacks and scale-free networks under attacks behave similarly. For small f, clusters of different sizes break down, although there is still a large cluster. This is supported by the cluster size distribution: although we see a few fragments of sizes between 1 and 16, there is a large cluster of size 9,000 (the size of the original system being 10,000). At a critical f_c (see Fig. 3) the network breaks into small fragments between sizes 1 and 100 (**b**) and the large cluster disappears. At even higher f (**c**) the clusters are further fragmented into single nodes or clusters of size two. Lower panels, scale-free networks follow a different scenario under random failures: the size of the largest cluster decreases slowly as first single nodes, then small clusters break off. Indeed, at $f = 0.05$ only single and double nodes break off (**d**). At $f = 0.18$, the network is fragmented (**b**) under attack, but under failures the large cluster of size 8,000 coexists with isolated clusters of sizes 1 to 5 (**e**). Even for an unrealistically high error rate of $f = 0.45$ the large cluster persists, the size of the broken-off fragments not exceeding 11 (**f**).

NATURE | VOL 406 | 27 JULY 2000 | www.nature.com

decreases the ability of the remaining nodes to communicate with each other.

When nodes are removed from a network, clusters of nodes whose links to the system disappear may be cut off (fragmented) from the main cluster. To better understand the impact of failures and attacks on the network structure, we next investigate this fragmentation process. We measure the size of the largest cluster, S, shown as a fraction of the total system size, when a fraction f of the nodes are removed either randomly or in an attack mode. We find that for the exponential network, as we increase f, S displays a threshold-like behaviour such that for $f > f_c^e \simeq 0.28$ we have $S \simeq 0$. Similar behaviour is observed when we monitor the average size $\langle s \rangle$ of the isolated clusters (that is, all the clusters except the largest one), finding that $\langle s \rangle$ increases rapidly until $\langle s \rangle \simeq 2$ at f_c^e, after which it decreases to $\langle s \rangle = 1$. These results indicate the following breakdown scenario (Fig. 3a). For small f, only single nodes break apart, $\langle s \rangle \simeq 1$, but as f increases, the size of the fragments that fall off the main cluster increases, displaying unusual behaviour at f_c^e. At f_c^e the system falls apart; the main cluster breaks into small pieces, leading to $S \simeq 0$, and the size of the fragments, $\langle s \rangle$, peaks. As we continue to remove nodes ($f > f_c^e$), we fragment these isolated clusters, leading to a decreasing $\langle s \rangle$. Because the ER model is equivalent to infinite dimensional percolation[22], the observed threshold behaviour is qualitatively similar to the percolation critical point.

However, the response of a scale-free network to attacks and failures is rather different (Fig. 3b). For random failures no threshold for fragmentation is observed; instead, the size of the largest cluster slowly decreases. The fact that $\langle s \rangle \approx 1$ for most f values indicates that the network is deflated by nodes breaking off one by one, the increasing error level leading to the isolation of single nodes only, not clusters of nodes. Thus, in contrast with the catastrophic fragmentation of the exponential network at f_c^e, the scale-free network stays together as a large cluster for very high values of f, providing additional evidence of the topological stability of these networks under random failures. This behaviour is consistent with the existence of an extremely delayed critical point (Fig. 3) where the network falls apart only after the main cluster has been completely deflated. On the other hand, the response to attack of the scale-free network is similar (but swifter) to the response of the exponential network to attack and failure of the exponential network (Fig. 3b): at a critical threshold $f_c^{sf} \simeq 0.18$, smaller than the value $f_c^e \simeq 0.28$ observed for the exponential network, the system breaks apart, forming many isolated clusters (Fig. 4).

Although great efforts are being made to design error-tolerant and low-yield components for communication systems, little is known about the effect of errors and attacks on the large-scale connectivity of the network. Next, we investigate the error and attack tolerance of two networks of increasing economic and strategic importance: the Internet and the WWW.

Faloutsos et al.[6] investigated the topological properties of the Internet at the router and inter-domain level, finding that the connectivity distribution follows a power-law, $P(k) \sim k^{-2.48}$. Consequently, we expect that it should display the error tolerance and attack vulnerability predicted by our study. To test this, we used the latest survey of the Internet topology, giving the network at the inter-domain (autonomous system) level. Indeed, we find that the diameter of the Internet is unaffected by the random removal of as high as 2.5% of the nodes (an order of magnitude larger than the failure rate (0.33%) of the Internet routers[23]), whereas if the same percentage of the most connected nodes are eliminated (attack), d more than triples (Fig. 2b). Similarly, the large connected cluster persists for high rates of random node removal, but if nodes are removed in the attack mode, the size of the fragments that break off increases rapidly, the critical point appearing at $f_c^1 \simeq 0.03$ (Fig. 3b).

The WWW forms a huge directed graph whose nodes are documents and edges are the URL hyperlinks that point from one document to another, its topology determining the search engines' ability to locate information on it. The WWW is also a scale-free network: the probabilities $P_{out}(k)$ and $P_{in}(k)$ that a document has k outgoing and incoming links follow a power-law over several orders of magnitude, that is, $P(k) \sim k^{-\gamma}$, with $\gamma_{in} = 2.1$ and $\gamma_{out} = 2.45^{3,4,24}$. Since no complete topological map of the WWW is available, we limited our study to a subset of the web containing 325,729 nodes and 1,469,680 links ($\langle k \rangle = 4.59$) (ref. 3). Despite the directedness of the links, the response of the system is similar to the undirected networks we investigated earlier: after a slight initial increase, d remains constant in the case of random failures and increases for attacks (Fig. 2c). The network survives as a large cluster under high rates of failure, but the behaviour of $\langle s \rangle$ indicates that under attack the system abruptly falls apart at $f_c^w = 0.067$ (Fig. 3c).

In summary, we find that scale-free networks display a surprisingly high degree of tolerance against random failures, a property not shared by their exponential counterparts. This robustness is probably the basis of the error tolerance of many complex systems, ranging from cells[8] to distributed communication systems. It also explains why, despite frequent router problems[23], we rarely experience global network outages or, despite the temporary unavailability of many web pages, our ability to surf and locate information on the web is unaffected. However, the error tolerance comes at the expense of attack survivability: the diameter of these networks increases rapidly and they break into many isolated fragments when the most connected nodes are targeted. Such decreased attack survivability is useful for drug design[8], but it is less encouraging for communication systems, such as the Internet or the WWW. Although it is generally thought that attacks on networks with distributed resource management are less successful, our results indicate otherwise. The topological weaknesses of the current communication networks, rooted in their inhomogeneous connectivity distribution, seriously reduce their attack survivability. This could be exploited by those seeking to damage these systems. □

Received 14 February; accepted 7 June 2000.

1. Hartwell, L. H., Hopfield, J. J., Leibler, S. & Murray, A. W. From molecular to modular cell biology. *Nature* 402, 47–52 (1999).
2. Claffy, K., Monk, T. E. *et al.* Internet tomography. *Nature Web Matters* [online] (7 Jan. 99) 〈http://helix.nature.com/webmatters/tomog/tomog.html〉 (1999).
3. Albert, R., Jeong, H. & Barabási, A.-L. Diameter of the World-Wide Web. *Nature* 401, 130–131 (1999).
4. Kumar, R., Raghavan, P., Rajalopagan, S. & Tomkins, A. in *Proc. 9th ACM Symp. on Principles of Database Systems* 1–10 (Association for Computing Machinery, New York, 2000).
5. Huberman, B. A. & Adamic, L. A. Growth dynamics of the World-Wide Web. *Nature* 401, 131 (1999).
6. Faloutsos, M., Faloutsos, P. & Faloutsos, C. On power-law relationships of the internet topology. *ACM SIGCOMM '99. Comput. Commun. Rev.* 29, 251–263 (1999).
7. Wasserman, S. & Faust, K. *Social Network Analysis* (Cambridge Univ. Press, Cambridge, 1994).
8. Jeong, H., Tombor, B., Albert, R., Oltvai, Z. & Barabási, A.-L. The large-scale organization of metabolic networks. *Nature* (in the press).
9. Erdős, P. & Rényi, A. On the evolution of random graphs. *Publ. Math. Inst. Hung. Acad. Sci.* 5, 17–60 (1960).
10. Bollobás, B. *Random Graphs* (Academic, London, 1985).
11. Watts, D. J. & Strogatz, S. H. Collective dynamics of 'small-world' networks. *Nature* 393, 440–442 (1998).
12. Zegura, E. W., Calvert, K. L. & Donahoo, M. J. A quantitative comparison of graph-based models for internet topology. *IEEE/ACM Trans. Network.* 5, 770–787 (1997).
13. Williams, R. J. & Martinez, N. D. Simple rules yield complex food webs. *Nature* 404, 180–183 (2000).
14. Maritan, A., Colaiori, F., Flammini, A., Cieplak, M. & Banavar, J. Universality classes of optimal channel networks. *Science* 272, 984–986 (1996).
15. Banavar, J. R., Maritan, A. & Rinaldo, A. Size and form in efficient transportation networks. *Nature* 399, 130–132 (1999).
16. Barthélémy, M. & Amaral, L. A. N. Small-world networks: evidence for a crossover picture. *Phys. Rev. Lett.* 82, 3180–3183 (1999).
17. Barabási, A.-L. & Albert, R. Emergence of scaling in random networks. *Science* 286, 509–511 (1999).
18. Barabási, A.-L., Albert, R. & Jeong, H. Mean-field theory for scale-free random networks. *Physica A* 272, 173–187 (1999).
19. Redner, S. How popular is your paper? An empirical study of the citation distribution. *Euro. Phys. J. B* 4, 131–134 (1998).
20. Lawrence, S. & Giles, C. L. Accessibility of information on the web. *Nature* 400, 107–109 (1999).
21. Milgram, S. The small-world problem. *Psychol. Today* 2, 60–67 (1967).
22. Bunde, A. & Havlin, S. (eds) *Fractals and Disordered Systems* (Springer, New York, 1996).
23. Paxson, V. End-to-end routing behavior in the internet. *IEEE/ACM Trans. Network.* 5, 601–618 (1997).
24. Adamic, L. A. The small world web. *Lect. Notes Comput. Sci.* 1696, 443–452 (1999).

letters to nature

Acknowledgements

We thank B. Bunker, K. Newman, Z. N. Oltvai and P. Schiffer for discussions. This work was supported by the NSF.

Correspondence and requests for materials should be addressed to A.-L.B. (e-mail: alb@nd.edu).

Name Index